MW01194651

Christian Worldview
and the Academic Disciplines

McMaster Divinity College Press
General Series

VOL. 1   Deane E. D. Downey and Stanley E. Porter, eds.
Christian Worldview and the Academic Disciplines: Crossing the Academy

Christian Worldview
and the Academic Disciplines

Crossing the Academy

edited by

DEANE E. D. DOWNEY

and

STANLEY E. PORTER

PICKWICK *Publications* · Eugene, Oregon

CHRISTIAN WORLDVIEW AND THE ACADEMIC DISCIPLINES
*Cross*ing the Academy

McMaster Divinity College Press General Series 1

McMaster Divinity College Press
1280 Main Street West
Hamilton, Ontario, Canada
L8S 4K1

Pickwick Publications
A Division of Wipf and Stock Publishers
199 W. 8th Av.e, Suite 3
Eugene, OR 97401

www.wipfandstock.com

ISBN 13: 978-1-60608-529-5

Cataloging-in-Publication data:

Christian worldview and the academic disciplines : *cross*ing the academy / edited by Deane E. D. Downey and Stanley E. Porter.

xxxvviii + 504 p. ; 23 cm.

McMaster Divinity College Press General Series 1

ISBN 13: 978-1-60608-529-5

1. Christianity and culture. 2. Religion and science. 3. Christianity and literature. I. Downey, Deane E. D. II. Porter, Stanley E., 1956– . Title. III. Series.

B823.3 C537 2009

Manufactured in the U.S.A.

Contents

Contributors

Senyo Adjibolosoo obtained a BA from the University of Ghana, an MA from York University, and a PhD in Economics from Simon Fraser University. An econometrician by training, Dr. Adjibolosoo devotes most of his research time to economic development, particularly the human factor aspect. The originator of the human factor perspective on development theory and practice, he is the founder and executive director of the International Institute for Human Factor Development and the editor of the *Review of Human Factor Studies*, the multidisciplinary journal of the IIHFD. His numerous publications include approximately 50 journal articles and book chapters. He has written seven books and edited or co-edited nine others. He has helped to create the Human Factor Leadership Academy in the Volta Region of Ghana, which is slated to admit its first freshman (university level) class in the fall of 2009.

John A. Anonby completed his BA (Hons.) and MA in English at the University of British Columbia and his PhD at the University of Alberta. He has published articles in a wide variety of fields beyond his specialty in Milton and has presented a number of papers at conferences in North America, Britain, and Africa. He chaired the English and Modern Languages department at Trinity Western University for a number of years. He and his wife took four years off to teach at Pan Africa Christian College (now University) in Kenya. Having published several essays on the novels of the Kenyan writer Ngugi wa Thiong'o, Professor Anonby had a book, *The Kenyan Epic Novelist Ngugi: His Secular Reconfiguration of Biblical Themes*, published in 2006. Now Professor Emeritus, he has completed another year of teaching at Trans-Africa Theological College, Kitwe, Zambia, and Pan Africa Christian University, Nairobi, Kenya.

Lloyd A. Arnett holds a BA in Performance (Fairmont State College), an MA in Theater History, Literature, and Criticism, and a PhD in

Theater Arts (both from the University of Pittsburgh), with additional divinity studies at Asbury Theological Seminary. He has taught at the University of Pittsburgh and for the Pennsylvania State University. His professional performance career includes over forty roles for stage and screen, directing, dramaturgy, and work in radio, television, and film. As a playwright he has created *Drama for Christian Seasons*, an anthology of original short plays, and adapted the *Hippolytus* of Euripides and the *Paphnutius* of Hrotswitha. He has written a survey history of American playwriting manuals (1890–1995), has presented over 40 guest lectures, and has taught playwriting seminars for professional theater companies. In 2001 he placed discovered documents of Austrian Hollywood-Connection actor Ludwig Stoessel with Filmarchiv Austria in Vienna. Most recently he wrote *Taking the Bible Seriously*, a contribution to the *Anglican Agenda* Series. Currently he is the senior lecturer in dramatic literature at Trinity Western University, where he has also produced over 130 shows in fifteen years.

Robert Burkinshaw completed his BTh (Vancouver Bible College) in New Testament Studies before turning to history. He completed a BA (University of British Columbia), an MA (University of Waterloo), and a PhD (University of British Columbia), all in Canadian and American history. He has authored one book, over twenty articles, many book reviews, and a number of presentations at scholarly conferences. Most of his research and writing deals with Canadian religious history. He has taught courses in Canadian and American history at Trinity Western University for 25 years. He currently serves as Dean of the Faculty of Humanities and Social Sciences and Director of the Master of Arts in Interdisciplinary Studies program.

John Byl completed BSc (mathematics) and PhD (astronomy) degrees at the University of British Columbia. He has taught astronomy at the University of British Columbia, physics at Dordt College in Iowa, and, for the last thirty years, physics and mathematics at Trinity Western University. He currently serves as Chair of the Mathematical Sciences Department, which includes the disciplines of mathematics, physics, and computer science. He has written articles on a range of topics including mathematics, astronomy, physics, and interactions between science and theology. He is the author of two books, *The Divine Challenge: On Matter,*

Mind, Math and Meaning (2004) and *God and Cosmos: A Christian View of Time, Space and the Universe* (2001).

Mark Charlton completed his BA in History at Messiah College. After a term of service with the Mennonite Central Committee as a teacher in Zaire, he obtained his MA in Political Science from the University of Western Ontario in London and his PhD from Laval University, where he studied as a Quebec–Ontario Fellow. Charlton has taught Political Science at the Universities of Saskatchewan, Windsor, and Western Ontario, and at Trinity Western University, where he also served as Dean of Research and Faculty Development. He is currently Vice President (Academic) and Dean of St. Mary's University College in Calgary, Alberta. Professor Charlton's primary research interest has been in the area of international food aid policy, which led to the publication of his book, *The Making of Canadian Food Aid Policy*, by McGill–Queen's University Press. He has also co-edited three political science textbooks and published a number of articles in various Canadian political science journals.

Deane E. D. Downey did a BA at McGill University, an MA at the University of Toronto, and a PhD in English at the University of Alberta. In 1973 he joined the faculty of Trinity Western College, where he served until his retirement in 2004. He wore several administrative hats, the last of which was Associate Academic Vice President in what became Trinity Western University. In addition to his administrative duties he developed and supervised first-year and senior Christian worldview courses and also taught an upper-level English course each semester. Co-editor of the Canadian edition of *The Little, Brown Handbook*, he has also given papers and/or written articles on Canadian fiction, the Bible as Literature, and teaching literature from a Christian perspective. He has taught short-term or part-time courses at the Universities of Regina, Ottawa, Alberta, and British Columbia in Canada; at Tianjin Foreign Studies University and Tianjin University of Technology in China; and in Atlantic Baptist University's World Drama semester located at Oxford University.

Harold W. Faw completed undergraduate degrees in theology (BTh, Emmanuel Bible College) and in psychology and mathematics (BA, Wilfrid Laurier University) and graduate degrees in experimental psychology (MA, PhD, University of Waterloo). He is currently Professor of

Psychology at Trinity Western University, where he has taught for over 25 years. His first book (published by Baker Books) was entitled *Psychology in Christian Perspective: An Analysis of Key Issues*. His second book explores links between faith and the more focused topic of remembering; it is entitled *Sharing our Stories: Understanding Memory and Building Faith*. Faw's research interests include applied human memory and the integration of psychology and theology.

Erica Grimm-Vance, Assistant Professor of Art at Trinity Western University, is represented in galleries across Canada, has had over 25 solo exhibitions, and is in numerous private and public collections, including the Vatican Art Collection, Canada Council Art Bank, and the Richmond Art Gallery. In 2002, she was the Distinguished Nash Lecturer at the University of Regina. In 2007 she was the First Prize recipient of the Imago National Juried Art Competition and was also honored as the Distinguished Alumna from the University of Regina. She is currently working on a series of sixteen larger than life-size female saints for Seabury Western Theological Seminary in Chicago. Grimm-Vance has recently installed a collaborative multimedia project called (im)Balance that includes a 20' x 5' encaustic and steel panel, three digital film sequences projected on steel and scrim, and soundscape triggered by viewer interaction. She has a BFA from the University of Regina and has done additional study at the Banff School of Fine Arts and Akademie der Bildenden Künste in Munich, Germany. She is currently enrolled in a PhD in Art Education program at Simon Fraser University.

Murray Hall, Associate Professor of Physical Education at Trinity Western University, has been chair of the department of Physical Education and Recreation and, for the past ten years, Director of Athletics. After earning a BPHE (Hons.) at Laurentian University and a BEd at Queen's University, he spent four years teaching and coaching in Ontario before earning an MSc from the University of Saskatchewan. Professor Hall has been teaching, coaching, and administering at the college and university level for 21 years. He has published articles on the effects of jet lag on athletic performance, the selection of coaches, ethics in sport, nutrition, and women's fitness. Other areas of his academic interest include leadership in sport, sport management, educational technology, organizational behavior and managing change, and strategic planning. He teaches several National Coaching Certification Program courses each year to community and school coaches. He is literally outstanding in his field as 1998 World Nike Games gold medalist in discus and current Canadian Masters' track and field champion in shot put and discus.

Kelsey Haskett completed her honors BA in French at the University of Western Ontario and her MA and PhD in French Literature at Laval University in Quebec City. Following eleven years' involvement in inner-city mission work in Quebec City, she taught French for three years at St. Stephen's University in New Brunswick before accepting an invitation to develop a French program at Trinity Western University. In 2003 she was appointed Chair of the newly created Modern Language Department, which offers courses in six languages. Her main areas of research interest are French women's literature and twentieth-century French literature. She has recently completed a major study of the novels of Marguerite Duras. An active participant in the North American Christian Foreign Language Association, of which she was secretary for three years, Haskett has published articles in the *Journal of Christianity and Foreign Languages* and in *Intégrité: A Faith and Learning Journal.* She is currently editor of a work in progress entitled *French Woman Authors: The Significance of the Spiritual.*

Craig Montgomery received his BSc from McMaster University and his PhD from the University of Western Ontario. After a stint at the University of British Columbia as an NSERC Postdoctoral Fellow, he joined the faculty of Trinity Western University in 1988. At TWU he serves as Professor of Chemistry and Chair of the Chemistry Department while also acting as an adjunct professor at Simon Fraser University. His research interests include synthetic inorganic and organometallic chemistry, and he has authored a number of articles and conference papers in these areas.

Don Page is currently a Senior Fellow and Professor Emeritus of Leadership Studies at Trinity Western University. Prior to joining the University in 1989 as Academic Vice President, he spent sixteen years with Canada's Department of Foreign Affairs and International Trade. Before that he taught history at the University of Saskatchewan. His PhD is from the University of Toronto. For most of his years in Ottawa, Page was deputy director for research on foreign affairs. From 1985 to 1989, he served as senior policy analyst in the department's Policy Development Bureau. In this role, he was involved in drafting the Government's foreign policy and writing foreign policy speech notes for five of Canada's foreign ministers and three of its prime ministers. He has been an adjunct professor at the Canadian Centre for Management Development in Touraine. He is recognized in *Canadian Who's Who* as the author of over six dozen published works in such diverse fields as public history, foreign policy, and leadership. His most recent book, *Effective Team Leadership: Learning to Lead through Relationships*, focuses on how to put Jesus' leadership principles into practice in an organization. In Christian circles, he is recognized as the founder of the Public Service Christian Fellowship and Trinity Western University's Laurentian Leadership Centre in Ottawa, and project director for the Executive Leadership Development Institute of the Council for Christian Colleges and Universities.

Richard Paulton received his PhD in microbiology and biochemistry from the Imperial College of Science and Technology, University of London, England. He was a professor at the medical school at the University of Saskatchewan for ten years, then a visiting scholar at Regent College, Vancouver, from 1979 to 1981. He began teaching at Trinity Western University in 1983. Dr. Paulton's recent research has included the epidemiology of malaria in Haiti and the spread of antibiotic resistance in "superbugs"—bacteria that have developed resistance to antibiotics—among animals. He recently retired as Professor of Biology and Chair of Biological Sciences at Trinity Western University. He is currently working with the American Society of Microbiology to publish a multimedia project, "Laboratory Microbiology on DVD."

Joanne L. Pepper completed undergraduate studies in both theology (Western Pentecostal College) and social Sciences (BA, Southern California College) before enrolling in the Graduate School of World Mission at Fuller Theological Seminary, where she obtained an MA in cross-cultural studies. As a Rotary International Exchange Fellow, she did extensive study and field work in Portugal and Brazil on the role of women, poverty, and the growth of non-conformist churches, leading to a PhD (University of Warwick). Pepper continues to apply anthropological principles through various cross-cultural teaching and ministry assignments in Canada and overseas. For eight years she taught at least one semester per year in republics of the former Soviet Union. In the past decade, she has been devoted to work in the former Soviet Union as well as in various regions in Latin America. She is currently coordinator of the Intercultural Religious Studies program within the Religious Studies Department of Trinity Western University. Her current areas of expertise are Eastern Europe, world religions, global theologies, missiology and contextualization, Women of the Bible, and Women in the Developing World.

Stanley E. Porter completed BA (Point Loma College) and MA (Claremont Graduate School) degrees in English before being "converted" to biblical studies, where he did an MA (Trinity Evangelical Divinity School) in New Testament and a PhD (University of Sheffield) in biblical studies and linguistics. An award-winning writer, Porter has authored or co-authored fourteen books and edited over fifty volumes. He is also the author of over 250 journal articles, chapters in books, and dictionary entries, and has delivered over 170 papers at conferences worldwide. Porter has taught at Biola University, Trinity Western University, and the University of Surrey Roehampton, and, since 2001, has been President and Dean, and Professor of New Testament, at McMaster Divinity College in Hamilton, Ontario. He researches and writes on a wide range of topics, including Greek language and linguistics, Pauline studies, the Gospels, papyrology and epigraphy, and ancient rhetoric. His recent research interest is the future of Christian higher education.

Julia Quiring-Emblen completed her BS (University of Oregon) and both her MN (in Medical Surgical Nursing) and PhD (in Nursing Education— Curriculum and Instruction) at the University of Washington. She has authored one book, four major chapters in texts, and 25 articles. She writes on a variety of nursing education topics, clinical aspects related to grief, and spiritual nursing care. She has taught most areas of undergraduate nursing, medical-surgical courses, and nursing theory and education courses at the graduate level. After retiring from Trinity Western University she worked in Oregon. Currently she is serving as a Parish Nurse and writing materials to be used by congregational members to assist them in visiting the homebound.

David W. Rushton holds a BMus with distinction (McGill University), an MMus in music theory (University of Alberta), an EdD in music education (University of British Columbia), and an A.R.C.T. diploma in piano performance (Royal Conservatory of Music in Toronto). In addition, he has studied choral and orchestral conducting with several of Canada's respected conductors. A member of Trinity Western University's faculty since 1973, Rushton served as Chair of the Music Department for fourteen years and is currently the senior professor of music in the department. From 1988–1998 he served as conductor and musical director of the Fraser Valley Symphony. He was recently appointed to the position of conductor and director of music of the Gloria Dei Chorale commencing with the 2008–2009 season. His current research interests include music curricula and program evaluation in higher education as well as the study of trends in the music and worship life of the church. He remains active as a church musician, accompanist, and guest lecturer.

Craig E. Seaton completed a BA degree (California State University, Long Beach) in psychology. He earned master's degrees in sociology (California State University, San Jose) and in educational psychology (University of Southern California). His PhD, also from the University of Southern California, was based upon the combined disciplines of psychology and sociology. He has authored three books: *Altruism and Activism* (1996), *Northern Ireland: The Context for Conflict and for Reconciliation* (1998), and *Self-Understanding through Guided Autobiography* (1999). His other writings include chapters in books, research reports, journal articles, and book reviews. His professional life includes service as a social worker, a U.S. naval officer, counselor, government policy researcher in California, dean of students, academic dean, study abroad director, and university professor. His primary academic interests have centered on adult development, conflict resolution, and human services training. He currently is Adjunct Professor of Behavioral Science at Western International University in Phoenix, Arizona. Seaton is also engaged in several research projects for the U.S. Census Bureau.

Douglas H. Shantz, with a PhD in history from the University of Waterloo, is Professor of Christian Thought at the University of Calgary, Canada. His recent publications examine Pietist historical writing, autobiography, conversion, and migration. His book, *Between Sardis and Philadelphia:*

The Life and World of Pietist Court Preacher Conrad Bröske, appeared in 2008 from Brill in Leiden, The Netherlands.

Bill Strom earned a BA in speech communication (Wheaton College, IL), an MA in communication theory (Northern Illinois University), and a PhD in communication research (University of Iowa). He has served for two decades as Chair of the Communications Department at Trinity Western University, where he teaches communication theory, intercultural communication, and relational communication. In addition to publishing several academic and popular articles, Strom has also written a faith-and-field text, *More Than Talk: Communication Studies and the Christian Faith* (3rd edition, Kendall/Hunt, 2008).

Rick Sutcliffe, with a BSc and MSc in mathematics (Simon Fraser University), is Professor of Mathematics and Computing Science at Trinity Western University. His interests are in combinatorics and the philosophy of mathematics, system design, programming languages, and the social and ethical aspects of technology. He has authored a text on introductory programming, a second on social and ethical issues in technology, and five novels exploring the latter themes in alternate history science fiction settings. He is also a frequent speaker, panelist, and conference guest. Sutcliffe was instrumental in developing the computing science major at Trinity Western University. He has served the institution in a variety of capacities, including Assistant Dean of Natural Science, Acting Dean of Natural Science, and Faculty Chair.

John R. Sutherland completed a BComm (Hons.) and an MBA at Queen's University (Kingston, Ontario). After a stint in the steel industry, he completed an MA in Biblical Studies at Trinity Evangelical Divinity School. His professional activities have included twenty-seven years of post-secondary instruction and administration, including Dean of the Faculty of Business and Economics and Professor of Business at Trinity Western University and Vice President (Academic) at King's University College, Edmonton, Alberta. He served for five years as Director of Public Relations for the Christian Labour Association of Canada. He does consulting in marketing research, strategic management, and leadership development. Sutherland has published many articles dealing primarily with business ethics issues from a biblical perspective. His first book, *Going*

Broke: Bankruptcy, Business Ethics and the Bible, won three international awards. His second, *Us and Them: Building a Just Workplace Community*, is an edited volume on labor relations. Sutherland has recently been appointed as General Manager of Vancouver's Pacific Theatre, a professional theatre company founded by Christians interested in exploring human spirituality.

Carl J. Tracie received a BEd in English (University of Alberta) before switching to the discipline of geography (MA and PhD, also at the University of Alberta). His professional interests lie in the field of historical geography, especially pioneer agricultural settlement, and, more specifically, settlement by religious and ethnic groups. His book *"Toil and Peaceful Life": Doukhobor Village Settlement in Saskatchewan, 1899–1918* and several articles reflect these interests. His recent receipt of Professor Emeritus in Geography status will allow him to pursue those interests in retirement. Dr. Tracie taught for nine years at the University of Saskatchewan before coming to Trinity Western University in 1981.

Harro Van Brummelen earned his MEd from the University of Toronto and EdD from the University of British Columbia. A Professor of Education at Trinity Western University since 1986, he has also served as dean of a number of faculties and schools, including Dean of Undergraduate Studies and Dean of the School of Education. His best known books are *Walking with God in the Classroom: Christian Approaches to Learning and Teaching* (3rd edition 2009) and *Steppingstones to Curriculum* (2nd edition, 2002) which have been published in ten and five languages, respectively. Many of his numerous journal articles have focused on Christian approaches to education and the role of religion in education. Van Brummelen currently serves on the British Columbia Degree Quality Assessment Board and the British Columbia Council for Admissions and Transfer.

Dennis R. Venema earned his BSc in Cell and Developmental Biology and his PhD in Genetics and Cell Biology from the University of British Columbia. He is currently Chair of the Biology Department at Trinity Western University, where he teaches upper-level courses on genetics, immunology, cell biology, and the interaction between biology and Christian theology. He has published articles on epithelial patterning as well as genetics education, the latter earning him a teaching award from the National Association of Biology Teachers in 2008.

Michael Walrod completed a diploma in theology and missions at Prairie Bible College in Three Hills, Alberta, before doing both an MA and a PhD in linguistics and humanities at the University of Texas at Arlington. He has authored two books on discourse analysis as well as many other articles on linguistics and cross-cultural work. Walrod has also produced many books, including some Scripture translations, in the Ga'dang language of the northern Philippines (where he worked for 17 years). He has served as Associate Director for Academic Affairs of the Summer Institute of Linguistics in the Philippines and on the Board of Directors of Wycliffe Bible Translators of Canada and of the Graduate Institute of Applied Linguistics (GIAL) in Dallas, Texas. Dr. Walrod is currently Chair of the Linguistics Department at Trinity Western University, program director for the Master of Applied Linguistics and Exegesis degree at ACTS (Associated Canadian Theological Schools) on Trinity Western University's campus, and director of the Canada Institute of Linguistics.

Richard Walters' undergraduate education led him, by the rather circuitous route of a diploma at Trinity Bible College, a semester at Trinity Seminary, and additional study at the University of Minnesota, to a BSc with high honors from Wheaton College (Illinois). After earning an MA in Science Education at the University of Minnesota (which included studying with one of North America's preeminent glacial geologists, H. E. Wright), Walters spent several years in cancer research at that university's Mayo Memorial Hospital and then taught for four years at St. Paul Bible College (now Crown College). In 1962, he and his wife moved to British Columbia, where he became one of the founding faculty members of Trinity Junior College in Langley, the forerunner of Trinity Western University. He taught biology (including comparative anatomy, embryology, genetics, and plant biology) and geology (both physical and historical) there until his retirement in 1991.

Phillip H. Wiebe completed BA and MA degrees at the University of Manitoba, then took a Commonwealth Scholarship to Australia to complete his PhD in philosophy at the University of Adelaide. He has authored *Theism in an Age of Science* (1988), *Visions of Jesus: Direct Encounters from* *the New Testament to Today* (1997), *God and Other Spirits: Intimations of Transcendence in Christian Experience* (2004), and "Religious Experience, Cognitive Science, and the Future of Religion," in *The Oxford Handbook of Religion and Science* (2006). He is currently working on a book on intellectual vision, a particular kind of religious experience celebrated by St. Augustine for the intuitive certainty it gives about religious matters without involving either the senses or the imagination. Wiebe taught at the University of Manitoba and Brandon University before coming to Trinity Western University, where he is a Professor of Philosophy.

Preface

It is our considered conviction that any Christian college or university whose administration and faculty do not have an ongoing and explicit commitment to the active integration[1] of biblical truth with that institution's learning/teaching/scholarly activities perhaps has no adequate reason to exist. Regardless of all the other benefits that are deemed to give most of such institutions an advantage over their public, secular counterparts—smaller class size, superior student/teacher ratios, commitment to whole student person development, not just intellectual growth—we believe this concern to foster critical reflection on the implications of a Christian worldview for both student learning and faculty teaching and scholarship is the *sine qua non* of a Christian college or university's mandate.[2]

This basic premise is shared by the contributors to this volume of essays. They have all been participants, at one time or another, in a one-semester-hour interdisciplinary studies course entitled "Introduction to Christian Worldview Thinking" required of all new students at Trinity

---

1. Heie and Wolfe, eds., *The Reality of Christian Learning: Strategies for Faith-Discipline Integration*, vii, provides a very good definition of "integration" in the sense that we are intending: "the fundamental search for commonalities between the Christian faith and the substantive, methodological, and value assumptions that underlie activity in the academic disciplines, as well as attempts to systematize academic learning into an overarching Christian schema."

2. We would prefer to believe that this active engagement in Christian worldview integration by Christian colleges and universities is the norm; unfortunately, it appears to be the exception. Almost a decade ago Larry Lyon and Michael Beaty quoted Robert Sloan, who was then President of Baylor University, as observing that most Christian colleges and universities in the USA took a "two-tier approach" to integration, assuming that religious beliefs and practices "had no essential relationship" to the main educational mission of their institution—which in effect left them only a step away from full secularization as they strove to not be essentially different from their secular counterparts ("Integration, Secularization, and the Two-Spheres View at Religious Colleges," 73–74). Lyon and Beaty continue with their quite astonishing assessment: "While hundreds of Protestant and Catholic colleges remain [speaking solely of the American scene], only a few in practice attempt to relate their religious identity to their academic practices" (75).

Western University in Langley, British Columbia, Canada, since the spring of 1992. The mandate for these discipline-specific speakers (all save the first three essayists in this volume) was first to describe some of the key issues or aspects of their respective academic subject area and then to outline some of the ways in which a biblically-informed Christian worldview impacts and affects their involvement in and approach to that discipline. For obviously pragmatic reasons, given the level at which this course was to be taught, these faculty colleagues initially developed their presentations with a rather introductory, foundational focus. In this respect, at least, such presentations differed considerably from some of the very helpful but much more erudite treatments of a Christian perspective and the academic disciplines that have appeared in such periodicals as the *Christian Scholar's Review* or in the superb volumes in the *Eyes of Faith* series fostered by the Christian College Coalition (now called the Council of Christian Colleges and Universities) and published by Harper and Row.

During the last decade or so, a veritable deluge of fresh considerations of a Christian worldview and its impact on the various academic disciplines has flooded (to extend the "deluge" metaphor) the academic marketplace, principally in the USA—in both monograph and periodical form.[3] Some of these works have been discipline-specific (e.g., Henk Aay and Sander Griffioen's 1998 book of edited articles, *Geography and Worldview: A Christian Reconnaissance*, or David Entwistle's *Integrative Approaches to Psychology and Christianity: An Introduction to Worldview Issues, Philosophical Foundations, and Models of Integration* [2004]). Other works have endeavored, like the present volume, to cover a wide range of academic subject areas[4] (e.g., the David Dockery and Gregory Thornbury-edited 2002 collection *Shaping a Christian Worldview: The Foundations*

---

3. In his 2004 book, *Christianity in the Academy*, Harry Poe noted that many academics, in the previous fifteen years, had talked about the importance of faith/learning integration, but few had shown how to "think Christianly" in relation to specific disciplines (13). The present volume is attempting to address that perceived shortfall, but our contributors are also drawing attention to the fact that much good work is being done in the various disciplines in the academy to demonstrate the nature of Christian-perspective thinking.

4. Please consult the "For Further Reading" bibliography at the end of this Preface for a more complete listing of these multiple-discipline monographs. Most of these works are also referred to, as appropriate, in the discipline-specific chapters in this volume, as are the many recent treatments of a Christian worldview applying to specific subject areas.

of *Christian Higher Education* or Arlin Migliazzo's *Teaching as an Act of Faith: Theory and Practice in Church-Related Higher Education*, also published in 2002).[5]

We as editors concluded, therefore, in consultation/collaboration with our contributors, that the focus of this volume's articles should be broadened to reflect a reasonably extensive (albeit not exhaustive) encounter with these more recent materials—certainly in terms of the content but particularly with respect to the "For Further Reading" bibliographies at the end of each chapter. Unlike most of the treatments of a Christian worldview and its implications for the academy, however, which are addressed principally to the professoriat, the essays in our volume are directed primarily at students. Also, as already indicated above, our contributors have tried to provide a basic introduction to some of the key topic areas or issues in their subject areas, something that is taken for granted, in large measure, in most of these other discussions.

Our hope is that these essays will be helpful both for students who are relatively recent arrivals on the post-secondary academic scene and for more advanced undergraduates and possibly even graduate students, mainly because of the reasonably extensive bibliographies provided at the end of each chapter. We would also like to somewhat impertinently posit that these treatments of a Christian worldview in relation to a broad range of academic disciplines (broader in terms of the sheer number of same, we have the temerity to assert, than any of the other essay collections on this theme that we have so far encountered) will prove useful to our academic colleagues who are either integrating Christian worldview considerations into their teaching activities or who are engaged in various forms of scholarly endeavor along these lines of integrative thought.

Speaking of impertinence, we would like to suggest that the "Canadian" perspective, usually implicit but occasionally explicit in the present volume, complements the great wealth of illuminating Christian worldview material emanating from both American and European scholars. The majority of contributors to this volume are either Canadians by birth or by choice (i.e., landed immigrants). We believe the addition of these voices to the Christian worldview conversation will enhance and enlarge the reader's perspective on this seminal issue. Many of the insights of American Christian academics apply very readily to the much smaller

5. Heie and Wolfe, eds., *The Reality of Christian Learning: Strategies for Faith-Discipline Integration* is a good example of a somewhat earlier multi-discipline treatment of a Christian worldview.

but rapidly growing Christian college and university academic scene here in Canada, something of which many of our American counterparts may be unaware. We have also attempted to acknowledge some of the fine work on integrative thinking produced outside of North America—especially in Great Britain. A number of these works appear in the bibliographies appended to each chapter.

We are trusting that these treatments of the impact of a Christian worldview on the principal academic disciplines of a liberal arts university or college will be helpful not only for students and faculty in Christian post-secondary institutions or even for teachers in Christian elementary and high schools, but also for Bible-affirming and believing students and professors pursuing their respective vocations at secular institutions.[6] This is not to say that we promote a dogmatism that seeks to impose one particular viewpoint. We consciously use the term "*a* Christian worldview" throughout, not "*the* Christian worldview," for adoption of the latter article would be both presumptuous and blind to the wonder of theological diversity extant within the body of Christ. Our contributors are, in effect, inviting their readers, whether undergrads or at a more advanced stage of academic endeavor, to reflectively engage in a conversation that has been initiated by these attempts to demonstrate what a Christian worldview looks like when applied to these various academic disciplines.

We are aware that inevitably some of these essays touch upon controversial issues at times. Probably the one topic that dominates application of a biblical worldview to many of the natural science disciplines has to do with the issue of origins—especially of the cosmos and of humankind. We have asked our contributors dealing with this issue to outline their personal "take" on it forthrightly, but also willingly to acknowledge (at least in the "For Further Reading" bibliography) that there may be a great range of responses to this issue—from Young Earth Creationism to Theistic Evolution (with Intelligent Design holding a position somewhere in between these polarities). One of our contributors holds to the Young Earth Creationist perspective, for example, and another subscribes to a Theistic Evolutionist viewpoint. Both would maintain that their perspective is in accord with both the biblical record and the scientifically-perceived natural world. In spite of the fact that a more narrowly-defined viewpoint on the origins issue sometimes constitutes the *shibboleth* of theological

6. For an elaboration of this suggestion, see the following chapter, "How to Use This Book."

orthodoxy in some Christian academies, both in North America and abroad, we are respectfully advocating the espousal of a more balanced response along the lines that Ted Peters and Martinez Hewlett enjoin:

> A healthy curriculum will provide room for discussion of the cultural controversy that includes scientific creationism and intelligent design as well as theistic evolution. Because the swirl of controversy whelms all our children on a daily basis, a nonanxious discussion of the spectrum of beliefs should be made available.[7]

The contributors to this volume very much represent that broad spectrum of outlook, partially reflected in the considerable range of denominational affiliations they represent—from Anglicans (the approximate equivalent to Episcopalians in the USA) to Pentecostals—and many other denominations in between those two denominational poles! (Trinity Western University was founded by the Evangelical Free Church of America and continues to enjoy close ties with the American and Canadian embodiments of that denomination, but few of the current faculty members actually attend EFC churches. The Statement of Faith that faculty and senior administrators sign annually, however, is in fact the EFC faith statement.) Few of our contributors would profess anything more than a rudimentary grasp of Christian theology, but we do consider it important not to rationalize evading a conscientious investigation of the implications of a biblical world and life view for our particular academic discipline because of that lack of theological expertise. Fortunately, as the bibliographies at the end of each chapter imply, we can learn much from colleagues both in our own fields and in related fields about the implications of an *a priori* commitment to the task of Christian integration.

Our secular colleagues—as well as some of our faith-affirming colleagues, unfortunately—would sometimes have us believe that a biblical perspective in academia has at best a narrowing, restrictive effect on the pursuit of study and learning—and at worst is completely incompatible with such activity.[8] On the contrary, we believe the contributors to this

---

7. Peters and Hewlett, *Can You Believe in God and Evolution*, 73.

8. Harry Poe effectively captures the sentiments of such critics: "The terms *Christian perspective, integration of faith and learning*, and *Christian worldview* [emphasis is Poe's] all conjure up images of fundamentalism, Creation Science, Bible colleges, indoctrination, and ignorance draped in piety" (*Christianity in the Academy*, 43). Later in his book, Poe gives short shrift to the complaint by some Christian academics that they have no time to learn philosophy and theology and apply those concepts to their discipline: "Once people claim faith in the Lord Jesus Christ, their obligation already exists to understand what

volume would all hold the opposite to be the case: that a biblical foundation for scholarly study and investigation—and indeed a trust in and love for the God who has chosen to reveal himself to humankind through his Word, through his world, and ultimately in the person of Jesus Christ—has a wonderfully liberating, expansive effect upon all such activities—one realization, indeed, of Jesus' promise to his followers recorded in the Gospel of John 8:32, "[Y]e shall know the truth, and the truth shall make you free." As Douglas Shantz notes in the first of the three opening essays in this volume, such functional compatibility between learning and faith was foundational to the university enterprise as originally practiced by Thomas Aquinas and others as early as the thirteenth century.

TWU's statement on academic freedom rather succinctly but we think accurately describes the flawed approach to this laudable value evident on most North American secular campuses in our day: it is a view of academic freedom that

> arbitrarily and exclusively requires pluralism without commitment; which denies the existence of any fixed points of reference; which maximizes the quest for truth to the extent of assuming it is never knowable; and which implies an absolute freedom from moral and religious responsibility to its community.

This statement goes on to affirm, however, that, while the University is intentionally involved in teaching "from a stated perspective, i.e., within parameters consistent with the confessional basis of the constituency to which the University is responsible," it strives to do so

> in an environment of free inquiry and discussion.... Students also have freedom to inquire, a right of access to the broad spectrum of representative information in each discipline, and assurance of a reasonable attempt at a fair and balanced presentation and evaluation of all material by their instructors.

Ideally, such an approach to the pursuit of knowledge should help both students and their instructors resist such contemporary pressures to academic conformity as "political correctness," interpretational subjectivism, ethical neutrality, and religious agnosticism—although probably at

---

they have taken upon themselves" (183). David Clearbaut demonstrates that he shares Poe's perspective when he says, "Not to engage the challenges, not to answer the call, not to shine the light of Christian insight across our disciplines, is to make the education we offer indistinguishable from the artificial lighting of the secular mainstream" (*Faith and Learning on the Edge*, 24).

the cost of being identified by such pathetically inadequate signifiers as "neo-conservative" or "homophobic" or "sexist"!

Another common thread uniting this otherwise quite diverse set of discussions about Christian worldview thinking and the academic disciplines is our indebtedness to the important insights into the nature of a Christian approach to a post-secondary liberal arts education embodied in Wheaton College philosophy professor emeritus Arthur Holmes' *The Idea of a Christian College*. Reliance on this relatively brief but seminal work, which for many years served as the sole textbook for the above-referenced "Introduction to Christian Worldview" course, is always implicit and frequently explicit throughout this volume. Our debt to this inspiring Christian thinker is enormous.

We also wish to acknowledge our indebtedness to another important Wheaton College figure, former president Hudson T. Armerding, whose long out-of-print collection of edited essays on Christian worldview thinking and the academic disciplines, *Christianity and the World of Thought*, has been another catalyst to this present collection. Our goals have been similar. Our sincere hope is that this collection will be as helpful to some as Armerding's volume was to many in the late sixties and early seventies.

We are not only indebted to our 26 colleagues, several of whom have either retired or moved on to other institutions in both the USA and Canada after a temporary association with TWU, whose thinking forms the substance of this volume, but also to TWU librarians Ted Goshulak and Ron Braid for help in enhancing many of the "For Further Reading" selected bibliographies at the end of most chapters. We are also grateful for the support and encouragement of our former colleague from the Religious Studies Department, Dr. Craig Evans, in this project.

Deane E. D. Downey
Formerly Associate Academic Vice President
Currently Professor Emeritus (English)
Trinity Western University, Langley, BC

Stanley E. Porter
President and Professor of New Testament
McMaster Divinity College, Hamilton, Ontario

WORKS CITED

Aay, Henk, and Sander Griffioen, eds. *Geography and Worldview: A Christian Reconnaissance*. Lanham, MD: University Press of America, 1998.

Armerding, Hudson T. *Christianity and the World of Thought*. Chicago: Moody Press, 1968.

Claerbaut, David. *Faith and Learning on the Edge: A Bold New Look at Religion in Higher Education*. Grand Rapids, MI: Zondervan, 2004.

Dockery, David S., and Gregory Alan Thornbury, eds. *Shaping a Christian Worldview: The Foundations of Christian Higher Education*. Nashville: Broadman & Holman, 2002.

Entwistle, David N. *Integrative Approaches to Psychology and Christianity: An Introduction to Worldview Issues, Philosophical Foundations, and Models of Integration*. Eugene, OR: Wipf and Stock, 2004.

Heie, Harold, and David L. Wolfe, eds. *The Reality of Christian Learning: Strategies for Faith-Discipline Integration*. Grand Rapids, MI: Eerdmans/Christian College Consortium, 1987.

Holmes, Arthur. *The Idea of a Christian College*. Rev. ed. Grand Rapids, MI: Eerdmans, 1987.

Lyon, Larry, and Michael Beaty. "Integration, Secularization, and the Two-Spheres View at Religious Colleges: Comparing Baylor University with the University of Notre Dame and Georgetown College." *Christian Scholar's Review* 19.1 (1999) 73–112.

Migliazzo, Arlin C., ed. *Teaching as an Act of Faith: Theory and Practice in Church-Related Higher Education*. New York: Fordham University Press, 2002.

Peters, Ted, and Martinez Hewlett. *Can You Believe in God and Evolution? A Guide for the Perplexed*. Nashville: Abingdon Press, 2006.

Poe, Harry L. *Christianity in the Academy: Teaching at the Intersection of Faith and Learning*. Grand Rapids, MI: Baker Academic, 2004.

FOR FURTHER READING

Anderson, Paul M., ed. *Professors Who Believe: The Spiritual Journeys of Christian Faculty*. Downers Grove, IL: InterVarsity Press, 1998.

Blamires, Harry. *The Post-Christian Mind: Exposing Its Destructive Agenda*. Ann Arbor, MI: Servant Publications, 1999.

Cooper, Monte V. "Faculty Perspectives on the Integration of Faith and Academic Discipline in Southern Baptist Higher Education." *Religious Education* 94 (Fall 1999) 380–95.

Glanzer, Perry L., and Todd Ream. "Whose Story? Which Identity?: Fostering Christian Identity at Christian Colleges and Universities." *Christian Scholar's Review* 35.1 (2005) 13–27.

Henry, Douglas V., and Michael D. Beaty, eds. *Christianity and the Soul of the University: Faith as a Foundation for Intellectual Community*. Grand Rapids, MI: Baker Academic, 2006.

Holmes, Arthur F. *Contours of a World View*. Studies in a Christian World View Series 1. Grand Rapids, MI: Eerdmans, 1983.

Jacobsen, Douglas, and Rhonda Hustedt Jacobsen, eds. *Scholarship and Christian Faith: Enlarging the Conversation*. Oxford: Oxford University Press, 2004.

Klassen, Norman, and Jens Zimmermann. *The Passionate Intellect: Incarnational Humanism and the Future of University Education.* Grand Rapids, MI: Baker Academic, 2006.

Marsden, George. *The Outrageous Idea of Christian Scholarship.* Oxford: Oxford University Press, 1997.

Noll, Mark A. *The Scandal of the Evangelical Mind.* Grand Rapids, MI: Eerdmans, 1994.

Ringenberg, William C. "The Faith and Learning Discussion in the Academy at the Turn of the Century." *Christian Scholar's Review* 34.2 (2005) 251–58.

Sire, James W. *Discipleship of the Mind: Loving God in the Way We Think.* Downers Grove, IL: InterVarsity Press, 1990.

How to Use This Book

STANLEY E. PORTER *and* DEANE E. D. DOWNEY

INTRODUCTION

STUDIES OF WORLDVIEW HAVE become increasingly important in recent discussions, both on campuses of universities and colleges, and off campus within various Christian theological traditions. The reformed theological tradition has long emphasized the importance of formulating and living out a Christian worldview. Even those outside the reformed tradition recognize today the fundamental importance of worldview thinking. In our self-reflective age— in which there is no longer, even in the Western world, a single (Christian or otherwise) worldview that dominates public life—there has been increasing recognition of the role that worldview plays. One's worldview influences how she or he approaches the world, thinks about it, and responds to it.

In recent times there have been several contributions to worldview studies within evangelical Christian circles. One of the first major attempts to address the issue was by Arthur Holmes, whose several works, especially *The Idea of a Christian College* and *Contours of a World View*, are cited extensively in the essays in this volume. His *Contours of a World View* explored the questions asked in worldview thinking, but his approach revolved mostly around philosophical issues raised in formulating a coherent and cohesive perspective on the world. Since then, a number of other books have been published in the area of Christian worldview (see the Preface to this volume), many written by a single author,[1] though a few have multiple contributors.[2] None of these books, to our knowledge,

1. For example, Claerbaut, *Faith and Learning on the Edge*; Poe, *Christianity in the Academy*.

2. For example, Dockery and Thornbury, eds., *Shaping a Christian Worldview*; Heie and Wolfe, eds., *The Reality of Christian Learning*; Henry and Beaty, eds., *Christianity and the Soul of the University*.

has the range and scope of coverage of the current volume, however. Each essay in our volume—and there are twenty-six subject-specific essays included (there could have been more!), besides the three introductory essays—tackles a definable subject area in the liberal arts[3] college or university curriculum. Each scholar writing here teaches and researches in that particular area. The essays were written specifically for this volume, with the author addressing the issue of how the particular subject area relates to the notion of developing a Christian worldview. These are some of the most important distinctives.

In light of the nature of this book, it is appropriate to suggest a number of ways in which it might be used most effectively.

THE AUDIENCE FOR THIS BOOK

This volume is designed to be used by both students and faculty members. Many will use it as a required textbook in a course on developing a Christian worldview. Such courses, especially in Christian liberal arts colleges and universities, are becoming increasingly recognized as fundamental to the purpose and organization of the entire liberal arts curriculum. They constitute either a foundational or a capstone learning experience that encourages students to think of how the liberal arts curriculum, and their area of major and/or minor study within it, work together within a Christian framework to help develop the next generation of Christian thinkers and leaders.

Students using this book in such a context will be pleased to know that it was specifically written with them in mind, for virtually all the essays included were actually presented by their respective authors to similar groups of undergraduate liberal arts students. Stanley Porter remembers when he first delivered his essay to such a group of students and had the opportunity to answer questions raised by the presentation. He found that some of the questions and issues that he considered of vital importance to his subject area were completely new to many, if not most, of the students. Some saw the potential of such subject areas for further thought and consideration, while others clearly did not see such issues as having any importance at all. Some students wished to go into more depth on the subjects raised, while others indicated that they thought

---

3. The term "liberal arts" of course includes a wide variety of subjects in the arts and humanities, social sciences and hard sciences, and not just "arts."

these were arcane matters of little importance to them. These responses helped Porter to re-think and re-formulate his conception of the subject, so that the topics discussed from his specific field were ones that, whether students had heard of them or not, proved to have genuine significance for them within the wider spectrum of Christian liberal arts study.

This volume is not designed for undergraduate students in worldview studies courses alone, however. It is also designed for use by any student at any level of study—whether undergraduate, graduate, or even postgraduate—who wishes to explore issues in worldview studies. As noted above, the essays here address subjects typically taught in the liberal arts curriculum of Christian colleges and universities. Some students may not have a course in worldview studies available to them, or are not attending or did not attend a Christian liberal arts institution that had worldview studies. This book should prove useful to them as well. Because its content is organized around the standard liberal arts curriculum, such students should find ready access to their subject areas in the book. The content essays should push these students to contemplate, perhaps for the first time or in more detail, how these subject areas relate to their own thinking about developing a Christian worldview. The three introductory essays may prove especially important in this regard, as they provide a foundational platform for such worldview studies and the rest of the essays in the book.

Professors will also find this volume of use in a variety of ways. Professors who are new to the field of worldview studies will find a broadly based and sufficiently detailed volume to encourage their own broad and informed study of a Christian worldview. Each essay identifies and then treats an academic area in sufficient detail that those unfamiliar with developing a Christian worldview, and the relation of specific subject areas to one's worldview, will have adequate information to begin to think through such issues. Each essay is followed by helpful bibliography, including works cited in the essay and usually other works for further reading.

We would like to think that readers who do not share our Christian worldview will find the essays in this volume useful as guides to the kind of thinking and approaches to the various subject matters that Christians hold. However, this volume was not specifically written with such accidental enquirers in mind. It was, rather, written for those who hold to a Christian belief system and wish to go further in developing a coherent and cohesive Christian worldview. Professors who teach at Christian colleges and universities may read such a volume, either individually or as part of a group (perhaps as a faculty discussion book during one semester or year), as a means of promoting and encouraging their own worldview studies perspective. Christian professors who teach at secular institutions may also find profit in a book such as this, as it encourages them to think about their own Christian worldview and how it relates to the worldviews of their colleagues. While this volume may not prove suitable as a textbook in such a secular context, it may provide a useful reference tool for the professor who is interested in developing further understanding in this area.

We hope this book will be used by students and professors as they seek to grow in their own knowledge of what constitutes a Christian worldview, especially one that specifically responds to and develops in regard to the major curricular areas of the liberal arts college or university.

THE ORGANIZATION OF THIS BOOK

The organization of this book encourages a wide range and type of uses. The first noticeable organizational principle is that the book is divided into two sections of unequal length. The first section—Prolegomena—includes three essays foundational to the organization of the volume. Each of these tackles one of the essential issues in worldview studies. The first positions the topic within the larger university context; the second historically defines what constitutes a Christian worldview; and the third encourages development of the characteristics of a Christian mind. In many ways, these essays constitute necessary preliminary reading to the subject-specific essays in the second part. However, they might also be read at the conclusion of studying the rest of the volume, as a means of bringing together and unifying what has been read regarding the specific subject areas.

The second part of the book includes twenty-six essays on the individual academic disciplines themselves. When the two parts are combined, the total of twenty-nine essays constitutes sufficient material to form the basis of a number of different configurations of courses. If a course meets once a week for a year, a different essay could be discussed each week. For courses that meet twice a week, one could either complete the entire book in a single academic term of about fifteen weeks, or still meet for the entire year, with the individual essay of the week providing the basis for reading, discussion, and even writing over two meeting sessions. There are, of course, other configurations that could make use of this volume as well.

The academic disciplines treated in this volume are arranged in alphabetical order. This makes it possible for a reader either to read the essays sequentially and thereby to cover the entire curriculum of the liberal arts institution, or easily to find the particular essay in which he or she is interested and read it on its own. Some courses may simply go through the areas in alphabetical order because this, in some ways, mirrors the arrangement of the liberal arts curriculum, where individual subject areas usually each have their own place in the academic curriculum.

Many institutions, however, arrange their curriculum in groups of allied subjects. These groupings often include the arts and/or humanities, the social sciences, the hard sciences, and the like. There is an advantage in reading essays on similar or related curricular areas together, as they share some common methodological assumptions. For those who want to read the essays in terms of their affiliated subject areas, the following chart of groupings might be helpful (the categories are not easily determined, but this is one way of viewing them):[4]

> *Arts and Humanities*: art, biblical studies, English literature, history (if not in social sciences), modern languages, music, philosophy, theater art

> *Social Sciences*: business, communications, cultural anthropology, economics, history (if not in arts and humanities), linguistics, physical education, political science, psychology, sociology, teacher education

> *Sciences*: biology, chemistry, computing science, geography, geology, mathematics, nursing, physics.

Some courses might wish to focus on a particular sub-set of the essays, perhaps organized according to their major curricular affinities. The individual essays within a category can help one to appreciate both what these various areas have in common and what distinguishes them from each other.

---

4. Some institutions might single out business or teacher education as separate areas, while others might single out biblical studies as part of a larger theological curriculum. There are other configurations as well.

A number of common factors uniting these subject areas can provide a useful means of approaching this book. The subjects in the arts and humanities are often text-based disciplines, usually with the common denominator of an interest in humanity, and have a variety of concurrent methods and approaches that are often applied to these subjects. There is often an emphasis on appreciating aesthetics, form, expression, and related areas of interest, as well as use of what is sometimes called qualitative appreciation and analysis. The social sciences subject areas typically focus on the patterns of behavior of human beings either individually or in groups, and usually draw attention to quantitative data for examination and study, gathered through a variety of field-based methods. The results of such study are often expressed in terms of quantitatively measurable distinctions. The so-called hard sciences usually focus on inanimate subject matter that can be subject to data gathering and the experimental method. The varying scientific methods tend to emphasize repeatability, regularity, measurement, and experimental design as scientists attempt to understand and explain their data.

The characterizations above, whatever merits they may have as rough distinctives, are subject to numerous qualifications. For example, does history as a subject area belong in the arts and humanities or in the social sciences? To some extent, this depends on the approach taken to historiography, and whether it is more concerned with texts or people. Nevertheless, there is significant overlap between them. Similarly, there are literary texts analyzed by linguists in ways that are similar to the approaches used by some English literature scholars. What these areas all have in common, at least as illustrated in this volume, is that each subject area—despite its manifest and important individual characteristics—deals with a significant part of the world in which we live, has approaches to these subject matters, and falls within the larger purview of God's creation. Falling within the domain of the Creator means that each subject has a common purpose in helping us to understand and appreciate from a particular viewpoint the larger world that God has created.

THE CONTENT OF THIS BOOK

The most important factor in the use of this book is arguably its content. Whatever configuration and organization is used to teach or use it, its distinctive is its content as a whole, and more particularly of each individual essay.

There are at least four distinctives of the content of the volume that are worth noting.

Authors as Experts

Each of the contributing authors, a recognized authority in his or her field, writes out of research and teaching experience accumulated over a number of years. The organizers of the project chose scholars who had distinguished themselves because of their professional expertise as well as their ability to relate to students at the undergraduate level. As the Preface mentions, when this project began, all of the authors were teaching at Trinity Western University (TWU). Most of the authors still teach at TWU, though a few have left and gone on to other institutions, and some have retired. In every case, these authors have continued to make profitable contributions to their field, and in the writing of these essays they draw on that professional competence accumulated over years of teaching and research.

Common Worldview

One of the distinguishing features of Trinity Western University is that it has retained the Christian principles it was founded upon as it has developed into one of Canada's premier educational institutions and a university of widespread significance. From the start, TWU based its undergraduate programs on a liberal arts curriculum. It was believed from the outset that this curriculum would provide the necessary foundation for developing and promoting a distinctly Christian worldview and the kind of subject competence needed for establishing recognized areas of expertise in major and minor areas of study. The results, both in terms of the graduates produced and the teachers and scholars attracted to the University, attest to the strength of this model.

From the start, TWU was founded upon a strong Christian worldview that informed and directed curricular decisions and development. What started as a modest two-year institution grew to a four-year college and then a university, now with multiple schools and graduate programs. A fundamental Christian worldview still stands at the heart of this development, so when it was thought appropriate to instigate a course in

Christian worldview, it was not difficult to recruit faculty members to be a part of it. They were usually already used to doing their teaching and research from such a perspective. That perspective forms the basis for and thoroughly informs each of the essays in this volume.

Essay Content

Each of the essays is written by an established scholar writing from a Christian worldview standpoint and with reference to two major factors: subject content and integration.

In terms of subject content, each essay attempts to lay out the major perspectives, methods, and issues within each of the disciplines found in most liberal arts institutions. These are different for each discipline, even compared to those closely allied to it, but it is significant that some of the same issues recur in the various essays. Thus, arts and humanities essays often return to issues of how one appreciates the subject matter of the respective disciplines, while essays in the hard sciences often interact with questions concerning theories of the origins of humanity and the universe.

A second factor in each essay is that it attempts to integrate the subject-specific content with larger issues regarding a Christian worldview. As these essays make clear, it is not enough to have a person of Christian faith teaching a subject to guarantee that a distinctly Christian worldview is being promoted and developed. Conscious and intentional integration of the subject area with a Christian perspective is required. That is the benefit of these essays, as they are written by scholars and teachers who have had years of such integrative experience in the classroom and in their own professional work of research and writing. This perspective is then presented in each essay in a way that shows how the subject-specific material functions along with and can be thought of in terms of a Christian worldview.

Differences of Perspective Joined by a Common Theme

A final distinctive of the content of this book is that, with two exceptions, each of the content and subject-specific essays is written by a different scholar. Whereas in some books on Christian worldview a number of subjects are lumped together, or one author writes on all of the topics—and some of these volumes are very good—this book has the virtue of allowing each author to address his or her own area of expertise. It is a strength of this volume that, as a result, there are noticeable differences of perspective to be found in it. All the authors are scholars with their own opinions and experiences to draw on in discussing a Christian approach to their subjects. If we had asked other members of the same departments to write on the same topics, the results would perhaps have been different. Nevertheless, what joins all the authors together is the common theme and purpose of writing about how their subject matter plays a significant role in worldview studies, and how a Christian worldview can inform that particular discipline—in fact, not just how a Christian worldview can inform that discipline, but how it has and continues to inform the Christian worldview of the individual author as a scholar and teacher. It is this common integrative theme that is able to join each essay to the larger topic of developing a Christian worldview, thereby providing a rationale for bringing them together into a common volume.

CONCLUSION

There are many potential uses for a book like this. It can be used by students and faculty members at almost any place in their academic career and development. A book such as this can be organized and re-organized in a variety of ways to make access to the material more conducive to a variety of course configurations. Its content draws on the best available Christian scholarship, united by a common emphasis on the development of a unifying and integrative Christian worldview.

This book does not pretend to be the final word in Christian worldview studies. However, it has many features that certainly represent significant advances in the treatment of the subject matter, and a number of features that the editors and authors believe will prove useful as discussion of worldview studies continues to grow and develop. This book is put forward as an important and serious contribution in the exploration of such a valuable topic. One of the distinctives, or at least potential distinctives, of the Christian liberal arts curriculum is its ability to integrate faith and learning within the purview of a Christian perspective. This volume is designed as a major voice to aid and encourage the development of such a fully integrative Christian worldview.

WORKS CITED

Claerbaut, David. *Faith and Learning on the Edge: A Bold New Look at Religion in Higher Education*. Grand Rapids, MI: Zondervan, 2004.

Dockery, David S., and Gregory Alan Thornbury, eds. *Shaping a Christian Worldview: The Foundations of Christian Higher Education*. Nashville: Broadman & Holman, 2002.

Heie, Harold, and David L. Wolfe, eds. *The Reality of Christian Learning: Strategies for Faith-Discipline Integration*. Grand Rapids, MI: Eerdmans/Christian College Consortium, 1987.

Henry, Douglas V., and Michael D. Beaty, eds. *Christianity and the Soul of the University: Faith as a Foundation for Intellectual Community*. Grand Rapids, MI: Baker Academic, 2006.

Holmes, Arthur F. *Contours of a World View*. Studies in a Christian World View Series 1. Grand Rapids, MI: Eerdmans, 1983.

———. *The Idea of a Christian College*. Rev. ed. Grand Rapids, MI: Eerdmans, 1987.

Poe, Harry L. *Christianity in the Academy: Teaching at the Intersection of Faith and Learning*. Grand Rapids, MI: Baker Academic, 2004.

PART ONE

Prolegomena

1

The Christian University in Contemporary Culture

The Distinctive and the Challenge

DOUGLAS H. SHANTZ

T HE CHRISTIAN COLLEGE OR university has a two-fold identity. On the one hand there is the historical distinctive: it is part of a great tradition of Christian scholarship that has explored truth wherever it may be found, confident that it is all God's truth. On the other hand there is the contemporary challenge: it is called to confront the pressing questions and challenges of our day from the perspective of Christ and the Christian tradition.

My aim in this chapter is to offer an historical perspective on how the Christian university has been understood in the past, and then to consider what its place should be in the world of the twenty-first century. I will highlight two scholars who devoted their lives to the Christian university, Thomas Aquinas and John Henry Newman, and two more recent scholars, Jaroslav Pelikan and Charles Malik, who have much to teach us about the challenge facing Christian higher education today.

THE HISTORICAL DISTINCTIVE OF THE CHRISTIAN UNIVERSITY

Thomas Aquinas, 1225–1274

Living in the thirteenth century, Thomas Aquinas was part of the first beginnings of the Christian university as it took shape in the high Middle Ages. The term *universitas* first appeared in a papal document in AD 1208–1209. It referred to the total body of teachers and students, a kind of academic union or guild. It also connoted the totality of the sciences (*universitas litterarum*) in four faculties: arts (philosophy), law, medicine, and theology. The university in Thomas's day had three characteristics. First, it was independent of church control, yet felt obligated to act responsibly in serving the church. Second, the medieval university sought to serve the whole Christian world. It welcomed students from all over Europe, offering an education that prepared students for life in that world. Finally, the universities in Thomas's day "stood in the current of urban life." They were not sheltered from the real world but prepared students to make their mark in church and society.[1]

From Thomas Aquinas we learn something of the character of the Christian university as well as the calling of the Christian university professor and student. Thomas characterized the university as a place where students consider the great questions of life in a way that takes both God's Word and God's world seriously. Thomas advocated a "Christian worldliness" that avoids two pitfalls: an unworldly spirituality and a secularistic worldliness.[2] Thomas opposed both a supra-naturalistic Biblicism that ignored the creation and an exclusive reliance on Aristotle that ignored the Bible. To Christian traditionalists, Thomas insisted that "the autonomy and effectiveness of created things prove the truly creative powers of God." The world was a legitimate sphere for human study and learning.[3] To extremist Aristotelians, he said, "You are right; the natural world is a reality in its own right, but there would be no such independent reality if the Creator did not exist."[4] In Thomas, we observe a speculative mindset that prompted him to investigate truth in all areas of life, to be open to truth wherever and whatever it might be. He sought an equal marriage of his faith with his reason. Aquinas's Christian worldliness provides a wonderful model for Christian universities today. They too should demonstrate an intellectual curiosity that takes both God's Word and God's world seriously.

From Thomas, we also learn something of the calling of Christian university professors and students. Thomas considered teaching his first vocation: "I feel that I owe it to God to make this the foremost duty of my life: that all my thought and speech proclaim Him." It could be said

1. Pieper, *Guide to Thomas Aquinas*, 59–62.

2. Ibid., 129–30.

3. Ibid., 122.

4. Ibid., 130.

of Thomas that "he was one of those who teach as they grow and grow as they teach."[5] For him, teaching involved two relationships and activities: his relationship to the truth in silently listening to reality; and his relationship with his pupils in clarifying, presenting, and communicating that truth.[6]

The *Summa Theologica* illustrates Thomas's understanding of the teaching task. He devoted his best energies not to a work of scholarship for fellow professors but to a textbook for beginners. His *Summa* was essentially that: *ad eruditionem incipientium* ("for instruction of beginners"). For Thomas, the teacher should possess the art of approaching his subject as if he were encountering the material for the first time. Successful teaching requires "loving identification with the beginner." "He sees reality just as the beginner can see it, with all the innocence of the first encounter, and yet at the same time with the matured powers of comprehension and penetration that the cultivated mind possesses." Thomas knew that the greatest challenge in teaching is to keep the material fresh and alive, to avoid the disinterest that often comes to teachers because of over-familiarity and constant repetition. As with Plato, for Thomas learning and teaching begin with "amazement" and questioning. He sought to lead the learner to recognize the *mirandum*, the wonderment, the novelty of the subject under discussion. In this way the teacher "puts the learner on the road to genuine questioning . . . [that] inspires all true learning."[7] Christian professors today must likewise make it a priority to keep their teaching current and fresh: to read, write, and stay abreast of the latest research in their fields and to keep alive the wonder of discovery.

Thomas Aquinas also presents a challenge to today's busy students. Thomas was no cloistered medieval monk; he was a member of the Dominican order of mendicants, a "youth movement" in the cities that challenged a church that was too comfortable with worldly wealth and power. The order was dedicated to imitating Christ's poverty, to preaching, and to study of the Bible, science, and philosophy.[8] In the midst of his busy urban life Thomas learned how to find inner seclusion, how to "construct a cell for contemplation within the self to be carried about

---

5. Ibid., 92–93.
6. Ibid., 94.
7. Ibid., 96.
8. Ibid., 23–29.

through the hurly-burly of the *vita activa* [active life] of teaching and of intellectual disputation."⁹ Thomas's academic achievements and writing were completed in the midst of constant distractions. When he arrived in Paris in AD 1252 to teach theology, he faced considerable opposition simply because he was a Dominican. Many Paris scholars thought that the mendicant orders were becoming too influential at the university. The Pope himself finally intervened to lift the boycott against him. Yet in his works during this period, "the smooth flow of not a single sentence appears to have been ruffled by all these troubles."¹⁰

Throughout his life, Thomas experienced constant interruptions to his chosen intellectual task of presenting "the whole of the Christian view of the universe." These interruptions included the following: (1) He was sent from Paris to Italy by the Dominican Order on commissions related to the organization of studies; (2) Pope Urban IV called him to his court in Orvieto for three years to work on defining the theological basis for union between the Eastern and Western branches of Christianity; (3) for two years Thomas served as head of the Dominican academy at Santa Sabina in Rome; (4) he was then recalled to the University of Paris, spending the next three years in theological debates between conservative and radical thinkers; (5) in 1272 the superiors of his order recalled him from Paris to found an academy in Naples; (6) after just a year in Naples, Thomas received another papal assignment asking him to participate in the General Council in Lyons, which began its sessions in the spring of 1274. On the way to Lyons, he fell ill and died on March 7, 1274, not yet fifty years of age.¹¹

What Thomas wrote in the midst of all of this, especially in the last three years in Paris, "seems almost beyond belief": commentaries on virtually all the works of Aristotle; commentaries on the Book of Job, on the Gospel of John, and on the Epistles of Paul; commentaries on the great disputed questions of the day such as the problem of evil and the virtues; and the second part of the *Summa Theologica*. All of this was accomplished in the midst of constant distractions.¹²

9. Ibid., 13, 97.

10. Ibid., 13, 64.

11. Ibid., 12–16.

12. Ibid., 97–98.

In more recent times, the prolific C. S. Lewis (an admirer of Thomas) kept house for Mrs. Moore, the retired mother of an army buddy who was lost in the war. Lewis wrote the *Narnia Chronicles* and many academic works in the midst of her demands and the daily tasks of cleaning and doing dishes.[13] The ivory tower does not exist—except in the space we make for it in our busy lives.

There is a lesson here for today's university students with the distractions they face and the many competing demands on their time. Thomas presents the challenge to somehow clear a space for study in the midst of a busy life, to faithfully nurture one's God-given intellect. If this is not a top priority, it simply will not happen.

John Henry Newman, 1801–1890

John Henry Newman wrote what has come to be a classic book on Christian university education, *The Idea of a University*. The first half of Newman's book consists of nine discourses he delivered in 1852 to the Catholics of Dublin to convince them of the importance of *Catholic* university education and the need to build a Catholic university in Ireland. Newman went on to successfully launch the new University of Ireland, in Dublin. The second half of *The Idea*, published in 1859 as "Lectures and Essays," is comprised of talks and articles that Newman produced while Rector at that Catholic university.

Ian Ker, the premier interpreter of Newman in our day, observes that Newman's *The Idea of a University* contains three themes that are at least as significant today as in his time. Ker suggests that we can learn from Newman something about the practical outworking of the Christian university in terms of its goal, its intellectual community, and its curriculum.[14]

In *The Idea of a University*, Newman wrote that the goal of university education is to produce thinking people. It is not the liberal arts themselves that make an educated person; it is the discipline and "mental cultivation" that result from the study of the liberal arts that constitute a liberal education. Newman observed that in everyday life and conversation most people are "illogical, inconsistent, 'never seeing the point,' hopelessly

---

13. Carpenter, *The Inklings*, 13, 166.
14. Ker, *The Achievement of John Henry Newman*, 33–34.

obstinate and prejudiced."[15] A proper education must nurture "the force, the steadiness, the comprehensiveness and the versatility of intellect, the command over our own powers, the just estimate of things as they pass before us."[16] He continued:

> When the intellect has been properly trained it will display its powers . . . in the good sense, sobriety of thought, reasonableness, candour, self-command, and steadiness of view which characterize it. In all it will be a faculty of entering with comparative ease into any subject of thought, and of taking up with aptitude any science or profession.[17]

Newman's emphasis fell on training the mind to be accurate, consistent, logical, and orderly. This training also promotes clear-sightedness, imagination, and wisdom. Newman did not equate a liberal education merely with breadth; breadth alone was no guarantee of a trained mind.

Newman illustrated his point by imagining a choice between two extremes: a university that had no residences but gave degrees to any person who passed an examination in a wide range of subjects, or a university that had no professors or examinations at all but brought young people together for three or four years in a residential setting. Newman chose the latter because the residence offered a place where a genuine and spontaneous learning environment might exist. When bright and eager students come together, they are sure to argue and discuss among themselves. The result will be that "they are sure to learn one from another, even if there be no one to teach them."[18]

Newman's educational goals have lost none of their relevance for today. Ker observes that the ability to think clearly and without prejudice is, if anything, even more essential in our day. The proliferation and specialization of knowledge, as well as the media's powers of persuasion and manipulation, demand that Christian people be capable of clear thinking and articulate criticism of ideas.[19] The Christian university can provide the setting for honing these skills.

---

15. Ibid., 5–6.

16. Newman, *The Idea of a University*, xv–xvi.

17. Ibid., xvii–xviii.

18. Ibid., 146.

19. Ker, *The Achievement of John Henry Newman*, 33.

For Newman, the Christian university was essentially an intellectual community, an association of individual minds personally interacting. Newman described the mutual duties and obligations of students and professors within this community. The duty of students was to meet their professors half-way, to engage with the material and make it their own. "A [person] may hear a thousand lectures and read a thousand volumes and be at the end of the process very much where [he or she] was as regards knowledge. It must not be passively received, but actually and actively entered into, embraced, mastered."[20] Newman argued that "the whole mind needs to be educated through active participation in a community of intellectual formation, not just the memory through passive attendance at lectures."[21] He challenged students: "Do not hang like a dead weight upon your teacher, but catch some of his life; handle what is given to you, not as a formula, but as a pattern to copy and as a capital to improve; throw your heart and mind into what you are about."[22]

The teacher too has a responsibility to make sure that teaching is not merely lecturing but a conversation or dialogue between teacher and student. Newman compared university instruction to the church's catechism, which proceeds by questions and answers. The professor "tells you a thing, and he asks you to repeat it after him. He questions you, he examines you, he will not let you go till he has a proof, not only that you have heard, but that you know."[23]

A third theme that we find in Newman's *The Idea of a University* is his conviction that the curriculum should include all the various branches of knowledge, with each holding its proper place. Newman referred to the fullness, wholeness, and unity of knowledge. This conviction has two implications. First, while a university may not in fact teach all the branches of knowledge, he believed that it must in theory be open to doing so. A university "by its very name professes to teach universal knowledge."[24] Second, Newman warned that one branch of knowledge must not intrude into the others. He opposed academics who become "bigots and quacks, scorning all principles and facts that do not belong to their own pursuit,"

---

20. Newman, *The Idea of a University*, 489.

21. Ker, *The Achievement of John Henry Newman*, 33.

22. Ibid., 21.

23. Newman, *The Idea of a University*, 489.

24. Ibid., 20.

who regard their own specialty as the key to all knowledge. He insisted that the various sciences should only speak out of their own particular perspective on reality. Each field of knowledge should recognize its need for the others. "As the sciences are but aspects of things, they are severally incomplete in their relation to the things themselves, though complete in their own idea and for their own respective purposes."[25]

This idea of the fullness and unity of knowledge is perhaps the most difficult theme for today's universities to understand, accept, and put into practice. With the exponential growth of research knowledge and the fragmentation of academic fields into ever smaller units, a person's ability to regain a sense of the whole, of what constitutes a properly educated person, becomes ever more difficult. This sense of the fullness, wholeness, and unity of knowledge remains elusive in our day.

THE CONTEMPORARY CHALLENGE FACING
THE CHRISTIAN UNIVERSITY

Besides acknowledging these historical traditions and distinctives, Christian higher education in the twenty-first century must also address the challenges and questions of contemporary society. In his 1980 speech at the opening of the Billy Graham Center at Wheaton College, Charles Malik argued that Christians face two tasks: saving the soul and saving the mind.[26] The Christian university has a mandate that is second in importance only to Christ's great commission to preach the gospel: the challenge to bring the mind of Christ to bear on the issues of our day, to confront our world from the perspective of the Christian tradition and revelation.

There is a practical aspect to this challenge. According to Malik, seven institutions constitute "the substance of Western civilization": the family, the church, the state, the economic enterprise, the professions, the media, and the university. He argued that the university "dominates more than any other institution" because its influence is pervasive in all the others. He asked rhetorically, "Where in the texture of modern civilization

25. Ker, *The Achievement of John Henry Newman*, 25; Newman, *The Idea of a University*, 137–38.

26. Malik, *The Two Tasks*, 34.

is the university absent?"[27] Saving the university is critical to saving the Christian mind.

Malik showed that Western universities have a twofold foundation: Greek curiosity, with its insatiable quest for universal knowledge, and Jesus Christ. "The universities which set a pattern for all other universities were all founded on Jesus Christ." Malik lamented that today most universities have lost their Christian foundation. He considered it a pressing task to launch a Christian critique of the university, calling the universities back to their foundations. At stake, he believed, are the mind, spirit, and character of our children, "the entire fabric of Western civilization," and the fate of the world.[28]

Malik's call for universities to acknowledge their twofold foundation, and to bring the mind of Christ to bear on the issues of our day, is a daring one. Such a university and such an education are like a garden whose fruits have great potential for nurturing intellectual and spiritual health but an equal potential for nurturing pride and unbelief. Exposure to the ideas and issues that belong to the university educational experience can lead students away from childhood faith and towards a secular outlook on life. But as Jaroslav Pelikan observes, a university education can also lead reflective students to engage with western traditions of faith and reason in new and positive ways. Some students, "having come to observe and criticize, remain to pray."[29]

CONCLUSION

Christian colleges and universities have a two-fold identity, a historical distinctive and a contemporary challenge. Christian colleges and universities in North America would do well to remember that they have a great heritage exemplified in Thomas Aquinas, the medieval universities, and John Henry Newman. These models have much to teach about the cooperative use of faith and reason, the disciplined pursuit of knowledge, the clarity of mind, and fullness of knowledge that mark a true education and community of learning. Only then are Christian universities prepared to confront the issues of our day on the twofold foundation of the gospel of Christ and Greek curiosity and openness to new truths.

27. Malik, *A Christian Critique of the University*, 15, 19–21.
28. Ibid., 20; Malik, *The Two Tasks*, 30–33.
29. Pelikan, *The Idea of the University: A Reexamination*, 40.

WORKS CITED

Carpenter, Humphrey. *The Inklings: C. S. Lewis, J. R. R. Tolkien, Charles Williams, and their Friends*. London: Unwin, 1981.

Ker, Ian. *The Achievement of John Henry Newman*. Notre Dame, IN: University of Notre Dame Press, 1990.

Malik, Charles Habib. *A Christian Critique of the University*. Downers Grove, IL: InterVarsity Press, 1982.

———. *The Two Tasks*. Westchester: Cornerstone Books, 1980.

Newman, John Henry. *The Idea of a University*. London: Longmans, Green, 1925.

Pelikan, Jaroslav. *The Idea of the University: A Reexamination*. New Haven: Yale University Press, 1992.

Pieper, Josef. *Guide to Thomas Aquinas*. Translated by Richard and Clara Winston. San Francisco: Ignatius, 1991 (1962).

FOR FURTHER READING

Colish, Marcia L. *Medieval Foundations of the Western Intellectual Tradition 400–1400*. New Haven: Yale University Press, 1997.

Erb, Peter C. *Newman and the Idea of a Catholic University*. Atlanta: Aquinas Center of Theology, 1997.

Henry, Douglas V., and Michael D. Beaty, eds. *Christianity and the Soul of the University: Faith as a Foundation for Intellectual Community*. Grand Rapids, MI: Baker Academic, 2006. (See especially David Lyle Jeffrey, "Faith, Fortitude, and the Future of Christian Intellectual Community," 85–99.)

Leclercq, Jean. *The Love of Learning and the Desire for God: A Study of Monastic Culture*. New York: Fordham University Press, 1974.

Noll, Mark. *The Scandal of the Evangelical Mind*. Grand Rapids, MI: Eerdmans, 1994.

Pegis, Anton C., ed. *Introduction to Saint Thomas Aquinas*. New York: Modern Library, 1948.

Polkinghorne, John. *Faith, Science and Understanding*. New Haven: Yale University Press, 2000.

Shantz, Douglas H., and Tinu Ruparell, eds. *Christian Thought in the Twenty-first Century: Agenda for the Future* (forthcoming).

2

What Is a Christian Worldview[1]?

BILL STROM

INTRODUCTION

BEFORE ASKING "WHAT IS a Christian Worldview?" it is important to ask "What is a worldview?" It is also important to ask "Where do we acquire our worldview?" and "How do worldviews function in everyday life?" If we answer these three preliminary questions, we will be in a better position to ask what a Christian worldview is, how it functions, and how it works in daily experience.

WHAT IS A WORLDVIEW?

Definitions

Anthropologist Michael Kearney sees this concept as an outlook shared with others when he asserts, "The world view of a people is their way of looking at reality. It consists of basic assumptions and images that provide a more or less sensible, though not necessarily accurate, way of thinking about the world."[2] More recently, Regent University philosophy professor

---

1. In worldview literature, this term is rendered as either one word or two. In this book we have chosen the former, save where authors referred to employ the two word form in either direct quotations or titles (e.g., as in the next footnote).

2. Kearney, *World View*, 41. Sire echoes—and indeed broadens—the somewhat equivocal proviso in Kearney's definition when he describes a worldview as "a commitment, a fundamental orientation of the heart, that can be expressed as a story or in a set of presuppositions (assumptions that may be true, partially true or entirely false) which we hold (consciously or subconsciously, consistently or inconsistently) about the basic constitution of reality, and that provides the foundation on which we live and move and have our being" (*Naming the Elephant*, 122). Earlier in his discussion, Sire asserts that

Michael Palmer defines worldview as "a set of beliefs and practices that shape a person's approach to the most important issues of life, [helping one to] determine priorities, explain [one's] relationship to God [or other supreme being, presumably] and fellow human beings, assess the meaning of events, and justify [one's] actions."[3]

James Olthuis provides a more nuanced but down-to-earth definition of worldview in David Naugle's important book, *Worldview: The History of a Concept*:[4]

> A worldview (or vision of life) is a framework or set of fundamental beliefs through which we view the world and our calling and future in it. This vision need not be fully articulated: it may be so internalized that it goes largely unquestioned; it may not be theoretically deepened into a philosophy; it may not even be codified into a creedal form; it may be greatly refined through cultural-historical development. Nevertheless, this vision is a channel for the ultimate beliefs which give direction and meaning to life. It is the integrative and interpretive framework by which order and disorder are judged; it is the standard by which reality is managed and pursued; it is the set of hinges on which all our everyday thinking and doing turns.[5]

Therefore, put in a summary way, a worldview is the set of assumptions we hold about the nature of life, the purpose of life, and the relation of people to the cosmos. While Olthuis points out that these assumptions often go unarticulated, that has not stopped people from making attempts to describe worldviews through philosophy, creeds, and cultural-historical

---

most exponents would see worldviews as "beliefs . . . (1) rooted in pre-theoretical and presuppositional concepts that are the foundation for all one's thought and action, (2) comprehensive in scope, (3) ideally though not necessarily logically coherent, (4) related in some positive way to reality . . . [and] (5) though not necessarily irrational, nonetheless fundamentally a matter of commitment that is not finally provable by reason" (36).

3. Palmer, *Elements of a Christian Worldview*, 24.

4. The importance of Naugle's book is conveyed by the following statement of his objective in the "Preface": "no work in English has been written that amasses a substantial portion of the literature on worldview from the various disciplines—theology, philosophy, religion, the natural sciences, the social sciences, etc.—and reflects upon it in a comprehensive, systematic way. . . . This book is designed, therefore, to reverse this present situation through an extensive, interdisciplinary study of the worldview concept" (*Worldview: The History of a Concept*, xviii).

5. Olthuis, "On Worldviews," cited in Naugle, *Worldview: The History of a Concept*, 349.

analysis. This book is an attempt in that direction, but not with the goal to produce *the* Christian worldview or *the* Christian perspective, but to bear testimony to the diverse ways believers who are scholars have engaged *a* worldview or *a* perspective of our faith to make sense of their academic disciplines. This chapter bears a similar testimony, as I attempt to describe a Christian worldview broadly shared in Christendom, but it is not the "final chapter."

An Example from Anthropology

Before we jump into this task, however, I want to provide an example that briefly contrasts western and eastern cultural ways of thinking so you can appreciate the value of articulating one's worldview. By "western" I mean the dominant way western civilizations have thought about life from the ancient Greeks to modern-day North Americans. By "eastern" I mean the way oriental civilizations have thought about life in China, India, and many countries in the African continent. Keep in mind, however, that these are general observations and may not apply to each individual you may know from these places, particularly as globalization, easy travel, and international media continue to blur cultural distinctions.

Among several contrasting values is the tendency for westerners to be individual-centered, while easterners tend to be group-centered. Westerners put high priority on the *me, mine,* and *I*; easterners on the *we, us,* and *our.* People in the west value self-actualization (a psychological term), inalienable rights of the individual (a political term), and free choice of the individual (a philosophical idea about human nature). Easterners believe in group-actualization, rights of the group, and group choice.

For example, consider Leo Chan, an undergraduate friend of mine from Hong Kong studying in the United States. When I asked him what he had planned after graduation he answered that he was going home to work in his father's electronics company and live with his aging uncle. Leo could have taken his degree and found employment almost anywhere in the U.S. or with many other companies in Hong Kong. He could have chosen to live in his own apartment, separate from his uncle. But so strong was his sense of family, the only reasonable thing was to work and live with relatives. Most North Americans who move back in with relatives after graduation would be regarded as immature cling-ons. Westerners typically act out behavior that gives them independence as individuals; Easterners behave to show interdependence in a group. Thus people who ascribe to western individualism might assert, "I am an autonomous individual here on earth to gain personal potential before I die and return to dust." People who ascribe to eastern collectivism might respond, "I am a self-in-community working toward group goals with the ultimate purpose of higher reincarnation."

Individualism in the west and group-centeredness in the east is but one example of contrasting values between these complex worldviews. Here are six other common distinctions:[6]

Western Mindset	Eastern Mindset
Tasks come before people	People come before tasks
People are basically good	People are basically evil
Faith should not interfere with public life	Sacred and public life are intertwined
People should rule over the earth	People should revere the earth
Life/time is linear	Life/time is cyclical
People control their destinies	Fate or God controls people's destinies

As you interact with these lists you might resonate with some yet not with others, and that's good. Few people are pure and pristine prototypes of their home-culture worldview. Rather, we piece together our worldviews through various social filters—other people who also are not cookie cutter clones of their culture's prevailing worldview. Let me describe a few.

WHERE DO WE ACQUIRE OUR WORLDVIEWS?

Where do we get these ideas that make up our worldview? Most obviously, we get them from people around us. Feral children, those raised by animals or deprived of normal human socialization, rarely learn to speak, much less handle the abstract thinking language affords. Arnold Gesell, the noted Yale University child specialist, has commented how "mentally naked" we are at birth and dependent on others to shape our personhood. While we eventually develop the capacity to think our own thoughts and to think about our thinking, we still begin that journey on a road map

6. For a well-received analysis of cultural values, see Hofstede's *Culture's Consequences*.

printed and distributed by four primary sources: first, from our parents or whoever raises us; second, from our peers with whom we socialize; third, from authority figures who are not our parents; and fourth, from distant personalities we encounter through media such as television, movies, books, and the Internet. Consider these examples:

Parental Influence on the Child

Parents are the strongest and most determining influence on us as children. Their beliefs and worldview largely become our beliefs and worldview. How they treat us even as infants reflects worldview and the values they hold.[7] Consider how in western families children are typically weaned from their mothers onto a bottle before they are one year old. At bedtime, one-year-old children are typically placed in their own room, in a personal crib, and allowed to cry a little before falling asleep. In Japan, a child is typically weaned from his/her mother later than age one. The child often sleeps in the parents' bedroom, between the parents in their bed, and cooed to sleep by an ever-present mother. The western family is already nurturing life-on-one's-own and the Japanese family is nurturing what they call "sweet dependency."

Peers

We have all heard of peer pressure. It is the expectation to think and behave like others of our age and status. Especially as adolescents, we are acutely aware of what is acceptable and what is not. Our peers might dress emo, skater, or gangster. My peer group indirectly pressures me to wear a tie on a day when I would rather wear jeans and a sweater. Peer pressure cues you to dress up in formal attire for your college's Christmas banquet! Peers influence not only our fashion choices but also deeper assumptions and values.

Other Adult Authorities

I believe that I would not be a communications professor at a Christian liberal arts university today if it were not for Byron Emmert, a Youth for Christ director, and Em Griffin, a professor at Wheaton College. One convinced me to study communication; the other inspired me to be a

---

7. See, for example, Kraehmer, *Heroes: Shaping Lives through Family and Culture.*

professor of communication. Of note, however, is that my parents instilled my foundational worldview before Byron or Em got hold of me. The two assumptions that these men affirmed in my life were that God had a larger purpose for me in his Kingdom, and that I am most free when I exercise the gifts and talents God gives me. In particular, these men helped me find a way to live out my worldview in an area of interest and occupation. Adult authorities usually *strengthen* assumptions and values already laid down by our parents.

The Media

One day when my eldest son was four and a half years old, he asked my wife if he could watch a video he got for Christmas—*Snow White*. My wife explained that she was concerned about the evil queen in the story and how Taylor might respond to her. Taylor replied, "Don't worry, Mom. She just represents evil. I won't be afraid." If you think he figured this out by himself, don't be too impressed. Two days earlier as Taylor and I looked at the video package, I explained how people in movies usually symbolize one of two major forces: good and evil. My point is this: if you develop a Christian worldview for your child, he or she will be able to use it to critically analyze and evaluate media fare. But if you fail to instill a particular worldview into your children, they will largely default to the media's depiction of secular liberal democracy, which tends to marginalize God from public discourse, glorifies individual achievement and political processes, and puts faith in technology and funding to solve life's problems. When parents fail to parent, media programmers and corporations gladly fill the gap.[8]

While parents, friends, authorities, and the media shape our worldview, this is not to say that we soak up their offerings like passive sponges and follow in lock-step order. Proof of this is in the simple observation that people leave their faith, join a new one, sometimes change their major or political party, and take up new causes with fresh conviction throughout their lifespan. But the bigger point just made still holds: any new vision of the world comes from some source, and those sources are usually the people around us.

---

8. An excellent book on this subject, *Children and Television* (edited by Manley-Casimir and Luke) is worth looking into.

HOW DO WORLDVIEWS FUNCTION IN EVERYDAY LIFE?

One more helpful task, before we describe a Christian worldview, is to note ways a worldview helps us perceive the world around us in everyday life. These benefits, suggested by missiologist Charles Kraft of Fuller Theological Seminary,[9] are true of any worldview, not just a Christian worldview, but I will make several Christian applications.

First, our worldview helps *explain* why the world is like it is. It explains how things got to be as they did and why they continue that way. For example, how did the world get here? The theist says, "God did it by design"; the atheist says, "Natural forces did it by chance." Neither can prove it, but both believe their foundational statement based on the faith assumptions of their worldview.

Second, our worldview also helps us *evaluate* things as good or bad. For example, is British Columbia's Coquihalla Highway good? The average Canadian would say, "Yes, because it gets me to Kamloops more quickly; I value time." The average First Nations Canadian would say, "No, because it disrupts the mountains and rivers we believe hold the spirits of our ancestors." As Olthuis noted earlier, a worldview "is the integrative and interpretive framework by which order and disorder are judged."[10]

Third, our worldview gives us *mental and emotional peace* in times of personal crisis. For example, how do people account for near-fatal accidents, such as flipping one's car? The Christian often says, "It was God's will, or his protection, or his angels, or something of him." The naturalist says, "I just have to thank my lucky stars; I can't explain it except to say I'm glad to be alive." For the Christian, God explains the crisis and gives relative peace. For the naturalist, luck or chance explains it and similarly gives relative peace.

Fourth, our worldview also helps us *integrate* things that seem inconsistent. For example, how can one believe that God is good and yet admit that there is evil in the world? A believer might respond that we know God is good from what the Scriptures tell us and from the blessings we receive from him daily. The Scriptures also tell us that evil is a result of our disobedience to his moral law. Just because God is good does not mean he forces us to be good. God still gives us the freedom to exercise free will, and, unfortunately, we often choose evil. With this reasoning

9. In Kraft, "Worldview in Intercultural Communication."

10. See Naugle, *Worldview: The History of a Concept*, 349.

God's goodness and the existence of evil in the world may be integrated within a Christian worldview.

Finally, our worldview helps us *adapt* to change. For example, consider your transition from home to university. Some of you have left the comfortable home of your parents in cities where your high school friends live to travel hundreds of miles to a university campus with its own subculture of crazy schedules, cafeteria food, and new friends. (Did you know that a number of your first-year colleagues did not return this spring? They did not adapt, but you did.) Why? Perhaps it is because in your Christian worldview you hold to Christ's claim that he will never leave you or forsake you; the knowledge that Christians are called to love and help those around them—especially fellow brothers and sisters; and the belief that God has called you to this school. All of these are beliefs which encourage you to hang in there while you make adaptations on the surface to a busy schedule, new food, and new friends. Your worldview has helped you to adapt.

WHAT IS A CHRISTIAN WORLDVIEW?

Now that we have defined worldviews generally, explained how they function in everyday life, and given some cultural examples, let us turn to a Christian worldview. We can define a Christian worldview as the beliefs, values, behaviors, and assumptions we as biblically informed Christians hold that guide our perceptions about who we are, what the world is like, and why we are even here in the first place.

In order to piece together my own version of this Christian vision, I use two methods. The first is to rely on three traditional documents that Christians have respected since the fourth century after Christ, attempting to pull from them several worldview elements. Later I use a more theoretical approach that asks four key questions for discerning any worldview, and I attempt to answer them Christianly.

A Traditional Perspective

From the time of Saint Augustine (around AD 300) to today, most believers—no matter what their stripe—will affirm (a) the Apostles' Creed, (b) the Ten Commandments, and (c) the Lord's Prayer. The first reflects what we believe, the second instructs us how to live,[11] and the third suggests

---

11. Palmer, *Elements of a Christian Worldview*, 49, describes this as the "norms" element in a Christian worldview. For him, a Christian worldview is not merely an

how Jesus saw his life mission, as well as our own.[12] I have chosen these statements, and not others, because they are (1) historically well-accepted throughout Christendom, (2) diverse in scope, (3) scriptural and theological, and (4) richly pixilated and ripe for analysis. Taken together, I believe these statements represent a dynamic, guiding vision for believers under God's lordship as they seek his will, engage their culture, and strive to bring people and his creation into closer covenantal communion with him. These statements do not represent mere ideas on paper to memorize for an exam, but a vision of life that results in both personal and cultural transformation.

The Apostles' Creed

The Apostles' Creed reads as follows:

> I believe in God the Father Almighty, Maker of Heaven and Earth, and Jesus Christ, God's only Son, Our Lord, conceived by the Holy Spirit, born of the Virgin Mary, suffered under Pontius Pilate, was crucified, dead, and buried. He descended into Hell; the third day he rose again from the dead; he ascended into heaven. He sits at the right hand of God the Father Almighty; from thence he shall come to judge the quick [i.e., living] and the dead. I believe in the Holy Spirit, the holy catholic [i.e., universal] church, the communion of the saints, the forgiveness of sins, the resurrection of the body, [and] the life everlasting.

This creed signals worldview as it represents a theology that assumes God's existence, Christ's incarnation, humanity's sinfulness, and heaven's

---

intellectual construct; rather, a person's worldview will govern one's behavior and essentially determine the elements in a person's character. Pearcey, in a chapter entitled "True Spirituality and Christian Worldview," in her book *Total Truth*, 361, underlines the practical implications of professing to have a Christian worldview: "having a Christian worldview is not just about answering intellectual questions. It also means following biblical principles in the personal and practical spheres of life. Christians," she warns, "can be infected by secular worldviews not only in their *beliefs* but also in their *practices*" [emphasis hers].

12. Palmer, *Elements of a Christian Worldview*, 75, makes the interesting observation that one's Christian worldview should be dynamic—i.e., it should be a growing and changing phenomenon, not a static credo of some kind. Sire makes a similar point when he says that a person's worldview will frequently change over time (*Naming the Elephant*, 93). The prayer model that Jesus taught his disciples on this occasion (see below) clearly indicates that prayer is to be a daily experience for his followers ("Give us *today* our *daily* bread [emphasis mine]").

hope. The creed also captures the story of God's engagement with us and the cosmos—a story of creation, fall (sin), and redemption. This big theme of good-over-evil plays out in everyday life as we work to reconcile with friends following conflict, or when we nurture justice and peace at work through redemptive business policies. This big theme of God redeeming us and the world through Jesus Christ also gives us an interpretive lens for understanding popular media, such as when we see a movie character bringing hope or salvation to an impossible situation.[13] Other worldviews, for example Marxism, assume no God, deny the possibility of incarnation (a spirit coming in the flesh), presume evil is the abuse of power, and ignore the likelihood of heaven.

The Ten Commandments

Palmer describes the Ten Commandments, given to Moses by God on Mount Sinai during the journey of the Israelites from Egypt to the Promised Land, as "the heart of Christian ethics." He continues, "Far more than a simple set of legal proscriptions, the Decalogue is a covenant . . . structured in the covenantal language of the ancient Near East . . . [that] calls for a response of disciplined love and gratitude to the Lord, not a tedious legalistic system."[14] He notes that the first four commandments have to do with a person's vertical relation to God, while the last six focus on one's horizontal relationships with others. Here are the commandments in paraphrased form:

1. You shall have no other gods before me.

2. You shall not make idols or worship any such idol.

13. Palmer speaks about the role of narrative in any well-developed worldview (*Elements of a Christian Worldview*, 28). It occurs to me that one way of looking at the Apostles' Creed is to consider not only its theological import but also the extent to which it essentially embodies the whole narrative history of God's interaction with humankind, from Creation to the Incarnation to the Final Consummation. In this connection I would take respectful issue with Palmer's comment later in his book, "Creeds tend to be abstract and philosophical. They therefore appeal mainly to educated adults interested in distilling and transmitting the key theological pillars of faith" (95). He goes on to speak of the "colorful, dramatic, and easily remembered" narratives of the Bible that contribute to the vitality of the scriptural record. True enough, but the narrative elements in the Apostles' Creed—and other similar creedal statements, I would maintain—constitute a fundamental aspect of their significance. As we have already noted, Sire makes a similar point—that our worldview can be described as "the story we live by," not merely a "conceptual scheme" (*Naming the Elephant*, 98).

14. Palmer, *Elements of a Christian Worldview*, 97.

3. You shall not misuse the name of the LORD your God.

4. Remember the Sabbath day and keep it holy.

5. Honor your father and your mother.

6. You shall not commit murder.

7. You shall not commit adultery.

8. You shall not steal.

9. You shall not give false testimony against your neighbor.

10. You shall not covet your neighbor's house, wife, servants, ox [or car!], or anything that belongs to your neighbor (see Exodus 20:1–17).

These commands are packed with assumptions, values, and outright behavioral directives that sharpen our Christian worldview. They assume monotheism (the belief that there is only one God), direct our worship toward the spiritual rather than the physical, respect the legitimate authority of parents, encourage monogamy (a one-spouse lifestyle), favor truth-telling over deception, and preach contentment with simple possessions. At first blush they may seem top-down and heavy stones to carry, but when understood in the context of a covenantal relationship with God, we see that they represent his love-message to us as he makes clear the good life when we embrace him and free ourselves from the hassles and heartaches of sin.

The Lord's Prayer

The Lord's Prayer (see Matthew 6) serves a similar function to represent Christian worldview thought and practice. Theologian N. T. Wright, in *The Lord and His Prayer*, writes, "The more I have studied Jesus in his historical setting, the more it has become clear to me that this prayer sums up fully and accurately, albeit in a very condensed fashion, the way in which he read and responded to the signs of the times, the way in which he understood his own vocation and mission and invited his followers to share it."[15] As to the prayer's current relevance, he writes, "We live, as Jesus lived, in a world all too full of injustice, hunger, malice and evil. This prayer cries out for justice, bread, forgiveness and deliverance. If anyone

---

15. Wright, *The Lord and His Prayer*, 2.

thinks those are irrelevant in today's world, let them read the newspaper and think again."[16] Here is how Jesus modeled prayer for his followers:

> Our Father, in heaven, hallowed be your name.
> Your kingdom come, your will be done on earth as it is in heaven.
> Give us today our daily bread.
> Forgive us our debts, as we also have forgiven our debtors.
> And lead us not into temptation, but deliver us from the evil one
> (see Matthew 6:9–13).[17]

This prayer is worldviewish in that it assumes an intimate relationship with a personal, loving God whom we can approach just as children approach their earthly parents. It assumes that God really cares about the "injustice, hunger, malice and evil" in the world, and that we ought to seek his wisdom and strength as agents of his kingdom here and now to redeem it after the heavenly pattern. However, this vision is not for us to carry out on our own, but with God's grace and strength as we receive daily sustenance for ourselves and others, engender redeemed relationships through forgiveness, and break free from Satan's charms or our own undoing. So different is this vision of life from, say, deism, which teaches that God created the world and then stepped away from it to let us make things up as we go along, or from various forms of animism, which assume that many gods—both good and evil—inhabit people, objects, and nature, and require buying off through prayers or good works. Jesus' prayer signals that God is for us as he works his good purposes in us toward his plan to redeem us and the world.

A Theoretical Perspective

The Apostles' Creed, the Ten Commandments, and the Lord's Prayer provide a traditional doctrinal and scriptural footing for understanding a Christian worldview. In addition, we might consider a broader theoretical approach. To help us, I refer to a book entitled *The Transforming Vision: Shaping a Christian World View*. In it Walsh and Middleton suggest that someone's worldview can be determined by asking him or her four key questions. Let us ask those questions and describe how Christians have often responded. These questions are as follows:

16. Ibid., 2.

17. All Scripture quotations in this chapter are from the New International Version (NIV) of the Bible unless otherwise indicated.

- Who am I?

- What's wrong?

- Where am I?

- What is the remedy?

1. Who am I? (or What is the nature, task, and purpose of human beings?)

(a) Nature: My reading of Scripture indicates that I am a creation of God and he is my Creator. He has made me in his image—in his likeness—in that I am a moral, historical, and valuable creature (Genesis 1:27). I am the pinnacle, the zenith, the masterful apex of his creation, and for that I am eternally in awe and forever grateful. I also have a free will, and so did Adam. Unfortunately he blew it— like any one of us would have—and because of him, we are all born into sin. It doesn't sound fair, but God has said that this is the effect of sin (1 Corinthians 15:21–22; Romans 3:23). Fortunately through Christ I can become a new creature, with new motives and a desire not to sin and a heart that is willing to serve others. In short, I can be redeemed (Romans 3:22–24; 2 Corinthians 5:16–21).

(b) Task: My task on earth is to serve people, society, and creation to the glory of God. Better put, my task on this globe is to *develop and preserve* the culture and creation around me. I am in the world, but not of the world in the negative sense (John 17:14–16). Some Christians say we should flee society and live in colonies, but most Christians understand that to be human is to be cultural; the question is who will influence the other more. Will I serve and redeem others and culture to God's glory, or will I embrace the world?

(c) Purpose: My purpose is to love God and enjoy him forever. My goal is not to come up with my own reason for living (as an existentialist might say) and it is not simply to survive and pass on my gene pool (as a natural evolutionist might say). Admittedly, serving others and serving God is not very flashy—it is not like the goal of winning the Super Bowl. But only humans have the ability to rise above their own creature needs to recognize that God is the Creator, we are created, and our purpose is to bring glory to him through service and leadership of those around us (Philippians 4:20).

2. Where am I? (or What is the nature of the world and universe I live in?)

As Christians we believe the creation—from invisible quarks to the expanding universe—is God's doing, his masterpiece (Genesis 1:1—2:3). But in Christian thought, the world and the animals are not made in God's likeness. Unlike many New Age and eastern religious views, the Bible does not teach that the world is our mother who gave us life, nor is it God emanating, nor is it God. However, creation shouts a loud testimony that God exists, and the earth metaphorically sings praises to God for his creativity and power (Psalms 96:11–13; 97:6). As Naugle concisely asserts, "God . . . is that ultimate reality whose trinitarian nature, personal character, moral excellence, wonderful works, and sovereign rule constitute the objective reference point for all reality," including how we understand the cosmos.[18]

Unfortunately, the entire created order has also fallen due to Adam's sin. The most obvious sign to humans is the presence of weeds everywhere, and the fact that people must work hard to gain a harvest. The Scriptures say that the whole world groans for redemption (Romans 8:22). It groans for its original perfect state; it groans for us that we may be redeemed so we will stop abusing it. As already noted, we are called to have dominion over the earth, but this means to develop and preserve it, not rape and exploit it.

3. What's wrong? (or What is the basic problem or obstacle that keeps me from attaining fulfillment? In other words, how do I understand evil?)

The Christian would say that what is wrong is us. Not the oceans or mountains. Not the blue jays or jaguars. But us. What is the nature of our problem? The rub is that we really enjoy being creatures with free wills. And ultimately, before we are redeemed, we prefer to live by our own rules. Even after we come to Christ and claim that we need him, we still often like to try it on our own (Romans 7:14–20). This made possible the ploy of Satan in the Garden of Eden. He promised Eve she could be like God, if she ate of the fruit, and that option was too deliciously tempting to ignore. So Eve caved, then Adam buckled, and ever since we have relied on ourselves along an achingly lonely journey apart from God (Genesis 3:1–5).

18. Naugle, *Worldview: The History of a Concept*, 261.

Walsh and Middleton suggest that if we get sucked into relying on ourselves—the created ones in love with the created ones—then we commit idolatry. We become our own little gods, adoring either ourselves or our Oprahs and Obamas. Many things clamor for our attention, for our worship, such as wealth, wheels, prestige, and our own accomplishments. The problem is that these idols distract us from the Creator.

4. What is the remedy? (or How is it possible to overcome this hindrance to my fulfillment? In other words, how do I find salvation?)

The remedy to this mess is redemption: redemption of us through Christ, and redemption of society and earth as well. By "redemption," I mean being bought back from destruction and being made new. If you were raised in an evangelical church, the idea of personal redemption through Christ is well understood, namely, that God saw that we had blown it, and according to his law a perfect sacrifice had to be made for payment. In the Old Testament that payment was a perfect animal; in the New Testament that payment was the perfect God-man Jesus Christ, the one who was with God in the beginning of the world, the one who lived a perfect life despite experiencing all temptations you and I experience. With Christ we have new life as spiritual beings (Romans 3:24; 1 Corinthians 1:26–31). This experience of a personal response to Christ's redemptive grace is critical. Nancy Pearcey expresses the matter well—along with some appropriate words of caution:

> Ultimately, this experience is the goal of developing a Christian worldview—not just studying and debating ideas, but dying and rising again in union with Christ. Without this inner spiritual reality, everything we have said about worldviews can become little more than a mental exercise—a way to solve intellectual puzzles, or, worse, a way to impress others by sounding smart and well-educated. Virtually anyone can learn to parrot high-sounding phrases, pronounce certain shibboleths, repeat a few punchy quotations, in order to craft an image of being cultured and sophisticated. Even worldview studies can become a seedbed for pride

instead of a process of submitting our minds to the Lordship of Christ.[19]

In addition to personal conversion, Christians also speak of cultural and creational renewal. If you were raised in a reformed tradition, you are familiar with these ideas. Not only are humans redeemed, but now we, through Christ, can help redeem our schools, businesses, and mass media, as well as our gardens, landfills, and emission policies. Second Peter 3 and Revelation 21 refer to the passing of the old and the coming of "a new heaven and a new earth." Redemption is more than personal and spiritual; it is cultural and creational too.

So, redemption is both *here and now*—Jesus' Spirit in you and me while writing papers or working at Starbucks—and it is also *futuristic* in that some day, as Colossians 1:20 says, he will reconcile to himself all things, whether things on earth or things in heaven. Everything fell when Adam fell; everything groans for renewal.

WORLDVIEW DETRACTORS

While most evangelical Christian thinkers are big fans of the worldview concept, investing considerable effort to develop Christian worldview statements (such as the one you just read), not everyone in the university environment values such convictions. In fact, some intellectuals object to worldview thought and life altogether, Christian perspective or not. These intellectuals have come to be known as the postmodernists. As you probably know, anyone who grew up from 1970 onward lives in what we now call the postmodern age, but this term does not make sense unless you understand its predecessor, the modern age. Let's consider what modern-

---

19. Pearcey, *Total Truth*, 354. Clark goes considerably beyond Pearcey's word of caution when he suggests that a focus on developing a Christian worldview can actually act as a deterrent to true Christian faith: "when evangelicals articulate their faith in terms of worldviews, they make philosophy foundational to their theology, and this philosophy prevents them from grasping the literal message of Scripture" ("Nature of Conversion," 202). He adds, at the end of his article, ". . . if a person is to convert to Christianity, one must stop using the language of worldviews and begin using the language of the church. One must abandon argument and risk prayer" (218). I, along with most Christian worldview advocates, find Clark's either/or (Naugle's term, *Worldview: The History of a Concept*, 339) viewpoint extreme (Naugle uses the more diplomatic "overstated"), but his warning about the importance of seeing Christianity as requiring a heartfelt commitment to Christ, not merely an intellectual assent to a set of Christian propositions, is unquestionably apt.

ists and postmodernists value so we can understand why postmodernists are down on worldview thinking.

Modernism grew out of the Enlightenment (AD 1650–1750) as the optimistic view that human reason and scientific research could answer the world's problems better than the Catholic church's leaders and teachings. This optimism was fueled by, as well as contributed to the fueling of, spectacular scientific discoveries, nation-states replacing feudal kingdoms, the rise of capitalism, and the Industrial Revolution. Modernists promoted the idea that people were primarily rational creatures—not image-bearers of God—and that if left alone by religious authority structures would solve social, economic, and even moral issues through their own "smarts" and the natural course of history. French philosopher René Descartes' famous adage, "I think, therefore I am," for example, celebrated the rationality of the free individual.

Today, a lot of people still think like modernists because they place their faith in science and politics to correct human ills. But a few "big rock" predictions that modernism made have not panned out, and this is why postmodernists decry the modernist worldview. Modernists predicted that rejecting the teachings of the church and embracing scientific progress would usher in a peaceful world where no one went hungry and reasonable dialogue would reign. But the ugly atrocities of two world wars and the Holocaust squashed this optimism, and the failure of Communism as a political (modernist) system convinced a lot of people that Marx was wrong when he thought we could socially engineer an ideal society. The cold war between the USA and the USSR also signaled modernism's failure as each superpower amassed weapons of mass destruction created through the science that was supposed to bring world peace. Finally, most modernists thought the advance of reason and science would cause religion to shrivel away worldwide, when in fact it continues to flourish.

So postmodernists have rejected the modernist worldview that our own reason and science and politics can determine the grand meaning of history and fashion solutions to human problems. Postmodernists are especially incredulous toward any group or authority that sets itself up as having the whole picture for everyone. As Christian philosopher Heath White explains, "Postmoderns call these visions 'metanarratives'—big, overarching stories that explain and justify and place in context the other smaller stories that make up most historical writing."[20] White continues to describe the postmodern attitude, and especially that of one key thinker, Jean-Francois Lyotard: "In other words, postmodernism, for Lyotard, was the intellectual state one had reached when one no longer believed *any* big story about history whether religious or secular. Postmodernism involves the loss of any hope that some larger-than-human-force—be it God or History or Progress or Science or Reason—is going to come to the aid of humanity and make everything all right in the end."[21]

It is the postmodern person's rejection of even a God-story for humans that is especially troubling for us Christians. Their negativism can lead to nihilism (the idea we cannot come up with solutions because there are none), as well as personal and cultural relativism (the idea that your truth is yours and mine is mine, or, more broadly, my people believe X, and your people believe Y, but you can't force your ideas on me). Postmoderns believe that when we buy into a traditional worldview such as Christianity or modernism or even liberal democracy we essentially give up unique thinking and personal freedom. They are convinced that the powerful elite of these pre-established big stories (such as successful scientists, or historians, or theologians and pastors) necessarily mute minority people through gentle or sometimes not-so-gentle persuasion. And they think that holding a particular worldview will tint how you see everything else in life (in a biased and bad way). This is why so many postmoderns are passionate about diversity, tolerance, and respect—values which they believe guarantee individual and group freedom. And it's why you grew up with the phrase "Whatever."

This last point is critical. It appears that postmoderns are primarily motivated by freedom *from* reigning worldviews of any sort, rather than being *for* another worldview alternative. Similarly, even modernist thinkers rejected the authority of the Church so as to be free *from* the reigning order of their day. Both modernists and postmodernists abhor the notion that any person or institution has the right to encumber anyone's personal freedoms.

So what do Christians say to this charge that embracing God's ways constrains us? Limits our thinking? Quashes our freedoms? One response is *wonderful*. Once again I rely on White, who puts it well:

20. White, *Postmodernism 101*, 150.

21. Ibid., 153.

> Christianity is fundamentally at odds with the project of seeking human freedom by eliminating constraints, whether the constraints are political, social, intellectual or moral. For Christians understand themselves *both* as under the all-encompassing authority of God, who lays claim to every sphere of life, and *also* as supremely free, freer than non-Christians could be.[22]

If you find this position paradoxical, it might be because you have been raised in a culture that is a beef stew mix of modern and postmodern ideas. However, this paradox might lessen if you consider that our relationship with God is similar to relationships with girlfriends and boyfriends and spouses, where we accept their influence because we know they have our best interests at heart. In biblical language, these are covenantal relationships where two people agree to love each other, forever, and hold each other accountable to standards for living. In a similar way, when we are in love with God, we assume that his guidelines, such as "love me, love others, and don't steal or commit adultery," are not there to quash personal choice or enforce mind-control, but to bring freedom within boundaries and ultimately well-being (i.e., life really is better that way).

CONCLUSION

So if we accept our relationship with God as lovingly covenantal, then our endeavor to create elaborate worldview accounts of the whole of life may not be quite so important. To be sure, as you read the chapters in this book you will encounter Christian scholars who seek to understand their disciplines from a Christian perspective, and yet you should not anticipate a grand theory to burst upon your mind. If the postmodernists are right about anything, I believe it is that we are limited and biased creatures, and this means we piece together the big picture bit by bit. Scientists and philosophers and theologians—as well as the rest of us—can be duped. Why, even postmodern advocates can be duped.[23]

22. Ibid., 163.

23. In 1996, New York University physics professor Alan Sokal submitted a fraudulent article to the postmodern journal *Social Text*. His intent was to show that preposterous claims about the physical world would be acceptable if cast in postmodern jargon. For example, one claim he made was that "physical reality is at bottom nothing more than a social and linguistic construct." The editors of *Social Text* published the paper without submitting it for blind review among people knowledgeable about quantum physics. Sokal published another article simultaneously in another journal making his point that some postmoderns trade academic rigor for what sounds good. See Sokal, "Transgressing

So, while this introductory chapter has outlined a Christian worldview, I hope I have done so with appropriate humility, for as the apostle Paul wrote, we "see through a glass darkly" (1 Corinthians 13:12). Moreover, God himself has told us, "my thoughts are not your thoughts, neither are your ways my ways" (Isaiah 55:8). To be sure, God has revealed much to us through his Word, his creation, and his Spirit. But to think we can know everything about the world or about God is impossible, if not simply arrogant.

I hope too you can appreciate the postmodernists' rejection of modernism's insistence on discovering truth solely by means of science and reason. If you look at the biblical record, you will see that Jesus' views of truth were not expressed in terms of reason and science but in terms of life, liberty, and spirit. Jesus said:

"I am the way, the truth, and the life." (John 14:6)

"You will know the truth, and the truth will set you free." (John 8:32)

"But when he, the Spirit of truth, comes, he will guide you into all truth." (John 16:13)

A biblical way of knowing understands truth as the dynamic bondage-breaking work of God the Holy Spirit in our lives. Facts and theories might enliven, but unless knowledge leads to wisdom and right living, it may only puff us up. And some things must simply go unknown. The late theologian Stanley Grenz put it this way:

We must acknowledge that intellectual reflection and the scientific enterprise alone cannot put us in touch with every dimension of reality or lead us to discover every aspect of God's truth. . . . [W]e must make room for the concept of "mystery"—not as an irrational complement to the rational but as a reminder that the fundamental reality of God transcends human rationality.[24]

So what, then, is a Christian worldview? I believe a Christian worldview begins as a commitment to God in a covenantal relationship which assumes he cares deeply for us and has great things in store for us. Given these two assumptions, we enter into life with him to acknowledge that he

the Boundaries," for the hoax article and Sokal, "A Physicist Experiments with Cultural Studies," for the article exposing it.

24. Grenz, *A Primer*, 169, 170.

made us in his image, that we sinned, but he has offered us redemption. Once in restored relationship with him we will seek to serve his purposes in sharing his love and act as agents of justice on this earth. In the middle of this vision is the centrality of Jesus who, as Saint Paul describes him, "is the image of the invisible God, the firstborn over all creation. For by him all things were created: things in heaven and on earth, visible and invisible, whether thrones or powers or rulers or authorities; all things were created by him and for him. He is before all things, and in him all things hold together. And he is the head of the body, the church; he is the beginning and the firstborn from among the dead, so that in everything he might have the supremacy" (see Colossians 1:15–27). A Christian worldview begins in a relationship of trust and weaves together beliefs, values, assumptions, and behaviors which ultimately acknowledge Jesus Christ as Lord over, under, and through everything created, and the hope that in him we may find reconciliation with ourselves, with each other, with the world, and with God.

WORKS CITED

Clark, Gregory A. "The Nature of Conversion: How the Rhetoric of Worldview Philosophy Can Betray Evangelicals." In *The Nature of Confession: Evangelicals and Postliberals in Conversation*, edited by Timothy R. Phillips and Dennis L. Okholm, 201–18. Downers Grove, IL: InterVarsity Press, 1996.

Grenz, Stanley. *A Primer on Postmodernism*. Grand Rapids, MI: Eerdmans, 1996.

Hofstede, Geert. *Culture's Consequences: Comparing Values, Behaviors, Institutions and Organizations across Nations*. 2d ed. Thousand Oaks, CA: Sage Publications, 2001.

Kearney, Michael. *World View*. Novato, CA: Chandler & Sharp, 1984.

Kraehmer, Steffen T. *Heroes: Shaping Lives through Family and Culture*. Minneapolis: Fairview Press, 1995.

Kraft, Charles H. "Worldview in Intercultural Communication." In *International and Intercultural Communication*, edited by Fred L. Casmir, 407–28. Washington, DC: University Press of America, 1978.

Manley-Casimir, Michael E., and Carmen Luke, eds. *Children and Television: A Challenge for Education*. New York: Praeger, 1987.

Naugle, David K. *Worldview: The History of a Concept*. Grand Rapids, MI: Eerdmans, 2002.

Olthuis, David. "On Worldviews." *Christian Scholar's Review* 14 (1985) 153–54.

Palmer, Michael D., ed. *Elements of a Christian Worldview*. Springfield, MO: Logion Press, 1998.

Pearcey, Nancy R. *Total Truth: Liberating Christianity from Its Cultural Captivity*. Study Guide Edition. Wheaton, IL: Crossway, 2005.

Sire, James W. *Naming the Elephant: Worldview as a Concept*. Downers Grove, IL: InterVarsity Press, 2004.

Sokal, Alan. "A Physicist Experiments with Cultural Studies." *Lingua Franca* (May/June 1996) 62–64.

———. "Transgressing the Boundaries: Towards a Transformative Hermeneutics of Quantum Gravity." *Social Text* 46/47 (1996) 217–52.

Walsh, Brian J., and J. Richard Middleton. *The Transforming Vision: Shaping a Christian World View*. Downers Grove, IL: InterVarsity Press, 1984.

White, Heath. *Postmodernism 101: A First Course for the Curious Christian*. Grand Rapids, MI: Brazos, 2006.

Wright, N. Thomas. *The Lord and His Prayer*. Grand Rapids, MI: Eerdmans, 1996.

FOR FURTHER READING

Colson, Charles, and Nancy Pearcey. *How Now Shall We Live?* Wheaton, IL: Tyndale House, 1999.

Holmes, Arthur F. *Contours of a World View*. Grand Rapids, MI: Eerdmans, 1983.

Nash, Ronald H. "Introduction—Worldview Thinking." In *Life's Ultimate Questions: An Introduction to Philosophy*, 13–33. Grand Rapids, MI: Zondervan, 1999.

Sire, James W. *The Universe Next Door: A Basic Worldview Catalog*. 3d ed. Downers Grove, IL: InterVarsity Press, 1997.

Walsh, Brian J., and J. Richard Middleton. *Truth Is Stranger than It Used to Be: Biblical Faith in a Postmodern Age*. Downers Grove, IL: InterVarsity Press, 1995.

3

Developing the Characteristics of a Christian Mind

Donald M. Page

INTRODUCTION

FOR THE LAST TWO decades, universities in both Canada and the United States have been criticized by (a) *employers*, who do not think that universities are providing the kind of education that is relevant to today's business and professional needs because their graduates cannot think relationally; (b) *governments*, who resent pouring so many taxpayers' dollars into universities that are producing graduates unable to make a positive contribution to society; and (c) *students* themselves, who are concerned about the poor quality of undergraduate instruction because most universities are devoting too much of their professorial expertise to graduate studies and research.

To find out more about what was wrong with universities in Canada, for example, the country's university presidents set up a commission in 1990 to enquire into the state of university education. Among many concerns that were noted, the commission faulted the universities for being multiversities rather than universities. The term university comes from the Latin *universitas*, which means *the whole*. Historically, universities were designed to prepare the intellectual, spiritual, and moral leaders of society by giving them broad, deep, ethical, unified minds. Students were educated to think beyond their individual disciplines to a wholeness of knowledge that united all learning and out of which meaning in life could be found. The epitome of this unified thinking was usually contained in a compulsory course on moral philosophy. This course, often taught by the university president, was designed to draw together and synthesize the entire undergraduate body of learning as well as the ethical sensitivities that students needed to enter the marketplaces of life. Students resented being told what was good and bad in a free society, however, so this senior course gradually disappeared in most universities by the turn of the nineteenth century. Unfortunately what was lost in the process was not only the theological and moral underpinnings of education but the unity of thought that held it together.

At the same time, universities took on the task of upgrading apprenticeships by establishing professional graduate schools like medicine, engineering, and law, which also detracted from the pursuit of intellectual wholeness. With the rise of the elective system and the rapid growth in specialization, the notion of a common core of learning, or a core set of fundamental disciplines, disappeared except at some liberal arts focused institutions. The Commission pointed out the negative consequences of this deterioration into a smorgasbord of electives that were taken for amusement or for job skill acquisition. Allan Bloom, in his classic, *The Closing of the American Mind*, describes how, in such a process, "the student must navigate among a collection of carnival barkers, each trying to lure him[/her] into a particular sideshow."[1] Not only are students not encouraged to construct a broad educational program, but there is no place where they can see their world of ideas as a unified whole, where the variety of disciplines can be seen as fostering integrative, interdisciplinary learning. The sad fact is that, despite this call for curriculum reform, very little was actually changed in subsequent years beyond the introduction of a pre-graduation token integration course.

Let me illustrate what is meant by interdisciplinary studies in the most commonly thought-of field of physical education—sport. If you want to understand sport you need to study at least some of the following:

- the history of sport
- the sociology of sport
- the politics of sport
- the psychology of sport
- anatomy, kinesiology
- the literature of sport

1. Bloom, *Closing of the American Mind*, 339.

- the art, drama, or music of sport
- the business of sport
- showmanship of sport
- sport as religion

Obviously knowledge from a wide variety of disciplines can help to illuminate a person's understanding of sport. Each discipline also has a context in which it interfaces with sport. If you want to understand Olympic sports, for example, you must learn something about the ancient Greek politics that gave birth to the Olympics. In more recent periods, you would have to know something about race relations or apartheid, Cold War politics, and drug abuse. My point is that you cannot become a qualified physical education instructor by just learning how to shoot a basketball or operate a computer-produced wellness program. There is a similar diversity of knowledge to be learned in virtually all academic disciplines.

THE CONTEMPORARY MINDSET

According to *Time* magazine, the members of your student generation

> have trouble making decisions. They would rather hike in the Himalayas than climb a corporate ladder. They have few heroes, no anthems, no style to call their own. They crave entertainment, but their attention span is as short as one zap of a TV dial. They hate yuppies, hippies and druggies. They postpone marriage because they dread divorce. They sneer at Range Rovers, Rolexes and red suspenders. What they hold dear are family life, local activism, national parks, penny loafers and mountain bikes. They possess only a hazy sense of their own identity but a monumental preoccupation with all the problems the preceding generation will leave for them to fix.[2]

There is also a very significant trend present in millennials (people born beginning in the late 1970s) and throughout contemporary society that I call the *spirit of anti-intellectualism*. For all of our modern accomplishments in advanced education, in today's culture of text messaging and learning through googling, *thinking is no longer as important as it*

---

2. Gross and Scott, "Proceeding with Caution," 57.

used to be. I believe there are at least five trends that contribute to this spirit of anti-intellectualism:

1. *Pragmatism*: In today's world, the first question about any idea is not "Is it true or right?" but "Does it work?" Pragmatism rules over both values and thought. Result-oriented social activists are often supporters of a cause without always inquiring too closely whether their cause has a good end or whether their action is the best means to pursue it.

2. *Focus on Results*: We have become an *impatient generation*. Students quickly become bored if there is not a lot of action. "Don't talk about it—just do it" seems to be the byword. They want to get it done, get results the instant way, or give up on it if it requires extensive thought.

3. *Preoccupation with Feelings*: We have also become a *feeling genera-tion*. Feeling triumphs over reason in our decision-making. "If it feels good, do it" is too often the principal criterion for behavior. A subjective experience becomes more important than revealed truth or absolutes in what has been described as our post-secular univer-sity thinking.[3] We are admonished to get in touch with our feelings. This is good, especially for males, but requires that a balance with reason also be struck.

4. *Ritualism*: Ritualistic attitudes have encumbered our intellectual imagination and creativity. In the church it has become an escape route to avoid our God-given responsibility to use the minds that God has given us. In educational circles, it can be identified with rote learning, learning from the professor merely to pass the exam or to be politically correct. The danger of ritualism is that it is mere performance in which ceremony has become an end in itself, a meaningless substitute for intelligent consideration.

5. *Intellectual Isolationism*: Profound thinkers are being increasingly *isolated* from the mainstream of human activity. I was once intro-duced to a very prolific writer who had written several dozen books. He spent all his time thinking about what the world should be like. He sought to inspire others through his writings, but he was so out of touch with where his readers were in the real world that there were

3. Carter, "When 7 X 5 = 75."

few readers to inspire. As a foreign policy planner, I found it relatively easy to write policy; the critical issue was the test of relevance in the light of current events. If the intellect is left on its own, it may become dry and humorless, leading to an academic intellectualism that is devoid of emotion, drive, and meaningful action.

THE IMPORTANCE OF MIND DEVELOPMENT

"For as [a person] thinketh in his heart, so is he" (Proverbs 23:7; all Scripture NIV, unless otherwise indicated). The world is shaped by ideas. How can you understand what happened to end the Cold War and recent Russian developments without reading Gorbachev's *Perestroika* or Yeltsin's *Against the Grain*? These works are similar in importance to Hitler's *Mein Kampf*, Marx's *Das Kapital* or *The Thoughts of Chairman Mao*. Or in contemporary youth culture, consider the impact that pop culture and the mystical Harry Potter have had. Alfred North Whitehead summed up the importance of mind development well when he wrote:

> The great conquerors, from Alexander to Caesar, and from Caesar to Napoleon, influenced profoundly the lives of subsequent generations. But the total effect of this influence shrinks to insignificance, if compared to the entire transformation of human habits and human mentality produced by the long line of men of thought from Thales to the present day, men individually powerless, but ultimately the rulers of the world.[4]

That is why Saint Paul wrote that "Our war is not fought with weapons of flesh, yet they are strong enough, in God's cause, to demolish fortresses. We demolish sophistries and the arrogance that tries to resist the knowledge of God; every thought is our prisoner, captured to be brought into obedience to Christ."[5]

The fact that God has chosen to reveal himself both through Scripture and through nature shows us how important our minds are. The ability of men and women to know what God has revealed in the universe is extremely important. It is the basis for all scientific research, which assumes that there is a rational correspondence between the character of what is being investigated and the mind of the investigator. Thus humans are able

---

4. Cited in Blackham, *Humanism*, 101. Thales was a sixth century BC Greek philosopher who was regarded as one of the original seven wise men of Greece.

5. 2 Corinthians 10:4–5, Jerusalem Bible.

to comprehend the processes of nature in terms of cause and effect. It is our mind that enables us to receive and respond to God. We are told in Scripture that we can have the mind of Christ. We are capable of thinking God's thoughts after him. If we denigrate the mind, we are undermining the very power of God that he has made available to us.

In the Old Testament people were admonished to love the Lord their God with all their heart, soul, and strength (Deuteronomy 6:5). Jesus said not only with our heart, soul, and strength but added with all our mind (Mark 12:30). The mind is important. That is why in both the Old and the New Testaments there is such a heavy emphasis on the acquisition of knowledge and wisdom. People were destroyed for their lack of knowledge. Paul prays that the believers in Ephesus may have wisdom and knowledge; for discernment and knowledge for the believers in Philippi; and for knowledge, wisdom, and understanding for the Colossians. The development of the mind is considered very important in both Testaments.

University education accentuates the development of the mind, which is why the foundation for that development is so important. Whether I buy a Pepsi or a Coke may impact my taste buds and stomach, but it does not affect my thinking. If I buy a computer from a pagan, it will not impact my inner being. If I work in an office I may have to listen to vulgar or blasphemous talk, but I am not compelled to absorb that way of thinking into my mind. Regulations and laws may affect how I conduct my business affairs, but they will not necessarily alter me personally. "The university, in contrast, is where thinking is altered and brought into line with the world."[6]

It is at university where you develop or alter your worldview, the basis upon which you make decisions in life and find meaning. As pointed out by Walsh and Middleton in *The Transforming Vision: Shaping a Christian World View*, it is our worldview that answers the fundamental questions of life such as, Who am I? Where am I? What is wrong with this world? and What is the remedy?[7] How one approaches these questions, from an atheistic, a secular, or a Christian perspective, profoundly influences how one sees the world and the purpose of a university education. In our public systems of higher education, for the most part, the only acceptable intellectual starting point has been in secularism, or, in the increasingly

6. Linnemann, *Historical Criticism of the Bible*, 40.

7. Walsh and Middleton, *Transforming Vision*, 35. For a fuller discussion of these four questions, see the preceding chapter by Strom, "What is a Christian Worldview?"

post-secular era, in our feelings. Oh, individual Christians are permitted to retain their faith in their private lives and may on occasion even be allowed to share their convictions. But the sovereign God and his redemptive Son are deemed to have no place in academic thinking. As Sommerville has pointed out throughout his book *The Decline of the Secular University: Why the Academy Needs Religion*, religion is seen as retrograde on the hot-button issues of the day. If you retain Jesus in your feelings but deny him in your thinking, then your education is being based upon anti-Christian principles. That is why at a Christian university we must begin from a Christian perspective and develop a mindset that reflects a Christian view of creation, redemption, and the final consummation.

ESSENTIAL CHARACTERISTICS OF THE CHRISTIAN MIND

Blamires describes a Christian mind as "a mind trained, informed, equipped to handle data of secular controversy within a framework of references which is constructed of Christian presuppositions."[8] These presuppositions include the existence of the supernatural, the pervasiveness of evil, the supernatural foundation of truth, the acceptance of divine authority, and the value of the human person as God's creation.

After defining the Christian mind, Blamires reaches the sobering conclusion that it no longer exists in today's world. "There is no longer a Christian mind," he writes. "There is still, of course, a Christian ethic, a Christian practice, and a Christian spirituality. . . . But as a thinking being, the modern Christian has succumbed to secularization."[9] The human ego has edged God out. This mindset excludes God and thereby limits enquiry to the observable. It is a fragmented mindset because there is no basis for unity of thought. It is also a confused mindset because it has no basis for value beyond the transitory present of human wisdom. What then are the traits of the Christian mind? I would like to suggest several, drawn from Gill's book *The Opening of the Christian Mind*,[10] in what follows.

The Christian Mind is Open

This means it both widens the field of vision and focuses on God within that wider field. "The Christian mind must be supremely open and broad,

8. Blamires, *The Christian Mind*, 43.

9. Ibid., 3.

10. Gill, *Opening of the Christian Mind*, 63–75.

oriented not only to the range of natural material, empirical and imma-
nent factors, but to the supernatural, supra-temporal, eternal and invisible possibilities."[11] Jesus is the supreme example. When he walked on this
earth he showed his concern for people, nature, human institutions, hunger, peace, and justice, but he also lived and thought with a consciousness
of both angelic and demonic forces as well as his heavenly Father. Thus
healing and disease were seen in relation to both physical suffering and to
the surrounding spiritual battle.

Today many people seek to exclude God from their consciousness.
You do not have to be an atheist to bracket God out of most seminars,
corporate planning sessions, court room proceedings, operating rooms,
and university classrooms. This represents a *narrow- or close-mindedness
that is little more than tunnel vision.* Ideas of truth and reality are all too
often based upon materialism, an ideology, a movement, or a relativism
that excludes the supernatural.

The Christian mind must be open to the quest for knowledge and
certitude in the context of a variety of viewpoints. Knowing God opens
the door to all knowledge and wisdom. As Proverbs 9:10 affirms, "For the
fear and reverence of God are basic to all wisdom. Knowing God results in
every other kind of understanding." Therefore, what God says in Scripture
about law, justice, money, health, history, sex, leadership, and so forth, is
more fundamental and important, in the end, than anything our scientific, rational, and technical methods might suggest. God not only adds
to our factual knowledge base but illuminates the values and meaning in
which these facts have significance for us. Thus we are enjoined to set our
minds "on things above, not on earthly things" (Colossians 3:2). Jesus was
not oblivious to what was all around him; rather, he saw these things in
the light of creation, redemption, and eternity. And so must we, even in a
technologically driven world of learning.

I offer several illustrations of the value of a biblical context for the
pursuit of knowledge. Sociologists may provide all the statistical explanations for urban growth, but they will never fully comprehend cities unless
they understand God's revelation with respect to the origin, history, and
development of cities, based on people's need to live in community.

11. Ibid., 65.

Similarly, how can you as a Christian work in finance or the banking industry without understanding something of what God says in the Scriptures about property, usury, and the purpose of wealth?

Openness to God changes the perspective of literary criticism in the study and teaching of English, for God is the source not only of language but of human creativity and imagination.

The natural sciences cannot deny his creation because they are structured around it. It was from the wasp that we learned how to make paper out of wood, from birds that we learned the principles of aeronautics, and the dragonfly inspired the invention of helicopters. This was not human genius but the application of God's genius as revealed in creation.

On May 18, 1974, India exploded a nuclear device. What was Canada to do? The key question for me as the chief historical researcher involved in assessing the case was "Should innocent people be deprived of their basic education, health, and food because of the actions of their government?" Revenge against those who had betrayed Canada's trust that India would make only peaceful use of nuclear technology was uppermost in the minds of the policy makers. The atheistic and the Christian responses were quite different in determining our nation's foreign policy. I thought about what Jesus would have done in this situation, how he helped those who lived under the rule of a cruel and despotic government, before I made the recommendation that was to become our government's policy.

In short, having a Christian mind means going beyond the narrow field of vision in the world around us. It means spatially enlarging and enriching our vision to see the world from the Creator's perspective.

The Christian Mind Learns from History

Second, having a Christian mind means using the past to increase our knowledge of the present and obtain guidance for the future. The apostle Paul wrote to the believers in Corinth: "These things [meaning Israel's past] happened to them as examples and were written down as warnings for us, on whom the fulfillment of the ages has come" (1 Corinthians 10:11). Reality is not mere cyclical repetition for the Christian, but life is seen to have a beginning and a purposeful end. God created the world, then entered into it in human form—in the person of Christ—and by so doing provided direction from creation to the apocalypse.

Jesus lived fully in the present while on earth, but drew on the past to explain the present and to offer warnings about the future. His temporal range of vision stretched from creation to the final judgment and God's eternal kingdom.

As Christians, we cannot make sense out of life and existence without looking at our past. For example, a computer major will never fully understand the effects of computer technology on society without first examining the significance of the Industrial Revolution and its impact on society. A law student cannot limit his/her perspectives to today's legal technicalities but must study the origins of Jewish law from which most of our laws are derived.

The Christian Mind is Humanistic

The Christian mind must go beyond the pursuit of mere abstract facts, studies, and theories, beyond impersonal or predatory relationships, to the development of a deep concern for persons. Individuals are important, for as Jesus stated, "[E]ven the very hairs of your head are all numbered. So don't be afraid; you are worth more than many sparrows" (Matthew 10:30–31). Psalm 139:1–16 points out that we were known and important to God while we were still in our mother's womb. And in Ephesians 1:18 we are told that God considers saints as riches that he will one day inherit, through his Son's atoning death for our redemption.

Christian humanism, focused as it is on the welfare of others, not ourselves, must be sustained and not forgotten. Left to itself, the human mind can become a tool for dominating nature, society, or other people. Today we see that abstraction, specialization, and impersonalization can all become dehumanizing—people becoming impersonal statistics manipulated by faceless bureaucracies using the latest technology. The speed, complexity, and competitiveness of modern life give too little room for personal concerns. Our neighbors, clients, students, patients, and colleagues can remain substantially anonymous. Left to itself, the mind cares most for itself.

It is God who attributes to his creatures worth and value. He is no respecter of persons. All people are created in his image and are the focus of his redemptive love. Jesus showed concern over people's needs, relationships, and future. He reached out to the adulterer, the Samaritans, the hungry, the poor, and the children, thereby stunning his contemporaries.

Jesus had a caring mind as he sought to touch people. He commanded his followers to be servants to others as he was a servant to them. This is a radically different appreciation of human worth than that presented by much post-secular feeling-motivated thinking.

We live in an era of narcissistic individualism and selfishness. When we do think of people, they are too often reduced to statistical abstractions and numbers. It is not just the reported numbers who have been killed through street violence or war that are important, but also the tragic impact on their families and society. In God's redemptive plan we have individual human worth established for all time.

The Christian Mind is Ethical

The fourth characteristic of a Christian mind is its ethical sensitivity to good and evil. "Hate what is evil; cling to what is good. . . . Do not be overcome by evil, but overcome evil with good" (Romans 12:9, 21).

Our public educational system has tried to provide a value-neutral education, but it has not succeeded. It has not been a question of all values being equal but of whose non-religious values would be pushed to the point, in extreme cases, of indoctrination. In part, this accounts for today's frequent reversal of values. What once was regarded as good is now evil and what was once shunned is now accepted as we cast off the values and the basis for them in our Judeo–Christian heritage in favor of a smorgasbord of secular values, where ethical behavior becomes a matter of personal preference and feelings rather than biblical principle. Opinions become little more than fashionable moralizing that changes as easily as the dress fashions of our day.

Let me illustrate this reversal of values from one of my experiences on Parliament Hill in Ottawa. When certain citizen groups and police forces in our largest cities were complaining about the increase in teenage female prostitution, the Justice and Legal Affairs Committee of the House of Commons decided that it was time to bring in some appropriate legislation to stem the tide. They were prevented from doing so, however, because two members of this committee argued that to curb teenage prostitution would be a denial of the then popular notion of Equal Opportunity for Employment! This constitutes a complete reversal of traditional values. Since when did employment opportunities take precedence over immoral conduct and the degradation of our God-given sexuality? As theologian

Carl Henry so cogently points out, "We now must cope with a segment of society for whom abortion is good under any circumstance, for whom adultery and divorce are good, the nuclear family restrictive, incest therapeutic, and crime justified as social necessity."[12]

One effect of this abandonment of a consensus about ethical norms is that facts are separated from values. Facts are objective subject matter for making decisions, but values are considered relative to communities or individuals. Thus good and evil are viewed as purely emotional and non-normative statements of personal preference.

The Christian mind exhibits a persistent, sensitive, ethical passion for what is right in accordance with God's laws. God's moral standards are absolute and permanent insofar as they reflect his character and are identified as ongoing standards and virtues in Scripture. As Tinder has pointed out, it is hard to find the reason for goodness in human actions apart from recognizing God as the source for a universal standard of goodness.[13]

The Christian biology student may be able to pass judgment on a particular course in genetic engineering, but must also understand how, if at all, it will contribute to God's purposes for human life.

Christian psychologists cannot be content with a disinterested, value-free analysis of why a husband beats his wife but must also seek to assist their clients in "overcoming evil with good" (Romans 12:21).

Having an ethical Christian mind provides us with the measuring stick to use in evaluating ideas, people, and products that come across our path each day. It also makes us less susceptible to advertisers, propagandists, and demagogues. Without such a measuring stick we would live in hopeless chaos and uncertainty. And we must never forget that ultimately we are accountable to a sovereign, all-knowing God for the ethical decisions we make.

The Christian Mind is Aesthetically Sensitive

Whatever is lovely, whatever is admirable . . . think about such things. (Philippians 4:8)

---

12. Henry, *The Christian Mindset in a Secular Society*, 15.
13. Tinder, "On the Political Meaning of Christianity," 85.

> The Lord God made . . . trees that were pleasing to the eye and good for food. (Genesis 2:9)

Creation is good—*and it was God who made it beautiful.* By the way, it is worth noting that both of these scriptural passages implicitly presuppose that the recognition of the lovely, the admirable, and the beautiful is in large part objectively ascertainable and consensual. Blamires very forthrightly describes how such assumptions no longer exist for many present-day artists: "The post-Christian mind has operated to persuade the public that there are no boundaries of good taste or decency which cannot be crossed in the name of 'art.' There is plenty of evidence that the public can be bamboozled into acceptance of any profanity, absurdity or obscenity if self-assumed artistic authority so decrees."[14] The pop culture of the millennials has also demonstrated this trend.[15]

Today our emphasis is more often on what something is *good for* rather than whether it is *intrinsically good.* We can miss the beauty of the lilies in the field or the snow on the mountains. The pressures of modern life and utilitarian prejudices from our technology-engendered stress on efficiency have often caused us to neglect smelling the roses. In so doing, we have forgotten a major purpose of creation. Creation reflects God's nature to us.

> For since the creation of the world God's invisible qualities—his eternal power and divine nature—have been clearly seen, being understood from what has been made, so that men are without excuse. (Romans 1:20)

> By the word of the Lord were the heavens made, their starry host by the breath of his mouth. He gathers the waters of the sea into jars; he puts the deep into storehouses. Let all the earth fear the Lord; let all the people of the world revere him. For he spoke, and it came to be. (Psalm 33:6–9)

Thus all creation is established to communicate to us who God is and what he is like. Natural beauty is God's beauty reflected back to us through a rose bud or a mountain reflecting in a lake. Thus it could be said that university education is really learning and seeing what God has put into this world and then giving it back to him in our use of what he has given to us.

14. Blamires, *The Post-Christian Mind*, 159.
15. See Howe and Strauss, *Millennials and the Pop Culture*, 237.

For the artist, art is not to glorify the artist or to conceptualize reality but to reflect the artist's stewardship and appreciation for God's creation.

In some Christian circles, there has been a mistaken notion that it is more spiritual to be austere and ascetic. We need a balance. The impoverishment of our poetic and artistic sensibilities impinges on our capacity to worship, to play, and to care for the environment and people. One's truly inner self is more often expressed in art and music and drama than in sterile words. Indeed, art may be therapeutic as we see ourselves before God and in juxtaposition with his creation. Just take time to examine the fine points of God's creation.

The Christian Mind is Truthful

"You will know the truth, and the truth will set you free"
(John 8:32).

"I am the way and the truth and the life" (John 14:6).

In today's world, truth has two popular meanings: (1) accurate, scientifically verifiable descriptions of facts, and (2) the authenticity with which you share your personal opinions. "It's true for me." Truth, however, is more than merely subjective opinion. There is also *objective truth*—truth which is true whether everyone accepts it or not, a truth that is defined by its relationship to an objective reality, whether that reality is popular or not. Gaede, in his 1993 book *When Tolerance Is No Virtue*, reveals how post-modernist thought has dispensed with a concern for objective truth and made "[unequivocal] tolerance of a plurality of truths a virtue. . . . Having no truths worth defending, [post-moderns] have made non-defensiveness a mark of distinction." He goes on to remind his readers of G. K. Chesterton's wise observation, "tolerance is a virtue of the man without convictions."[16]

Truth also implies that the knower has a *responsibility* to act upon that truth once it is known to be true—e.g., scientists have a responsibility for what they create in their labs and cannot carelessly pass on that responsibility to politicians or those who would misuse the discovery. Jurors must act on what they know to be true in a given presentation to the jury. Knowledge of the truth brings responsibility. If you know what is true, how can you in all honesty consciously act on what is untrue?

16. Gaede, *When Tolerance Is No Virtue*, 27.

There is also a *unity* to truth, a wholeness that leads to deeper understanding because Christ offers meaning and hope for the future through redemption. Jesus is the truth in whom all partial truths have their unity. A Christian mind strives to know the truth in and of Jesus Christ and then relates everything to him. "If you hold to my teaching . . . then you will know the truth, and the truth will set you free" (John 8:31–32). Thus the truth is ultimately known to us in Christ. It is that truth within us that makes a difference in our thinking. Professor Mark Noll of Notre Dame University captured this idea when he wrote:

> To a Christian, the mind is important because God is important. Who, after all, made the world of nature and then made possible the sciences through which we find out more about nature? Who formed the universe of human interactions and so provided the raw material of politics, economics, sociology, and history? Who is the source of harmony, form, and narrative patterns and so lies behind all artistic and literary possibilities? Who created the human mind in such a way that it could grasp the realities of nature, of human interactions, of beauty, and so make possible the theories on such matters by philosophers and psychologists? Who, moment by moment, sustains the natural world, the world of human interactions, and the harmonies of existence? Who, moment by moment, maintains the connections between what is in our minds and what is in the world beyond our minds? The answer in every case is the same: God did it, and God does it.[17]

A Christian has a renewed mind (Romans 12:1–20), a prepared mind (1 Peter 1:13), a self-controlled mind (1 Peter 4:7), and a pure mind (2 Peter 3:1). As Paul says, "We have the mind of Christ" (1 Corinthians 2:16). With God's help we are able to think as Christ thinks. His mind was full of Scripture, constantly aware of the heavenly Father, and sensitive to the Holy Spirit's guidance while at the same time observing and ministering to the world around him.

Minds are always subject to change. Christian psychologist Gary Collins observes,

> We can fertilize our minds with enriching ideas, positive attitudes, and biblical concepts. We can determine to let our minds dwell on things that are pure, positive, and praiseworthy. We can resist the tendency to let our minds grow wild and to be filled with the

17. Noll, "The Scandal of the Evangelical Mind," 30.

weeds of bitterness, cynicism, immoral thoughts, impure fantasies, self-centered ambition, revenge, and anger.[18]

This is not something that we can do on our own, but God can cause this transformation of the mind to take place.

The Christian mind, then, is truth affirming. God wants all men and women to come to a knowledge of the truth (1 Timothy 2:4): that is, to an awareness of God's truth in the real world that we live in. And God has promised, in the words of the writer of Proverbs, that the earnest seeker of divine wisdom shall not only find that supernatural gift but also discover the source of that understanding, God himself:

> My son, if you accept my words and store up my commands within you, turning your ear to wisdom and applying your heart to understanding, and if you call out for insight and cry aloud for understanding, and if you look for it as for silver and search for it as for hidden treasure, then you will understand the fear of the Lord and find the knowledge of God. For the Lord gives wisdom, and from his mouth come knowledge and understanding (Proverbs 2:1–6).

CONCLUSION

Our call to have a Christian mind is not some dry, dusty, outmoded obligation to become some kind of armchair intellectual. It ought to be an exciting and joyful adventure in personal growth. It should enable you to experience joy and contentment that passes all understanding. The Christian alone knows that quality of spiritual reality "so that [God's] joy may be in you and that your joy may be complete" (John 15:11). We do this by bringing every thought into obedience to Christ. As Harry Lewis of Harvard University points out in *Excellence without a Soul: How a Great University Forgot Education*, there can be no excellence unless it is connected to the basic longings of our souls.[19] And that longing must connect us to our Creator through a religious experience.

It is also *a call to action*. In his book, *The Post-Capitalist Society*, the late Christian business guru Peter Drucker explained that knowledge can only be productive when it is applied to make a difference.[20] But we must

18. Collins, *Your Magnificent Mind*, 228–29.

19. Lewis, *Excellence without a Soul*, 159–60.

20. Drucker, *The Post-Capitalist Society*, 50.

start from a sound knowledge base before we try to apply it. There is little purpose in developing a Christian mind that does not lead to Christian action. Wisdom is the art of being successful, of forming the correct plan to gain the desired results through which God will be glorified. Therefore the truly Christian mind will not be a useless appendage but one that engages in debate and enters intentionally into life. As you enter into life, may you always remember the words of Matthew 5:16: "In the same way, let your light shine before men, that they may see your good deeds and praise your Father in heaven." The delivery of higher education will indeed be changed by today's generation of technologically sophisticated students, but it can also be enriched if we focus on the one who gave us a Christian mindset in the first place.

WORKS CITED

Blackham, H. J. *Humanism.* New York: Penguin, 1968.

Blamires, Harry. *The Christian Mind.* Ann Arbor, MI: Servant Publications, 1978.

————. *The Post-Christian Mind: Exposing Its Destructive Agenda.* Ann Arbor, MI: Servant Publications, 1999.

Bloom, Allan. *The Closing of the American Mind: How Higher Education Has Failed Democracy and Impoverished the Souls of Today's Students.* New York: Simon and Schuster, 1987.

Carter, Stephen. "When 7 X 5 = 75." *Christianity Today* (December 2006). http://www.christianitytoday.com/ct/2006/december/21.61.html.

Collins, Gary. *Your Magnificent Mind: The Fascinating Ways It Works for You.* Grand Rapids, MI: Baker, 1988.

Drucker, Peter F. *The Post-Capitalist Society.* New York: HarperCollins, 1993.

Gaede, S. D. *When Tolerance Is No Virtue: Political Correctness, Multiculturalism & the Future of Truth and Justice.* Downers Grove, IL: InterVarsity Press, 1993.

Gill, David W. *The Opening of the Christian Mind: Taking Every Thought Captive to Christ.* Downers Grove, IL: InterVarsity Press, 1989.

Gross, David M., and Sophfronia Scott. "Proceeding With Caution." *Time* 136.3 (July 16, 1990) 56–62.

Henry, Carl F. H. *The Christian Mindset in a Secular Society: Promoting Evangelical Renewal and National Righteousness.* Portland, OR: Multnomah Press, 1984.

Howe, Neil, and William Strauss. *Millennials and the Pop Culture.* Great Falls, VA: Life Course Associates, 2006.

————. *Millennials Go to College: Strategies for a New Generation on Campus.* 2d ed. Washington, DC: American Association of Collegiate Registrars, 2007.

Lewis, Harry R. *Excellence without a Soul: How a Great University Forgot Education.* New York: Public Affairs, 2006.

Linnemann, Eta. *Historical Criticism of the Bible: Methodology or Ideology?* Grand Rapids, MI: Baker, 1990.

Noll, Mark. "The Scandal of the Evangelical Mind." *Christianity Today* 37 (October 25, 1993) 28–32.

Sommerville, C. John. *The Decline of the Secular University: Why the Academy Needs Religion*. Oxford: Oxford University Press, 2006.

Tinder, Glenn. "On the Political Meaning of Christianity: Can We Be Good Without God?" *Atlantic Monthly* 264.6 (December 1989) 69–85.

Walsh, Brian J., and J. Richard Middleton. *The Transforming Vision: Shaping a Christian World View*. Downers Grove, IL: InterVarsity Press, 1984.

FOR FURTHER READING

Elshtain, Jean B. "To Serve God Wittily, in the Tangle of One's Mind." In *Christianity and the Soul of the University: Faith as a Foundation for Intellectual Community*, edited by Douglas V. Henry and Michael D. Beaty, 37–47. Grand Rapids, MI: Baker Academic, 2006.

Heskett, Jim. "How Will Millennials Manage?" *Harvard Business School Working Knowledge for Business Leaders* (August 2, 2007). http://hbsk.hbs.edu/item/5736.html.

Howe, Neil, and William Strauss. *Millennials Rising: The Next Great Generation*. Toronto, ON: Random House of Canada, 2000.

Sire, James W. *Habits of the Mind: Intellectual Life as a Christian Calling*. Downers Grove, IL: InterVarsity Press, 2000.

PART TWO

The Academic Disciplines

4

A Christian Perspective on Art

Reflections from an "Ocean Dweller": Art as Mimesis, Form, Sign, and Philosophical Inquiry

ERICA GRIMM-VANCE

WHY STUDY ART? AN OCEAN DWELLER'S RESPONSE

WHEN LUDWIG WITTGENSTEIN WAS released from a prisoner of war camp in 1919, he emerged a changed man.[1] In his knapsack he carried a manuscript, newly finished, that he had worked on throughout his incarceration. Now famous, the book is known as the *Tractatus*.[2] In it, he analyzes how language works; he holds that language expresses things like facts clearly, but that the structure of language limits what can be spoken of. That the structure of language itself influences what can and cannot be said was, and is, an amazingly prescient idea. Most importantly, Wittgenstein's exploration of the limits of language was largely due to his interest in what language *cannot* express.[3] A friend of his explained, "Wittgenstein passionately believes that all that really matters in human life is precisely what, in his view, we must be silent about."[4] Wittgenstein spent his entire life thinking about language; he took great care to define what in the end he viewed as "unimportant," since "it is not the coastline of

1. What contributed to Wittgenstein's change was experiencing the horrors of war but also, according to Grayling, reading Tolstoy's account of the Gospels, *The Gospels in Brief*. See Grayling, *Wittgenstein*, 8.

2. Controversial and infamous, some would contend, since Wittgenstein himself reconsiders many of the conclusions he comes to in the *Tractatus* in his later writings.

3. Grayling, *Wittgenstein*, 16–19.

4. Zijlstra, *Language, Image and Silence*, 12.

that island which he is bent on surveying with such meticulous accuracy, but the boundary of the ocean."[5] The ocean that Wittgenstein is drawn to but remains silent about is religion, ethics, and aesthetics. Art, unlike descriptive or propositional language, can show that which is paradoxical and unspeakable, beyond language.[6] For Wittgenstein, furthermore, art can show what is most important in life.[7]

The majority of university courses concern themselves with the shoreline of logical facts, scientific investigations, and propositional theories: knowledge of a discursive (i.e., reasoning) kind. Art making explores the "unspeakable" ocean. It shows rather than tells, and although art making certainly entails reason, it uses a "language" of a different sort and taps into ways of knowing that extend beyond the discursive. Art has great respect for the shoreline since it requires theories, plunders other disciplines for insight and content, and is deeply connected to philosophy. Surprisingly, amongst its many methodologies are those that echo the mystical traditions, whose ancient technologies hone practitioners' attentiveness and seek to dislodge the ego. Like a contour line following the edge of an island, it also shapes the negative space around it; the line is equally of the negative space and of the positive form. What follows is an attempt to understand the ocean that is visual art, organizing its powerful energies, waves, and currents into some sort of coherent pattern. This attempt to understand the "ocean" that is visual art is probably insufficient to the task, knowing the chaotic unpredictability of the ocean (its primary appeal, after all). The attempt is akin to holding back the tide, since the language with which it is described is necessarily a second one.

As a provisional means of charting the ocean that is visual art, I have used four paradigms: Art as Mimesis, Art as Form, Art as Sign, and Art as Philosophical Inquiry. Obviously other constructs exist, but I have chosen these four paradigms because they have generated significant bodies of divergent work, igniting artists across continents and times; taken togeth-

5. Ibid.

6. Here I owe a debt of gratitude to Dr. Stuart Richmond, who introduced me to Wittgenstein's work and suggested this connection with the visual arts during the course of my Ph.D. program in Arts Education at Simon Fraser University. The metaphor of the ocean and the shore provides a unifying frame for this entire chapter. Also valuable was the generous feedback and lively conversation regarding the chapter from Timothy Long, head curator at Regina, Saskatchewan's MacKenzie Art Gallery, and Maggie Milne, my colleague at Trinity Western University.

7. Zijlstra, *Language, Image and Silence*, 29.

er, these purposes widen our horizons, bringing us closer to deciphering the complex discipline of art today. Like the oceans that circumscribe the earth, these purposes are permeable, for they flow and intermingle and certainly are not mutually exclusive. Possibly it is this very unpredictable fluidity that has both drawn and sadly repelled Christians from these watery depths. But before considering these four paradigms of art-making practice, let us start by grounding our conversation in the Creation and the Incarnation.

"IT WAS GOOD": CREATION AND INCARNATION

> We say that Christianity is a religion of the word, but it is the word made flesh. Perhaps we have forgotten the message contained in the foundations of this religion, that of the permanent joining of the body and signs. (Julia Kristeva)[8]

Julia Kristeva is on to something here. Belief in the Incarnation is a radical affirmation of the material realm. If one believes that God, in the person of Jesus, indwelt flesh and walked in our midst, then this has radical implications regarding our attitude towards the material "stuff" around us. It also has implications for what it means to be a molder of material. It suggests that the material realm is amazingly good since, in Martin Luther's words, it can "bear the infinite."[9] And even more amazingly, if the material realm *once* bore the infinite, then it is, even now, hallowed; it can, in a sense, bear the infinite again, especially "if we have eyes to see"[10] and if we live our lives with a particular kind of attentiveness.[11] To call oneself a Christian has implications for how one attends and what one attends to. Rilke puts it this way: "For all things sing you: at times we just hear them more clearly."[12] *All* things. Ordinary stuff can, unexpectedly and in the most unusual places, "flare out like shining from shook foil." For Gerard Manley Hopkins this is because the world is "charged with the grandeur of God."[13]

8. Cited in Penwarden, "Of Word and Flesh," 26.

9. Martin Luther is, in this well-known phrase, speaking of the Eucharist.

10. These are ee cummings' famous words, which echo the biblical text.

11. Conversation with Loren Wilkinson, Professor of Interdisciplinary Studies at Regent College, Vancouver, BC.

12. Rilke, *Book of Hours: Love Poems to God*, 81.

13. Hopkins, "God's Grandeur," 66.

Creation is good—very good in fact. Often I begin my first year art foundations classes by reading the first chapter of Genesis. We read in this ancient Hebrew text of a God that orders, separates, organizes, speaks, makes, gathers, calls, sees, blesses, and creates *ex nihilo*, out of nothing, bringing creation into existence. In the refrain, "It was good," repeated again, and again, and again—an astonishing seven times throughout this first chapter—we are assured that God likes what God has made.[14] Dorothy L. Sayers points out in the *Mind of the Maker* that it is at this point, in verse 27 of the *first* chapter of the biblical text, that a remarkable statement is made: men and women are made in God's image, when really, all that has been said about God is that God makes stuff, God creates.[15] Just what it means to be made in God's image has had a long history of speculation, but Sayers' point, that it has something to do with one's capacity to be creative in the first place, is compelling. Now admittedly, I hasten to add, God creates *ex nihilo*, and artists create, as the students discover as the semester progresses, out of matter: often recalcitrant, frustrating, sometimes weighty, awkward, resistant matter. And although I suspect that God did not experience frustration at the time of creation, we as human artists most certainly will. The creation narrative is a profound affirmation of the material realm that retains God's fingerprint. It also provides a penetrating insight into what it means to be made in the *Imago Dei* (image of God).

ART AS MIMESIS

Students often arrive in my first-year art foundations course holding that art making is about representing the world around them in a realistic manner. This common perception of art is known as Art as Mimesis or Art as Imitation. As we shall see, realistic reproduction is certainly not the only intent behind art making, but it has fuelled an enormous body of visual work. At the most basic level, mimesis responds to the energy of existence by attempting to breathe life into images, whether on paper,

14. Aldrich, "Through Sculpture," 104.

15. Sayers, *The Mind of the Maker*, 17. The ability to create is not the only interpretation of this verse; reason and moral choices are frequently cited. In an e-mail exchange with me, Timothy Long (cf. footnote 6) suggested that the verse be taken literally. Based on his reading of French anthropological philosopher Rene Girard, he explained, "Humans are images, end of story. That is to say, it is our essential nature to be mimetic. We create, but never originally, only by imitating something or somebody else."

in three dimensions, or in a digital image. Artists respond to something in the world outside themselves, and their visual work cajoles, criticizes, critiques, honors, questions, screams, or hints at a response. It is not just verisimilitude but reanimation that is being pursued. The struggle is to recreate, using visual form, that which has been seen,[16] to communicate without words—although it has to be said that many artworks, even of the imitative kind, contain words. This reanimation is, of course, not simply rote representation; it amalgamates reanimation of the visible with the maker's unique, personal expression. This is attested to in every drawing class as, consistently, drawings of the same form are astonishingly different by virtue of each mark being a result of each maker's perceptions translated through each maker's body. See Figure 1. The much celebrated cave paintings, the progressively honed Renaissance discovery of naturalism and linear perspective, and a whole host of contemporary manifestations of imitation mediated by numerous media technologies are but a few examples.

Besides rendering spaces and objects, mimetic work often represents other living entities, whether rendered in two-dimensional, three-dimensional, or digitally simulated forms. Images of the body are significant because they reveal and play a role in identity construction; images of another confront and simulate a mirror encounter. Referring to Rene Girard's seminal insights regarding human beings' propensity for mimesis, curator Timothy Long holds that being made in God's image means that we are images; we imitate. Images tell us "who we are" or perhaps "who we might be." Images are powerful since they exert a formative pressure on us. Images "hail us," as Marxist theorist Louis Althusser puts it.[17] Put another way, we become what we contemplate. We see this impulse evidenced in young people who seem particularly keen to surround themselves with images of other people, whether sports heroes, supermodels, or rock stars. Art history is filled with this type of encounter. The Egyptian Fayum portraits (funerary portraits dating from the Roman period [first to fourth centuries] found in Egyptian tombs), Greek and Russian icon paintings, the Northern and Italian Renaissance figurative tradition, the Postimpressionists, British figurative art (e.g., Lucien Freud), are rightly

16. For a discussion of this important philosophical issue, see Gombrich, *Art and Illusion.*

17. Sturken and Cartwright, *Practices of Looking,* 358. Althusser held that images form us unconsciously; then, sometimes years later, we recognize ourselves in them.

loved since the best work in each of these systems of imitating is infused with an almost tangible presence. They are successful in fixing in material a breathing life force, something palpable even today.[18]

Of course, in the twenty-first century, we are flooded with visual images that imitate, all too often, in a manipulative way. In twenty-four hours we typically see more images than a medieval person saw in a lifetime. Debord has identified ours as a visual society of spectacles in which consumer driven images mediate relations between people.[19] Advertisers unrepentantly manipulate mimetic imagery to create desire, influencing far more than product sales. For example, the saturation of images of everthinner female bodies coexists with a societal epidemic of eating disorders as young women try to recreate themselves in this impossible image. This is especially problematic for Christians, given, as we have seen, the belief that every human being is created in the *Imago Dei*. Obviously, contemporary visual images that imitate can also be used to subvert this manipulation, as publications like *Adbusters* have done brilliantly for almost twenty years. The objectifying gaze[20] damages, dehumanizes the "other" (given its attendant position of power), as numerous cultural theoreticians[21] have persuasively argued.

Significantly, the system of imaging that is employed—*how* figures are structured, *what* is included and what omitted, and *how* space is rendered—tellingly reveals what is vital in the society and culture in which the artist is doing the imaging. Humans have therefore been called meaning-making beings. Thus, images also reveal ideological biases. An imitative work may seem naturalistic, pure or unmediated, but it always contains a particular system of representation whose conventions are not neutral. Ways of imaging have historically been linked to the values and ideas that people hold and the assumptions about life that are common in a particular place and time. Artworks reflect the shared understandings, meanings, and biases of the culture in which they were created. Let

---

18. Berger, *The Shape of a Pocket*, writes with a sense of urgency about cave paintings, the Fayum Portraits, Michelangelo, Rembrandt, Degas, Vincent Van Gogh, and others from the vantage point of an artist rather than an art historian.

19. Debord, *The Society of the Spectacle*.

20. Sartre identified the "gaze" as the objectifying, alienating vision of strangers.

21. See Jay, *Downcast Eyes: The Denigration of Vision in Twentieth-Century French Thought*; Said, *Orientalism*; and Mulvey, "Visual Pleasures and Narrative Cinema."

us now look at some examples of how systems of rendering bodies and spaces are linked to meanings.

By scanning vastly different systems of imitating the body that emerge out of different cultures, we see how these systems reflect societal beliefs. Egyptian figures from the third millennia BCE ("Before the Common Era," used to denote years before the traditional date of the Birth of Christ—and thus an alternative to "BC") were based on the square due to its mathematical association with the Golden Ratio and the equiangular logarithmic spiral seen commonly in nature (the direction that water drains, the shape hurricanes take, the spiral core of the sunflower). Seeing it everywhere in nature, the Egyptians connected it with eternity and the afterlife. By shaping images of the figure using an amalgam of profiles, frontal views and squares, they attempted to fix for eternity the person's identity. Byzantine art also portrayed spiritual, symbolic resemblances rather than physical ones, but through the imitation of archetypal "holy images." Greek art improved on the individual by attempting to portray the ideal, creating elaborate mathematical formulas to achieve an image of the perfected human body as a suitable vehicle to express the divine. In the Renaissance this is translated into a humanistic celebration of "man as a measure" of all things.[22] Northern Renaissance painters portrayed physiognomic particularities and surface detail as material evidence of claims to piety, frugality, and hard work. Oddly, this trajectory culminates in the present day by imaging people through the single lens of the objectifying sexual gaze; however, it is in real flesh that these ideals are being carved as young people recreate themselves in Calvin Klein's image. In contemporary art Lucien Freud, Betty Goodwin, and Magdalena Abakanowicz[23] convey simultaneously a sacred presence and the existential brutality of global (in)humanity in their moving portrayals of human beings. Given how fundamentally grounded Christianity is in the flesh, as Julia Kristeva reminded us earlier, how the body is imitated is inseparable from an

22. Bro, *Figure and Form*, 123–29.

23. Most readers will probably not recognize many of the artists I refer to here. I recommend that a quick image search, even on Google, be done with each unrecognized name to see the type of visual form that is being discussed. This will make more obvious what otherwise might seem complicated because communication is being done verbally rather than visually. Some types of knowledge are poorly communicated with words but are quite apparent when the visual images themselves are seen.

exploration of spiritual questions.[24] As in archaeology, observing *how* a culture imitates the body gives significant clues to the "maker's" values. The system used to imitate conveys content; mimesis is always mediated and is never neutral.

Similarly, how space is depicted also reveals societal meanings and assumptions. Linear perspective, for example, is a system that is predicated upon what one eye sees at one moment in time. The view is fixed; the person drawing must not move, and the viewer is placed at the apex of the cone of vision, often described as a position of power. In "Scopic Regimes of Modernity," Martin Jay connects Renaissance notions of perspective with Cartesian ideas of subjective rationality in philosophy, whereas Northern art reflects more closely the observation-based empirical philosophical tradition.[25] In contrast, cubism shatters a single perspectival view by putting together many views of the same object simultaneously. Russian iconography displaces the viewer from a singular point of view, reversing the perspective so that the viewer is included in the widest apex of the cone of vision, as seen in Andrei Rublyev's famous "Icon of the Trinity." Surrealist work creates a dreamlike perspective, clearly paralleling theories of the unconscious articulated by Freud. Ways of rendering the visible world are thus inextricably linked to ideas bubbling up amongst philosophers; both shape as well as reflect the assumptions held by the culture in which they live.

Art as imitation has been around a long time. Plato, writing in an age that celebrated the arts, roughly 400 BCE, simply assumes "imitation" is what artists do. Ironically, Plato suggests banishing many artists, escorting them to the outskirts of the ultimate utopian city-state that he plans in conversation with Socrates and others in the dialogue of the *Republic* (398a). But why might Plato come to ostracize artists when his description of moments of insight echoes the artist's own working process? The answer lies in what Plato holds to be reality and what vehicle he thinks can reliably get at it. Contained in the *Republic* is Plato's famous allegory of the cave,[26] loved particularly for its potent description of "aha!"

---

24. See Prescott, ed., *A Broken Beauty,* for thoughtful essays regarding the contemporary depiction of the human body in art. The text accompanies an exhibition of art, conceived of by Bruce Herman and curated by Gordon Fuglie, of contemporary artists of faith, myself included, whose work depicts the body.

25. Jay, "Scopic Regimes of Modernity."

26. Plato, *Republic*, Book VII, 177–202. In the cave, people are held captive looking at shadows cast against the back wall of a cave. They assume these shadows are real and

moments of enlightenment that everyone will recognize from experience. Films such as *The Matrix* are contemporary retellings of the cave episode. Plato compares the material world to the cave's shadows/illusions, holding that the physical material realm is an imitation of the real world of unseen Forms or Ideas. A table made of wood, for example, is an imitation of the invisible, ultimate Idea or Form of Table, the real Table. The arts are therefore imitations of imitations, three times removed from "reality"; they are therefore dispensable, even dangerous due to their enormous potential to influence. Plato implies that art distances the individual from reality, whereas philosophy (thinking or contemplating) takes one closer to reality and truth.[27] One might suspect Plato of playing with his readers (he himself started life as a poet but turned to philosophy after meeting Socrates) since, despite his vehement dismissal of the artist's imitative tools, he still powerfully employs narration and poetry in the *Republic* itself. Perhaps one might best imitate Plato's methods rather than his words.[28] What is clear is that Plato suggests banishing certain types of

---

come up with elaborate attempts at interpreting them. But the shadows are merely cast by a fire behind them. Turning around reveals the shadows to be mere illusions, not realities at all. This realization requires an effort and entails difficulties, as does the subsequent ascent out of the cave to see the sun and the "real" world.

27. Thus began the long quarrel between philosophy and poetry extending notably through Hegel, Nietzsche, Murdoch, and Martin Jay.

28. My experience of the drawing process is that it is a honing of the gaze, but this gaze is very different from the objectifying gaze that produces much media and popular culture. The manipulative bombardment of images of a certain sort of over-sexualized superficial beauty by media and popular culture are dangerous because they influence the attitudes, the self-images, and the actions of entire generations of young people. I wonder if these were the kind of stereotypic images—images that do not tell but distort the truth—that Plato was objecting to so strenuously in the *Republic* (written around 380 BCE) when he suggested that this sort of artist would be politely escorted to the outskirts of the city. The disciplining of the eyes and exquisite attentiveness developed while drawing requires self-forgetfulness. Unselfconsciousness while drawing is usually the experience of those who love to draw. The pencil is indwelt in the same way that Polanii famously describes a dentist indwelling the tool. I think that the same happens with sight. When one is unselfconscious, the self, with its multiple, complex grids of gender, sexuality, culture, etc., falls away. Stereotypes also fall away. Like Plato's famous description of prisoners looking at shadows cast against the wall of a cave, then turning to see the fire that generates the shadows, and then eventually ascending out of the cave to see the sun itself, so a sequential clarifying of sight occurs as one learns to draw. The other is seen without the reified distortion of form born out of the visual prejudice produced by living in such a visually saturated society. Like the chained prisoners seeing the fire, then reflections of the sun, and then gradually the sun itself, vision is cleansed and beauty is

artists simply due to their potential power to not only influence but also deceive.[29]

Aristotle, who was Plato's student, suggests that artists do not recreate the visible world but improve upon it via imagination and intuition. They arrive at an ideal representation; they present the invisible[30] by representing that which is beyond words, the ineffable or intangible. Artists by virtue of their imaginative powers do not hinder, but, like philosophers, help to reveal reality and truth. Art and philosophy are potent vehicles of understanding and, as is the case with powerful tools, have the potential to lead to reality (or truth or the Good) but also to lead astray. Now why might artists today care what Plato or Aristotle believed? Most, in fact, do not. The reason I include them is that a surprisingly large number of assumptions (including some false ones) that people today hold regarding the work, value, and place of art and artists originate with Plato and Aristotle.

In *The Shape of a Pocket,* John Berger draws on French social philosopher Simone Weil when he suggests that the chief attribute of art as imitation is the cultivation of attentiveness. "To forget oneself, however briefly, to identify with a stranger to the point of fully recognising her or him, is to defy necessity, and in this defiance, even if small and quiet . . . there is a power which cannot be measured by the limits of the natural order. It is not a means and it has no end. The Ancients knew this."[31] The practice of art as imitation hones one's capacity for attentiveness, providing perceptual tools to see through the flood of stereotypic images that "are to the eye what prejudices are to the brain,"[32] By heightening perceptual awareness, the artist is like an antenna or open wound, unsatisfied

---

recognized in each human face. Seeing in this way affects a great deal more than one's drawings. It is the first step in putting aside not only cultural constructs but in transcending the ego. Iris Murdoch and Simone Weil both describe the importance of developing attentiveness. For Weil it is the real purpose for studying anything since it directly corresponds to one's ability to pray. Murdoch describes honing one's attentiveness as the first step in the de-selfing or unseating of the ego, the first step in living a moral and ethical life. For further reading see Murdoch's *The Sovereignty of Good* and Weil's "Reflections on the Right Use of School Studies."

29. For further reading, see Murdoch, *The Fire and the Sun: Why Plato Banished the Artists.*

30. See Clarke, *The Nude: A Study in Ideal Form,* 12.

31. Berger, *The Shape of a Pocket,* 179.

32. Matisse quoted in Flam, *Matisse on Art,* 148.

with stereotype, asking, through the medium of art, hard questions and aiming at truth telling. And the best work has the glimmer of truth about it. Something is communicated that one recognises, feels, but cannot quite name. Art, as both Plato and Aristotle recognised, is a powerful tool that can be used positively or negatively. In the process of art as imitation, one's attentiveness is sharpened in a particular kind of way. One can participate in the "gaze" that Sartre likened to the objectifying vision of strangers, or, to use Martin Buber's terminology, one can see the other not as an I–It, but as an I–Thou.[33] Art as mimesis can be an objectifying act or an empathetic act; the work of art always shows the difference. Perhaps this was part of what Wittgenstein recognised as being beyond the limits of language.

ART AS FORM

> I think everyone starts out by seeing a few works of art and wanting to do something with them. You want to understand what you see, what is there, and you try to make a picture out of it. Later you realize that you can't represent reality at all—that what you make represents nothing but itself, and therefore is itself reality. (Gerard Richter)[34]

At the opposite end of the spectrum of representational practices from art as imitation, art as form experiments with lines, tones, textures, shapes, edges, light, surfaces, forms, scale, and colors, unhinging representation from the imitation of recognisable natural appearances. Although art as imitation does employ visual form in order to imitate, this paradigm uses form as a potent communicator of content without imitating something. Dyrness, discussing the value of abstract art works, remarks that they "defy translation into data, information, entertainment, rational image or any kind of narrative. [They] present an ineffable balance of sensation, experience, and knowledge."[35]

A mark or backwash of pigment can be expressive (can create meaning) without having also to imitate something other than what it is. See, for example, Figure 2 (p. 82), Makoto Fujimura's *Still Point—Evening*, which employs no mimetic devices but yet communicates powerfully via

33. Buber, *I and Thou*.
34. Richter, *The Daily Practice of Painting*, 72.
35. Dyrness, *Visual Faith: Art, Theology, and Worship in Dialogue*, 16.

the contrasts and graduations between light and dark, through marks and materials. Form, rather than imitation, becomes the primary vehicle for expression. Of course, even art as imitation uses visual form to imitate and to express meaning. Brand and Chaplin explain that "[t]he form of a work of art conveys meaning which goes beyond that of its subject matter. It can convey a general sense of, for instance, order or disorder, balance or imbalance, warmth or coldness, cheerfulness or gloom, fluidity or rigidity. The whole point about art is how this form transforms the subject matter."[36] Art as form can be profoundly expressive and meaningful even when the subject matter is not imitative.

In 1912, Kandinsky radically proposed, in *Concerning the Spiritual in Art*, that color harmony ought to reflect a direct correspondence with the human soul rather than illustrate the local color of an object.[37] He announced a "spiritual revolution" in painting by calling artists to express their interior life directly through abstract visual form. Analogous to music, abstract compositions draw heavily on mathematical sequences, rhythm, repetition, and the illusion of motion.[38] Art as imitation had, over time, been drained of energy; it had become systematized, ceasing to be a challenge and losing its ability to communicate. Art reduced to polished technique failed to give life to either artist or viewer. The energy that came from "fixing in material stasis an imitation of what is seen" failed. Instead, the spark came from the freedom of throwing off the confines of imitative form, as a musician would, if, after simply imitating sounds in nature, she could suddenly create with sound itself, with notes, chords, octaves, harmony, rhythm, and counterpoint to communicate a whole range of feelings and musical ideas directly.

In 1913, amidst the anticipation of the Russian Revolution, Kasimir Malevich, writing similarly of the struggle to free art from the burden of representation, painted a square form on a white field. He related this radical reduction to the elegant simplicity of theories such as Einstein's Theory of Relativity and, like Einstein, relied on intuition and the imagination, his work containing "both scientific and mystical overtones."[39] Thus began the Suprematist movement, which looked to geometric non-objective forms

---

36. Brand and Chaplin, *Art and Soul*, 142.

37. Kandinsky, *Concerning the Spiritual in Art*, 26.

38. Ibid., 6–20.

39. Cited in Jansen, *History of Art*, 786.

to portray "supreme" reality, essences of scientific and spiritual purity, as a means to imagine a new revolutionary *Zeitgeist*.

Influenced by surrealism, existentialism, and Jungian psychology and developed in a context shaken by World War II, Abstract Expressionism explores non-objective form in two stylistic variations known as Action Painting and Color Field Painting. Championed by art critic Clement Greenberg, the retention of the two-dimensional flatness of the canvas and celebration of "materials as materials" became a canonical mantra. "Content is to be dissolved so completely into form," said Greenberg, "that the work of art or literature cannot be reduced in whole or in part to anything not itself."[40] For Greenberg paintings were not windows on the world but were canvas and paint; imitations of any kind were dishonest and limiting. It is hard to imagine now, with the current plethora of stylistic possibilities, how hegemonic (i.e., generally unquestioned ideologically and put forward as common sense) this viewpoint was and how thoroughly marginalized were those who persisted in other practices.

This investigation fuelled work in Europe and North America from 1912 through the entire modernist era, roughly into the 1950s and 60s. Individuals like Gerhard Richter have continued, intermittently from 1960 through to the present, to make abstract paintings, many characterized by images that are absolutely "paint" but with a remarkable spatial logic.[41] As powerful as abstraction was as a generator of artistic energy in the modernist period, it too has gradually cycled down to be eclipsed by other concerns. And of course 1912 was not the first time artists have explored inner feelings and abstract rather than naturalistic form. Pre-Cycladic Greek figures, Coast Salish carvings, Kwa'kwak'kwak ceremonial masks, Iranian Khatam-kari, traditional African art, and North American quilting traditions are all highly sophisticated non-objective ways of working. Pattern, color, material, and surface are their common vocabulary. It was, of course, the influence of seeing these cultural forms (whose vastly different intentions were later labelled art—evidence of a modernist construct in action) that enabled western artists to "discover" abstraction.

Technically speaking, *abstract* refers to art that retains a connection to what is seen in the world, a simplification of reality, for example, whereas non-objective work is fully independent of *realistic* subject matter. Both

40. Greenburg, "Avant-Garde and Kitsch," 51.

41. See www.gerhard-richter.com/art/.

can be understood from a different vantage point as being more firmly rooted in the real world than art as imitation ever was. Both abstract and non-objective work is profoundly connected to what is—the material world. Both abstract and non-objective works exhibit a profound respect for materials themselves—the pigments, wood, clay, fibre, or metal that make up the work. Materials are attended to with care. Paint is paint, wood is wood, metal is metal. Pigments, all by themselves, speak—given, as we have seen, that they still are embedded with the stamp of the Creator. So also do clay, steel, and limestone speak. Each has inherent characteristics that are to be celebrated, not made to imitate something else. To force materials into an imitative role is to not respect what they are. Seen from the vantage point of the practitioner, putting aside imitation is not an escape from the material realm (as many philosophers and theologians mistakenly believe) but is, in fact, an indication of profound respect for the miracle that materials are. Respect for material is a tradition with long roots stretching back to Aristotle and his profound, meticulous attentiveness to the material world. In medieval times, Aquinas extended this, holding that God cannot be approached directly but reveals God's self through material "corporeal similitudes."[42]

The artist lives jammed in a pool of materials (as Annie Dillard so eloquently put it in *Holy the Firm*).[43] To be an artist is to profoundly trust those materials. Aldrich suggests in her essay, "Through Sculpture: What's the Matter with Matter," that materials are not neutral; materials change both content and ideas.[44] Given the proclaimed "goodness" of creation that we saw earlier, the embedded wisdom within materials is what artists discover, respect, and then fashion from.[45] The material realm is the visual artist's alphabet, but it is more. The artist does not just project intelligence into material but, for Aldrich, "uses material to think with."[46] For Simone Weil, the created realm has the potential of being *Metaxu*, a "bridge between us and God."[47] This idea is perhaps best expressed by Rilke in a

---

42. Cited in Eco, *Art and Beauty in the Middle Ages*, 63.

43. Dillard, *Holy the Firm*, 22.

44. Aldrich, "Through Sculpture," 98–117.

45. Begbie, "Christians and the Arts in a Post-Modern Age."

46. Aldrich, "Through Sculpture," 104.

47. Weil, "Metaxu," 363.

poetic form: "All things sing you."[48] Similarly for the Canadian poet Susan McCaslin, "the avoidable and appropriate path lies in descending into [material] rather than in escaping prematurely to a transcendence outside or beyond the world. . . . [T]here is an insistence that things are both themselves and mean beyond themselves."[49] Hence to be an artist and to be a Christian is to absolutely reject the Manichean separation of spirit and matter and the dualistic privileging of spirit over matter. In *Radical Orthodoxy*, Milbank, Pickstock, and Ward's perspective of participation (*methexis*) insists on the material and the spiritual existing in tension. "Materialism and spiritualism are false alternatives";[50] material is not to be denigrated or denied. It is the conduit through to the spiritual. Materials properly are to be respected and attended to with a grammar of self-emptying listening, a letting-go of preconceived notions.

Neither abstract nor non-objective images are generated in a vacuum; rather, the artist is communicating something. Whether by an emotional, analytical, mathematical, intuitive, or spiritual insight, an interior experiential reality is being conveyed. Subject matter is not representational, although lived experience is clearly responded to. Rudolf Otto believes non-objective art can convey transcendent experiences that can "impress the observer with the feeling that the void is depicted as the main subject of the picture."[51] For Otto there is a direct correlation between pictorial emptiness and the void spoken of by the mystics. He mentions Asian work connected to the contemplative traditions, and clearly the work of Kandinsky, Mark Rothko, Barnett Newman, and, more recently, Makoto Fujimura, also participate in this attempt. Newman described his work as creating a "modern mythology concerned with numinous ideas and feelings . . . it is concerned with metaphorical implications, with divine mysteries."[52] Expressionism like that produced in Germany and England prior to and after the World Wars powerfully translates "sheer anguish into visual form."[53] For Richter the intent is less ambitious: "What counts

48. Rilke, *Book of Hours: Love Poems to God*, 81.

49. McCaslin, *A Matter of Spirit: Recovery of the Sacred in Contemporary Canadian Poetry*, 17.

50. In Milbank, Pickstock, and Ward, eds., *Radical Orthodoxy*, 4.

51. As quoted in Howes, *The Art of the Sacred*, 157–58.

52. See Baigell, "Barnett Newman's Stripe Paintings and Kabbalah: A Jewish Take," 617.

53. Jansen, *History of Art*, 816.

is always just one thing: how I am to cope in this world, with myself and with painting."[54] Abstract, Expressive, and Non-objective traditions communicate the interior life powerfully without words (using the vocabulary of line, tone, form, texture, and color). These art works convey everything from the silence of spiritual rapture to the elegant "aha!" of scientific discovery, from fervent ecstasy to cool detachment, from angry outrage to the grief and lament generated by the insane brutality of war. As Wittgenstein experienced firsthand, words are ultimately insufficient for some communicative tasks. In these cases, art can show what words cannot tell.[55]

ART AS SIGN

> The creative act is not performed by the artist alone; the spectator brings the work in contact with the external world by deciphering and interpreting its inner qualifications and thus adds his contribution to the creative act. (Marcel Duchamp)[56]

Jean-Francois Lyotard was the first to theorize the term *Postmodern*. He did so in a publication, *The Postmodern Condition: A Report on Knowledge*, commissioned in 1979 in Quebec. (The very first person to use the term *Postmodern* was Leo Steinberg in his 1972 essay "Other Criteria," a defence of painter Robert Rauschenberg). Lyotard describes the effect of postmodernism in his report as "a transformation of the game rules for science, art, and literature since the end of the 19th century."[57] What might he have meant by this? And what might have instigated such a paradigm shift? Dunning describes, in *The Roots of Postmodernity*, how a metaphor of language as sign begins to captivate artists, eclipsing interests in imitation and formalism. He notes that American scientist-philosopher

54. Richter, *The Daily Practice of Painting*, 231.

55. Mulder notes that many Christians tend to reject such non-representational artistic creations out of hand, with little or no forethought. "In my opinion, instilling the 'response' instinct rather than allowing the 'reaction' response to overrule ought to comprise a key principle of Christian education. It ultimately distinguishes truly educated Christians from milk-fed Puritans trained up with platitudes and superficial attitudes from the safe subculture of [evangelical] Christianity" ("Christian Worldview and the Arts," 198).

56. Duchamp, from Session on the Creative Act, Convention of the American Federation of Arts, Houston, Texas, as reported in Wikipedia, "Marcel Duchamp."

57. Lyotard, *Postmodern Condition*, xxiii.

Charles Sanders Peirce, the developer of semiotics, literally the science of signs, held that meaning is not found in the perception of a sign but in the interpretation of the sign. This thesis influenced Saussure, whose analysis of language structures has transformed many fields in the humanities, not just art.[58] Together with interest in Wittgenstein's notion of "language games," we see a growing interest in language itself. The insight that captivated artists, and so profoundly changed their art-making practices, was that all meaning-making activities or forms of communication are composed of signs, whether "painting, religion [or] the clothes we wear are embedded in an overall linguistic structure and are guided by all the rules, organizations, and relationships between parts that are characteristic of linguistic structures."[59] Signs are not limited to words; signs can be visual, gestural, aural, or performative. Meaning is parsed, decoded, or read within a context; it is interpreted. The context is crucial for the operation of the sign. For example, some gangs signify membership by wearing certain clothes, but someone outside the gang is unaware that communication is taking place. Lists of numbers and anachronisms listed daily in the newspaper have great import to a stock broker but have less meaning to someone not able to decode this information. Meaning is contingent upon the interpreter recognizing the code. Meanings can change in different contexts and/or when interpreted by someone with a different code. Red, for example, has entirely different meanings in Western and in Asian contexts. Quite simply, it means that painting and other activities can be understood as a kind of language whose meanings are bound up with a context and a viewer.

Art as sign expands the conversational complexity by taking seriously, or playing with, the context and the viewer. The "game" is no longer just between the artist and the object he or she creates, but equally takes into consideration what the spectator brings to the interpretative table and how the context influences the meanings that are made. Meanings are constructed through signs and are not pre-existent. Furthermore, meanings are made not just by the artist, but also by complex interactions between artist, object, viewer, and context. Like art that imitates and art as

58. As Dunning goes on to outline, the linguistic metaphor was applied to psychiatry by Jacques Lacan, to anthropology by Claude Levi-Strauss, to other social sciences by Michel Foucault, and to philosophy by Jacques Derrida, who developed deconstruction (*The Roots of Postmodernism*, viii).

59. Ibid.

form, art as sign is layered with meanings that require decoding. But art as sign extends this decoding practice by explicitly shifting or questioning those readings. The viewer's interpretive function, phenomenological experience, and the cultural context are explicitly part of the artist's "toolbox." This opens art-making practices up to a wide array of methods and strategies that had not previously been considered.[60]

Let's look at some examples. Bill Viola's profound multimedia installation work functions as a sign, surrounding the spectator; through video and film he shifts scale, destabilizing the viewer, invoking mythic themes, and provoking new perceptual awareness.[61] Tim Rollins collaborates with marginalized, poverty-stricken inner-city kids (K.O.S. stands for Kids of Survival) by reading canonical pieces of literature, then layering the actual text as the first step in making artworks that are now in most contemporary Art Museums in the Western world.[62] Social interaction is at the heart of their practice; many of those neglected Bronx kids are now in university. Jana Sterbak's *Vanitas: Flesh Dress for an Albino Anorectic* was a dress sewed from flank steaks that brilliantly and controversially critiqued the fashion industry's position of power.[63] Her use of material (the meat) is a sign. Each of these artists incorporates context and collaborates with the spectators in remarkable ways. See Figure 3 (p. 83), Lynn Aldrich's *Baptistery*, which uses pages of pool design images from glossy coffee table books. The pools are isolated by gold paint, after which all the pages are assembled, creating a "text" that describes a contemporary architecture for the sacrament of baptism.

Whereas art as imitation can be seen to focus on subject; art as form explores the expressiveness of visual form unhinged from illusion; art as sign mines the shared meanings within culture and deconstructs content. The work requires interpretation by a viewing community that will recognize the conventions, have the shared background to decode the signs, and read the meaning. For example, Canadian artist Brian Jungen uses ordinary consumerist objects (a practice known as bricolage) like Nike Air Jordan running shoes, and cuts, reconfigures, and hand-sews them to resemble traditional aboriginal masks in a double appropriation,

---

60. See Sturken and Cartwright, *Practices of Looking*, and Hall, ed., *Representation: Cultural Representations and Signifying Practices*.

61. See Bill Viola's website.

62. Pedulla, "Fulfilled in Your Seeing."

63. See Jana Sterback's website.

critiquing simultaneously corporate corruption and cultural assimilation.[64] To appropriate is to steal a code from one context and use it in another. The interest here is not to find a universal language but rather a context-dependent one. One needs to know of the historical appropriation of aboriginal work, the meaning associated with objects like Nike running shoes, and the fact that Jungen is from First Nations roots to fully "get" his work.[65] Jungen's art can be read as a wittily scathing Postcolonial critique of culture.

Art as sign explores all meaning-making practices within a culture, freely deconstructing and decoding, to mine their metaphoric potential. Images and objects from all walks of life enter the gallery, and, conversely, art moves out of the gallery and into the public sphere. Boundaries between "high," "low" (e.g., tattoos), popular (cartoons), and anti-art (graffiti) are blurred. Images from media, advertising, medical, scientific, and consumer culture are freely used, critiqued, and appropriated; collaborative and collective practices challenge the understanding of artist as individual genius; the ocular-centric nature of culture is exposed and challenged; and theory is used to mine the textual meanings of visual signs.[66] Like art that imitates and art as form, artists that "sign" work with all kinds of materials—graphite, paper, clay, stone, pigments, steel, wood, cathode ray tubes, video, film, drywall, and digital tools. But they also work with pure light, sound, space, time. Their tools are signs and what they signify; their materials ordinary objects and the assumptions of cultural contexts.

Art as sign has therefore made possible a new kind of ethical art practice. In *Mapping the Terrain: New Genre Public Art*, Lacy considers 90 artists, Tim Rollins and K.O.S. amongst them, whose engaged, caring, public art or art activism is fuelled by issues of our time (eco catastrophe, race, homelessness, aging, gang warfare, cultural identity, etc.). These artists use both traditional and non-traditional mediums, but all structure their work to engage and collaborate with their audiences. New Genre refers to art that combines media with numerous methodologies to promote audience engagement and rigorous social critique.[67]

---

64. See "Brian Jungen," on the website of the Canada Council for the Arts.
65. Burnham, "The Instant 'I Get It' of Brian Jungen's Art."
66. Sturken and Cartwright, *Practices of Looking*, 6.
67. Lacy, *Mapping the Terrain*.

Art as sign is, of course, not new. In *The Teacher*, written in AD 389, Augustine analyzes the purpose of language, parsing differences between sign, signifier, and signified.[68] Signs are combinations of signifiers (the literal word, sound, or image) and what is signified (meaning). In 1957, Roland Barthes brought Ferdinand de Saussure's linguistic metaphor together with Augustine's insight to reveal signs as dependent on underlying codes and conventions that are constructed, dependent on social, historical, and cultural context, and, therefore, able to function like myths.[69] His work, revealing the ideologies that permeate images and the viewer's unconscious participation in making meaning, has been enormously influential in film and art criticism. Bro calls images that carry significance, whose potency goes beyond their literal meaning, *charged images* or *icons*. They depend on the viewer understanding the coded significance, whether of a cultural, religious, or political kind. All kinds of images, she continues, whether religious icon, political slogan, or advertising billboard, derive their power from this process.[70] Artists can hold up these meanings or deconstruct them, and viewers can accept the dominant images or resist them through a range of oppositional readings.[71]

Dunning traces similar signing interests in the Middle Ages, in the fifteenth-century Netherlands, in the art of Duchamp, and in a great deal of non-western art. Surrealism, pop, minimalist, performance, and feminist art all function as signs. Some recurrent characteristics of art as sign are: the use of symbols, theories, text, social concerns, plurality of styles, charged images, identity issues, ordinary materials, and a waning of interest in concerns of perception, form, and illusory techniques. When Wittgenstein formulated his notion of the "multiplicity of language games"[72] in his late work, I am sure he never would have anticipated the influence he, and others with a fascination with language, would come to have on the development of the visual "language game."

---

68. Augustine, *Against the Academicians* and *The Teacher*, 94–117.

69. Barthes, *Mythologies*, 109–36.

70. Bro, *Figure and Form*, 185–205.

71. Sturken and Cartwright, *Practices of Looking*, 55–70.

72. Cited in Grayling, *Wittgenstein*, 83.

ART AS PHILOSOPHICAL INQUIRY

When Duchamp signed a urinal and exhibited it in the 1917 exhibition of the New York Society of Independent Artists, he caused considerable consternation. He also challenged the widely held assumptions of what constitutes art.[73] By what some described as a cheeky, disrespectful act, he provoked people to ask a serious question of a philosophical nature: "What is art?" If Duchamp's *Fountain* is not art, why wouldn't it be art? Would it be art if it were drawn, or meticulously reproduced in clay? Is the idea art, or is it art when it is exhibited in a gallery? This requires one to think about the boundary between what is and what is not art. Whereas art as sign blurs contextual boundaries and requires the interpretive collaboration of the spectator, art as philosophical inquiry inhabits the boundaries between what is and is not art.

Art, like all disciplines, engages in conversations amongst its practitioners, historians, and theorists regarding cutting edge research, new developments or directions in the field, taking the next step. Often this means contesting the boundary of art-making practice. It can also entail blurring interdisciplinary boundaries by utilizing new technologies and new artistic forms. Canadian installation artist Janet Cardiff's *40 Part Motet* is often described as an audio piece (see Figure 4, p. 84). Forty speakers, mounted at head height on music stands and arranged in an oval, transmit individual tracks of forty separately recorded singers. Each is singing one of the forty parts of Thomas Tallis's polyphonic choral masterpiece *Spem in Alium*. From the centre of the oval, viewers hear individual voices and physically feel sound waves when the entire forty voices are singing the famous polyphonic music. She says, "I am interested in how sound may physically construct a space in a sculptural way and how a viewer may choose a path through this physical, yet virtual, space."[74] The piece is not about the virtuosity of either the speakers or the individual singers but about the sculptural potential of sound to create a corporeal experience of the body as receptor and about questions of identity mediated through technological means.

Mona Hatoum, a Palestinian artist from Lebanon, uses the body as a metaphor for social struggle. *Corps etranger* uses an endoscopic camera to survey the interior of the body. The movements of the endoscopic camera

73. Bro, *Figure and Form*, 216, and Sturken and Cartwright, *Practices of Looking*, 353.
74. See the website of Janet Cardiff and George Bures Miller.

are projected on the floor, which is encased in a womb-like space. The camera, becoming a symbol for political invasion and violation, is a means of exploring achingly tragic, seemingly irresolvable human histories. Boundaries are blurred in these two pieces between art, music, medical imaging systems, and tragic lived experiences for which no easy solutions exist. Can sound constitute sculptural space? Can human anguish be made potent using the contested tools of science and medical imaging? Do we recognize a truth about our own reality and identity through seeing speakers and hearing human conversation and voice through them?

Orlan is a controversial artist who, through surgical interventions, restructures her own face as her art. Recent collaborations between genetic engineers and artists have raised real dilemmas regarding the ethical boundaries of what is allowable in either the name of research or art making. Art on the edge of the discipline inquires into the technological complexities and ideological uncertainties of meaning making, an activity that can sometimes change our perception of the world. Through the philosophical process of asking "What is art?" and by exploring new means of inquiring about the experiences of being alive, art as philosophical inquiry extends both the means and the ends of art.

Both art and philosophy examine inquiry itself. Philosophy, at its most basic level, is concerned with understanding knowledge, reality, and existence. It means literally "the love of wisdom." Widely respected historian of ancient philosophy Pierre Hadot said, "I've always believed that philosophy was a concrete act, which changed our perception of the world, and our life: not the construction of a system. It is a life, not a discourse."[75] By Hadot's definition, it is not only written philosophical texts that can change our perception of the world. Art qualifies as well. Neilsen comes to a similar conclusion when he says, "Words aren't the only symbols and books aren't the only [meaning-making] texts."[76] The artist Gerhard Richter calls painting "a kind of applied epistemology."[77] Similarly, Karl Rahner describes the non-verbal arts as vehicles of human self-expressions, embodying the process of human self-discovery, having therefore "the same value and significance as the verbal arts."[78] He believes

75. Hadot, *Philosophy as a Way of Life*, 279.
76. Neilsen, "Are Paintings Texts?" 289.
77. Richter, *The Daily Practice of Painting*, 68.
78. Cited in Howes, *The Art of the Sacred*, 160.

that art communicates truth regarding being human that cannot be translated into verbal theology. Taylor charts the epiphanic nature of much modern art in *Sources of the Self*. The equation of metaphysics and art is echoed by Hart in *Unfinished Man and the Imagination* and by Hadot, who refers to Wittgenstein:

> But everything that touches the domain of the existential—which is what is most important for human beings—for instance our feeling of existence, our impressions when faced by death, our perceptions of nature, our sensations, and *a fortiori* the mystical experience, is not directly communicable. The phrases we use to describe them are conventional and banal; we realize this when we try to console someone over the loss of a loved one. That's why it often happens that a poem or a biography is more philosophical than a philosophical treatise, simply because they allow us to glimpse this unsayable in an indirect way. Here again, we find the kind of mysticism evoked in Wittgenstein's *Tractatus*: "There is indeed the inexpressible." This shows itself; it is the mystical.[79]

Art as philosophical inquiry asks "What is life?" and contests "What is art?" redefining its boundaries. By stretching and interrogating the boundaries of what is and is not art, visual art can show what words cannot tell.

As I said at the beginning of this chapter, the majority of university subject areas concern themselves with the shoreline of logical facts, scientific investigations, propositional theories—knowledge of a discursive or "reasoning" kind. Art-making explores the ocean. In *Art Practice as Research: Inquiry in the Visual Arts*, Sullivan argues for art being a legitimate way of knowing and the kind of practices in which artists engage in their studios being valid research that contributes to new knowledge. Sullivan grounds visual art research in its own practices, rather than those borrowed from the social sciences, and in its own cognitive capacities that inherently inform visual making and thinking. Sullivan is beginning the groundbreaking task of identifying and legitimizing the practices that are inherently unique to the thinking, knowing, and making of the non-verbal arts.[80] The articulation of visual practices, like the exploration of the ocean, has only just begun.

---

79. Hadot, *Philosophy as a Way of Life*, 285.
80. Sullivan, *Art Practice as Research*, 115–22.

THE CHRISTIAN VOCATION OF ART-MAKING[81]

The Christian artist can obviously and unhesitatingly participate in each of these art-making practices, differences in personality and temperament largely being the determining factors in whether an artist chooses the more contemplative internal exploration of non-objective art as form or the rather more extroverted art as sign activism that prophetically deconstructs societal ills and justice issues. Art as imitation celebrates the created order, and its practice hones the practitioner's attentiveness. The process encourages the displacement of the ego and parallels the process of prayer. Art as philosophical inquiry extends the definition of art, asks questions common to theology, and can communicate what verbal theology cannot.[82]

Artists live their lives with a certain kind of attentiveness and listen in a particular way. Like the religious cultivation of ancient technologies that hone the contemplative's capacity to listen, amongst artists are developed methodologies to hone one's capacity to be attentive, although these practices usually have mundane labels like drawing. Visual artists listen, being simultaneously attentive to their materials, to the work as it unfolds before them, to the history and theory of their discipline via

81. CIVA (Christians in the Visual Arts), an international network of Christians in the arts, with membership drawn principally from artists in the USA and Canada, and the journal *Image: A Journal of the Arts and Religion*, now called *Image: Art Faith Mystery*, edited by Gregory Wolfe and published by the Center for Religious Humanism, both foster conversations about faith and art. In Canada, the organization Imago does similar work. In the UK, Jeremy Begbie has established the Institute for Theology, Imagination and the Arts, with similar goals.

82. A good example of this capacity seems to have been evident in the general public's response to the "Seeing Salvation—The Image of Christ" art exhibition at the National Gallery in London during the summer of 2000. Graham Howes remarks that the event saw an average of 5,000 visitors a day over a four and a half month period, breaking box office records for any British art exhibition of the previous two decades and demonstrating that modern, largely secular audiences "can engage with the masterpieces of Christian art at an emotional as well as a purely aesthetic or historical level" (*The Art of the Sacred*, 48). One observer commented that in spite of the crowded conditions of the National Gallery rooms, a quiet, respectful hush dominated the atmosphere as people moved past the pictures: "Despite the queues and the heat there was no jostling and no noise . . . as if the pictures and the artifacts exerted a powerful hold on the visitors." It was analogous to "going into a cathedral" where people were "full of awe, sorrow and reverence" (54). In Canada, the *Anno Domini: Jesus through the Centuries* exhibition curated by David Goa at the Provincial Museum of Alberta at the end of 2000 received similar overwhelmingly positive responses.

the visual discoveries of artists before them, to the givenness of their own bodies and creative capacities fearfully and wonderfully made in the *Imago Dei*, to the creation, to the biblical text, and to silence where, when they listen very closely, they discern a "small still voice." In a CBC "North by Northwest" radio interview, the poet Lorna Crozier spoke of silence as beginning and ending every work of art. She quoted Nietzsche as saying people do not like to be alone as they are afraid that something will be whispered in their ears. By contrast, visual artists wait with fierce attentiveness for that whisper.[83] For poet Tim Lillburn, listening is also a compositional methodology. Echoing the practice of listening prayer that originated in the fourth century with John Cassion and the Desert Fathers and Mothers, he offers self-emptying listening as a compositional device suggesting that the artist listens not only at the beginning and end but also all the way through creating a work of art.

But the cultivation of this interior silence is tough work in western culture. Internet, Facebook, MP3 players, game cubes, all manner of digital culture and technological breakthroughs make it possible to experience a great deal in a simulacrum of sorts with no connection to the real world. It is possible to have the volume turned up to such an extent and degree that interior awareness is impossible; moments when it is experienced are inadvertent and are therefore frightening and awkward. Listening to the "teacher within" might be a skill with an unprecedented few practitioners. Therefore, the cultivation of methodologies like drawing that introduce interior awareness and silence can be likened to a moral imperative, an apprenticeship in attentiveness, a precursor to the ability to pray.

I do recognize that the majority of you reading this chapter will not likely end up becoming practising artists. You would not have read to this point in the chapter, however, if you did not wish to understand art better—as well as to have a better idea of how one's Christian faith can illuminate both the purpose and the practice of art. Siedell provides both helpful advice on these questions and an appropriate word of caution when he says:

> Art can shape us, reveal new aspects of experience, deepen our understanding of common experiences, and embody transcendence. This is why so much evangelical thinking about the visual arts, and particularly about modern and contemporary art, is pro-

83. Interview with Lorna Crozier on CBC radio program "North by Northwest," December 2007.

foundly iconoclastic [hostile to images]. One gets the sense that
it must never be experienced on its own, for its own sake. It must
be screened through the filter of "worldview thinking" or at the
safe distance of some philosophy or history of art that keeps the
material specificity of the work of art from doing anything other
than serving as an object lesson or confirmation of what I already
believe.[84]

Not that the inquiry into the worldview conveyed by a work of art is a
pointless pursuit. For Brand and Chaplin, indeed, worldview need not
"reduce art to an ideological tract" but is "an inescapable ingredient in all
works of art. This is not to say that all art works wear their worldview on
their sleeve. For most it is far more subtle. Of course it works best if it *is*
subtle."[85] Later, they add the important exhortation that "Our appreciation
of a work of art should not depend on whether it happens to share our
worldview. Rather, art is about a shared experience of what it means to be
human."[86]

The visual work in each of the four paradigms of art discussed in
this chapter *shows* what words cannot *tell*. Expressiveness, creativity, intention, imagination, and aesthetic acumen are required in each of these
paradigms. And each deserves more attention than space here allows.
Visual art imitates that which is seen; explores form in all its communicative and expressive power; is parsed as sign, in a complex interaction between object, artist, context and viewer; and contributes to philosophical
inquiry, asking questions about the nature of existence, knowledge, and
reality. Each of these forms of art-making practice gives visual voice to the
"unsayable," inviting us to venture from the safe discursive shoreline into
an unpredictable, chaotic ocean where language fails but the Creator calls
(each by name) from deep unto deep. Why study art? What else could be
more important?

84. Siedell, "Art and the Practice of Evangelical Truth," 131.

85. Brand and Chaplin, *Art and Soul*, 141.

86. Ibid., 146.

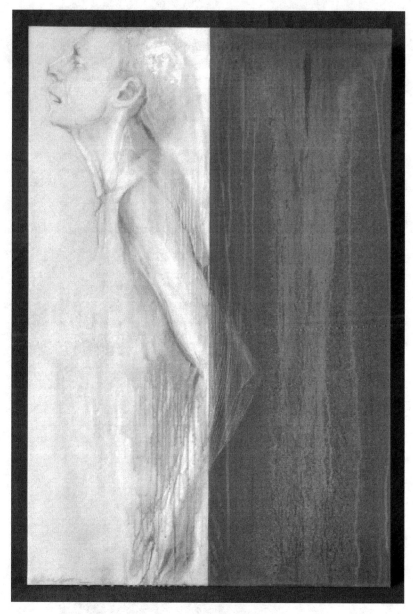

FIGURE 1: Erica Grimm-Vance, *Procession–Lament*, 2002. Steel, encaustic and graphite on board, 48 x 30 inches, private collection.

FIGURE 2. Makoto Fujimura, *Still Point—Evening*, 2002–2003. Mineral Pigments, Gold, Tarnished Silver on Kumohada, six 36 x 90 inch panels, collection of Kikkoman Corporation, Tokyo. Used with the permission of Makoto Fujimura.

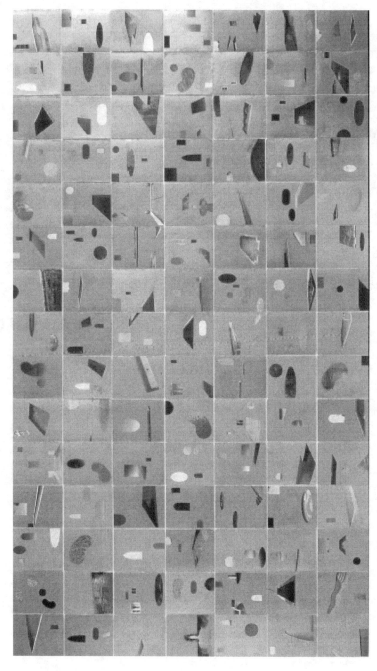

FIGURE 3. Lynn Aldrich, *Baptistery*, 2003. Gold leaf paint on pages from pool design books. 78 x 140 inches. Used with the permission of Lynn Aldrich.

83

Figure 4. Janet Cardiff, *Forty-Part Motet*, 2001. 40 loud speakers mounted on stands, placed in an oval, amplifiers, playback computer, 14 min. loop with 11 min. of music and 3 min. of intermission. Used with the permission of Janet Cardiff.

WORKS CITED

Aldrich, Lynn. "Through Sculpture: What's the Matter with Matter?" In *Beholding the Glory: Incarnation through the Arts,* edited by Jeremy Begbie, 98–117. Grand Rapids, MI: Baker Academic, 2000.

Augustine. *Against the Academicians* and *The Teacher.* Translated by Peter King. Cambridge: Hackett, 1995.

Baigell, Matthew. "Barnett Newman's Stripe Paintings and Kabbalah: A Jewish Take." In *Reading Abstract Expressionism: Context and Critique,* edited by Ellen Landau, 615–25. New Haven: Yale University Press, 2005.

Barthes, Roland. *Mythologies.* Translated by Annette Lavers. New York: Hill & Wang, 1972.

Begbie, Jeremy. "Christians and the Arts in a Post-Modern Age." Taped lectures delivered at Regent College in 1992.

Berger, John. *The Shape of a Pocket.* New York: Vintage, 2001.

Brand, Hilary, and Adrienne Chaplin. *Art and Soul: Signposts for Christians in the Arts.* 2d ed. Carlisle, UK: Piquant and Downers Grove, IL: InterVarsity Press, 2001.

Bro, Lu. *Figure and Form,* vol. I. Dubuque, IA: Brown & Benchmark, 1992.

Buber, Martin. *I and Thou.* Translated by Walter Kaufmann. New York: Scribner, 1970.

Burnham, Clint. "The Instant 'I Get It' of Brian Jungen's Art." *The Vancouver Sun,* Saturday, 28 January 2006, F1 and F3.

The Canada Council for the Arts. "Brian Jungen." Online: www.canadacouncil.ca/aboutus/artistsstories/visualarts/Jungen.

Cardiff, Janet, and George Bures Miller. Janet Cardiff and George Bures Miller website: www.cardiffmiller.com.

Clarke, Kenneth. *The Nude: A Study in Ideal Form.* Princeton: Princeton University Press, 1956.

Crozier, Lorna. Interview by Cheryl McKay on CBC radio program "North by Northwest," December 2007.

Debord, Guy. *The Society of the Spectacle.* Detroit: Black & Red, 1983.

Dillard, Annie. *Holy the Firm.* New York: Harper & Row, 1977.

Duchamp, Marcel. Session on the Creative Act, Convention of the American Federation of Arts, Houston, Texas, April 1957.

Dunning, William V. *The Roots of Postmodernism.* Englewood Cliffs, NJ: Prentice Hall, 1995.

Dyrness, William A. *Visual Faith: Art, Theology, and Worship in Dialogue.* Grand Rapids, MI: Baker Academic, 2001.

Eco, Umberto. *Art and Beauty in the Middle Ages.* Translated by Hugh Bredin. New Haven: Yale University Press, 1986.

Flam, Jack D. *Matisse on Art.* London: Phaidon, 1973.

Gombrich, Ernst. *Art and Illusion.* Oxford: Phaidon, 1960.

Grayling, A. C. *Wittgenstein: A Very Short Introduction.* Oxford: Oxford University Press, 2001.

Greenberg, Clement. "Avant-Garde and Kitsch." In *Pollock and After: The Critical Debate,* edited by Francis Frascina, 48–59. New York: Harper & Row, 1985.

Hadot, Pierre. *Philosophy as a Way of Life.* Oxford: Blackwell, 1995.

Hall, Stuart, ed. *Representation: Cultural Representations and Signifying Practices.* London: Sage, 1997.

Hart, Ray L. *Unfinished Man and the Imagination: Toward an Ontology and a Rhetoric of Revelation*. Louisville, KY: Westminster John Knox Press, 2001.

Hopkins, Gerard Manley. "God's Grandeur." In *The Poems of Gerard Manley Hopkins*, edited by W. H. Gardner and N. H. MacKenzie, 66. 4th ed. Oxford: Oxford University Press, 1970.

Howes, Graham. *The Art of the Sacred: An Introduction to the Aesthetics of Art and Belief*. London: I. B. Tauris, 2007.

Jansen, H. W. *History of Art*. 6th ed. New York: Prentice Hall, 2001.

Jay, Martin. *Downcast Eyes: The Denigration of Vision in Twentieth-Century French Thought*. Berkeley: University of California Press, 1993.

———. "Scopic Regimes of Modernity." In *Visions and Visuality*, No. 2, edited by Hal Foster, 4–15. Discussions in Contemporary Culture Series (Dia Art Foundation). Seattle: Bay Press, 1988.

Kandinsky, Wassily. *Concerning the Spiritual in Art*. Translated, with an Introduction, by M. T. H. Sadler. New York: Dover, 1977.

Lacy, Suzanne. *Mapping the Terrain: New Genre Public Art*. Seattle: Bay Press, 1995.

Lyotard, Jean Francois. *The Postmodern Condition: A Report on Knowledge*. Minneapolis: University of Minnesota Press, 1984.

McCaslin, Susan, ed. *A Matter of Spirit: Recovery of the Sacred in Contemporary Canadian Poetry*. Victoria, BC: Ekstasis, 1998.

Milbank, John, Catherine Pickstock, and Graham Ward, eds. *Radical Orthodoxy*. London: Routledge, 1999.

Mulder, Karen L. "Christian Worldview and the Arts." In *Shaping a Christian Worldview: The Foundations of Christian Higher Education*, edited by David S. Dockery and Gregory Alan Thornbury, 192–217. Nashville: Broadman & Holman, 2002.

Mulvey, Laura. "Visual Pleasures and Narrative Cinema." In *Art in Theory 1900-1990: An Anthology of Changing Ideas*, edited by Charles Harrison and Paul Woods, 963–70. London: Blackwell, 1992. Originally published in *Screen* 16.3 (1981) 6–18.

Murdoch, Iris. *The Fire and the Sun: Why Plato Banished the Artists*. London: Oxford University Press, 1978.

———. *The Sovereignty of Good*. London: Routledge, 1970.

Neilsen, Allan. "Are Paintings Texts? Making the Strange Familiar Again." In *The Art of Writing Inquiry*, edited by Lorri Neilsen, Ardra L. Cole, and J. Gary Knowles, 283–91. Halifax, NS: Backalong, 2001.

Pedulla, Albert. "Fulfilled in Your Seeing: The Life and Work of Tim Rollins and K.O.S." *Image: Art Faith Mystery* 45 (Spring 2005) 21–34.

Penwarden, Charles. "Of Word and Flesh: An Interview with Julia Kristeva." In *Rites of Passage: Art for the End of the Century*, 21–27. London: Tate Gallery Publications, 2000.

Plato. *The Republic*. Translated by Benjamin Jowett. New York: Dover, 2000.

Prescott, Theodore L., ed. *A Broken Beauty*. Grand Rapids, MI: Eerdmans, 2005.

Richter, Gerard. *The Daily Practice of Painting: Writings and Interviews 1962-1993*. Edited by Hans-Ulrich Obrist. Translated by David Britt. Cambridge, MA: MIT Press, 1995. (See also www.gerhard-richter.com/art/.)

———. Gerard Richter's website: www.gerhard-richter.com/art/.

Rilke, Rainer Maria. *Book of Hours: Love Poems to God*. Translated by Anita Barrows and Joanne Macy. New York: Riverhead, 1996.

Said, Edward W. *Orientalism*. London: Routledge & Kegan Paul, 1978.

Sayers, Dorothy L. *The Mind of the Maker.* London: Methuen, 1959 (1941).

Siedell, Daniel A. "Art and the Practice of Evangelical Truth." *Christian Scholar's Review* 34.1 (2004) 119–31.

Sterbak, Jana. Jana Sterbak's website: www.janasterbak.com.

Sturken, Marita, and Lisa Cartwright. *Practices of Looking: An Introduction to Visual Culture.* Oxford: Oxford University Press, 2001.

Sullivan, Graeme. *Art Practice as Research: Inquiry in the Visual Arts.* London: Sage Publications, 2005.

Taylor, Charles. *Sources of the Self: The Making of the Modern Identity.* Cambridge, MA: Harvard University Press, 1989.

Viola, Bill. Bill Viola's website: www.billviola.com.

Weil, Simone. "Metaxu." In *The Simone Weil Reader,* edited by George Panichas, 363–65. New York: David McKay, 1977.

———. "Reflections on the Right Use of School Studies with a View to the Love of God." In *The Simone Weil Reader,* edited by George Panichas, 44–52. New York: David McKay, 1977.

Wikepedia, "Michel Duchamp." wikepedia.org/wiki/Marcel_Duchamp.

Zijlstra, Onno. *Language, Image and Silence: Kierkegaard and Wittgenstein on Ethics and Aesthetics.* Bern: Peter Lang, 2006.

FOR FURTHER READING

Apostolos-Cappadona, Diane, ed. *Art, Creativity and the Sacred.* New York: Continuum, 1995.

Arthurs, Alberta, and Glen Walloch, eds. *Crossroads: Art and Religion in American Life.* New York: New Press, 2001.

Bernstein, J. M. *The Fate of Art: Aesthetic Alienation from Kant to Derrida and Adorno.* University Park: Pennsylvania State University Press, 1992.

Brown, Frank B. *Good Taste, Bad Taste, and Christian Taste: Aesthetics in Religious Life.* Oxford: Oxford University Press, 2000.

Claerbaut, David. "How Do We Look at Art through Christian Eyes?" and "Some Guidelines for the Christian Artist." In *Faith and Learning on the Edge: A Bold New Look at Religion in Higher Education,* 181–87, 188–93. Grand Rapids, MI: Zondervan, 2004.

Edwards, Betty. *Drawing on the Right Side of the Brain.* Los Angeles: Tarcher, 1989.

Harries, Richard. *Art and the Beauty of God: A Christian Understanding.* London: Mowbray, 1994.

Jensen, Robin M. *The Substance of Things Seen: Art, Faith, and the Christian Community.* Grand Rapids, MI: Eerdmans, 2004.

Ryken, Philip G. *Art for God's Sake: A Call to Recover the Arts.* Phillipsburg, NJ: Presbyterian & Reformed Publishing, 2006.

Seerveld, Calvin. *Bearing Fresh Olive Leaves: Alternative Steps in Understanding Art.* Willowdale, ON: Tuppence Press, 2000.

Sherry, Patrick. *Images of Redemption: Art, Literature and Salvation.* London: T. & T. Clark, 2003.

5

A Christian Perspective on Biblical Studies

STANLEY E. PORTER

WHAT IS A CHRISTIAN PERSPECTIVE ON BIBLICAL STUDIES?

Matters of Definition

The Uniqueness of Biblical Studies as a Discipline

SPOKESPEOPLE FOR THE OTHER disciplines represented in this volume, all enthusiastic about their subject, try to say something about how their discipline is a reflection of the principles and values of Christianity or how their discipline helps us to understand God and his world better. But rather than getting at God through secondary means, the biblical studies student attempts to go to the primary source, the Scriptures, for knowledge of him. No other discipline has been entrusted with the same responsibility for interpreting God's revelation. It demands the finest minds working at their most diligent level.

The Importance of Attitude and Method

A Christian perspective in the academic study of the Bible first requires the proper attitude—an intellectually honest search for the truth—and secondly involves the proper method and academic orientation.

"ACADEMIC" STUDY OF THE BIBLE. Let me clarify two concepts. First, I use the word "academic" to distinguish what is done in the university and similar settings (and ideally what will be done by informed Christians everywhere) from what is often called personal Bible study. The latter can include anything from a very free-form, emotive, personal response to a biblical passage to dogmatic assertions about what the Bible supposedly says, to discussion of the biblical text informed by what professional students of the Bible are saying. Bible study can often be enhanced by consideration of the work of biblical scholars, most of whom are attempting to convey reasonably complex concepts in a form accessible to a diverse and often untrained audience. The popular ministries of such well-known expositors of the Scriptures as Charles Swindoll, Robert Schuller, Chuck Smith, and John MacArthur often reflect the beneficial effects of their encounter with the work of such scholars, although such men would probably not claim to be biblical scholars themselves.

ACADEMIC "STUDY" OF THE BIBLE. We often think of studying as something that we choose to do. For example, did you "study" for the exam? The study of the Bible, however—at least for those who claim to be followers of Christ—is not an option that one can choose not to take. It is a requirement for the course called the Christian life. There may be disciplines one can omit from the Christian college/university curriculum, but the study of the Bible is not one of these. I wish to discuss the kind of orientation that I believe a Christian should have to this field as an academic discipline, but I am not addressing only those considering a career in biblical studies. Every Christian, in striving for a more informed knowledge of the Bible, can benefit from this kind of attitude and procedure.

Education, Honesty, and the Quest for Truth

Being Educated versus Simply Acquiring a Degree

Too often education is equated with earning a college or university degree. I would be the last person to minimize the importance of completing a rigorous course of higher education. There is no substitute for disciplining oneself to complete a program of study that exposes one to the major texts in a field, that compels one to think and write critically about these texts, and that forces one to think creatively about his/her own approach to the discipline. In biblical studies, the course is quite rigorous, requiring intensive knowledge of ancient history, several ancient languages, linguistics, theology and philosophy, rhetoric and world literature, sociology, and anthropology. Fortunately, being educated is more than simply earning degrees. It is about developing an inquiring approach to one's subject, whatever it may be. This is, I believe, the sense in which Holmes speaks of being educated in *The Idea of a Christian College*.[1] Educated persons seek after truth both for its own sake and in order to live up to their fullest potential as created by God and serving a redemptive purpose in this world. There are no shortcuts to hard work in reading, writing, and, most of all, thinking about not only one's particular subject but larger questions as well.

Education and Attitude

These tasks must all be performed with honesty, integrity, and humility. Without abandoning our presuppositions, we must be willing to look candidly at the evidence, put aside personal prejudices, recognize our own limitations, and follow arguments through to their honest conclusions. If all truth is God's truth,[2] then we must seek to discover it and be willing to respond to it appropriately. Although I affirm the doctrine of inerrancy and work as a biblical scholar from that standpoint, I do not think that this position is essential for a Christian perspective in biblical studies. I do believe, however, that a high view of Scripture is an essential prerequisite for the serious biblical studies student. We must believe that there is something worth interpreting, and we must be willing to subject ourselves to it, even if it seems to say something that pulls us in new or uncomfortable directions. Scripture, then, constitutes the focal point of our interpretation. More than that, it is also an essential part of our orientation, the belief that God has revealed in his Scripture a reliable and trustworthy word, one worth interpreting because revealed by a God whose character both evokes worship and deserves emulation. Any of these procedures has the potential for causing personal discomfort as we examine issues and subjects from new perspectives and in the light of new evidence that may cause us to question what we have been led to believe are unimpeachable truths. But positions held in ignorance are not positions honestly held. The process might cause some discomfort but our integrity will be intact, and we will genuinely know why we believe what we believe because we will have ourselves examined the evidence, not just accepted what our religious tradition or what our parents or other authority figures have told us. A concern for intellectual integrity should be foundational in all disciplines, but I have emphasized this point

1. See Holmes, *Idea of a Christian College*, especially chapters 3 and 9. See also his *Contours of a World View*.

2. Holmes, *Idea of a Christian College*, 17.

because it is no less important for academic biblical study, where many unexamined ideas float around regarding how the Bible ought to be read and interpreted.

Presuppositions and a Method of Interpretation

The Necessity of Presuppositions

DEFINITION OF PRESUPPOSITIONS AS "FUNCTIONAL ABSOLUTES." It is not enough to share the common goal of seeking after truth; one must also develop a method for interpretation of the data or evidence. This begins with a deliberate effort to think about one's own presuppositions—those fundamental beliefs that undergird how we view the world around us. Sometimes presuppositions are characterized as unanalyzable or even as irrational beliefs that humans hang onto despite the evidence. No attitude could be more detrimental. Christianity is not a leap into the dark without some faith that God will catch us! Presuppositions are perhaps best thought of as "functional absolutes";[3] that is, basic beliefs that are not negotiated every time a subject is approached but are always in place when one is going about the interpretive task. It is not that these absolutes cannot be changed, but they are not constantly "up for grabs." These presuppositions, arrived at through various means and the product of a number of cultural, religious, educational, and psychological factors, can be changed once one is convinced by a significant amount of competing data.

ONE'S VIEW OF SCRIPTURE AS A "FUNCTIONAL ABSOLUTE." One of my presuppositions is a high view of the authority and integrity of the Bible. For me, this view of Scripture not only motivates what I do, but it is a fundamental assumption about how I do my study. I am not always sure how such a presupposition will manifest itself in a given interpretive context, but it reflects something about my belief in God, his nature, and the kind of revelation such a God would give. Could this presupposition be overthrown? Possibly, if enough evidence were marshalled to undermine my belief in God, his character, and the kind of revelation that is fitting for him, but it would certainly take more than a few difficult passages. Instead, this presupposition gives me a position and a reason for trying to gain a better grasp on those difficult passages.

---

3. The terminology is adapted from Carson, "Redaction Criticism," 141–42.

THE NECESSITY OF SELF-CRITICISM. In his article, "Is Exegesis without Presuppositions Possible?" Rudolf Bultmann gives us a sense of what is required in this interpretive task.[4] He recognizes that there is no such thing as analysis or exegesis of the Bible without a methodological framework. For example, at various times in church history, various methods have been followed. Augustine and Origen practiced an allegorical method, in which they saw every passage of Scripture as having several levels, including historical, figurative, and theological. At the time, this was seen to be the best method of biblical interpretation. Bultmann makes us aware of the necessity of being self-critical, being ever aware of the presuppositions that we bring to the text. For Bultmann, a product of the naturalism of the nineteenth century, this meant that there was no place for direct supernatural intervention in his strictly cause-and-effect world; consequently, he emphasized the priority of personal or existential experience. Most evangelical scholars work from a different set of presuppositions, however. They believe that there is a God who is active in the universe. Some of the ways that he has functioned in the past are perhaps not quantifiable scientifically but are perfectly compatible with a universe as Einstein defined it, one open to the role of the imagination in scientific method, where light bends and time is not absolute. Presuppositions are an inevitable part of what it means to interpret not only the Bible but all of life. Interpreters must make an effort to acknowledge and control their presuppositions; otherwise, the presuppositions inevitably control them.

The Necessity of an Interpretive Method

There is an unhealthy tendency, however, to become so enamored with questions of method and presuppositions that one never gets down to the task of actual interpretation. The second part of Bultmann's essay describes the historical-critical method, which he considered the best way to minimize the unjust intrusion of presuppositions into the interpretive process.[5] The historical-critical method is an attempt to find an objective procedure for arriving at what the biblical text meant in its original context. (It does not mean simply being critical of the Bible!) In the last several decades it has been expanded and augmented to include

4. Translated and reprinted in *Existence and Faith: Shorter Writings of Rudolf Bultmann*.

5. Bultmann, "Is Exegesis without Presuppositions Possible?" 291. Cf. Krentz, *The Historical-Critical Method*.

an appreciation of social description, anthropology, modern linguistics, literary theory, and discourse analysis. This is only to say that, even if the historical-critical method is one that still requires constant refinement, it allows for all biblical scholars, whether they are conservatives or liberals, believers or non-believers, from any part of the world, to enter into the same arena and engage in a mutually beneficial dialogue regarding the biblical text. Currently the historical-critical method, rightly defined, provides such a means, since it places important emphasis on the original languages of the documents as they were used in their initial social, cultural, historical, and theological contexts. To use the language of recent interpretive theory, one must establish the horizon of the original text—in other words, what the text meant then—before one can move to the second horizon to say what the text means for today.[6]

The Advantages of Christian Interpreters

The conservative Christian's distinct advantages in this entire process are perhaps the most difficult to define. It begins with one's fundamental orientation. The Christian, probably having a greater sympathy for the text as God's word, is less skeptical and thus more willing to give difficult passages the benefit of the doubt. They tend to be evidential maximalists. For example, it is fairly common in Pauline studies to argue that Paul is contradictory in several passages—e.g., in Romans 2 he seems to entertain the idea that someone can gain salvation by works whereas in Romans 3 he says faith without works is the sole means of salvation.[7] A Christian interpreter might be willing to go to extra effort to understand these perceived contradictions; certainly one's Christian faith should not blunt one's critical faculties by ignoring such problems, resulting in exegesis that brings glory neither to man nor to God.

Furthermore, we must consider the influence of God's Spirit in maintaining the right attitude of humility and acquiescence before the text. I would not want to over- or underestimate this relationship. On the one hand, to overestimate is to run the risk of sloppy exegesis, in which reliance upon the Spirit's inspiration takes the place of the hard work of interpretation of the written text or results in an overconfidence regarding one's conclusions. One must be careful of making statements about

6. This language draws upon the work of Thiselton, *The Two Horizons*, esp. section 1.

7. For those who find Paul to be contradictory or problematic at points, see, e.g., Sanders, *Paul, the Law, and the Jewish People*.

what God has "told" us, especially when that runs contrary to what has been clearly stated in the Bible.[8] The results of exegesis are not a matter of private inspiration and revelation and must be subject to assessment by others, particularly fellow academics in the scholarly community. On the other hand, to underestimate the role of God's Spirit is to run the risk of undue self-reliance, perhaps even leading to a messiah complex in which one believes that all interpretation—in fact, all of God's program—relies upon what I and I alone accomplish. Not only might this result in burnout, but it almost certainly reflects an incredible lack of humility, something not good for either God's kingdom or the field of biblical studies.

The Importance of Perspective

Once one gains some knowledge of biblical studies, one soon realizes that not all is bliss. Even where interpreters concur on a method, have many broad perspectives in common, and even agree on many interpretations, there are inevitable and often quite significant differences of opinion, where no apparent resolution is forthcoming. How does a Christian approach such disputes, especially in terms of a subject where one is dealing with such important topics as God and his revelation to humanity?

Historical Causes of Division

Early in the last century in North America, many splits in denominations occurred between people perceived to be more liberal and those deemed to be more conservative (the Fundamentalists).[9] As a result, a number of new institutions were founded that claimed to be preserving and protecting traditional biblical truths, while those founders abandoned their previous institutions to what they deemed to be the encroachment of liberalism. Until fairly recently there has been a tendency in the United States for a division between institutions with fairly conservative, evangelical faculties and those with faculties perceived to be otherwise. These more conservative institutions have done much good, especially in training of pastors and church workers, but in many ways they have left serious scholarship to others, abandoning or denigrating a very important calling within the church. Fortunately this situation is changing. One of the ma-

8. A classic example of this is cited by Carson in *Exegetical Fallacies*, 13 n. 2.

9. On the history of this debate, see Marsden, *Fundamentalism and American Culture*; as well as his *Understanding Fundamentalism and Evangelicalism*. See also Noll, *Between Faith and Criticism*, and especially Noll's *The Scandal of the Evangelical Mind*.

jor reasons is that conservative scholars are more willingly entering the academic arena and are gaining credibility through their hard work. But they have much work to do to overcome the negative effects of minimal communication between liberal and conservative biblical scholars over much of the twentieth century.

Areas of Possible Further Improvement

MINIMALIZATION OF ANTI-INTELLECTUALISM. There is a longstanding tradition in North America to fear things cognitive. This is often translated into a misguided emphasis on practicality, as if ideas do not have a usable value or as if practical implements come about without ideas. I believe that this attitude reveals a fundamental mistrust of the intellect, often heightened by the perception that those who engage in thinking are liberals and cannot be trusted.

MINIMALIZATION OF SIMPLISTIC THINKING. Some Christians have the mistaken notion that interpretation of the Bible is self-evident and that too much learning gets in the way of godly living. This kind of dichotomous thinking again grows out of an attitude of mistrust of those who have a wealth of learning but who are perceived to have little positive to say about the Bible. All that this reveals, however, is simplistic thinking that is not a credit to the biblical witness.

PROVIDING A CONSERVATIVE VOICE IN BIBLICAL STUDIES. The greatest detriment of the division between liberal and conservative scholarship on the study of the Bible is that conservative biblical scholars, having a more limited audience, have had greater difficulty gaining acceptance and finding a voice in the academic community. As a result, they have sometimes not been able to provide as good an education for their students. These consequences need not have come about. But this situation works both ways. On the one hand, there is still persistent mistrust of what is perceived to be the insidious force of liberalism. I would not want to defend all that has been done in biblical studies over the last century, but the reactionary response that gave up fine academic institutions to the liberals and crusaded to ensure doctrinal purity, even at the expense of individuals, has suffered a noticeable backlash. Today in the academic study of the Bible, a significant number of scholars, even in their relatively mature years, continue to work out of a sense of rebellion against their conservative upbringings.[10]

AREAS OF DISCUSSION IN CONTEMPORARY BIBLICAL STUDIES

Having introduced some of the major issues regarding a Christian perspective in biblical studies, I now turn to some of the major topics and issues in the discipline. Here I have made a subjective choice from a number of issues that could have been selected. What I have chosen are not only those that are, I believe, of the greatest interest but also those where evangelical Christian scholarship has played a significant role. I am also suggesting areas where the implications for study of these topics might have the most significance for a believing community.

The Quest for Ancient Israel

The Issue regarding the Existence of Ancient Israel

If one were to approach the Old Testament without knowing any better, one could be excused for thinking that there was such a thing as "ancient Israel." Nothing is as simple as it first appears. In recent work the historicity of ancient Israel as a nation before the time of the monarchy (that is, before Saul, David, and Solomon, around 1000 BC) has been questioned. To summarize briefly, the major issue is the fact that, before the monarchy, the quantifiable extra-biblical evidence, for example archaeological and documentary evidence, for the existence of ancient Israel, is negligible. The existence of ancient Israel in Egypt, of the exodus, of their living in the desert, of a conquest as described in Joshua by such a people, are all undocumented apart from the biblical text. Similarly, the period of the Judges is full of both manifest chronological and historical problems. In all, this evidence compels some scholars to distinguish among biblical Israel (the Israel depicted in the Bible), historical Israel (the inhabitants of Palestine during this time) and "ancient Israel" (a construct out of biblical and historical Israel).[11]

10. This point is made well in Evans, *Fabricating Jesus*.

11. For a recent work by one of those skeptical about the historicity of the biblical accounts, see Van Seters, *Prologue to History*, especially 24–44. For a summary of discussion, see Ahlstrom, *The History of Ancient Palestine from the Palaeolithic Period to Alexander's Conquest*, especially chapter 4.

A Christian Perspective on the Existence of Ancient Israel

This revisionist interpretation of ancient Israel has not caught on with all scholars, and for good reasons.[12] But this discussion does raise some serious issues for a Christian perspective in biblical studies. For example, it raises the question of how dependent one's Christian experience needs to be upon actual historical events. One might well ask how the possibility that Abraham never existed would affect one's interpretation of Paul's use of Abraham in Romans 4 and Galatians 3. Would Paul's discussion of Abraham being justified by faith before the coming of the law have the same meaning if Abraham never existed? Furthermore, by all reckonings it appears that Paul believed that Abraham existed. Would Paul's supposedly mistaken understanding affect how we regard his use of Abraham and what he is saying about justification? The answer is obviously "Yes, profoundly."

Of benefit to Christian interpreters is the recognition that the Bible is not simply a history book but also a theology book. The grounds for ancient Israel's existence are to my mind still firmly established in the light of not only the biblical evidence, which must be given its due place (here is where my presupposition regarding the authority of Scripture enters into the discussion), but also in the light of the surrounding historical context.[13] It is much more probable in terms of the evidence to believe that ancient Israel existed as it is depicted in the biblical text and in the light of the surrounding milieu than to believe that it did not. But I can also appreciate that ancient Israel as depicted in the Bible has theological significance regarding a God who can and will form a people to serve him, the obligations of obedience for this people, and the fact that this people need not be the biggest or most powerful in the area. Furthermore, this revisionist view helps me to appreciate the literary dimension of the Bible. The Bible is not merely a book that narrates history and expounds theology, but it is a piece of ancient literature that needs to be interpreted with a full understanding of how literature was written and understood in the ancient world. For example, is the story of creation meant to be a strictly historical account, or is there some other literary genre to which it belongs, such that it says something about the kind of God who creates and the orderliness with which he creates?

12. See, e.g., Kitchen, *Ancient Orient and Old Testament.*
13. On this issue, see Younger, *Ancient Conquest Accounts.*

The Languages of the Bible

The Old Testament was originally written in Hebrew and Aramaic, and the New Testament in Greek. Bultmann in "Is Exegesis without Presuppositions Possible?" makes the point that the historical-critical method relies upon understanding the original languages of the Bible for accurate interpretation.[14] If one wants to be an accurate interpreter of the Scriptures one must understand the languages in which they were written. For all their value, translations are almost inevitably a committee's interpretation of the original text. One can appreciate the difficulty of calling oneself an expert in the Bible without having studied the original languages by comparing it to an expert in German or French literature who has never studied either of those languages. Yet the study of Hebrew and Greek has been persistently neglected by biblical scholars, especially in recent times. This stems from several causes, one of them probably being the assumption that ancient languages do not change. Since the languages do not change, some might think, the grammars of the languages do not change either.

It is true that the biblical languages do not change, but discoveries are always being made of other documents that might enhance our knowledge of the original languages, such as Greek papyri and manuscripts like the Dead Sea Scrolls. But even though the languages do not change, our understanding of them should be developing. In the study of Hebrew, there has not been a full-scale reference grammar in English since the translation from German of a grammar from the middle of nineteenth century. In Greek only one reference grammar has been written since the Second World War. Another cause of the neglect of biblical languages is the failure of biblical scholars to appreciate the insights and advancements of modern linguistics. Only recently has the revolution in study of language encouraged by the Swiss linguist Ferdinand de Saussure been appreciated in biblical studies.

The Search for the Historical Jesus

It might come as a surprise to find out that there is controversy over the historical Jesus. A distinction is often made in scholarship between the Jesus discoverable by historical enquiry and the Christ worshipped by the Christian church. Here is a classic example where evangelical scholarship

14. Bultmann, "Is Exegesis without Presuppositions Possible?" 291.

has made significant inroads in recent work, although a good portion of the conservative church is probably unaware that there are even any issues for discussion.

The Traditional Characterization of the Search for the Historical Jesus

The history of historical Jesus research is often characterized by a four-fold development. The tale is frequently told in the following way.[15] As a result of the Enlightenment and the rise of rationalism in the eighteenth century, scholars began anew and in a revitalized way to assess the Gospels. This, the first quest for the historical Jesus, wanted to provide an explanation for the development of the Gospels, probably from oral sources, into the documents that we have in our canonical text. Several factors became obvious, such as the interdependence among the Gospels, in which sizeable portions of wording are shared; differences in depiction of Jesus, where certain events are included in some Gospels but not others; and differing structures of the Gospels, which raise the question of how chronologically and historically reliable they are. A number of scholars undertook to discover as much as they could of the "historical Jesus" behind these varying Gospel accounts, written, so they posited, much later and reflecting the theological concerns of the early church. This movement continued for a number of years, until early in this century Albert Schweitzer brought the entire quest for the historical Jesus to a temporary close (the "no quest" period) by his depiction of the history of previous research as simply reflecting the times and the character of the investigators.

For about the next fifty years scholarship refrained from engaging in this kind of study of the historical Jesus, shifting its emphasis toward the process by which the Gospels came into being and downplaying the significance of the historical Jesus as if it didn't really matter whether one could know anything about him. In the early 1950s, however, scholarly interest in the historical Jesus revived and a second quest for the historical Jesus was begun. Previous scholarship, such as that of Bultmann, assumed that data regarding the historical Jesus were not a factor to be considered in discussion of the Christ of faith worshipped by the later church. One of Bultmann's students, however, re-opened the discussion by positing that there may be a closer relation between the historical Jesus and the Christ of faith, since the two are depicted together in the Gospels. This

---

15. For a brief history of this discussion, see Evans, "The Historical Jesus and Christian Faith," 48–63.

second quest soon gave way to a supposed third quest, which, in the light of twentieth-century developments such as the discovery of the Dead Sea Scrolls, emphasized four distinguishing features: (1) locating Jesus firmly in terms of his Jewish background, (2) asking the question of why Jesus was crucified rather than simply noting the fact that he was, (3) integrating political and theological issues rather than distinguishing them, and (4) bringing together scholars with various backgrounds.[16]

Alternative Views of the Search for the Historical Jesus

One of the noteworthy features of historical Jesus research throughout this period of over two hundred years is that scholars—despite pronouncements to the contrary—have continued to be interested in and write about Jesus.[17] On the basis of this continuing work, there is little real reason for designating these epochs in historical Jesus research. The four-part description of historical Jesus research may only have applied to a small group of German scholars highly influenced by form criticism, and perhaps not even them, as people like Bultmann himself, as well as others, wrote lives of Jesus even during the so-called "no quest" period. Thus, the supposed third quest that is said by some to have begun in the 1980s seems to be merely a continuation of the second quest begun in the 1950s. As Stein states, "The same historical-critical method remains foundational for many of the researchers involved in the so-called 'third quest.'"[18] What is more important to note is that this historical method goes even further back, at least to the time of the so-called "no-quest" period, if not earlier to the time of the "first quest." In other words, there is none other than a single multi-faceted quest for the historical Jesus, with various modifications and adjustments in approach, some of them perhaps influenced by method and others perhaps by personality or nationality. There certainly is, to my mind, no clear way to characterize a given epoch in a singular and uniform way, and there is certainly no clearly discernible or definable break between epochs that anyone can turn to.[19]

One might well argue that this single quest began with the earliest interpreters of Jesus' life, death, and resurrection, such as the apostles and

16. Neill and Wright, *The Interpretation of the New Testament*, 397–98.

17. See Porter, *The Criteria for Authenticity*, 28–62, where a number of the key writers are noted.

18. Stein, *Jesus the Messiah*, 13.

19. See Porter, *The Criteria for Authenticity*, part one.

then the early church Fathers, and has continued down through Christian history until the present. At times such studies have waxed, while at others they have waned. Their various proponents have held to a variety of views regarding the major critical questions regarding Jesus, such as whether he thought of himself as Messiah, and have written in a variety of languages throughout especially the western world. Their common theme is the desire to know more about this Jesus of history, and there is still much more to learn as scholars discover more about the ancient world in which Jesus lived. This line of continuity from the Gospels to present exploration of Jesus gives credence to those who wish to note that the historical Jesus and the Christ of Christian confession are one and the same—and this one Jesus is found in the Gospels. The Jesus of the Gospels is, in this sense, the only Jesus to be found.[20]

The New Outlook on Paul

Traditional interpretation of Paul depicts him as the apostle to the Gentiles, arguing vociferously against all opponents, especially Judaizers, that justification is by faith alone, not by works of the law. This consensus was changed over thirty years ago when E. P. Sanders concluded that the traditional stereotype of first-century Jews as works-oriented was wrong. He argued instead for a concept he called "covenantal nomism," which meant that there was a covenantal and law-oriented relationship that the Jews saw between themselves and God, in which one entered the believing community by means of the covenant and remained there by obeying the law.[21] The admission requirement was not obedience but God's gracious act in establishing his covenant with his people. This looks very much like what Paul is talking about in Romans and Galatians. Some say that for Paul Christianity and Judaism were essentially the same except that the latter did not have a clear place for Christ, something that was crucial to Paul after his Damascus Road conversion.

Many Christians have been actively involved in formulating this reassessment of Paul, so it would be unfair to characterize this position as less Christian than another.[22] This recent assessment of Paul has opened

20. See Johnson, *The Real Jesus.*
21. See, e.g., Sanders, *Paul and Palestinian Judaism.*
22. See, e.g., Dunn, "The New Perspective on Paul," 95–122; and exemplified in his commentary, *Romans.*

up several new areas of exploration, but it has also illustrated that one must be careful not simply to follow the latest fads. The discussion of anti-Semitism in the New Testament is an example. Frankly, I find it a bit difficult to call someone like Paul, a Jew and former member of the Pharisees, anti-Semitic, as some argue, when he offers his critique of Judaism. But that certainly does not mean that abuses of various racial groups, including the Jews, on the basis of the documents of Christianity can be tolerated either, so perhaps this discussion has helped us in understanding each other better and in coming to terms with the distinctives of Christianity and Judaism. Here Christians have been aided by Jewish scholars, who have resisted the characterization of Christianity as simply a modified version of Judaism by pointing out fundamental differences.[23]

There are, nevertheless, two major problems with this revised view of Paul. Even among Christians seeking to exegete Scripture as faithfully as they can, there is a place for disagreement and charity, since no side can make a claim to knowledge of all of the truth in all matters. The first is that the evidence from the documents of the Old Testament and of later Judaism simply does not clearly support the position that is claimed for them. The documents reveal a much higher emphasis on the fundamental requirement of obedience to the law than proponents of this position are willing to admit. Second, a number of passages in Paul make it clear that he is not simply saying that Judaism and Christianity conform to the same covenantal model. From Paul's perspective he saw Judaism as endorsing a works-based righteousness.[24] This issue shows that there is often a fundamental disagreement regarding how much weight to give to the biblical documents themselves. In this instance, what role do Paul's writings play in reconstructing and offering a critique of the world of the time? Some are skeptical of Paul's contribution, whereas others put Paul's writings at the heart of this endeavor. Discussion on this topic continues, with evangelicals having made significant contributions to both sides of the debate.

23. See, e.g., Neusner, *Death and Birth of Judaism.*

24. For these criticisms, among others, see Westerholm, *Israel's Law and the Church's Faith*, part 2.

The New Literary and Rhetorical Criticism

Historical criticism of the twentieth century has been seen by many to have over-emphasized the Jewish origins of Christianity and its documents, and in its study of both the Old and New Testaments to have failed to consider the literary environment out of which these documents emerged. As a result, many scholars, abandoning some of the traditional concerns of historical criticism, describe themselves as literary critics of the Bible.[25] Typically in these treatments there is a shift from asking historical questions, such as "When did this happen?" to more literary questions, such as "Who are the major and minor characters? What is the plot? What is the setting?" Literary criticism emphasizes that the biblical documents are not primarily theological or historical but are in the first instance literary, capturing the aspirations and reflections of the Jewish people and the first writers of Christianity. Rhetorical criticism has emphasized that the New Testament documents are products of rhetorical situations, especially those where an author desires to persuade his audience for a particular purpose. To do this, he must package his message according to accepted standards of rhetoric.[26]

Literary and rhetorical criticism has had a significant impact on recent work in the Old and New Testaments. First, it has helped scholars become more sensitive to the literary dimensions of the documents, appreciating that they are not simply manuscripts created by faceless communities or through a process of cut-and-paste but by actual writers with motives, purposes, and perspectives. Second, it has forced scholars to appreciate not only what is said but how it is said. The message is inextricably united to the way the biblical text was written. To read what many literary/rhetorical critics have to say, however, one could be excused for thinking that a radical disjunction exists between traditional historical criticism and these new literary/rhetorical methods. In their extremes this is true, although both sides probably neglect elements of the other in their method.

25. For an insightful article that utilizes several of the approaches of literary criticism, see Clines, "Reading Esther from Left to Right," 31–52.

26. For a collection of essays that discusses the range of issues, see Porter and Olbricht, eds., *Rhetoric and the New Testament.*

CONCLUSION

In defining a Christian perspective in Biblical Studies, I have refrained from putting Christian interpreters into another category entirely, with all sorts of resources and tools at our disposal that simply are unavailable to non-Christians. I recognize that I have not emphasized the role of the Holy Spirit in interpretation as much as others might have. The Holy Spirit does have a role in interpretation, but it is very difficult to quantify this function. The part that we can quantify and in some sense describe and assess is the traditional hard work of interpretation, which many people can do, whether they are Christians or not. I would like to believe that Christian interpreters will work more diligently, will have higher integrity, will think through their presuppositions more thoroughly, and will apply their methods more fairly and more rigorously, but I am not sure that those superior qualities will always be in evidence. Instead, I would like to emphasize that as Christians we have an obligation to read and interpret the Bible, an option for most non-Christians but essential for believers. Since we are called to undertake this task, it is our God-given responsibility to do it to the very best of our ability, since we will be accountable to him for how we use the intellectual resources he has given us. As much as I like to get phone calls from my students after they graduate, I hope and pray that I will never receive one that accuses me and my colleagues of ever giving our students less than what they deserve in their serious-minded study of the Bible.

WORKS CITED

Ahlstrom, G. W. *The History of Ancient Palestine from the Palaeolithic Period to Alexander's Conquest*. Sheffield: JSOT Press, 1993.

Bultmann, Rudolf K. "Is Exegesis without Presuppositions Possible?" In *Existence and Faith: Shorter Writings of Rudolf Bultmann*, translated and edited by S. M. Ogden, 289–96 and 314–15. Cleveland: World, 1960.

Carson, D. A. *Exegetical Fallacies*. Grand Rapids, MI: Baker, 1984.

————. "Redaction Criticism: On the Legitimacy and Illegitimacy of a Literary Tool." In *Scripture and Truth*, edited by D. A. Carson and John D. Woodbridge, 119–42. Grand Rapids, MI: Zondervan, 1983.

Clines, David J. A. "Reading Esther from Left to Right: Contemporary Strategies for Reading a Biblical Text." In *The Bible in Three Dimensions*, edited by David J. A. Clines, Stephen E. Fowl, and Stanley E. Porter, 31–52. Sheffield: JSOT Press, 1990.

Dunn, James D. G. "The New Perspective on Paul," *Bulletin of the John Rylands Library* 65 (1983) 95–122.

————. *Romans*. 2 vols. Dallas: Word Books, 1988.

Evans, Craig A. *Fabricating Jesus*. Downers Grove, IL: InterVarsity Press, 2007.

———. "The Historical Jesus and Christian Faith: A Critical Assessment of a Scholarly Problem." *Christian Scholar's Review* 18 (1988) 48–63.

Holmes, Arthur F. *Contours of a World View*. Grand Rapids, MI: Eerdmans, 1983.

———. *The Idea of a Christian College*. Rev. ed. Grand Rapids, MI: Eerdmans, 1987.

Johnson, Luke T. *The Real Jesus: The Misguided Quest for the Historical Jesus and the Truth of the Traditional Gospels*. San Francisco: HarperCollins, 1996.

Kitchen, K. A. *Ancient Orient and Old Testament*. Downers Grove, IL: InterVarsity Press, 1966.

Krentz, Edgar. *The Historical-Critical Method*. Philadelphia: Fortress Press, 1975.

Marsden, George M. *Fundamentalism and American Culture: The Shaping of Twentieth Century Evangelicalism 1870–1925*. New York: Oxford University Press, 1980.

———. *Understanding Fundamentalism and Evangelicalism*. Grand Rapids, MI: Eerdmans, 1991.

Neill, Stephen, and Tom Wright. *The Interpretation of the New Testament 1861–1986*. 2d ed. Oxford: Oxford University Press, 1988.

Neusner, Jacob. *Death and Birth of Judaism: The Impact of Christianity, Secularism, and the Holocaust on Jewish Faith*. New York: Basic, 1987.

Noll, Mark A. *Between Faith and Criticism: Evangelicals, Scholarship, and the Bible in America*. San Francisco: Harper & Row, 1986.

———. *The Scandal of the Evangelical Mind*. Grand Rapids, MI: Eerdmans, 1994.

Porter, Stanley E. *The Criteria for Authenticity in Historical-Jesus Research: Previous Discussion and New Proposals*. Sheffield: Sheffield Academic Press, 2000.

Porter, Stanley E., and Thomas H. Olbricht, eds. *Rhetoric and the New Testament: Essays from the 1992 Heidelberg Conference*. Sheffield: JSOT Press, 1993.

Sanders, E. P. *Paul and Palestinian Judaism: A Comparison of Patterns of Religion*. Philadelphia: Fortress Press, 1977.

———. *Paul, the Law, and the Jewish People*. Philadelphia: Fortress Press, 1983.

Stein, Robert H. *Jesus the Messiah: A Survey of the Life of Christ*. Downers Grove, IL: InterVarsity Press, 1996.

Thiselton, Anthony C. *The Two Horizons: New Testament Hermeneutics and Philosophical Description with Special Reference to Heidegger, Bultmann, Gadamer, and Wittgenstein*. Grand Rapids, MI: Eerdmans, 1980.

Van Seters, John. *Prologue to History: The Yahwist as Historian in Genesis*. Louisville, KY: Westminster/John Knox, 1992.

Westerholm, Stephen. *Israel's Law and the Church's Faith: Paul and his Recent Interpreters*. Grand Rapids, MI: Eerdmans, 1988; repr., Eugene, OR: Wipf & Stock, 1998.

Younger, K. Lawson, Jr. *Ancient Conquest Accounts: A Study in Ancient Near Eastern and Biblical History Writing*. Sheffield: JSOT Press, 1990.

FOR FURTHER READING

Bultmann, Rudolf K. *Theology of the New Testament*. 2 vols. New York: Scribners, 1951.

Evans, Craig A. "Authenticity Criteria in Life of Jesus Research." *Christian Scholar's Review* 19 (1989) 6–31.

———. "Life-of-Jesus Research and the Eclipse of Mythology." *Theological Studies* 54 (1993) 3–36.

Käsemann, Ernst. "The Problem of the Historical Jesus." In his *Essays on New Testament Themes*, 15–47. London: SCM Press, 1964.

6

A Christian Perspective on Biology

DENNIS R. VENEMA *and* RICHARD J. L. PAULTON[1]

INTRODUCTION: SELECTING KINGS AND MAKING RIGHT DECISIONS

> But the Lord said to Samuel, "Do not consider his appearance or his height, for I have rejected him. The Lord does not look at the things human beings look at. People look at the outward appearance, but the Lord looks at the heart."[2]

YOU NO DOUBT REMEMBER the story. The handsome, tall king Saul of Israel had disgraced himself by his disobedience to God. Shortly thereafter, God sent the prophet Samuel to select and anoint a new king for Israel from among the sons of Jesse of Bethlehem. In the selection process, God directed Samuel to reject, in turn, each of Jesse's seven older sons—though they, like Saul, were tall and handsome—and to select David, the eighth and youngest son. The message to Israel was clear: relying on outward appearance is a deceptive guide for finding a leader after God's own heart.

To study biology as a Christian is both a wonderful journey of investigation and discovery, as well as a potential quagmire of deeply contentious and divisive issues. I recall one of my colleagues in Religious Studies once lamenting that each of his students arrives for the first class already a

---

1. Richard Paulton wrote the initial version of this chapter; his colleague Dennis Venema has been responsible for updating and revising it. Unless otherwise indicated, all first person statements are to be attributed to Dr. Venema.

2. 1 Samuel 16:7. All Scripture quotations are from Today's New International Version unless otherwise noted.

theologian.[3] So too in biology: far and few between are Christian students with no opinions whatsoever on biological topics such as evolution, stem cell therapies, genetically modified organisms, environmentalism, and the like. Often the approach to the science of biology in evangelical Christian circles is one of suspicion and mistrust. My pastor (at the time when I left home for my first year of university) put it thus: leading the congregation in prayer, he thanked God for all those bound for Bible college, and petitioned that those going to secular schools not lose their faith.[4]

The primary issue for many Christian biology students is that of evolution. This area of biological study has been accused of being incompatible with, and hostile to, Christianity to an extent that few other areas in the sciences experience.[5] I can recall a time in my own thinking as a youth when the word *evolution* was inextricably linked to *atheism*—and where I viewed any scientific data that was purported to support evolution with deep suspicion.

IN THE BEGINNING: SCIENCE AND THE QUESTION OF BIOLOGICAL ORIGINS

It must have been simpler to have been a biologist long ago. In the absence of relevant scientific evidence[6] or an understanding of the social and literary contexts for the book of Genesis,[7] most seventeenth- and eighteenth-century biologists took what the Bible had to say about creation at what they perceived to be its face value. They saw their work as in concert with the principle Paul had in mind when he affirmed, "For since the creation of the world God's invisible qualities—his eternal power and divine nature—have been clearly seen, being understood from what has been made" (Romans 1:20). Early European biologists thus developed a

3. Having experienced this issue *mutatis mutandis* with biology students, I was naturally empathetic.

4. Perhaps not surprisingly, the choice of Bible college versus secular higher education was not a reliable predictor of "losing one's faith" for my cohort.

5. Short perusal of a web site such as www.answersingenesis.org will make the point easily.

6. The science of biology for this period was largely descriptive, focusing on categorization rather than experimentation.

7. For an excellent discussion of these issues as they pertain to the Genesis 1 creation narrative, see Watts, "On the Edge of the Millennium: Making Sense of Genesis 1," and Lamoureux, "Lessons from the Heavens: On Scripture, Science and Inerrancy."

paradigm of natural theology, viewing the remarkable adaptation of each living organism to its own particular environmental niche as evidence for the wisdom of the Creator. In the creation, they believed, God had designed each living organism for a unique purpose. The concept of design with purpose is known as teleology (Greek: *telos* = end). Many seventeenth- and eighteenth-century biologists also believed that extant organisms were part of the original creation. Their view did not allow for changes in living organisms that might have occurred through time.

It was this societal and scientific context that the work of Charles Darwin would change dramatically. It should be noted that Darwin did not set out *a priori* to seek natural explanations for biodiversity, but rather that he was increasingly unable to square his observations with the idea that all species had existed unchanged since their (essentially) simultaneous creation. Rather, the data suggested gradual change over long time periods. In 1859, Charles Darwin published *The Origin of Species*, followed in 1871 by *The Descent of Man*. Darwin's theme was evolution: that populations of living organisms change over time, and that this process accounts for present biodiversity. Darwin based his idea on two key concepts: that there is heritable variation within populations, and that such variation will experience differential reproductive success through natural selection.[8] Darwin thus offered an alternative interpretation for variation and adaptation. He wrote:

> As many more individuals of each species are born than can possibly survive, and as consequently there is a frequently recurring struggle for existence, it follows that any being, if it vary in any manner profitable for itself, under the complex and sometimes varying conditions of life, will have a better chance of survival and thus be naturally selected.[9]

Darwin's ideas, unlike the teleological biology that preceded them, were open to experimentation: they made testable predictions. In the 150 years since *Origin of Species* was published, repeated experimentation has borne Darwin out—with the result that his hypotheses are now consid-

---

8. Indeed, the biological basis for evolution is so simple that some students feel something of a "letdown" upon learning it, having expected something much more complex, and perhaps sinister.

9. Darwin, "Introduction," in *Origin of Species*, 21.

ered scientific theory.[10] Indeed, evolutionary theory unites biology into a cohesive science[11]—it would otherwise be mere "stamp collecting" of dissociated facts.[12]

While "Darwin's dangerous idea"[13] has won great scientific acclaim, it has had much less success in Christian circles. Various theological responses to Darwinism have been formed. Like Samuel before you, you have several options to choose from.

Some Christian groups, including *Answers in Genesis* (AiG)[14] and the *Institute for Creation Research* (ICR),[15] believe that Scripture, as the ultimate authority, is the best source of *scientific* information about the natural world. They espouse a very literal interpretation of the first several chapters of Genesis, including the creation and great flood narratives. They also believe in a young earth and do not accept the evolutionary changes or time scale suggested by the fossil record. They argue that if we erode our view of Scripture, even slightly, subordinating it to science, we are left with non-biblical standards for all of life's decisions.

However, in their attempts to affirm this view of Scripture, these groups are obliged to reject an overwhelming amount of scientific data. For example, Ken Ham of AiG holds that, in accord with Genesis 1, the earth must have been created prior to stellar formation. In a similar vein, he argues that the universe was created less than 10,000 years ago despite being billions of light-years in size—and speculates, as follows, that the speed of light was vastly greater in the past to account for the apparent discrepancy: "It is usually assumed that the speed of light is constant with time. At today's rate, it takes light (in a vacuum) about one year to cover a distance of 6 trillion miles. But has this always been so? If we incor-

10. There is persistent confusion between the scientific use of "theory"—that of a hypothesis that has withstood repeated experimentation—and the popular use of the term "theoretical." I, of course, intend the former. To call evolution "only a theory" is in fact high praise from a scientific viewpoint.

11. Dobzhansky, "Nothing in Biology," is a well-known essay among biologists that makes this point well.

12. The quotation is from physicist Ernest Rutherford: "All science is either physics or stamp collecting." As a biologist, I would contend that biology has collected some very fascinating stamps of late.

13. The allusion is to a book by Daniel Dennett with that title.

14. See www.answersingenesis.org.

15. See www.icr.org.

rectly assume that the rate has always been today's rate, we would end up estimating an age that is much older than the true age."[16]

The position that phenomena scientists today observe as constants were once vastly different is also needed to explain why the earth appears so old when using radiometric dating:

> It is hypothesized . . . that at some time in the past much higher rates of radioisotope decay have occurred, leading to the production of large quantities of daughter products in a short period of time. It has been suggested that these increased decay rates may have been associated with the rock-forming processes on the early earth, and possibly one of the results of God's judgment upon man following Creation . . . large amounts of radioactive decay may have occurred during the first two and a half days of Creation as part of the supernatural Creation process. The jury is still out and, until we complete our research phase, this thesis remains tentative.[17]

Creationist groups such as these have little if any credibility with the vast majority of scientists, who conclude that there simply is no science in so-called "scientific" creationism. At worst, AiG and ICR bring Scripture itself into question. Given the choice between this interpretation of Genesis and the broad sweep of current scientific consensus, it is not surprising that most scientists choose the latter. In so doing, many understand themselves to have rejected Scripture altogether. This is regrettable, and as one commentator has put it, "a literal mistake."[18]

Other Christians claim a high regard for science as well as Scripture. They affirm that God is Creator, and see evolution as the mechanism used by God in the creation process. Known as *theistic evolution*,[19] this viewpoint affirms the scientific method and is a respected worldview paradigm among many educated Christians. Many Christian biologists are theistic evolutionists. A notable theistic evolutionist is Kenneth Miller, a cell biologist and Roman Catholic. His book, *Finding Darwin's God*, is both an

---

16. Retrieved from http://www.answersingenesis.org/articles/nab/does-starlight-prove.

17. Vardiman, et al., "Radioisotopes and the Age of the Earth." An excellent overview of the trustworthiness of several dating techniques can be found in a two-part review by Young entitled "How Old Is It? How Do We Know?"

18. Fischer, "Young-earth Creationism."

19. Recently, Denis Lamoureux has put forward the term *evolutional creation* as an alternative label for this view. His approach has appeal in that it avoids the common misconception that theistic evolution is in fact *deistic* evolution. See Lamoureux, *Evolutionary Creation*.

accessible read for a lay audience and a thoroughgoing presentation of theistic evolution. Miller makes a strong case, contending that theistic evolution does not diminish God's role as Creator but rather celebrates it. Miller's God (and, he argues, Darwin's God) is not a watered-down deity with nothing left to do, but a master architect who set in place the conditions and mechanisms required for evolution. If Darwin can be credited with allowing for "intellectually fulfilled atheism,"[20] Miller has made good progress towards a theologically fulfilled Darwinism.

Perhaps the most well-known theistic evolutionist in Protestant circles is Francis Collins, the former head of the Human Genome Project. In his recent book, *The Language of God*, Collins rightly brings his obvious expertise to bear in discussing recent genomic findings based on whole-genome sequence comparisons between mammals. One striking example is comparisons between the human genome and the chimpanzee genome, the latter having been available since 2005.[21] The scientific facts are not in dispute: the chimp genome is nearly identical to our own, including nonfunctional, repetitive sequences that are present at the same locations in both genomes. Collins concludes that the simplest explanation for this genome-wide correspondence is that we share a common evolutionary ancestor with chimpanzees. Also present in the human genome are *pseudogenes*[22] that retain function in the chimp. To suggest that genetic errors were independently created in us but not in chimps is a proposition Collins finds difficult from a theological point of view.[23] Recent comparative genomic analyses continue to amass evidence for common ancestry between mammals. An example is the discovery of egg yolk *vitellogenin* pseudogenes in placental mammals, replete with identical inactivating mutations present in armadillos, dogs, and humans.[24]

---

20. Dawkins, *Blind Watchmaker*, 6.

21. The Chimpanzee Sequencing and Analysis Consortium, "Initial Sequence of the Chimpanzee Genome."

22. A *pseudogene* is a DNA sequence that is easily recognizable as once having been a functional gene but that has been inactivated through mutation.

23. See Collins, *Language of God*, 133–41. The likelihood of the remaining option, that these striking correspondences are the result of mere chance, is of course tiny to the point of absurdity. For an excellent overview of the challenges that chimpanzee–human genomic comparisons present to the thesis of *de novo* creation of humans, see Wood, "The Chimpanzee Genome."

24. Brawand, Wali, and Kaessmann, "Loss of Egg Yolk Genes in Mammals."

Theistic evolution is not without its theological tensions, of course. One of note is its seeming rejection of the Genesis 2–3 narrative concerning the creation of Adam and Eve and their subsequent Fall into disobedience. As Newman points out, the theistic evolutionist is obliged to consider what appears to be historical narrative in these chapters as myth.[25] Even among theistic evolutionists there is considerable variation in belief at this and other points. In their recent book, *Origins: A Reformed Look at Creation, Design and Evolution,* Deborah and Loren Haarsma discuss various theistic evolutionary positions on Genesis in a balanced way.[26]

In the mid-1990s, a third approach arose to the question of origins that sits in opposition to both young-earth creationism and theistic evolution.[27] The principal doctrine of this group was the evidence of intelligent design throughout the natural world; as such, these scholars are commonly referred to as exponents of the "Intelligent Design" (or simply "ID") movement. The principal spokespersons for this group are Phillip Johnson,[28] Michael Behe, and William Dembski. Dembski's work is primarily mathematical in nature,[29] whereas Behe, as a biochemist, has carried the brunt of the biological argument for design. Behe outlined his argument in two books: *Darwin's Black Box: The Biochemical Challenge to Evolution* and *The Edge of Evolution: The Search for the Limits of Darwinism.* Briefly stated, the biochemical argument for ID is that biological systems exist that cannot be accounted for by naturalistic mechanisms. These systems (protein complexes comprised of numerous interrelated parts dependent

25. Newman, "Some Problems for Theistic Evolution," 124. Of course, seeing Genesis 1–3 as "mythic literature" is not equivalent to viewing it as false. See also Watts, "On the Edge of the Millennium: Making Sense of Genesis," and especially Lamoureux, *Evolutionary Creation,* for a thorough treatment of these issues.

26. See especially chapter 12. This book is an excellent overview of creation science, Intelligent Design (see below) and theistic evolution, outlining the theological strengths and weaknesses of each.

27. Early on, the ID movement attempted to include young-earth creationists within its ranks through its so-called "Big Tent" policy, though apparently with only minimal success.

28. Johnson's book, *Darwin on Trial,* published in 1991, was a seminal book for the ID movement.

29. For example, Dembski, *The Design Inference.* Dembski, like Behe, has had little success in winning a hearing for his arguments in his area of expertise. For thorough critiques of Dembski accessible to non-specialists, see Nichols, "Scientific Content, Testability, and Vacuity of Intelligent Design Theory," and especially Felsenstein, "Has Natural Selection Been Refuted?"

on each other for function) are rendered functionless by the removal of any one component. Such an "irreducibly complex" system, Behe argues, cannot arise by the successive accumulation of parts (i.e., by Darwinian gradualism) since only the complete complex has function that can be selected for.[30] Furthermore, irreducibly complex systems cannot acquire a new function through random mutation and selection.[31]

The question of ID as science literally had its day in court in 2005 as Kitzmiller versus Dover Board of Education.[32] The trial, in some respects, was akin to a scientific peer review of the central claims of ID. Specifically, Behe's assertion that irreducibly complex biological systems cannot arise or be modified to acquire new functions by natural selection[33] was countered effectively with several examples, most notably in the testimony of Kenneth Miller.[34] Interspersed between the scientific details presented in the Kitzmiller case, a larger issue consistently arose: defining the nature of scientific inquiry and evaluating ID in light of that definition.[35] The testimony of several ID advocates during the trial asserted that the intent of the ID movement was to broaden the definition of science to accept supernatural causation, and that such a re-definition was necessary for ID to be considered science. Under cross-examination, Scott Fuller, an expert witness in the philosophy of science for the defense, put it thus:

> Q. And here you're talking about broadening that definition beyond natural causation . . . to supernatural causation?

30. The main thesis of *Darwin's Black Box* is the argument for irreducible complex-ity.

31. This idea is defended at length in Behe, *The Edge of Evolution*.

32. Complete transcripts of the Kitzmiller case are available online at several locations including http://www.talkorigins.org/faqs/dover/kitzmiller_v_dover.html and http://www2.ncseweb.org/kvd/. Chapman's *40 Days* is both a popular account of the Kitzmiller affair (authored by the great-grandson of Darwin himself) and a useful guide to orient oneself within the court transcripts.

33. Behe's assertion that irreducibly complex biological systems cannot arise through evolutionary mechanisms has been critiqued in detail in the literature as well. See Gishlick, "Evolutionary Paths," and Musgrave, "Evolution of the Bacterial Flagellum."

34. "Kitzmiller et al. v. Dover Area School District," Trial Transcript: Day 1 (September 26), AM Session Part 1–AM Session, Part 2. Nonetheless, Behe went on to publish *The Edge of Evolution* in 2007, to be met with several scathing reviews, e.g., Levin, "The Edge of Evolution."

35. Indeed, both the plaintiffs and the defense requested that Judge John Jones III rule on the question of whether ID was science.

> A. Yes. And what I'm talking about . . . is going beyond the taken-for-granted categories . . . [T]his has happened in the history of science and does periodically, where things that people regard as occult forces and things that cannot be observed and are not detectable by ordinary experimental means, people postulate them, use them as the basis for research, and eventually you do come up with something that can then be assimilated within naturalistic science.[36]

Fuller thus seems to value ID as a sort of "fringe science"—on the edge, exploring new avenues of productive research that eventually may find a home within naturalistic science. It is interesting to note that Fuller sees the value of ID as (eventually) contributing to *natural* explanations, which is hardly the intent of the ID movement. Also noteworthy is that the ID movement, to date, has not produced original research but has focused on reinterpreting work published by others.[37] Fuller's view is an interesting one. ID certainly has prodded evolutionary science to clarify its arguments, more carefully define its terms, and close gaps in evolutionary understanding. Still, I question Fuller's readiness to deliberately include something non-naturalistic within science to further science's naturalistic aims.[38]

The Kitzmiller case ended badly for proponents of ID. In his ruling, Judge Jones ruled that ID was not science but inherently creationist in content, and thus unconstitutional to teach in the Pennsylvania public school system.[39] He also chastised the defendants for holding to a false dichotomy with respect to evolutionary science and theology:

> Both Defendants and many of the leading proponents of ID make a bedrock assumption which is utterly false. Their presupposition is that evolutionary theory is antithetical to a belief in the existence of a supreme being and to religion in general. Repeatedly

36. "Kitzmiller et al. v. Dover Area School District," Trial Transcript: Day 15 (October 24), PM Session Part 1.

37. This has led to the accusation that the ID community is more concerned about gaining scientific status than doing science.

38. I have made every effort to read Fuller's comments in the context of his complete and rather nuanced testimony. Fuller, called as an expert witness to defend ID as science, nonetheless openly described ID as not yet a full-fledged scientific theory. His testimony strikes me as among the least biased of the Kitzmiller expert witnesses.

39. The complete Kitzmiller decision is available online at http://www.pamd.uscourts.gov/kitzmiller/kitzmiller_342.pdf.

in this trial, Plaintiffs' scientific experts testified that the theory of evolution represents good science, is overwhelmingly accepted by the scientific community, and that it in no way conflicts with, nor does it deny, the existence of a divine creator.[40]

It is over the issue of redefining science that most scientists (Christian, atheist or otherwise) reject ID. Science demands no philosophical or theological allegiance; furthermore, it is by convention barred from asserting philosophical or theological positions. Science, by its very nature, is limited in scope and cannot empirically investigate the supernatural.[41] Broadening the definition of science to consider the supernatural *scientific* cannot limit which theological or philosophical positions are acceptable. When pressed on this point under cross-examination, Behe conceded that astrology could count as acceptable scientific inquiry under the ID definition of science.[42] The conclusion that atheism—itself a theological position—would thus also qualify as acceptable science is inescapable. To accept the ID definition is in fact to open science to all comers of any philosophical or theological bent, and to simultaneously deprive scientists of the means to falsify their claims. Small wonder most biologists (and prominent Christian biologists among them) resist such a redefinition.

ALREADY/NOT YET: FAITHFUL LIVING IN THE AGE OF GENOMICS

Certainly the question of origins is a topic of much debate among Christians, but it is by no means the only issue of concern to Christian biologists (nor even, I would contend, the most important). In the last decade, scientific advances in biology and biotechnology have engendered many ethical issues on which, for obvious reasons, there is no direct biblical teaching. As we have seen with respect to origins, a simple cut-

---

40. Kitzmiller decision, 136.

41. The Kitzmiller testimony of Barbara Forrest provides an excellent discussion of this issue. See "Kitzmiller et al. v. Dover Area School District," Trial Transcript: Day 6 (October 5), AM Session–PM Session.

42. "Kitzmiller et al. v. Dover Area School District," Trial Transcript: Day 11 (October 18), AM Session Part 1. Behe has since argued that he was misinterpreted—that he intended to assert merely that astrology was once considered science before maturing into astronomy. The context does not seem to support Behe's claim; indeed, it would seem to follow from Behe's interpretation that ID should not yet be considered science until, like astrology, it "matures" by divesting itself of supernatural explanations.

and-paste approach will cause more harm than good; we require responses deeply rooted in both the relevant science and the Christian faith that speak to the issues of the day. New Testament scholar N. T. Wright analogizes faithful Christian living in the present age as an act of Spirit-inspired improvisation.[43] Wright asks us to imagine a scenario where the fourth act of a five-act play is missing. How might the missing act be improvised? Quite simply: the first three acts set the stage for the fourth, and the fifth act shows where the entire play is going. What is required are actors, thoroughly versed in the available material, who faithfully improvise the intervening act.[44] This is a useful analogy as we consider what "faithful improvisation" might mean in light of recent biological advances.

As a graduate student, I remember watching the movie *Gattaca*[45] and chuckling at the Hollywood characterization of the process by which an individual "got sequenced"—his or her genomic secrets laid bare in a matter of minutes, replete with the knowledge of how the details would play out in life. In 1997, such an idea truly was in the realm of science fiction. In the intervening decade, this technology has increasingly moved from fiction to fact,[46] bringing with it a host of ethical issues. The key advances in this area were the sequencing of the human genome[47] and the International HapMap project,[48] which sought to identify all common single-nucleotide sequence variations in the human genome. Simply put, we now know where to look for genetic differences between humans, and where we can be quite certain no common differences exist—at a genome-wide level. This simplifies genomic analysis considerably, to the point where whole-genome analysis of an extended family now can be accomplished in a matter of days[49] (since it is not necessary to sequence the entire genome of any given individual). This powerful method has already identified numerous variations correlated with disease by a whole-

43. Wright, "Creation and New Creation in the New Testament."

44. Wright of course notes that what counts as *faithful* improvisation may be contentious among the actors, who then examine the extant acts to argue their case.

45. Released October 24, 1997, by Columbia Pictures.

46. Blow, "The Personal Side of Genomics."

47. More properly, the first sequencing of a representative human genome: the initial sequence was determined from a randomized sample of several donors.

48. See www.hapmap.org for an overview of the HapMap project.

49. Gibbs and Singleton, "Application of Genome-wide Single Nucleotide Polymorphism Typing."

genome statistical approach: by simply examining the entire genome of numerous affected individuals, comparing them to the genomes of non-affected individuals, and looking for variations that are significantly over-represented in the affected group. Examples of early successes include the identification of risk factors for common cancers[50] and macular degeneration, among others.[51] The rate at which such discoveries will take place will almost certainly grow exponentially in the next few years—and, in the not-too-distant future, likely result in the technological capacity effectively equivalent to the scene in *Gattaca*. Already it is possible to have one's genome evaluated privately for approximately $1000, the results of which may be compared against current knowledge of disease risk factors as well as future discoveries.[52] As Christians, we have much to celebrate here, not least that those at risk of genetic diseases may learn of their predispositions long before disease onset and alter their lifestyles to mitigate their risks. Moreover, we can expect this approach to greatly advance human understanding of many common diseases, especially since it requires no *a priori* hypotheses about what genes might contribute to a specific condition.[53]

As with any new discovery, however, this knowledge is open to abuse. At its most elementary level, genomic technology is a discriminatory tool—discriminating between what genes influence a given condition and what genes do not, for example—but this information also can be used for discrimination in the popular sense. It is likely only a matter of time before this approach identifies genetic variation that influences complex human traits such as intelligence, predisposition to violence, religious devotion, or sexual orientation.[54] Indeed, widespread genomic sequencing of the human race could allow for discrimination at an unprecedented level of detail. Insurance companies might deny health claims

50. For example, Sun et al., "Haplotypes in Matrix Metalloproteinase Gene Cluster."

51. Klein et al., "Complement Factor H Polymorphism." In this instance the result was a surprise in that an immune system protein variant was identified as a risk factor, suggesting macular degeneration to be an autoimmune disease.

52. See Goetz, "23AndMe."

53. Indeed, it is likely that genome-wide polymorphism analysis of individual patients will be the standard of care in western medicine in the not-too-distant future.

54. Following his 2007 keynote address at the National Association of Biology Teachers Annual Conference, Francis Collins was specifically asked about variation contributing to religious experience. His response was to the effect that while it was likely such variation would be found, subtle predisposition was not to be viewed as deterministic.

for individuals with disease-predisposing genotypes. Companies might only hire individuals with favorable genomics. Universities might require applicants to submit a DNA sample along with an SAT score. Parents of the future may choose genetic testing to screen prospective embryos for a veritable "laundry list" of predispositions—and abort (or elect not to implant) those who fail their criteria.[55] The view driving these potential abuses of genomic technology is genetic determinism: the notion that traits are, in the main, controlled by genes.[56] This view is erroneous, in that it overlooks or downplays the vital role of environmental influence on complex characteristics. A growth of genetic determinism in popular opinion has followed scientific advances in genetics before,[57] so this is not necessarily surprising.

In light of these complex issues, what might faithful improvisation look like? The key issue, that of discrimination, is a major theme in the New Testament. Division along Jew–Gentile lines was a problem for many of the Pauline churches, and Paul was vigilant against it, for he knew it negated the gospel of Christ. Consider his swift response when Peter and Barnabas withdrew from table fellowship with Gentiles at Antioch: "When Cephas came to Antioch, I opposed him to his face, because he stood condemned" (Galatians 2:11).[58] The reason for this no-holds-barred approach is clearly based on Paul's conviction about the unifying work of Christ on the cross.[59] While the Jew–Gentile schism is the primary division at issue in the New Testament, Paul's theology of unity cuts across every potential basis for division of the day:

> So in Christ Jesus you are all children of God through faith, for
> all of you who were baptized into Christ have clothed yourselves
> with Christ. There is neither Jew nor Gentile, neither slave nor free,

55. Pre-implantation genetic diagnosis is already a widespread practice for couples known to be carriers for certain recessive diseases.

56. *Gattaca* depicts a society that has bought into genetic determinism wholesale.

57. The most notorious example is of course that of Nazi Germany, where racial discrimination and genocide was rationalized, in the words of Rudolf Hess, as "nothing more than applied biology." That Hess could appeal to biology in this way is indicative of popular perception at the time. The rediscovery of Mendel's work and its repeated confirmation in other species, including our own, defined the scientific climate of biology in the early 1900s.

58. Note also Paul's statement in v. 14 that Peter was out of line with respect to the "truth of the gospel."

59. For example, see Paul's argument in Ephesians 2:11–22.

> neither male nor female, for you are all one in Christ Jesus. If you
> belong to Christ, then you are Abraham's seed, and heirs according
> to the promise. (Galatians 3:26–29)

The point, of course, is not that these categories cease to exist:[60] women will remain women, Gentiles will remain Gentiles, *et cetera*. Variation does not vanish into uniformity. The point is that these categories, in the light of Christ, cease to have social significance or divisive power. To re-invest these categories with such significance is to return to viewing one another *kata sarka*—that is, according to the flesh.[61] Note too how the categories include what the ancients would have considered differences in heredity.[62] What shall we say then? Paul rejected and vigorously opposed all contemporary means of discrimination and division in his day as antithetical to the gospel. Though genomics might permit an ever more detailed means by which some may advocate discrimination, we should do no less than he.[63]

"RAPTURE ME AND LET IT BURN": WHAT PLACE CHRISTIAN ENVIRONMENTALISM?

We now turn to an issue that, while it concerns faithful living in the present age, is influenced by *eschatology*: what one believes about the age to come.[64] Christian environmentalism, once viewed with great suspicion as too pantheistic by evangelicals,[65] has made great advances in recent

---

60. There is an exception: Paul advocates that slaves obtain their freedom, if possible. Cf. 1 Corinthians 7:17–24, where freedom from slavery is the one departure from Paul's general admonition for the Corinthians to remain in the station they were in when they came to faith.

61. For example, 2 Corinthians 5:16: "from now on we regard no one from a worldly point of view" (*kata sarka*).

62. Even with the slavery issue, there would have been overtones of heredity present, as slaves were often born into their station or were captured members of other races.

63. One might contend that Paul was focused only on these issues *within* the church. This is to miss the point entirely: Paul's view was that the church was the "colony" of the future worldwide Kingdom of God. It was for good reason that Paul was accused of heralding "another king, one called Jesus," in direct opposition to Caesar (Acts 17:7).

64. Truesdale, "Last Things First."

65. Tony Campolo's 1992 book promoting Christian environmentalism entitled *How to Rescue the Earth without Worshiping Nature* gives a good picture of the mindset of the intended audience at that time. Ample evidence of this mindset can also be seen in the interlocutor to whom DeWitt responds in "Preparing the Way for Action" (see below).

years.[66] Another viewpoint has also made great strides in the last decade, however: that of premillenial "rapture" theology. Having begun with origins, and holding to our premise of present faithful living, we now turn our attention to "the end."

As part of an introductory biology course for non-majors, I lecture on the biblical basis for environmental stewardship. As an introduction to the lecture, I query students about their own environmental views. One student's response, though not unique, was particularly telling: she expressed an interest in environmentalism but wondered how such interest could have a biblical basis given that the earth was going to be destroyed in the end times, and Christians raptured up to heaven to escape its destruction. The particular version of eschatology this student assumed ran roughshod over biblically-motivated environmentalism by removing the non-human creation from God's redemptive plan.[67] This set of beliefs regarding the end times, though popularized in the last few years through hugely successful novels,[68] is not easily reconciled with Paul's use of *parousia* imagery.[69] Despite the popularity of the *Left Behind* series, several theologians argue instead that Christian environmental stewardship finds its true motivation in the view that the final dwelling place of God, and those who are redeemed by him, is a renewed earth.[70]

Even within the Christian environmental movement there is a regrettable lack of consensus on the final fate of the created order. Calvin DeWitt, noted Christian environmentalist, educator, and author, makes a case for conservation in spite of the earth's impending destruction. Primary in his list of "stumbling blocks" to Christian environmentalism lies the key question: "Since we're headed for heaven anyway, why take

66. The success of Christian environmental organizations such as A Rocha and the Au Sable Institute are good examples of how the issue has penetrated the evangelical consciousness.

67. Truesdale, "Last Things First."

68. As of this writing, the novels in the *Left Behind* series have sold more than 65,000,000 copies.

69. Wright, "Farewell to the Rapture." Paul's description of meeting Jesus in the air upon his return has the concept of *parousia* as its cultural referent: the welcoming of an emperor into one of his cities by going out to meet him. The original recipients of Paul's letter would not have expected the emperor to whisk the welcoming party away.

70. For example, the announcement in Revelation 21:3 that the dwelling place of God will be "among the people" that precedes the description of the new Jerusalem descending to earth.

care of creation?"[71] DeWitt argues that even objects destined to be destroyed are maintained and cared for until their designated end. Notably, he includes the human body in his examples: "But temporal as our bodies are, we still take care of our appearance and health. . . . Thus, even structures *whose destruction is planned* are still protected and maintained with . . . custodial care [emphasis mine]."[72]

DeWitt's argument concurs with the view that "Heaven is my home, I'm just a-passing through"—and that creation itself is to be destroyed. Thus, in want of a practical theological motivation for environmental stewardship, he frames his argument merely in terms of obedience: "Biblical teachings reinforce our responsibility for the care and keeping of creation. They include teachings for a stewardly life, [and] they give grave warning that those who destroy the earth will themselves be destroyed. . . ."[73]

Others contend that the New Testament vision for the coming new creation is strikingly different and vastly more appealing. Theologians such as Gordon Zerbe and N. T. Wright have made a strong case for a renewed earth as the final dwelling place of God and his kingdom.[74] Zerbe frames the crucial question in much the same way as DeWitt: "Why preserve the present earth when it is headed for collapse and a new heaven and new earth will replace it? Why be concerned with the earth at all? Are not spiritual concerns more important?"[75] In the course of his arguments, however, Zerbe arrives at a radically different conclusion:

71. DeWitt, "Preparing the Way for Action," 81.

72. Ibid., 81.

73. Cf. Revelation 11:18. DeWitt does modify his position somewhat in a later publication, asserting that "Creation is not a lost cause" in a discussion of the work of Abraham Kuyper (DeWitt, *Caring for Creation*, 37–40). He does not elaborate on what "not a lost cause" might mean or retract his previous arguments, however.

74. This vision is not unique to the New Testament, but runs right through Scripture from Genesis 1 (the creation declared *good* by God) to Isaiah's prophetic visions of the earth rejoicing at the return from exile (e.g., Isaiah 55:12–13) and on to the grand vision of the new Jerusalem coming down from heaven to a renewed earth in Revelation 21. See Wright, "Creation and New Creation in the New Testament"; also, Zerbe, "The Kingdom of God and Stewardship of Creation."

75. Zerbe, "The Kingdom of God and Stewardship of Creation", 83, with the irony duly noted that this fine essay appears in a book edited by DeWitt and published several years before DeWitt's "Preparing the Way for Action."

> [T]he New Testament vision of the kingdom is first that of the
> new order in the age to come. That reality results when the rule of
> Christ and of God is realized in all creation. . . . [T]his future vision
> shows that God is concerned not only with the world of humanity,
> but with the entirety of creation. All creation is good and is the
> object of God's ultimate redeeming act.[76]

Zerbe thus answers his original question of whether earth-keeping is a Christian believer's responsibility with a resounding "Yes"—not merely in terms of obedience, but with the insight that the earth will not be replaced, but redeemed. This is a crucial issue: there is continuity and discontinuity between the earth of this age and the age to come.[77]

Despite this overarching theology in the New Testament, there is little direct teaching therein on creation care. The reason for this is simple: in New Testament times there was not widespread environmental degradation of the earth, nor were humans considered to have much control over, or impact on, nature. We do, however, have an appropriate parallel in one of Paul's letters to the Corinthians: an example of creation abuse that Paul actively corrected. Paul's letters, though masterpieces of sustained logical argument, are *occasioned* documents, addressed to the specific needs (often we might say errors) of the recipient congregation.[78] The Corinthian church fell into erroneous, dualistic thinking about the treatment of the human body: by asserting the body to be temporary, some in the congregation held that sexual union with prostitutes was acceptable (1 Corinthians 6:12–20). Paul's blunt and forceful correction is based on his theology of bodily continuity: "In particular, the argument . . . depends on Paul's belief that what is done with the present body *matters* precisely because it is to be raised. The *continuity* between the present body and the future resurrection body is what gives weight to the present ethical imperative."[79] Thus the future resurrection life informs ethics in the present age predicated on its continuity with the present embodied life. This

76. Ibid., 83.

77. Wright, "Creation and New Creation in the New Testament." This lecture series includes an excellent discussion of continuity/discontinuity imagery in the Pauline corpus.

78. Indeed, if not for the errors of the New Testament church we would lack clear teaching on several topics considered central to Christian faith.

79. Wright, *The Resurrection of the Son of God*, 289 (emphasis mine). That DeWitt selects the human body as an example of a temporary object is especially regrettable in light of the New Testament theology of resurrection continuity.

theme is a major chord in Paul: that Christians, through the indwelling power of the Holy Spirit, live the life of the coming age in the present one.[80] That is, after all, what *zōē aiōnios*, commonly translated as "eternal life," means: "the life of the coming age."[81] What, then, would be Paul's response to the environmental crisis? In the coming age all creation will be renewed and liberated by God (Romans 8:18–19).[82] There is continuity between the present creation and the renewed creation to come, just as there is continuity between our present bodies and our future resurrection bodies.[83] How then shall we live with respect to the environment in the present? Shall we await the rapture to whisk us away from the earth's destruction? God forbid. To do so runs counter to the theology of the New Testament, recapitulating the dualistic Corinthian error with respect to the planet as a whole.

CONCLUSION

The call to a scientifically informed, thoughtful Christian interaction with contemporary culture is not a new one. As you prayerfully consider your calling as a potential student of biology, consider well the words of Saint Augustine:

> Usually even a non-Christian knows something about the earth, the heavens, and the other elements of this world, about the motion and orbit of the stars and even their size and relative positions, about the predictable eclipses of the sun and moon, the cycles of the years and the seasons, about the kinds of animals, shrubs, stones and so forth, and this knowledge he holds to as being certain from reason and experience. Now, it is a disgraceful and dangerous thing for an infidel to hear a Christian, presumably giving the meaning of Holy Scripture, talking nonsense on these topics; and we should take all means to prevent such an embarrassing situation, in which people show up vast ignorance in a Christian and laugh it to scorn. The shame is not so much that an ignorant individual is derided, but that people outside the household of faith think our sacred writers held such opinions, and, to the great loss of those for whose

80. Fee, *Paul, the Spirit, and the People of God,* 51–52.

81. Wright, *The Resurrection of the Son of God,* 246.

82. It is tragic that Paul's central and majestic vision of the new creation in Romans 8 has often been viewed as something of an aside by Reformation theologians, among others.

83. Wright, "Creation and New Creation in the New Testament."

salvation we toil, the writers of our Scripture are criticized and rejected as unlearned men. If they find a Christian mistaken in a field which they themselves know well and hear him maintaining his foolish opinions about our books, how are they going to believe those books in matters concerning the resurrection of the dead, the hope of eternal life, and the kingdom of heaven, when they think their pages are full of falsehoods on facts they themselves have learnt from experience and the light of reason? Reckless and incompetent expounders of Holy Scripture bring untold trouble and sorrow on their wiser brethren when they are caught in one of their mischievous false opinions and are taken to task by those who are not bound by the authority of our sacred books. For then, to defend their utterly foolish and obviously untrue statements, they will try to call upon Holy Scripture for proof and even re-cite from memory many passages which they think support their position, although they understand neither what they say nor the things about which they make assertion.[84]

WORKS CITED

Augustine. *The Literal Meaning of Genesis*. In *Ancient Christian Writers: The Works of the Fathers in Translation*, No. 41, translated by John Hammond Taylor. New York: Newman Press, 1982.

Behe, Michael J. *Darwin's Black Box: The Biochemical Challenge to Evolution*. New York: Free Press, 1996.

———. *The Edge of Evolution: The Search for the Limits of Darwinism*. New York: Free Press, 2007.

Blow, Nathan. "The Personal Side of Genomics." *Nature* 449 (October 2007) 627–30.

Brawand, David, Walter Wali, and Henrik Kaessmann. "Loss of Egg Yolk Genes in Mammals and the Origin of Lactation and Placentation." *PLoS Biology* 6 (March 2008) 0507–0517.

Campolo, Anthony. *How to Rescue the Earth without Worshiping Nature*. Nashville: Nelson, 1992.

Chapman, Matthew. *40 Days and 40 Nights: Darwin, Intelligent Design, God, OxyContin® and Other Oddities on Trial in Pennsylvania*. New York: Harper Collins, 2007.

The Chimpanzee Sequencing and Analysis Consortium. "Initial Sequence of the Chimpanzee Genome and Comparison with the Human Genome." *Nature* 437 (September 2005) 69–87.

Collins, Francis S. *The Language of God: A Scientist Presents Evidence for Belief*. New York: Free Press, 2006.

Darwin, Charles. *The Origin of Species*. New York: Modern Library, 1998 (1859).

84. Augustine, *The Literal Meaning of Genesis*, Book One, Chapter 19. This passage, though over 1600 years old, is so timely I quote it here at length. See also the discussion of portions of this passage in Miller, *Finding Darwin's God*, 255–59.

Dawkins, Richard. *The Blind Watchmaker: Why the Evidence of Evolution Reveals a World without Design.* New York: Norton, 1996.

Dembski, William A. *The Design Inference: Eliminating Chance through Small Probabilities.* Cambridge: Cambridge University Press, 1998.

Dennett, Daniel C. *Darwin's Dangerous Idea: Evolution and the Meanings of Life.* New York: Simon & Schuster, 1995.

DeWitt, Calvin B. *Caring for Creation: Responsible Stewardship of God's Handiwork.* Grand Rapids, MI: Baker Books, 1998.

———. "Preparing the Way for Action." *Perspectives on Science and Christian Faith* 46.2 (June 1994) 80–89.

Dobzhansky, Theodosius. "Nothing in Biology Makes Sense Except in the Light of Evolution." *American Biology Teacher* 35 (March 1973) 125–29.

Fee, Gordon. D. *Paul, the Spirit, and the People of God.* Peabody, MA: Hendrickson, 1996.

Felsenstein, Joe. "Has Natural Selection Been Refuted?" *Reports of the National Center for Science Education* 27 (May–August 2007) 20–26.

Fischer, Dick. "Young-earth Creationism: A Literal Mistake." *Perspectives on Science and Christian Faith* 55.4 (December 2003) 222–31.

Gibbs, J. Raphael, and Andrew Singleton. "Application of Genome-wide Single Nucleotide Polymorphism Typing: Simple Association and Beyond." *PLoS Genetics* 2 (October 2006) 1511–17.

Gishlick, Alan D. "Evolutionary Paths to Irreducible Systems." In *Why Intelligent Design Fails: A Scientific Critique of the New Creationism,* edited by Matt Young and Taner Edis, 58–71. Piscataway, NJ: Rutgers University Press, 2004.

Goetz, Thomas. "23AndMe Will Decode Your DNA for $1000. Welcome to the Age of Genomics." *Wired Magazine* 15 (November 2007). Available online at www.wired.com/medtech/genetics/magazine/15-12/ff_genomics.

Haarsma, Deborah B., and Loren D. Haarsma. *Origins: A Reformed Look at Creation, Design and Evolution.* Grand Rapids, MI: Faith Alive Christian Resources, 2007.

Johnson, Phillip F. *Darwin on Trial.* Downers Grove, IL: InterVarsity Press, 1991.

Klein, R. J., et al. "Complement Factor H Polymorphism in Age-related Macular Degeneration." *Science* 308 (April 2005) 385–89.

Lamoureux, Denis O. *Evolutionary Creation: A Christian Approach to Evolution.* Eugene, OR: Wipf & Stock, 2008.

———. "Lessons from the Heavens: On Scripture, Science and Inerrancy." *Perspectives on Science and Christian Faith* 60.1 (March 2008) 4–15.

Levin, David E. "The Edge of Evolution." *Reports of the National Center for Science Education* 27 (March–April 2007) 38–40.

Miller, Kenneth R. *Finding Darwin's God: A Scientist's Search for Common Ground between God and Evolution.* New York: HarperCollins, 1999.

Musgrave, Ian. "Evolution of the Bacterial Flagellum." In *Why Intelligent Design Fails: A Scientific Critique of the New Creationism,* edited by Matt Young and Taner Edis, 72–84. Piscataway, NJ: Rutgers University Press, 2004.

Newman, Robert C. "Some Problems for Theistic Evolution." *Perspectives on Science and Christian Faith* 55.2 (June 2003) 117–28.

Nichols, Ryan. "Scientific Content, Testability, and Vacuity of Intelligent Design Theory." *American Catholic Philosophical Quarterly* 77 (2003) 589–609.

Sun, T., et al. "Haplotypes in Matrix Metalloproteinase Gene Cluster on Chromosome 11q22 Contribute to the Risk of Lung Cancer Development and Progression." *Clinical Cancer Research* 12 (December 2006) 7009–17.

Truesdale, Al. "Last Things First: The Impact of Eschatology on Ecology." *Perspectives on Science and Christian Faith* 45.2 (June 1994) 116–22.

Vardiman, Larry, et al. "Radioisotopes and the Age of the Earth." In *Proceedings of the Fifth International Conference on Creationism*, edited by R. Ivey. Pittsburgh, PA : Creation Science Fellowship, 2003. Accessed online at www.icr.org/pdf/research/RATE_ICC_Vardiman.pdf.

Watts, Rikki E. "On the Edge of the Millennium: Making Sense of Genesis 1." In *Living in the LambLight: Chistianity and Contemporary Challenges to the Gospel*, edited by Hans I. Boersma, 129–51. Vancouver, BC: Regent College Publishing, 2001.

Wood, Todd C. "The Chimpanzee Genome and the Problem of Biological Similarity." *Occasional Papers of the Baraminology Study Group* 7 (February 2006). Available online at http://www.creationbiology.org/.

Wright, N. T. "Creation and New Creation in the New Testament" (audio recording). Regent Audio, 2003. Available online at www.regentaudio.com.

———. "Farewell to the Rapture." *Bible Review* 17.4 (August 2001) 8.

———. *The Resurrection of the Son of God*. Christian Origins and the Question of God, III. Minneapolis: Fortress Press, 2003.

Young, Davis A. "How Old Is It? How Do We Know? A Review of Dating Methods—Part One: Relative Dating, Absolute Dating, and Non-Radiometric Dating Methods." *Perspectives on Science and Christian Faith* 58.4 (December 2006) 259–65.

———. "How Old Is It? How Do We Know? A Review of Dating Methods—Part Two: Radiometric Dating: Mineral, Isochron and Concordia Methods." *Perspectives on Science and Christian Faith* 59.1 (March 2007) 28–36.

Zerbe, Gordon. "The Kingdom of God and Stewardship of Creation." In *The Environment and the Christian: What Can We Learn from the New Testament?* edited by Calvin B. DeWitt, 73–92. Grand Rapids, MI: Baker, 1991.

FOR FURTHER READING

Anderson, Paul M. "A Common Thread." In *Professors Who Believe: The Spiritual Journeys of Christian Faculty*, edited by Paul M. Anderson, 14–27. Downers Grove, IL: InterVarsity Press, 1998.

Coalition of Scientific Societies. "Evolution and its Discontents: A Role for Scientists in Science Education." *FASEB Journal* 22 (January 2008) 1–4.

Cobb, John B., Jr., ed. *Back to Darwin: A Richer Account of Evolution*. Grand Rapids, MI: Eerdmans, 2008.

Colling, Richard G. *Random Designer: Created from Chaos to Connect with the Creator*. Bourbonnais, IL: Browning Press, 2004.

Dembski, William A., ed. *Uncommon Dissent: Intellectuals Who Find Darwinism Unconvincing*. Wilmington, DE: ISI Books, 2004.

Falk, Darryl R. *Coming to Peace with Science: Bridging the Worlds between Faith and Biology*. Downers Grove, IL: InterVarsity Press, 2004.

National Academy of Sciences and Institute of Medicine. *Science, Evolution, and Creationism*. Washington, DC: The National Academies Press, 2008.

Peters, Ted, and Martinez Hewlett. *Can You Believe in God and Evolution? A Guide for the Perplexed*. Nashville: Abingdon Press, 2006.

Pigliucci, Massimo. *Denying Evolution: Creationism, Scientism, and the Nature of Science*. Sunderland, MA: Sinauer Associates, 2000.

Ratzsch, Del. *The Battle of Beginnings: Why Neither Side Is Winning the Creation–Evolution Debate*. Downers Grove, IL: InterVarsity Press, 1996.

Ross, Hugh. *The Creator and the Cosmos: How the Greatest Scientific Discoveries of the Century Reveal God*. 3d ed. Colorado Springs, CO: NavPress, 2003.

7

A Christian Perspective on Business

JOHN R. SUTHERLAND

INTRODUCTION

WHEN I ARRIVED AT what was then Trinity Western College in 1978 to teach in the Division of Business, I encountered two very surprising attitudes, conveyed to me with greater or lesser degrees of tact by certain colleagues of that day. The first was that a professional business administration program constituted something of an intrusion into what had been, until recently, a purely liberal arts college. Second, some professors felt that it was virtually impossible to be a success in business life while retaining a Christian worldview and value system.[1] My purpose in what follows is to share with you the fruits of my struggle—a process that in some respects continues to this day—to resolve these two questions. I wish briefly to review the usual understanding of what constitutes the liberal arts and then speculate as to whether adding a business administration program represents a significant departure from that kind of education, or if it can be seen as consistent with it. Then, I will try to illustrate how business administration courses differ when taught in a Christian university or college as compared to a public one, where religious perspectives are typically ignored.

---

1. Fortunately, there has been a sea change in this perspective, particularly in North American Christian colleges and universities over the past decade or so, fostered to a significant degree by the development, in the mid-nineties, of the Christian Business Faculty Association, and shortly thereafter, in 1995, the establishment of that organization's peer-reviewed journal, *Journal of Biblical Integration in Business*, published annually.

THE LIBERAL ARTS AND BUSINESS ADMINISTRATION

The Nature of a Liberal Arts Education

In *The Idea of a Christian College* by Wheaton College philosophy professor emeritus Arthur Holmes, the author considers two ways of understanding a liberal arts education. The first is to define the liberal arts in terms of a set of academic disciplines. This is the standard dictionary definition—a broad, general education consisting of courses in the natural sciences, the social sciences, and the humanities, including religious studies, with the intention of developing students' general intellectual capacities as opposed to their professional or vocational skills.

If you were to think of a liberal arts education as being first and foremost the study of these traditional disciplines, then there is no question that the introduction of business courses such as marketing, management, finance, accounting, statistics, management information systems, and so on would not fit the mould.

However, Holmes goes on to discuss what I think is a much more useful way of looking at a liberal arts education. He defines it in terms of a type of education that is appropriate to persons as whole persons, rather than to a more narrowly trained specialist such as an accountant, a nurse, a teacher, even a scholar. Holmes speaks of liberal learning as concerned with truth and beauty and goodness, which have intrinsic worth to people considered as well-rounded persons rather than as workers whose perspective might be limited to how an education relates only to certain practical functions in the workplace. I suspect he means by that statement that an accountant, for instance, would see limited use for philosophy in preparing a financial statement, although that same accountant as a human being might come to certain philosophical conclusions about the integrity that lies behind human endeavors, including the evaluation of a business's affairs.

Holmes hastens to add that usefulness is not a crime, but the practical uses of the things we learn are limited and changeable. This is unquestionably true. Most of the jobs you will occupy once you graduate from college probably did not exist when you entered kindergarten, at least not in their present form. That is why Holmes sees the necessity of a liberal learning that takes a long-range view and concentrates on what shapes students' understanding and values rather than on what they can use in various vocational roles they might find themselves performing from time to time.[2]

The Liberal Arts' Contribution to the Making of Persons

Holmes goes on to reflect on how the liberal arts contribute to the making of persons. He notes first of all that a person trained in the liberal arts is, or should be, a reflective, thinking being.[3] Thus, we should be helped by our education to be analytical, to organize ideas into an ordered whole, to be systematic. In addition, we must examine our own worldview and that of others whose theories we evaluate.

Second, he sees a liberal arts educated person as a valuing being.[4] He maintains that in the curriculum you study you should be exposed to aesthetics and other areas involving value formation, as well as to the logical structure of value judgments.

Finally, Holmes sees a liberal arts educated person as a responsible agent, accountable ultimately to God, for life is a stewardship of what God has created, but also to other people with whom that individual has a relationship.[5]

The Current Decline of Liberal Arts Institutions

Universities were originally founded to teach students the liberal arts. Those days are "long gone" in many cases. A 1991 study in the United States estimated that only about 200 liberal arts colleges are left among America's 3,400 colleges and universities.[6] The definition of a liberal arts college in this case was one that granted at least 40 percent of its under-graduate degrees to students who had majors in traditional liberal arts fields.[7] A number of years ago I heard a speaker characterize the trend this way: "In the [19]60s students studied sociology because they wanted to change the world; in the [19]70s they enrolled in psychology in order

2. Holmes, *Idea of a Christian College*, 27–29.

3. Ibid., 29–31.

4. Ibid., 31–32.

5. Ibid., 32–33.

6. By 1998, this total had risen to 3,913, 1,644 of which were public and 2,269 private. Of the latter, 919 had some sort of religious affiliation (from Poe, *Christianity in the Academy*, 35).

7. Putnam and Stevens, "Management as a Liberal Art," B1.

to change themselves; and in the [19]80s students took business administration because they wanted to find a job!" In 1991, 24.2 percent of all bachelor's degrees and 23.7 percent of all master's degrees awarded in the United States were in business.[8] The Canadian post-secondary educational scene has exhibited a similar dominance of business graduates over all other categories. A report from Statistics Canada dated 7 February 2008 noted that for the fourth year in a row, the business, management, and public administration field, in 2005, ranked above all others, with the field accounting for 21 percent of all qualifications granted (including both undergraduate and graduate studies degrees). (The social and behavioral sciences ranked a close second, with 20 percent of all degrees awarded.)[9] In the light of Holmes' perspective on the best kind of education, have we been witnessing a troubling trend?

Business Studies in the Past

I cannot say that traditional business studies were always concerned with issues of ultimate truth, ethics, social problems, and stewardship, especially stewardship on God's behalf. An interview conducted more than two decades ago with a number of business faculty at the University of Michigan (ranked fifth out of 700 schools of business in the United States), for example, revealed the following:

> Prof. A: In the strategy courses we do tend to take a longer term horizon than the functional area courses, but I maintain that we are not going far enough. When we think about what a manager's job will be in the future, it is important that that person have a broader focus than we are imparting in the business school. A narrow definition of business problems is going to be very dangerous in the future. What is business? Where does it fit into society? We might be broad in the policy area, but we are not broad enough.

> Prof. B: I guess there's some question as to whether that topic fits in the policy area, or in the philosophy department.

8. The American Assembly of Collegiate Schools of Business, "Number of Undergraduate Business Degrees Awarded Continues to Plummet." Interestingly, however, by 1995/96 the number of U.S. undergraduate business degrees as a percentage of all undergraduate degrees had declined to 19.4%, and MBA degrees as a percentage of all master's degrees was down to 23.1%.

9. Statistics Canada, "University Degrees, Diplomas and Certificates Awarded."

Prof. C: Are we as a business school faculty qualified to teach those kinds of issues? The role of the corporation in society? The corporation as a social organization?

Prof. A (a little later): In teaching MBAs in their fourth term here we did one or two cases in social responsibility, and it didn't seem to me that students had been thinking about these sorts of issues prior to that time. I found that they were very passive. . . .

Prof. D: I have tried to raise certain social responsibility issues in courses that I teach. It is not my intention to teach ethics, but just to have students start thinking about the broader role of management in our society. I think many students are leaving the school without giving any thought to the social responsibilities that they will have.

Prof. D again: A lot of people teaching in business schools around the country think that what we are talking about here has no place in the curriculum.

Prof. B: Probably a lot of our faculty feel that way.[10]

The professors interviewed went on to say that employment recruiters did not show any interest in whether the graduating students had been exposed to broader philosophical questions of ethics and social responsibility.

There is no question that the business administration curriculum, until very recently at least, lacked what we could consider a grounding in the liberal arts. Business professors did not include a significant liberal arts component in their own career preparation, their teaching, or their research.

More Recent Business Developments in the 1980s and Beyond

The decade of the 1980s is not one on which the business world can look back with pride. A 1983 Gallup Poll done for the *Wall Street Journal* reported that 49 percent of those surveyed thought that business ethical standards had declined in the preceding ten years. Only 9 percent thought they had risen. Matters got worse as the decade went by—and, indeed, into the last decade of the century, as the infamous Enron debacle illustrated.

It would appear that the ethical and social challenges confronting the business world in the early years of this new millennium are likely to

10. "What's the Mission?" 10–11.

force business executives, professors, and students to focus as they have not done in the past on ethics, values, indeed on the very mission of economic activity. Consider this prediction by ethicist John Langan, a Jesuit priest:

> In societies as different as the United States and Poland, the United Kingdom and Mexico, greater reliance is steadily being put on the private sector to meet a wider variety of personal and social needs. This ensures that even more of the vexing problems of contemporary societies will come to be ethical problems for business. But business itself is constantly being subjected to new strains and new pressures for change as markets and production processes become global, as technology makes vast quantities of information more readily available, and as demands for rapid decisions are intensified.[11]

The response of schools of business to the public outcry for a broader mandate for business institutions in society has been twofold: one, to broaden the traditional business subject areas to include more liberal arts courses and emphases, and two, to begin to incorporate ethics into its programs.[12]

In 1991, the American Assembly of Collegiate Schools of Business, the accrediting body for North American business schools, altered its

11. Langan, "The Ethics of Business," 81–82.

12. Some commentators are very dubious about a secular academic institution's ability to legitimately teach ethics because of their relativistic ethical presuppositions. Charles Colson, guest speaker in a Harvard Business School course, asserted, "Harvard could never teach business ethics because the school did not believe in absolute values— the best it would do would be to teach pragmatic business judgments" (quoted in Beckett, *Loving Monday*, 62). I suggest that the illusive nature of secular attempts to define a foundation for morality is perhaps reflected in an opus like the 1995 textbook by Trevino and Nelson, *Managing Business Ethics: Straight Talk about How To Do It Right*, for their definition of ethics in business is "behavior that is consistent with the principles, norms and standards of business practices that have been agreed on by society," as influenced, they go on to say, by the character of the individual and the characteristics of the organization (14). Earlier in their book, they opine that "most people aren't guided by a strict and consistent internal compass. Rather, they look outside themselves for cues about how to behave, particularly when the circumstances are ambiguous or unclear as they are in many ethical situations. At work, the organizational culture transmits many of these cues" (9). Sounds a lot like situational ethics to me—which are as difficult to ascertain and define as attempting to nail a piece of jello to the wall! Indeed, Dalla Costa goes so far as to assert that "[t]here are no neutral decisions or actions in business. Every outcome expresses a set of values and presumes (or neglects) some ethical commitment" (*Magnificence at Work*, 15).

accrediting standards to require that new topics such as ethics, global business, and the impact of demographic diversity on the workplace become mandatory. The new rules also stress a desire for creativity and innovation.[13]

Business schools now routinely refer to the liberal arts as a necessary part of a business major's preparation for a career. The University of Denver, for instance, in listing the objectives for its undergraduate business core curriculum, includes this statement:

> Build a foundation for life-long learning: clear thinking and communication, problem solving, research and team skills, analytical prowess, computer competence, and the ability to enrich both personal and business life through relating to and appreciating the liberal arts.[14]

Such a perspective is strongly seconded in the previously-cited article by Putnam and Stevens. The authors begin by noting that at the same time as traditional liberal arts institutions are expanding their professional programs, the corporate world is increasingly placing a high value on skills one learns in liberal arts courses such as the ability to write effectively, to ask probing questions, and to devise structured solutions to complex problems. The writers urge educators to focus on how to integrate liberal arts courses more effectively into management programs.[15]

It would appear that this new attention to the liberal arts has expanded even to that hallowed ground, the funny pages of the daily newspaper. In my favourite comic strip, *Calvin and Hobbes*, Calvin stands moodily beside his faithful pet while waiting for his arch enemy, the school bus. He remarks, "I hate going to school. I wish *I* was a tiger. Tigers don't need to know anything." Somewhat miffed at this opinion, Hobbes replies, "Hey! Attacking running animals involves a lot of physics. There's velocity, gravity and laws of motion, not to mention all the biology we have to know. Then there's the artistic expression of it all, and a lot more!" "Gosh," says a chastened Calvin, "I never realized killing was so grounded in the liberal arts." "Yes," replies Hobbes, "my dissertation on ethics was *very* well received."

---

13. Fuchsberg, "Under Pressure," B1, B14.

14. "A New Undergraduate Business Core Curriculum at the University of Denver" (rough draft), September 1992.

15. Putnam and Stevens, "Management as a Liberal Art," B2.

By 1988, only 11 percent of American MBA programs did not have an ethics course in the curriculum. Such initiatives are very much in accord with Holmes' perspective on liberal arts as career preparation. He refers to the necessity of developing the appropriate attitude toward work itself, the need to acquire cognitive and communication skills, the importance of stimulating one's ability to think in fresh, creative ways, and the necessity of value development.[16] Most business schools concur, either incorporating these emphases into their own courses or utilizing available liberal arts courses to meet these needs in business majors' programs.

THE VALUE OF BUSINESS PROGRAMS IN A CHRISTIAN CONTEXT

It is legitimate to conclude, therefore, that a business administration major is an appropriate offering in a Christian college or university. Dunn makes this comment:

> The [Christian] college serves as an instrument to help adults prepare to bring about societies characterized by righteousness and social justice. . . . The business department is created in the Christian college to prepare individuals to move into positions of influence in business. Business leaders have an important role to play as they help shape the economic future of the country, as they provide working environments for their employees, and as they become social leaders in their communities. As these business leaders influence their companies, their communities, and their industries for good, they are helping the Christian college meet its ultimate goals.[17]

Departures from the Ideal: No Difference Observable

How should a business administration program at a Christian postsecondary institution differ from one offered at a public institution? I once heard of a student recruiter from a Christian liberal arts college (that shall obviously be nameless) who, when asked that question by a high school student, replied, "There is no difference." I shudder to think that this could be so, but apparently just such a situation exists more often than we would like to think.

16. Holmes, *Idea of a Christian College*, 38–41.
17. Dunn, "The Strategic Importance," 113–14.

Regrettably, there is evidence. Lyon and Beaty, in a 1999 *Christian Scholar's Review* article reporting on a comparative study of attitudes to integration of the Christian faith with academic subject material at three professedly Christian institutions (Baylor University, the University of Notre Dame, and Georgetown College) discovered, in the case of Baylor, that the majority of faculty felt that their distinctive task was to offer a good university education "in a caring environment," but that the university should not be considering Christian perspectives more than others.[18] More specifically, when asked to respond to the statement, "If I wished to do so, I could create a syllabus for a course I currently teach that includes a clear, academically-legitimate Christian perspective on the subject," 56 percent of Baylor's responding faculty disagreed—with approximately three out of ten disagreeing strongly. Some added comments suggesting that attempting to do so within the class context would be absurd—and would ruin the academic credibility of the course.[19] They were open to discussions of "faith" questions outside of class, especially if such discussions were initiated by individual students. Early in their article, Lyon and Beaty declare that the above situation is, unfortunately, the rule rather than the exception: "While hundreds of Protestant and Catholic colleges [in the USA, the focus of their interest] remain [as ostensibly "Christian" institutions], only a few in practice attempt to relate their religious identity to their academic practices."[20]

I legitimately possess a letter written by a fourth year business student to the chair of the Business Department of a well-known U.S. Christian liberal arts college. I quote from its contents to illustrate the scenario I strongly believe we must attempt to avoid:

> I am writing to you as Chairman of the Business Department to express a great concern of mine. While speaking with several other students, we realized that something was missing from the classes we had taken . . . a strong integration of Christian and business principles. In my time here, I can remember only two occasions when we discussed Christian principles in business during class time. I remember these because of their rarity. . . . As I speak with students of other disciplines, I find they are not in the same situa-

18. Lyon and Beaty, "Integration, Secularization, and the Two-Spheres View at Religious Colleges," 76.

19. Ibid., 81.

20. Ibid., 75.

tion. The Science department consistently presents God in nature. There is a great deal of social awareness and involvement in the English department. And Sociology and Social Work eagerly present Christian principles and duties. . . . As I tell others my major, I am surprised to find that I am held in lower esteem because of it. One student even said, "I avoid business students like the plague." The reason, they say, is that business students are unaware of or unconcerned about God's work. Business students have a reputation for being very self-seeking. I do not believe this is entirely true, but I also do not think we are adequately training students to make responsible decisions in light of Christian principles.

Business Programs with a Difference: Three Examples

Fortunately the above situation is not representative of a number of Christian liberal arts colleges in North America. Let me give you a few brief illustrations from three fine Christian institutions (all, as it happens, in the USA):

1. Goshen College, a Mennonite liberal arts college in the American Midwest. Guiding business education there is the College's mission statement, which views education as "a moral activity that produces servant leaders for the church and the world." The crux of business education as a moral activity is its reflection on business practices and structures from social, theological, and ethical perspectives.

2. Dordt College, a Christian Reformed institution, also in the Midwest, asserts: "We want you to understand that Christianity is more than just a 'religion' in the narrow sense of the word. Rather, it is a comprehensive view of the world which seeks to understand all areas of life in light of the truth of God's word, the Holy Scriptures. This world-and-life view is radically different from other pictures of reality, and hence gives us a very different interpretation of what we see around us, including our economic system, our business structures, goals, practices, etc."

3. Seattle Pacific University: "[The School of Business's third goal is] to provide an educational environment for the achievement of academic competence, professional excellence, and ethical decision making that is intellectually honest and biblically based."

A CASE IN POINT: BANKRUPTCY FROM A CHRISTIAN PERSPECTIVE

I wish to illustrate in a practical way how a Christian perspective can be brought to bear on a business issue. In the early 1980s, bankruptcies began to rise very rapidly as a severe recession gripped the North American economy. With the economic recovery of the middle and later part of the '80s, bankruptcies declined slightly, but then began to rise again and continue to set records as each year went by. A few years ago, we witnessed three venerable Canadian retailers—Woodwards, western Canada's major department store chain; Eaton's, a nation-wide department store conglomerate; and Birks, one of Canada's oldest and largest jewelers—take desperate steps to avoid business failure. The International Credit Association in the United States estimated in 1990 that 24 million Americans were in financial trouble and that 3 million were on the verge of filing for bankruptcy.

The effects of bankruptcies on employees, lenders, and the families of bankrupt individuals can be devastating emotionally, financially, and spiritually. Many Christians, having gone through this same difficult experience, have encountered the additional problem of finding themselves ostracized by their churches and abandoned by their Christian friends because it was felt that declaring bankruptcy is a sin.

In 1983, I was approached by Trinity Western's academic dean about writing an article from a biblical perspective on the subject of bankruptcy. That article eventually grew into a book entitled *Going Broke: Bankruptcy, Business Ethics and the Bible*. To the best of my knowledge, it is the only book in existence that analyzes the legal, financial, emotional, and moral aspects of bankruptcy and business failure from a Christian viewpoint.

Writing the book was not easy. As is the case with most business problems, the Bible has nothing to say about bankruptcy. In fact, many professing Christians involved in business life have concluded that the Scriptures have no relevance whatsoever to their economic activities. For example, the chairman of the board of one of America's largest dry goods corporations, known for having read the Bible through at least 70 times, was interviewed by a biographical story writer for a major evangelical publication. He exclaimed, "I never mix the Bible with business. Good business is good business. There's no Christian way of doing business."[21]

21. Cited in Krutza, "The Nearsighted Ethics of Christian Businessmen," 15.

One of Canada's most famous Christian businessmen was asked if his corporation was an expression of his kind of Christian witness. He replied, "Not at all. . . . I never let . . . religion affect my business knowingly."[22]

The authors of an excellent casebook on business ethics have analyzed this rather surprising point of view very well, as follows:

> A popular type of Christianity holds that faith in Jesus Christ is primarily a private affair. One belongs to a church and prays with a community of believers, perhaps even participates in church social events and gives money in the collection for the poor. The Gospel message is taken to be a call for a change of heart, for a new trust and love, yet for many this conversion plays itself out solely in churchly activities and family life.
>
> Although the major portion of each week for many Christians is spent in the business world, this world may be insulated from the values of the Gospel.
>
> It is often taken for granted that Christian faith is not really meant to change the world, and certainly not the business world. This may result from a sober judgment that, after all, business is business, and its rules and ethos must hold sway . . . if an enterprise is to survive. The business world is a highly complex phenomenon, and some very competent people suggest that it is not at all clear that the simple stories of the Bible are relevant to twentieth century economic life.[23]

Fortunately, there are refreshing exceptions[24] to such dualistic perspectives on the part of professing Christian entrepreneurs. John Beckett, CEO of the R. W. Beckett Corporation in Ohio, the world's largest producer of oil burners for residential heating (by the mid-1990s employing over 500 people and generating approximately $100 million in annual sales), says that the Bible serves as a kind of "corporate compass" for his business activities, adding, "The more I spend time with it, the more I am instructed, challenged, and encouraged by timeless truths that reach into

22. "Jimmy Pattison," 31.

23. Williams and Houck, *Full Value*, 3–4. Dalla Costa illuminates this point more than twenty-five years later: "All too often, business people today experience the opposite of integration, having to self-divide moral judgment from managerial expertise to serve the overriding expediencies of efficiency" (*Magnificence at Work*, 12).

24. Lester and Padelford mention two other American corporations: Service Master and Polaroid, whose company leaders also attempted to operate their businesses on Christian principles ("Christian Worldview and the World of Business," 342.)

every area of my life—including day-to-day aspects of my work."[25] For example, he sees his employees as people made in God's image. He therefore attempts to exhibit a "profound respect for the individual," doing all he can to ensure that they will see their work as "dignified, challenging, rewarding, and enjoyable."[26] Beckett sees "compassion plus accountability in balance" as a key principle of doing business successfully.[27] Supervisors are intentionally trained to serve their employees, "facilitating, not demanding; teaching, not criticizing." He adds, "We keep a very flat organizational structure with a total of four levels to encourage lateral transactions and discourage hierarchy."[28]

Biblical principles also serve as the foundation for his firm's dealings with its customers. Its corporate mission, clearly embodying an unequivocal embracing of biblically-based servant leadership principles, is expressed as follows: "We commit to being very attentive to our customers, going beyond servicing them to satisfying their highest expectations. We pledge to be responsive, following through on commitments while avoiding any kind of arrogance or indifference. We desire to be predictable, reliable and trustworthy, willing to go the extra mile for something we believe in."[29] The Corporation's vision statement makes its biblical foundation explicit: "Our Vision is to build a family of exceptional companies, each of which serves its customers in distinctive and important ways—and each of which reflects the practical application of biblical values throughout."[30]

In examining a modern business problem from a Christian perspective, I first had to decide whether the Christian Scriptures were relevant. As a Christian, I thought I had no choice but to believe that my faith applied to all areas of life; still, I had to decide in what fashion the Bible can be used to address economic issues.

I concluded that the Bible functions in three ways as I critique business life Christianly. First of all, it gives us a worldview or a life perspec-

---

25. Beckett, *Loving Monday*, 79–80.

26. Ibid., 89.

27. Ibid., 110.

28. Ibid., 119.

29. Ibid., 117–18.

30. Ibid., 146.

tive. In a classic article in *Harvard Business Review,* Johnson makes this point very well:

> The application of religion's ultimate insights to specific situations is . . . a tremendously difficult task. There are no blueprints, no simple rules to go by. Christianity does not present the executive with a tool kit of easy-to-use rules and precepts by which problems can be solved. The doctrines are not bound up in a simple list of "do's" and "don'ts" somewhat in the style of a book of etiquette, which if followed will result in harmonious, gentlemanly relations within and without a business. But it does offer a *frame of reference*, a universe view, which instead of giving peace of mind and easy success in human relations often breaches the barricade of self-assurance, focuses on difficulties, and erases naive hopes of business progress ever onward, ever upward.[31]

The Bible teaches us to view society as God does, from a bird's eye perspective, as it were, above and outside our culture. It forces us, if we let it, to break through our cultural conditioning. For example, the fact that our North American culture highly prizes *individualism* affects many aspects of our society, including how we view our role in a business organization. We have had to learn the important management strategy of *teambuilding* from the Japanese. We could have learned it from the Scriptures. The Bible places high stress on community, on using one's gifts to the benefit of others, on building one another up, and on putting aside one's own interests for the sake of our colleagues. North American Christians have, by and large, reserved this biblical perspective for the local church. The Japanese, whose culture highly values teamwork and organizational loyalty, have applied these scriptural notions to business life with great success. How pathetic that a non-Christian nation had to model biblical emphases (without realizing that is what they were doing, of course) to people with a Judeo-Christian tradition.

Second, the Bible teaches us values, including those that can be applied to business life. Values represent our ideals concerning how things ought to be (i.e., ends or goals), and how things ought to be done (i.e., means). You will find that biblical values may stand at times in stark contrast with private enterprise values. For instance, in our capitalistic economy wealth and property are valued as a measure of a person's worth. From a Christian worldview, wealth and property are seen, on the

---

31. Quoted in Sutherland, *Going Broke,* 98.

one hand, as an opportunity for increased service for humankind, and on the other hand as a possible obstacle to salvation ("It is easier for a camel to go through the eye of a needle than for a rich person to enter the kingdom of heaven" [Luke 18:25]).[32] In private enterprise, one might see the value of justice as the protection of property one already possesses. For the Christian, justice is regarded as the right of every person to the means of leading a meaningful human life.

Third, the Bible provides us with general ethical principles that guide our thinking in fundamental ways, helping us to devise our own value system. These principles include such things as the solidarity of the family unit or the purpose of economic life.

Having concluded that the Bible was relevant to evaluate this ethical dilemma of bankruptcy, I next looked for specific scriptural material that might be of use. As I said, there is nothing explicitly on bankruptcy, just as there are no specific data on pricing, labor unions, or stock markets, but I did find some help.

I concluded that in order to deal with a specific economic issue, I should try to see if the Bible could at least give the problem an economic context. While the biblical writers never directly addressed my particular concern, they were inspired to provide us with certain fundamental principles describing what economic life should be like and what its goals should be.[33] If I could determine those things, then I could perhaps decide where the bankruptcy issue consistently fit in. Thus I spent a great deal of time uncovering the timeless economic principles which lie behind biblical teaching on private property, the key economic resource in biblical days.

Our modern capitalistic notion of private holdings such as land, capital, and other resources that individuals privately own is based on

32. Bandow comments on this two-sidedness of capitalism as follows: "By generating abundant wealth and spawning transformational technologies, capitalism has created new avenues for sin.... Although capitalism promotes virtues in some ways—rewarding thrift and hard work, for instance, it also multiplies temptations" ("The Conundrum of Capitalism and Christianity," 309). Succumbing to those temptations—such as the "unseemly desire for wealth and material pleasure and a distressing lack of concern for the good and virtuous life," adds Bandow later in his article, "reflect[s] human, not economic failings" ("The Conundrum of Capitalism and Christianity," 326).

33. Again, Bandow makes a helpful comment: "There is no explicit endorsement of any type of economic system in the Bible, no equation of capitalism or socialism with the Kingdom of God. Old Testament Israel placed some restrictions on debts, interest, and property transfers, but it allowed for relatively free economic exchange and obvious wealth inequality" ("The Conundrum of Capitalism and Christianity," 310–11).

the ancient Roman idea that private property is available to *use*, or even *abuse*, as the owner sees fit. This notion of private property, including the right to use it any way we choose, is so important to us as Canadians that we have been clamoring for years that this principle be enshrined in our constitution.

But the biblical view of private assets, I learned, is much different. God retains ultimate ownership, considering us to be stewards of his property. Self-indulgent or self-interested use of private property is ruled out. Rather, we are to use private holdings to further the interests of justice. The primary purpose of economic life is not to maximize profits for the shareholders but to do justice.

Is the pursuit of profit illegitimate? Not at all. Nowhere is the accumulation of wealth denounced in Scripture. Material resources are even at times an indication of God's favor. But are profits an end in themselves, as the typical free enterprise position holds? Absolutely not. Material resources are means to further godly ends; they are not ends in themselves. How does one use these resources? To do justice.

What does justice mean? I studied a good deal of philosophical material as I wrote my book in order to examine the various ways in which business decisions can be made. Distributive justice, as it is called, is certainly one such way. But I found that the usual philosophical definition of justice was not exactly the same as the biblical understanding of the term. This latter view of justice has to do with what is fair for all parties affected by a decision. The category of justice called distributive justice refers to the fair distribution of society's benefits and burdens. Equal pay for work of equal value is a question of justice, as is the wage rates paid to men versus women. In capitalistic economies, the prevailing view is that society's benefits should be distributed primarily on the basis of a person's contribution to society's well-being. This contribution would be measured in terms of such things as effort and productivity. Socialists are more inclined to see benefits going in the direction of need.

While space does not permit an exploration of the biblical material, I can tell you briefly that justice is seen first and foremost as an *activity*.[34] One did not *get* justice, one *did* justice. The form it took was to care particularly for the needs of the vulnerable and the disadvantaged, or as one

---

34. I discussed this principle more fully in "Justice: The Key to Business Ethics and Goals," 11–21.

commentator[35] put it, to defend the cause of people on the margins of society. Justice in biblical terms involves fairness plus mercy.

Such a view of the way business should be done has significance for a host of business issues,[36] including such matters as:

1. The firm's responsibility toward customers, competitors, and the community
2. Just compensation and treatment of employees
3. Affirmative action
4. Elimination of discrimination connected to race, sex, disabilities, and age
5. Responsibility toward the environment[37]

---

35. Dr. Elmer Martens of Fresno Pacific University, from notes I took in a course of his offered at Regent College, Vancouver, in the early 1980s.

36. A phenomenon that has come to be known as the Spirit at Work movement, birthed in the USA in the 1980s but also making an appearance, albeit quite independent of its American predecessor, towards the end of that decade, first in the United Kingdom and later in other parts of Europe as well as Canada, Australia, and New Zealand, was founded on similar concerns to these—as important complements to a traditional preoccupation with the financial bottom line (Howard and Welbourn, *The Spirit at Work Phenomenon*, 184). Unifying the numerous manifestations of this movement is a belief in a spiritual reality of some kind—not necessarily God—that must be considered in order for a business to be successful (*The Spirit at Work Phenomenon*, 41). Michel Joseph, an important American apologist for this phenomenon, listed, in a 2000 *Faith in Business Quarterly* article, "Spirituality in the Workplace: What are We Talking About?" the following four dimensions of this new understanding of "spirituality": (1) some connection with a higher power (possibly God, but not necessarily God); (2) connection with other people (including people across the dividing lines of rank at work as well as customers and, indeed, the larger community); (3) a new awareness of self; and (4) awareness of our connection with nature and the environment (discussed in Howard and Welbourn, *The Spirit at Work Phenomenon*, 45). This movement has attracted a wide range of advocates, from people with no religious faith whatsoever to those who hold to a biblically-based personal faith in God and the necessity for personal salvation (Howard and Welbourn, *The Spirit at Work Phenomenon*, 42). Catalysts to the growth of the Spirit at Work movement have been such factors as rapid growth in technological innovation, the negative consequences of globalization, concern for environmental degradation by industry, and, last but by no means least, the scandalous evidence of corruption at the highest levels of corporate management. While it is regrettable that the meaning of "Spirit" often has nothing to do with the Holy Spirit in many instances, it is interesting that such admirable Christian entities as the Ridley Hall Foundation in Cambridge England, founded in 1989, whose Director, Richard Higginson, co-edits the movement's journal, *Faith in Business Quarterly*, identifies with the movement's basic concerns (Howard and Welbourn, *The Spirit at Work Phenomenon*, 195).

37. Kise and Stark suggest a very appropriate and balanced way of expressing a firm's profit-making objective that also reflects these laudable ancillary concerns: "The direc-

With respect to the issue of bankruptcy, I had one last area of biblical teaching to draw upon, that being the material on debts and the forgiveness of loans. This was of immeasurable help in coming to conclusions about the just treatment of bankrupt individuals.

Turning our attention to a new topic as a final illustration of the application of biblical principles to the world of business, in 1999 I edited a book on labor relations entitled *Us and Them: Building a Just Workplace Community*. We contributors to the volume considered questions of justice and reconciliation in finding a Christian approach to healing the labor–management rift,[38] so wide-spread in North America, that stands in the way of greater economic competitiveness. My particular interest was in the issue of strikes and alternative dispute resolution strategies. My goal was to find ways to protect the legitimate concerns of individual workers in dealing with their employers, while at the same time respecting the rights of innocent third parties who are often harmed by strikes. General biblical principles and values, especially those involving justice and reconciliation, had a significant impact upon my research.

SOME ADVANTAGES OF STUDYING BUSINESS IN A CHRISTIAN CONTEXT

My purpose in all this is to illustrate three things. First, in a Christian college or university, a business faculty can intentionally explore issues in ways that are uniquely biblical. At public universities, such ways of dealing with topics are considered to be inappropriate. For instance, a business ethics professor at Simon Fraser University in Burnaby, BC, wrote what is in many ways quite a good article entitled "Should Universities Teach Business Ethics?" The author concludes that a language of applied ethics,

---

tors and officers of [the] corporation shall exercise their powers and discharge their duties with a view to the interests of the corporation and of the shareholders, *but not at the expense of the environment, human rights, the public safety, the communities in which the corporation operates, or the dignity of its employees*" (*Working with Purpose*, 74; emphasis mine).

38. Dalla Costa gives one very practical suggestion as to how managers can not only significantly reduce management–labor tension but also contribute to the effectiveness of their whole business enterprise: "workers whose wisdom is respected and used tend to feel much more loyalty to their company and deeper ethical commitment to customers, shareholders and other stakeholders" (*Magnificence at Work*, 59).

one providing a logical and *secular* mode of making sense of the moral minefield hidden beneath conventional wisdom, is an imperative.[39]

Second, good business research and teaching in a Christian institution can draw upon the wealth of knowledge and skills that all of the liberal arts, including biblical studies and theology, provide. Samuel Dunn is absolutely correct when he says, "With respect to knowledge, the business disciplines may be viewed as applied liberal arts, as they are direct applications of psychology, sociology, economics, philosophy, mathematics, and religion."[40] Most public universities would place limitations upon my academic freedom by denying me the use of my religious perspective in the courses I was assigned to teach.

I anticipate what some of you might be thinking: "Why don't we hear more of this kind of teaching at church?" I wish we did. But Christian businesspeople have not often found the church to be of much help in dealing with ethical issues that are peculiar to economic life. For example, in one study several hundred executives were asked whom they usually consult on ethical matters related to their work. They listed clergy last, behind even "No one; I work it out myself."[41]

The results of this study were not a surprise to me. As part of my research for the book on labor relations mentioned above, I wrote to every Christian denomination in Canada, asking them for denominational statements, historic church positions, rules of thumb, or anything else they might provide to indicate their views on labor-related topics. Fewer than twenty bothered to answer, all but five to say that they had nothing, but felt that something was desperately needed. Here are a few representative replies.

1. The Associated Gospel Churches: "I agree that the [labor] movement does function with little critique from the church and from Christian leaders. . . . [W]ithin our Association I do not know of any documents that would be of value to you."

2. The Quakers: "Canadian Yearly Meeting has made no statements on labor-related matters."

---

39. Wexler, "Should Universities Teach Business Ethics?" 13–15.
40. Dunn, "The Strategic Importance," 116.
41. Maltby, "The One-minute Ethicist," 26–29.

3. Evangelical Lutheran Church in Canada: "Congratulations on your project to edit a book on labor relations in biblical perspective. Neither our church, nor its predecessor bodies, have done much work in this area."

4. Evangelical Free Church: "I affirm the work you are doing on the proposed book on labor relations in biblical perspective. The evangelical church has so specialized in 'religious' things that it has abdicated its responsibility in terms of the practical. It is only as we bring the relevance of Scripture to the broad cross section of life and address mankind in an integrated, holistic manner that we will gain a hearing for the Gospel."

5. The Canadian Council of Churches: "This is a most timely study, and we would be eager to learn of your findings."

This brings me to my third point about the way in which we as a business faculty can do our task differently in a Christian institution. For the kingdom of God to extend into the economic realm, Christian businesspeople must take a leadership role. It will be primarily the businesspeople, not the clergy, who will bring the redemptive Word of God to bear upon business matters. As Dunn puts it so well:

> It is critical that business leaders in our society be well grounded in theology, philosophy, ethics, history, and political science. It is also critical that they understand how decision-making in business management is replete with opportunities to apply Christian moral and ethical principles. In a world characterized by rapid change, by information technologies, and by ethical diffusion, and where the physical environment is so easily and so often degraded, there is a critical need for business leaders with a high vision of humankind and of God's physical creation. The business department in the Christian college can help prepare the kinds of leaders needed.[42]

CONCLUSION

In conclusion, I pass on to you an important biblical truth I continually strive to follow in my own life and in all my business teaching: "Trust in the Lord with all your heart, and do not rely on your own understand-

---

42. Dunn, "The Strategic Importance," 114.

ing. In all your ways acknowledge Him, and He will direct your paths"
(Proverbs 3:5–6).

WORKS CITED

The American Assembly of Collegiate Schools of Business, "Number of Undergraduate
  Business Degrees Awarded Continues to Plummet: MBA and Some Business
  Doctoral Degrees on the Increase." *Newsline* (Fall 1998). No pages. Accessed at www
  .aacsb.edu/publications/printnewsline/NL1998/fandegrees_1.asp.

Bandow, Doug. "The Conundrum of Capitalism and Christianity." In *Wealth, Poverty,
  and Human Destiny*, edited by Doug Bandow and David L. Schindler, 307–45.
  Wilmington, DE: ISI Books, 2003.

Beckett, John D. *Loving Monday: Succeeding in Business without Selling Your Soul*. Downers
  Grove, IL: InterVarsity Press, 1998.

Dalla Costa, John. *Magnificence at Work: Living Faith in Business*. Toronto: Novalis, 2005.

Dunn, S. L. "The Strategic Importance of the Christian College Business Department."
  Faculty Dialogue 13 (Winter 1990) 105–18.

Fuchsberg, G. "Under Pressure, Business Schools Devise Changes." *Wall Street Journal* (23
  April 1991) B1, B14.

Holmes, Arthur F. *The Idea of a Christian College*. Rev. ed. Grand Rapids, MI: Eerdmans,
  1987.

Howard, Sue, and David Welbourn. *The Spirit at Work Phenomenon*. London: Azure,
  2004.

"Jimmy Pattison: The Man Behind Expo '86." *Faith Today* 4.4 (September/October 1986)
  31.

Joseph, Michael. "Spirituality in the Workplace: What Are We Talking About?" *Faith in
  Business Quarterly* 4.3 (2000) 3–5.

Kise, Jane, and David Stark. *Working with Purpose: Finding a Corporate Calling for You and
  Your Business*. Minneapolis: Augsburg, 2004.

Krutza, W. J. "The Nearsighted Ethics of Christian Businessmen." *Eternity* 27.9 (September
  1976) 15–17, 40.

Langan, J. "The Ethics of Business." *Theological Studies* 51.1 (March 1990) 81 100.

Lester, Donald L., with Walton Padelford. "Christian Worldview and the World of Business."
  In *Shaping a Christian Worldview*, edited by David S. Dockery and Gregory D.
  Thornbury, 335–45. Nashville: Broadman & Holman, 2002.

Lyon, Larry, and Michael Beaty. "Integration, Secularization, and the Two-Spheres View at
  Religious Colleges: Comparing Baylor University with the University of Notre Dame
  and Georgetown College." *Christian Scholar's Review* 19.1 (1999) 73–112.

Maltby, D. E. "The One-minute Ethicist: Can Business School Ethics Courses Really Make
  Us Better?" *Christianity Today* 32.3 (19 February 1988) 26–29.

Poe, Harry L. *Christianity in the Academy: Teaching at the Intersection of Faith and
  Learning*. Grand Rapids, MI: Baker Academic, 2004.

Putnam, B. H., and E. I. Stevens. "Management as a Liberal Art." *Chronicle of Higher
  Education* 37.45 (24 July 1991) B1–2.

Statistics Canada. "University Degrees, Diplomas and Certificates Awarded." *The Daily*
  (February 7, 2008). No pages. Accessed at www.statcan.ca/Daily/English/080207/
  d080207c.htm.

Sutherland, John R. *Going Broke: Bankruptcy, Business Ethics, and the Bible.* Waterloo, ON: Herald Press, 1991.

————. "Justice: The Key to Business Ethics and Goals." *CRUX* 31.1 (March 1995) 11–21.

————. *Us and Them: Building a Just Workplace Community.* Toronto: Work Research Foundation, 1999.

Trevino, Linda Klebe, and Katherine A. Nelson. *Managing Business Ethics: Straight Talk about How To Do It Right.* New York: John Wiley & Sons, 1995.

Wexler, M. "Should Universities Teach Business Ethics?" *Simon Fraser Alumni Journal* (Spring 1992) 13–15.

"What's the Mission?" *Dividend: The Magazine of the* [University of Michigan] *Graduate School of Business* (Winter 1982) 8–14.

Williams, Oliver F., and John W. Houck. *Full Value: Cases in Christian Business Ethics.* San Francisco: Harper & Row, 1978.

FOR FURTHER READING

Alford, Helen J., and Michael J. Naughton. *Managing as if Faith Mattered: Christian Social Principles in the Modern Organization.* Notre Dame, IN: University of Notre Dame Press, 2001.

Bakke, Dennis W. "Joy at Work Postscript: 'Enter into the Master's Joy.'" *Journal of Biblical Integration in Business* (Fall 2006) 10–41.

Brook, Stacey. "A New Testament Perspective on Wage Determination Using the Principle of Spiritual Rewards." *Journal of Biblical Integration in Business* (Fall 2005) 6–12.

Catherwood, Fred. *The Creation of Wealth: Recovering a Christian Understanding of Money, Work, and Ethics.* Wheaton, IL: Crossway, 2002.

Chewning, Richard C. "Relativistic Synthesis: Thwarting the Mind of Christ." *Journal of Biblical Integration in Business* (Fall 1997) 22–42.

Chewning, Richard C., John W. Eby, and Shirley J. Roels. *Business through the Eyes of Faith.* San Francisco: Harper & Row, 1990.

Clouse, Robert G., and William E. Diehl, eds. *Wealth and Poverty: Four Christian Views of Economics.* Downers Grove, IL: InterVarsity Press, 1984.

Goossen, Richard J., ed. *The Christian Entrepreneur: Insights from the Marketplace*, I. Langley, BC: Trinity Western University, 2005.

Hardy, Lee. *The Fabric of This World.* Grand Rapids, MI: Eerdmans, 1990.

Kreuger, David A., with Donald W. Shriver, Jr., and Laura L. Nash. *The Business Corporation and Productive Justice.* Nashville: Abingdon, 1997.

Martinez, Richard J. "Defining and Developing a Space for Business Scholarship at the Christian Academy." *Christian Scholar's Review* 34.1 (2004) 55–73.

————. "Editorial: What's Wrong with the Christian Business Faculty Association?" *Journal of Biblical Integration in Business* (Fall 2006) 1–9.

Mitroff, Ian I., and Elizabeth A. Denton. *A Spiritual Audit of Corporate America.* San Francisco: Jossey-Bass, 2001.

Moreau, Gary L. *The Ultimate MBA: Meaningful Business Analogies for Business.* Minneapolis: Augsburg, 2004.

Nash, Laura. "The Evangelical CEO." *Across the Board* 31.2 (February 1994) 26–33.

Nash, Laura, and Scott McLennan. *Church on Sunday, Work on Monday: The Challenge of Fusing Christian Values with Business Life.* San Francisco: Jossey-Bass, 2001.

Naylor, Thomas H., William H. Willimon, and Rolf Osterberg. *The Search for Meaning in the Workplace*. Nashville: Abingdon, 1996.

Novak, Michael. *Business as a Calling: Work and the Examined Life*. New York: Free Press, 1996.

Pollard, C. William. *The Soul of the Firm*. New York: Harper Business and Grand Rapids, MI: Zondervan, 1996.

Rae, Scott B., and Kenman L. Wong. *Beyond Integrity: A Judeo-Christian Approach to Business Ethics*. Grand Rapids, MI: Zondervan, 1996.

Spohn, William C. *What Are They Saying about Scripture and Ethics?* New York: Paulist, 1984.

Stackhouse, Max L., and Lawrence M. Stratton. *Capitalism, Civil Society, Religion, and the Poor*. Wilmington, DE: Intercollegiate Studies Institute Books, 2002.

Tucker, Graham. *The Faith-Work Connection*. Toronto: The Anglican Book Centre, 1987.

Vander Veen, Steve. "Let's Quit *Thinking* about Integration for a Change." *Journal of Biblical Integration in Business* (Fall 1997) 7–18.

Winston, E. Bruce. *Be a Manager for God's Sake: Essays about the Perfect Manager*. Virginia Beach, VA: Regent University, 1999.

8

A Christian Perspective on Chemistry

CRAIG D. MONTGOMERY

INTRODUCTION

ONE OF THE OBJECTIVES of this collection of articles is not only to present you with an introductory look at the various academic disciplines offered at a liberal arts and sciences college or university, but also to give you some thoughts on how one might approach each particular discipline as a Christian.

Such a goal might seem to be reasonable when it comes to history or psychology or English, but what about a physical science such as chemistry? Surely it makes absolutely no difference whether I am a Christian or not when it comes to studying chemistry. Doesn't mixing hydrogen gas and oxygen gas in the presence of an electrical spark result in an explosion regardless of the belief system of the person doing the mixing? Do electrons not have a charge of 1.6022 X 10-19 coulombs for atheistic and theistic scientists alike? How can there be a "Christian approach" to chemistry?

The goal of this article is to establish that there is indeed a Christian approach to chemistry, and therefore that it makes a difference whether you are studying chemistry at a Christian liberal arts college rather than at a secular institution. But before turning to that it is first necessary to consider the question of why one should study chemistry at all.

WHAT IS CHEMISTRY?

Chemistry is the study of matter, or more precisely, the structure of matter and the transformations that can be observed in matter. One of the ways that we as chemists classify ourselves is by the types of materials that we study. Chemists who study materials based on carbon are called organic chemists. Those who work with materials based on other elements are called inorganic chemists. (As an inorganic chemist myself, I like to say that the organic chemists are capable of handling only one element while we look after the remaining 102!)

Another branch of chemistry that used to be considered as part of the organic realm, because it also deals with carbon compounds, in recent years has developed into a legitimate field of its own. This is the area of biochemistry, the chemistry of life. Perhaps one of the most significant scientific discoveries of the last (or any other) century occurred in this field in the 1950s when Watson and Crick determined the structure of DNA, a biological chemical that carries the genetic code.

Other chemists are "pigeon-holed," not by the types of materials they work with, but by what it is about the materials that interests them. Those that study the *physical* properties of materials, such as conductivity, are considered *physical* chemists while those who attempt to determine the *composition* of the materials are *analytical* chemists.

To see what sorts of problems chemists are currently interested in, all one needs to do is follow the daily news. A casual perusal of Internet news or print media will inevitably turn up a variety of articles illustrating current chemical research. One topic about which we hear a great deal today is the environment. Unfortunately chemistry has been a contributor to some of the problems that face us in this realm, but it is also providing us with solutions.

In addition, we are all aware of the millions, indeed billions, of dollars being poured into medical research to find cures for cancer, AIDS, and high blood pressure, to name just a few of the high profile ones. Virtually each day one hears of a new drug to combat these and other medical conditions. Again, chemists are right at the center of these efforts as they try to synthesize new drugs in the hope that they will be effective against these diseases.

Another research area about which we are hearing a great deal these days is "nanotechnology." Indeed a quick search of the Internet yielded about 17,000,000 hits using the term "nanotechnology." While highly interdisciplinary in nature, this area clearly continues to demand contributions of chemists as "molecular machines," medical "nanorobots," "nanotubes," and other new materials are being developed.

Computing technology itself may be revolutionized in the not too distant future by work being done currently on "molecular switches" as well as materials such as "high temperature superconductors." These are but a few of the more high profile areas of research where chemists are currently involved.

WHY STUDY CHEMISTRY AT A LIBERAL ARTS COLLEGE?

In attempting to illustrate what chemistry is, the sorts of things that chemists do, and the problems that interest them, I have also laid the foundation for the first two reasons why I believe some understanding of chemistry is an important "brick" in a liberal arts education.

Notice I say *some* study of chemistry is important. I am not proposing that all of you sign up as chemistry majors (although I am certainly not opposed to such an idea). Rather, the following reasons why it is of value to study chemistry apply equally to the philosophy major, the history major, the religious studies major—indeed any subject major you might find at college or university.

The first reason is that we live in a society where science and technology play an extremely important role. I don't think any one of us would deny that this is the case. In comparing contemporary society with that of two hundred, one hundred, or even fifty years ago, the first and most striking difference would likely be a technological one. We skip to and fro across the globe via high-speed aircraft, communicate using the amazing microchip, and live to a ripe old age due to surgical and medical techniques unknown oftentimes a few months ago, let alone a lifetime ago.

Therefore, surely some understanding of science is of great value. How else is one to function in such a society, let alone act as a responsible citizen who makes wise, informed decisions on matters that are so often rooted in science?

The second reason why it is desirable to know something about chemistry is that not only do we live in a scientifically-oriented society, but chemistry specifically permeates virtually every area of our daily lives. I have already noted how a casual perusal of the newspaper will usually turn up many articles involving chemistry; these could involve new technologies, environmental problems, developments in medicine, etc. I would challenge you to mentally walk yourself through a typical day and take note of all the ways your life has been affected (perhaps both positively and negatively) by chemistry.

Look down at the pen you are using to take notes on this textbook. More than likely it is not a quill drawn from one of the many geese that inhabit our North American climes but rather some sort of construct that employs a number of different synthetic polymers. There may be a nylon jacket draped over the back of your chair as well as dyes in the clothes you are wearing that are all products of chemists' work.

You may have driven to class today in a car that illustrates in both a positive and negative sense how chemistry touches your life. Few of us would deny the fact that a car is a very convenient timesaving device. It is another example of something constructed from materials developed by modern chemistry. (Even the fuel is refined from the original crude oil by a complex chemical process.)

But in addition, the car (and the chemistry of the car) has also brought us a great deal of pollution and environmental harm. The problem of global warming is a topic of much discussion today, with many suggesting that "greenhouse gas" emissions are a significant contributor to the problem. This chemical problem is being countered in part with chemical solutions such as fuel cell technology.

Just by scratching the surface (what about the food you eat, the medicine you take, and so on?), hopefully I have impressed upon you that your life today is very different from that of your grandparents or even your parents because of modern chemistry. You are constantly rubbing shoulders with the products of chemical research.

One more reason why the study of chemistry is valuable is its ready application across the board to other liberal arts disciplines. There are skills that are developed by a study of chemistry that are of great benefit to any person, chemist or not, quite apart from the knowledge gained. Chemistry is very much an experimental science. One does not learn chemistry so much in the library (although library resources are important) as in the lab. As a result of the "hands-on" nature of the science, an ability to solve problems is crucial. These problem-solving skills are one of the many benefits of studying chemistry.

More specifically, how does a chemist go about solving problems? The chemist needs an analytical mind, one that can dissect the problem and in a logical, stepwise fashion construct a solution. This way of thinking is an invaluable benefit of studying chemistry.

WHY STUDY CHEMISTRY AT A CHRISTIAN INSTITUTION?

Having examined some of the benefits of studying chemistry, we now must return to the original and central question: Why study chemistry at a *Christian* college or university? What difference does a Christian perspective make on a hard, well-defined, physical science such as chemistry?

Arthur Holmes, in *The Idea of a Christian College*, identifies three different approaches to integrating one's faith with a particular academic discipline. They are a *foundational* approach, an *attitudinal* approach, and an *ethical* approach. To these helpful categories for discussing the nature of a Christian approach to chemistry I wish to add a fourth, the *motivational approach*.

The Foundational Approach[1]

As Christians, we have a different starting point for the scientific task. Holmes points out that one must examine the basic presuppositions or assumptions of any academic discipline, looking for points of contact with one's Christian faith. Interestingly, as one examines the presuppositions of chemistry (or indeed any of the physical sciences), one finds that both Christians and non-Christians share at least three basic assumptions:

1. *The universe is orderly.* By order we mean structure as opposed to chaos. This is the basic starting point of *all* science. Unless there is order in the universe there is no way of doing science, for science is the discovery and defining of that order.

2. *The universe is consistent.* This assumption goes hand in hand with the first assumption. What is meant here is that, all factors being equal, systems behave in the same manner each time. For example, in the introduction I mentioned the violent reaction of hydrogen and oxygen. If on two occasions hydrogen is reacted with oxygen and all the conditions are kept constant (same temperature, same amounts of each gas, same concentration, same spark to catalyze the reaction, etc.), then the same reaction should occur, at the same rate, giving the same products, giving off the same amount of heat, etc.

    From these first two assumptions stems the idea of the "laws of nature." We shall discuss the role of these "laws" more a little later. These two assumptions then lead logically to the third assumption.

---

1. Holmes, *Idea of a Christian College*, 52–57.

3. *The universe is knowable.* Since there is order and consistency in the universe, then logically, as one studies the physical universe, one should be able to know or understand it.

Being able to understand the physical world involves at least two ideas. First, it suggests an understanding of the cause behind an effect or phenomenon. For example, it is possible for me to understand that two elements react together because of their individual atomic structures, their electron configuration. (Please note that at this point I am not referring to ultimate causes; ultimate causes lead back to God and are not in the mind of the non-Christian scientist. They will be considered later.)

This leads then to the second aspect of "understanding" the creation: prediction. Once I understand the cause behind a particular chemical reaction, I can begin to predict and ultimately control when this reaction occurs. (This actually is a fundamental question that is debated by philosophers of science: What is the purpose of science? Is it to understand the true nature of the physical world or is it merely to develop models that "work" in the sense that they allow us to predict and control?) Again this task of understanding the physical universe is made possible by the first two assumptions, that it is both orderly and consistent.

These then are three assumptions or presuppositions with which all scientists, whether Christian or not, approach the scientific task. There are, however, some assumptions, again at least three, that are held by the Christian scientist alone. These three assumptions are really even more foundational then the earlier three. The non-Christian scientist assumes the first three and then as a result launches himself into the task. The Christian scientist, on the other hand, asks, "On what basis can I make these three assumptions? What are the assumptions necessary for these assumptions?"

The three biblically-based underlying presuppositions of the Christian chemist are:

1. *God created the universe* (Genesis 1:1; Isaiah 42:5; 45:8; John 1:3). This is the starting point for science as performed by Christians. The entire universe and all that it contains were created by him *ex nihilo* (from nothing). This assertion reminds me of an incident that was related to me recently regarding a children's class in a church. Each child was given a cookie and one of the teachers, wondering which kind mother had done the baking, asked the children who had made

the cookies. "God did" came the reply from one miniature theologian, clearly advanced beyond her age of two years.

In a humorous way this illustrates the mindset of both the apostle John ("All things were made by him and without him was not anything made that was made") and the Christian scientist. What we study as chemists is the creative work of God.

2. *God sustains and upholds his creation* (Colossians 1:17). God did not abandon his creation, but even after creating it *ex nihilo,* he continues to be intimately involved with it, upholding and sustaining it. Notice that it is not some set of impersonal "laws of nature" that run things; it is God. The Christian scientist, unlike the deist, does not view creation like a watch that some cosmic watchmaker (God) carefully made, wound up, and then left ticking away on its own. Rather, s/he believes that God created and continues to be intimately involved with his creation. This is why the universe is consistent and ordered and therefore understandable.

3. *God is revealed in his creation* (Romans 1:20; Psalm 19:1–6). In understanding the creation, so the Christian chemist maintains, one can understand something of the Creator, in the same way that a painting tells us something about the artist or a novel tells us something of the writer. This is more than just an acknowledgement that there is a creator, but a quest to understand what he is like. When we view creation, whether we are looking at the majesty of a mountain scene or, as chemists, considering the structure of a DNA molecule, we recognize it as the handiwork of the Creator. However, Paul in Romans 1:20 does not merely say that the existence of a creator is evident in the creation, but that "God's invisible qualities—his eternal power and divine nature—have been clearly seen" in his creation.

As chemists, who view and study the creation at the molecular and atomic level, we see clearly that God is a God of order, of consistency, of faithfulness, and of power. As we seek to understand his creation, we can understand more of him.

The Motivational Approach

As Christians, we have different reasons for undertaking the scientific task. If you were to ask individual chemists (not necessarily Christian ones) why they study chemistry, they might initially have difficulty answering the question. I suspect that given enough time to think about it, however, there might be two responses that would frequently be given.

Some might suggest that they have pursued a career in chemistry because "they are good at it." In other words, their natural inclinations and abilities led them into that discipline even perhaps without their consciously considering it.

Should this honest response be immediately eliminated as a legitimate reason for a Christian to study chemistry? I don't think so. We as Christians should recognize all that much more that God has gifted us individually for specific tasks. To function as a responsible steward requires that one consciously seek to best utilize these gifts.

Another reason that I suspect would be given for studying a science like chemistry might involve the "thrill of discovery," of coming to a new understanding of a particular phenomenon or system. Again we must not be quick to discard this reason either. Scripture greatly elevates as an ideal the concept of "truth" and the pursuit of truth. This is really what is being talked about in such a response, though perhaps using slightly different terminology.

These two aforementioned reasons are then common to both the Christian and non-Christian chemist. There are also, however, a couple of reasons for studying chemistry that are applicable to the Christian only.

1. Humankind's ability to know and worship God is enhanced by study of the creation.

    It might be argued that this point is really the same as the one above about the pursuit of truth. What I am emphasizing here is the *result* of that pursuit. Because of the different presuppositions of the Christian chemist (Recall: God has created the universe and is revealed in it), truth is not to be viewed as an end in itself. Instead, it is a way to understand and appreciate God to a degree not otherwise possible.

    Consider the Psalms and notice how often the psalmist reflects on the creation in his adoration of God, or read Job 38–41 as Yahweh speaks of the glory of the creation. Note how Job responds: "My ears have heard of you but now my eyes have seen you."

2. Humanity has the role of ruler and steward of creation.

In the so-called "cultural mandate" of Genesis 1:26, 28, and 2:15, God makes it clear that humankind is to have dominion over, to be a steward of, and to care for the creation. In order to properly fulfil that mandate, it is obviously necessary for humanity to understand the creation. This principle, as a motivation for the Christian chemist, cannot be emphasized too much. Virtually all that such a chemist does, whether developing new drugs or analyzing water samples, can and ought to be viewed as service to God and humanity and as fulfilling the mandate to have "dominion."

The Attitudinal Approach[2]

As Christians we go about the scientific task in a different way. Christian chemists need to approach their research with an attitude that places great value on truth and integrity. This is not to suggest that the non-Christian scientist is necessarily lacking in these values. Rather, Christians should as much or more so emphasize integrity in their work simply as a reflection of the emphasis that Scripture places upon this character trait.

While this clearly is a valid point of integration for any academic discipline, it is especially relevant in the sciences. There is always a temptation in research to "fudge" the data, to manipulate the numbers to support your hypothesis. Perhaps some of you have even heard reports of such fraudulent research. Again, it is clear that the Christian chemist needs to approach his/her work with an attitude that places supreme value on truth and integrity.

In addition, there ought to be an attitude of reverence in the Christian scientist. In the same way as the art lover might approach the work of Leonardo da Vinci or Michelangelo with a respect bordering on reverence, so the scientist ought to respectfully approach the handiwork of the Creator. Such an attitude would manifest itself in how scientists view and conduct their investigations. They do not poke and prod, viewing the study of the creation merely as a means to their own satisfaction. Rather, their study of the creation, even at the molecular level as is the case for the chemist, demonstrates a love and reverence for God's creation. Clearly this attitude of reverence is closely related to the motivation discussed above, which recognizes humankind's role as steward. Here, however, the emphasis is not so much on the action of ruling and stewarding as it is upon their recognizing that scientists are *merely* stewards, not masters.

2. Holmes, *Idea of a Christian College*, 47–50.

The Ethical Approach[3]

Christians pursue the scientific task with different values. Secular science maintains that such study needs to be value-free; that is, truth can only be arrived at if one approaches one's study with no encumbering set of values that might cloud one's ability to discern truth. "We can understand the world," they maintain; "we can come up with the answers simply by unbiased observation."

As Christians, on the other hand, we recognize that the possibility of such value-free investigation is a myth. All scholarship is value-laden. The question is not "Do I have values as I conduct my research?" but rather "What are the values that I need to carry with me into my work?" For the Christian those values need to be biblical ones that permeate one's scholarship and not be merely what Holmes calls "moralizing tacked on to the end." Rather, Holmes says Christian scholars "must explore the intrinsic relationship between the facts and the values of justice and love."[4]

For the Christian chemist (as well as other Christian scientists), then, there is an obvious need for this kind of ethical approach to integration in the area of the environment. We bring a unique set of values to this problem. The value God places upon his creation is evident from the first chapter of Scripture, when God viewed what he had made and said it was "good." In addition, we recognize, as mentioned before, that God has placed humanity in the role of steward, of caretaker of his creation.

The environment is not the only area where Christian values and thinking can be applied. Earlier I made the point that chemistry touches our lives in many ways—that the results of chemical research are evident all around us, affecting us mostly positively but sometimes negatively. These results of our chemical research ought to be consistent with our Christian values. The reader may wish, as a helpful exercise, to consider the work in developing, say, a new anticancer drug, or in analyzing water samples, or in doing weapons research, and ask what values are implicit in such work.

Christian values—and a Christian way of thinking—need to permeate our approach to our chemical research. Such a perspective should provide us with an ethic with which we can perform our tasks.

3. Holmes, *Idea of a Christian College*, 50–52.
4. Ibid., 51.

CONCLUSION

I trust I have convinced you that it does indeed make a difference what my worldview is, even when I approach a hard physical science such as chemistry. If I approach the task as a Christian then I have different presuppositions to begin with, based on God as Creator. I also have a different motivation for studying chemistry as I see chemistry as a way of enhancing my understanding of and appreciation for my God. I also have a different attitude, as the results that I get are secondary to pursuing them in a manner that reflects integrity and places a high value on truth. Finally, a different ethic permeates the scientific task, one that is based on biblical values.

I mentioned above that both the Christian and the non-Christian scientist can experience the joys of scientific investigation and discovery. I wish to conclude by considering the words of a seventeenth-century scientist (albeit an astronomer, not a chemist), Johannes Kepler, a devout Christian, who discovered the laws that govern the motion of the planets. Upon making this discovery, he was said to have exclaimed, "O God, I am thinking thy thoughts after thee."

Another famous believing scientist, this one a contemporary, Francis S. Collins (with both a PhD in Physical Chemistry and an MD) expressed a similar sentiment when recalling the success, announced in June, 2000, of the international multidisciplinary Human Genome Research Institute project team he was leading. In a 2006 book recounting his journey to Christian faith, he states, "for me the experience of sequencing the human genome, and uncovering this most remarkable of all texts [the human DNA structure], was both a stunning scientific achievement and an occasion of worship."[5] Collins devoted this entire book to answering the following question: "In this modern era of cosmology, evolution, and the human genome, is there still the possibility of a richly satisfying harmony between the scientific and spiritual world views? I answer with a resounding *yes!*"[6]

However thrilling it was to make such discoveries, both Kepler and Collins were led beyond those personal thrills to the joy of understanding and appreciating God in a deeper way. That is the reward that comes

5. Collins, *Language of God*, 3.

6. Ibid., 5–6.

to those who study the creation, whether at the planetary level or at the atomic and molecular level: they recognize it as the handiwork of God.

WORKS CITED

Collins, Francis S. *The Language of God: A Scientist Presents Evidence for Belief.* New York: Free Press, 2006.

Holmes, Arthur. *The Idea of a Christian College.* Rev. ed. Grand Rapids, MI: Eerdmans, 1987.

FOR FURTHER READING

Ashby, E. C. "Gene." "God Is Faithful." In *Professors Who Believe: The Spiritual Journeys of Christian Faculty,* edited by Paul M. Anderson, 55–64. Downers Grove, IL: InterVarsity Press, 1998.

9

A Christian Perspective on Communications

BILL STROM

INTRODUCTION

My bet is that today you woke up to the music of a clock radio, conversed over breakfast with roommates, listened to music on your iPod, and have already listened to one or two lectures. You probably did not think twice about these events. They seemed natural and easy.

Even though we communicate every day and all through the day, one might be hard-pressed to define "communication," or explain what Communication Departments teach and why. Furthermore, few people have asked how being a Christian should influence our study and appreciation of this marvelous ability. By reading this chapter, I hope you come to understand what we in Communication Departments do, and for a brief time think about the complexity and importance of communicating.

WHAT IS COMMUNICATION?

If you ask ten friends "What is communication?" you will likely get ten different answers. Two of our scholars canvassed communications research thirty years ago, and even then discovered over 120 definitions![1] So, while communication may be common, it is also complex, for we have not agreed on a single definition of it. For starters, however, the *word* "communication" comes from the Latin *communis*, which means "to share, or to make common." But what are we sharing in common? Most agree that we create and share *meanings*—ideas, emotions, and images associated with

---

1. Dance and Larson, *The Functions of Communication*, 171–92.

symbols (e.g., simple words such as "dog") or complex symbols (such as "antiestablishmentarianism"), and nonverbal signals (such as a "thumbs-up" sign) or complex ones (like a Japanese tea ceremony). Along the way, we might create different meanings due to trouble with homonyms (words that sound the same but are spelled differently; you heard me say "fairy" but I meant "ferry"), or diverse cultures (ferries in Washington State are common, but not in Nevada), or outright physical noise (e.g., the diesel engine of the ferry overrides our conversation). We also understand that communication occurs along channels such as electronic ones like e-mail or film, and personal ones like a conversation or public speech. So a standard definition of communication is that it is a process by which two or more people use symbolic means and channels to create shared meaning with the likelihood of some interference.

Because this theoretical *process* of communication is central to what we study, we examine it part by part. For example, we study the nature of people as senders and receivers. People vary in their personalities and their habitual styles of interacting. People pick up rules for interaction from their birth families, showing their ethnic stripes through cultural habits. You can therefore better understand what I mean if know that I tend toward exaggeration, learned to respect my elders when I was young, and hold moderately conservative values.

We also study how the channels of communication shape and tint our interpretation of messages. Consider how e-mail is terrific at conveying lots of information through written words, but poor at capturing one's emotions and humor because it lacks nonverbal cues such as our voice and appearance. In contrast, a conversation with a friend over a coke might convey much emotion and humor but lose focus on details because our presence overwhelms our words.

After establishing how the process works theoretically, we then look at how it works in different contexts and *applications*. Some of our departments are called Communication *Studies* because scholars study communication in diverse places. For example, the National Communication Association (the largest academic organization in the United States) recognizes over seventy specialties within our field, including:

- African American Communication and Culture
- Communication Ethics
- Family Communication

- Mass Communication

- Peace and Conflict Communication

- Performance Studies

- Religious Communication

- Visual Communication[2]

The historical study of communication, going as far back as Plato and Aristotle (350 years before Christ), was integral to schooling during the Middle Ages. Today, the study of communication has diversified to homes in humanities departments, social science departments, and the performing arts. It finds resonance with these three areas because people are symbolling creatures, and these departments study our symbolic expressions. A humanities approach might examine themes in the *Lord of the Rings* film trilogy or the rhetoric of Barak Obama. A social science approach might consider the hurtful pain of verbal abuse in a family or how leaders inspire in organizations. Performing arts professors create and comment on creative communication such as plays and web designs.

When we say humans are symbolling creatures, we mean we have the ability to use symbols (i.e., language, behavior, images, and sound) to express complex and abstract messages. Animals may communicate, but they do so in closed systems with only a handful of symbols and a few rules for combining those symbols. In contrast, humans begin with hundreds of thousands of symbols which we combine to create billions of interpretable messages. The honey bee may be able to wiggle with varied intensity and duration to convey "Pollen 50 meters south," but only people can speak rationally about honey, record the history of the bees' honey production, and argue for the value of honey in one's diet, all through symbols.

Some students take communications as a major because, unlike philosophy or history, they say, "You can do something in the 'real world' with communications." Yes, a communications major may appear to prepare you for a specific job (such as being a journalist or web designer), but hopefully you value the bigger picture of the liberal arts. As Holmes says, "Education should . . . prepare us to adapt, to think, to be creative."[3]

---

2. See the National Communication Association website at www.natcom.org.

3. Holmes, *Idea of a Christian College*, 24.

"The *human* vocation is far larger than the scope of any job a person may hold because we are human persons created in God's image, to honor and serve God and other people in all we do, not just in the way we earn a living" [emphasis mine].[4]

Studying communication gives us an appreciation of this complex human activity we take for granted, helping us to think critically about the barrage of messages we receive daily from other people and the media. Yes, you may learn how to write a newspaper article using the inverted-pyramid technique, but more importantly, you will learn to be more fully human through the art and science of communication.

WHAT IS CHRISTIAN COMMUNICATION?

If you Google "Christian communication" you will find everything from guidelines for ethical interaction to video production agencies run by Christians to websites for how to give an evangelistic talk. We can make sense of this diversity by noting that Christian communication is defined by its people, its principles, and its purpose.

I think it is fair to say that if you want to understand Christian communication then you should watch Christians communicating. Of course, this is a risky claim because as sinful and limited creatures Christians do not always communicate Christianly. But the core assumption should hold: Christ redeems and renews those who believe and depend on him, and as we submit ourselves to his will, the renewed condition of our heart spills over into how we treat others as well as how we show our creativity. As Jesus said when he chastised the Pharisees, "Make a tree good and its fruit will be good, or make a tree bad and its fruit will be bad, for a tree is recognizable by its fruit. You brood of vipers, how can you who are evil say anything good? For out of the overflow of the heart the mouth speaks" (Matthew 12:33–34).[5]

Christian communication starts with God's people and then conforms to certain principles. That is, to communicate like Christ means shaping our interaction to biblically-based ethical guidelines. The Scriptures brim with exhortations to do this. Notice Jesus' word. He said: "A new commandment I give you: Love one another. As I have loved you, so

4. Holmes, *Idea of a Christian College*, 25.

5. All Scripture from the NIV unless otherwise indicated.

you must love one another" (John 13:34). We communicate love to others when we:

- Forgive them—Ephesians 4:32 and Colossians 3:13
- Serve them—Galatians 5:13
- Show them hospitality—1 Peter 4:7–10
- Encourage or edify them—Romans 14:19 and 1 Thessalonians 5:11
- Confess our sins to them—James 5:16
- Avoid evil talk about them—James 4:11
- Counsel or admonish them—Romans 15:14 and Colossians 3:16
- Yield or submit to them—Ephesians 5:21–22

While this list could be doubled or tripled, the point should be clear. If communication is to be "of Christ" it will align with his ways and his commands. It will also align with his purposes.

What are God's purposes for us? What was Christ's purpose on earth? How do we purpose to respond? In broad relief we know God made us for his pleasure, and that our call is to "love him and enjoy him forever" (The Westminster Catechism). Through Christ we know that God is reconciling the world unto himself, person by person, relationship by relationship, and one day this will be made complete (Romans 5:10; 2 Corinthians 5:18; Colossians 1:19–21). Between now and then it seems our call is to enter in with God to be his ambassadors of peace and justice this side of heaven.[6] Consider the work of one parachurch organization, Peacemaker Ministries. It purports "to equip and assist Christians and their churches to respond to conflict biblically."[7] Peacemakers train individuals to help others reconcile their differences and come to restitution and resolution. Another group, Taproot Theatre, exists to "create theatre that explores the beauty and questions of life while providing hope to our search for meaning." They claim to "value faith, respect people, and celebrate theatre."[8] When Peacemaker staff work to heal broken relationships and Taproot Theatre gives hope for the human condition, they share the goal of

---

6. See Wolterstorff, *Until Justice and Peace Embrace.*

7. Peacemaker Ministry website. See www.peacemaker.net.

8. Taproot Theatre website. See www.taproottheatre.org.

redeeming people to God and to others. Redemption is at the heart, then, of Christian communication.

THREE APPROACHES TO STUDYING COMMUNICATION

I arrived at this description of Christian communication through a process called *inquiry*. Inquiry is the asking and answering of significant questions. In communication departments we do inquiry three primary ways: the objectivistic, the interpretivistic, and the practical (praxis). Let's look at each.

The Objectivistic Approach

The objectivistic (or scientific) approach is similar to the one used in psychology and sociology. All three are social sciences, and all three assume that truth is best discovered via the scientific method. The scientific method assumes that reality is "out there" (outside of us), is relatively stable, and is accessible to our senses. Thus communication scientists attempt to measure how communication *is* by sampling hundreds of people with questionnaires or involving them in experiments. After gathering their data, scholars attempt to make sense of it all by constructing theories. Their theories are said to be true when they explain the data well, and can predict how others will act in similar situations. Most important is that a scientific theory can be tested by other scholars who agree on the methods used and the interpretation of answers given. Scientific theories about communication can help us solve practical problems in everyday life (such as how might one create credibility in a speech or how a politician might time a media campaign).[9]

This objectivist approach results in statistics that *describe* communication. For example, from a study using this approach, we have found that the time university students spend communicating during an average day breaks down into listening (53%), reading (17%), speaking (16%), and writing (14%).[10] Another discovery was that during a college or university lecture, an average of only 20% of students will actually be listening to what the instructor is saying. Unfortunately, approximately 20% will be reminiscing about something else, another 20% will be pursuing erotic

9. See Bostrom, *Communication Research*, and Griffin, *A First Look at Communication Theory*, for a discussion of scientific inquiry and theorizing.

10. Barker et al., "An Investigation."

thoughts, and the rest will be daydreaming, worrying, or, perhaps very positively, thinking about God.[11]

By using the scientific approach, we also know that women are better than men at perceiving other people's emotions as well as communicating emotion.[12] We have learned that some immigrants to North America interact more with television than with real live Canadians or Americans, and that they can even improve their English by so doing.[13] We also know that adolescent girls who watch a lot of body-image shows (such as *Friends* or *The O.C.*) and soap operas, read teen magazines (such as *Seventeen*), and/or watch music videos tend to be dissatisfied with their bodies, especially when they strongly identify with the celebrities in these media.[14]

These social science facts describe communication. From them, we can ask questions about redemption, justice, and peace. For example, is it right for a Christian university not to offer a course in listening if we do so much of it and if Scripture commands us to be slow to speak and quick to listen? What changes might Christian men make to their interpersonal relational abilities to become more in touch with the emotional needs of their girlfriends or wives? Or is it good for Christians just to sit back idly as immigrants from all over the world come to our doorstep to be acculturated by Jerry Springer and the *Ultimate Fighter*? Finally, how should Christians respond to young women wrapped up with sexualized media and warped with body dissatisfaction? How might Christians redeem the content of teen magazines or music videos? How should we counsel women who cave to these images so they may find peace with themselves and their bodies?

My own training is in the social-science tradition, and my research has examined how married couples perceive and express human virtues such as self-control and humility. One could say my goal is to discover empirically what the Scriptures claim authoritatively, namely, that the fruit of the Spirit brings life. My questions of inquiry were (1) Do spouses tend to marry people of equal virtue, (2) What meanings do couples attach to

11. Adler and Towne, *Looking Out/Looking In*, 251.

12. See Wood, *Gendered Lives: Communication, Gender, and Culture*, 186–88.

13. See, for example, Kim, "Communication Patterns of Foreign Immigrants," 66–77.

14. Hofschire and Greenberg, "Media's Impact on Adolescents' Body Dissatisfaction," 125–52.

the terms "self-control" and "humility," and (3) Does being virtuous make a difference in the quality of one's marriage?[15]

To answer these questions, I developed a survey that tapped husbands' and wives' perceptions of their own virtue and their spouse's virtue as well as questions about their communication and their satisfaction with their marriage. I did so among 70 couples and then loaded their answers into SPSS—Statistical Package for the Social Sciences. With another set of people, I did interviews and asked what "self-control" and "humility" meant to them, and how they communicated each to one another. I also read what other scholars were saying about these virtues. Together the statistical results and the narrative ideas gave a fuller answer to my research questions.

I found that people do tend to be married to people whom they perceive as having the same moral make-up as themselves. That is, the more virtuous husbands perceived themselves, the more virtuous they perceived their wives, and the same was true for wives' perception of themselves and their husbands. This finding brings to mind the proverb, "As iron sharpens iron, so one man [or woman] sharpens another" (Proverbs 27:17). My narrative research indicated that "self-control" means having one's cool head rule over hot emotions, not indulging in activity harmful to oneself, and regulating how one interacts with others so both parties benefit. I learned that "humility" means having an accurate understanding of one's gifts and shortfalls, recognizing one's creatureliness before God, and putting others first through small acts of kindness. Given these positive relational expressions of these two virtues, it was not surprising that the survey data confirmed that the more husbands and wives thought the other to be virtuous, they also rated their marriage as highly satisfying.

These examples show how we can use research from the social science approach to respond Christianly to the world around us. We can use these facts to ask important questions for application, and we can structure our research to discover confirmatory proof for biblical values and insights.

---

15. See Strom, "Communicator Virtue and Vice," 84–103, and Strom, "Communicator Virtue and its Relation to Marital Satisfaction," 23–40.

The Interpretive Approach

The second way scholars study communication is the interpretive approach. Interpretive scholars do not measure communication; they *interpret, explain,* and *evaluate* it. Interpretive scholars are more likely to study texts, artifacts, and discourses such as films, speeches, plays, and art. To do so they begin with their own set of assumptions about symbolic culture and how people make truth claims about it.

Interpretivists assume that reality is "in here," or within us, and it is this reality that we bring to interpret the world around us. An interpretivist scholar argues for a valid interpretation of a film or speech by relying on a *governing paradigm* through which to make a critique. A paradigm is a set of assumptions about God, knowledge, and living that is shared by a community of people. Common paradigms include Marxism and Christianity. Interpretivists believe they have arrived at a compelling paradigm when a significant community of scholars agree with them, when the paradigm articulates what is important in life, when the paradigm sheds light on the human condition (or what it means to be human), and when the theory can help reform society.[16] Interpretivists also write well, and their ideas take on force through lucid prose. In our field, these para digms help us make sense of communication as diverse as advertising and fashion to sports and *The Simpsons*. Let us briefly examine Marxism and Christianity and how scholars use them to interpret popular culture and media.

A Marxist/Critical Paradigm

Karl Marx believed that most of the ills of society were due to the struggle between groups of people, namely the rich and the poor, or, to use his terms, the bourgeoisie and the proletariat. He believed that the group that controlled the material goods of a country (normally the rich), and its communication media (normally the elite), could control the worldview—or thinking—of the people. The ideas of Marx continue to influence a wide range of communication studies, but now more commonly under the label "critical tradition." Littlejohn and Foss capture the critical tradition's key concerns:

---

16. See Griffin, *A First Look at Communication Theory*, for a discussion about interpretivist inquiry and theorizing.

The questions of privilege and power have assumed importance in communication theory, and it is the *critical* tradition that carries this banner. If you have privilege, or lack it, because of the color of your skin, your nationality, your language, your religion, your sex, your sexual orientation, your regional affiliation, your income level, or any other aspect of your identity, then you are facing the kind of social difference that assumes great importance to critical scholars. These theories show that power, oppression, and privilege are the products of certain forms of communication throughout society, making the critical tradition significant in the field of communication theory today.[17]

These authors go on to identify the three essential features of the critical approach: (1) scholars point out power structures in society and identify who benefits and who loses from them, (2) scholars promote new structures that empower marginalized and oppressed people of a society, and (3) scholars attempt to put feet to theory by changing communication or language habits so as to reform society.[18]

In order to get a handle on the Marxist/critical approach at work, let's examine the ABC News website located at www.abcnews.go.com. As a media artifact, it is comprised of large-font headlines, photos of newsmakers, and lists of story titles to click on. What we might miss is that a website doesn't exist on its own but represents an entire industry of producers, editors, writers, and photographers who have two primary motives: (a) to tell the news and (b) to tell it in a way that attracts hits on the website. Critical scholars would observe that the motive to attract hits is directly connected to the political economy of the industry, namely, that one must package the news in such a way that will increase viewership so that ABC may sell advertisements and generate income.

As I clicked on story titles, I read ads or watched videos for a number of specific products or services: toothbrush technology, a wireless hand-held device, a wedding planning service, auto insurance, and a mortgage package. Some of them were "pop up" and unavoidable, while other ads were posted in side- or bottom-bars. The spokesperson for the toothbrush was a beautiful mid-30s Caucasian brunette, and the hand-held device advocate was an attractive mid-50s CEO-like woman. In both cases, the message was clear: my life would be much better with the science behind

---

17. Littlejohn and Foss, *Theories of Human Communication*, 47.

18. Ibid., 47–48.

that toothbrush in my mouth or the freedoms implicit in having wireless e-mail and internet access in my hand. From these simple examples, a critical scholar might argue that being white—or whiteness—is privileged, as is being middle or upper class, and most certainly being attractive. They might point out that only the rich can afford wedding planners or buy automobiles on a regular basis, thus privileging the wealthy, their values, and their agenda.

But what about the news? How can news privilege one group over another, or represent the interests of some but not others? As I write this in December 2007, the top stories read like this:

- "It's a Holly Jolly Holiday for Congressional Parties"
- "Dogs Bring New Hope to Cancer Research"
- "CIA Spy Speaks, Calls Waterboarding Necessary But Torture"
- "Colorado Church Gunman Had Been Kicked Out"
- "Watch the World News Webcast: 12/12/07"
- "Photos: Still No Power; More Ice Coming"
- "Videos: Inside the White House; Obama Hit[s] Hollywood; Sumatra's Elephants"
- "Christmas Recalled: No Toys for Poor Kids?"
- "A Journey Down the Yangtze"
- "O My: Oprah Extravaganza on '08 Trail"
- "Oprah Answer? Clinton Taps Mom, Daughter"
- "Feds Launch Inquiry over CIA Tapes"

A critical theorist might first point out the role of ABC news producers as gatekeepers of world information. Gate-keeping is the limiting of all news items to a workable, salable set based on "newsworthy" criteria such as relevance, magnitude, and visual appeal. Any day of the week ABC staff might learn of one- to two-hundred possible stories, but post only five to ten percent of them. (Of note, newspapers generally publish about ten percent of known stories, and broadcast news covers about one percent.) So if ABC cannot shine a light on all news, what news does it choose to cover?

From the above list, the answer is most obviously "U.S. news." Eleven of the thirteen stories feature American interests. That is eighty-five percent. If the reader thinks that I may have entered ABC's "US" site, the answer is no. These results came from ABC's "World News" page. Even when one enters the "World News Webcast" show, the picture is much the same. Stories featured here in video format dealt with the Federal Reserve, CIA tapes, a Midwest ice storm, a day in the life of President Bush (approximately a quarter of the entire cast), drug use by US teens, Obama's campaign in Hollywood, and the CIA's use of "waterboarding." Three non-US items concerned an Al-Qaeda bombing in Algeria, better relations between North and South Korea, and those Sumatran elephants again. A critical scholar might infer that the producers of ABC News believe that *American* news is *world* news and thus deserves center stage in viewers' consciousness.

Much enlightenment might be gained by comparing the ABC News site with the British Broadcasting Corporation site (www.news.bbc.co.uk). A quick glance indicates regional news for Africa, the Americas, Asia-Pacific, Europe, the Middle East, and South Asia. A click on the "Middle East" yielded fifteen stories alone. On the main page again, the top stories dealt with a Lebanon bombing, the Algerian bombing, Federal Reserve and European bank loans, Ike Turner's death (Tina Turner's husband), and stories from Nigeria, the Caribbean, the Middle East, Switzerland, Russia, and South Africa. A critical theorist could make comparisons between the BBC and ABC corporate culture, values, and policies to explain why the BBC gives voice to diverse news events compared to ABC. A result might be a paper on how ABC can reform its policies to be less American-centric.

The collapse of communism in the USSR and eastern Europe in the late twentieth century caused many conservatives to declare Marxist ideas invalid and passé. However, many communication scholars still find the ideas and ideals of critical theory compelling for interpreting, explaining, and evaluating cultural communication, especially in media and entertainment industries.

We now turn to a Christian worldview that enjoys similar lively application.

A Christian Paradigm

Just as Marx's ideas have diversified and matured under the umbrella of "critical studies," so too have Jesus' teachings and the biblical record blossomed into multiple Christian perspectives on communication. Earlier I argued that a Christian paradigm requires an eye for how communication redeems relationships through justice and peace. We turn now to a theology of communication articulated by reform scholars, and, in particular, William Romanowski of Calvin College. Romanowski has written *Eyes Wide Open: Looking for God in Popular Culture*, and *Pop Culture Wars: Religion and the Role of Entertainment in American Life*, among other publications.

Reform scholars believe God has put us on earth for a purpose, namely, to be stewards of his natural creation and of culture. Romanowski defines culture as the "collection of ideals and beliefs, values and assumptions that makes up a kind of master plan for living and interpreting life."[19] So, while God may have created humans and the natural world, he has given us the role to create culture. "God's co-creators [people] have used the stuff of creation to develop imaginative art forms—literature, poetry, painting, sculpture, theater, music, and film—and incredible means for human communication, including languages, printing, photography, sound recordings, radio and television broadcasts, satellite transmissions, and the Internet."[20] "Culture represents human responses to God's first and foundational command: 'Be fruitful and increase in number; fill the earth and subdue it' (Genesis 1:28). God entrusts ordinary human beings with continuing the process of creation. That we are God's co-creators is a fundamental assumption and overarching theme in Scripture."[21]

Reformers sit between the one extreme of shunning and damning culture (what Richard Niebuhr called the "Christ *against* culture" position) and the other extreme of mindlessly embracing everything culture presents to us.[22] Rather, in a position-of-the-center, reformers believe that culture is basically good but fallen, just as we are made in God's image but have chosen to sin. Thus both humankind and culture require the redeeming grace of Jesus Christ for ultimate restoration.

Romanowski's theory of communication, or theology of culture, places God's lordship and our stewardship front and center. When we understand these two realities, we are able to engage, interpret, and transform culture with our "eyes wide open." Romanowski proposes eight principles in a Christian approach to popular culture and media. They include:

19. Romanowski, *Eyes Wide Open,* 49.

20. Ibid., 45.

21. Ibid., 44.

22. For a classic answer to how Christians have responded to cultural life, see Niebuhr, *Christ and Culture.*

[1] God made *everything*—visible and invisible—and claims ownership of *everything*. Further, all things were made with a purpose—to serve in God's creation—and so all things are God's servants. 2) To be God's image bearer is to be human, and to be human is to be a cultural agent, carrying on God's creative work by *doing* culture. This is known as the *cultural mandate*. 3) *Culture* is our common, historical endeavor to define and live in God's world, but because of the human fall in sin, culture became a complex affair because the effects of sin are not limited to the human heart but involve culture, society, and creation. 4) Symbolizing [naming culture through communication] is a key to living because it is the means by which we establish meanings for all things done in God's world. 5) The fact that culture reveals what humans believe about "things" shows the close relation between faith and culture. 6) Culture is communicated through *texts*, which are human actions, events, and material works [such as movies, TV shows, rock concerts, etc.] that embody meaning and are widely shared. 7) The term *religion* refers to an innate condition of human existence that is both fundamental and universal. Being religious is not restricted to confessional life [such as attending church, praying, reading the Bible], but we are religious in every dimension of life. 8) The popular arts are cultural representations or texts that give substance to cultural values and perspectives. Creating and evaluating popular art is one way we turn faith into a vision both of and for life.[23]

As one might guess, Romanowski encourages Christians to use a wide range of criteria for making wide-eyed assessments of popular culture. He is eager to see students become excellent critics and consumers of culture, as well as Christian in their perspective. When you pick up a favorite novel or rent your next DVD, you might ask yourself questions such as the following: For whom was this media product targeted? What age, race, or class of people most identify with it? What does it glamorize and value? Who are its heroes and villains? How do these depictions compare with Christian values and beliefs? How are symbols and names used to create compelling meaning? How is visual style or cinematography used to capture the producer's message? Is God depicted at all in the work? If so, how? If not, why not? How is nature depicted? The universe? Is the world a friendly or evil place according to the work? How are people depicted? Are they inherently good or evil, simple or complex, redeemable or incorrigible? How are men (and masculinity) and women

23. Romanowski, *Eyes Wide Open*, 55–56.

(and femininity) portrayed? Are they in stereotype? With which characters do you most identify? Can you figure out why? What is the nature
of evil, and is it personal, social, or cultural? Is evil considered sin, or is it
normalized as desirable? Do characters in the story find hope or redemption? Do they reconcile with each other? With God? How are sexuality
and violence portrayed? Are sex and violence thrown in gratuitously, or
do they play a significant role in the storyline or development of the characters? How do depictions of sex and violence align or clash with your
Christian understanding and values? Who has authority in the work? Is
authority in the hands of strong individuals, or do social institutions such
as the church, government, or business exercise authority for or over the
individual? And finally, does this work of art apply to your real world, or
is it simply escapist? Does this piece of art paint a map of reality that you
can embrace, reject, or adopt in part? Can you figure out why?

Let's take, for example, an episode of *Wheel of Fortune*. If we take a
reform perspective seriously, we will engage the show with a critical eye
rather than one simply looking for a way to blow thirty minutes. The show's
host, Pat Sajak, and assistant, Vanna White, represent traditional male (in
control) and female (helping men) roles. Vanna is objectified as a sexual
person with meager intelligence who performs a role unnecessary to the
game or its outcome (that is, the technician in the back room could light
up the puzzle's letters). The show likely identifies most with a middle-aged
audience as contestants are drawn from the 30–60 year range, but more
women than men, and more whites than blacks or Hispanics. The show
glamorizes the American Dream that suggests anyone can hit the jackpot
with a little luck and a little skill. The program parades as a shopping
mall for sponsored products cast amidst planned applause, oohs, and aahs
as solutions to one's middle-class doldrums. God and his creation don't
frequent the show except for panel-sized photos of white-sand beaches by
destination resorts. The dominant message is that little people (like you
and me) may find happiness through consumption if assisted by the good
people at King World Productions.

You may not agree with every item of my *Wheel of Fortune* appraisal,
and that's fine. Romanowski doesn't think that "being one in spirit and
purpose" (Philippians 2:2) guarantees unanimous agreement in how
we read popular culture. His hope, however, is that you engage it with
some Christian principles so you become a thoughtful steward. Doing so

also serves as the basis for creating your own redeemed slice of culture, whether that be in how you write, edit, or act.

We turn now to the applied or practical approach to communication.

A Practical (Praxis) Approach

Whereas the objectivist (scientific) and intepretivist (humanities) approaches help us understand and evaluate communicative facts and theory, *praxis* is putting these to work with our creativity and skill. To have good ideas without applying them is like having faith but no works. Just as good works are a sign of true faith, so too excellent skills are a sign of good theorizing and critical thinking.

Of course, we apply more than just facts or theories. We employ our gifts. Perhaps already you have discovered your knack for writing or speaking, film production or interpersonal relating. Your abilities seem natural and easy. Or perhaps you don't consider yourself particularly gifted in any one area—you're a jack of all trades, if you will. We know from the Scriptures that God gives us gifts for his purposes. First Corinthians 12:27–29 reads:

> Now you are the body of Christ, and each one of you is a part of it. And in the church God has appointed first of all apostles, second prophets, third teachers, then workers of miracles, also those having gifts of healing, those able to help others, those with gifts of administration, and those speaking in different kinds of tongues. Are all apostles? Are all prophets? Are all teachers? Do all work miracles?

The Apostle Paul understood that God's kingdom is giftedly diverse and that the exercising of our gifts builds the kingdom.

Attending college provides opportunity for you to explore your gifts and try them out. Don't be afraid to try, for in trying you learn about yourself and your gifts. Each year at my university about thirty students experience internships through our communications program. Four times a semester they meet for an entire evening with each other to share stories, compare notes, and find out whether their experiences are normal or not. Recently two students interned at local television stations with starkly different responses, one loving it and the other hating it. Meg found a fit because she loves people and enjoys hobnobbing with celebrities. She enjoys acting and expressing herself on-the-spot. She remains in control when the center of attention. Meg could see her potential for on-camera work some day. Tina, in contrast, simply could not identify with all the pomp and frenzy. She needed her space and time to think. She felt herself more gifted for administrative work in a slower-paced environment. Neither may have known of their fit, or lack thereof, if they had not stepped out in faith and taken the internship.

Elsewhere I have noted basic assumptions that communication practitioners hold.[24] The first is that we can improve our communication gifts; we are not locked in at one level. "While it is true that God gives gifts variably according to the grace given us (Romans 12:6), the apostle Paul also says, 'Since you are eager to have spiritual gifts, try to excel in gifts that build up the church' (1 Corinthians 14:12). His admonishment to *try to excel* in certain gifts indicates that we can improve on our talents and reduce our deficiencies."[25] Students who enroll in our basic public speaking class see huge gains in their confidence and skill when they *try to excel*. Some enter quite unsure of themselves, but today serve as pastors, lawyers, and teachers.

The second assumption is that improvement takes hard work; it isn't going to be easy.[26] It is easy to envy a singer or writer, believing perhaps that their talent is natural and unrehearsed. Joseph Moxley, in his book on getting published, points out how hard writers work. His research shows that published authors work hard, are not necessarily brilliant, and don't enjoy the rigors of writing![27] This is much like a Glasbargen cartoon I once saw: a supervisor is coaching a colleague by saying, "Actually, success is 2% inspiration, 97% perspiration, and 1% deodorant."

The third principle is that enhanced skills can transform our personal world.[28] As we exercise a gift, we may see ourselves in a new light. People give us feedback, shaping our identity. My own hobby as an amateur ventriloquist bears this out. My first performances were on the steps of my family home, and as I saw the kids laughing I figured I must be doing something right. Later I did a skit at church, and eventually at my

---

24. Strom, *More than Talk*. See Chapter 14: "Building Temples: Engaging Communication Gifts."

25. Ibid., 367.

26. Ibid., 368–69.

27. Moxley, *Publish, Don't Perish*, 3–14.

28. Strom, *More than Talk*, 369–70.

high school. I soon became known as the "guy with the dummy" and began receiving phone calls that began with, "Hi, are you the ventriloquist?"
As my confidence and skills improved I came to believe I could perform
anywhere, and for the most part this is true. Recently I began teaching
other adults this ancient craft, thus molding my image of myself as ven-
triloquism *instructor*. And the cycle continues.

A final assumption about putting our skills to work is that by doing
so we serve others and build covenantal culture.[29] A covenantal culture is
a community where believers openly dialogue about a moral vision for
what will benefit all its members. A local church assembly is a covenantal
culture when, in the spirit of 1 Corinthians 12 (quoted above), each member offers his or her gift in order to build up others and contribute to the
discussion of first things. We may not understand the full impact of an
encouraging word, a cantata well-sung, or a video trailer at the moment,
but the offering of these gifts to others under God's lordship makes us
responsible stewards. They serve as sweet-smelling sacrifices to him.

CONCLUSION

At the beginning of this chapter, I defined communication as the process
by which two or more people use symbolic means and channels to create
shared meaning, with the likelihood of interference. By now you should
also understand that communication is more than meaning-creation. As
James Carey, a much respected scholar in our field, has observed, communication is "a process whereby reality is created, shared, modified, and
preserved."[30] Carey understood the potential of our talk and media to
creatively express our worldview, share our innermost selves, mold how
others see us and the world, and preserve first things. Studying communication connects you to all of life. As a liberal art, communication educates
you for work, for leisure, for becoming better citizens, and for being better
witnesses for Christ. Like all education, studying communication is "an
open invitation to join the human race and become more fully human."[31]

29. Ibid., 370–73.

30. Carey, *Communication as Culture*, 33.

31. See chapter 8 in Holmes, *Idea of a Christian College*.

WORKS CITED

Adler, Ronald B., and Neil Towne. *Looking Out/Looking In.* 6th ed. Toronto, ON: Holt, Rinehart & Winston, 1990.

Barker, L., R. Edwards, C. Gaines, K. Gladney, and F. Holley. "An Investigation of Proportional Time Spent in Various Communication Activities by College Students." *Journal of Applied Communication Research* 8 (1981) 101–9.

Bostrom, Robert N. *Communication Research.* Prospect Heights, IL: Waveland Press, 1998.

Carey, James W. *Communication as Culture: Essays on Media and Society.* Boston: Unwin Hyman, 1989.

Dance, Frank E. X., and Carl E. Larson. *The Functions of Communication.* New York: Holt, Rinehart & Winston, 1972.

Griffin, Em. *A First Look at Communication Theory.* 6th ed. Toronto, ON: McGraw-Hill, 2006.

Hofschire, Linda J., and Bradley S. Greenberg. "Media's Impact on Adolescents' Body Dissatisfaction." In *Sexual Teens, Sexual Media: Investigating Media's Influence on Adolescent Sexuality,* edited by Jane D. Brown, Jeanne R. Steele, and Kim Walsh-Childers, 125–52. Mahwah, NJ: Lawrence Erlbaum Associates, 2002.

Holmes, Arthur. *The Idea of a Christian College.* Rev. ed. Grand Rapids, MI: Eerdmans, 1987.

Kim, Young Y. "Communication Patterns of Foreign Immigrants in the Process of Acculturation." *Human Communication Research* 4 (1977) 66–77.

Littlejohn, Stephen W., and Karen A. Foss. *Theories of Human Communication.* 8th ed. Belmont, CA: Wadsworth, 2005.

Moxley, Joseph. *Publish, Don't Perish: The Scholar's Guide to Academic Writing and Publishing.* Westport, CT: Greenwood Press, 1992.

National Communication Association. See www.natcom.org.

Niebuhr, Richard. *Christ and Culture.* New York: Harper and Row, 1951.

Peacemaker Ministries. See http://www.peacemaker.net.

Romanowski, William D. *Eyes Wide Open: Looking for God in Popular Culture.* Rev. ed. Grand Rapids, MI: Brazos, 2007.

———. *Pop Culture Wars: Religion and the Role of Entertainment in American Life.* Downers Grove, IL: InterVarsity Press, 1996.

Strom, Bill. "Communicator Virtue and its Relation to Marital Satisfaction." *Journal of Family Communication* 3 (2003) 23–40.

———. "Communicator Virtue and Vice: Neglected Constructs of Relational Communication?" *The New Jersey Journal of Communication* 10 (2002) 84–103.

———. *More than Talk: Communication Studies and the Christian Faith.* 2d ed. Dubuque, IA: Kendall Hunt, 2003.

Taproot Theatre. See www.taproottheatre.org.

Wolterstorff, Nicholas. *Until Justice and Peace Embrace.* Grand Rapids, MI: Eerdmans, 1983.

Wood, Julia T. *Gendered Lives: Communication, Gender, and Culture.* Belmont, CA: Wadsworth, 1997.

FOR FURTHER READING

Anker, Roy. *Catching Light: Looking for God at the Movies*. Grand Rapids, MI: Eerdmans, 2004.

Ellul, Jacques. *The Humiliation of the Word*. Grand Rapids, MI: Eerdmans, 1985.

Fortner, Robert S. *Communication, Media, and Identity: A Christian Theory of Communication*. Lanham, MD: Rowman & Littlefield, 2007.

Griffin, Emory A. *The Mind Changers: The Art of Christian Persuasion*. Wheaton, IL: Tyndale House, 1976.

Hendershot, Heather. *Shaking the World for Jesus: Media and Conservative Evangelical Culture*. Chicago: University of Chicago Press, 2004.

Johnston, Robert K. *Reel Spirituality: Theology and Film in Dialogue*. 2d ed. Grand Rapids, MI: Baker Academic, 2006.

Kraft, C. *Communication Theory for Christian Witness*. Nashville: Abingdon, 1983.

Mayers, M. K. *Christianity Confronts Culture: A Strategy for Cross-cultural Evangelism*. Grand Rapids, MI: Zondervan, 1987.

Mallard, Kina. "Christian Worldview and Media." In *Shaping a Christian Worldview*, edited by David S. Dockery and Gregory A. Thornbury, 25–40. Nashville: Broadman & Holman, 2002.

Nida, Eugene. *Message and Mission: The Communication of the Christian Faith*. Rev. ed. South Pasadena, CA: William Carey Library, 1990.

Rogers, Juan D. "The Integration of Theological Perspectives in Communication Studies." *Transformation* 19.4 (October 2002) 233–43.

Schultze, Quentin J. *Christianity and the Mass Media in America: Toward a Democratic Accommodation*. East Lansing: Michigan State University Press, 2003.

———. *Communicating for Life: Christian Stewardship in Community and Media*. Grand Rapids, MI: Baker Academic, 2000.

Schultze, Quentin J. et al. *Dancing in the Dark: Youth, Popular Culture and the Electronic Media*. Grand Rapids, MI: Eerdmans, 1991.

Silk, Mark. *Unsecular Media: Making News of Religion in America*. Public Expressions of Religion in America Series. Urbana: University of Illinois Press, 1995.

Smith, D. K. *Creating Understanding: A Handbook of Christian Communication across Cultural Landscapes*. Grand Rapids, MI: Zondervan, 1992.

Stout, Daniel A., and Judith M. Buddenbaum, eds. *Religion and Mass Media: Audiences and Adaptations*. Thousand Oaks, CA: Sage Publishers, 1996.

10

A Christian Perspective on Computing Science

RICK SUTCLIFFE

INTRODUCTION

THE FOURTH CIVILIZATION (FOLLOWING the hunter-gatherer, agricultural, and industrial ones), in which humankind currently lives, is energized by microelectronic technologies, the core disciplines of which fall into two groupings: (1) *computing sciences*, concerned with the theory and practice of building new hardware and software systems to solve specific problems (electrical and software engineers, compiler writers, specialty programmers, and chip designers being the principal professions of this group); (2) *information systems*, whose professionals employ computing systems to solve problems relating to the functions of organizations. They apply existing hardware and software, provide connectivity solutions, and make use of applications packages to solve problems, usually business-related, particularly those involving the storage and manipulation of data.

Because the tendency of humankind is to build first and ask questions later, and because the latest technologies have developed in little more than a single generation, there has been little careful consideration of the epistemological, ethical, and social issues generated by these techniques.

PHILOSOPHICAL ISSUES

The questions most fundamental to any discipline are the *meaning* ones. What exactly are the computing and information sciences, and what do their practitioners mean when they refer to knowledge or truth? That the answers are fundamentally different from those in other disciplines ought to be expected. Indeed, these disciplines do not commonly refer to knowledge questions so much as they do to correctness and reliability, because they are engaged in problem solving, a process not unlike the scientific method:

- understand the problem,

- specify the requirements for a solution,

- analyze the steps of the problem,

- formulate a detailed solution and refine it into a program,

- translate the solution into a notation that can be machine-read,

- execute the solution,

- scrutinize the results for conformity to requirements,

- document everything.

A computer program is correct if the solution conforms to the formal requirements developed in the analysis. It is reliable if the program embodying the solution can go on operating indefinitely. In more common terms, the epistemology here is like that of any technology—truth conflates with functionality, and the key question is: "Does it work?"

A related question is "Is the computing system reliable?" Most of us have had the experience of going to our local bank and discovering that we are unable to transact our business or use the ABM machine because "the computers are down." Sometimes the resulting inconveniences are relatively minor; at other times a technical breakdown can have more serious and far-reaching consequences. In November 2007, the *National Post* reported the following scenario under the headline "Air Canada Glitch Causes Flight Chaos":

> Air Canada experienced flight delays and cancellations after a computer glitch wiped out its check-in system around the globe yesterday morning.
>
> While the country's largest carrier cancelled only 16 of its more than 600 scheduled flights, hundreds of others were delayed throughout the day.
>
> ... Air Canada was treating the computer glitch as an isolated incident yesterday and had no immediate plans to compensate the travelers for the delays. ...

> The outage was caused by a programming problem that pre-
> vented the check-in system from communicating with the reserva-
> tion system and other such customer-service functions as baggage
> check in.[1]

Obviously the tremendous changes that computerization has made have not always resulted in smoother sailing—or flying!

Any understanding involved in the computing process—any intentionality, purpose, or meaning—lies not with the software or with the symbols in which it is written, but is developed by the programmer when the specifications are written and communicated to the user by the running of the resulting program. The only difference between this process and what happens in mathematics is that what is written down are not the symbols embodying a logical proof but a set of directions for an automaton. Here, the communication of meaning is not done directly by one human to another in symbols; rather, an intervening synergistic interaction with a directed mechanical process occurs. However, the machine does not create meaning, even when it is used as an organizing tool; it is just a device for transmitting and manipulating abstractions.

Similarly, a collection of raw data, however large, and gathered from whatever source, is not necessarily information. The latter term implies that the things it describes have meaning, significance, or relevance. Meaning in turn requires two things: (1) intentional and intelligent organization, and (2) the capacity for being communicated.

Thus, because information is a product of purposeful organization and design, not simply an assemblage of facts, it is necessary to do more than just store it. To be of much use, it has to be interpreted (given meaning) and disseminated to others. This is of particular importance to cultural or religious groups such as Christians, whose continued existence depends upon transmitting its essential ideas and practices to the next generation, for failure to do so is the precursor to almost certain extinction.

ETHICAL ISSUES IN THE COMPUTING AND INFORMATION SCIENCES

The computing professional is faced with the same kinds of pressures and decisions as any other professional—demands to do quality work and

1. Deveau, "Air Canada Glitch Causes Flight Chaos," FP7.

finish it on time, to provide adequate customer support and service, to keep proper records, and to follow appropriate legal and professional codes. In the process, there is always the temptation to take shortcuts—to copy unattributed work from others, mislead the customer about the finished product, overcharge for the goods, or do poor accounting. If there is no commitment to an underlying set of absolute values, no standard exists to censure such behavior. In such ethical matters, Christians need to speak authoritatively to all professions. There are other issues, however, unique to this arena.

Information Services and the Professions

Doctors, dentists, lawyers, engineers, realtors, and accountants not only have local client databases in which to file histories, treatments, recall dates, project designs, and billings, but they also have access to local or remote expert systems on which they can diagnose, determine treatments, look up case law, find parallel situations, and so on. These tools allow a single professional to handle a much larger number of clients more efficiently and more accurately than previously. These tools also reduce dramatically the number of facts that the professional must learn and retain in personal memory in order to work competently.

Researchers and translators of the Bible and other specialized literature have reference materials, manuscripts, parallel writings, commentary, and language aids readily available because of the computer. They are therefore able to produce translations into new languages in a fraction of the time it previously took.

Other organizations already maintaining specialized databases include government (taxation, geologic, geographic, demographic, and other statistical information), law-enforcement agencies (arrests, fingerprints, DNA records, and stolen property records), retailers and wholesalers (market trends, inventory, accounts, and customers), credit card issuers, libraries (loans, books on hand and in print), newspapers (articles by subject), and stock market and brokerage houses (prices, press releases, and transactions).

Scientists and engineers can look up the physical properties of substances or locate journal articles or books. Researchers in all fields can do periodical searches and keep up-to-date on the most current work in their field. Such facilities will gradually become major information utilities in their own right, and the professionals who rely on them now will find their dependence growing to the point where they cannot work at all without them.

These considerations readily show that professionals of all callings are rapidly being transformed from being personal repositories of information into people who are skilled at finding and applying that information as they need it. This will profoundly affect both the way they actually work and the way they are educated for their professions in the first place. Those who fail to understand and take advantage of this new reality will not be effective practitioners in the fourth civilization, if indeed they work at all.

Sex, Violence, and the Internet

On a less enlightening note, the purveyors of explicitly violent and sexual materials have also used electronic media. There are three possible responses:

1. Censor the electronic media and remove such materials.

2. Employ filtering programs to prevent access to such materials.

3. Do nothing, on the grounds that since someone must decide what ideas are allowed expression and what are not, there is as much potential for "good" ideas to suffer as "bad" ones.

Unfortunately, the third course may not adequately protect groups that find themselves targeted, such as women, children, and minorities, for the mere existence of depictions of abuse lends credence to its actual perpetration. That is, fictitious or potential abuse portrayed in violent or sexual materials seems likely to increase real abuse of real people. In the same manner, false denials of the Holocaust inflict great psychological pain on the survivors of the death camps and their families.

Moreover, this view is based on the liberal feeling that good ideas and their use should overwhelm bad ones. This in turn implies that those expressing such a hope have the ability to know which are which. Based on actual human history, not only is this hope vain, but such abilities appear to be wanting. At some point and in some manner, it seems necessary to decide to what extent the good of freedom of speech/information must be set aside for the greater good of preventing threats to people's lives. There must be a balance between the right to freedom of speech/action and the right to enjoy peace, order, and good government. It is essential for Christians to understand and participate in such debates, for they have the critical truth of the uncensored gospel to communicate.

Privacy

It seems at times that one must not only anticipate that government and private companies will know every intimate detail of the lives of ordinary citizens, but also must make the same assumption about the nine-year-old down the street with the computer and modem in her bedroom. Although it may be possible to establish safeguards to require permission of the subject before personal information is formally obtained, the spread of such data may not ever be controlled entirely, for it exists in many locations. Some of these are less secure than others—or have less than scrupulous owners. However, any system sufficiently comprehensive to enforce rules for personal data access would by its very existence pose a threat to privacy greater than it could prevent.

Jacques Ellul draws attention to another threat inherent in the very existence of data banks: the vulnerability of such systems to unlawful access by criminals and/or fraud artists:

> One of the greatest problems of data banks and other memory systems is that they guarantee the [accuracy of the] information contained in them. But simple manipulations can result in swindles.... Those who handle computers have to take serious steps to protect themselves: codes and passwords.... Codes and passwords help, but they have to be changed frequently.... Without pressing the point, I would emphasize that there is no sure protection of data. We have here a vast and uncharted territory of possibilities of fraud and data exploitation.[2]

There was a time when such information was not readily available. A prime minister of Canada or president of the United States could be a notorious womanizer and the news media collectively choose not to report it. A member of Parliament or Congress could be reasonably confident that an old police record would never surface. A vice-presidential candidate could keep hidden a stay in a mental institution, and a would-be senator could keep secret a string of shady business deals or underworld connections. The past could be hidden and forgotten, whether it included

---

2. *The Technological Bluff*, 281.

unusual sexual practices, divorce, illegitimate children, molestation, abuse, bankruptcy, tax fraud, a criminal record, failure in school, a dishonorable discharge, cowardice, bad judgment, the misappropriation of funds, or traffic violations.

Today, people have to assume that all details of their past life are a matter of record—part of a universally accessible data store or *Metalibrary*. Those in the public eye, whether as government, corporate, or union leaders, or as professionals in positions of trust, have had to realize that an individual's life has become much more an open book than it was in the past. Whether anyone will care about another's moral judgment is a separate question. When such information is so readily available, the result could well be a cynical, jaded public that, hearing about the private lives of the rich and famous, turns a blind eye to their moral lapses altogether.

What would be left of a right to privacy in such a world? Only that which leaves no record. Since many people would choose to have their home Metalibrary terminal monitor activities inside the house as well as their use of what is available in the outside world, there might be very little human activity left unrecorded. At the place of work, performance monitoring would increase. It is not difficult to imagine the state obtaining the power to continuously record all activities of every person. This could initially be justified in terms of law-and-order enforcement efficiencies, for each criminal's activities would be documented. One cannot ignore, however, a corresponding prospect for absolute state control over every citizen. The system of universal surveillance portrayed in George Orwell's *Nineteen Eighty-four* may no longer be a remote possibility.

If all that were done was the elimination of cash, it would be impossible to hide anything significant. An institution (governmental or not) that could know everything could also control everything. In such a scenario, one could easily imagine that a "universal person code" could be placed on the hand of every citizen, to be passed over the supermarket scanners along with the beans and bread—permanently recording not only human activity but humanity itself. That such a society would one day exist was predicted by the apostle John writing in the first century AD: "He also forced everyone, great and small, rich and poor, free and slave, to receive a mark on his right hand or on his forehead, so that no one could buy or sell unless he had the mark" (Revelation 13:16–17a NIV).

Big Brother and Little Brother

On the other hand, while there is the potential for increased government control of information, individual access to knowledge of government activities has also been improved. So too have opportunities for citizens to express themselves and change the course of government. Some envision a participatory democracy in which citizens would have daily opportunities not just to express opinions but also to learn facts and decide issues. Thus, even while people might lose some ability to act as "private" citizens, governments would also lose their capacity to operate arbitrarily and in secret. That is, loss of personal privacy does not necessarily mean a gain in centralized power—it just means that nothing can be hidden from anyone.

This could frighten away from public office those with a seamy history—seemingly more a boon than a bane. However, since no one has a perfect past, perfect judgment, or perfect morality, the effect upon the aspirations of society's leaders might not be great. People would have to judge others (including their leaders) for who they are in the present and what they might be in the future rather than for their past.

Two more extreme responses are possible. On the one hand, a swing of the pendulum towards a comprehensive moral legalism of the type attributed to the Victorian era could not be ruled out. On the other, a variation of antinomianism is already prevalent among modern liberals—in this case the notion that in many areas of human activity the idea of morality is simply irrelevant. This is usually phrased in terms of tolerating alternate life-styles, but there is no effective difference between permitting all moral systems as equals and saying that none are valid. Although this position includes the logical contradiction that it tolerates everything except disagreement with itself, it has nonetheless become a popular response to the "outing" of information with moral overtones. Indeed, this appears to have become the control belief in the public ethical arena of many western democracies, threatening the freedom and in some cases the very existence of those who hold that moral issues are indeed important—especially if, as Christians do, they say they are absolute.

Turning from the action of individuals to those of the state, there are similar tensions between the desire for secrecy and the need to gather and manage information. Although most people in the western world do not want comprehensive statism, the opposite extreme—no government, only daily electronic democracy—may well be too unstable and discontinuous to work.

Likewise, if the state has control over the strong encryption of data, forcing vendors of such products to give the state "keys" to decode any data back to plain text, there could be no privacy of data or communication. In this instance, however, the technology for message and file encryption was sufficiently widespread by the late 1990s that it can no longer be controlled—government officials simply had not realized this fact as yet.

The most likely outcome is a situation involving gains and losses to both privacy and democracy—not a swing of power to either the individual or the state, but a realignment that changes both. Information availability creates the potential for a new kind of tyranny, but it also creates checks and balances by giving the individual citizen greater knowledge and therefore more power. The two trends may not simply cancel each other out, because an open information society will be very different, but these trade-offs between privacy and knowledge may well become generally accepted and thus little remarked upon.

The ethical question here relates to the fundamental basis for the human desire for privacy. Is privacy a fundamental human right, or is it merely a culturally derived preference? One could argue on religious grounds, for example, that since human dignity and self-esteem are at stake, the greatest possible amount of privacy ought to be granted other people in order to affirm their value. On the other hand, one could argue that the New Testament requires the people of God to join together in open and transparent communities that would foster keeping no secrets from one another. One could even argue that both of these principles are true and that they do not contradict each other.

ISSUES IN BUILDING THINKING MACHINES

Can a machine ever be regarded as intelligent? British mathematician and theoretical computer scientist Alan Turing proposed in 1950 what he called the "imitation test," in which a person has two computer terminals. One is connected to a room where a human will respond to questions, and the other has a computer generating responses. The tester engages in a lengthy conversation with both concerning topics such as the weather, sports, politics, mathematics, and so on, and then decides which is the human and which is the computer.

Turing proposed that one regard the computer as intelligent when it was no longer possible to distinguish between the two any more reliably than by chance—that is, when the tester guessed correctly which respondent was human only 50% of the time.

Although no device comes close to this ability yet, there are four common tasks that lie in the realm of "artificial intelligence":

1. *Simulations*, which are used in the design of expensive components or systems—e.g., using a supercomputer to run a graphical simulation of a wind tunnel and picture the stresses on an airframe. Expensive though such machines are, they are cheaper than building the wind tunnel and testing a prototype. Also, medical schools have found that artificial cadavers connected to a computerized analyzer can both foster safer practice for many types of operations and provide a detailed summary for the instructor.

2. *Expert tasks*, for instance, in the field of medical diagnosis. A program uses a search scheme to take a list of symptoms provided by a doctor and suggest tests that can be performed to narrow down the possible causes. Once the results of a series of tests have also been entered, a probable diagnosis is made and treatment suggested. Similar software is used in other fields, including the law, metals and minerals prospecting, and chemistry.

3. *Logical and inference tasks*, where the database is not so much a pool of facts as a history of the success or failure of previous decisions. Moreover, the program is designed not so much for the analysis of data as it is to follow a collection of rules. For instance, a chess program uses board rules, the heuristics (rules of thumb collated from expert players), and the history, together with brute force computational methods that can examine millions of combinations that may arise from any possible legal moves. Even though chess playing machines are now capable of defeating internationally rated players[3] and could soon be able to win a world championship, the type of logic used is based entirely on fast computation and does not

3. This first occurred on May 11, 1997, when an IBM supercomputer, nicknamed "Deep Blue," defeated chess master Gary Kasparov in a six-game match.

approximate human thinking. In short, it does not have human intelligence, even if it achieves similar results.

4. *Design tasks*, which draw on a knowledge base and sometimes use rules for analysis and inference to assist in the design of both manufacturable products and the machines to make them. Computers are already employed to develop new designs for more complicated devices such as three-dimensional integrated circuits. It is a short step from this point to the design of more powerful computers using software alone. Better design software could be generated by a computer for installation in the next machine, with the history of the first program downloaded as the initial data base for the second. Thus, computers will design their successors' hardware and software, and each machine in the sequence will be smaller, faster, and a better designer of the next. Supposedly, the process could be continued until the processing power and memory exceeded that of the human brain.

At some point along this trail, enough will also become known about the chemical construction of large molecules to design new ones, and these new molecules could in turn be programmed to design others. Some researchers have suggested that people may one day be able to employ virus-sized machines for such tasks as studying brain functions neuron by neuron, locating and repairing arteries blocked by strokes, destroying toxins, bacteria, and viruses in the body, and even editing DNA.

ISSUES IN SIMULATING HUMAN INTELLIGENCE

Some researchers believe that the totality of what it means to be human will be known when they can fully describe the activity of the brain. So far, it is known that nerve complexes called neurons respond to electrochemical signals in the brain by means of a complicated switching operation known as a synapse. The speed at which a synapse operates and the rate at which signals move through the brain turn out to be substantially slower than in electronic switches. Even though the mechanism by which these responses take place is not clearly understood, some researchers are confident that the functions of the human brain can be duplicated in a smaller and faster electronic device.

If a functional equivalent of the human brain can be built, two things could be done with such a device. The first is to program it or "teach" it so that it can perform a few simple tasks. Then it could act as an "intelligent" controller or designer capable of making decisions and acting upon them in an electronic equivalent of the fashion in which the human brain works. Perhaps it would be possible to build an ambulatory body for this thinking machine and thus create the mobile robot of science fiction—the perfect servant/slave that could be given instructions like

"Let the cat out."

"Bathe the kids."

"Go to the grocery store."

Indeed, it should be possible to let the machine decide when the house or office routine dictates that something needed doing, and go ahead without asking or being told. Whether it will be possible to discuss child rearing, philosophy, or one's emotions with such a machine is another matter.

The motivation to spend the enormous sums of money to develop such machines would have to be powerful indeed. While making the ideal butler, maid, secretary, lover, or factory worker might be interesting, it is not clear that such a versatile machine is necessary for all these tasks, or that it needs either a human shape or the equivalent of a human brain. Perhaps such devices would be necessary in very hostile environments where humans could not go—such as on the ocean floor, in space, on the moon, underground, or in a nuclear reactor. To do a necessary job that cannot be done otherwise, machines will be built. They need not look or act anything like a human being for such purposes, and it is uncertain that many robots ever will. Moreover, such devices will not be used at all in the home unless there is a substantial benefit to recover the cost.

The most optimistic of artificial intelligence (AI) researchers are confident that not only can such a machine be built, but that a human brain can eventually be scanned and its activity duplicated in the artificial version. Thus, they believe, the totality of the human's thinking could be downloaded into the mechanical construct. Since the duplicate would now reside in a more easily repairable body, or in no body at all, and since backups could be made at any time, the body of flesh could be discarded. The net result: immortality in a mechanical form. The artificial human ceases to be blood and bone and is instantiated partly or fully as a machine—with electronic capabilities projected to be many times as great as those of the current models we inhabit.

The result of this line of research is supposedly nothing less than the ultimate in man-made salvation from death—eternal life in a manufactured body and brain, here on earth, with no need for any heaven. Quite apart from other ethical problems that may come to mind, this goal raises an old conundrum, the answer to which may in part determine whether such goals can ever be achieved.

"Is the mind more than the brain?" If, on the one hand, the human mind and soul can be expressed unambiguously as the sum of the brain's electrical parts, then downloading its activities to a functional equivalent produces a copy of the personality from a "machine made of meat" to one made of electronic parts. This would be regarded by many as offering a final proof that the empirically verifiable material world is the sum total of all existence, and that the spiritual and supernatural are fantasies. On the other hand, if such things as intentionality, self-awareness, emotions, friendship, anger, fear, intuition, poetic appreciation, conscience, and the ability to seek God cannot be expressed as sets of electrochemical impulses (a position I believe any Christian computer theorist is obliged to adopt), this endeavor will fail, for because the mind is then demonstrably more than the brain, the automaton will always fall short of intelligence.

John Seely Brown, chief scientist at the time at Xerox Corporation and director of the Xerox Palo Alto Research Center, and Paul Duguid, a historian and social theorist affiliated with the University of California at Berkeley, responding to what they called the "Doom-and-Gloom" prognostications of technofuturist Bill Joy, the developer of the Java Programming Language, in a very famous article entitled "Why the Future Doesn't Need Us,"[4] sounded a similar dubious note about the possibility of robots taking over control of their human creators when they observed,

> [Robots] that search, communicate, and negotiate for their human masters may appear to behave like *Homo sapiens*, but, in fact, [robots] are often quite inept at functions that humans do well—functions that call for judgment, discretion, initiative, or tacit understanding. They are good (and useful) for those tasks

4. This article, originally appearing in the Spring 2000 issue of *Wired*, was reprinted in Teich, ed., *Technology and the Future*, 115–37. Joy warned that, as early as 2030, the human species could be supplanted by intelligent machines, which would surpass their creators both qualitatively and quantitatively in both intelligence and consciousness.

that humans do poorly. So they are better thought of as comple-mentary systems, not rivals to humanity. Although [robots] will undoubtedly get better at what they do, such development will not necessarily make them more human.[5]

They go on to argue that even apparently intelligent fictional talking robots (like *Star Wars'* C-3PO [my comparison, not theirs]) tend to "avoid the full complexities of human language" and are "profoundly hampered by their inability to learn in any significant way." They acknowledge the many successes of robot developers but conclude that "computer science is still about as far as it ever was from building machines with the learning abilities, linguistic competence, common sense or social skills of a five-year-old child."[6]

Because such issues impinge on the very essence of what it means to be human, attempts to achieve practical immortality by these means are sure to touch many raw nerves. Those who oppose such research may say that there are some things that ought never to be tried. To those who support it, the potential prize is great enough to pursue at all cost. Furthermore, there is no stopping such an idea once it has been proposed. It would be impossible for society to forbid such research and make the prohibition stick, so long as qualified researchers were not yet satisfied that the question had been answered.

Even if the attempt to do this succeeded, questions would still remain. Would the downloaded person's thinking and memories really constitute the person? Or is this a simulated person and not a full duplicate of the original one? It would be reasonable to assume that the soul would have departed when the flesh-and-blood body was discarded, and would not have been transferred along with the contents of the brain. Could we ever be certain that such a "copy" was fully human—or even alive?

It may be many years before such questions need to be asked seriously, for research on the activity of the brain is moving very slowly, and it seems unlikely that it can soon be computationally, much less functionally, duplicated. In the meantime, computer and communications research may take other turns, the products of which could also render the production of artificially intelligent brains unnecessary.

5. Brown and Duguid, "A Response to Bill Joy," 140.

6. Ibid., 141.

ISSUES IN AUGMENTING HUMAN INTELLIGENCE

A more immediately fruitful path for intelligence technology is related to the ongoing development of substantial improvements to the human/machine interface and to the portability of computing devices. It is not difficult to envision a small but powerful computational device that can be carried about in much the same way as a contemporary engineer totes a multi-function calculator. Indeed, there are already pocket computers, but the device envisioned here, though not having a simulated intelligence, is so much more that it has been called a pocket brain, though it might properly be termed a Portable Intelligence Enhancement Appliance, or PIEA.

Initially, a PIEA will be a powerful computer, possibly utilizing voice input, together with a means of communicating on demand with larger machines for information query and data transfer. Such devices could before long be sold with memory in terabyte quantities—they would be personal secretary, diary, dictation machine, and calculator/computer all in one.

Eyeglasses could be devised that contained a small video screen at the periphery of vision combined with an earphone. This would allow rapid transmission of audio and graphical information to the wearer of the appliance, though at first some manipulation by voice and electronic signals would be required for the reverse transmission. Perhaps voice control could be achieved with a throat patch that picked up sub-vocalization. A wearer could control the device without anyone else even knowing it was there, and would eventually become almost unconscious of its presence and use.

Once the memory store of the PIEA was made sufficiently large, it would be able to store the pictures it showed to the user in a digitized form and in very large quantities. Communication through the Metalibrary or directly with another individual could be achieved by triggering the PIEA to send an appropriate picture or text to be shown to the intended receiver (picting). Gradually, communications would take on the form of a stream of images rather than of text. Individuals would send personal messages to each other as they happened to think of them. The PIEA would from time to time interrupt its wearer's activity to inform him or her of waiting mail.

This concept has a number of advantages over other proposed future data/communications systems. A substantial amount of what an individual did, thought, and contributed could be stored in the PIEA. Because material would be sent to the Metalibrary only if the individual so directed, some privacy could be retained. As far as the Metalibrary itself is concerned, it could be fitted with the best available expert system and logical/inference software and become a "smart" omnipedia, capable to some extent of doing its own research.

Devices on the market by late 2007, including the higher end Treo and iPhone, have begun to show that this vision of future technology is at least feasible, if not probable. This contrasts sharply with the state of "hard AI" prospects, which have no obvious technological path to follow.

Those who see immortality in cyborg form as their goal will be disappointed if the PIEA/Metalibrary link does turn out to be the result of research into intelligence and the workings of the human brain. However, it may be a more achievable goal from a technical point of view, for elements of it exist now in primitive form in hardware, services, and software. The downloading scenario, however, has no immediately realizable aspects.

OTHER ISSUES IN ARTIFICIAL INTELLIGENCE

Playing God?

One objection raised against AI work is that the researchers are "playing God." Although this is on the surface a comprehensive and definitive objection to such work, it is one whose meaning and validity are very difficult to analyze. Presumably the objector is claiming acquaintance with the preferred agenda that God has in such matters and the statement means that such research is known to be a usurpation of rights and privileges that God reserves to himself. But, from a logical point of view, this argument can no more be sustained than "If God had meant us to fly, he would have given us wings." If God is the all-knowing one, does not this imply that searches for knowledge about his creation are, in general, good, because they are searches for something that ultimately derives from God?

"But," the response could be, "it is not just knowledge at stake, but its application. Only God has the right to make intelligent beings." The first part of this new statement is one few people would argue with, for whatever "good" and "evil" are defined to be, their meaning takes substance in the effects of applications, not in theory alone, even when theory seems to lead to action rather directly. However, the last part of the statement is a rather large presumption, for even if only God has the power to create *ex nihilo*, it does not follow that only he can create. Indeed, the fact of having been created "in God's image" would seem to imply that humans have the ability to create in turn.

Those who make this objection also have two practical obstacles to overcome. The first is to demonstrate that they do have the credentials to speak for God in such matters, and the second is to devise an effective means of preventing the research they propose to forbid. There does not, at this point, seem to be a way to do either. First, there seems little evidence to offer that God is at the present time in the habit of divulging new revelations to modern prophets, and second, the control of research on an international scale is effectively impossible. It would seem more practical to control products that might emerge from such work than to ban it and thereby drive it underground.

There may be something to the objection that AI researchers are "playing God," for the pronouncements made in the name of "Science" do often have that ring to them, but even this is a comment on the motivations of the people involved and not directly on the legitimacy of their work. A similar comment can be made in reverse if the objectors are excessively presumptuous in their claims to know the mind of God, or if they subscribe to eastern mysticism and believe they are gods. The spokespersons/objectors for God may also be judging motivations by their perceptions of the work in question, but perhaps inappropriate motivations are matters to be taken up with God. The objection may also focus directly upon what the products of the AI work are to be used for, but again, such possibilities do not in themselves invalidate the work itself.

This objection may be accurate and well-taken if the goal is to become immortal, "like gods," or to build a tower of knowledge and abilities to reach heaven and become "all-knowing ones." Nor would the acceptance of such an objection invalidate all AI work, for there may well be other motivations and applications. This discussion does lead one to wonder, however, about those motivations and potential applications. Would the benefits of AI be confined to the creators and controllers, who would indeed become "gods" and "lords" over the rest of humanity? Or would they be shared with all? Because history would suggest that the former outcome is more likely than the latter, a considerable degree of caution would seem appropriate.

Perhaps the "playing God" objection is instructive, for it forces reflection on the relationships among motivation, technique, and society. Some argue that pure technique is morally neutral, and so is all knowledge, but because technique always has a social and motivational context from which it cannot be extracted pure and value free, this argument is impractical. Thus, while work on AI devices does not automatically imply an attempt to usurp God's creative powers, the motive for their development and their actual use may well constitute usurpation of God's authority.

Are such entities to be regarded as subordinate to humans or as equals? At what point would they be given the status of persons? For instance, if it were considered that an AI device were alive and had semi-human status, would turning off or destroying one be murder? Would they be regarded as more human than a child in the mother's womb, or less so? No ready answers exist to such questions. They only become worse if the thinking machine is housed in an ambulatory robot body, for then their qualities become even more human-like. Moreover, if AI researchers really are prepared to download themselves into an artificial brain and hope still to be regarded as human, it may be difficult for them to withhold the same label from one of the same devices that has been programmed without a human download. This subject is already the focus of considerable controversy, for whatever the resolution, it touches upon the definition of what a human being is as well as the extent to which human beings wish to retain their current definitions or change them.[7]

Rights of AI Devices

If devices are to be made that are "intelligent" in a meaningful fashion; if they are to share the essence of thinking humanly, must they then be accorded equal rights with humans? Should they have freedom of speech, the right to liberty, and the right to own property? If so, could they by

---

7. Donald Norman, Vice President of Apple Research at Apple Computer and founding chair of the Department of Cognitive Science at the University of California (San Diego), makes the interesting point (related to the comment by Brown and Duguid quoted earlier) that "computers will not replace humans until they acquire the important social capacity to deceive—for telling a white lie [e.g., "I just *love* your new outfit" or "Your speech yesterday was *fantastic!*"] smooths over many otherwise discomfiting social clashes" ("Why It's Good that Computers Don't Work Like the Brain," 109–10).

virtue of superior computational ability capture ownership of the entire economy, all the stocks, bonds and properties, and place the original and slower humans entirely in their debt? What of the right to bear arms or for that matter to marry each other (or human beings) and to have offspring?

Indeed, one might even ask, "Are artificially intelligent devices moral agents?" This question could be answered as early as the time such artifacts are first programmed. At one extreme, if "downloading" were to succeed, some would say that the answer would be "yes," for the argument would be that a human being had simply transferred residence in recording and replaying a tape of brain activities. Others would counter by saying that the device is an animated dead creature or zombie and accuse all participants of murder if the original human body were destroyed after an apparently successful transfer. The tape with the recording of the human brain scan also has a doubtful status. It would manifestly not be alive, yet it would contain the pattern not to grow a human body as does DNA, but to reconstitute what is purported to be the essence of humanity. Would such a tape, if it could ever be made, also have to be regarded as a moral agent?

But even though this is one of the express goals of AI research, it is still highly speculative and there are more immediate likelihoods. Some, however, lead to very similar questions. The simplest way of arriving at essentially the same place is to program an AI device in such a way that it can make errors—not just those due to data problems, but deliberate choices to ignore what the program indicates is the right choice based on the data analysis. Given for a moment that the word "know" has a meaning in this context, the question now becomes "Will AI devices be able to knowingly make wrong choices?" The mere presence of this possibility is a key issue in AI work, regardless of the nature of the device, for if the artifact is intelligent and has volition by human standards, it follows that it is a moral agent, regardless of whether or not it is in fact human. Does this mean that such devices would be capable of doing "good" or "evil" at billions of times the rate of human beings?

How would human beings respond to volitional machines? Would they try to destroy them? Would protective societies come into being, labeling such actions "genocide" and vowing to establish legal rights for their mechanical "brothers and sisters"? Should not some such questions be considered at the time decisions are being made to build such machines, not after the fact?

Christians would also face some interesting problems with respect to machines that were capable of choosing to do wrong. Granting that such a machine were regarded as "alive," that is, had a soul—the breath of life—would it also be considered to have inherited a fallen nature from its creator? If so, could it be said to have a spirit, that is, the ability to relate to God? If so, does salvation apply to it equally as to humankind?

The possibility of such a notion being seriously entertained is not as unlikely as one might initially think. Futurist and inventor (of, among other things, a reading machine for the blind) Ray Kurzweil had this to say about robots eventually claiming to have spiritual experiences: "Machines, derived from human thinking and surpassing humans in their capacity for experience, will claim to be conscious, and thus to be spiritual. They will believe that they are conscious. They will believe that they have spiritual experiences. They will be convinced that these experiences are meaningful."[8] Mathematician and philosopher of science William Dembski, one of the original founding Fellows of Discovery Institute (an agency devoted to the promotion of the Intelligent Design view of origins), gave short shrift to such an argument, pointing out that Kurzweil, a committed materialist, defines "spirituality" as a consciousness of self, not a capacity to reach out to a non-physical divine being or to exhibit moral virtue. He suggested that Kurzweil had moved from discussing a scientific issue to a metaphysical, ontological one.[9]

The answers to most of the questions raised in this section are simple if AI devices are to remain mechanical expressions of subsets of human thinking patterns—not to be thought of as actually intelligent or "alive" in the human sense. Given the present-day agenda of the AI research community, however, the difficult questions seem likely to re-surface, with increasing complexity. At some point, it seems likely that a careful definition of "human" and "intelligent" will have to be agreed upon. It is not at this time clear what that definition will eventually include. Neither

8. *The Age of Spiritual Machines*, 153.

9. Dembski, "Kurzweil's Impoverished Spirituality," 113. This article is contained in the volume entitled *Are We Spiritual Machines? Ray Kurzweil vs. the Critics of Strong AI*. "Strong AI," according to Herzfeld, "has as its goal the production of full human-like intelligence in a computer, intelligence that functions as a human mind functions, in a wide variety of areas" (*In Our Image*, 42).

is it clear that Christian thinking will have any influence on the process of AI research or the interpretation of its outcomes, unless Christian people are intimately involved with the design, implementation, and application of it at all stages.

CONCLUSION

None of the issues raised here are simple. If the next generation of Christians is to have anything to contribute to resolving some of these debates in a manner compatible with their beliefs, increasing numbers of gifted Christian students will need to recognize the critical importance of mastering the challenges of computing technology and facing its issues. It is my earnest hope and prayer that many will do so.

WORKS CITED

Brown, John S., and Paul Duguid. "A Response to Bill Joy and the Doom-and-Gloom Technofuturists." In *Technology and the Future*, edited by Albert H. Teich, 138–43. 10th ed. Belmont, CA: Wadsworth, 2006.

Dembski, William A. "Kurzweil's Impoverished Spirituality." In *Are We Spiritual Machines? Ray Kurzweil vs. the Critics of Strong AI*, edited by Jay Richards et al., 98–115. Seattle, WA: Discovery Institute, 2002.

Deveau, Scott. "Air Canada Glitch Causes Flight Chaos." *National Post*, Saturday, 17 November 2007, FP7.

Ellul, Jacques. *The Technological Bluff*. Translated by Geoffrey Bromiley. Grand Rapids, MI: Eerdmans, 1990.

Herzfeld, Noreen L. *In Our Image: Artificial Intelligence and the Human Spirit*. Minneapolis: Fortress Press, 2002.

Kurzweil, Ray. *The Age of Spiritual Machines: When Computers Exceed Human Intelligence*. Harmondsworth, England: Penguin, 1999.

Norman, Donald A. "Why It's Good that Computers Don't Work Like the Brain." In *Beyond Calculation: The Next Fifty Years of Computing*, edited by Peter J. Denning and Robert M. Metcalfe, 105–16. New York: Copernicus, 1997.

Orwell, George. *Nineteen Eighty-four*. Harmondsworth, England: Penguin, 1964.

Teich, Albert H., ed. *Technology and the Future*. 10th ed. Belmont, CA: Wadsworth, 2006.

FOR FURTHER READING

Asimov, Isaac, and Karen A. Frenkel. *Robots—Machines in Man's Image*. New York: Harmony, 1985.

Burke, James. *The Day the Universe Changed*. Rev. ed. Boston: Little Brown, 1995.

Denning, Peter J., and Robert M. Metcalfe. *Beyond Calculation—The Next Fifty Years of Computing*. New York: Copernicus, 1997.

Drexler, K. Eric. *Engines of Creation*. Garden City, NY: Anchor Press, 1986.

Drexler, K. Eric, with Chris Peterson and Gayle Pergamit. *Unbounding the Future—The Nanotechnology Revolution*. New York: Simon and Schuster, 1991.

Eden, J. Gary. "Unseen Realities." In *Professors Who Believe: The Spiritual Journeys of Christian Faculty*, edited by Paul M. Anderson, 74–79. Downers Grove, IL: InterVarsity Press, 1998.

Ellul, Jacques. *The Technological Society*. New York: Knopf, 1973.

Fjermedal, G. *The Tomorrow Makers*. New York: Macmillan, 1986.

Hardison, O. B., Jr. *Disappearing through the Skylight—Culture and Technology in the Twentieth Century*. New York: Viking Penguin, 1989.

Henson, H. Keith. "Memetics and the Modular Mind—Modelling the Development of Social Movements." *Analog* (August 1987) 29–42.

Horton, John, and Susan Mendus, eds. *Aspects of Toleration*. London: Methuen, 1985.

Inose, Hiroshi, and John R. Pierce. *Information Technology and Civilization*. New York: W. H. Freeman, 1984.

Kuhn, Thomas S. *The Structure of Scientific Revolutions*. 3d ed. Chicago: University of Chicago Press, 1996.

Naisbitt, John, and Patricia Aburdene. *Megatrends 2000: Ten New Directions for the 1990's*. New York: William Morrow, 1990.

Popper, K. R. *The Logic of Scientific Discovery*. London: Hutchinson, 1959.

Postman, Neil. "The Ideology of Machines." In *Technopoly: The Surrender of Culture to Technology*, 107–22. New York: Vintage Books, 1992.

Project Gutenberg. See www.prairienet.org/pg/.

Rogers, Everett M., and Judith K. Larsen. *Silicon Valley Fever—Growth of High Technology Culture*. New York: Basic Books, 1984.

Roszak, Theodore. *The Cult of Information*. New York: Random House, 1986.

Tavani, H., ed. *The Tavani Bibliography of Computing, Ethics, and Social Responsibility*. Palo Alto, CA: Computer Professionals for Social Responsibility January 15, 1997. See www.siu.edu/departments/coba/mgmt/iswnet/isethics/biblio/index.html.

Taylor, Richard. *Ethics, Faith and Reason*. Englewood Cliffs, NJ: Prentice-Hall, 1985.

11

A Christian Perspective on Cultural Anthropology

JOANNE L. PEPPER

WHAT IS ANTHROPOLOGY?

THE DISCIPLINE OF ANTHROPOLOGY is comprehensive—or *holistic*—in many respects. That is, anthropology consists of an all-embracing examination of human conditions couched in the broadest possible geographical and historical contexts. No aspect of human lifeways in prehistoric, historic, or contemporary societies is beyond its purview. Anthropology bridges the gulf between the sciences and the humanities because of its subject matter and methodology.

The field of anthropology includes four major sub-disciplines, namely: anthropological linguistics, archaeology, physical anthropology, and cultural anthropology. The unifying concern of these differing specializations is *humankind* and *culture* (in their origins and their variations through time and space).

Specifically, *anthropological linguistics* deals with the development of language itself, as well as language's role in the development of differentiation among human cultures. Linguistics attempts to reconstruct historical changes that have led to the formation of individual languages and families of languages. Also, linguistics is concerned with the way in which languages influence and are influenced by aspects of contemporary society, early discussions of which can be found in the work of Edward Sapir and Benjamin Whorf.[1] (For a fuller treatment of the essentials of

---

1. See Whorf, *Language, Thought and Reality*; as well as the work of his mentor, Sapir, *Language: An Introduction to the Study of Speech.*

205

linguistics as well as a Christian perspective thereon, see Michael Walrod's chapter later in this collection.)

Archaeology studies the social and cultural evolution of ancient civilizations. Analyzing the remains of past human activity recovered from on-site excavations is especially crucial in the work of this discipline. *Physical anthropology* seeks to describe the distribution of variations among contemporary human populations. It attempts to measure the relative contributions made by heredity, environment, and culture to human biology.

While archaeology directs its attention toward extinct or antiquarian societies, *cultural anthropology* focuses upon the dynamics of human interaction with and within culture. Careful attention is given to examining and explaining the processes by which worldview is formed and transmitted within given societies. Cultural anthropology attempts to account for how and why cultural change takes place, even in the face of deep-seated human belief and behavior. As well, cultural anthropology monitors the effect of such change upon individuals within society and upon society as a whole.

In addressing these issues, anthropology is at least partially interdisciplinary with psychology, sociology, and history. Contemporary anthropology borrows concepts from these fields as freely as it loans its own to them. The most essential contribution that anthropology makes in the social sciences—and also in religious studies—is the habit of viewing human phenomena cross-culturally, or studying the institutions of human society comparatively. Biblical Studies and History of Anthropology Professor Louise Lawrence of the University of Glasgow elaborates upon this point as follows:

> [Anthropology] begins with the simple, but effective, assumption that one type of behaviour can only be properly understood when it is placed among comparative examples of similar behaviours in other contexts and situations. Anthropologists observe the totality of relationships between people within a social unit. . . . They are characteristically "interpretive" in their methodology, conducting participant observation, description and comparison.[2]

In essence, then, anthropology is the social science that studies peoples, languages, and cultures. Relatively narrow and time-bounded "snap-

2. Lawrence, "Introduction—A Taste for the Other," 10.

shots" of a particular society or people group are frequently compared and contrasted with those of other societies, in order to develop analytical case studies that seek to deduce wider principles of human social interaction. Psychology, sociology, history, and even economics have specialized in observing, analyzing, and interpreting certain phases of the culture of western civilization. However, it is precisely beyond the limits of western horizons that anthropologists must see if they are to gain a significant understanding of the human condition.

WHAT IS CULTURE?

Culture may be defined as the system of integrated patterns of learned and shared beliefs and behaviors characteristic of the members of any society. It is a complete design for living for those members. Some anthropologists also distinguish between material and non-material culture. In this model, non-material culture consists of humankind's beliefs and patterns of behavior, while material culture consists of the artifacts created by the members of individual cultures.

Belief, the inner core of culture, defines and describes the deepest convictions of an individual. Belief many be conceptualized on three sublevels: knowledge, feeling, and values. While each of these dimensions aids individuals in the establishment of a personal worldview, they also create and maintain barriers that interfere with the individual's ability to effectively communicate and interact across cultures. In the cognitive (knowledge) level of culture, a lack of sensitive interchange between individuals of different societies is likely to lead to confusion and misunderstanding about what are "logical" conceptual frameworks and *a priori* assumptions about the nature of life and existence. On the affective (feeling) level, cross-cultural confusion is manifested by ethnocentrism, the action of rating and scaling the cultural traits of another society in comparison to our own in such a way that our culture is always seen in the more favorable light. A normal emotional response most people experience when they confront another culture for the first time, ethnocentrism provides individuals with the belief that their culture is logical, desirable, and "civilized," while other cultures are presumably lacking the same levels of sensibility or refinement. On the evaluative level of culture, societal and interpersonal clashes occur when individuals attempt to reinforce their ethnocentrism with strong approval or disapproval of the beliefs and behaviors of others. Problems of cultural interpretation arise because individuals tend to judge the unknown before they have learned to understand or appreciate it. This prejudging causes many difficulties in relating responsibly to other people groups. Prejudice—a behavior often born out of ignorance or fear—closes the door to further understanding and communication between cultures. As a matter of fact, anthropological research confirms that such premature judgments are usually false.

Anthropology points to the fact that in the face of increasing globalization, both cultural borrowing and cultural variety are universal phenomena. Those persons desiring to interact as "world citizens" must acknowledge and seek to understand differing perceptions of reality, differing preferences for social organization and lifestyle, and differing values for judging what is and what is not worthwhile in life, as expressed through the world's varied cultures.

WHAT ARE THE FUNCTIONS AND RELEVANCE OF CULTURAL ANTHROPOLOGY FOR THE SOCIAL SCIENTIST?

Anthropology is committed to the use of the scientific method that most other sciences employ. However, because it is a social science, anthropology also includes specific techniques for learning about people and their cultures. Scientific tools for such investigations are controlled experiments, surveys, case studies, interviews, and participant-observation studies.

The careful study of anthropology and its application within the realm of the social sciences can provide significant insight into the meaning of both individual and collective human behavior. Through anthropological research, source materials and analyses of specific societies are made possible. Anthropology also provides an orientation to the relevance of symbolic communication within societies. While it does not provide prescriptive means whereby all barriers to intercultural communication may be overcome, anthropology can point out and help resolve some of the major difficulties inherent in cross-cultural interaction. For the individual, the study of different cultures provides a much better understanding of one's own culture. From a societal point of view, the understanding of different cultures can contribute to the solution of pressing social problems.

WHAT ARE THE FUNCTIONS AND RELEVANCE OF CULTURAL ANTHROPOLOGY FOR THE CHRISTIAN?

As the most encompassing of the social sciences, anthropology presents the Christian with holistic perceptions of peoples and cultures. Anthropology studies social structures in relation to the intertwined roles played by government, religion, economics, education, and family. This emphasis upon the integration of all facets of culture supports the Christian contention that religion cannot be isolated or marginalized from the mainstream of life. While the tendency to compartmentalize religious practice and make it peripheral to everyday life is an ostensible characteristic of North American culture, this is not typical of most other societies in the world. When the Christian asserts that religious belief and devotion are to be the central defining characteristics of human existence, he or she stands on firm ground, anthropologically speaking.

Furthermore, the discipline of anthropology has a great deal to offer the Christian church and its leaders in a time of rapid social change. Anthropology stresses the necessity of understanding the dynamics of culture and worldview change as a prerequisite to meaningful interaction within any society. This aids Christians in preparing to be effective as "salt and light" within their social sphere, for it stresses the fact that all professional religious advocates (pastors, priests, evangelists, missionaries, teachers) should take seriously the far-reaching ramifications of the changes that they seek to introduce, by way of religious persuasion, to a society. Anthropology emphasizes that it is neither logical nor ethical to say "I disagree" (with a cultural belief or practice) before being able to assert, with integrity, "I understand."

Also, anthropology can serve as a yardstick for measuring the accurate, sensitive, and effective transmission of the gospel message. The communication of Christianity based upon a perceptive understanding of a culture can provide the means by which biblical truth may be shared in a meaningful context with the people of a given society. Although a study of cultural anthropology will not guarantee that a message communicated to any group of people will be accepted, anthropology helps to guarantee that the message, when communicated, is likely to be understood. As such, anthropological insights assist Christian communicators in their quest to make contact with their target audiences, helping to stimulate members of a given culture to consider the claims of Christ.[3]

Indeed, it is difficult to imagine a life vocation in which a knowledge of anthropological concepts and data would not be beneficial for Christians. As one studies humans, not only as *spiritual* but as *cultural* beings, more is learned about God. Humans are created in the image of God. Christ was incarnated into a human culture. It is apparent both from Scripture and from history that God uses human cultural relationships to reveal himself to his creation. As human culture is studied, it is possible to gain a fuller understanding of the nature and purposes of a deity who delights in endless variety among both natural and human phenomena.

TOWARDS A BIBLICAL WORLDVIEW: BIBLICAL AUTHORITY AND CULTURAL RELATIVITY

The anthropological concept of "cultural relativity" is the position that ideas, actions, and objects should be evaluated by the norms and values of the culture of which they are part, rather than by another culture's norms and values. Also, this principle holds that the norms and values of each culture should be evaluated in the light of the culture to which they belong. Cultural relativists would maintain that "good" cultural traits are those which prove to be well adapted to a particular situation, while those that are "bad" are so labeled because they are not so adapted.[4]

While the majority of both Christian and non-Christian anthropologists hold to the position of cultural relativity, at least as a methodological approach, there has been some criticism of the position. For example,

---

3. Take, for example, the case study of Phil Parshall, an American missionary who worked for several years among Muslims in Bangledesh. After several seasons of fruitless and frustrating ministry among his target group, Parshall took daring steps of cultural contextualization. Buttressed by his training in anthropology and cross-cultural communication, Parshall began to rethink, reorder, and reorganize his entire mission structure. He concentrated on developing Christian *forms* that paralleled Muslim symbols and practices, while maintaining the integral biblical *meaning* of Christian theology. As the noted missionary statesman Donald McGavran was renowned for saying, the greatest barriers to Christian conversion are not *theological* but *social*. It is not so much that Christ has been tried and found wanting—it is that he has not been truly tried at all! See McGavran, *Understanding Church Growth*; and Parshall, *New Paths for Muslim Evangelism: Evangelical Approaches to Contextualization*.

4. See two works of Franz Boas, who championed this viewpoint: *Race, Language and Culture* and *The Limitations of the Comparative Method of Anthropology*.

the concept itself is said to be ethnocentric, reflecting the western bias of judging something to be "good" only if it is functional and efficient (by western standards, of course!). In addition, cultural relativity would seem to have little value in resolving cross-cultural conflict. If two equally "good" cultures are in competition or conflict, the only way to arrive at conclusions about which culture is "better" may well be to see which people group succeeds in establishing a cultural or military domination over its rival. Pushed to the extreme, cultural relativity would seem to suggest that might makes right, or that the doctrine of the survival of the fittest is moral. Indeed, it might be argued that cultural relativity leads to ethical relativity. That is, cultural relativism precludes the belief that some values may be good for all humanity. To the Christian social scientist, cultural relativism raises issues that call for both sensitivity and caution when researching and/or ministering in a cross-cultural setting. With respect to the latter context, anthropologist Louise Lawrence reminds her readers that "[t]raditionally . . . anthropologists [are] very skeptical of missionaries, not least because they [are] seen to disregard native worldviews and pursue colonialist strategies and initiate cultural change."[5] As indicated above, a fundamental tenet of this social science discipline is that the anthropologist is typically expected to be the objective observer of a people group's behavior, rather than someone promoting cultural change among that group. Lawrence does comment, however, on how an understanding of anthropological principles can do much to help missionaries gain in-depth understanding of the culture in which they are working.

It might appear that cultural relativity is in strong opposition to the concept of biblical authority. Can Christians claim a universally applicable morality in the face of obvious diversity among the world's cultures? Christian anthropologists would say "Yes." However, certain factors must modify this assertion. To begin with, it is important to remember that all cultures are relative, even those in which the Scriptures were written. Just as an anthropologist is careful not to absolutize a cultural form in his or her own culture and make that the standard for other cultures, so the Christian anthropologist must be careful not to absolutize the cultural forms found in the Scriptures and make them the standard for all other cultures. Although the "seeds" of the gospel may be planted by a sower from but a single homogeneous cache, the environmental conditions of

---

5. Lawrence, *Reading with Anthropology*, 23–24.

different "gardens" will determine the particular physical adaptations of the "plants" that are ultimately produced. That is, the *message* of the gospel is supracultural (i.e., "above culture," speaking universally to all peoples), but the cultural *forms* in which the message exists are not sacred.

Furthermore, it is important to realize that the members of any culture will emphasize certain teachings of the Scriptures, while members of another culture will tend to emphasize other aspects of biblical doctrine congruent with their societal concerns. Therefore, a working knowledge of culture and its role in human society is important to both interpreting the Bible in the light of its cultures as well as in applying biblical principles cross-culturally to people living today. As Lawrence asserts, "Cross-cultural understanding is needed like never before, in this post-September 11th 2001 world. Anthropology can teach us that we too are 'others,' culturally strange and different in the perspectives of many thousands across the globe."[6]

Christian anthropologists would contend that biblical authority and cultural relativity can be integrated concepts. Indeed, it may be argued that only a person who holds to biblical authority can truly practice cultural relativity and yet maintain a commitment to universal morality. That is, since no person is free of the constraints and ethnocentric biases of culture, the values of a person's culture will always influence the determination of what is "good" or adaptive in a culture. However, the position of biblical authority makes possible the potential for a non-biased cultural relativity. This is so because the basis for what is good does not come from the values of any one culture but rather from the supra-cultural principles found in God's Word.

WORKS CITED

Boas, Franz. *The Limitations of the Comparative Method of Anthropology*. New York: Free Press, 1966.

———. *Race, Language and Culture*. New York: Macmillan, 1940.

Lawrence, Louise J. "Introduction—A Taste for 'The Other': Interpreting Biblical Texts Anthropologically." In *Anthropology and Biblical Studies: Avenues of Approach*, edited by Louise J. Lawrence and Mario I. Aguilar, 9–25. Leiden: Deo, 2004.

———. *Reading with Anthropology: Exhibiting Aspects of New Testament Religion*. Milton Keynes, UK: Paternoster, 2005.

McGavran, Donald A. *Understanding Church Growth*. Grand Rapids, MI: Eerdmans, 1970.

6. Lawrence, "Introduction—A Taste for 'The Other,'" 20.

Parshall, Phil. *New Paths for Muslim Evangelism: Evangelical Approaches to Contextualization.* Grand Rapids, MI: Baker, 1984.

Sapir, Edward. *Language: An Introduction to the Study of Speech.* New York: Harcourt & Brace, 1921.

Whorf, Benjamin L. *Language, Thought and Reality.* New York: John Wiley, 1956.

FOR FURTHER READING

Bowie, Fiona. *The Anthropology of Religion: An Introduction.* 2d ed. Malden, MA: Blackwell, 2006.

Cannell, Fenella, ed. "Introduction." In her *The Anthropology of Christianity*, 1–50. Durham: Duke University Press, 2006.

Conn, Harvie M. *Eternal Word and Changing Worlds: Theology, Anthropology, and Mission in Trialogue.* Grand Rapids, MI: Zondervan, 1984.

Grunlan, Stephen A., and Marvin K. Mayers. *Cultural Anthropology: A Christian Perspective.* 2d ed. Grand Rapids, MI: Academie Books, 1988.

Hefner, Robert W., ed. *Conversion to Christianity: Historical and Anthropological Perspectives on a Great Transformation.* Berkeley: University of California Press, 1993.

Hesselgrave, David J. *Communicating Christ Cross-culturally: An Introduction to Missionary Communication.* 2d ed. Grand Rapids, MI: Zondervan, 1991.

Hiebert, Paul G. *Anthropological Insights for Missionaries.* Grand Rapids, MI: Baker, 1985.

Howell, Brian. "The Anthropology of Christianity: Beyond Missions and Conversion: A Review Essay." *Christian Scholar's Review* 34.3 (2005) 353–62.

Kraft, Charles H. *Anthropology for Christian Witness.* Maryknoll, NY: Orbis Books, 1996.

Luzbetak, Louis J. *The Church and Cultures: New Perspectives in Missiological Anthropology.* Maryknoll, NY: Orbis Books, 1988.

Mayers, Marvin K. *Christianity Confronts Culture: A Strategy for Crosscultural Evangelism.* Grand Rapids, MI: Academie Books, 1987.

Naugle, David K. "A Disciplinary History of 'Worldview' II: The Social Sciences." In his *Worldview: The History of a Concept*, 238–49. Grand Rapids, MI: Eerdmans, 2002.

Nida, Eugene A. *Customs and Cultures.* Pasadena, CA: William Carey Library, 1975.

Richardson, D. "Do Missionaries Destroy Cultures?" In *Perspectives on the World Christian Movement: A Reader*, edited by Ralph Winter and Steven C. Hawthorne, 482–93. 3d ed. Pasadena, CA: William Carey Library, 1992.

Smalley, William A, ed. *Readings in Missionary Anthropology II.* Pasadena, CA: William Carey Library, 1978.

Smith, Donald K. *Creating Understanding: A Handbook for Christian Communication across Cultural Landscapes.* Grand Rapids, MI: Zondervan, 1992.

Taylor, Mark C. *Beyond Explanation: Religious Dimensions in Cultural Anthropology.* Macon, GA: Mercer University Press, 1986.

12

A Christian Perspective on Economics

Senyo Adjibolosoo

INTRODUCTION

IN AN ATTEMPT TO present economics to others who may never have had anything to do with the subject, it is very important to first establish the meaning of the subject. Different economists have coined a series of reasonable definitions for economics. Samuelson, for example, lists the following as possible definitions:

1. Economics is the study of those activities that involve money and exchange transactions among people.

2. Economics is the study of how people choose to use scarce or limited productive resources (land, labor, capital goods such as machinery, and technical knowledge) to produce various commodities (such as wheat, beef, overcoats, concerts, roads, and yachts) and to distribute them to various members of society for their consumption.

3. Economics is the study of people in their ordinary business of life, earning and enjoying a living.

4. Economics is the study of how humankind goes about the business of organizing its consumption and production activities.

5. Economics is the study of wealth.[1]

More often than not, individual economists usually prefer one of these definitions for teaching/study purposes. Yet if these five different definitions of the discipline are pieced together, a more complete descrip-

---

1. Samuelson, *Economics: An Introductory Analysis*, 5.

tion of the subject emerges. Economics can be seen as the social science that studies humanity's attempts to distribute scarce resources to achieve maximum returns. It is principally concerned about alternative uses of scarce resources in order to satisfy human wants and/or needs. Mansfield explains the importance of a basic grasp of this discipline as follows:

> [E]conomics helps us to understand the nature and organization of our society, the arguments underlying many of the great public issues of the day, and the operation and behavior of business firms and other economic decision-making units. To perform effectively and responsibly as citizens, administrators, workers, or consumers, most people need to know some economics.[2]

A careful analysis of economics reveals that as a social science, the discipline is mainly concerned with four key problems that face all people. First, economics is concerned with what is to be produced for society and how it will be produced (the resource allocation issue). Second, the discipline concerns itself with what is consumed and by whom (the issue of distribution). Third, economics deals with the problems of inflation and unemployment. That is, there is a need to know about the level of employment and also what general price levels are (i.e., very high or very low). Fourth, the discipline is concerned with how the productive capacity of an economy changes over time (economic growth and development).

Central to all these economic problems are the issues of scarcity and choice. Economists argue that although the needs, desires, and wants of men and women are numerous, the means (i.e., resources) for achieving/attaining these needs/desires/wants are very limited. Thus, one basic and binding consequence of scarcity for humanity is that every desirable thing cannot be easily acquired at the same point in time. For example, suppose that you have just finished high school and have planned to go to college or university to study economics. In order to have a good experience, you decide that you need books, a television set, a DVD, a ghetto-blaster, a computer, recreation and/or entertainment money, an iPod, a cellular phone, a table, and a desk.

Even though all these may make your stay in the university enjoyable and memorable (and possibly short-lived!), your financial resources will likely not allow you to acquire all of these items at the time of your entrance to the university. Therefore, you will need to draw up a priority

2. Mansfield, *Microeconomics*, 1.

list. On this list, the most pressing (i.e., items you cannot do without) have to be listed first, then the less pressing ones (i.e., those you can do without or at least postpone). Thus, your list becomes what economists call the scale of preference, which then serves as your guide (or priority list) as you go about acquiring these items.

As you can see, you have to behave this way because your resource (i.e., money) for acquiring these needs/wants is scarce. Thus, the central problem of economics, scarcity, forces you to make choices among many alternatives. Also, when you make the choice, you may impose some non-monetary costs upon yourself. That is, your decision to buy the television set may preclude you from purchasing the cellular telephone. Alternatively, if you decide to buy the cellular telephone, you might have to go to university without a DVD player for your television set. In a sense, your decision to purchase any one of the items listed on your scale of preference likely makes you forego some other item(s). This cost you incur due to the choice you make is usually referred to in economics as "the opportunity cost." It does not necessarily have anything to do with the true value and/or cost of items. For example, when you finally decided that you would buy the cellular telephone and go without the DVD player for a short period of time, then the opportunity cost for buying the cellular telephone was the DVD player you had to forego (even though both items might have different monetary values).

Another illustration of the opportunity cost concept can be drawn from how you use your time resources. If you decide to go and play a game of squash at 2:10 in the afternoon instead of attending my lecture on the principles of economics, the opportunity cost to you for playing squash during that time is the economics lecture you miss (or forego). This concept is very useful to us as we contemplate making decisions. Economists use it to remind us that because our resources are scarce, every choice we make imposes an opportunity cost on us. It is always very crucial for us (as individuals or nations) to learn to use our scarce resources prudently (i.e., being good stewards of our scarce resources and means).

Since every individual or country is confronted by the problem of scarcity, great consideration is usually given to the development of procedures and/or mechanisms for dealing with the scarcity problem. In human history two major economic systems have been developed to help deal with scarcity and the four key economic problems described above: capitalism and socialism. Each of these systems is just a means and/or method for providing answers to the basic economic problem of scarcity. Each system makes rules and regulations concerning property ownership and how property can be used to improve the welfare of society. Whereas capitalism, by subscribing to the freedom of the individual principle, allows for private ownership, socialism normally does not.

That is, capitalism (also known as the free enterprise economic system, the market economic system, or the *laissez-faire* system) is the economic system that encourages people to own property and the various means of production privately. In this system, the means of production (i.e., land, labor, capital, technology, etc.) are mostly privately owned. Resource allocation is usually accomplished without any massive central government direction. Ideally, all individuals, both consumers and producers, independently pursue their own self-interests, making their own decisions to either maximize satisfaction or protect their interests in society. These individual decisions are indirectly coordinated by the price mechanism. In a sense, an invisible hand (or an impartial observer) is said to lead individuals to act in such a way that by providing for themselves, they will unconsciously produce an improved society in general. Since such a system is said to uphold individual liberty, it is subscribed to by most Western democracies.

On the other hand, socialist or command economic systems are planned and usually centralized. They do not necessarily allow for private ownership. The means of production are normally owned by the government. Unlike the free market system, where private individuals make production and consumption decisions, socialism is based on extensive planning by government. For example, in the former Soviet Union, Gosplan was the government arm that gave oversight to a complicated system of production. This system was subscribed to by mostly eastern European countries and some countries in Asia and Africa. Since it almost inevitably stifles individual liberty, Western democracies have usually looked down upon it. Of course, we need to be aware that some countries have had great success with some variations of socialism (e.g., the Scandinavian countries).

There is, however, a third alternative, usually referred to as a mixed economic system. This system, a blend of capitalism and socialism, combines elements of both private and public property ownership. As a matter of fact, few countries can boast of being either purely capitalist or purely socialist. Most countries, by combining elements of capitalism and social-ism, are more accurately described as mixed economic systems.

In an attempt to deal with the economic problem of scarcity, each of these three economic systems attempts to serve as a means for achiev-ing desirable ends for individuals and their countries. Prominent among these desirable ends are:

1. The attainment of an increasing standard of living

2. Maintaining and protecting the environment

3. Achieving reasonable economic growth and progress

4. Economic stability—the attainment of full employment with little or no inflation

5. A favorable balance of payments with the rest of the world

6. Efficient resource allocation

7. Economic freedom for every person

The pursuit of these goals usually generates a lot of conflicts and de-bates in that while a country may wish to achieve one or a group of these goals, other objectives may be jeopardized. Similarly, individuals have dif-ferent preferences. These differences sometimes generate a great deal of heated debate among politicians and different interest groups.

ASPECTS AND BRANCHES: THE CONTENT OF ECONOMICS

Positive versus Normative Economics

Economists have for many years tried to show that their discipline is a science. However, as noted by Lipsey and others,

> [T]he success of modern science rests partly on the ability of scientists to separate their views on what does happen from their views on what they would like to happen. . . . Distinguishing what is true from what we would like to be true depends on recognizing the difference between positive and normative statements. Positive statements concern what is, was, or will be. Normative statements concern what one believes ought to be. Positive statements, asser-tions, or theories may be simple or complex, but they are basically about matters of fact.[3]

3. Lipsey et al., *Economics*, 18.

While disagreements over positive statements can be dealt with by appealing to real life observable data and/or facts, this is not easily so with normative statements because the latter are colored by our values, religious beliefs, and cultural context. Similarly, while most positive statements can be tested, normative statements cannot always be tested. The statement "When money supply increases, interest rates decline" is a positive statement because any disagreements over its validity can easily be tested by appealing to real life data and observations about money supply and interest rates. On the other hand, the assertion "Every government ought to see to it that every citizen is well cared for" is a normative statement. Any disagreements over the validity of this statement cannot be easily settled and/or resolved, for obvious reasons. The demarcation of statements as either positive or normative automatically divides economics into positive economics and normative economics.

Positive Economics

The *HarperCollins Dictionary of Economics* defines positive economics as follows:

> [T]he study of what can be verified rather than what ought to be. For example, the statement that a cut in personal taxes increases consumption spending in the economy is a statement that can be confirmed or refuted by examining available empirical evidence on the effects of taxation on spending. Positive economics seeks to identify relationships between economic variables, quantify and measure these relationships, and make predictions of what will happen if a variable changes.[4]

The pursuit of this kind of economics forces economists to concern themselves solely with variables that can easily be measured and/or quantified. This desire to *scienticize* economics has led to an increased use of mathematics in the discipline. It has also narrowed the focus of many modern economists.

Normative Economics

The *HarperCollins Dictionary of Economics* describes normative economics as the study of what ought to be in economic theory, rather than what is provable. For example, the statement that people who earn high

4. Pass et al., *HarperCollins Dictionary of Economics*, 397.

incomes ought to pay more income tax than people who earn low incomes is a normative statement. Normative statements reflect people's subjective value judgments of what is good or bad, depending on ethical considerations such as fairness rather than on strictly economic rationales.

Normative economic analysis has been frequently ignored by many modern economists because they are mainly interested in the mathematicization of economic theory. In order to formulate and develop economic theories, some economists maintain that the relevant variables must be quantifiable. Value judgments that affect individual economic behavior are swept under the carpet as if they did not exist. Many modern economists, by concentrating on positive economics, have often exorcized ethics—moral, religious, or cultural principles—out of economics. As we shall see later when discussing a Christian perspective on economics, modern economic thought often tends to be barren because, by focusing on positive economics, it ignores a whole dimension of economic analysis that takes into account ethical value judgments.

Microeconomics and Macroeconomics

The prefix *micro* implies small or little, whereas the prefix *macro* designates large or big. The use of these prefixes does not imply that economics is either a small or a large discipline. Rather, they denote what each particular demarcation of economics concerns itself with.

Microeconomics

This branch of economics concerns itself with the study of the behavior of firms (producers) and households (consumers) and the determination of prices. Microeconomics studies the utility-maximization behavior of households, for example. It suggests that consumers maximize utility by using their income to buy those goods and services they like. In a sense, it is an inquiry into the allocation of scarce personal resources. It also studies the profit-maximizing behavior of firms. Firms use scarce factor resources in the best ways to achieve efficiency. By so doing, they are able to maximize profits—usually referred to as *Price Theory* because this phenomenon concerns itself with the determination of prices (for goods, services, and inputs).

Microeconomics, by focusing on the concepts of demand and supply, is able to explain how the prices of goods, services, and inputs are determined in the free-market system. In addition, it helps us both to comprehend how frequent changes in market-determined prices and individual incomes affect consumer and producer behavior and to develop powerful theories that have strong predictive powers. For example, microeconomic theory is capable of predicting the impacts on prices of goods, services, and inputs when demand and supply conditions change in the marketplace. Its concept of the price mechanism provides insight into the behavior of consumers and producers.

Macroeconomics

This branch of economics studies aggregate economic behavior, investigating how the whole economy works in general. In its analysis macroeconomic theory attempts to understand and explain the reasons for changes in the levels of national output (or income), employment/unemployment, and the general price level (inflation). Macroeconomists are concerned with the formulation of theories to explain the fluctuations in these economic variables. They also try to put forward theories to explain how changes in each of these variables affect a nation's welfare. Macroeconomists depend on aggregate demand and supply tools to explain how changing conditions in the world affect the whole economy.

Keynesian economic theory (named after John Maynard Keynes, an important English economist) subscribes to the use of macroeconomic policy to solve any disequilibrium in the economy. These policies are grouped into two categories: fiscal and monetary. While fiscal policy is solely concerned with changing taxes and government expenditures in order to influence national output (income), prices (inflation), and employment levels in the economy, monetarists advocate monetary policy, which suggests that the government must change the size of the money supply in order to influence these variables. Unending debates occur among all shades and brands of macroeconomists regarding the success or failure ratio of such policies. In macroeconomics we also study money, banking, government budget deficits and their impact (on both individuals and a country's economy as a whole), exchange rates, and balance of payments issues.

Other Branches of Economics

Microeconomics and macroeconomics are not only two simple demarcations of economics but also the core of economic theory. Other branches of the discipline draw heavily on theories developed in these main components of the field. Space does not permit more than a brief listing of some of the other branches of economics: (a) history of economic thought; (b) monetary economics; (c) industrial organization; (d) mathematical economics; (e) econometric theory; (f) international trade; (g) economic development; (h) population economics; and (i) economics of specific fields, such as forestry, transportation, fisheries, labor, and many others.

A CHRISTIAN WORLDVIEW IN ECONOMICS

As noted earlier, economic and business activities permeate every sphere of our lives, for we devote a reasonably large proportion of our discretionary time trying to achieve certain economic goals and/or meet certain economic needs. People's needs generally include the desire for self-actualization, self-esteem, belonging, safety, and the ability to house, clothe and feed (i.e., meet the physical needs of) themselves and their dependants. It is the legitimate desire to meet these needs that moves an individual to engage in business and economic activities in order to make money. Self-interest is clearly a great motivator of human economic/business behavior. A basic question is whether or not these activities should be pursued for their own sake—for the individual's own self-actualization. Christian economist Charles Wilber, for example, who has taught at both the American University in Washington, DC, and the University of Notre Dame, notes that one could consider the primacy of self-interest as an evidence of human fallenness.[5]

Wilber's view is, however, only partially correct, for the simple reason that self-interested behavior must be viewed from two distinct perspectives. First, when self-interest pursuits are subjected to and are in line with the dictates of God's universal principles, they are in consonance with God's desires for our lives and expectations of us. Viewed in this light, there is nothing wrong with our pursuit of self-interests in our everyday lives. (Ensuring that such basic necessities as food, clothing, and shelter are secured for ourselves and our dependants, for example, is one type of

5. Wilber, "Teaching Economics while Keeping the Faith," 3.

self-interest that is entirely legitimate.) The pursuit of our self-interests in this case does not reflect human fallenness.

On the other hand, when self-interests are pursued on the basis of acute personal greed and ruthlessness, they contravene the dictates of God's universal principles and his expectations of us as our Father in Heaven. When our self-interests are carried out in this manner, they truly reflect human fallenness. Though Adam Smith, the Father of Economics, made this distinction clear in his book, *The Theory of Moral Sentiments*, in 1759, most scholars have missed it. We need to be aware of this distinction so we do not make the mistake of thinking that every kind of self-interested pursuit violates universal divine principles and, therefore, is wrong. When we think in this manner, we will be guilty of what economists refer to as the fallacy of composition.

It is very necessary, then, to recognize the usefulness of economics in understanding many aspects of what it means to be human. Another Christian economist, J. P. Wogaman, notes:

> [E]conomics is of critical importance to the whole human enterprise. It involves our access to goods and services without which we would perish, along with most of the other things needed to enrich and ennoble—as well as degrade—humanity. It is inconceivable that humankind, placed on this limited planet as it is, could ever be able to ignore economics altogether—although there might come some happy time in the future when abundance would so overtake scarcity as to make competition for scarce goods less a preoccupation. Plainly we are not there yet; and even if that day of abundance should arrive we would doubtless find that much of life still must revolve around what to do with and about economic goods and services.[6]

As Christians, we must not, therefore, leave the field of economics to people operating solely from secular presuppositions. We need to allow the Lord to use us to help others realize the great contributions the Christian faith can make towards developing and improving modern economic science in both theory and practice.

I would like to discuss several elements of a Christian perspective on economics, based on biblical principles, by applying normative economic analyses to an imaginary Christian community. Economics professor James Halteman uses this approach as the underlying thesis for his

6. Wogaman, *Economics and Ethics*, 3.

recent book, explaining his rationale as follows: "[T]he economics of the Bible can best be understood in the context of a community of faith. . . . Market capitalism can deliver goods and services in amazing quantities, but it cannot guarantee caring communities that sustain [both] body and spirit."[7] He goes on to argue—and I would heartily endorse this—that Christian believers should also attempt to infiltrate and positively influence the secular society of which they are necessarily a part by practicing such Christian economic behaviors as restrained consumption, concern for the poor and disadvantaged, respect for and stewardship of creation, and so forth.[8]

Craig Gay, in his very perceptive analysis of both positive and negative effects of money in Western market economies, is even more outspoken about Christians' frequently unreflective adoption of secular economic values when he states, "The capitalist process delivers certain material and political benefits . . . but at the cost of all meaning and belief that extends very far beyond creature comforts and strictly material progress." Indeed, he warns that capitalism "buttresses the plausibility of secularism, materialism, utilitarianism and, ultimately, nihilism."[9]

It goes without saying that though this pronouncement is a powerful indictment against us as humans, we must also keep in mind that the capitalist system is an inanimate economic organization. As such, it has no life of its own. The life it has is what we humans give to it. Viewed in this light, the real problem of the capitalist economic system is not necessarily inherent in it as an economic system *per se*. Instead, the problems evident in the operation of the capitalist economic system are the result of severe human factor decay. This human depravity is what we also refer to as the fallen aspect of our being human.[10]

This normative analytical approach will allow us to postulate how issues *should* be seen and/or how human behavior *ought* to proceed when considering economic principles from a biblical perspective. Since every economic and/or business activity involves dealings with other people, it is very important to establish relevant and workable rules of conduct regarding such activities and contractual arrangements. These stipulations

7. Halteman, *Clashing Worlds of Economics and Faith*, 10–11.

8. Ibid., 174–80.

9. Gay, *Cash Values: Money and the Erosion of Meaning in Today's Society*, 61.

10. See Adjibolosoo, *Human Factor in Developing Africa*, *Human Factor in Leadership Effectiveness*, and *Developing Civil Society*.

have to speak to and deal with, among other factors, the inappropriateness of totally self-interested behavior. That is, in a Christian economic setting, individuals must learn to subject their self-interests to the interests of others, under the power and leading of the Holy Spirit. By so doing, these members of the community can learn to engage in economic activities with the view of not necessarily promoting their own self-interest at the expense of the welfare of others, but also recognizing that they are stewards of the resources entrusted to them by the Creator and Owner of this world. They must learn to manage these resources in prudent ways.

In a Christian economic community, producers and consumers must not only be profit and utility maximizers respectively, but must also hold to Jesus' eternal principles concerning life and work. For example, a Christian economic context must make it possible for individuals to uphold and promote the mission of Jesus Christ in the world. When Jesus entered into this world two thousand years ago, he made it known to all his contemporaries that he was concerned about the welfare of the downtrodden, the helpless, the hopeless, the poor, hungry, afflicted, sick, terminally ill people, the oppressed, and the abused (see Luke 4:18–19).

In his lifetime, he ministered to these kinds of people, making sure that they were emotionally, psychologically, and/or physically healed. Most of his activities were designed to achieve these ends. His main desire of course was that people would seek the Kingdom of God and its righteousness (Matthew 6:33 and Romans 14:17). Similarly, Jesus did everything to the glory and honor of his Father in heaven (John 17:1–6). His all-consuming love for his Father and his property in this world meant that he could not do otherwise but glorify his Father in everything he did. Jesus did not seek to exploit and/or manipulate anyone. Selflessness and a willingness to seek and promote the welfare of others were always strongly evident. Accordingly, meaningful Christian economic values should be based on Jesus' eternal principles of life, of which the following are especially relevant:

The Principle of God-Centeredness

As noted earlier, Jesus' life was solely God-centered. He did everything to the glory of God. In a Christian economic community, individuals must be encouraged to place God first in everything they do (1 Peter 4:11). Economic principles and theories must make individuals aware that they are responsible not only to themselves and society for their economic and business activities, but also ultimately to God (Ecclesiastes 12:13–14). God's role in the life of people must be paramount in this type of economic setting. Things must not be done as if God does not exist or at least does not matter. In addition, people in this economic community must let others know the ability and willingness of God to care for them when they cast all their cares upon him. The absence of this principle may cast doubts on the legitimacy of any economic community that purports to be Christian in orientation.

The Principle of the Greatest Commandment

Jesus taught that we must not only love God with all our heart, soul, and mind, but also love our neighbor as ourselves (Matthew 22:37–40). As a foundational principle for a Christ-centered economic group, this second principle allows for self-interested pursuits (behavior) subjected to the will and leadership of the Holy Spirit, but it also promotes altruistic behavior. In a Christian economic community, the love for both God and neighbor must serve as a moral compass to guide the economic and business activities of individuals. In contrast, as Wilber observes, secular economic theory generally conceives of people, at least in the West, as wanting to "maximize pleasure and minimize pain" and (as assuming) that "pleasure comes primarily from the consumption of goods and services"—that people, in short, are in essence materialistic, with "having" being superior to "being."[11]

Because the members of this imaginary Christian economic community love each other, they will be careful not to inflict harm on one another. They will always want to ensure that the stipulations of any contractual arrangements and/or agreements they participate in are carefully constructed to be not only useful to them and/or the rest of society but also acceptable to God. When this principle is closely adhered to, a Christian economic community will voluntarily foster and promote modern economic and business activities free of greed and extortion (1 Corinthians 6:10; Proverbs 15:27), overemphasis on self-enriching pursuits of material things to the detriment of the welfare of others (Luke 15:12; 1 Timothy 6:1–11), unjust economic relationships and contractual

11. Wilber, "Teaching Economics while Keeping the Faith," 15.

agreements (Micah 6:8), and swindling the means of sustenance away from others (Job 24:2–11; Exodus 22:25–27).

This concern for the welfare of others, not just ourselves, should flow out of a sense of gratitude to God for the abundance of his material blessings—especially for those of us living in North America. In many cases those blessings come to us in spite of, not necessarily because of, our economic decisions. Craig Gay makes reference to an important state- ment by Richard John Neuhaus about the importance of a thankful heart in response to God's bounty: "A theologically informed appreciation of economic life and the production of wealth should be marked by a sense of whimsy and wonder in the face of the fortuitous, contingent, chancy, and unpredictable realities of economic behavior." Gay goes on to remark that, in accordance with Christ's comments about the lilies of the field in Matthew 6, a Christian's approach to economic matters should be marked by a freedom from anxiety, emanating from a deep trust in God.[12]

The Principle of Justice

In this imaginary, ideal Christian economic community, the pursuit of equity and fairness must prevail. Every individual must be given what s/he is due. Our Lord's desire is that we deal with each other with complete justice and fairness (Psalm 82:3). If this principle were adhered to by all Christians, the great deal of inequity and injustice we see in our modern economic systems could easily be minimized. Any economic grouping that fails to encourage its members to pursue justice cannot qualify to be called Christian. Wilber comments that the Bible defines justice by how the powerless—widows, the homeless, the poor—are treated.[13]

Given that we are now living in what Marshall McLuhan described as a global village (in his *Understanding Media*), we as North American Christians cannot avoid an awareness of profound human need in the Third World, not just closer to home. When reassessing, in 1996, his very critical 1976 analysis of the significant economic gap between Christians in the West and most of the Third World, *Rich Christians in an Age of Hunger*, Ron Sider asserted that over one billion people still lived in des- perate poverty, with virtually no education, health care, or even enough

12. R. J. Neuhaus, "Wealth and Whimsy: On Economic Creativity," *First Things* (Aug./ Sept. 1990) 23–30, cited in Gay, *Cash Values*, 90.

13. Wilber, "Teaching Economics while Keeping the Faith," 10.

protein and other food to develop healthy bodies. That translates into massive global pain and anguish that could largely be prevented.[14]

The Principle of Stewardship and Service

A Christian understanding of economics must also be based on a commitment to stewardship and service. Economic and business activities must be directed to the service of God and one's fellow human beings. We are stewards of all resources that come into our possession since it is God who gives strength to acquire possessions and riches (Deuteronomy 8:17–20). It is only when people are willing to assist and/or serve others that they can realize what it means to serve the Lord with a true and sincere heart. In addition, our service to others is also to God and must therefore be cognizant of the prospect of eternal accountability and, hopefully, reward as faithful stewards (1 Corinthians 15:58; Matthew 25:31–46).

The Principle of Individual Freedom and Democracy

God forbids the oppression of others (Psalm 62:10). Since each individual is made in the image of God, s/he must be respected and treated as such. Whatever economic activities we find ourselves pursuing, we must always make sure that we do not do so at the expense of others' freedom. In a democratic way, we must give careful and reasonable consideration to the thoughts, activities, and functions of others. Our Christian economic outlook must promote this principle, the pursuit of which may, without contradiction, still support the idea of individual private property and the right to exist and be free. God not only hates those who oppress and kill but also punishes economic and business activities that perpetrate dehumanization (Psalm 72:4).

The Principle of Welfare Promotion

Christians also need to pursue their individual economic goals so as to promote the welfare of all, not just themselves. While Christian business entrepreneurs should not indulge in their activities to the detriment of the individual consumer, our imaginary Christian economic community should promote the establishment of government policies that are designed, pursued, and implemented with meticulous care so that they

14. Sider, "*Rich Christians in an Age of Hunger*—Revisited," 333.

do not hurt people. When governments lose track of the fact that their policies are to be developed for the welfare of citizens, they run into enormous problems. In modern government policy formulation and implementation planning, things are sometimes done without keeping people in mind. For example, governments may put policies in place in order to maximize future votes in the next election, even when it hurts another section of the society. A Christian economic community should encourage the development of government policy to avoid these pitfalls. Welfare payments and/or grants should be made available for those who need them (Deuteronomy 15:11). Chances of abuse should be effectively minimized.

Although these Christian principles are not exhaustive, their pursuit can lead to improvements for all in any economic system. In a secular system, these principles may be very difficult to implement. For this reason, those of us who crave for such a biblically-based economic community must be willing to be used of the Lord to advocate and be models of the proper conduct of our economic activities, whatever the context.

THE PRACTICAL RELEVANCE OF ECONOMICS

Economics permeates and saturates every sphere of our lives. Whatever your vocation, you daily face not only economic decisions and issues to deal with but also the problem of selecting and using your scarce resources in the best manner possible. Whether you are a government official or an individual who is engrossed in some other vocation or profession, you need to understand how the economy works and the various issues involved. Similarly, you also need to understand how our society is organized and how businesses and governments make decisions that impact your life.

Your basic knowledge of economics can help you follow most of the current issues of today's modern economy. Economics helps you understand the behavior of financial institutions, the gravity of poverty, the uses and abuses of riches, the importance of interest rates, the reasons behind why governments cannot do everything for their citizens, and why prices of goods, services, and materials change. This knowledge will also help you learn to use your own personal resources in the most efficient ways. In a sense, equipped with economic theory, one is able to critically analyze and assess daily behavior of consumers and producers in the marketplace. The study of economics enlightens one about the organization and types of economic and business activities in different parts of the world. Adequate knowledge of meaningful and productive opportunities encourages the best use of one's resources. Similarly, armed with basic knowledge in economic theory, one is able to understand the preferences of people, why they indulge in activities, the choices they make, how they spend their income and other resources, buying and selling behavior, decision-making under uncertainty and risks, and why an individual may want to exchange one item for another.

With such information, one can hardly deny that for every college and university student, the study of economics *should be obligatory*. Whatever discipline these students plan to specialize in, a basic knowledge of economics is a solid asset. Since no individual can escape economic issues and problems in his/her everyday life, it is important for one to acquire a basic economics education. As pointed out by Arthur Holmes,

> [A] considerable degree of specialization is of course appropriate in any major field of concentration . . . but the liberal arts college has no business producing narrow specialists who see no further than their laboratory, have no larger sense of responsibility and little understanding of science as an essentially human cultural undertaking.[15]

It is important, in short, for the Christian student to have some knowledge of other disciplines outside his/her own specialty.

Jobs and positions abound for economists. They are found in every sphere of a country's economy. Economists work in government, business, teaching, consultancies, research institutes, International Monetary Fund (IMF), the World Bank, and non-governmental organizations. In many instances, governments usually seek the opinions of economists before embarking upon elaborate national policies and projects.

CONCLUSION

Economics is not only an interesting academic discipline but also a very relevant and meaningful body of knowledge that can help us improve the situation of both ourselves and others. The careful study of economics and the application of the relevant knowledge gained can, if subject to the principles of God's Word, benefit humanity. As we become more and

15. Holmes, *Idea of a Christian College*, 35.

more aware of the finiteness of the earth's resources, we now realize that there is a dire need for conservation and very prudent utilization of these natural resources. Our knowledge in economics can lead to the design of policies that will help us know how to use these resources wisely. Since our lives depend on economic principles, we need to understand these principles so that we can use them to our best advantage—and for the benefit of others. The economic systems we have in the modern world do not seem to have the power to deal effectively with the major economic problems of the day. It is my firm belief that by subscribing to Christian economic principles, we would be able to deal effectively with some of these problems. Since economics permeates every aspect of our lives, it is a reasonable investment for every university student to take a few basic courses in this discipline. By so doing, we will all equip ourselves to deal biblically with everyday economic problems and issues of the modern world. May God help us to that end.

WORKS CITED

Adjibolosoo, Senyo. *Developing Civil Society: Social Order and the Human Factor.* London: Ashgate, 2006.

——. *The Human Factor in Developing Africa.* Westport, CT: Praeger, 1995.

——. *The Human Factor in Leadership Effectiveness.* Mustang, OK: Tate, 2005.

Gay, Craig M. *Cash Values: Money and the Erosion of Meaning in Today's Society.* Grand Rapids, MI: Eerdmans, 2004.

Halteman, James. *The Clashing Worlds of Economics and Faith.* Waterloo, ON: Herald Press, 1995.

Holmes, Arthur F. *The Idea of a Christian College.* Rev. ed. Grand Rapids, MI: Eerdmans, 1987.

Lipsey, R. G., D. Purvis, and P. O. Steiner. *Economics.* New York: HarperCollins, 1991.

Mansfield, E. *Microeconomics: Theory and Applications.* London: Norton, 1991.

McLuhan, Marshall. *Understanding Media: The Extensions of Man.* New York: McGraw-Hill, 1964.

Pass, Christopher, Bryan Lowes, Leslie Davis, and Sidney J. Kronish. "Positive Economics." In *The HarperCollins Dictionary of Economics,* 397. New York: HarperPerennial, 1991.

Samuelson, P. *Economics: An Introductory Analysis.* 5th ed. Toronto, ON: McGraw-Hill, 1961.

Sider, Ronald J. "*Rich Christians in an Age of Hunger*—Revisited." *Christian Scholar's Review* 26.3 (1996) 322–35.

Wilber, Charles K. "Teaching Economics while Keeping the Faith." In *Teaching as an Act of Faith: Theory and Practice in Church-Related Higher Education,* edited by Arlin C. Migliazzo, 3–20. New York: Fordham University Press, 2002.

Wogaman, J. P. *Economics and Ethics: A Christian Inquiry.* Philadelphia: Fortress Press, 1988.

FOR FURTHER READING

Bandow, Doug. "The Conundrum of Capitalism and Christianity." In *Wealth, Poverty, and Human Destiny*, edited by Doug Bandow and David L. Schindler, 307–45. Wilmington, DE: ISI Books, 2003.

Beed, Clive, and Cara Beed. "An Evangelical Christian Response to Naturalistic Social Science." *Christian Scholar's Review* 34.1 (2004) 21–41.

Claerbaut, David. "Economics: Some Christian Views on the 'Dismal' Science." In his *Faith and Learning on the Edge: A Bold New Look at Religion in Higher Education*, 295–306. Grand Rapids, MI: Zondervan, 2004.

Gay, Craig M. *With Liberty and Justice for Whom? The Recent Evangelical Debate over Capitalism*. Grand Rapids, MI: Eerdmans, 1991.

Grelle, B., and D. A. Krueger, eds. *Christianity and Capitalism: Perspectives on Religion, Liberalism and the Economy*. Chicago: Center for the Scientific Study of Religion, 1986.

Hay, D. A. *Economics Today: A Christian Critique*. Grand Rapids, MI: Eerdmans, 1989.

Jones, A. *Capitalism and Christians*. New York: Paulist Press, 1992.

Pemberton, P. L., and D. R. Finn. *Toward a Christian Economic Ethic*. Minneapolis: Winston Press, 1985.

Schlossberg, H., V. Samuel, and R. J. Sider, eds. *Christianity and Economics in the Post-Cold War Era*. Grand Rapids, MI: Eerdmans, 1994.

Sider, Ronald J. *Rich Christians in an Age of Hunger*. Rev. ed. Dallas: Word, 1997.

13

A Christian Perspective on English Literature

JOHN A. ANONBY

INTRODUCTION

WHILE I WAS IN the process of writing this chapter, a telephone call abruptly interrupted my reveries. "Is this Dr. Anonby?" a woman's voice inquired. I replied in the affirmative. "I am in desperate need of a neck treatment," she responded, "so I wonder if I can come in this after-noon?" I gently informed her that she had contacted the wrong kind of doctor.

This incident forcefully drew to my attention that my particular spe-cialization, English literature, had some limitations. I was more qualified to stretch minds and expand hearts than to treat necks. Other limitations must also be acknowledged. The intricate conventions of English gram-mar cannot easily be adapted to automotive mechanics or most other aspects of our highly industrialized and computerized age (though it *may* be helpful to understand English vocabulary when following instructions relating to the assembling of products of modern technology). The fact remains that expertise in English language and literature is not a trade but an art—an art that employs words as its medium of expression instead of pigments as in painting, notes as in music, or stone as in sculpture. The supreme Creator, God himself, has endowed human beings with creative propensities which reflect, in a small measure, his image in us. The wonder of spoken language (though it cannot treat necks) is that it has the capacity to stretch minds by allowing direct communication from one person to another or to an entire assembly or, by means of electronic devices, potentially to the entire world. Spoken language can also expand hearts by communicating words of comfort and joy. The wonder of written language is even greater, as legacies of ideas can be passed on from people who have disappeared into the mists of antiquity to generations yet unborn.

Literature frequently captures, in the words of the nineteenth-century literary giant, Matthew Arnold, "the best which has been thought and said in the world."[1] Particular forms of literary artistry have varied throughout the ages, with differing cultures expressing themselves in diverse forms. The ancient Hebrews reached their highest literary excellence in the lyric poetry we now categorize as the Psalms and in brilliant encapsulations of wise sayings known as the Proverbs. In the classical world of the Greeks, the genres (or types) of literary art that stood apart in their excellence were the dramatic forms of tragedy and comedy, as well as the long narrative heroic poem we define as the epic. The great tragedians of ancient Greece such as Aeschylus, Euripides, and Sophocles were largely unrivalled for 2,000 years, until the "Sweet swan of Avon," Shakespeare, appeared with such masterpieces as *Hamlet* and *King Lear*. *The Iliad* and *The Odyssey*, attributed to the great epic poet, Homer, have been models for envious emulators, of whom only a few geniuses such as Virgil in his *Aeneid*, Dante in his *Divine Comedy*, and Milton in his *Paradise Lost* can be considered serious contenders. The power of the proverb, so adeptly handled by the Hebrews, has been modestly tapped by the late eighteenth-century mystic, William Blake, in his *Auguries of Innocence*, but the laurel of acclaim could also go to the Ibo people of West Africa, whose rich oral tradition, spiced with pithy proverbs, has been conveyed by the brilliant Nigerian novelist, Chinua Achebe.

THE PRINCIPAL GENRES OF ENGLISH LITERATURE

English literature throughout the world has been dominated by four genres: poetry, drama, the short story, and the novel. Each of these artistic forms is characterized by some unique advantages as well as corresponding limitations.

Poetry

With the exception of the epic, poetry aspires towards brevity, compactness, resonance, and evocative imagery. Whether rhymed (as with much

---

1. Arnold, *Culture and Anarchy*, 6.

traditional poetry) or in the form of free verse (unrhymed and flexible, as in much modern poetry), a poem's excellence is inextricably tied to the power, sound, and imagery (word pictures) of a poet's judiciously selected vocabulary. A good poem unites sound with meaning, with every word in its proper place, like each stroke of the brush in a good painting.

Drama

Drama, powerfully blending verbal with visual effects (or spectacle), has traditionally taken one of two forms: comedy or tragedy. The former frequently elicits laughter and, on occasion, scorn; the central issues involve social expectation, with derision heaped on violators of social decorum and manners. Since customs in society are constantly in flux, comedies often tend to become outdated. Tragedy is a form of dramatic art that focuses on intensely serious concerns, often of an existential nature, bringing into sharp relief dilemmas that appear irresolvable. The precariousness of human existence, the harsh irony of circumstances beyond an individual's control, and the conflicting propensities for good and evil in people are explored in tragedy, arousing such emotions as fear and awe in the spectators.

The Short Story

The short story and the novel both demonstrate the power of prose narrative, but on differing scales. The short story, whether adventurous, psychological, or symbolic, relies on its capacity to produce an intense, single effect, its purpose being to penetrate deeply into a single incident or aspect of human experience, sometimes defined as a "slice of life." This art form has been attempted in many different cultures. Particularly influential short story writers were Edgar Allan Poe of the United States, Anton Chekhov of Russia, Guy de Maupassant of France, and Katherine Mansfield of New Zealand.

The Novel

If the short story can be defined as a "slice of life," the novel can presumably be considered an entire loaf. A novel, unlike the short story, tends to be panoramic, though the historical and geographical setting can be as broad or narrow as the author chooses. Regardless of its breadth, however, a good novel will likely funnel its plethora of incidents through the consciousness of a central character, or protagonist, who thereby becomes a pivotal unifying device in the novel. The potential power of the novel has been demonstrated in fascinating detail in a work by Canadian novelist Hugh MacLennan. In *Voices in Time*, he chillingly portrays a ruthlessly oppressive dictatorship that

> had not worried about ideas, knowing that there were so many ideas of all kinds floating around that they were bound to cancel each other out. But novels deal with individual lives, and they had hunted them down and destroyed them as though they were carriers of a plague.[2]

MacLennan's anti-utopian bureaucracy fails to eradicate all of these precious literary legacies, but it has nevertheless grasped a most significant point: much of what we know as civilization is embodied in the accumulated literary remnants of the ages.

THE VALUE OF LITERATURE

Literature as a "Vision of Life"

The value of literature is explicitly affirmed in Henry Zylstra's *Testament of Vision*, as cited by Professor Beatrice Batson in a 1968 essay entitled "The Christian and Modern Literature." Great authors, Zylstra asserted,

> are more than makers, that is fabricators, of stories: they are also seers and prophets. Such are the Hugos and Balzacs and Flauberts. . . . Such are the Goethes . . . the Kafkas and Manns. . . . Such are the Tolstoys and the Dostoevskis and the Turgenevs. Such in England are the Fieldings and Jane Austens and Scotts, the George Eliots and Thackerays. . . . And such in America are the Melvilles . . . and the William Faulkners. . . . To come from the *Moby Dick* of Melville . . . the *War and Peace* of Tolstoy, the *Brothers Karamazov* of Dostoevski . . . or yet again from *The Plague* of Camus . . . is to know that one has touched powerfully on life at many points. It is to have seen the chaos of life transmuted into the order of significant form. . . . To read such a novel is to have entered a universe comprehensive in scope and intensive in quality. It is to have confronted the moral issues of men, not in the skeleton of theory or the bones of principle, but in the flesh and body of concrete

---

2. MacLennan, *Voices in Time*, 123.

experience.... It is a vision of life profoundly seen, greatly embodied and valid.[3]

Literature as Vicarious Experience

In a similar vein, Ricke postulates that because of the brevity of our lives
and the narrowness of our own experiences in relation to the magnitude
of the world, our "eyes are not enough"; hence, our "encounter with literary texts widens our grasp of truth."[4] Exposure to significant literature is a
useful component in liberal education generally, which, as Arthur Holmes
contends, "provides an opportunity to steward life more effectively by becoming more fully a human person in the image of God, by seeing life
whole rather than fragmented, by transcending the provincialism of our
place in history, our geographic location, or our job."[5] The essential feature
of these citations is their affirmation of the vicarious value of encounters
with the experiences and impressions of other people, other minds, and
other times and places. On both an intellectual and an emotional level, perceptive readers can multiply their experiences; their understanding of the
human condition will not merely expand but will grow exponentially.

THE NATURE OF LITERATURE

Literature as Intrinsically Interdisciplinary

Of all the branches of the arts and sciences, literature is arguably the most
intrinsically interdisciplinary. Keeping in mind Batson's safeguard against
"the two extremes of studying the mechanics and hunting the 'message'"
since "literature is truth in vital form,"[6] let us briefly survey how wide-
arching the literary rainbows over the academic world really are.

As Philosophical Quest

We have noted how the art form of tragedy tends to depict humans in
their most acute dilemmas—encounters that raise crucial philosophical
questions about the meaning, purpose, or value of existence, or whether
the human quest for understanding can ever arrive at truth. Such ques-

3. Zylstra, *Testament of Vision*, 34.

4. Ricke, "Perspective, Dialogue, Interpretation," 9.

5. Holmes, *Idea of a Christian College*, 36.

6. Batson, "The Christian and Modern Literature," 34–35.

tions, central in philosophy, frequently appear in poetry, drama, short stories, and novels. When they do, these questions move us from the level of abstract theory into the very experiential pulse of the protagonists we encounter between the covers, as in Camus' *The Plague* and Kafka's *The Trial*. Not only our minds but our hearts are engaged in the process.

It is precisely these questions that biblical revelation, with its proclamation of the hope offered in Christ, seeks to address. A while ago, bumper stickers displaying the slogan, "Christ is the Answer," appeared on many automobiles. Under one of these, some witty person had scratched, "What is the question?" I would argue that many of the questions to which Christ is the answer are asked in literature. Whether literature is sympathetic or antagonistic towards a Christian affirmation is not the point. The concerned believer attempting to reach his or her fellow human beings with the crucial message that Christ is the way, the truth, and the life must listen to the questions that are being asked before applying the "Balm of Gilead" to aching hearts and searching minds.

As Dynamic Dialogue with History

Literature also often engages in a dynamic dialogue with history. As Ricke contends, "[L]iterature is both a strong ally of the study of history and one of the primary . . . means of 'doing history.'"[7] An historian studying the Renaissance may carefully record, assess, and analyze such concepts, for instance, as the popular idea of the divine right of kings, but this concept leaps into life when embodied in a dramatic work like Shakespeare's *Richard II*. In this gripping tragedy, the reader or spectator is confronted by the dilemma posed by two utterly incompatible positions: a legitimate king who does not know how to rule and a most capable usurper who understands statecraft. This political impasse is given further resonance in Shakespeare's subtle infusions of the imagistically antithetical properties of fire and water associated with each of these contenders for power. There is also another implication here. The concept of "divine right" is clearly tied into the Christian backdrop of the entire issue, frequently taking the form of Christ imagery, as when Richard compares the treachery of his subjects to Judas's betrayal of Christ. While it is not universally true of all literature, it is noteworthy that almost all literature written in English throughout the world has been permeated with the historical

7. Ricke, "Perspective, Dialogue, Interpretation," 12.

influence of Christianity. This is as much the case with the novels of Ngugi wa Thiong'o of Kenya as it is with the novels of Margaret Laurence of Canada or those of Tim Winton of Australia.

As Psychological Exploration

The centrality of character in literature, particularly in drama, the short story, and the novel, brings literature into realms inhabited by psychology. The complex factors that motivate human actions had been explored by literary authors long before Freud's attempt to categorize, systematize, and offer a workable terminology for explaining human behavior. Psychology and literature illuminate each other, as the seemingly inexhaustible endeavors to psychoanalyze complex characters such as Shakespeare's Hamlet illustrate. Christian perspectives can enter this arena very profitably also, as they not only acknowledge the fallen condition of humankind but also affirm humanity's redeemability, for people have not merely evolved by random natural forces but have been intentionally created in God's image.

As Sociological Investigation

The perpetual potential for tension between individuals and their society—which functions as a catalyst for sociological change—has attracted the attention of poets and dramatists throughout the ages. Depicted in Sophocles' drama, *Antigone*, for example, performed in ancient Greece, conflict between the individual and societal norms has also been a major concern of numerous novelists. The ostracism of Hester by the Puritan society of New England in Hawthorne's *The Scarlet Letter*, the attempts of Thom to separate the chaff from the wheat in the traditional values of the Mennonite community in Rudy Wiebe's *Peace Shall Destroy Many*, and the personal struggles of the Mexican "whisky priest" caught in a wave of anti-Catholic persecution in Graham Greene's *The Power and the Glory* are representative depictions of sociological phenomena that should engage the careful scrutiny of a perceptive Christian reader. To what extent are Christian practice and behavior prompted, promoted, and protected by a nominally Christian society? Conversely, to what degree is real Christianity jeopardized in a deliberately secular one?

As a Bridge to the Sciences

While recognizing the felicitous affinities between literature and philosophy, history, psychology, and sociology, are we at the same time obliged to concede that the imaginary rainbows of literature cannot be painted on the real skies inhabited by the sciences? Can a bridge ever be built between the domains of fiction and fact? This is a large and open-ended topic, but a few basic reflections can demonstrate that, metaphorically speaking, the "Jews" of literary expression and the "Gentiles" of scientific investigation often speak a similar language. While every discipline acquires a body of preferred terms, there is nevertheless considerable overlap as the sciences reach out for new terms that can portray more precisely the "actual" world—with every "image" being, of course, a word picture. In addition to their mutual dependency on the tools of imagistic language, literature and science are, in fact, continually illuminating each other. Poets celebrating the beauty of a flower, a tree, a forest, or a landscape will not find their subject matter diminished by looking into a scientist's microscope; indeed, this device will in all probability enhance the poet's sense of wonder. The expanding world of nineteenth-century science, particularly in the areas of geology and paleontology, had a profound effect on the penning of *In Memoriam*, the greatest poem of the period, by motivating Tennyson to affirm his faith in God in spite of the apparently random changes seeming to characterize all observable phenomena. The scientist has something to learn from the poet, too. The intricacies of this world and the universe represent the environment where humankind lives, breathes, thinks, and responds—and these responses are often most eloquently articulated by literary artists.

As a Companion to Theological Studies

But what about the queen of the curriculum, theology? In *The Idea of a Christian College*, Arthur Holmes carefully distinguishes between "Christian theology" and a "Christian worldview":

> Christian theology is a study of the perspective itself as disclosed by the biblical revelation. It looks within, whereas a Christian worldview looks without, at life and thought in other departments and disciplines, in order to see these other things from the standpoint of revelation and as an interrelated whole.[8]

8. Holmes, *Idea of a Christian College*, 59.

Like Sophocles, "who saw life steadily, and saw it whole" (in the words of Matthew Arnold's "To a Friend"[9]), the literary artist strives for a panoramic vision as well as verbal intensity—a process that may be enhanced by a wide reading of the Scriptures, the classics, and works from many other fields.

While the Christian literary scholar must readily acknowledge the supremacy of Scripture, constantly exploring biblical influences, allusions, and motifs in literature, there should be a simultaneous and reciprocal process at work. A familiarity with the power of metaphorical and imagistic language, as well as an understanding of literary forms, can also significantly enhance one's appreciation of the Scriptures themselves. The Bible is not only the behavioral guidebook and final court of appeal, as it were, for Christians; it is also a literary masterpiece whose beauties have been largely preserved, even in spite of many translations. Of these, it is an historical—I am tempted to also say providential—fact that the Authorized Version of 1611 has influenced English literature, more than any other source, for over 300 years. Many of the Psalms are among the finest lyrics ever written; the Proverbs have never been surpassed in their wisdom—so frequently expressed in the form of trenchant antitheses; Jesus Christ's sermons and messages are conveyed by simple yet astonishingly compelling imagery such as bread and water, rock and sand, light and darkness.

One's appreciation of Scripture is almost always enhanced by exposure to great literary works. After reading Sophocles' *Oedipus the King* and Shakespeare's *King Lear*, I was able to read the ancient book of Job with new eyes; I found in the latter all of the essentials of tragedy—encased, however, in a silver lining. Milton's *Paradise Lost*, while profoundly influenced by Scripture, has paid its debt by enabling the reader to *see* the beauty of Eden in a fresh way and to *feel* the power of Satan's temptation with new heart-strings. We vicariously re-live the fall, acknowledging our own implicit involvement in the process—and suddenly discover the theological significance of Paul's declaration in 1 Corinthians 15:22 that in Adam we all died. And is it not ironic that many secular academics who have dismissed Christianity as a relic from the past still keep an underlined copy of *Paradise Lost* on their front bookshelf? Even further ironies appear as quasi-believers attempt to analyze the sophisticated literary

---

9. In Culler, ed., *Poetry and Criticism of Matthew Arnold*, 7.

insights of Christian scholars like C. S. Lewis, raised up by God as Milton's successors to continue his attempt to "justify the ways of God to men."

Literature as Potentially Dangerous

Our emphasis up to this point has been on some of the intellectual, emotional, and even spiritual advantages of literary awareness. In view of all of these benefits, are there any dangers? We do a disservice to ourselves and others if we seek to evade this question. Since it is clearly evident that many powerful and articulate writers are not Christians and may even be abusive in their beratings of Christians and cherished Christian beliefs, we need to be mindful of the challenge this hostility presents to us. While it is certainly the case that the long tradition of literature written in English has been penetrated, and in some works saturated, by Christian beliefs, this situation has greatly altered in the last two centuries, partly fostered initially by the iconoclasm and individualism of the Romantic writers of England and the United States, who frequently challenged traditional values by a plethora of individualistic perspectives. These tendencies have gathered great momentum in our so-called postmodern age.

A positive approach to these developments has been suggested by Ricke, who advocates the need for our "interpretive response" as we dialogue with other perspectives.[10] A slightly more cautious approach has been offered by one of the greatest literary giants of the last century, T. S. Eliot, who did not embrace the Christian faith until well into his literary career. Eliot warns against "a false sense of security in leading [people] to believe that books which are *not* suppressed are harmless."[11] It is important, Eliot argues, not to "separate our literary from our religious judgments."[12] We are living in an age of thoroughgoing secularism that simply cannot understand the Christian's primary concern, "the primacy of the supernatural over the natural life."[13] Given this current scenario, Eliot does not advocate retreat, however. He affirms that Christians *should* read the best that appears, but "we must tirelessly criticize it according to our own principles" and not by the standards of the popular media.[14]

10. Ricke, "Perspective, Dialogue, Interpretation," 15–16.

11. Eliot, "Religion and Literature," 36.

12. Ibid., 35.

13. Ibid., 40.

14. Ibid., 42.

This places a heavy load of responsibility on perceptive Christian scholars who, while recognizing the power of literature, are able to utilize the same critical tools as their secular counterparts in their challenging task of moral as well as literary scrutiny.

EXAMPLES OF SIGNIFICANT CURRENT LITERARY ISSUES

Deconstructionism

The multiplicity of conflicting views about virtually everything in our age has led to two significant trends in literary fashion in the last few decades, both of which offer challenges to the Christian author or critic. One of these, termed "Deconstruction" (which I prefer to call "Deconstructionism") arises out of the work of the French philosopher, Jacques Derrida. *Of Grammatology* (1967) has had an extraordinarily disproportionate influence on literary criticism since its initial appearance as an attack on the rigidity of French intellectual life.[15] In his brilliant exposé of Deconstructionism, Ellis contends that the slogan "all interpretation is misinterpretation,"[16] while in a certain sense true, has become a pseudo-sophisticated tactic for depriving all literary texts and literary criticism of any significance. It is a kind of *reductio ad absurdum* that relentlessly exposes the limitations of language and the inadequacies of any critical approach to such an extent that words and interpretations lose their meaning. Another key term in deconstructionism is "textuality," which means that "the text has a life of its own," without any tie to the author or his or her intentions.[17] The difficulty with this position is that no two critics are likely to agree on an understanding of the text, nor arrive at even a general consensus as to its meaning. In one sense, every interpretation becomes equally legitimate—or perhaps more accurately, illegitimate.

While it must be conceded that language is always changing (though seldom as blatantly as in the word "gay," once a neutral term indicating light-hearted happiness), it does not follow that words have no meaning. And just because critics may not arrive at unanimity in their interpretations of any text does not prove that significant illumination is impossible. Literary criticism is a procedure enhanced by constant ongoing

---

15. See Ellis, *Against Deconstruction*, 83.

16. Ibid., 97.

17. Ibid., 114–15.

refinement with whatever linguistic, historical, and intellectual tools are available. Scholarship advances as critics build on the work of others. This is constructive, whereas merely tearing down is, well, deconstructive. Claerbaut observes that one of the regrettable consequences of this reduction of literary analysis to mere personal opinion is that "we are left floating on an ocean of subjective reactions, with literature losing much of . . . its moral and didactic value."[18]

The amazing feature of this fad was its appeal, somehow paralleling that of the dogmatic agnostic who can neither believe nor will allow anyone else to. Upon further reflection, however, we can see that deconstructionism was one of the bizarre manifestations of what some have aptly termed a "value-neutral education." An education without values will inevitably lose its value altogether. Dynamic communication will be stultified, including the vital transmission of human experience by means of the verbal art we term literature, along with the reflective and judicious responses of discriminating literary criticism.

The Revision of the Literary Canon

There have, of course, always been shifts in literary taste. Many works that were highly popular at one time have fallen into obscurity and even oblivion; other works, while not particularly popular when they first appeared, have eventually gained the admiration of many readers. This is demonstrated, for instance, by the novels of Jane Austen, most of whose works did not reach a second edition during her lifetime, whereas the "twentieth century [and continuing on into the twenty-first] has atoned for the neglect of most of the nineteenth."[19] In contrast, popular contemporaries of Jane Austen such as Jane Porter and prolific writers like Maria Edgeworth are now virtually forgotten.

The process of literary re-evaluation has intensified in the last few years, resulting in an ongoing revision of the "literary canon" of previously highly esteemed great works of literature. There is both a positive and a negative side to this phenomenon. One benefit of reassessing the "canon" is that it provides ongoing opportunities to bring into critical focus meritorious literary works that have not been adequately considered heretofore due to accidents of history or vagaries of fashionable taste. A negative

18. Claerbaut, "How Do We Teach Literature in a Postmodern World?" 195.

19. Baugh, *Literary History of England*, 1206.

consequence of canonical revisionism is its tendency to assess the merits or defects of writings on sociological rather than literary grounds. Ritchie succinctly summarizes the two polarities in this modern-day "battle of the books" when he observes that the proponents of the new ideology describe "ancient literature" (usually works from the "canon") as reflecting their authors' (most of them "dead white males'") racism, sexism, and/ or classicism, while the defenders of a more traditionally orthodox approach to literary analysis accuse the new ideology of "relativism, the loss of standards, and political correctness."[20] He goes on to point out that most of the proponents of canon revision have been influenced by one or more of such contemporary ideological agencies of social change as multiculturalism, feminism, and deconstructionism.

To be sure, a variety of critical perspectives can greatly enrich critical dialogue, whether it be Freudian, Marxist, historical, feminist, biographical, or Christian. Regardless of the critical approach, however, aesthetic criteria must apply: a poem, story, drama, or novel is not necessarily fine or great, for example, because it conveys a Christian message or is written by a Christian, a principle that applies to every valid critical approach. Good literature, to reiterate Batson's citation, is "truth in vital form,"[21] or in the words of the poet Archibald MacLeish, literature "should not [merely] *mean*, but *be*."[22] And, one might add, good literature is also designed to give the reader *pleasure*—not just freedom from oppression (perceived or real).

CONCLUSION

Although critical approaches and preferences may vary according to time and place, the value and wonder of literature will remain as a vital component of any culture that recognizes the indispensability of verbal and written communication and also appreciates the unique capacity of literary art to shape human experience into memorable form. These factors account for the firmly entrenched policies of the many universities that require students to take at least one full-year course in literature, regardless of their program of study. Many students, thus enlightened, discover how fascinating and resonant literary study can be, not only in the subject

20. Ritchie, *Reconstructing Literature*, 1.
21. Batson, "The Christian and Modern Literature," 35.
22. MacLeish, "*Ars Poetica*," 1064.

matter itself, but in the diverse manner in which it can be taught, and are thereby enticed into pursuing minors, concentrations, majors, and even honors programs in English.

WORKS CITED

Arnold, Matthew. *Culture and Anarchy*. Cambridge: Cambridge University Press, 1966 (1869).

Batson, Beatrice. "The Christian and Modern Literature." In *Christianity and the World of Thought*, edited by Hudson T. Armerding, 31–51. Chicago: Moody Press, 1968.

Baugh, A. C. *A Literary History of England*. New York: Appleton-Century-Crofts, 1948.

Claerbaut, David. "How Do We Teach Literature in a Postmodern World?" In his *Faith and Learning on the Edge: A Bold New Look at Religion in Higher Education*, 194–99. Grand Rapids, MI: Zondervan, 2004.

Culler, A. Dwight, ed. *Poetry and Criticism of Matthew Arnold*. Boston: Riverside, 1961 (1849).

Derrida, Jacques. *Of Grammatology*. Baltimore, MD: Johns Hopkins University Press, 1976, translation of *De la Grammatologie*. Paris: Les Éditions de Minuit, 1967.

Eliot, T. S. "Religion and Literature." *Selected Prose*, edited by John Hayward, 31–42. Harmondsworth, Middlesex: Penguin, 1953.

Ellis, John M. *Against Deconstruction*. Princeton: Princeton University Press, 1989.

Holmes, Arthur. *The Idea of a Christian College*. Rev. ed. Grand Rapids, MI: Eerdmans, 1987.

MacLeish, Archibald. "*Ars Poetica*." In *The Norton Introduction to Literature*, edited by Jerome Beaty et al., 1064. 8th ed. New York: Norton, 2001.

MacLennan, Hugh. *Voices in Time*. Toronto: Macmillan, 1980.

Ricke, J. M. "Perspective, Dialogue, Interpretation: An Approach to Faith and Literature." *Faculty Dialogue* 16 (Winter 1992) 5–16.

Ritchie, Daniel E. *Reconstructing Literature in an Ideological Age: A Biblical Poetics from Milton to Burke*. Grand Rapids, MI: Eerdmans, 1996.

Zylstra, H. *Testament of Vision*. Grand Rapids, MI: Eerdmans, 1958.

FOR FURTHER READING

Anderson, Chris. *Teaching as Believing: Faith in the University*. Waco, TX: Baylor University Press, 2004.

Barratt, David, Roger Pooley, and Leland Ryken. *The Discerning Reader: Christian Perspectives in Literature and Theory*. Leicester, UK: Apollos, 1995.

Edwards, Michael. *Towards a Christian Poetics*. Grand Rapids, MI: Eerdmans, 1984.

Gallagher, Susan V., and Roger Lundin. *Literature through the Eyes of Faith*. San Francisco: Harper & Row, 1989.

Hawley, J. C. *Through a Glass Darkly: Essays in the Religious Imagination*. New York: Fordham University Press, 1996.

Jeffrey, David L. "On Being a Slow Learner." In *Professors Who Believe: The Spiritual Journeys of Christian Faculty*, edited by Paul M. Anderson, 217–24. Downers Grove, IL: InterVarsity Press, 1998.

Meyer, Arlin G. "Teaching Literature as Meditation: A Christian Practice." In *Teaching as an Act of Faith: Theory and Practice in Church-Related Higher Education*, edited by Arlin C. Migliazzo, 253–76. New York: Fordham University Press, 2002.

Poe, Harry L. "The Influence of C. S. Lewis." In *Shaping a Christian Worldview: The Foundations of Christian Higher Education*, edited by David S. Dockery and Gregory A. Thornbury, 92–108. Nashville: Broadman & Holman, 2002.

Ryken, Leland. *Triumphs of the Imagination: Literature in Christian Perspective*. Downers Grove, IL: InterVarsity Press, 1979.

Walhout, C., and Leland Ryken. *Contemporary Literary Theory: A Christian Appraisal*. Grand Rapids, MI: Eerdmans, 1991.

14

A Christian Perspective on Geography

INTRODUCTION

WHAT I WISH TO present to you in this chapter is divided into two parts. First, I would like to give a sampling of some of the distinctives of geography and attempt to answer the question, "What is a geographer?" Then I would like to attempt to answer a second question, "What is a Christian geographer?" In this latter section, I will outline what I believe to be the three tasks of a Christian scholar and relate them to the discipline of geography—thereby giving a better understanding of what a college or university education informed by biblically-based presuppositions and Christian commitment is all about.

THE DISCIPLINE OF GEOGRAPHY

Most of us are geographers intuitively. We want to know the location of places, we sometimes draw rough maps to guide someone else to a particular place, and when we arrive in a new place, we "get our bearings" or "orient" ourselves (both interesting terms that describe the activity of locating oneself in reference to direction—the first comes from a compass bearing or direction; the second comes from the early practice of locating oneself in relation to the East, the Orient, since early maps had east, rather than north, at the top). But a university discipline is distinguished by a set of concepts and perspectives that must be learned. It is just what the word means—a discipline, a molding of the mind.

Definitions

The Two Subdivisions of Geography: Physical and Human

Perhaps more than most disciplines, geography wrestles with the perennial problem of being misunderstood. Some people remember their experience in the social studies of an earlier era and equate geography with learning the capitals of countries and the names of physical features. Others, perhaps most, have a vague understanding of geography as having something to do with the physical landscape, confusing it with geology. If you were to attend a lecture on the geography of British Columbia, for example, I suspect most would anticipate a discussion of landforms and life forms, climates, and vegetation. You would be right in expecting those topics to be treated—physical geography is basic to our discipline—but it is only half our concern. We also study the groupings and culture of *people* in human geography. Put another way, keeping in mind the literal meaning of "geography" as "earth description" or "earth writing," geographers are concerned with two kinds of inscriptions on the surface of the earth: the inscriptions of God, in the physical realm; and the inscriptions of humans, in the cultural realm. The ways in which these two types of inscriptions interact with each other form one of the strongest themes in geography. I will explore a specific example of this interaction later.[1]

All elements of the physical and human realm are, in fact, grist for the geographer's mill. This very diversity and inclusiveness creates other problems in coming to a clear understanding of geography as a discipline. Many disciplines are defined by a discrete body of material that is at least largely that discipline's private domain. Botanists study plants; zoologists study animals; geologists study rocks. But no such private domain exists for geography. We share the physical field of our activity with geologists, biologists, soils scientists, meteorologists, and many others. We share the cultural arena with sociologists, psychologists, anthropologists, and other social scientists. What, then, is the basis for identifying geography as a discipline of knowledge? It is in the *perspective* that geography takes on the diverse range of phenomena it studies.

---

1. State University of Utrecht geography professor Gerard Hoekveld reveals the interaction of these two elements in his description of geographers as people who pursue "the study of peoples, places and environments from a spatial perspective and who appreciate the interdependent worlds in which we all live" ("Alien in a Foreign Land," 84).

Distinction by Perspective, not Content: A Spatial Perspective

Preston James defines geography as being concerned about *arrangements* and *associations* of things on the surface of the earth that give character to particular places.[2] Another geographer, Richard Hartshorne, defines the major thrust of geography as "areal differentiation"—the study of distinctions among things on the basis of their areal expression.[3] The geographer's task has been defined also in response to certain key questions: "Where is it? What is it like? What does it mean?"[4] Geographers study any element, physical or human, that has spatial expression (although some are more significant or central than others). We are concerned about the distributions of, and the connections and associations among, an endless variety of phenomena in order to understand both the processes that have created the uneven distributions and the landscapes that have been produced by the interaction among these phenomena.

To illustrate, suppose we consider the uneven distribution of people on the globe. The creation of a population distribution map is a response to the first key question: Where is it? In other words, where are people located on the globe? Once made, the map immediately raises the question: What does it mean? What accounts for the irregular distribution of people on the globe? What factors explain the areas of population concentration and the "empty" areas that the map depicts? If we compare this map with one depicting the global distribution of climates, we could begin to make some simple areal associations that would provide partial answers to the question. Very dry places (deserts), very cold places (northern areas) and very high places (mountainous areas) tend to be associated with low population densities. On the other hand, moderate climates, rich soils, and level terrain correlate with some areas of high population density. Of course, this example deals with people in terms of numbers only. If we were concerned with other aspects of population, we would be responding to the second question: What is it like? In other words, what is the distribution or location of different kinds of people in terms of race, economic activity, educational level, or some other population characteristic?

---

2. James, "Introduction: The Field of Geography," 4.

3. Hartshorne, *Perspective on the Nature of Geography,* 12.

4. James, *All Possible Worlds,* 4–9.

The central focus of geography, then, is concerned with description, assessment, and explanation of the spatial components of physical and cultural phenomena, of their associations and interactions in space, and of the landscapes that those interactions create.

The Major Traditions in Geography

A variety of themes and concerns have characterized geographic research and explanation. William Pattison suggests four major traditions in geography: the area studies, spatial, earth science, and human–land or ecological traditions.[5] These traditions or themes, reflecting differing emphases rather than discrete entities, merge frequently in practice.

The Area Studies Tradition

Area or regional studies consider the distributions of, and interplay among, a wide variety of physical and cultural components that together create segments of the earth's surface that "hang together"—that is, have identity—because of similarity of features or functional connections. A regional study of British Columbia's Fraser Valley, for example, would consider this physical region, a river floodplain and delta, as the unifying feature, and would go on to consider variations within this broad region that reflect the settlement sequence, the cultural variations among the settlers, the development of communications systems, and so on. By coming to understand these various components and their interactions within the region, we begin to understand the region as a unified, interacting region that differs from other regions surrounding it. This kind of study tends to focus on the rich complexity of human perception and behavior as a sense of the region is developed. The regional tradition stresses the concept of "place," which, as Houston notes, is an important part of our sense of order and usefulness, standing in contrast to a focus on mere "space."[6]

The Spatial Tradition

The spatial tradition emphasizes space as an attribute of any element on the earth's surface. Every phenomenon can therefore be assessed in terms of location or position, relationship to other phenomena (direction,

5. Pattison, "The Four Traditions of Geography," 211–16.

6. Houston, "The Concepts of 'Place' and 'Land' in the Judaeo-Christian Tradition," 224–37.

distance), and movement (flows). Geographers working in this tradition are interested in describing, analyzing, and explaining these relationships in space. They often use economic-geographic generalizations in simplified models of reality to clarify these relationships. For example, Walter Christaller's central place theory modelled the pattern of agricultural service centers and their trade regions as a series of nested hexagons of varying sizes.[7] Simplifying the real-world complexity of factors involved in the distribution of service centers by assuming the unreal characteristics of equal access on a completely featureless plain, he thus created a pattern ruled by space rather than place.[8]

The Earth Sciences Tradition

The earth sciences tradition is concerned with the characteristics of form, distribution, and relationships among the earth's physical components and with the processes that continually modify them. Thus the geomorphologist analyzes variations in the characteristic shapes of the land (landforms), seeking to understand the processes that account for those variations. Similarly, the climatologist describes and analyzes the way long-term elements of weather vary from place to place, attempting to account for those differences by analyzing large and small-scale atmospheric processes. It is this tradition that defines geography in many people's minds.

The Ecological Tradition

The ecological tradition is the earliest as well as the most persistent theme in geography. As people and their environment interacted, two emphases came to dominate the interpretation of the resultant physical and cultural landscapes: environmental determinism and possibilism. *Environmental determinism* stressed the primacy of the environment in understanding the characteristics and distributions of people and their activities. Beginning with the classical explanations of variations in peoples by reference to the intimate link between climatic elements (hot, cold, wet, dry) and bodily humors (phlegm, yellow bile, black bile, and blood), this

---

7. Christaller, *Central Places in Southern Germany*, 66.

8. Calvin College Professor of Geography and Environmental Studies Janel Curry-Roper notes that "The field of geography . . . has always struggled with the tensions of space verses [*sic*] place; the search for universals verses [*sic*] the recognition of the unique . . ." ("Christian Worldview and Geography," 51).

tradition carried on through to early twentieth-century interpretations of settlement, economic activities, and innovations based on certain environmental constituents (including a persistent interest in the influence of heavenly bodies on human affairs). *Possibilism* gave emphasis to the near-endless human capacity to create distinctive landscapes based on cultural values and skills, relegating environment to a secondary role. (In extreme cases, an emphasis on cultural determinism almost completely denied the environmental influence.) The two streams have come together as we understand both our ability to drastically alter global environmental systems and our inability to escape the environmental consequences of those actions.

These four traditions are clearly discernible in today's geographical literature. The ways in which the traditions are carried out, however, varies considerably. In the spatial analysis and earth-science traditions, geographers have increasingly taken a quantitative approach, attempting to reduce the complexity of the real world by identifying value-free components that operate in an idealized world model. This is done in order to reveal law-like relationships among things and processes that will then facilitate analysis and explanation. The same quantitative approach has been applied to the area studies and the ecological traditions, but in a much more restrained manner. A return to a detailed consideration of the richness and complexity of the real world has marked much recent work in these areas.

In summary, then, geographers make varied and complex contributions to the search for knowledge, seeking understanding of both the earth and its inhabitants, especially as components of each interact and are distributed unevenly in space.

WHAT DOES IT MEAN TO BE A CHRISTIAN GEOGRAPHER?

This question focuses on the ways by which a Christian geographer brings together discipline and faith, in essence asking, "What distinguishes a Christian geographer from a non-Christian one?" Let me begin to reply to this by outlining what I deem to be the major tasks of a Christian scholar. The Christian scholar is, I believe, faced with three tasks: to apply revealed truth to work and life; to uncover "embedded" truth; and to explore how these two sets of truths inform each other. The first, concerned primarily with living Christianly, is the necessary context for the other tasks. The second is concerned primarily with scholarly investigation within one's discipline. The third, perhaps the most delicate, is concerned with finding the edges of revealed and embedded truth and devising a fit that violates neither. While the word "integration" is used generally to cover all three tasks, I would suggest that it applies particularly to the first. The second task emphasizes the contributions of a scholarly discipline, in this case geography, in revealing truth, although the context of integration plays a significant role in the assumptions and presuppositions that influence our work. The third task, the one to which we are most likely to apply the concept of integration, involves what I prefer to call synthesis. I wish to explore these three tasks as they relate to the discipline of geography.

The First Task: Application (Integration)

The first task of the Christian scholar is to apply revealed truth (biblical truth mediated by the Holy Spirit) to all areas of our lives. It is to this most fundamental and significant task that the word "integration" most properly applies. I would define integration as the process by which the quality of integrity is allowed increasing expression in all areas of our lives. "Integrity" comes from the root word "integer," which means "whole," and from this comes the connotation of completeness, consistency, undivided unity, or thoroughgoing and habitual honesty. In the antiques trade, for example, the integrity of a piece of furniture designates a wholeness, a harmony of purpose and design that is inherent in the piece. From every perspective, the unifying purpose is evident in every part. That "integrity" is destroyed if the piece is modified, even for useful and practical reasons. We speak more commonly of integrity in other contexts—the integrity of a structure, of a plan, of an agreement—but refer still to the same quality of wholeness, of undivided, unfragmented intactness.[9]

A person of integrity, then, is a "whole" person characterized by consistency despite changing circumstances, turning the same face to every

---

9. Alvin Plantinga expanded on this cross-disciplinary understanding of "integrity" while addressing a 1984 faith and philosophy conference at the University of Notre Dame, when he asserted, "Christian philosophers must display more integrity—integrity in the sense of integral wholeness, or oneness, or unity, being all of one piece. Perhaps 'integrality' would be the better word here." Interestingly, this statement by Plantinga was quoted by Sweeney in his September 22, 2006, presidential address to the Conference on Faith and History entitled and later published as "On the Vocation of Historians to the Priesthood of Believers: Faithful Practices in Service of the Guild," 10.

situation. For Christians, the biblical basis for such wholeness is a single-minded allegiance to Christ. The "single" eye, filling the whole body with light (Matthew 6:22), and "singleness of heart" (Ephesians 6:5; Colossians 3:22) speak of wholeness. This is contrasted with double-mindedness, which creates instability and inconsistency in everything a person does. Matthew notes that "no man can serve two masters" (Matthew 6:24), and James underlines the impossibility of a double-minded allegiance by saying that "friendship with the world [identifying with the goals and aspirations of the world] is enmity with God" (James 4:4). The basis of integrity, single-minded allegiance to Christ, must be applied to every area of our lives, a process that is the essence of integration.

Our discipline of geography is one important segment of our life through which our allegiance to Christ is made visible. But the question is not so much "What aspects of geography are most likely to be informed or transformed by my allegiance to Christ?" but more broadly, "What does it mean to be a geographer of faith?" For me, it means that we first nurture the life of integrity; then we put our minds to what that life means in our discipline: to the content of our discipline, to the way we advance it through research and writing, to the way we communicate it to students, and to the kind of lives we live while engaged in these activities.

Often we talk about integration as though it was essentially concerned with finding a Lego-like "fit" between faith and our academic discipline, with an emphasis on those content areas in our discipline that are most able to reflect our faith. Coming to grips with the relationships between revealed and embedded truth is clearly part of our task—I would see this as the essence of the third task, synthesis—but it is not, in my view, the essence of integration.

Integration, then, is the process by which revealed truth (as encapsulated by a single-minded allegiance to Christ) is allowed to permeate every area of our lives, including our academic discipline. The result is a discipline practiced by persons of integrity, ensuring that the second task, the search for embedded truth, is accomplished within the context of Christian faith.

The Second Task: Investigation

The second task of the Christian scholar is the search for truths that are inherent or "embedded" in the created order, both physical and human.

Here the Christian scholar brings to bear a mind educated in the perspectives, concepts, and skills of a specific discipline, in this case, geography. I have already discussed the special perspective that geographers bring to their investigation of both the physical and human components of the created world.

The Third Task: Synthesis

This third task consists of determining the ways in which revealed truth and embedded truths inform each other. I have suggested that the task involves identifying the boundaries of the two sets of truths and then attempting to ascertain how they fit together. The applied limits of both sets of truth are often ill-defined or varyingly interpreted. Truth, of course, is not variable, but the interface between the truths of faith and discipline is pocked with differences in interpretation and application from both sides of the dichotomy, making a seamless fit quite difficult. Free University (Amsterdam) social philosophy professor Sander Griffioen makes the important observation that, for both the Christian and the secular academic, "Worldviews do not just represent empirical tendencies, but instead, are normatively laden. They harbor [truth] claims."[10]

In many areas of research in geography, the task of synthesis is irrelevant in any but the broadest context. It is unlikely that revealed truth and embedded truth will interact with each other in, for example, research into the soils geography of British Columbia's lower Fraser Valley, or in the assessment of the spatial structure of the transportation systems in San Francisco. But the fact that there is little scope for Christian "synthesis" in these areas has no bearing on the responsibility for, and practice of, Christian integration in these and all other topics explored by the Christian geographer. It is in these areas of study that a distinction between integration and synthesis in the Christian scholar's work is most useful.

An open question, of course, is whether the Christian mind should direct us to some topics in geography and not others. Should we focus our attention on those tasks where revealed and embedded truths *do* inform each other—and where the product of a Christian geographer's research is likely to be quite different from that of a secular researcher? I believe scholars must answer that question individually, but I would like to direct

10. Griffioen, "Perspectives, Worldview, Structures," 133.

our attention to a particular segment of the ecological tradition in geography where Christian synthesis is both possible and necessary.

In considering the interrelations between humans and their environment in order to assess environmental impact, a Christian geographer brings together the revealed truth of humans created in the image of God, occupying a unique place within the created order, and the embedded truth that people are an intricate part of a web of life within which ignorant or greedy or arrogant behavior brings disaster, swift or slow. The synthesis of these truths compels us to develop and live by a Christian environmental ethic. Let me "unpack" the detail and implications of this generalization.

A good deal of research has explored the relationship between a people's belief system and the way in which that people view and affect their environment. One of the most influential articles of the past forty years has been Lynn White's "The Historical Roots of our Ecological Crisis," in which he argues first that what people do about their ecology (their relationship to the environment) is, in large part, conditioned by their beliefs about their nature and their destiny, that is, their religion. He goes on to contrast the Judeo-Christian belief of humans created in the image of God and given rightful dominion over the rest of creation with pagan animism, whose proponents believe that every part of creation is indwelt by a guardian spirit. The first belief system led, White maintains, to an arrogant, exploitative attitude toward creation, which, coupled with the technological advances of the scientific revolution, wreaked havoc on the natural order and resulted finally in the problems that are of global scope in our own time. The second belief system did not prohibit environmental modification, but the scope of it was restrained, says White, by the feeling of regard for the elements of the natural environment. (While I have considerably compressed the substance of White's paper, the essence of his argument reflects an area of study in which revealed and embedded truth certainly interact in coming to terms with understanding ecological relationships.)

Francis Schaeffer, in *Pollution and the Death of Man*, expresses this synthesis in a quite different light.[11] Creation, he argues, *does* have value in and of itself because God made it. Humans, while made in the image of God and therefore enjoying a unique relationship with God, are nonethe-

---

11. Schaeffer, *Pollution and the Death of Man*, 46–47.

less part of the created order and share their createdness with all other elements of creation. The fact that humans are made in the image of God and enjoy a unique relationship with him endows them with a responsibility unique in the created order, one that is absent in a more pantheistic view. After all, if humans are no different from trees (i.e., both are imbued with divinity), how can they be responsible for environmental care?

The fact that humans share their createdness with all other elements of creation should lead not only to an intellectual assent to that fact but also to a genuine empathy for all other components of the created order. Ecological theologian Ruth Page sees this awareness of our oneness with all of creation as a crucial modifying element in our creation care and stewardship activities, "to prevent that management from becoming anthropocentric and as manipulative as the practices that gave rise to our [ecological] problems."[12] This attitude of fellowship with all creation, she observes, is portrayed in Saint Francis of Assisi's well-known hymn:

> All creatures of our God and King,
> Lift up your voice and with us sing,
> Alleluia!

I believe a similar theme is inherent in such eschatological scriptural passages as "the mountains and hills will burst into song before you, and all the trees of the field will clap their hands" (Isaiah 55:12 NIV) and "let the fields be jubilant, and everything in them. Then all the trees of the forest will sing for joy" (Psalm 96:12 NIV), where these inanimate elements of God's creation are endowed with anthropomorphic capabilities to render praise.

Humans look two ways, then, according to Schaeffer: upward in a relationship to a personal God that is absolutely unique in all of creation; and downward in a relationship to all the created order as fellow-creatures, created by an infinite God. It should be noted that Schaeffer acknowledges that Christians have not always *acted* upon these truths, but they are truths nonetheless.

These are only two "models" that illustrate the thrust of synthesis. White's "dominion" model stresses the role of belief in human separateness from, and supremacy over, creation, which leads to environmental damage. Schaeffer's model stresses both the roles of human separateness and human connectedness in a creation of worth, which leads to

12. Page, "The Fellowship of All Creation," 98.

responsible stewardship from a position of authority. Other models of the past have stressed intermediate positions. The "partner" model of the Benedictines, for example, stressed the responsibility of people working together with God in the task of improving the earth and making it more productive. The Franciscan model, which White suggests as a possible solution to our need for a new religious perspective, stresses the fellowship and unity of all creation and, according to some, comes uncomfortably close to a pantheistic perspective, although in context, this appears to be a distortion of his belief.[13]

Whatever the variations in the perspectives represented in these models, it is clear that the boundaries between revealed truth and embedded truth are seldom sharply defined, owing to differences in the interpretation of both revealed truth and embedded truth and in the progressive findings of embedded truth. In many areas of geography, then, the task of synthesis is one involving challenges in the areas of integration and investigation.

GEOGRAPHY AS A COMPONENT OF A LIBERAL ARTS EDUCATION

In his *The Idea of a Christian College*, Wheaton College philosophy professor emeritus Arthur Holmes points out that a liberal education makes many worthwhile contributions to career preparation: work attitudes, breadth of education, cognitive and communications skills, imagination, and value development. I believe this to be as true about geography as any other discipline, but I would point out that geography contributes two other components as well. First, it provides a natural bridge between the physical and social sciences. The two facets of geography, physical and cultural, are so intertwined that one cannot do either without a thorough understanding of the reciprocal field. It would be impossible to understand the rural settlement patterns in the Fraser Valley of British Columbia, for example, without knowing about variations in climate, soils, landforms, and groundwater. By the same token, it would be impossible to assess the

13. For a well-crafted, biblically sound, and widely endorsed summation of a proper Christian understanding of environmental stewardship, see "Appendix I—An Evangelical Declaration on the Care of Creation," in Brandt, ed., *God's Stewards*. As footnote 1 explains, "The *Declaration* was launched in 1994 as one of the first products of the Evangelical Environment Network . . . and has since been endorsed by several hundred church leaders throughout the world" (94).

landforms of this area without considering human activity as one of the agents that shape the land.

Second, geography encourages one's ability to see things "together," "whole," as interacting systems, each part influencing and being influenced by a multitude of factors. The integrative skill of being able to synthesize a variety of factors and see the unity in them is valuable in many occupations, not least in various planning activities, so it is not surprising that many geographers find their way into urban, regional, and municipal planning.

CONCLUSION

I have presented what I believe to be a helpful structure within which to pursue our academic work as Christians (regardless of whether we are students or professors), but, as the example I have used in the synthesis section illustrates, there are many difficulties and challenges in carrying out our tasks. There may appear to be more questions than answers, but those questions are significant, and the pursuit of their answers will help us to sharpen the task of synthesis. For example, what is the revealed truth of Scripture concerning our attitude toward the environment? What does it mean, in practice, to have "dominion" over the created order? Does this mean we can do what we please? What responsibilities are inherent in humans being created "in the image of God?" Is biblical stewardship utilitarian and human-centered, or is it to be undertaken because creation has a value in and of itself? And to what extent do we apply the findings of our discipline, the "embedded" truth, to apprehend more clearly what is meant in revealed truth and, more particularly, to how we apply that revealed truth?

These distinctions I believe to be much more than semantic exercises. To separate the geographer's activities and responsibilities in this manner helps us to maintain a balance between the extremes of a hyper-spiritual view and a hyper-pragmatic view of our work. In the case of a Christian professor, the first would have us engage only in those areas of research where a Christian perspective is going to produce different results or conclusions when compared to a secular scholar's research. The second would have us focus on scholarship alone with little or no regard for the Christian perspective. The structure I have suggested emphasizes the need for integration, the thoroughgoing infusion of the lordship of

Christ in every part of our academic responsibilities (as in all other areas of our lives), a responsibility for which all Christian academics—both students and instructors—are equally accountable. But it also recognizes that in some disciplines or parts of disciplines, we have little scope for synthesis except in the most general terms. Thus, while the task of synthesis may have little relevance to many parts of physical geography but will be the natural conclusion of many other aspects of geography, the task of integration cuts across all disciplines and all parts of disciplines. Thus I must be a geographer (or historian, or psychologist) of *integrity* no matter what my area of research, but the scope for synthesis may be limited or absent for specific areas of research.

Historian Mark Noll has suggested two broad approaches to the task of bringing together faith and discipline: the Reformational view (where the *content* of a discipline is reformulated in the light of Christian revelation) and the Wesleyan view (in which emphasis is on the transformed *life* of the student or scholar bearing witness to Christian revelation in any and every task).[14] I see these views applying to the various facets of the Christian academic's task, not mutually exclusive, but not wholly overlapping. Integration, in the structure I have presented, would correspond to the Wesleyan perspective, while synthesis would encompass the Reformational perspective.

In sum, I would say that in our activity as geographers these three remain: integration, investigation, and synthesis, but the greatest of these is integration.

WORKS CITED

Brandt, Don, ed. *God's Stewards: The Role of Christians in Creation Care*. Monrovia, CA: World Vision Publications, 2002.

Christaller, Walter. *Central Places in Southern Germany*. Translated by C. W. Baskin. Englewood Cliffs, NJ: Prentice-Hall, 1966.

Curry-Roper, Janel M. "Christian Worldview and Geography: Positivism, Covenantal Relations, and the Importance of Place." In *Geography and Worldview: A Christian Reconnaissance*, edited by Henk Aay and Sander Griffioen, 49–60. Lanham, MD: University Press of America, 1998.

Griffioen, Sander. "Perspectives, Worldview, Structures." In *Geography and Worldview: A Christian Reconnaissance*, edited by Henk Aay and Sander Griffioen, 125–43. Lanham, MD: University Press of America, 1998.

Hartshorne, Richard. *Perspective on the Nature of Geography*. Chicago: Rand McNally, 1959.

14. Summarized in Yandell, "Evangelical Thought, 1987," 346.

Holmes, Arthur F. *The Idea of a Christian College*. Rev. ed. Grand Rapids, MI: Eerdmans, 1987.

Hoekveld, Gerard A. "Alien in a Foreign Land: Human Geography from the Perspective of Christian Citizenship." In *Geography and Worldview: A Christian Reconnaissance*, edited by Henk Aay and Sander Griffioen, 83–101. Lanham, MD: University Press of America, 1998.

Houston, James M. "The Concepts of 'Place' and 'Land' in the Judaeo-Christian Tradition." In *Humanistic Geography: Prospects and Problems*, edited by David Ley and Marwyn S. Samuels, 224–37. Chicago: Maaroufa Press, 1978.

James, Preston E. *All Possible Worlds: A History of Geographical Ideas*. Indianapolis: Odyssey Press, 1972.

————. "Introduction: The Field of Geography." In *American Geography: Inventory and Prospect*, edited by P. J. Jones and C. Jones, 3–18. Syracuse: Syracuse University Press, 1954.

Page, Ruth. "The Fellowship of All Creation." In *Environmental Stewardship: Critical Perspectives—Past and Present*, edited by R. J. Berry, 97–105. London: T. & T. Clark International, 2006.

Pattison, W. "The Four Traditions of Geography." *Journal of Geography* 63 (1964) 211–16.

Schaeffer, Francis A. *Pollution and the Death of Man: The Christian View of Ecology*, expanded with additional chapter by Udo Middelmann. Wheaton, IL: Crossway, 1992.

Sweeney, Douglas. "On the Vocation of Historians to the Priesthood of Believers: Faithful Practices in Service of the Guild." *Fides et Historia* 39.1 (Winter/Spring 2007) 1–13.

White, Lynn. "The Historical Roots of our Ecological Crisis." *Science* 155 (1967) 1203–1207.

Yandell, K. E. "Evangelical Thought, 1987." *Christian Scholar's Review* 17 (1988) 341–46.

FOR FURTHER READING

DeWitt, Calvin B. *Caring for Creation: Responsible Stewardship of God's Handiwork*, edited by James W. Skillen and Luis E. Lugo. Grand Rapids, MI: Baker, 1998.

Gersmehl, Philip J. "This Calls for a Map." In *Professors Who Believe: The Spiritual Journeys of Christian Faculty*, edited by Paul M. Anderson, 178–91. Downers Grove, IL: InterVarsity Press, 1998.

Gottfried, Robert R. *Economics, Ecology, and the Roots of Western Faith Perspectives from the Garden*. Lanham, MD: Rowman & Littlefield, 1995.

Hessel, Dieter T., and Rosemary R. Ruether, eds. *Christianity and Ecology: Seeking the Well-Being of Earth and Humans*. Cambridge, MA: Harvard University Press, 2000.

James, Preston E. "Toward a Further Understanding of the Regional Concept." *Annals of the American Association of Geographers* 47.3 (1952) 195–222.

Livingstone, David N. "Science and Religion: Toward a New Cartography." *Christian Scholar's Review* 26.3 (1996) 270–92.

Plantinga, Alvin. "Advice to Christian Philosophers." *Faith and Philosophy* 1.3 (October 1984) 253–71.

Toly, Noah J. "Climate Change and Climate Change Policy as Human Sacrifice: Artifice, Idolatry, and Environment in a Technological Society." *Christian Scholar's Review* 35.1 (2005) 63–78.

Van Dyke, Fred, et al. *Redeeming Creation: The Biblical Basis for Environmental Stewardship*. Downers Grove, IL: InterVarsity Press, 1996.

15

A Christian Perspective on Geology

RICHARD R. WALTERS

WHAT IS GEOLOGY AND WHAT DO GEOLOGISTS DO?

GEOLOGY IS A SCIENTIFIC discipline that studies the earth and its earlier inhabitants. I say "earlier" to anticipate any argument over what is or is not a fossil. Geologists have been known to say that if it still smells it is not a fossil! Geologists study the materials of the earth, the processes occurring there, the forces or causes responsible for these events, and the resulting configurations or structures, whether they be the shape of the continents or the intergrowth of adjoining crystals in a rock as viewed under a microscope. Obviously the scope of geologists' interests is very wide.

In more specific terms, geologists study minerals and rocks, plate movements of the earth's crust, volcanism (molten rocks), metamorphism (altered rocks), weathering, sedimentation (layered rocks), surface and ground water, mass wastage, the work of the wind, glaciation, marine geology, earthquakes, rock deformation, and ancient life—all sub-sciences of the discipline. Even planetary geology is largely directed at furthering our understanding of the earth and its history. Many of these geologic specialties have an historical dimension rather than just the study of present processes emphasized in physical geology. Expanding on this point, Alexander and White assert that geologists are engaged in

> reconstructing historical events from data collected many millions of years after the events. But geology, like other sciences, uses present-day experiments, analogues or theoretical models to deduce the conditions that would have given rise to particular types

of rocks, or environmental conditions, in the past. As with other sciences, it is a fundamental tenet of geology that the way in which matter behaves is consistent and predictable: one particular way in which this is often expressed in geological research is that "the present is the key to the past."[1]

THE MOTIVATION FOR GEOLOGY

The study of geology is multi-faceted in its motivation. (That would be a pun if you were a gemologist!) Many geologists are governed by economic motives as they work for industries that depend on a constant supply of raw materials, including everything from gold, petroleum, copper, coal, and building stone to not-so-lowly gravel. Other geologists are concerned with the prediction and/or the alleviation of geologic hazards that are a threat to life, property, and/or industry. These hazards may include earthquakes, slope failures with or without quakes, floods, volcanic eruptions, sandstorms, or even the advance of glaciers on valuable mine sites. This second category of geological activity may include attempts to control the forces of nature such as regulating earthquakes or counteracting the effects of gravity.

Many of these geologic pursuits are not ends in themselves but are important adjuncts to other human endeavors. Highway construction, for example, is often concerned with rock and slope stability and drainage. The erection of major facilities such as power and flood control dams and nuclear power plants must avoid active fault zones. Dams and reservoirs must be constructed over suitable bedrock material. Geologists have also long been involved in resource management, and more recently with environmental stewardship. For example, the tapping of underground thermal energy for power sources may alter the ecology of sensitive areas such as Crater Lake or Yellowstone Park. Prospecting by satellite, another recent development in the field of geology, can reveal the existence of resources safely distant from environmentally controversial areas.

Underlying the study of historical geology is humankind's great curiosity about our own origin and that of the earth, our home. We wonder about the "when" and the "how." The rock record has long been known to contain clues about the earth's past and about earlier life forms. Fossils of recognizable sea dwellers found in high mountain strata clearly indi-

---

1. Alexander and White, *Science, Faith, and Ethics*, 5–6.

cate that major topographical changes have taken place. Historically, not all explanations are reasonable, but they provide a beginning. Aristotle's response about a fossil fish was that "a great many fishes live in the earth motionless and are found when excavations are made."[2] The task of unraveling the record continues.

Generally, the work of scientists is designed to uncover or discover the underlying working relationships governing their disciplines. When these relationships are determined it is assumed they will be intelligible. A scientist's never-ending task is to arrive at more encompassing explanations that will account for more of the events and observations in their field of study. For example, in the science of physics, the law of gravity applies to a wide range of phenomena. In geology, plate tectonic theory accounts for many major occurrences, both preserved in the record and still happening today. As the scientist builds onto a pyramid of knowledge, each new level of generalization is given a name like principle, law, or theory, depending on its range of applicability and how well it has withstood repeated testing or can account for new data. Some people find it intriguing to debate whether scientific knowledge (content) is created or discovered. Scientists in general act as if the information in the part of natural reality they are investigating was there all the time and that they are merely finding it. The real creativity comes in the ingenious, improvisational, insightful ways in which scientists arrive at their conclusions. Often the brilliance of their creativity comes through in the experimental design or the particular test system selected.

THE ROLE OF GEOLOGY IN A CHRISTIAN LIBERAL ARTS INSTITUTION

Why is geology appropriate for the liberal arts curriculum in a Christian college or university? Arthur Holmes, in *The Idea of a Christian College*, describes a liberal arts education as involving students in a broad encounter with the natural sciences, the social sciences, and the humanities, including religion, helping them seek fulfilment as persons, not just as employees, especially in terms of their potential as reflective, valuing, and responsible human beings.[3]

---

2. Cited in Lutgens and Tarbuk, *Essentials of Geology*, 2.
3. Holmes, *Idea of a Christian College*, 25–33.

For many persons, geology taps a well, a mine arousing deep curiosity, inquisitiveness, and natural interest. Others don't seem to notice things geological. Contrary to the child's bedtime prayer, "If I should die before I wake," maybe such people should pray to wake up before they die, for they miss so much of what is going on all around them. Geology is everywhere; it impinges on our experience every day. Once one is sensitized to the myriad of possible interests, ranging from pebbles in the surf to the orientation of mountain ranges, one begins to appreciate the scope of this subject area and experience the excitement that it can engender, especially when a person has that spark of "native inquisitiveness" that can ignite the passion to know.[4]

If, as Holmes maintains, the liberal arts are designed to foster those qualities appropriate to a person's uniqueness as a thinking, reflective being, then certainly the science of geology exhibits this characteristic. In the process of developing the geologic account, the thought processes commonly proceed as follows: "What am I seeing here?" "What is the explanation?" "What are the forces underlying the causes?" "How does this relate to the broader framework of my understanding?" At each step, analysis, organization of a sequence of cause and effect relations, evaluation of the rationality of causal explanations, and ascertaining the fit or congruity with the larger principles of the discipline must all take place. In searching for those broader, more encompassing explanations referred to earlier as part of the scientific task, the geologist will develop hypotheses to be tested. In fact, multiple working hypotheses may exist until they are narrowed down through the progress of those pursuing the study. For example, the plate tectonic theory involving movement of large portions of the earth's crust now holds sway over former competing ideas.

THE VALUE OF AN INTERDISCIPLINARY APPROACH TO GEOLOGY

The study of geology, which should be approached culturally as well as scientifically and vocationally, lends itself well to an interdisciplinary approach. First of all, it relates to other sciences, traceable historically to the classic liberal art of astronomy and currently to a broad range of related fields. Chemistry is involved in mineral formation, since minerals are the constituents of all rocks. Many aspects of weathering phenomena have a

---

4. Ibid., 30.

chemical basis as do matters of solution and transport. Biology and geology are highly interrelated. A paleontologist (a fossil expert) must know the anatomy and classification of organisms. As there is a contemporary ecology, so there is paleoecology, the study of ancient environments and their resident organisms. All of the out-of-doors sciences encompassed by biology, such as marine biology, forestry, wildlife management, fisheries, and agriculture draw on the study of geology at some point. Geology and physical geography have much in common, the geographer emphasizing the response of humans within their physical setting while the geologist focuses on the natural processes.

Much of humankind's history as we know it has been woven on the loom of time, with geology as the warp and our own measure of self-determination the woof, creating a fabric sometimes brilliant, sometimes drab and despicable. From life in caves, battles on broad river plains, pursuit of salt deposits, first discovery of metals, selection of defensible dwelling sites, choosing of trade routes over land and water, settlement of new lands, historic encounters of armies, and on and on to landing on the moon, human history has been played out in a geologic setting. The props for the stage have been mountains or plateaus, mesas or buttes, fertile flood plains or blistering deserts. The raw materials to be found, the fertility of the soil, the climatic determiners, the availability of water, and the access to transportation routes have been part of the plot, all of which have a basis in geology. Humankind's creation of our own history, always in a geological setting, should illustrate the interdisciplinary connections that are possible between this science and the study of history.

Besides the contribution of geology to the character of humankind as reflective and historic beings, the subject area clearly shows up in our writings, our literature. It is here, to use Holmes' words, that one's "valuational orientation to life" shows itself. "The value [a person] places on various aspects of life comes out in the literature he writes [or reads]."[5] Clearly we are not dealing with professional scientific literature here, with its established style and well-supported content that defends a value of objectivity. (I once had an instructor who said that we scientists are so strong on objectivity that we only become emotional in defense of that objectivity!) Rather, the literature referred to here is that which reveals people's thinking, their feelings about themselves, their self-awareness,

5. Ibid., 31–32.

and their sense of origin and destiny. Since feelings, emotions, and beliefs are supposedly not the domain of objective science, we must make a transition to considering worldview content and ultimately religious belief because this is the essence of worldviewishness.

If we accept that a liberal education allows us to become whole persons, to see life more completely, and to find meaning in what we do,[6] then we must ask such larger questions as "Why do I feel related to the earth?" "Has it affected me more than just in physical provision?" "Why does my mood change when I find solitude in some of earth's secluded places, until then a secret kept from me?" "As I learn more and more, why do I feel that earth is a specially prepared place?" (Astronauts have reported this on return to our planet.) "Why are homes with a view in demand?" It cannot be that they are more easily defended (although present societal trends may take us back to that!). The following literary examples support my point.

Writers, either in their chosen literary genre or in their personal musings, often reveal the values they place on their particular earthly heritage. James A. Michener devotes extensive sections, in his historical novels, to the history of the land itself, to the development of the surface features, and to the total setting. As in true life, he recognizes that, for his characters, the drama of their lives is played out in a setting that largely determines what each character will become. Michener's Paul Garrett struggles with his own penchant for loneliness and its part in American history, but he sees the rewards for the development of strong, principled character. When early ranches were thirty miles apart it required more ingenuity and inventiveness to survive.[7] The reason for the isolation is spelled out by writers like Walter Prescott Webb[8] and John Wesley Powell.[9] It just required that much land to graze enough stock to support a family. The realities of climate and life on the land were not adequately matched with the provisions of various land grants to settlers.

The English poet William Wordsworth adds support to my point here about the role of landscape and geological formations in human life. He was born and spent much of his life in a mountainous district of Britain known as the Lake District. Geikie states, "Thence he drew the inspira-

---

6. Ibid., 36.

7. Michener, *Centennial*, 1020.

8. Webb, *The Great Plains*.

9. Powell, *Lands of the Arid Region of the United States*.

tion which did so much to quicken the English poetry of the nineteenth century.... The scenes familiar to him from infancy were loved by him to the end with an ardent and grateful affection."[10] Wordsworth recognized his debt to his natural setting in life when he wrote:

> If, mingling with the world, I am content
> With my own modest pleasures, and have lived
> With God and Nature communing, removed
> From little enmities and low desires,
> The gift is yours.... (*The Prelude*, Book Second, ll. 428–32)

Wallace Stegner, writer, historian, and literary critic, refers to his "absence of roots" due to his moving some sixty times after living in eight states and in Canada. His essay "At Home in the Fields of the Lord" explains how and why he selected Salt Lake City, Utah, as his adopted hometown, out of all the possibilities he might have chosen. Stegner explains his discovery that "much of my youth is there, and a surprising lot of my heart." He relates things that would interest sociologists, physical education teachers, and church historians, but always there were the mountains, the north-south trending representative of the Rockies, the Wasatch Range. His Wasatch Mountains are described as a "rampart, insulating from the stormy physical and intellectual weather of both coasts." After not always being complimentary to Salt Lake City, he asks, "But what is a hometown if it is not a place you feel secure in?" Stegner speaks of the city's setting as in the "lap" of someone whose reposing chest is those mountains again, mountains accessible to any boy through seven canyons, leading to all the things boys love to do. In case we have forgotten the point, literature both reveals and influences values. Later, if not sooner, people value their heritage, what helped to make their becoming a reality—and that heritage almost always involves an implicit geological context. Stegner clinches the point thus: "Up in the Wasatch is another world, distinct and yet contributory, and a Salt Lake boyhood is inevitably colored by it."[11]

Some of us have less time than others to become "whole persons," but life in its entirety was intended to be a learning experience. To learn is rewarding at any age. One aspect of wholeness is to be a thinking person, working on the big questions. Why do I feel related to the earth? It is because Earth is my created home and I am created, a unique being. I find

---

10. Geikie, "Landscape and Literature," 214.

11. Stegner, "At Home in the Fields of the Lord," 158, 159, 165.

the Creator's intentions and provisions to be perfectly matched. My capacity to experience earth's physical sustenance, to be soothed in spirit in its quiet places, and to understand the message of its revelation convinces me completely of his good intentions for humankind.

How better may one be a whole person than by becoming intellectually, volitionally, and emotionally involved in that which is fundamental to one's very existence? Scripture is not indulging in a mere literary play of word images when we are told of the origin from dust and the destiny of a return to dust for our physical bodies. It is possible to trace this dusty account from star dust, to rock dust, to earth's soil dust, to plants and animals, and ultimately to the very elements that compose the structure of the body and participate in its energy relationships.

SOME OF GEOLOGY'S DISTINCTIONS AMONG THE SCIENCES

The approach of geologists to their work is necessarily different than in other sciences. Humankind was not present to observe the occurrence of most of the geological phenomena now studied. Many aspects of the study of the earth cannot be duplicated and studied under controlled laboratory conditions. Recognizably, the length of time, the magnitude of forces involved, and primitive earth conditions are not duplicable. Nevertheless, modern laboratory capabilities are adding to our understandings of these issues.

In all sciences, we make certain assumptions about our task. For our work to be practical we assume that the same functional relationships, the same causes and effects, have continued throughout time. We assume the same physical, chemical, and biological laws to have persisted for all time. This is true for the geological realm as well; however, we must recognize that over time the dominating geological activities may have varied. Such geological occurrences as volcanic eruption or glaciation in the past leave ample evidence of their activity, all under the influence of the same natural laws that continue to operate today.

When geologists find preserved results in the geologic record similar to those effects being produced today, they attribute the recorded evidence to the same causes. Rivers still build deltas. Mountains continue to rise. Sediment deposits still require sources. Volcanoes cover the landscape with their fiery products. Organisms continue to be buried by everyday occurrences in nature. Glaciers continue to exist today in every size, from very small ones to those of continental scale which once covered much of North America and Europe. Earthquakes frighten us as plates of the earth's crust move against each other. The rock record carries ample evidence of these occurrences in the past. This method of interpreting the earth's natural history has been known as uniformitarianism. The major alternative explanation is that of catastrophism. Proponents of this latter view often attempt to crowd the whole geologic time scale into a very narrow time frame by attributing the geologic record to one or more short-term catastrophes with far reaching effects. These adherents seem unprepared to acknowledge that these occurrences may be only part of the repertoire of creation, whose concert of geologic changes is being conducted over what almost certainly appears to be a much more extensive time frame.

Due to the nature of the task and its inherent limitations, the work of geologists is heavily weighted to being that of observers. One must be keenly aware of natural processes and their effects, both the immediate and the long-term. The collection of current observations validates the observations about the past record. The preserved record is understandable when you know what nature is doing now. You must understand the language of the earth if you are to grasp its message. To be sensitive to the geologic account is to recognize the "wasness of the is."[12]

SOME IMPLICATIONS OF A CHRISTIAN APPROACH TO GEOLOGY

What else can be said about the approach of Christian geologists? As in many sciences, the working content, the day-to-day tasks, may not differ significantly from that of non-Christian geologists. What *will* vary are the former's presuppositions regarding the nature of creation, the ultimate origin of the earth, the governing power over the laws observed to be operating, and the personal meaning of the discoveries found that affects one's whole world and life view. Claerbaut affirms the critical importance of creation in all Christian worldview thinking as follows: "Not one shred of Christian thought has any validity apart from creation. Creation is the ball game. It establishes theism and leads to the Christian concept of God."[13] He goes on to observe that Christians may differ on issues like the

12. Harrington, *To See a World*, 57.

13. Claerbaut, "Why is Creation Central to the Faith-and-Learning Enterprise?" 147.

age of the earth, but they are all obliged to believe that God created the heavens and the earth.

Christian belief and experience based on both scriptural revelation and the revelation of the creation assert that God is not only the Creator and Originator of all that exists but that he is also exercising his control over creation in and through so-called "natural laws." To say that natural laws can account for the workings of our earth without the intervention of Deity disregards God's immanence and operation through those laws, although he may participate in a manner not obvious to humans.

Christian geologists find their role personally meaningful through an understanding that they are working with the part of God's revelation called the creation. The believing geologist does not expect any areas of such revelation to be self-contradictory. God will show himself consistently in both specific revelation (the Scriptures) and general revelation (the creation). God's repeated declaration in Genesis 1 about a "good" creation applies to all aspects of his creation (including the rocks!). The Scriptures affirm that creation itself praises God. (See, for example, Psalm 19:1–4.) In my opinion, a Christian geologist is necessarily one who believes that God must ultimately be seen as both the Creator and the Sustainer of the cosmos. But that does not mean that a Christian geologist thinks that his or her discoveries need be shrouded in interminable mystery. One does not need to wait for heaven to provide all the answers. Though God's ways are sometimes mysterious, his works through the creation are seen as ultimately intelligible, bringing glory to himself. Believing scientists understand themselves to be rational persons receiving meaningful information. This is the principal reason for revelation—to reveal, to deliver a message with important content. I believe the value of science is far more than just its application to technology. Christian geologists can also experience the deep satisfaction that comes from a growing understanding and appreciation of the marvelous universe brought into existence by our Creator, something lost on those who do not so believe.

One critical issue facing Christian geologists is reconciliation of the scientific and the biblical accounts of early earth history. They come to the issue with the unequivocal expectation that revelation will be non-contradictory. They must have no preconceived time frame into which earth history must be condensed, for the Bible provides none. Since theirs is an avowed Christian perspective, they must place the highest value on truthfulness. They must seek to handle their data honestly. Differences between scientific conclusions and biblical interpretations, when they occur, just tell us that some of our analyses are either incomplete or mistaken, either in our scientific reasoning or in our biblical understanding.

The biblical account of creation, due to the absence, obviously, of human observers, is what could be called retrospective revelation, or revelation that looks back, whereas prospective revelation, or prophecy, anticipates or looks ahead. The narrative is clear enough in answering questions such as who did it and why it was done. It sets the scene for an adequately fitting, worshipful situation for humans toward their Maker. To a pre-scientific culture little is said about the exact nature of the how and the when. It is interesting that a similar lack of temporal or modal precision is present in many of the eschatological passages of the Scriptures (e.g., in Daniel or Revelation), but some biblical interpreters seem more willing to grant this for a range of conclusions about post-historical (i.e., end times) events than about prehistorical (i.e., creational) ones. One of the Christian geologist's principal tasks is to attempt to "creatively" serve as moderator between the principals (and principles!) involved in these discussions (disputes?) about cosmological origins.

To be specific, some very disparate stances on these how and when questions have developed among commentators who otherwise share theistic presuppositions. Some (called "Young Earth Creationists") believe that the earth was created and populated over the course of six 24-hour days less than 10,000 years ago. Other believing scientists hold that there is scientific evidence for the earth being created something like 4.5 billion years ago. Two Cambridge University professors holding to this latter perspective, molecular immunologist Denis Alexander and geophysics professor Robert White, explain the basis for their position as follows:

> If there were only one or two scientific observations that suggested an age [of the earth] of thousands of millions of years, we could justifiably hold loose to the presumption of an ancient earth. But in fact, there are dozens of independent ways of measuring the age of the earth which give consistent results; furthermore, the same physical constants that are used in geological dating of rocks are lynchpins in disciplines as diverse as biology, biochemistry, astronomy, particle physics and chemistry. . . . We cannot . . . ignore one piece of evidence, such as the age of the rock, without bringing a huge interlocking area of quite diverse science crashing down.[14]

14. Alexander and White, *Science, Faith, and Ethics*, 74–75.

An increasingly accepted viewpoint that seeks to reconcile the Genesis account of the creation of the cosmos by God with an apparently "old" earth is the so-called "big bang" thesis. Christian theist and scientist Hugh Ross describes this viewpoint as follows: "According to the big bang, at the creation event all the physics (specifically, the laws, constants, and equations of physics) are instantly created, designed, and finished so as to guarantee an ongoing, continual expansion of the universe at exactly the right rates with respect to time so that physical life will be possible."[15] Later in his book, Ross acknowledges the considerable opposition to the big bang explanation of the universe's origin from both young earth creationists as well as people with agnostic or atheistic frames of reference, pointing out that the basis for this rejection is principally philosophical, not scientific:

> Though the case for the big bang, that is, a transcendent cosmic creation event, rests on compelling, some might say *overwhelming* [emphasis Ross's] evidence, the theory still has its critics. Some skepticism may be attributable to the communication gap between scientists and the rest of the world. Some of the evidences are so new that most people have yet to hear of them. Some of the evidences . . . are so technical that few people understand their significance. The need for better education and clearer communication remains. In fact, it motivates the publication of this book [i.e., *The Creator and the Cosmos*].[16]

Besides their contribution to understanding earth history, Christian geologists can assist other Christians toward more congruent and satisfying worldviews. One's world and life view is that perspective that unifies one's experience, provides answers to the major issues in life, and gives meaning and purpose from one end of life to the other. Humankind's most fundamental concerns have varied little over history. Issues of physical well-being, family and social relations, meaning and purpose in life, spiritual crises, and eternal destiny have long been with us. The experiential input to these concerns, however, varies from age to age. Our meaningful understanding of ourselves grows or shrinks as our worldview is able to absorb or categorize the incoming data and experience. Christians need an all-encompassing worldview. As Dye observes, without such a view Christians can only resort to defensive tactics, "able only to react

15. Ross, *The Creator and the Cosmos*, 25.

16. Ibid., 67.

irrationally against new scientific data [they] cannot reconcile with [their] religious views." Too often, he continues, some Christians attach the label "science falsely so-called" to scientific data (or their interpretation of it) that do not match their pre-formulated biblical interpretations.[17] This side-stepping of the issue satisfies only those who use it. Christian geologists with their sense of existing as rational beings should aspire to treat their evidence (data) as the content of an intellectually honest witness to the work of the Creator.

The acceptance of some observations made by geologists may cause considerable thoughtful struggles for some Christians. The rewards of an expanded or adjusted worldview will be worth the disruption of a too comfortable faith that results from closure of one's mind to new input. To be honest to our high commitment to truth requires that we take the risk. The following examples of potentially troubling observations may illustrate my point:

1. The early fossil record does not contain many of the organisms living today.

2. Up to ninety percent of the life forms that ever lived have become extinct. In view of point 1 above, this suggests a complex picture of the timing and origin of earth's various life forms.

3. Though the creation is unspeakably beautiful and satisfying to the human mind and senses, it is not now as it was, fresh from the Creator's hand.

4. The study of annual growth rings in trees has traced time backward for nearly 9,000 years. What does this mean regarding a recent creation when these details come to us only in the most recent of deposits?

5. God's creative activity did not happen instantaneously, if we mean his acts that brought the creation to the state we now know.

Support and clarification of the above examples would require a longer treatise—perhaps even a full book!

A third positive contribution of Christian geologists is to their own worship experiences and those of their fellow Christians. The contemporary church desperately needs a restoration of reverence and meaning-

17. Dye, *Faith and the Physical World,* 14.

ful content to its worship experience. The study and understanding of creation can sensitize worshippers to read their Scriptures and sing their hymns more meaningfully. "Were the whole realm of nature mine, that were a present far too small" is a far more significant expression of praise for those who know and understand that creation.

The last contribution of Christian geologists I wish to mention relates to their role in the creation mandate. Humankind's God-given responsibility over the earth is that of caretaker, not exploiter. We are charged with taking care of a valued asset or provision. When a geologist shares insights and understandings about a remarkably functioning creation, this should raise awareness of the threats to the earth, our created home. Particular contributions could include issues of soil conservation, world food supply, flood and erosion control, potential ground water contamination, and global warming concerns. Understanding promotes appreciation, which in turn leads to valuing, hopefully valuing enough to act in accordance with the Creator's intentions and desires.

WORKS CITED

Alexander, Denis, and Robert S. White. *Science, Faith, and Ethics: Grid or Gridlock? An Approach to Controversial Topics in Science*. Peabody, MA: Hendrickson, 2004.

Claerbaut, David. "Why Is Creation Central to the Faith-and-Learning Enterprise?" In his *Faith and Learning on the Edge: A Bold New Look at Religion in Higher Education*, 146–59. Grand Rapids, MI: Zondervan, 2004.

Dye, David L. *Faith and the Physical World: A Comprehensive View*. Grand Rapids, MI: Eerdmans, 1970.

Geikie, Archibald. "Landscape and Literature." In *Language of the Earth*, edited by Frank H. T. Rhoads and Richard O. Stone, 212–15. Toronto, ON: Pergamon, 1981.

Harrington, John W. *To See a World*. St. Louis: C. V. Mosby, 1973.

Holmes, Arthur F. *The Idea of a Christian College*. Rev. ed. Grand Rapids, MI: Eerdmans, 1987.

Lutgens, Frederick, and Edward Tarbuck. *Essentials of Geology*. 4th ed. Toronto, ON: Maxwell Macmillan, 1992.

Michener, James A. *Centennial*. New York: Fawcett Crest, 1974.

Powell, John W. *Lands of the Arid Region of the United States*. 2d ed. Boston: Harvard Common, 1983 (1879).

Ross, Hugh. *The Creator and the Cosmos: How the Greatest Scientific Discoveries of the Century Reveal God*. Colorado Springs, CO: NavPress, 2001.

Stegner, Wallace. "At Home in the Fields of the Lord." In his *The Sound of Mountain Water*, 157–69. Lincoln, NE: Nebraska University Press, 1985.

Webb, Walter P. *The Great Plains*. New York: Grosset and Dunlap, 1976 (1931).

FOR FURTHER READING

Collins, Francis S. *The Language of God: A Scientist Presents Evidence for Belief.* New York: Free Press, 2006.

Craig, William Lane, and Quentin Smith. *Theism, Atheism, and Big Bang Cosmology.* Oxford: Oxford University Press, 1993.

Gale, Barry G. *Evolution without Evidence: Charles Darwin and* The Origin of Species. Albuquerque: University of New Mexico Press, 1982.

Godfrey, Stephen J., and Christopher R. Smith. *Paradigms on Pilgrimage: Creationism, Paleontology, and Biblical Interpretation.* Toronto, ON: Clements, 2005.

Pigliucci, Massimo. *Denying Evolution: Creationism, Scientism, and the Nature of Science.* Sunderland, MA: Sinauer Associates, 2000.

Ratzsch, Del. *The Battle of Beginnings: Why Neither Side Is Winning the Creation–Evolution Debate.* Downers Grove, IL: InterVarsity Press, 1996.

16

A Christian Perspective on History

ROBERT K. BURKINSHAW

INTRODUCTION

I HAVE TO BEGIN with a confession. I did not like history in high school. In fact, I felt so antagonistic towards it that I refused to take History 12, something that most students on the academic stream in my high school chose to take.

As you might have guessed, my mind has changed a little since then. I would not have spent ten years studying history at university and spent the last twenty-five years trying to interest students in it if I hadn't become interested. In fact, the more I teach and study history, the more I am convinced it is something Christians should know more about.

Let me give you several reasons why I believe a Christian should study history. Then I will describe some of the ways in which a Christian approach to it is different from a secular approach.

WHY SHOULD A CHRISTIAN STUDY HISTORY?

Interest

What began to strike me after I left high school and was exposed to several post-secondary history courses was the range of subjects that can be studied. I was surprised that it could be something more than learning lists of the names of kings, queens, battles, and prime ministers or presidents. It was not the old "name and date idea" I had mistakenly picked up in junior high school, but *it involved any area that is important in human affairs*. In other words, history could be relevant to people with any one of a whole range of interests. Examples:

1. *Christianity*: Why and how has the church changed since the New Testament book of Acts was written? How has the church changed society? What are the issues the church faced in the past that we also face today? (It so happens that it was a course in the history of Christianity that first awakened my interest in the study of history.)

2. *Ideas and Values*: What has been the source of ideas and values in our culture? How have they shaped history—e.g., Darwinism and its impact on scientific, religious, economic, and racial views in North America?

3. *Society and Culture*: Issues such as changing views of the family, the developing ethnic mix in society, social reform movements, changing roles of women in society, the rise of industry and cities, and the development of public education are all interesting issues that historians study.

Influence Gained from an Understanding of History

I recently received notice of a newly released reprint of a book with the title *Ideas are Weapons: The History and Uses of Ideas*.[1] The wording of that title *Ideas are Weapons* is probably not too strong. It is extremely important what individuals think—their ideas are often the motivators of their actions. When *many* individuals in a society hold and act on certain ideas, those ideas become very powerful. It is not surprising that we have a saying, "The pen is mightier than the sword" (or, to employ more modern parlance, "The computer keyboard is mightier than the AK47"!).

When we study history, we form ideas about the past. These ideas are often based on interpretations, some of which are closer to the historical facts than others. Whether based on fact or not, those interpretations are often very influential in the present.

Examples:

1. *Soviet Union/Russia*: We are told that the history of the Stalinist period is being rewritten. Why? Because the older version was carefully tailored to glorify the Stalinist regime in order to attempt to create a positive attitude among the people towards their totalitarian system. Much of the authority of the old hardliners in the former

---

1. Lerner, *Ideas are Weapons*.

Soviet Union rested on their ability to convince the people of a certain view of history.

2. *Marxism in the Western World*: Many academics in Western universities still hold some sort of version of Marxism. They believe that economics (or material concerns) are the only real motivators of human action. Furthermore, in their view, there must always be conflict or struggle between different economic classes in society (workers/owners etc.). Real change only comes from that conflict.

   Marxists base their beliefs on a particular view of history. Karl Marx and Friedrich Engels, in the first sentence of the *Manifesto of the Communist Party*, wrote: "The *history* [emphasis mine] of all hitherto existing society is the *history* of class struggles."[2] As a result, much of the energy of the many Marxist historians is spent in establishing as fact the view that material concerns and class struggle or conflict are the most important factors in the nation they are studying—whether Britain, France, Canada, the United States or any other country. If they can establish that, through the study of history, their views can have much greater power *in the present*.

   Historians who are not Marxists try to highlight factors other than economic motives—whether political ideas or principles or religious beliefs and principles, for example—which have motivated people. They also point out periods in which classes have not been in conflict but have cooperated, sometimes for the benefit of many classes.

3. *Quebec, Canada*: Marxists and non-Marxists are not the only ones who see the study of history as important in establishing the legitimacy or influence of their own ideas. For example, the Canadian Parti Quebecois was first elected in Quebec in 1975, partly as the result of a certain view of Quebec history that had come to dominate in most universities, colleges, and high schools in that province. The document that the separatist government released at the time of the 1980 Sovereignty-Association vote spelled out that historical view— that most of Quebec's social and economic problems in the past and present were the result of the English conquest and continuous domination of Quebec. That was a powerful idea that almost won the day. It was defeated in part by another view of Quebec's history,

---

2. Marx and Engles, *Manifesto of the Communist Party*, 1.

that there were other sources of its problems that separatism could not solve.

4. *Reform Party of Canada*: In 1990, I heard then Reform Party of Canada leader, Preston Manning, speak on Trinity Western University's campus. The largest single part of his speech was historical. He traced the history of ideas and movements of political reform in Canada from the last century to the present. Why did he take so much time with history? He knew that if he could establish the fact in our minds that political reform was a legitimate part of our history, then we might be persuaded that the Reform Party was not a party of the "lunatic fringe" that so many thought it was at that time.

5. *The History of Abortion*: Certain historians have tried to overturn the commonly held view that most women in the past did not accept abortion as a viable option for them. These historians argue instead that women of the past commonly sought abortions. Therefore, they claim, the pro-choice view is more legitimate because abortion has always been accepted, at least by the women of our society. I don't believe for a moment that their history is very accurate, but their attempts do show how significant it is for Christians to know history.

6. *The Changing Face of the History of Christianity*: Always an important subdivision of history, the study of the history of Christianity continues to attract devotees in some places. My own research is in Canadian religious history. I am trying to explain why the province of British Columbia became, in the twentieth century, the most secular part of North America and yet, despite the hostile environment, the home of numerous thriving evangelical churches and institutions.

Research in Canadian religious history has shown tremendous growth in the last twenty years. It is gratifying to see that increasing numbers of academic historians are recognizing the importance of the Christian church in Canada's past.

The history of Christianity, while certainly not the only area of importance for Christians to study, does evoke some very probing questions. For example, in the face of great criticisms of Christians in public life (people like Canada's current Prime Minister, Stephen Harper), historians with Christian faith presuppositions ask questions such as:

- What has been the church's influence in society? Has it consistently degraded women, as so many critics claim? Is it inveterately and inherently homophobic because many of its members are opposed to sanctioning gay marriage?

- Has it made positive contributions to society in the areas of educational and medical reforms, the abolition of slavery, and the care of the homeless, orphans, and widows?

These questions are important. Whether we like it or not, many people judge the church on its past record—on its history, in short. That is not always as good a record as we would like, but it is important that it be understood as accurately as possible.

In addition, many Christians are interested in the history of the church because it gives us insight into the current situation. For example, what factors contributed to the decline of the church in certain periods in the past? And what factors contributed to great revivals of faith in the past?

Christianity: An Historical Faith

Christianity is based on facts of history, but it also speaks about the future. Therefore the study of history, biblical and non-biblical, is important to Christians because history is seen to have a purpose. We came from somewhere, it asserts, and are going somewhere. We believe that history is more than a collection of random events that happened by chance. As the New Testament writers said of Old Testament history, we can learn from events of the past. We can gain real insights that may help us as a society, as the Christian Church, and as individuals.

DOES A CHRISTIAN STUDY HISTORY DIFFERENTLY?[3]

Not always. Basic facts remain unchanged whether a Christian or a non-Christian is studying them. But studying history is much more than com-

3. This question was explicitly addressed when the Conference on Faith and History (CFH) was established in the U.S. in 1967 to both foster fellowship among Christian historians and challenge them to explore the relationship of their faith to their research and teaching. The following year the semiannual journal *Fides et Historia* was founded to provide a means for the scholarly exploration of this topic. In a 2001 article in *Christianity Today*, "Whatever Happened to Christian History," Tim Stafford points out that at the time CFH was established, there may have been only one prominent Christian historian

piling a list of facts. It is as much, or more, a process of selecting the most relevant facts and interpreting them. Why did a certain development take place? What were the factors at work? What was the significance of that development? In short, there is no single Christian interpretation of most events of history, but there should be some common features:

Honesty of Approach

Some historians now wonder whether it is even possible for historians to talk about "truth in history." However, I believe it is not only at least partially possible, but it is also something we must strive for. Our limited access to all of the facts as well as our own biases and perspectives will always make it difficult to say absolutely that we "have arrived at the truth" in our historical investigations. But, while that should make us humble in our claims, it should not stop us from making the attempt. Indeed, as Christians we are called to always tell the truth in every area of life. The need for an honest approach to history is extremely acute because of the potential for abuse that stems from the influence historical views can have. In fact, history is often used as a "tool" by people who dishonestly select and manipulate the facts to suit their purposes.

Examples:

1. *Misinterpretation of the Role of Christianity in History.* Some historians claim too much for the positive role of the church in society and ignore the problems Christians have sometimes created when they

---

(Timothy Smith at Johns Hopkins University) recognized and respected by his secular university colleagues. Some thirty years later, there were at least half a dozen (including Nathan Hatch and George Marsden at Notre Dame, Mark Noll at Wheaton College, and George Rawlyk at Queen's University, Ontario). Westmont College historian Shirley Mullen, in a 2005/06 *Fides et Historia* article "History, Virtue, and the Conference on Faith and History," reviewing the "history" of both the Conference and its journal, noted that religion is now a legitimate topic for mainstream historical study (not so 40 years ago) and that conservative historians are much less fearful about speaking forthrightly to the whole culture about religious implications of their historical investigations (2). However, in response to suggestions by some that the Conference on Faith and History organization was no longer needed, in that historians with a Christian worldview "have won the right to participate in secular conversations at the late modern, multicultural, academic table," CFH president Douglas Sweeney, in his September 22, 2006 address to delegates (published as "On the Vocation of Historians") asserted that more reflection was needed on the implications of their Christian faith for their roles as both scholars and teachers (2). For an informative account of the formation of the Conference on Faith and History, see Hart, "History in Search of Meaning."

did not follow Christ faithfully. More commonly, other historians do not acknowledge the tremendous influence the church has had in shaping our modern society.

2. *Ultranationalist Historians* (e.g., Germany, USA, Britain, etc.). Such historians often manipulate the facts to put their nation in the best possible light, highlighting "glorious" events and ignoring shameful ones.

3. *Anti-nationalist Historians* (e.g., USA). Such historians misuse history for purposes opposite to those of some nationalist historians. They carefully select facts to support their belief that the U.S. is "the evil empire" while ignoring very important facts that would balance the picture.

4. *Quebec Historians*. In the heat of the Canadian debate over Quebec separatism, both schools of historians (nationalist or federalist) were perceived by some to use history as a tool to support their cause. We Christian historians may feel tempted similarly to downplay or outrightly evade inconvenient historical facts because the issues are so important to us. However, we are accountable to God to be ruthlessly honest in making sure we don't manipulate history to make it teach the lessons we want it to teach.

Humility of Approach

Christians must always realize that we don't know everything with certainty. We often "see through a glass darkly" (1 Corinthians 13:12). In addition, because we are aware of the great influence historical views have, we must speak and write with great care. In regard to these two attitudes Wheaton College philosophy professor emeritus Arthur Holmes writes that a Christian academic must have a motive characterized by

> a love for the truth and then a concern for the common good of the community to which one belongs. *It implies care about attitudes* [emphasis mine], lest one grow heady and opinionated and cease to bow in humility and awe. It implies working loyally within the framework of reference to which one stands committed.[4]

4. Holmes, *Idea of a Christian College*, 69.

Subject Matter as Reflecting a Christian View of Human Nature

What we choose to study and emphasize says a lot about what we think is important about people and about human nature. Christians have a view of human nature that includes much more than do many non-Christian views. For example, Marxists de-emphasize, or even deny, the importance of ideas in history. Only material or economic forces are deemed to be significant. Christians, on the one hand, agree with the Marxist that economics can be an important factor, even most important sometimes. On the other hand, however, we believe that humankind is created such that ideas, beliefs, principles, and sentiments are also very important, even critical sometimes. We also believe that ethics and good relations between people and nations are important. Therefore, we choose to emphasize such matters in addition to the material and economic factors.

On a related issue, many secular historians believe that religion has played a very minor role in history. They are simply reflecting a certain modern belief about human nature—that religion is not of primary importance and therefore can be simply ignored in historical analysis. Professor Timothy L. Smith, one of the better known historians in the United States at the time, argued, however, that one cannot understand American history without understanding how religious ideas and movements have affected it. As a Christian, he knew that the religious side of human beings is very important to many people, in the past as well as the present, so he chose to emphasize that where appropriate. He has identified over twenty periods and events in the United States where religious beliefs and principles were so important that one actually distorts American history by ignoring them (as most high school texts tend to do).[5]

Wheaton College history professor Mark Noll provides an interesting additional insight into why "Christian history" has been gaining increasing acceptability by a heretofore skeptical postmodern audience, noting "the manifest failure of Marxism, Freudianism, and Social Darwinism, the principal 'grand theories' in earlier decades of this century [the twentieth, for he was writing in 1998], to provide satisfactory comprehensive explanations for human history."[6]

The trend among some historians today is to stress the study of marginal groups, usually minorities and women, that have been oppressed

5. Smith, "High School History Texts," 20–32.

6. Noll, "The Potential of Missiology for the Crises of History," 109.

in different periods. Certainly a Christian should be very interested in the study of such groups, but a Christian historian must also be wary of falling into the trap of thinking that *only* such groups are worthy of study. Several years ago a Jewish woman taking graduate history courses in a major American university wrote of her difficulty in trying to pursue her interest in medieval intellectual history. The problem in finding courses dealing with this area, she wrote, arose because most of the intellectuals of the Medieval period "happened to be [Christian] theologians and male." She was informed that nobody wanted to teach courses dealing with theologians who were male.[7] This kind of approach can lead to as much distortion as the old approach that ignored almost everybody who was not a powerful male leader.

Interpretation of History

Our view of human nature also affects how we understand history. Why did things happen the way they did? What were the intentions of the people? What caused them to act the way they did? Christian historians do not *always* differ from their secular counterparts, but there *often* are differences.

We believe that humans are noble, created in the image of God, and therefore capable of elevated thoughts and good deeds and intentions. Therefore, we try to avoid being cynical about people's motives and intentions in history. On the other hand, we also recognize that humanity is flawed by sin and capable of tremendous evil, greed, and self-interest. Thus we aren't surprised, as are some liberal historians, when we find less than honorable motivations behind certain historical developments.

In short, I believe Christians probably have an advantage when it comes to interpreting history. Our view of human nature allows for a great range of possible interpretations. Also, we who believe in the religious nature and needs of humanity also gain a better insight into how *most* people in history viewed themselves and their world. Since most people in history have been religious in some sense, we can understand them far better than a modern, secular historian who does not recognize that side of human nature and experience.

---

7. Nedell, "Religion in the Academy," 4.

A FINAL NOTE: GOD'S ROLE IN HISTORY

On a final note, we as Christian historians must be careful. The history we study and write is different than biblical history. The biblical writers were inspired, we believe, to understand God's perspective on certain events and issues. As mere historians we cannot claim that kind of inspiration or understanding. We can gain great insights into people and their beliefs and motivations, but we are dealing on a human level. We may conjecture what God's view of this or that period is, but we must remember that he has not always revealed to us exactly how he has worked in history. Christians *do* believe that God works in human history, but we have to be careful not to think we can always understand his working.

Let us take, for example, the American War of Independence. We can explore people's motives—whether they were fighting for what they felt was right or merely for their own self-interest or whether they were simply confused. We can even read what Christians on both sides of the Atlantic thought of it. But God has not revealed whether he favored Britain or the United States in that war. Therefore we cannot pretend to speak for him on that issue.

On some issues, such as the success of what appear to be genuine spiritual revivals or the elimination of an evil such as the slave trade, I believe that we can have a reasonably fair idea of God's view. He has revealed some biblical principles to us that can make us relatively certain of our interpretation of events. But because human motives and actions are almost always a mixture of good and evil, of selflessness and self-interestedness, we still must always exercise caution in our judgments.

This limitation should not discourage us from studying history, however. Certainly there is no problem with having our Christian faith perspective be an important factor in our choice of historical topics and in our interpretations. In addition, just because we cannot claim to completely comprehend God's actions and mind in most events does not mean we shouldn't do all we can to further our historical knowledge and understanding.

Because history deals with all the issues important to humankind, and because of the significance of views of history in shaping present-day attitudes, and because Christianity, more than any other religion, is based on historical facts, we of all people should be involved in studying history. We can't claim to study or write history perfectly, nor will our views always be different from those of non-Christian historians, but our insights into human nature and the Christian attitudes of honesty and humility can and do give us a great advantage.

WORKS CITED

Hart, D. G. "History in Search of Meaning: The Conference on Faith and History." In *History and the Christian Historian*, edited by Ronald A. Wells, 68–87. Grand Rapids, MI: Eerdmans, 1998.

Holmes, Arthur F. *The Idea of a Christian College*. Rev. ed. Grand Rapids, MI: Eerdmans, 1987.

Lerner, Max. *Ideas are Weapons: The History and Uses of Ideas*. New York: Viking Press, 1939.

Marx, Karl, and Friedrich Engels. *Manifesto of the Communist Party*. New York: International Publishers, 1948.

Mullen, Shirley A. "History, Virtue, and the Conference on Faith and History." *Fides et Historia* 38.1 (Summer/Fall 2005) and 38.1 (Winter/Spring 2006) 1–9.

Nedell, Emily. "Religion in the Academy." In "The Religion of Journalists." *First Things* 42 (April 1994) 2–6.

Noll, Mark A. "The Potential of Missiology for the Crises of History." In *History and the Christian Historian*, edited by Ronald A. Wells, 106–23. Grand Rapids, MI: Eerdmans, 1998.

Smith, T. L. "High School History Texts Adopted for Use in the State of Alabama: The Distortion and Exclusion of Religious Data." *Crux* 23.4 (December 1987) 20–32.

Stafford, Tim. "Whatever Happened to Christian History?" *Christianity Today* 45.5 (April 2, 2001) 42–49.

Sweeney, Douglas. "On the Vocation of Historians to the Priesthood of Believers: Faithful Practices in Service of the Guild." *Fides et Historia* 39.1 (Winter/Spring 2007) 1–13.

FOR FURTHER READING

Bebbington, David W. *Patterns in History: A Christian Perspective on Historical Thought*. Rev. ed. Grand Rapids, MI: Baker, 1990.

Bendroth, Margaret L. "Men, Women, and God: Some Historiographical Issues." In *History and the Christian Historian*, edited by Ronald A. Wells, 91–105. Grand Rapids, MI: Eerdmans, 1998.

Butterfield, Herbert. *Christianity and History*. London: G. Bell, 1949.

Hankins, Barry. "'I'm Just Making a Point': Francis Schaeffer and the Irony of Faithful Christian Scholarship." *Fides et Historia* 39.1 (Winter/Spring 2007) 15–34.

Harvey, V. A. *The Historian and the Believer*. Urbana, IL: University of Illinois Press, 1996.

Marsden, George M. "What Difference Might Christian Perspectives Make?" In *History and the Christian Historian*, edited by Ronald A. Wells, 11–22. Grand Rapids, MI: Eerdmans, 1998.

Marsden, George M., and Frank Roberts, eds. *A Christian View of History?* Grand Rapids, MI: Eerdmans, 1975.

McKenzie, Robert T. "Christians Teaching History: 'Sermons' for the Secular Classroom." *Fides et Historia* 36.1 (Winter/Spring 2004) 93–104.

Noll, Mark A. *The Scandal of the Evangelical Mind*. Grand Rapids, MI: Eerdmans, 1994.

Otto, Paul. "Teaching History as Creational Development." *Fides et Historia* 36.1 (Winter/Spring 2004) 118–24.

Sanders, Glenn E. "Christian Belief and History Teaching: Some New Opportunities." *Fides et Historia* 39.1 (Winter/Spring 2007) 75–84.

———. "Christian Faith and Teaching History: Tools and Communities." *Fides et Historia* 36.1 (Winter/Spring 2004) 105–10.

Yandell, Keith E. "Evangelical Thought, 1987." *Christian Scholar's Review* 17 (1988) 341–46.

17

A Christian Perspective on Linguistics

MICHAEL R. WALROD

INTRODUCTION

IN THIS DISCUSSION OF linguistics, the study of human speech, I shall outline the main categories or sub-divisions of this discipline before considering some of the differences that a Christian perspective makes in one's approach to linguistics. I shall conclude with a brief discussion of some of the reasons for a Christian devoting time to the study of linguistics, particularly on an applied or practical as opposed to a purely theoretical level.

IMPORTANT ASPECTS OF LINGUISTICS

Phonetics: The Sounds of a Language

Humans are capable of producing hundreds of speech sounds. Yet any given language uses only a small subset of all the sounds that humans are able to produce. The problem of going from one language to another is that each language uses a different subset of the possible sounds. Therefore, people who learn a second language, especially if they learn it when they are adults, usually speak the second one with an *accent*. This means that they try to pronounce the words of the second language according to the sounds used in their first language.

Linguistics includes the study of phonetics, involving the sounds of human languages in general. Linguists need to be able to recognize the sounds of another language, write them down, and reproduce them well, as free as possible from any "foreign" accent.

Phonology: The Sound System of a Language

The sounds of every human language are arranged in a system. Each language has its own restrictions on which sounds may occur, and in what order. For example, in English we do not have words that begin with the "ng" sound. (This is one sound, or phonetic segment, in spite of the fact that we write it with two letters.) Other languages do have words that begin with "ng," the sound at the end of the English word "sing." The word meaning "black" in some languages of the Philippines is "ngisit."

The speakers of a language recognize units of sound, called *phonemes*, and perceive these as the same in all instances. For example, in English there are different possible ways of pronouncing the sound *p*. It is common to pronounce *p* with a slight aspiration (puff of air) after it, and this is done whenever the *p* is at the beginning of a word or at the beginning of a stressed syllable. Elsewhere in words (e.g., following *s*, or at the end of a word), the *p* sound does not have aspiration. Yet English speakers think of both ways of making *p* as the same sound. (In other languages, these two might be seen as separate sounds.)

Another example of the system of English sounds is that it is possible to start a word with three consonants. Most languages do not permit this. However, even in English, there are very few possible combinations of sounds in words that do start with three consonants. The first sound must be *s*, the second sound must be *p, t,* or *k,* and the third sound must be *l, r,* or *w*. Examples are *split, strike,* and *scratch* (note that the *k* sound is sometimes written with a *c*).

The study of phonology enables the linguist to analyze the sound system of any language and to create a suitable orthography (alphabet) to represent the sounds of the language. Such an orthography, called a *phonemic* orthography, is an economical way of writing the language. Our English writing system is not a good phonemic orthography, because the spelling of words in English is very irregular. If our writing system were good from a phonemic perspective, then all words with the *f* sound, for example, would be written with "f." Instead, we write this sound at least three ways, as illustrated in the words *fun, phone,* and *rough.* There are many other examples in English of alternate spellings for the same sounds.

Grammar: Morphology, Syntax, Texts

The core of most linguistic analysis is the grammar or structure of a language. A linguistic approach to the study of grammar is not like a grade school approach. The way grammar is taught in grade school is usually *prescriptive*, that is, "This is the way you must construct a grammatical sentence." In linguistics, we are more concerned with the utterances that actually occur in human communication rather than just those that are considered to measure up to the standard rules of grammar teachers. Therefore, the linguistic approach to grammar is *descriptive*.

Grammar in linguistics refers to *morphology* (how words are formed using prefixes, suffixes, or even changes in the root form), *syntax* (the structure of phrases, clauses, and sentences), and *text grammar*, also called *discourse grammar* (the way longer utterances are constructed, either in monologue or in dialogue form).

Semantics: Meanings of Words, Propositions, and Relationships

Semantics is another level of analysis in linguistics. The linguist Noam Chomsky proposed the sentence "Colorless green ideas sleep furiously" as an example of a sentence that is grammatically correct but semantically anomalous. It is nonsense; it has no referent in the real world. Yet we recognize that there is no grammatical error. This shows that semantic structure is *somewhat* independent of grammatical structure. Phonology, grammar, and semantics are all somewhat independent of each other, and yet all occur simultaneously in human communication. The poem "Jabberwockey" by Lewis Carroll is an example of a text that is correct in grammar and phonology but is semantically irregular and inscrutable:

> 'Twas brillig, and the slithy toves
> Did gyre and gimble in the wabe;
> All mimsy were the borogroves,
> And the mome raths outgrabe.

Semantics is the study of the meanings of words, propositions, and the relationships between propositions. Words may be analyzed according to their semantic components. For example:

horse:	thing, animal, equine
stallion:	horse, male, adult
colt:	horse, male, young
mare:	horse, female, adult
filly:	horse, female, young

These are not all the semantic features of each of these terms; there are extended and peripheral meanings also. But these central features of meaning are sufficient to distinguish each term from the others in the set.

Pragmatics: Social Relationships, Attitudes, Intentions, and Worldview

Pragmatics is the study of all the information speakers of human languages know, consciously or unconsciously, that enables them to construct or decode utterances. It is the study of the data of the communication situation, that is, the social relationships between speakers and hearers, the attitudes and intentions of both, and their worldview and "knowledge structures."

Knowledge structures are sets of "facts" that we know, stereotypical combinations of bits of information or sequences of actions that enable us to generate expectations when we decode utterances that we hear. These knowledge structures, called scripts and frames, are what we know something about (for example, eating in a restaurant, attending church, or playing football). Because we know what to expect, we can decode utterances about these events, even though much of the information is left unsaid (implicit). For example, in relating an incident that happened at a restaurant, such as a waiter spilling coffee on a customer, we would usually feel free to omit details such as reading the menu, ordering, and paying the bill. All of these events will be assumed subconsciously by the listener.

Computational Linguistics: Artificial Intelligence

The sub-discipline of *artificial intelligence* is an area of intersection between psycholinguistics and computer science.[1] Computers are being programmed to simulate human thought and communication. The applications of artificial intelligence to linguistics are in text generating (e.g., producing stories) and text processing (e.g., "understanding" stories or other texts) as well as speech recognition and machine translation.

Computers are becoming increasingly important in linguistics, being used for managing databases of information about languages as well as for analysis and description of languages.

---

1. See pp. 183–204 of this volume for an extended discussion of artificial intelli-gence.

IMPLICATIONS OF A CHRISTIAN WORLDVIEW FOR LINGUISTICS

Some anthropologists describe human culture as having layers like an onion. The outermost layer is *behavior,* what people do, which may be observed and described. Beneath that is the layer of *taxonomy,* which includes the knowledge such as codes and categories of a group of people— such as economic, scientific, and/or political categories. A still deeper level of human culture is *ideology,* which includes a group's beliefs, mythology, ethics, and values. Finally, at the "core of the onion," the most basic level of all, is *worldview.* It is the least accessible and hardest to observe because it is largely subconscious. The group usually believes that it needs no explanation; it often defies explanation. Worldview may be thought of as the "articles of faith" of a society or a sub-group within a society. It is the set of the most basic assumptions, never questioned in the normal course of life (e.g., belief in the supernatural is this kind of basic assumption in most societies).

A Christian worldview, therefore, is a worldview that interprets all the data of perception and cognition from the perspective of the basic assumptions of Christian theism (belief in God as revealed to us in creation and the Christian Scriptures). That is to say, we may perceive by intuition and affirm by faith that there is an all-powerful, good God who created us and our universe, and that he did so according to his purposes, a master plan, revealed to us in the Scriptures. There is also a substantial revelation of God built into the universe and into us, such as our God-consciousness, our desire for meaning and purpose, and our sense of value (e.g., the concepts of right and wrong, good and bad, and the notion of should or ought). Philosophical arguments in the areas of cosmology (the universe), teleology (design and purpose), and axiology (values) strongly support the Christian worldview. Linguistics adds powerful evidence to these arguments.

Linguistics as an Extension of the Cosmological and Teleological Arguments

There is obviously complex design in language. One of the tenets of a Christian worldview is that the world is not randomly ordered. We would never accept that, given enough time, the molecules in a randomly ordered universe would come together by chance and form a Yamaha racing bike.

How much more preposterous to assume that without a specific purpose, without a master designer, the universe has produced human beings—living, breathing, conscious, rational, social, and spiritual. Humans seek a sense of larger purpose, pursue a relationship with creation, and have a sense of value, design, and beauty. God's involvement in all of this bombards our consciousness; it takes effort to ignore it (see Romans 1:18ff.). Yet humankind is naturally inclined to make the effort to do so.

Human language, in its orderly structure (design), its creative potential, its conceptual content of values and norms, and in the fact that all languages have all of these and many other features in common (i.e., they are universal features), strongly corroborates the Christian worldview. If all "creation" (cosmos) were random, why would there be *any* universals in language? There are, in fact, many universal features of sounds, grammar, and meaning in languages.

In addition, universal semantic relations exist between propositions, such as purpose, reason-result, cause-effect, and condition-consequence, that indicate the universal preoccupation with the larger context, the *why*, the reason for our existence.

Furthermore, there are value systems encoded in every human language: the concepts of should and ought, good and bad, right and wrong. I assert and maintain the validity of an "axiological argument," that is, why should *everyone* have these value concepts if it were true that the present universe were the result of chance? Why would there be words like good/bad, right/wrong, and why would there be any normative discourse (arguing or persuading others to believe/behave in certain ways)?

Everyone, regardless of national origin or language grouping, has concepts of value such as good and bad, as well as a relatively sophisticated vocabulary for talking about these concepts. *Normative discourse* is the use of language for evaluating and prescribing, for determining what is good or bad, better or worse, and for perpetuating the values and norms of the society.

Effects of a Christian Worldview on Linguistics

1. *Ethical Issues*: We must value all peoples, including their languages and worldviews. Other worldviews are not inferior to our own just because they are different. In fact, others may be closer to a Christian worldview in some respects than is a North American worldview. For example, among

the Ga'dang people of the Northern Philippines (where I did fieldwork for seventeen years), kinship and other social relationships are highly valued. There is a strong sense of community and solidarity. This is in contrast to the radical individualism valued in our Western context, as evidenced by all our books on self-actualization, self-fulfillment, and personal development.

2. *Pragmatic issues*: Because God is the author of human languages, and the whole process of human communication is one he designed, languages have many features and functions in common (e.g., sound systems, grammar, and semantics). There is conceptual transferability, for translation is always possible.

REASONS FOR STUDYING LINGUISTICS

Infinite Complexity and Creativity of Language: A Never-ending Challenge

Languages have the structure of mathematics but the beauty and creativity of art. Their variety and complexity seem infinite. For example, it is impossible to find in any language two exactly synonymous terms, that is, terms that have precisely the same meaning and can be distributed in exactly the same way, interchanged in every sentence/utterance in which they occur. The creative function of language is limitless. As one of the areas where humans can really exercise *creativity*, language is a significant part of the image of God in us.

Communicative Function of Language: A Means to a Worthwhile End

The phenomenon of expressing a meaning that exists in my mind by making some noises or some marks on paper, and the fact that another person can hear the noises or see the marks and then have the same or similar thoughts in his or her mind, is one of the most incredible phenomena in human experience. (I am not even focusing on the physical aspects of sound waves striking the ear drum or, in the case of reading, light waves striking the retina.) We are able to *communicate* meanings from one mind to another through language!

One very significant application of the communicative process with language is persuasive or normative discourse. Through language, we can effect cognitive and behavioral change in other people. This is a critical use of language, a means to a valuable end, since we believe that all people should hear and believe the message of the Christian gospel (even though we know that not all people will accept it).

Linguistics as a Tool for Removing Worldview Blinders

When we as infants learned a language and a culture, we came to view the world in the ways prescribed by our society. In a sense, the information we learned functioned as a set of blinders. It prescribed a manageable and comfortable number of categories of knowledge, prioritizing these in a way that guides our perception and attention.

Applied linguistics gives us a tool to remove those blinders to become familiar with another worldview. Once we have done so, we can never really put the blinders back on. We can never view the world in the restricted way we once did. For example, the Ga'dang people had to revise their worldview, through contact with my language and culture, when we brought a toy poodle to their village.

> "What's that?" they demanded to know.
> "A dog [*atu*]," I replied.
> "No possible way," they said, or words to that effect.
> "Well, what is it then?" I countered.
> "A sheep [*karnero*]," they said.

As a matter of fact, they had seen neither poodles nor sheep, but they had seen pictures of sheep and this poodle looked more like one of those than any dog they had seen. Then the poodle barked. At that moment the Ga'dang worldview was modified!

In similar ways, my worldview was modified as I learned to "see through their eyes." I learned the value of *atal*, which is sometimes translated "shame" but really means "an appropriate sense of reserve and respect." This beautiful value is all but ignored in Western society. *Atal* seeks to promote the well-being and happiness of others rather than the welfare of the individual.

Through applied linguistics, I was able to identify two kinds of first person plural pronouns in Ga'dang, whereas we have only one in English. In Ga'dang, there is an *exclusive* first person plural pronoun *ikkami*, which means "we, i.e., my companions and I, but not you (one or more people) to whom I am speaking." There is also an *inclusive* first person plural pronoun *ikkanetam*, which means "all of us (including you)." After many years of living in the Ga'dang community, I began to use the phrase "*ikkanetam a Ga'dang* [we Ga'dangs, inclusive]," implying that I was a member of their ethnic community. It caused only a momentary look of surprise the first time I said it. I had made a substantial claim to insider status, and they accepted it. I was able to communicate with them in their mother tongue, on a level that could never be achieved through a trade language.

Once I was viewed as an insider, I was able to use normative discourse effectively. I was able to communicate the Christian gospel and worldview, and it was well accepted.

The Timeliness of Linguistic Science in the Master Plan

Although languages have universal categories, there are enough differences in surface structure (phonetics, phonology, grammar), semantics, and pragmatics (social relationships, worldview, cognitive orientation such as concrete-relational versus abstract-conceptual) that cross-language communication has been difficult, often leading to serious misunderstanding. But now God has given us the technology to overcome the language and culture barrier. *The Babel effect is being reversed* through linguistics, cultural anthropology, and computer technology. When will the reversal be completed? The resources now exist. Linguistics is enabling us to be effective and successful in cross-cultural communication and is changing the world we live in.

FOR FURTHER READING

Fromkin, V., R. Rodman, and N. Hyams. *An Introduction to Language.* 7th ed. Independence, KY: Heinle, 2002.

Longacre, Robert E. *The Grammar of Discourse.* New York: Plenum Press, 1983. See esp. Ch. 8, "Toward Maximum Context," 337–56.

Lyons, John. *Introduction to Theoretical Linguistics.* Cambridge: Cambridge University Press, 1968.

18

A Christian Perspective on Mathematics

RICK SUTCLIFFE

INTRODUCTION

T HE STARTING POINT IN any discussion of the impact of the Christian faith on mathematics must of necessity be the nature of mathematical thought itself. What is mathematics? What does one mean when one says one "knows" that something is true in this discipline? How do the answers to these questions differ from those asked of science (or any other discipline, for that matter)? Once mathematical ideas have been properly classified in this sense and this classification has also been examined from a Christian perspective, the student of mathematics is in a position to make some applications to the more practical realm.

KINDS OF KNOWLEDGE

One of the most important of philosophical questions has to do with the meaning of "knowing." That is, what does one mean by such statements as "I know this is true," or "We hold these truths to be self-evident"? The answer to such meaning questions depends very much on the culture, on the discipline, and on the thought system of the one who is the alleged "knower," for there are a variety of ways to regard this concept.

Logical Knowledge

In the tradition represented by certain of the ancient Greek philosophers such as Plato, and as later re-interpreted by such thinkers as René Descartes (sixteenth century), the highest and most reliable form of knowing was the most abstract (including the mathematical), for knowing was equated with the results of reasoning.

A true idea, once it was appropriated from the realm of the divine and put into communicable form by logical argument and delivered with appropriate rhetoric, was termed *logos*, and even in this form had an element of the divine about it. Some of the Greek philosophers took this into their religious belief systems, anticipating that the unknown and unknowable God who had created the universe would one day send from the heavens the ultimate *logos* as a revelation of the divine nature to humankind—a task that John assured them had been fulfilled in Christ (John 1:1–3).

An example of logical knowing is the statement "Two plus two equals four." Because the truth of this statement seems to depend on universal ideas that are independent of language or the notation in which they are written, this truth is said to be knowable in an absolute sense. Such knowing also includes such lines of reasoning as:

> All women are mortal.
> Nellie Hacker is a woman.
> Therefore, Nellie Hacker is mortal.

The conclusion is held with confidence (given the premises) because the rules for such a logical process are regarded as infallible.

Logic *is* important in itself and its study a worthy one as a prerequisite for all disciplines, for all scholars need to be able to think clearly and correctly. However, if taken to extremes, valid thought might be seen to consist of logic alone, and its proponents might attempt to judge everything else, including the physical world, by its principles. What could not be brought into this process would then be deemed to be at least uninteresting, perhaps suspect, and might not be seen as knowledge at all. In the most radical view, applications of the pure science of thinking to the mechanics of the physical world, including the development of science technology, could be regarded as unimportant, even beneath the notice of the philosopher. Knowledge would be thought of as an end in itself rather than a means to generate practical applications or products. Why should the Greek thinkers build steam engines? Did it not suffice to demonstrate their theoretical possibility?

Empirical Knowledge

Another kind of knowing is that derived from experience. This kind of knowing is practical, not just theoretical. Such is the knowledge derived when the scientific method is applied to the physical world. One could also express this in terms of data and information. Data consist of the raw facts of a matter, so far as these can be ascertained. Information is the meaning attributed to those facts by some community of appropriately informed experts (e.g., that Canada has a $516+ billion debt [2008 figure] is a fact; whether one should conclude that the country is on the verge of bankruptcy is a matter of interpretation).

Empirical knowledge depends utterly on the ability to gather and interpret evidence from the physical world. It also depends on the ability to give meaning to that data and communicate the same reliably to other people. In short, the data and the consensus on the information it conveys together constitute "knowledge" in this realm (e.g., the fossils dug from the earth provide a factual record of dead organisms; the meaning of that record depends on its interpretation, for no human alive has actually seen the creatures that left those bones).

Thus, if by "knowledge" one wishes to insist upon not just a reasonable certainty that something is true but upon absolute truth, it is important to realize that the consensus of experts about what constitutes "knowledge" may in fact be wrong. Indeed, "knowledge shifts" are not at all uncommon. A theory might be taught as universally accepted fact for many years, only to be later (and perhaps suddenly) replaced by a contradictory theory. Denis Alexander and Robert White provide a helpful elaboration and useful example regarding this point:

> [T]he theories or models of how the universe works, developed by scientists, are always provisional, in the sense that better explanations often lie just around the corner. Even such an influential and successful body of work as Newton's laws of motion was shown by Einstein to be based on conceptually incorrect ideas. The point is not that Newton's laws were wrong, because they still provide a perfectly adequate and effective description of how things work in circumstances relevant to many of our daily activities, such as driving cars or playing snooker, or even for getting a man to the moon. But in more extreme cases, such as explaining black holes, Einstein's general theory of relativity is required.[1]

---

1. Alexander and White, *Science, Faith, and Ethics*, 6–7.

As long as one realizes that what is called knowledge in this data/information sense is both an approximation and a moving consensus, it is still possible for those involved in a particular field to say they "know" a lot of things about a subject. With some refinements, this is the model for knowledge actually used in the sciences today.

Mathematical Knowledge

The nature of knowledge in mathematics is particularly interesting, for its philosophers can take one of two extreme views:

- that mathematical ideas are solely theoretical/speculative, or
- that mathematics describes things with a real existence.

To put it another way: Do mathematical ideas come into being the first time someone thinks about them (created by thought), or are they pre-existent (already in the universe) and only being discovered as time goes on? For example, the equation $ax^2 + bx + c = 0$ (a, b, c are real numbers with a > 0) can be solved for x by use of the quadratic formula:

$$x = (-b \pm \sqrt{b^2 - 4ac}) / 2a$$

Did the quadratic formula exist before it was first written down by a human being, or has it always been inherent in the concept of number?

Although some would hold out for the absolute truth of one or the other of these positions, it should be evident that mathematics actually has both aspects, for while the entities with which it is concerned are on the one hand mental ones, these ideas clearly, on the other hand, have some relationship to the physical universe.

- In one sense the concept of number is universal and pre-existent. God has always existed in three persons, for example. However, the numerals employed for the communication of notation used to express this idea are cultural inventions, not universal truths. Thus, the ideas contained in the assertion that 2 + 2 = 4 are inherent in the concept of number and are not inventions. However, the notation in which the idea has been written is an artifact, for rather than "two" or "2" one could use "deux" or "II" without changing the meaning.

- The use of base ten numerals like 4645 to express the idea of 4000+600+40+5 is probably due to the vast majority of humans having ten fingers with which they began learning to count. There is no *a priori* reason why one should not use a system founded on a base of two, three, eight, sixteen, or some other number. Indeed, one does use base twelve (dozens and/or gross) to measure quantities of eggs, buns, or hours, and base sixty to measure degrees, minutes, and seconds. A consequence of this is that there never was any special significance to the year whose numeral we wrote as "2000."

- Pythagoras's theorem about right triangles is true regardless of the way in which it may be written out, and it unfailingly categorizes triangles as right triangles or not regardless of what any observer may think or how that observer might write the result down.

- Likewise, the interesting observation that the number 1961 reads the same right-side-up or upside-down is entirely a construct of the notation; it has no universal truth in itself. On the other hand, the notion of symmetry that this example illustrates *is* universal and can be found wherever some object can be rotated or flipped and still be a copy of itself.

- In a broader sense, this example illustrates the universal notion of complementarity found in such pairs of opposite ideas as: left/right, up/down, right/wrong, good/evil—all of which exist independent of the language that describes them.

Similar arguments can be made for the major ideas of such branches of mathematics as statistics, topology, algebra, analysis, discrete math, calculus, transfinite numbers, and set theory, not just number theory. On the one hand, many of these ideas have appeared on the human scene recently; on the other, the very rationality of their interconnectedness argues that they are in some manner inherent and inevitable (part of an objective reality) once one thinks long and deeply enough.

THE PROBLEM OF MATHEMATICS' INHERENT COMPLEXITY

The difficulties in understanding the nature of mathematical statements are compounded by the fact that in all but the simplest cases one must *be* a mathematician in order to perform its mental experiments. A grade ten student in remedial mathematics once said to me, "I know everything there is to know about mathematics already; why should I have to take this course?" The sad fact was that the student lacked the most basic vocabulary to understand the chasm that was his ignorance. He barely had acquaintance with the multiplication of fractions and had never heard of the aspects of mathematics mentioned above, much less of computational geometry, complex analysis, relativity, probability, combinatorics, or any of their applications.

In this realm, then, "truth" can only get informed consent—many times can only be understood—if one has sufficient training and experience in mathematical thinking to be qualified to be part of the consensus. Not just any person can comment meaningfully on mathematics, for grappling with its ideas often requires special knowledge. Even among highly qualified mathematicians, embarrassing errors take place. A proof for a widely accepted theorem is sometimes later shown to be incorrect. In one celebrated case in the 1960s and 1970s one theorem was purported to have been proven in published papers by three successive writers, but all three proofs were subsequently shown to be incorrect.[2]

Thus, mathematics relies on a community consensus of what is "true"—one that is not infallible but is at least a reliable determinant of what things are part of the discipline and constitute a properly derived result. In a way, the existence of this peer consensus is not unlike that of the high-diving or figure-skating judge who holds up a score card after each performance. The consensus of the group (i.e., the average score) becomes the final judgment on the dive or the skating routine.

The determination of what constitutes good mathematics takes more people and a longer time (perhaps generations), but nonetheless produces a determination of its value by the result of a community examination of the work in question. It is even possible to quantify this agreement somewhat by counting the number of times a paper or book is cited positively in the bibliographies of later works—the higher the number, the more firm the consensus of worth.

One could summarize by saying that whether mathematical truths are created or discovered[3] by mathematicians, they certainly cannot be

---

2. Among other places, this problem was described in Sutcliffe, "Vertex-transitive Graphs."

3. Christian mathematics professor (at both Gordon and The King's Colleges) Harold Heie believes it is both. See "Developing a Christian Perspective on the Nature of Mathematics," 107.

discerned apart from the collective experience, training, and beliefs of the mathematical community. This is not unlike the situation in the scientific community and indeed in other disciplines as well. That is, acceptance of mathematical and scientific results by most people, even those trained in another branch of the discipline, requires some degree of acceptance of the consensus of the expert part of the community. This consensus, because it is an interpretation, is not necessarily *true* in any absolute sense. For example, no matter how much a present-day mathematical model for the first few seconds of the existence of the universe may be consistent with present-day scientific observations, acceptance of the model as a fact involves a leap into faith, one that bears a great resemblance to the belief held by others in an all-powerful Creator who made everything in six literal days.

IS MATHEMATICS CERTAIN?

In the latter part of the nineteenth century, a number of logicians showed that the standard method of logic employed at the time led invariably to fundamental contradictions. For instance, consider this statement:

> *The barber of Seville shaves all the men of the city who do not shave themselves.*

or similarly,

> *S is the set of all sets that do not include themselves.*

Now does the barber shave himself or not? Is S a member of S or not? Unless one sneakily attempts to escape the logical trap by positing that the barber is a woman, a machine, or an alien, either answer leads to a contradiction. The existence of such contradictions introduces an uncertainty into mathematical logic itself, not just into the correctness of part of its consensus. That this uncertainty could not in any way be resolved was shown in 1931 by Kurt Gödel when he demonstrated that no set of axioms used to describe a mathematical system could prove both the consistency and completeness of the system.

Consider, for example, the natural numbers:

$$N = \{1, 2, 3, 4. \ldots\}$$

Gödel showed that, on the one hand, any set of axioms (rules) that could be used to prove all true statements about these numbers would necessarily be inconsistent (lead to contradictions like the one above). On the other hand, any consistent set of axioms (no contradictions possible) could never be complete enough to derive all true statements about the system. As Douglas Hofstadter puts it: "In short, Gödel showed that provability is a weaker notion than truth, no matter what axiomatic system is involved."[4]

MATHEMATICS AND SCIENCE

The concept of uncertainty is partly applicable to science as well, not only because science uses the language of mathematics, but also because Gödel's theorem applies to *all* logical analyses, not just mathematical ones. Science must also deal with the uncertainty that the more closely something is observed, the more the very act of observation changes the thing being examined, and so the less accurate the observations are.

Yet, the entrance of such uncertainties into the scientific realm does not create the difficulties for its practitioners that it might for theoreticians. After all, it is the assumption of potential predictability (and not theoretical consistency) that is the basic qualification for an investigation to be classified as scientific. A researcher in some other part of the world with similar equipment needs only to be able to duplicate a reported experiment and obtain essentially the same experimental results, within a reasonable margin of error. For science, duplicable results are the important thing, even where there is no agreement about the interpretation (meaning) of the results.

Indeed, questions about *ultimate* meaning are not really on the agenda of science, and scientists who speak of such matters are no longer talking about their own specialties but about those of others. The Nobel prize-winning physicist who goes on the talk show circuit to proclaim there is no God probably has no more qualifications to speak on that subject than most theologians do to declaim on gravitational field theory.

Some philosophers of science in the early part of the last century attempted to settle these questions about meaning by taking a very narrow view of knowledge that included only the empirical. To these logical positivists, either something was the result of reproducible human experience (science), or it was not knowledge at all.

---

4. Hofstadter, *Gödel, Escher and Bach: An Eternal Golden Braid*, 19.

This narrow view of knowledge would even exclude mathematics when it attempted to produce its results by logic alone. Yet mathematics not only provides the language, structure, and tools for systematic investigation, it also has reasons of its own to be applied to the real world. Mathematics is therefore inextricably intertwined with all scientific disciplines. Not only can no science exist without the language of mathematics to describe its investigations, but also the boundaries between applied mathematics and science are quite unclear. Is relativity, for example, applied mathematics or theoretical physics?

The term "mathematical sciences" has therefore become common today, reflecting the tendency of the general population to regard these disciplines as less an art and more a science. To many people, including some practitioners, it does not matter whether the definitions of science and mathematics are exact; their people are seen as inhabiting roughly the same world.

MATHEMATICS AND REALITY

There is no unanimity of perception among mathematicians themselves concerning their discipline. Perhaps the majority view among them is that mathematics is indeed primarily about ideas, with the issue of whether these ideas have any correspondence to physical reality being irrelevant. Let us pursue this further.

In this view, mathematics deals with abstractions, the truth or falsity of which is determined by a process of deduction from certain assumed first principles or axioms undertaken according to certain accepted rules of logic. In this "purist" view, there need not be either any correspondence with or any applications to a physical reality.

For instance, suppose one has a line, and a point not on that line, and then asks how many lines can be drawn through the point that are parallel to the line?

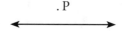

One could answer (i) one; (ii) none; (iii) more than one; but it turns out that a consistent geometry can be constructed using any one of the three answers. Whether one of these abstract geometries corresponds to the physical universe is not necessarily important to the geometer.

In this sense, mathematics is indeed fundamentally unlike science. The latter is firmly rooted in the physical world as its entire reason for existence and the natural world is its test bed. The hypotheses of science may be regarded as coming from experience (induction) or as free, unjustified, and unjustifiable notions that simply spring into existence from somewhere in the experimenter's mind. In either case the hypotheses can be established or refuted within certain limits of corroboration (that can themselves be precisely stated), using tests based on the actual physical world.

It can be argued that the truths of mathematics are not at all like that, but are instead about abstract systems that are capable of internal self-consistency within the abstract structure itself without having to be true of any physical reality. This principle is also true in the fine arts, where the artist must be free to devise a composition without any necessary references to anything called "reality."

The second (and nearly opposite) view is the more historically traditional one—that mathematics *is* about reality and not just about ideas. The famous eighteenth-century philosopher Immanuel Kant took the position that mathematics was both necessary and *a priori* (pre-existent). From its inclusion in or close relation to logic, he came to the conclusion that mathematics does indeed describe a reality that existed before and independent of the first human conception of it as an abstraction, and that this is so even if it must be conceded that the reality discovered is different from the one science investigates. He also concluded that mathematics is necessary in the sense that description of the physical world is impossible without it.

MATHEMATICS, SCIENCE, AND GOD

While some scientists might hold that both mathematical and all scientific ideas come into being only when they enter human thought, being constructed by the first action of perceiving them, I believe that a Christian must draw the opposite conclusion—that not just observable data but also all the correct interpretations and theories of science and mathematics pre-existed in the mind of God and that all are being discovered, not created. Indeed, a Christian must assert that a transcendent view of God requires this outlook, not only on mathematics but on any search for knowledge whatsoever. Otherwise, one is positing a

God limited in understanding or power and on whose works one can improve—and a limited God (as any wrong view of God) is as false an idol as any plaster statue.

One could argue that some conclusions of science are false and that some mathematical ideas may be irrelevant, even if they are not wrong— nothing more than amusing parlor games or chewing gum for the mind, but one is still left with the challenging problem of separating true mathematics from the illogical and the incorrect. I believe that such discernment is also the task of the Christian academic if s/he is to discover what God has truly wrought.

Producing criteria for knowing when a correct discernment has taken place is, of course, more difficult than saying that correct discernment must exist. One can say that the likelihood of a theory or idea being true increases with the degree to which it is in agreement with prior understanding of (in increasing order):

(a)   other theories and ideas already accepted as true

(b)   the knowledge God has revealed in his Word

(c)   God's own character

Thus a new idea that seemed to agree with prior human art but that apparently contradicted the revelation of Scripture would at best be suspect (perhaps the Scripture was being misunderstood), but one that considered God a liar, for example, could not possibly be true.

Moreover, the view of humankind as God's creatures in his image implies that humans have the capacity to think the very thoughts of God, even if this ability is limited, incomplete, and marred by the fall. Moreover, as God is Creator and humans are in his image, they have some power to "create" as well, but out of the raw materials of the universe as he made it, complete with all its laws and potentials, rather than *ex nihilo* as God alone can do.

Indeed, the parable of the talents suggests that one who finds understanding of the ways of God's universe has a responsibility to re-engineer the stuff of the physical and intellectual worlds (science and mathematics) in ways that bring even more glory to the God who not only created reality in the first place but made us to be its stewards. The human race is accountable to thoroughly, responsibly, and diligently tend, care for, develop, and produce fruit from both God's physical and his intellectual garden.

This principle is true whether these efforts produce a history essay, an airplane, a computer program, an abstract mathematical structure, a rose garden, or a solution to a problem using calculus. All may be regarded as "artifacts" from the hand of a human person, but all are made from what God first created, and their making employs the physical, mental, and logical realities whose potential he also created before any human being ever thought these thoughts.

APPLICATIONS

This way of thinking about mathematics has some important consequences:

1. While mathematics may well be about a different kind of reality than science, the fact that its ideas do describe something that existed (even if only potentially) before the ideas were formulated by humans means that mathematics is indeed more like science than it is unlike it. One could say that mathematics is an idea notation system for describing reality and is therefore both prior to and necessary for science in every important way. That is, mathematical ideas are part of God's design of physical reality and therefore are our principal means of describing that same reality. Even its notations represent human efforts to communicate the beauty and truth of God's reality. Mathematics professor Harold Heie calls this the "aesthetic" function of mathematics, pointing out that such constructs as mathematical theorems draw attention to the beauty, harmony, and elegance of the God-created natural world.[5]

    We should note in this connection that one does not usually have quite the same problem in mathematics as in science with the conflicting interpretations of data. That is, one much less often has to worry too much about such ideas as evolution—a metaphysical interpretation of real world data that is not necessarily scientific, much less reliable in any empirical sense.

2. If one does accept the proposition that mathematical reasoning is valid because its logical rules have a legitimacy that predates their

5. Heie, "Mathematics: Freedom within Bounds," 210.

mere expression in a formal notation, one is driven to the conclusion as a Christian that mathematical knowledge, like all other knowledge, derives entirely from God and is not, as humanists would claim, the sole invention and possession of the human mind without any external reference points. Indeed, one must consistently conclude that everything true comes from God, including the potential for all true knowledge, whether empirical or logical.

3. Although some elements of mathematics appear to be entirely abstract, something within mathematics seems to demand it be applied. Experience confirms this view. Most abstract mathematical structures have sooner or later been borrowed by physics to provide suitable models for describing perceived reality. Thus, actual experience supports the view that God has inspired mathematical thought, at least in part, in order for mathematicians to describe the physical reality that he created. One need not suppose, however, that all true mathematics is necessarily part of the nature of God (as is the Trinity); some of it (seven days to the week) may be part of his creation.

4. Neither mathematics nor its applications can, in this view, be regarded as merely neutral objects or thoughts with no values attached to them.

(a) Ideas are not neutral. If one is to seek objective truth, one must seek the mind of God who first is/was truth and who then created all truths other than himself. To find truth is to discover something about God. Of course, it is not enough merely to know, for as James 2:19 puts it, "You believe that there is one God. Good! Even the demons believe that—and shudder" (NIV). Rather, to apply truth well by using it to further God's will in glorifying and serving him is the highest of all goals. One must conclude that even the pursuit of abstractions without immediately apparent applications can be a redemptive activity if it is undertaken by redeemed people with the purpose of giving God the glory for all true knowledge.

(b) The applications of the ideas of mathematics are not neutral either. One thing of which one can be sure is that any knowledge, discipline, or technology that humankind may derive by thinking God's thoughts will be perverted by Satan to use against God.

Only the redeemed people of God who stand before him clothed in Christ's righteousness and in the power of his Holy Spirit can apply that knowledge to do God's will out of a proper motive of service to him.

Take computer science, for example. This offspring of the union of electrical engineering and mathematics deals with cybernetics—the processing of information in the broadest possible sense. Its hardware, in the Christian view, the product of humankind's discoveries about how God designed the universe, was implied within that design before the foundation of the world. Mauchley, Eckert, Atanasoff, and Wozniak did not invent the computer—they devised something God foreknew and built what God had already made provision for.

Likewise, computer science's software is, like all mathematics, written in a notation devised for expressing ideas and giving instructions, and foreknowledge of this too is implied in an omniscient Creator. Thus, even if humankind succeeds, through great effort, planning, and expense, in producing an intelligent, self-aware, mobile, self-replicating thinking machine, it will not somehow demonstrate that life came into being by accident. Quite the contrary—it will show the necessity of a sophisticated planning process. It will point out the necessity of the notation (or mathematics) to do the planning. It will point *to* God, not away from him.

CONCLUSION

Human beings are stewards of all things God has made, whether actual or potential, whether physical entities or ideas. Human beings are not owners of these things; they have instead the responsibility to give glory to God for what they have discovered, being accountable in every way for the manner in which they use what they know. In particular, mathematics should not be merely a narcissistic game that the human race plays with itself but a technique of thought to assist in discovering truth and thus knowing God.

This is so when one thinks of mathematics as the necessary prerequisite for all the sciences in their attempts to describe and understand the created order. It is also so when one realizes that its logical methods, though imperfect, are a prerequisite to clear thinking as a means to acquiring true knowledge in any discipline. These twin necessities press upon the student the urgency of coming to grips with the theory and applications of mathematics, regardless of the discipline, for its methods are as universal as its language.

God himself, rational in all his works, appeals to the reason he created in us: "'Come now, and let us reason together,' says the LORD. 'Though your sins are like scarlet, they shall be as white as snow; though they are red as crimson, they shall be like wool'" (Isaiah 1:18 NIV).

The enemies of God are sin, sickness, death, and ignorance. Those who do God's work fight against all four, pushing them back and reclaiming the ground lost in the Fall. The Christian academic has taken on the last of these as his or her special responsibility, though not ignoring the fight against the others.

Scripture tells us "that at the name of Jesus every knee should bow . . . and every tongue confess that Jesus Christ is Lord, to the glory of God the Father" (Philippians 2:10–11). It also says of him that "you [God the Father] crowned him with glory and honor and put everything under his feet" (Hebrews 2:7–8). This includes all knowledge; it certainly includes mathematics.

WORKS CITED

Alexander, Denis, and Robert S. White. *Science, Faith, and Ethics: Grid or Gridlock?* Peabody, MA: Hendrickson, 2004.

Heie, Harold. "Developing a Christian Perspective on the Nature of Mathematics." In *Teaching as an Act of Faith*, edited by Arlin C. Migliazzo, 95–116. New York: Fordham University Press, 2002.

———. "Mathematics: Freedom within Bounds." In *The Reality of Christian Learning: Strategies for Faith-Discipline Integration*, edited by Harold Heie and David L. Wolfe, 206–30. Grand Rapids, MI: Eerdmans/Christian College Consortium, 1987.

Hofstadter, Daniel R. *Gödel, Escher, Bach: An Eternal Golden Braid.* New York: Basic Books, 1979.

Sutcliffe, R. J. "Vertex-transitive Graphs." Unpublished M.Sc. thesis, Simon Fraser University, 1974.

FOR FURTHER READING

Barbour, Ian. *Issues in Science and Religion.* Englewood Cliffs, NJ: Prentice Hall, 1966.

Barbour, Ian, ed. *Science and Religion—New Perspectives on the Dialogue.* New York: Harper & Row, 1968.

Bibby, Reginald W. *Fragmented Gods—The Poverty and Potential of Religion in Canada.* Toronto, ON: Irwin Publishing, 1987.

Brophy, Donald, ed. *Science and Faith in the 21st Century.* New York: Paulist Press, 1968.

Byl, John. "From Mind to Math." In his *The Divine Challenge: On Matter, Mind, Math, and Meaning*, 111–32. Edinburgh: Banner of Truth Trust, 2004.

―――. "Mysteries of Mathematics." In his *The Divine Challenge: On Matter, Mind, Math, and Meaning*, 133–54. Edinburgh: Banner of Truth Trust, 2004.

Chase, Gene B. "Complementarity as a Christian Philosophy of Mathematics." In *The Reality of Christian Learning: Strategies for Faith-Discipline Integration*, edited by Harold Heie and David L. Wolfe, 231–46. Grand Rapids, MI: Eerdmans / Christian College Consortium, 1987.

Davis, Philip J., and Reuben Hersh. *The Mathematical Experience*. Boston: Birkhäuser, 1987.

Granberg-Michaelson, Wesley, ed. *Tending the Garden—Essays on the Gospel and the Earth*. Grand Rapids, MI: Eerdmans, 1987.

Green, Ronald M. *Religious Reason—The Rational and Moral Basis of Religious Belief*. New York: Oxford University Press, 1978.

Hammond, Phillip E. *The Sacred in a Secular Age—Toward Revision in the Scientific Study of Religion*. Berkeley: University of California Press, 1985.

Hawkin, David J. *Christ and Modernity—Christian Self-Understanding in a Technological Age*. Waterloo, ON: Wilfrid Laurier University Press, 1985.

Henry, Carl F. H., ed. *Horizons of Science*. San Francisco: Harper & Row, 1978.

Hummel, Charles E. *The Galileo Connection—Resolving Conflicts between Science and the Bible*. Downers Grove, IL: InterVarsity Press, 1986.

Kuhn, Thomas S. *The Structure of Scientific Revolutions*. The International Encyclopedia of Unified Science 2/2. 2d ed. Chicago: University of Chicago Press, 1970.

Schaeffer, Francis A. *How Should We Then Live—The Rise and Decline of Western Thought and Culture*. Old Tappan, NJ: Fleming H. Revell, 1976.

Stewart, Ian. *Concepts of Modern Mathematics*. New York: Penguin, 1975.

Tymoczko, Thomas, ed. *New Directions in the Philosophy of Mathematics: An Anthology*. Boston: Birkhäuser, 1986.

19

A Christian Perspective on Modern Languages

KELSEY HASKETT

A BIBLICAL VIEW OF LANGUAGE

To BEGIN OUR DISCUSSION of a Christian perspective on modern languages, I would like to consider the significant difference that viewing God as our Creator makes on language study. The perspective taken in most modern literature and linguistics post-secondary classrooms is radically different from the Christian perspective, tending increasingly to bring into question the whole idea of meaning and communication. On the other hand, having a worldview based on the fact of God's creation enables us to affirm the possibility of meaningful communication through language.

Aspects of God's Nature Imparted to Humans at Creation

When God made humankind in his image, he allowed some very fundamental aspects of his nature to become part of our human nature, making us unique in his creation and in particular different from the animals. In accordance with his immeasurable ability to create and to delight in that which he has created, God has also imparted to us as human beings a sensitivity to beauty, stemming from the perfection of his own nature, as referred to in Psalm 50:2: "Out of Zion, the perfection of beauty, God shines forth" (NIV, used throughout). This sense of aesthetic appreciation is a universal characteristic that allows us to appreciate not only the wonder of God's creation but also the beauty of human creation as embodied in art, music, literature, and other means of expression. As well as in the realm of aesthetics, God has differentiated us from the animal kingdom by giving us an ability to think verbally and communicate propositionally, that is, in a way that can propose and reflect upon meaning, truth, ideas, and action. These two dimensions of our being, aesthetic appreciation and verbal expression, are both involved in language study, being particularly significant in our ability to produce and enjoy literature or to communicate in a wide variety of ways.

The Importance of Form and Content in Language

The French speak of both the *forme* and the *fond* of literature, that is, the verbal form or shape of a piece of writing as well as its meaning or message. In humankind's aesthetic creations, as well as in God's created world, form is significant, whether it be verbal, visual, auditory, or other. Created form enhances meaning as it strikes both our conscious and our unconscious minds in conjunction with the ideas evoked by such elements as the words of a poem or the message of a song. Linguistic form, the use of words in terms of their sonority, rhythm, and intonation, is one of the creative tools God has given us by which we may express a sense of beauty or any perception of the senses coupled with a full spectrum of thoughts and emotions. Each language has its particular characteristics, which the writer or speaker may exploit to their fullest to create an aesthetic effect.

Language's primary function, however, is to convey meaning. In *The God Who Is There*, Francis Schaeffer underscores the fact that because we have received the linguistic side of God's nature, God has been able to communicate with us "in a linguistic, propositional form, truth concerning Himself and truth concerning man, history, and the universe."[1] We, in turn, can communicate verbally with God and with our fellow human beings on a complex, intellectual level.

Jesus Christ, the Enfleshed Word

God has not only spoken this truth to us verbally through his written Word, however, but also through his own Son, the Word made flesh. "In the beginning was the Word, and the Word was with God, and the Word was God," John states in the first chapter of his Gospel. Thus any study of language from a Christian perspective leads us to consider the very nature of God as a point of departure, for the verbal expression of God's character has come to us through Christ, the living Word, the perfect expression

1. Schaeffer, *The God Who Is There*, 93.

of God's nature. In fact, the essence of a verbally communicating God has become in a very real sense our essence as human beings, as reflected in Descartes' famous declaration, "I think, therefore I am." Thinking, of course, requires language.

The Role of Language Study in a Liberal Arts Education

Arthur Holmes, in his book *The Idea of a Christian College*, speaks of the role played by the humanities in a university education as "we grapple with ultimate questions and struggle to express our values and beliefs with a precision and beauty becoming the sanctity of this life."[2] These qualities of precision and beauty, as they relate to our search for truth, are of course functions of language, highlighting once again this aspect of our human nature that we have shown to be reflective of God's nature. The importance of language study to the humanities relates to the original purpose of the liberal arts, which are, in Holmes' words, "a group of disciplines having to do with language and thinking."[3] As we become people of understanding and not merely those who have acquired certain skills, we can cultivate our minds and broaden our vision by acquiring new modes of perception and reflection that different languages bring to us. In fact, only then can we speak of acquiring a liberal arts education, in the true sense. At the same time, this education will enable us to interact cross-culturally, reaching beyond the bounds of our limited experience to those of a different tongue and culture.

To summarize, I suggest that if language constitutes such an important part of our being, both aesthetically and as the very foundation of our thought processes, reflecting our Creator on both accounts, then it stands to reason that language study should have a prominent place in a Christian college or university curriculum where sound verbal communication is one of the principal goals.

God as the Author of Linguistic Diversity

Having ascertained that language is a crucial component of human identity and expression, we might well ask ourselves why so many languages exist in a world where verbal communication is essential. Surprisingly, perhaps, Scripture reveals that God himself is the author of the linguistic

2. Holmes, *Idea of a Christian College*, 15.
3. Ibid., 26.

diversity permeating our world. Genesis 11 portrays humans striving to reach heaven through their own means by building a tower (which was also meant to unify the human race). The Bible states that at that time "the whole world had one language and a common speech" (Genesis 11:1). Because God saw in this building enterprise a great potential for evil, he confused the language of the people so that they could not understand one another's speech and scattered them abroad over the face of the earth. God's judgment on language here reflects both its power to unite and its potential to bring about either devastation or a form of progress not consistent with his plan for the human race: "The Lord said, 'If as one people speaking the same language they have begun to do this, then nothing they plan to do will be impossible for them'" (Genesis 11:6).

From this point in time on, not only linguistic groups but nations began to form as part of God's design for our salvation, requiring us to reach out to him and to each other in new ways. Acts 17:26 states that "he made from one every nation of men to live on all the face of the earth, having determined the allotted periods and the boundaries of their habitation, that they should seek God." Prior to his ascent to heaven, Jesus Christ commissioned his followers to go and make disciples of all nations (Matthew 28:19). Implicit in this command is the fact that they would need to learn the languages of those nations if they were to communicate with them to make disciples. The book of Revelation reveals that some day a great multitude "from every nation, tribe, people, and language" will stand before the throne of God crying out, "Salvation belongs to our God, who sits on the throne, and to the Lamb!" (Revelation 7:9–10). Not one language but a multitude of languages will be represented before the throne of God on that great day, illustrating not only the richness of these languages originated by God and the pleasure he takes in hearing his praises sung in the language bequeathed to each one, but also the redemptive work carried out through their use. It behooves us, therefore, to consider seriously the study of modern languages, not only for our own pleasure and cultural enlightenment but also as a possible part of God's plan in our lives, for his glory.

IMPORTANCE OF LANGUAGE STUDY IN A CHRISTIAN COLLEGE OR UNIVERSITY EDUCATION

I believe that some form of exposure to modern languages should be a part of everyone's university experience, if not life experience. I would like to examine the various levels of involvement in language study that would be suited to different needs and purposes. No matter what level of language achievement you are striving for, language study will help you step out of a box, the box of your own culture and language, which necessarily limits your perception of the world, whether you realize it or not. The inexperienced visitor to the far north, for example, might speak of endless vistas of nothing but snow, while certain native languages offer an incredibly wide variety of words to describe the phenomenon we call "snow," revealing a much more complex reality for those whose language enables them to see in a particular way and to communicate their unique perceptions accordingly.

Basic Level of Language Study

If we begin at a very basic level of language study, a rudimentary knowledge of a language will enable you to travel, to meet people, and to show your friendliness and Christian goodwill in a way that not only is helpful to your getting around but also shows that you care about others. I have observed that people using even a few words of the language of the country or culture they are visiting—some elementary French in the province of Quebec, for example—will immediately evoke a sympathetic response and a willingness to help from the people around them. If we consider our own culture, we usually expect non-English-speaking people to try using some English and are much more open to those who do than to those who speak only in a foreign language. As both Christians and English speakers, we need to be wary of projecting an elitist attitude towards our language and try to overcome this real or perceived image we project by making an effort to speak the other person's language, particularly when travelling.

Understanding another people's language, even at an elementary level, will give you a measure of insight both into their modes of thinking and their ways of expressing themselves. Certainly a friendly, personal relationship is impossible unless there is some degree of communicating in the other person's language. If you are considering any kind of short term mission work, a certain amount of basic language study before you go is a must. An elementary grasp of a language may also enhance job prospects, as employers are often looking for someone with some knowledge of another language to help expand their business opportunities.

Intermediate Level of Language Study

The next level of involvement with a language implies broadening one's understanding and acquiring a deeper level of knowledge of a language, with the result that communication is greatly facilitated and more meaningful exchanges can take place. At this level, you can step even farther outside of your box, broadening your horizons by reading magazines and newspapers in another language, listening to news broadcasts with a point of view coming from sources other than those in English, and dialoguing to some degree with native speakers of the language on a wide variety of topics, even though you haven't yet become fluent. At this stage, you may also begin to appreciate literature written in the other language, gaining both a respect for the culture represented by this language and a greater understanding of the people. This level of interpersonal, multicultural understanding will be an asset to anyone desiring to make a meaningful impact for God in today's world.

If you are interested in education and also enjoy studying a particular language, you may want to consider teaching it. Business opportunities also increase with this level of understanding, and the possibility of working abroad becomes more realistic. International organizations and diplomatic work obviously require some language preparation. In Canada, an intermediate level of language acquisition in French is useful, if not mandatory, for anyone considering a career in politics, certain government positions, various social service jobs, journalism, aviation, or any field in which you may be communicating with francophones. French teachers are always in high demand in the English-speaking provinces of Canada. In addition, in a great number of countries in Europe, Africa, the Middle East, and Asia, French is the first or second language of the people. In fact, if you can speak both French and English, you will be able to get along in at least half the countries of the world. A knowledge of Spanish, of course, will open multiple doors in the Americas and elsewhere, while the ability to understand and speak an Asian language is becoming more and more significant as we increasingly build relationships with the East. Those going into an M.B.A. program in international business will find as well that there is usually a heavy foreign language requirement. Both inside and outside of the workplace, this level of interpersonal, multicultural understanding will certainly prove to be an asset. I believe that as Christians we can demonstrate Christ's love by going the extra mile in learning another person's language, rather than always expecting others to speak English. Of course the spiritual needs are very great in all language groups outside English, so you should consider the possibility of learning another language to the degree of competency that would be helpful in furthering God's kingdom.

Advanced Level of Language Study

The next stage of language acquisition to examine is that requiring a serious commitment to a language, entailing advanced studies in that language, either in literature or in linguistics. The literature of another language can open the door to a whole new world of experience. Through literature courses, students begin to understand the people whose language they are studying and to discern their spiritual needs as revealed in various ways through their writings. The study of literature from a Christian perspective gives us a greater sensitivity to the people represented by it. At the same time we discover how the world at large has changed through the influence of thinkers and writers of that language. We learn to critically evaluate their works in terms of Christian values and beliefs as well as to examine the aesthetic merits of these works. In a way we become world citizens, tasting of the fruit of a culture different from our own. It is those who are able to grasp the messages being transmitted through literature and other forms of culture and address the issues being raised from a well thought out biblical perspective who will make an impact on our world. Christian students who develop their oral and written skills to a proficient level will be able to take the offensive, speaking truth into our modern world and into the language and culture that they have studied.

We can also discover much about ourselves and our own cultural heritage by studying languages that have made an impact on our history and our civilization. At the same time, modern languages afford an exciting challenge to those who enjoy studying the structure of language, words and their meaning, and the complex set of laws governing language that we do not yet fully understand. Linguistic theory has greatly influenced other scholarly fields in recent times, and Christian theorists are much needed in this field that has often challenged a biblically-based Christian worldview.

To achieve a high degree of competency in a language requires a considerable amount of immersion in that language, preferably in a cultural setting where the language is spoken. This experience, however, without the preparation of serious language study in advance, can prove frustrating and incomplete. A Christian university can not only provide the necessary language background but also foster a love for the people involved and a concern for their spiritual well-being. We are fortunate that in Canada excellent bursaries can be obtained from the government to study the official language—either French or English—that is not our mother tongue, at a university where that language is spoken.

In fact, if your goal is to truly understand another people, then you will have to study their literature, immerse yourself in their culture and history, listen to their poets and songwriters, and dialogue with individuals in that culture. Christ has called us to lay down our lives for the sake of the gospel, and he may be calling you to lay down your personal language rights and privileges and become like a little child, learning the language of another people and taking on their culture, perhaps even laying aside your own, at least temporarily. In our own country, Quebec represents one of the greatest mission fields in the world, with evangelical Christians representing only half of one percent of the population, a statistic reflecting nonetheless the unprecedented growth of French-speaking evangelical churches during the 1970s and 1980s. At the same time, the practicing Catholic population has drastically declined, leaving a great spiritual void in Quebec, as in France and other French-speaking countries.

GLOBALIZATION AND ITS EFFECT ON LANGUAGE STUDY

With globalization having become an ever-present reality in our world, we need to seriously rethink the meaning of the Great Commission in terms of our careers and long-term goals. The church as a whole has a responsibility to proclaim the good news of the gospel to all nations. Each one of us needs to ascertain to which nation God wants us to go, even if it ends up being our own nation. No matter what your area of specialization, you may have thought of taking your skills abroad at some point in your life to help those in much greater need than we in North

America are. If you are considering this, then you should also be aware of the importance of modern language study, for the principles involved in learning one language can be readily applied to learning a second, third, or fourth language. Whether you are doing a major in the humanities, business, economics, the social sciences, the natural sciences, or any other field, why not consider doing at least a minor in a modern language with the thought of using your acquired language skills to serve others some day? As Christians, we should not expect others to learn our language if we are not willing to at least try to learn theirs. And unless God is specifically calling us to impact our own culture, should North American Christians continue to penetrate and perpetrate a culture that has had more exposure to the gospel than any other?

I encourage you to consider becoming a global citizen by taking Christ's commission to go into all the world seriously, by preparing yourself today through the study of modern languages, and by becoming available to God to live out his will for your life, wherever it might take you and whatever it might cost.

WORKS CITED

Holmes, Arthur F. *The Idea of a Christian College*. Rev. ed. Grand Rapids, MI: Eerdmans, 1987.

Schaeffer, Francis. *The God Who Is There*. Downers Grove, IL: InterVarsity Press, 1968.

FOR FURTHER READING

Roques, Mark. "Chapter 14: Modern Languages." In his *Curriculum Unmasked: Toward a Christian Understanding of Education*, 169–75. Eastbourne, E. Sussex, UK: Monarch, 1989.

Smith, David I., and Barbara Carvill. *The Gift of the Stranger: Faith, Hospitality, and Foreign Language Learning*. Grand Rapids, MI: Eerdmans, 2000.

Steensma, Geraldine J. "Language." In *Shaping School Curriculum: A Biblical View*, edited by Geraldine J. Steensma and Harro W. Van Brummelen, 62–71. Terre Haute, IN: Signal, 1977.

20

A Christian Perspective on Music

David W. Rushton

INTRODUCTION

In a recent book designed to provide students with insights and perspectives that will inform and enhance their experience with music, author Craig Wright begins as follows:

> Why do we listen to music? Because it gives us pleasure. Why does it give us pleasure? We don't know, though psychologists have spent a great deal of time trying to find out. . . . [M]usic has the power to intensify and deepen our feelings, to calm our jangled nerves, to make us sad or cheerful, to incite us to dance, and even, perhaps, march proudly off to war. . . . We in the modern world have made music a part of our most important religious, social, and artistic activities. Music adds to the solemnity of our ceremonies, activities, and entertainments, and thus "moves" or heightens the feelings of all those who watch or participate.[1]

Have you ever thought of watching a movie without the music or watching a parade without music? Music accompanies other ceremonies and celebrations that are important to us: birthdays, graduations, marriages, anniversaries, the Olympics, national celebrations. Sometimes music speaks a mysterious language—it does not need words or a "message."

In this chapter, I shall attempt to describe a Christian perspective on music. But what does that mean? Is there a uniquely Christian music? If there is, then what is non-Christian music? "Many non-Christians make

---

1. Wright, *Listening to Music*, 1.

music as well as—sometimes better than—Christians."[2] Is the sacred–secular distinction, as far as music is concerned, a valid one? We live in a complex, multicultural, pluralistic, technological age, characterized by diverse musical languages and practices. Is there one type of music that is uniquely Christian?

"The musical instinct is one aspect of [humankind's] creative curiosity. . . . To be human, then, is to be musical,"[3] writes Wheaton College music professor emeritus Dr. Harold Best. Human creativity proceeds from the image of God in us. Indeed, God is the ultimate source of all creativity. Wheaton College's philosophy professor emeritus Arthur Holmes, in *Contours of a World View*, states:

> (1) Human creativity derives its value from God's creativity and his creation mandate to us; I respond to the revelation of his creativity with mine.

> (2) Human creativity manifests God's image in our humanness: creative imagination is vested in a physical world, along with a capacity for sensory, intellectual, and emotive delight.[4]

Artistic productivity (whether in visual art, literature, theater, or music), therefore, is actually a human response (albeit often unconscious) to God's creativity. Bruce Lockerbie, in *The Timeless Moment: Creativity and the Christian Faith*, says "[E]ach of us is called by God to the vocation of artist, since being made in the image of God [Genesis 1:27] entitles each human being to image forth the Creator."[5] Our responsibility is to glorify God—the "Supreme Artist"—by developing the creative abilities he has placed within us. Martin Luther once stated that "music is an outstanding gift of God . . . next [in importance] to theology. . . . And youth should be taught this art; for it makes fine skillful people."[6]

God created the world *ex nihilo*; he thought it up, crafted it, and completed it to his own satisfaction, pronouncing all that he made good. Pursuit of the arts entails the application of the creation mandate (Genesis 1:26–28) in a particular medium. For the musician, that medium is sound. God has furnished the raw materials for the composer (the physical prop-

---

2. Best, "The Art of New Music," 10.

3. Ibid., 10.

4. Holmes, *Contours of a World View*, 106.

5. Lockerbie, *Timeless Moment*, 111.

6. Cited in Plass, comp., *What Luther Says*, 979.

erties of sound: pitch, duration, intensity, timbre). The musical instinct, the desire to manipulate sound (as both a composer and a performer—and in a real sense the performer is a re-creator and interpreter) reflects, I believe, a basic desire within us placed there by God.

THE BIBLICAL IMPERATIVE

Involvement with music, for the Christian—indeed for all Christians (and not just the so-called professional musician)—is not an option. The Scriptures literally command us to make music. The Psalms alone contain over 100 references to music (see, for example, Psalms 81, 92, 95, 96, 98, 100, 149, and 150). In the New Testament, the apostle Paul in two places (Ephesians 5:18, 19 and Colossians 3:16) exhorts us to "speak to one another [in the context of corporate worship] in psalms, hymns, and spiritual songs, making melody in your hearts *to the Lord* [emphasis mine]." Notice the primary direction of our music making in both the Psalms and the New Testament passages: to God.

THE NATURE OF MUSIC

Paradoxical

Leland Ryken, in his introduction to Part 7 of *The Christian Imagination,* states that "music is the most paradoxical of the arts. It is at once the most elusive and the most universal."[7] It is elusive because, unlike the visual and the spatial arts, it is less tangible in the sense that you can't see it or touch it; it is more abstract than words or colors on a canvas. Nevertheless, music exists in every culture, and in that sense it is universal. "No one culture, style, or medium has all the answers, however favored it might be at any given time or place."[8] Musical languages, in short, are extremely diverse and varied.

Music Defined

Music, like love, is perhaps easier to experience than to define because, like love, it is encountered on different levels and in different contexts. Nevertheless, I shall attempt a definition: "Music is the organization of sound in time into meaningful patterns created by certain successions

7. Ryken, *Christian Imagination,* 399.

8. Best, "The Art of New Music," 10.

and combinations of tones arranged rhythmically and texturally and presented by various media that endow those tones with unique timbres or colors."

Listening to Music

Music probably has a more universal appeal in our culture than any other of the so-called "fine arts." We need to *learn* to listen. You might ask, "Why do I need to learn to listen to music? I listen to it every day!" But *how* do the majority of us listen? We have become so accustomed to hearing music in our daily lives virtually everywhere we go that we usually pay very little attention to it. We are largely passive/inattentive listeners. Ironically, the very technology that surrounds us with music has tended to make us poor listeners. We need to contemplate (i.e., think about) what we see and hear if we are to more fully grasp the essence of a musical work. Also, a more active/thoughtful approach to listening will eventually help us become more discriminating, enabling us to distinguish varying levels of quality and make more informed value judgments about the worth of a particular piece. In music, this is challenging in that music is both an auditory and a temporal art. Because our response is largely aural, we cannot return at will to segments of a piece already heard (unless, of course, we replay a track on our CD player or iPod).

Subject Matter in Music

I suspect that many of you listen mostly to music that is accompanied by words, and perhaps most of it would be dubbed "Christian contemporary music." What makes it "Christian"? The subject matter (i.e., the lyrical content) may be Christian, but what of the music itself? Whereas literature and visual arts generally possess a clearly identifiable subject, music itself cannot make its subject clear, if indeed it possesses a subject at all. Apart from music accompanied by lyrics (and we must scrutinize lyrical content Christianly through the lens of Scripture), there is a great body of music of which we would say the subject is self-contained, that is, it is as though the composer was saying, "This combination of sounds *is* the subject. It exists only in this medium of expression and must be considered in that context." In other words, we must not burden it with pictorial or literary descriptions that the composer may never have intended. Music of this type is generally referred to as *absolute* music.

Much of this so-called absolute music is unparalleled, however, in its ability to evoke a mood, or outline an idea, or arouse a state of mind, or perhaps even draw one to an awesome, reverent, or joyous encounter with God. We might even say that "music takes over where words leave off" in the expression of the state of our innermost being. Moreover, much of this music potentially provides us with pleasure and joy that may be experienced on various levels. It need not have any other utilitarian function; it has intrinsic worth. In fact, Ryken points out that we may distort the arts when we "attempt to 'use' a work of . . . art rather than recognize that its beauty [even its abstraction] and craftsmanship are their own reason for being."[9] Stanislaw suggests that "the more abstract the art, the more it takes its reason for being from the innate creativity which infects every human being."[10]

CONTRIBUTION OF A CHRISTIAN PERSPECTIVE ON MUSIC

God as the Source of Human Creativity

A Christian perspective recognizes the source of musical creativity. Johann Sebastian Bach acknowledged this; he placed the letters S.D.G. (*Soli Deo Gloria*—"To God alone be the glory") at the end of all his compositions. Bach, responding to the creative urge placed in him by God, sought to produce the finest music of which he was capable. Bach is generally considered to be one of the greatest composers who ever lived. Christian musician Douglas Yeo, bass trombonist with the Boston Symphony Orchestra, asserts, "It is God alone who bestows on composers the mysterious gift of composition and on performers the unspeakable gift of interpretation."[11]

A truly Christian perspective recognizes God as the source of these gifts. In Philippians 4:8 the apostle Paul exhorts us with these words: "Finally brethren, whatever is true . . . honorable . . . right . . . pure . . . lovely . . . of good repute, if there is any excellence and if anything worthy of praise, let your mind dwell on these things" (NASB). What we have here is more than a remedy for evil thoughts. Rather, it is a positive injunction to encourage the good. Surely this scriptural imperative includes so-called "secular" music. For example, an orchestra performing a Haydn or Mozart

9. Ryken, *Christian Imagination*, 359.

10. Stanislaw, "The Fine Arts—Liberal Arts," 4.

11. Yeo, "The View from the Back Row," 40.

symphony is praising God in that the composer and the performers are imaging forth their Creator by virtue of the creative acts in which they are involved. Although non-Christian musicians may not think of their creative involvements in this way, the Christian (composer, performer, and listener) recognizes the source of this creativity and willingly acknowledges and worships God the creator. As C. S. Lewis stated, "[A]n excellently performed piece of music, as a natural operation which reveals in a very high degree the peculiar powers given to man, will thus always glorify God whatever the intentions of the performers may be."[12]

Music as an Act (or Offering) of Worship

The Christian life involves the freedom to express to God—as an offering—our creative expressions, including, I believe, our receiving of (i.e., hearing) creative expressions in music. As Christians, such involvement should be seen as an act of worship, an offering. God desires that we dedicate ourselves and our gifts to him in humble gratitude and service (see Romans 12:1). Best suggests that

> music, offered to God, is neither means nor end. If it becomes means, it is a form of legalism, because we use it to work our way to God or impress Him. If it becomes an end, it is a form of idolatry, because it displaces God [for we worship what we create]. Only God is both Means and End, Author and Finisher. Our role is to offer up and be at worship.[13]

That is a Christian view of the arts and artistry. Best goes on to say that "to be [a] Christian [musician] is not so much having a corner on music-making as having better reasons for making it [as an act of worship and because Scripture commands it (Psalms, Ephesians 5:18–19, Colossians 3:16)]."[14]

Some of you considering a major in music may well end up involved in the worship music ministry of a church, either as a leader or as a member of a worship team. The use of music in corporate worship has experienced a sea-change during the last couple of decades or so. Fuller Seminary professor (and church minister of music) Robb Redman observed, in his 2002 book, that there had been more innovation and

---

12. Cited in Hustad, *Jubilate II*, 5.
13. Best, "The Art of New Music," 10.
14. Ibid., 10.

change in (North American) Protestant worship practices in the past 25 years than in the preceding 75.[15] One of the key changes has been a reduction in the use of traditional hymns and the replacement thereof with contemporary praise and worship songs.[16]

Unfortunately such changes have frequently engendered rather strong disagreements among parishioners, often, though not always, along generational lines—with older folks tending to prefer "the traditional hymns of the faith" and the younger set the more contemporary music. Theologian Marva Dawn astutely observes, however, that conflicts over worship music styles tend to revolve more around "the opposition of objective and subjective, expressions of truth about God and feelings in response to God,"[17] for most hymns are doctrinally focused whereas the majority of contemporary worship songs reveal the song-writer's personal feelings about and/or experiences with God.[18]

Resolution of these differences is no easy matter. Some churches have sought to establish "blended" services where both traditional hymns and more contemporary praise songs are employed in directing the hearts and minds of those present to the worship of God—with a periodic appeal to the congregation to exhibit a spirit of generosity toward and tolerance for a wide variety of musical styles. Other congregations establish two or even three services, each of which will reflect a focus on a particular musical style: liturgical/traditional, blended, and contemporary. The apostle Paul seems to have been implicitly encouraging a balanced perspective when he urged the Ephesians, in a passage already referred to above, to

15. Redman, *The Great Worship Awakening*, xiv.

16. One could conceivably argue that advocates of these more contemporary expressions of praise and worship are literally fulfilling the psalmist's injunction in Psalm 96:1 (echoed in Psalm 98:1) to "sing unto the Lord a *new song*" (emphasis mine)! For a different take on this verse, however, see Best, "The Peculiarity of Music and its Unique Role," 145–46.

17. Dawn, *How Shall We Worship*, 7.

18. Redman makes a similar point, adding the interesting suggestion that this phenomenon may be a reflection of the postmodern mindset that questions the validity of all-encompassing explanations of reality and advocates instead "a respect for difference and a celebration of the local and particular . . ." (*The Great Worship Awakening*, 133 and 135). In contrast, Johansson eschews neutrality on this issue, observing that postmodernism's "emphasis on individual liberty, taken to radical extremes, along with a sweeping cultural egalitarianism and pluralism, has led musicians, church leaders, and congregations to believe that all music, regardless of style or quality, is equally valid in the church (*Music and Ministry*, x).

"[speak] to one another with psalms, hymns and spiritual songs. Sing and make music in your heart to the Lord" (Ephesians 5:20 NIV), showing his awareness not only of a need for a variety of musical expressions but also, significantly, of their two-fold focus: both to one another and to God.

The Problem of a Sacred–Secular Dichotomy

To be sure, any thematic (textual or associative) content must be critically scrutinized through the lens of Scripture, but music as music is essentially morally neutral. Music *per se* (i.e., the arrangement of pitches and durations in certain timbres and textures) cannot be categorized as either sacred or secular. It is only by association with certain occasions, places, and/or ceremonies, etc., *over time* that certain styles of music have been given such labels as sacred or secular. One writer states:

> [T]here is nothing "secular" about music. There are, however, at least two sinful things we do with it. First, we produce bad music as well as good music. Whenever through incompetence, slovenliness, insensitivity, personal pride, or egocentricity we approach this great gift of God with insufficient awe and gratitude, we produce bad music. Such music is indeed an offense to God . . . not because it is "secular"—all too often it is meant to be "sacred." It is an offense because it is bad. Another sinful thing we do is to worship our good music.[19]

Style in Music

The Bible says nothing specific about musical styles. A study of music history reveals, however, a multiplicity of musical styles. Wright defines style as follows:

> Style in music is the surface sound produced by the inner action of the elements of music: melody, rhythm, harmony, color, texture, and form. It is the shape of the melody, the arrangement of the rhythm, the choice of the harmony, the disposition of the texture, the treatment of form, and the use of instrumental color that, taken in sum, determine musical style.[20]

As Christians, we should be open to create, receive, celebrate, and participate in a variety of musical expressions. As Best notes,

19. "Church Music and the Sacred–Secular Syndrome," 41.

20. Wright, *Listening to Music*, 63.

Living in the Spirit means reveling in a whole world of music, cross culturally and historically. It is terribly wrong for anyone— any subculture or age group—to lock into one style of music and reject the rest as being out of date. . . . Each of us, young and old, should be . . . open to and enthused over a variety of styles and media. A good deal of musical preference is caused by peer pressure. Christianity takes us beyond peer pressure into personal freedom. . . . Not only should each Christian be open to the whole world of music, but the whole world of music needs Christians: symphony orchestras; opera companies; public schools; jazz and studio musicians; music librarians; [etc.]. . . . The narrowness of the Christian road is not the narrowness of doing one thing, but the narrowness of doing many things for one reason: the Glory of God and in the name of Jesus.[21]

Quality in Music

For the Christian musician a habitual vision of excellence should be the norm, whatever the style. All music is not qualitatively the same. We live in a society with the threat of mediocrity and aesthetic relativism hanging over it. This threat is perhaps greater in music than in the other arts. We mindlessly absorb "background music," which conspires against good musical taste. Gaebelein states, "Good taste is not expensive; it is just discriminating. And it can be developed."[22] Ryken observes, "What we habitually take into our minds and imaginations becomes a permanent part of us. If we consistently immerse ourselves in mediocre literature or painting or music, we become, in that sphere of our lives, mediocre people. . . . Christians are obligated to excellence because of who God is."[23] This is our "reasonable service" or, as the NASB states it, our "spiritual service of worship."

A biblical perspective sees God as the measure of all things. Excellence in artistic expression then becomes not a basis for public comparison but the grounds for personal evaluation before God. As Professor Harold Best observes, the biblical perspective is two-fold:

[1] Absolute, because it is the norm of stewardship and cannot be avoided or compromised; [and 2] Relative, because it is set in

21. Best, "The Art of New Music," 11.
22. Gaebelein, *The Christian, the Arts, and Truth*, 57.
23. Ryken, *Christian Imagination*, 429.

the context of striving, wrestling, hungering, thirsting, pressing on from point to point and achievement to achievement. Moreover, we are unequally gifted and cannot equally achieve. Consequently, some artists are better than others. But all artists [including musicians] can be better than they once were.[24]

Above all, as Gaebelein asserts, "The God of all truth looks for integrity in artistic expression."[25]

CONCLUSION: OUR TWO-FOLD RESPONSE TO MUSIC

Our response to music can be two-fold: subjective and objective. The objective (evaluative) response ("That is a good piece of music because . . .") is perhaps a difficult one to grasp but deals with things like balance, proportion, unity, variety, and order within a composition. As we examine God's creation, we observe form, order, variety, completeness, and purpose. The subjective (personal preference) response ("I like that piece of music because . . .") varies according to our background, training, taste, and experiences. A piece of music means different things to different people, inevitably resulting in different responses.

A basic problem with many of us is that we are in a musical rut. We say, "We know what we like," but in reality it would be more accurate to say, "We like what we know." Not only does culture affect musical style, it also conditions the listener. We each possess what Manoff calls "a cultural filter—a feeling filter which influences our perceptions [and responses to music]. . . . One way a cultural filter may function is by blocking out [or rejecting] the unfamiliar."[26] Let me challenge you to become acquainted with as much great music (in a variety of styles) as you can. Go beyond the simple, the immediate, and the easy-to-understand (though these can have value too). The arts, including music, are one of many ways to think, learn, and worship. Your life will ultimately be richer because you take the time and effort to involve yourself in creative musical expressions, certainly as a listener and perhaps even as a composer or performer.

---

24. Best, quoted in Hustad, *Jubilate II*, 69; see also Best, *Music through the Eyes of Faith*, 108–9.

25. Gaebelein, *The Christian, the Arts, and Truth*, 52.

26. Manoff, *Music: A Living Language*, 3.

WORKS CITED

Best, Harold. "The Art of New Music." Editorial. *Contemporary Christian Magazine* (March 1984) 10–11.

———. *Music through the Eyes of Faith*. New York: Harper, 1993.

———. "The Peculiarity of Music and its Unique Role." In his *Unceasing Worship: Biblical Perspectives on Worship and the Arts*, 143–51. Downers Grove, IL: InterVarsity Press, 2003.

"Church Music and the Sacred–Secular Syndrome." Editorial. *Church Music* 67.2 (1967) 40–41.

Dawn, Marva J. *How Shall We Worship? Biblical Guidelines for the Worship Wars*. Wheaton, IL: Tyndale House, 2003.

Gaebelein, Frank E. *The Christian, the Arts, and Truth: Regaining the Vision of Greatness*. Portland, OR: Multnomah Press, 1985.

Holmes, Arthur F. *Contours of a World View*. Grand Rapids, MI: Eerdmans, 1983.

Hustad, Donald P. *Jubilate II: Church Music in Worship and Renewal*. Carol Stream, IL: Hope Publishing, 1993.

Johansson, Calvin M. *Music and Ministry: A Biblical Counterpoint*. 2d ed. Peabody, MA: Hendrickson, 1998.

Lockerbie, D. Bruce. *The Timeless Moment: Creativity and the Christian Faith*. Westchester, IL: Cornerstone, 1980.

Manoff, Tom. *Music: A Living Language*. New York: Norton, 1982.

Plass, Ewald M., comp. *What Luther Says: An Anthology*. II. *Glory—Prayer*. St. Louis: Concordia, 1959.

Redman, Robb. *The Great Worship Awakening: Singing a New Song in the Postmodern Church*. San Francisco: Jossey-Bass, 2002.

Ryken, Leland, ed. *The Christian Imagination: Essays on Literature and the Arts*. Grand Rapids, MI: Baker, 1981.

Stanislaw, Richard. "The Fine Arts—Liberal Arts." Unpublished paper presented at a Christian College Coalition Deans Conference, San Francisco, March 30, 1990.

Wright, Craig. *Listening to Music*. 2d ed. St. Paul, MN: West, 1996.

Yeo, Douglas. "The View from the Back Row." *Christianity Today* 27.2 (January 21, 1983) 40.

FOR FURTHER READING

Begbie, Jeremy S. *Resounding Truth: Christian Wisdom in the World of Music*. Grand Rapids, MI: Baker Academic, 2007.

Darlington, Stephen, and Alan Kreider, eds. *Composing Music for Worship*. Norwich, UK: Canterbury Press, 2003.

Dawn, Marva J. *Reaching Out without Dumbing Down: A Theology of Worship for the Turn-of-the-Century Culture*. Grand Rapids, MI: Eerdmans, 1995.

DeMol, Karen. *Sound Stewardship: How Shall Christians Think about Music?* Sioux Center, IA: Dordt College Press, 1999.

Frame, John M. *Contemporary Worship Music: A Biblical Defense*. Phillipsburg, NJ: Presbyterian and Reformed, 1996.

Hustad, Donald P. *True Worship: Reclaiming the Wonder and Majesty*. Colorado Springs, CO: Shaw / Carol Stream, IL: Hope, 1998.

Johansson, Calvin M. *Discipling Music Ministry: Twenty-first Century Directions*. Peabody, MA: Hendrickson, 1992.

Kavanaugh, Patrick. *The Spiritual Lives of Great Composers*. Nashville: Sparrow Press, 1992.

Liesch, Barry W. *The New Worship: Straight Talk on Music and the Church*. Expanded ed. Grand Rapids, MI: Baker, 2001.

Miller, Steve. *The Contemporary Christian Music Debate: Worldly Compromise or Agent of Renewal?* Wheaton, IL: Tyndale House, 1993.

Myers, Kenneth A. *All God's Children and Blue Suede Shoes: Christians and Popular Culture*. Wheaton, IL: Crossway, 1989.

Pass, David B. *Music and the Church: A Theology of Church Music*. Nashville: Broadman Press, 1989.

Segler, Franklin M., and Randall Bradley. *Understanding, Preparing for, and Practicing Christian Worship*. 2d ed. Nashville: Broadman & Holman, 1996.

Towns, Elmer. *Putting an End to Worship Wars*. Nashville: Broadman & Holman, 1997.

Webber, Robert E. *Blended Worship: Achieving Substance and Relevance in Worship*. Peabody, MA: Hendrickson, 1995.

———. *Worship Is a Verb*. 2nd ed. Peabody, MA: Hendrickson, 1995.

Wienandt, Elwyn A., ed. *Opinions on Church Music: Comments and Reports from Four-and-a-half Centuries*. Waco, TX: Baylor University Press, 1974.

Wilson-Dickson, Andrew. *The Story of Christian Music: From Gregorian Chant to Black Gospel: An Authoritative Illustrated Guide to All the Major Traditions of Music for Worship*. Minneapolis: Fortress Press, 1996.

21

A Christian Perspective on Nursing

Julia D. Quiring-Emblen

INTRODUCTION: DEFINITION OF NURSING

How do people define nursing? How have they formed these definitions? Probably by contact with nurses when they or a family member may have been ill, by knowing family members working in nursing, by watching television, movies, or videos, or by reading books and/or other materials that have a nurse as a main focus. These avenues collectively influence the public's view of nursing.

With the careful work of Florence Nightingale (1859), who is often called the Founder of Modern Nursing, the scientific basis of care was established. The training program she set up incorporated principles she had found helpful to treat and restore patients to health. One of her key goals was to put patients in the best condition for nature to act upon them, primarily by altering their environment.[1]

According to Kalisch and Kalisch this image of a nurse that began as an Angel of Mercy (circa 1854–1919) had often eroded to the nurse as Sex Object by 1960.[2] Neither the MASH version of Margaret "Hot Lips" Hoolahan nor Kesey's depiction of the nurse as a hard-driving army sergeant[3] promotes the current professional emphasis on the nurse as a career person. Dworkin reported a nursing student study of "Get Well" greeting cards that found the same negative images—a young female with

---

1. Nightingale, *Notes on Nursing*, 6, 75.
2. Kalisch and Kalisch, "Anatomy of the Image of the Nurse."
3. In the novel by Kesey, *One Flew over the Cuckoo's Nest*, later made into a movie.

pronounced sexual characteristics or a uniformed old battle-ax threatening with a syringe.[4]

The profession has been working vigorously to restore a more positive image by focusing on nursing as a career. With the gradual change in the practice of nursing, the image is improving and the definition of nursing is expanding. Perhaps one of the most classic definitions of nursing, widely adopted by the profession because of its comprehensive scope, was created by Henderson: "The unique function of the nurse is to assist the individual, sick or well, in the performance of those activities contributing to health or its recovery (or to peaceful death) that he would perform unaided if he had the necessary strength, will or knowledge."[5]

Common elements in most definitions include a focus on service and provision of care designed to assist, support, and enable clients/patients to regain health. The term *client* is used when the person cared for is not in bed. *Patient* is used when the person is hospitalized, often in bed, when ill. According to some, indeed, the use of the term *patient* is inconsistent with the current nursing focus on health, not illness.

My own general definition of nursing reflects the ideas of these nursing leaders. I hold that nursing care must consider the values, beliefs, and symbols that characterize individuals and groups in order to improve the health of humans, treat diseases, manage disabilities, and prepare for death.

In a Christian context, I believe that life is a precious gift from God that nurses have the privilege of helping, maintaining, and protecting. In his first letter to the Corinthians, Paul indicated that our bodies are the temples of God (1 Corinthians 3:16). Human beings need to do all they can to promote their own health as well as the health of others.

In Mark 9:41, Jesus mentions the value of giving something as inconsequential as a "cup of cold water" to someone in need. Actions represented by the cup of water could be expanded to include all the skills nurses use in providing care for those in need. The story Jesus told about the Good Samaritan who cared for the immediate wounds of the injured man (Luke 10:30–35) reflects both the nurse's caring as well as his/her administrative roles.

---

4. Dworkin, "Cards Present Unrealistic Image of Nurses."

5. Henderson, *Nature of Nursing*, 15.

I believe Christian nurses can go into a home or hospital and by word and action provide care to the sick and suffering and their families. By their very presence Christian nurses can bring Christ's comfort and love to those for whom they care (Romans 8:9, 11).

KEY ISSUES

Nursing as a Discipline

The nursing profession has grappled with the difficulty of being recognized as a discipline in its own right. For years nursing has been caught on the coattails of the medical profession. The nursing profession has struggled to develop its own body of knowledge, using the arts and sciences as a foundation. Nursing leaders such as Nightingale, Henderson, and others have been instrumental in developing their ideas on professional nursing in such a way that nursing can be scientifically studied using research techniques.[6] Nursing has developed its own process of thinking about, planning, and providing care. It has also developed its own educational program, licensing body, ethical code, practice standards, and skills that help to define the basis of nursing competence. These efforts have also served to increase nurses' professional autonomy.

Role Confusion

Physician and Nurse

A related issue arises regarding the changing role of nursing in the health care milieu. In efforts to move toward professional recognition, nurses have sometimes been seen in the role of *junior doctors*. As nurses sought to increase their professional skills some became *nurse* practitioners. But sometimes the term *nurse* is a misnomer. Nursing aspects become obscured as nurses perform what traditionally were physician skills—for example, doing physical exams and prescribing medications. Such changes have confused the public, threatened physicians who were concerned that their traditional skills were being taken over by nurses, and frustrated nurses who could no longer clearly define their own role.

From the definitions cited earlier, it is clear that caring is the principal role of nursing. This is translated as 24-hour, seven-day-a-week care

---

6. Cresia and Parker, *Conceptual Foundations*, 5.

(not just by one nurse, but by several members of the profession working together). Nursing includes care for the whole person—biological, psycho-social, cultural, and spiritual. This holistic approach includes care for sick persons to restore health to the degree possible within the limits of the illness. As medical technology continues to develop, the potential exists for some overlap of skills and functions between physicians, other health care personnel, and nurses.

Once the medical and/or surgical diagnosis is made and specific treatment prescribed by the physician, nursing care can begin. In formulating each treatment plan nurses must include the physical, psychological, social, and spiritual concerns of the patient such as changed cardiac output, altered comfort, and spiritual distress. The nurse assesses a given patient with particular diagnoses to determine which problems have occurred or are present for that patient. Based on these assessments, specific plans are made to care for the patient. Nursing care involves coming alongside the person who has a diagnosis from one or several physicians, administering specifically ordered treatments such as medications, and then being ready to provide additional nursing care for changes in condition related to current problems or new and uncommon ones that occur due to the treatment's effects.

Nurse Administrator

Different roles of nursing administration may be confusing. In the past the nurse with the longest time in nursing usually became the supervisor. While this is still the practice in some places, a general change is occurring. Nurses with administrative responsibilities must generally have not only nursing competence but also academic preparation in business or some other administrative focus.

Nurse Educator

A similar pattern of role confusion has occurred in nursing education. While it is true that all nurses *teach* in the context of providing patients and clients with information on disease treatment, prevention, and care, it does not follow that this information-giving role is analogous to the type of educational background needed to teach a given specialty area within nursing. To become a nurse educator, a person needs academic preparation in both educational techniques and principles of learning. (I recall that because I had received an "A" in a nursing anatomy class, I was asked to teach it upon graduation. Since I had no advanced knowledge background or any educational preparation in the discipline, I concluded that I had no alternative but to decline.)

Professional Practice

Nursing involves more than the discipline itself, composed of its body of knowledge and pure or applied research. The nurse delivers a professional *service* that includes scientific aspects as well as intuition, creativity, and interpersonal communication or expressiveness in relationships with patients/clients. After acquiring this background in an educational program, the nurse uses it to provide professional nursing service as a member of what is termed the "helping" professions. The focus is to provide caring skills to assist others to maintain healthy lifestyles or decrease illness effects.

Because nursing is a profession as well as a discipline, it has a list of skills and competencies or expected standards of performance designated by a governing body for nursing. It also has its own ethical code that requires both professional autonomy and accountability.

Educational Preparation

The multiple routes to become licensed to practice nursing have presented an educational dilemma. Unlike physicians, who early separated themselves from hospitals and developed their own body of knowledge and educational programs, nurses remained in hospitals and received on-the-job training. Such a dependent role created an indentured servant relationship of the nurse with the hospital.

The nursing training period usually included three years of apprenticeship, with combinations of formal training and practical work. (A typical pattern was 7 to 11 a.m. work, 11 to 3 for training and lunch, and 3 to 7 p. m. work again.) Upon completion of the training period the apprentice was given a diploma to signify transition from trainee to graduate. Because the hospital gave the training, nurse graduates were expected to express their appreciation by working for a low salary in whatever positions the hospital had available.

The variation in the quality of education (classroom work and clinical practice) provided by different hospitals presented another concern. As the profession became more consolidated, it initiated a general examination to ensure minimal knowledge competence on graduation. Upon passing this exam the nurse became known as a *registered nurse*. Because the training hospitals did not want their graduates to fail the national exam, hospital administrations became more accountable for providing better education.

As the quality of nursing care improved, the demand for nurses increased. This increase was compounded by war—both World War II and, especially for the U.S., the Korean conflict. To meet the need for additional nurses Mildred Montag instituted a two-year associate degree or community college program in nursing.[7] This innovation met a need to supply more personnel quickly. But it added one more group to be licensed.

As the profession grew and became more autonomous, increasing numbers of nurses began to go to four-year colleges and universities to obtain their baccalaureate nursing degree. So the third educational route to becoming a registered nurse emerged. Nurses with very different academic backgrounds were required to take the same exam and demonstrate similar performance competencies. The two-, three-, and four-year educational program alternatives have created confusion and often some animosity within the profession.

Bioethical Issues

With the arrival of the twenty-first century, professional issues are beginning to take a back seat to bioethical issues created by science and medical technology such as stem cell and other types of laboratory research. Organ transplantation presents an example at the human level. Some illnesses can be treated by transplanting a new organ such as a heart, kidney, liver, lung, or pancreas into the sick person's body. Ethical dilemmas arise when there are insufficient donors available to provide the organs needed. If a baby is born without a brain (usually such babies live only a short time), the question may be asked if that body can be used to "harvest" organs for use as transplants.

Surrogate parenting is a related ethical issue. The usual scenario is that a female is impregnated with sperm from someone other than her legal spouse. This woman carries the baby to term and delivers the child, but the child is not the biological product of conception of the two married partners. The woman's uterus (womb) is essentially being used as an

---

7. Montag, *Community College Education for Nursing.*

incubator. There is a degree of social acceptance nowadays for this type of surrogate parenting. But sometimes this incubation process is taken a step further. When a pregnant woman is legally brain dead from accident or disease, her body can be kept alive by means of life support until the baby she is carrying is old enough to live outside the uterus. Sometimes the time requirement may be several months. Ethical questions arise as to whether this is right or justifiable for the social-emotional needs of the child and other family members and/or whether the economic cost can be justified.

There are bioethical problems at the other end of the age spectrum, too. Persons in the last stages of Alzheimer's disease deteriorate to the point where they are unable to swallow food. Since there is available technology to feed them either with a stomach/intestinal tube or intravenously, the question arises as to whether to use this capability. In providing care to such patients the nurse's role can vary in light of his/her religious values and beliefs about the use of medical technology. Often the nurse is the one whom the family approaches for help in thinking through such issues.

A difficult aspect of bioethics is the question about whether life should be maintained at all costs. These "costs" may become very high in strictly monetary terms as well as in the physical and emotional suffering involved for the ill person and for the family. One example that I recall involved a man who was only 27. He had developed a condition that destroyed his kidney tissue. The standard provision of dialysis (using fluid to wash out waste products) was limited at the time to persons who had a lot of rehabilitation potential. Because Mr. M. did not qualify as having high potential, he had to face the possibility of death.

A lot of patients have long waits for organs to become available for transplantation. Some medical professionals believe that human life must be maintained regardless of the fiscal or personal costs. Others believe that expensive medical technology should not be used when the disease condition is medically futile (with no potential for recovery). Persons should not be subjected to invasive insults in this case. Nurses are sometimes caught in the midst of such issues and conflicts result.

The nurse's accountability for chemically impaired colleagues poses a different type of ethical dilemma. It is difficult to get accurate statistics due to the confidential nature of chemical impairment, but those who work with professionals estimate that one out of every seven nurses has a problem with substance abuse. It is hard to know what steps to take when working with a badly impaired co-worker. The patient's care may be jeopardized so some action seems required. Yet impaired professionals could lose their licenses or be without a salary for an indefinite time. Often impaired persons confide in their colleagues and enlist peers as a support network, thus increasing the complexity of the ethical dilemma.

Legal Issues

Perhaps the issue I find most disappointing to have to identify is the legal one. All nurses should work competently, but this just does not always happen. As a result, legal parameters have had to be identified. Nurses are accountable and liable for their own actions. Even if a nurse gives ordered medication as specified that is incorrect, the nurse can be charged with malpractice. Nurses are expected to know normal dosages and to question deviations.

Furthermore, nurses have a professional responsibility for maintaining privacy of information. They must not talk about their clients or patients in elevators, cafeterias, or even in their own homes. The need for care in this latter area was highlighted for me on one occasion when my nurse roommate and I were discussing a patient. Through our discussion my aunt, who was visiting us from a city 200 miles away, learned that one of her cousins had been hospitalized with a sexually transmitted disease.

Clients and patients often ask nurses what to do regarding different types of treatment options: for example, should they have surgery or not? A nurse could be sued for malpractice by giving wrong counsel. One patient had a terminal disease and was only kept alive by his daily medication. He wanted to die and asked the nurse to help him. She refused but did tell him he would die if his wife did not give him his medication. Eventually he did decide to stop his medication and died. In one sense the nurse was responsible for his death.

Another legal issue involves censure of speech. In some health institutions nurses are not allowed to convey personal views and beliefs. Since patients are often highly vulnerable and certainly a captive audience, it is possible to say things that distress patients. Some institutional mandates prohibiting proselytizing prevent nurses from making comments to persuade a patient in favor of a particular religion.

Value Issues

With the introduction in North America of Eastern religions as well as novel philosophical outlooks such as New Age, a number of care modalities are being introduced that are incompatible with Christian values. Sometimes nursing care is modified to include these new treatments. For example, *therapeutic touch* is thought by some to promote healing. Because this introduces non-Christian beliefs and values, Christian nurses may have to compromise their values when called upon to provide such care.

On the other hand, the expansion of nursing practice in recent years to include a spiritual dimension has sometimes had the salutary effect of freeing Christian nurses to explore this heretofore forbidden territory in patient care. Verna Benner Carson, a member of the faculty at the School of Nursing at the University of Maryland until the mid-nineteen-nineties, was able to develop what became a very popular elective at the School of Nursing, "Spiritual Dimensions of Nursing." Her book by that very title, published in 1989, won two *American Journal of Nursing* Book of the Year awards.[8] Obviously she had to be careful not to give undue attention to her own spiritual version of Christian spirituality (Roman Catholic in her case), but the very fact that both the textbook and the course were deemed acceptable in a public institution signaled a rather unexpected expansion in the definition of orthodox nursing care.

Susan Jacob, Dean and Professor in the School of Nursing at Union University in Tennessee, draws attention to a further aspect of the spiritual dimension of health care when she observes that recent medical literature contains an increasing number of studies showing that "religious involvement prevents illness and helps people recover from illness and live longer."[9] Indeed, Jacob takes a surprisingly uncompromising stand on the issue when she asserts, "Documented empirical evidence of the correlation between faith and health make [*sic*] it imperative for Christian health care professionals to base personal and patient decisions on values emanating from the Christian worldview."[10]

Another innovation in the nursing profession that allows an even freer introduction of spiritual values was the development of what became known as "parish nursing." Introduced in Park Ridge, Illinois, by

8. Carson, "A Journey with Jesus," 98.

9. Jacob, "Christian Worldview and Health Care," 299.

10. Ibid., 301.

Lutheran clergyman Rev. Dr. Granger Westberg, parish nursing operates on the premise that spiritual care is central to nursing practice, although the meaning of "spiritual" became an umbrella term that integrated physical, psychological, and social, as well as strictly spiritual, dimensions. Parish nurses typically work in conjunction with faith communities—churches, temples, and synagogues—although sometimes they can work out of a hospital or a clinic. The parish nurse focuses on integrating faith and health by caring for the whole person. Faith aspects are integrated in health education, counseling, referrals, and other care functions.[11]

A CHRISTIAN WORLDVIEW AND NURSING CARE

In the midst of these critical issues within the profession, the Christian nurse can live out a number of values that are counter to existing professional norms. Christian nurses can have a profound impact on the profession by reflecting Christian values in their attitudes and responses. I would like to highlight eleven such values; they are similar to those that Shelly and Miller found Christian nurses considered to be "extremely important."[12]

Motivation

The Christian nurse's primary motivation is service to God through meeting the needs of other humans created in God's image. Such motivation does not eliminate the need for a salary or make all work pure joy, but it does change the focus of a particularly difficult task to make the nurse believe that performing it for another human being in need is in a real sense rendering service to God.

Sanctity of Life

Christians view all of human life as God-breathed and sacred, with human beings formed in the image of God. Christian nurses can therefore care for unlovely, sick, lame, cantankerous people (many at their lowest ebb in illness), not for mutual pleasure, but because it is a Christian mandate. Because such nurses consider life to be sacred, they believe humans do not have the right to take it even in the face of suffering and diminished

---

11. See Solari-Twadell and McDermott, eds., *Parish Nursing.*

12. Shelly and Miller, *Values in Conflict.*

quality of life. Christians believe that God is the originator and controller of both life and death, not other human beings. (Unfortunately, current advanced technology medicine holds the potential for drastically taking over the control of life and altering the span of life.)

Altruistic Love

In a Christian context love is of God. First John 4:10–11 indicates that because God loved us he sent Christ to die for our sins. Because of his great love for us we should express our love for God by loving one another. For the nurse this may imply acts such as physically touching and caring for those with ugly and dangerous diseases such as Hansen's Disease (leprosy) or AIDS in order to help reduce their pain and suffering. It could suggest figurative touch by being present during moments of great anguish over decisions to be made and even in moments of death.

Faith

Christian nurses need to have a faith that transcends human skill and technology. God is the Master Physician. The nurse can assist him as well as others who might become involved in the caring process. Faith in God must persist even when faith in humans is disappointed.

Hope

The ultimate hope of the Christian is to be in the presence of the Lord forever. This hope goes beyond the human hope that keeping a patient alive for one more day will provide more time for a cure to be developed. For the Christian nurse, anticipating the presence of the Lord provides the basis for renewing daily commitment toward what may seem to be hopeless efforts of care.

Trust

Sometimes Christians are considered to be naïve when they insist that God is in control in human affairs. Even when humans experience a series of health problems that require extensive treatment and long recovery, the Christian nurse maintains a steady trust in God and in the use of intermediaries to restore health. The nurse who trusts in God's sovereignty can communicate that trust by serving clients and patients with calm confidence.

Integrity

Integrity is a high value in nursing because it is based on the biblical principle that a yes is truly yes and no is no. Translated into nursing care, this equates with nurses keeping their word when, for example, they tell a patient they will return at a certain time. A nurse with integrity will in fact return as close to the time agreed on as possible. In addition, nurses often have highly responsible choices and options with respect to providing counsel as well as administering treatment. They must be careful to recognize the integral complexities associated with their actions.

Honesty

Honesty is a value closely related to integrity. Truth-telling is absolutely essential for Christian nurses. Covering or not admitting an omission (or other error of care), such as a medication not administered, could produce great harm for a patient. If normal expected changes are not apparent because of an error, a patient's treatment could be greatly prolonged and possibly even misdirected.

Genuineness

The Psalmist indicates that we cannot hide from the God who made us (Psalm 139), so attempting to disguise our responses is wasted effort. This understanding helps us because once we realize we are valued by God in spite of all our imperfections, we can then value others as they live out their own lives. Nurses can display authenticity with clients, expressing genuine feelings rather than superficial, hypocritical, or Pollyanna-like responses. Nurses can allow clients the freedom to express their angry feelings toward God and the world in general at points when their pain and suffering overwhelm them.

Empathy

Usually people do not want someone to pity them in their difficulty. Rather, they ask that someone be with them to listen to them express their feelings. Since Christian nurses have access to the constant comforting presence of the Holy Spirit, they are personally comforted by the Lord. In a response of gratitude they can come alongside another hurting person and offer some of the comfort they have received, extending themselves by listening and in other ways bearing the burdens of their clients and patients.

Courage

The Lord commanded Joshua to be strong and courageous because God would be with him (Joshua 1:6–9). Real courage for nurses comes from the awareness that because God's presence is with them they can depend on his strength rather than displaying mere human bravado in the face of difficult situations. Nurses frequently must do difficult tasks—administering treatments that result in degrees of harm in order to eventually produce positive outcomes; responding to people who are under stress and not in control of their words and emotions; and making decisions that require a degree of risk. Without the sense of God's enabling, human courage to step out would often falter.

In a broad sense these values, integral to those of the Christian faith, have provided the basic concepts on which professional codes of ethics are built. It is essential that Christian nurses live out these values in their nursing practice. It is certain that any failure to reflect them will be noted. Demonstrating these values does not always evoke appreciation from the human recipients, but there will be a time when what is done privately will be publicly revealed. Anticipating the "Well Done!" commendation from the Lord makes the effort to live out these values worthwhile.

CONCLUSION

The nursing profession must confront many challenges. On the national level there are political struggles to continue developing professional autonomy. The bioethical issues facing nursing, along with other professionals involved in health care, continue to expand with new scientific and technological developments. The nurse sometimes has to assist clients and families in decision-making regarding care choices. Not every patient care decision is consistent with a given nurse's personal, professional, and/or religious values. Caring in such times produces conflict. One Christian nurse told me that she was forced to ask to be excused from a home care case when the parents asked her to stop giving medication and physical treatments their paralyzed son needed to treat his pneumonia.

The challenge to Christian values is constantly present. The main focus for the Christian nurse is not directed at enhancing the profession by increasing the body of nursing knowledge, attaining greater professional power and autonomy, raising the scholarly level of nursing, or getting more acclaim from peers. For the Christian nurse the principal goal is to serve others—to provide care to human beings as if one were serving the Lord. The Christian nurse is aware of others' professional concerns and at times becomes involved in them, but such secondary goals do not become the directing force of one's professional life. For the Christian nurse the goal is to glorify the Lord in the profession—to live a life worthy and pleasing to the Lord (Colossians 1:9–10).

WORKS CITED

Carson, Verna B. "A Journey with Jesus." In *Professors Who Believe: The Spiritual Journeys of Christian Faculty*, edited by Paul M. Anderson, 94–104. Downers Grove, IL: InterVarsity Press, 1998.

Cresia, J. L., and B. Parker. *Conceptual Foundations of Professional Nursing Practice.* London: Mosby Year Book, 1991.

Dworkin, Andy. "Cards Present Unrealistic Image of Nurses." *Nursing Opportunities* 2 (February, 2003) 1, 6.

Henderson, V. *The Nature of Nursing.* London: Macmillan, 1966.

Jacob, Susan R. "Christian Worldview and Health Care." In *Shaping a Christian Worldview: The Foundations of Christian Higher Education*, edited by David S. Dockery and Gregory A. Thornbury, 298–316. Nashville: Broadman & Holman, 2002.

Kalisch, B. J., and P. A. Kalisch. "Anatomy of the Image of the Nurse: Dissonant and Ideal Models." In *Image-making in Nursing*, edited by C. Williams, 3–23. Kansas City: American Academy of Nursing, 1982.

Kesey, K. *One Flew Over the Cuckoo's Nest.* New York: Viking, 1977.

Montag, M. L. *Community College Education for Nursing: An Experiment in Technical Education for Nursing.* New York: McGraw-Hill, 1959.

Nightingale, Florence. *Notes on Nursing: What It Is and What It Is Not.* Philadelphia: Edward Stern, 1946 (1859).

Shelly, J. A., and A. B. Miller. *Values in Conflict.* Downers Grove, IL: InterVarsity Press, 1991.

Solari-Twadell, P. A., and M. A. McDermott, eds. *Parish Nursing.* St. Louis: Mosby, 2005.

FOR FURTHER READING

Carson, Verna B., and Harold G. Koenig. *Parish Nursing: Stories of Service and Care.* Philadelphia: Templeton Foundation Press, 2002.

Meyers, Margaret E. *Parish Nursing Speaks: The Voices of Those Who Practice, Facilitate, and Support Parish Nursing.* Toronto, ON: Opus Wholistic Publications, 2002.

22

A Christian Perspective on Philosophy

PHILLIP H. WIEBE

INTRODUCTION

THE WORDS "PHILOSOPHY" AND "philosopher" conjure up many images for people. Some think that philosophers are wise old men with
an unkempt appearance who meditate on the meaning of life and the
future of the human race. Some describe philosophy as a blind person's
search for the elusive black cat in an otherwise empty room. Others define it as a verbal activity in which people split hairs over the meanings
of words. Still others see in it an examination of the foundations of all
knowledge. An element of truth can be found in each of these images,
although philosophers would naturally take exception to any unflattering
connotations.

The *Oxford English Dictionary* defines philosophy as "love of wisdom
or knowledge, especially that which deals with ultimate reality, or with the
most general causes and principles of things." This definition incorporates
the literal meanings of the two Greek terms from which the English word
is derived, for *phileō* means "love" and *sophia* means much the same as
"wisdom." Philosophers indeed have sought to understand the principles
by means of which the universe operates and the place of humans within
it. The first philosophers in Western civilization, commonly known as Pre-
Socratics since they predated the first really famous philosopher Socrates,
lived in Asia Minor in the sixth century before Christ. They speculated on
such problems as the basic elements out of which everything is composed
and the principles upon which such elements operate. The few writings
that have come down to us from these earliest figures make reference

to such things as air, earth, fire, water, and ether as basic elements, and to compression and expansion as basic principles. These thinkers also speculated on the nature of human beings, on whether humans had immortal souls, on the basis for moral values, on the possibility of *certain* knowledge, and so on, and thus gave rise to the large and comprehensive discipline area known as philosophy.

It is generally agreed that philosophy originally included inquiries that we now recognize as specific sciences. Physics, for instance, now includes critical thought concerning the nature of the physical world and its principles of operation, but this kind of study was once part of philosophy. Psychology—another word derived from Greek, meaning literally "the study of the mind"—was often undistinguished from philosophy even 150 years ago, but it is now a large and expanding academic discipline. Similar remarks could be made about political science, biology, literary theory, and other discipline areas. What this means is that philosophy has been giving birth to many new fields of inquiry over the centuries, especially since the scientific revolution some four centuries ago. The main topics I wish to address are what philosophy is like now, and what difference a Christian perspective on life and the world makes to the study of it.

THE CONTENT OF PHILOSOPHY TODAY

In view of the fact that the content of philosophy gradually eroded as the sciences expanded, one might wonder if there are any subject matters that are distinctly philosophical. Five relatively distinct subject areas are commonly recognized, and a new group of topics has come into view in the last half-century. I will describe each of these in some detail and then discuss the relevance of a Christian worldview to some of these branches of philosophy.

Epistemology

This subject area is the study of *epistēmē*, a Greek word we translate into English as "knowledge." This branch of philosophy raises broad and far-reaching questions about whether knowledge is possible, and if it is, what can be known. Plato is one of the earliest philosophers whose writings have been preserved for us to read and study. He sought to define what it meant for someone to have knowledge, as opposed to mere belief, about some feature of the world. For instance, many people have believed and still believe the proposition that God exists, but the question philosophers have asked is whether these people also *know* that God exists. This is a stronger claim, in some important sense of the term "stronger," than saying people only *believe* that God exists. Plato argued that three conditions had to be satisfied in order for a person to legitimately claim to know a proposition: (a) that person had to believe the proposition, (b) the proposition had to be true, and (c) that person had to have justification or evidence for believing that proposition. Here we have one of the earliest attempts to understand and clarify the notion of knowledge. This contribution to philosophy from Platonic times has become part of the content of epistemology and hence of philosophy. Even if the view is mistaken, most philosophers think it is at least a good first approximation to the truth about knowledge. It is a starting point, at least.

An important epistemological view in the long history of philosophy is that there is nothing that can really be known for certain, that everything advanced as knowledge is ultimately beyond absolute proof and conclusive evidence, that everything is doubtful. This position, known as scepticism, has remained a perpetual favorite to which thinkers have gone from time to time. We live in an era in which scepticism is popular again, perhaps in part because of the fairly obvious fact that the sciences—those discipline areas supposedly giving us our best knowledge because they are based upon careful observation, demanding method, and repeatable experiments—continually revise their theories and assertions about what the world is like. It is tempting to think that if the sciences cannot give us certain knowledge, then surely the imprecise thinking which characterizes so much of ordinary life is even less trustworthy. So scepticism is a real alternative for many people living today.

But there are puzzling features of a scepticism that is not restricted in some way or other, for if everything is doubtful, then it appears that this very claim itself must also be doubtful. Moreover, what good argumentation could one ever offer in defense of such a claim? The claim itself does not appear to be self-evident in the way the claim "I now exist" appears self-evident to the person making it. Second, such a claim could not be the conclusion of a completely convincing argument, for the very premises on which such an argument rests would be undermined by the conclusion, "Everything is doubtful." And if we used a less than completely convincing argument, commonly called an "inductive" argument by philosophers, we would not have an absolute basis for advancing the view. But since such a view is either self-evident, or the conclusion of a completely convincing argument, or the conclusion of an inductive argument, it is clear that it cannot have a solid footing. Scepticism is one of the many topics that is discussed in the subject area known as epistemology.

Logic

The line of argument I have just traced has already introduced us to the use of logic or exact reasoning to defend a position. Philosophers are very concerned with logic, for it is one of the most important tools to examine propositions about the nature of the world, including human nature, for credibility or otherwise.

Logic is concerned with evaluating human argumentation or reasoning by discovering standards against which actual reasoning can be assessed. Aristotle was one of the first to give this topic careful attention, and his logic is still studied today by students who are introduced to this subject area. His achievement in logic is comparable to the work in geometry done by the Alexandrian Euclid around 300 BC, for these accomplishments of the Old World have been a standard part of education for 2,300 years. A great deal of work in logic and geometry has, of course, been done, especially in recent centuries, but the insights of these great thinkers still form part of the foundations of the two subject areas.

Aristotle was interested in determining what kind of inferences could be made from one, two, or more propositions. He wanted to know, for instance, what we could infer from the claim that all humans are mortal (or liable to die). Could we be confident that "No humans are mortal" is false? He thought so. Could we also be confident, given the claim mentioned, that "All non-humans (gods, for instance) are non-mortal"? He thought that we could infer neither the truth nor the falsity of this proposition. Aristotle also examined inferences from two propositions, for example, the inference that some Canadians are not patriots from the premises "No anarchists (people who advocate the abolition of government) are patriots" and "Some Canadians are anarchists." He thought (correctly, we might add) that this was a legitimate inference.

This brings us to an important question, namely, how can we say that an inference is correct? For couldn't this question of correct inference be just a matter of opinion rather than a matter about which one is correct or incorrect? Couldn't we find people who disagree about which propositions follow from others, and would there be any way to settle disputes between two parties making conflicting assessments on such a matter? The cluster of related questions just posed is very important—and one that philosophers continue to debate. Some suggest that logic reflects shared agreements about the way in which words will be understood by language users sharing similar languages and vocabularies. Others suggest that there is a deeper basis for logic, a basis found in the structure of the world itself. Still others offer the view that logic reflects thought patterns broadly shared by human beings because of similar neurological structures. Whatever the most plausible answer to this question might be, this much is clear: when we study logic we do not simply study the way in which people *do* think; we are also studying positions put forward by logicians about how people *ought* to think. When we study the ways in which people actually do think, we find that they sometimes draw inferences that are incorrect, inferences that logicians call "fallacies." Naturally, people also reason correctly a great deal, perhaps even most of the time. Inasmuch as logic is concerned with how people ought to think, we call it an evaluative or normative study, since it offers standards or norms by means of which specific instances of reasoning can be assessed. Logic is like epistemology in this respect, for epistemology is not content to record the fact that people make knowledge claims but wishes to examine the question of whether a knowledge claim is one which *ought* to be made.

An important advance in logic was made at the beginning of this century. Two British philosophers, Bertrand Russell and Alfred North Whitehead, published a book entitled *Principia Mathematica* that substantially changed the foundations and character of logic. Aristotle's logic was restricted to a limited number of propositions, and while the results he obtained were not put in doubt, the methods and symbolism that Russell and Whitehead introduced significantly extended our ability to examine the relationships between propositions. Their work also allowed the logical structure of key concepts to be made more explicit. One of the concepts that these authors analyzed was that of number. They showed, for instance, that the concept of number is capable of being defined using notions that make no use of number at all. In this way, they showed that mathematics makes use of concepts even more basic than that of number—hence the title of their book. An example using their symbolic notation which allows the number 2 to be expressed without using it or any other number is illustrated in the following "sentence," which is a "translation" of the English sentence, "There are exactly two senators from Idaho":

$$(\exists x)(\exists y)[Sx \cdot Ix \cdot Sy \cdot Iy \cdot \sim(x=y) \cdot (z)((Sz \cdot Iz) \supset ((z=x) \vee (z=y)))]$$

In this expression, "Sx" stands for "x is a senator" and "Ix" stands for "x is from Idaho," whereas the other symbols have a standard meaning in symbolic logic. This logical notation, along with appropriate rules of correct inference, has proved to be a powerful tool in analyzing argumentation and reasoning.

Metaphysics

The illustration just given of how numbers can be made to "disappear" raises important questions about what is really basic in our thought or what is fundamental in the universe. Perhaps numbers are constructions that intelligent humans have devised rather than discoveries that observant people have made. To begin to wonder what really exists is to engage in a study known in philosophy as metaphysics.

The term "metaphysics" is another Greek term, literally meaning "beyond physics." The boundary between physics and metaphysics has not always been a definite one, since certain views in physics have had direct and profound implications for what is thought to be basic or fundamental to the universe. Atomism, for instance, is a general metaphysical view that asserts that the world is ultimately composed of very tiny and hence individually invisible and intangible entities, perhaps varying in shape or size, that do not admit of further subdivision. The term "atom," used to describe these ultimate or foundational entities, meant the same as "uncuttable." Various atomistic views have been advanced in the long history of philosophic thought, and we of course in our modern civilization have made atomism the foundation of our research work in the physical sciences. This means that at this point in Western civilization, metaphysical views are significantly shaped by the scientific community.

The atomists of the fifth and fourth centuries BC wondered about the nature of the human soul, for they, like most the people living in Asia Minor, assumed that humans possessed souls. One of these thinkers, Democritus, suggested that the soul consisted of very small and smooth spherical atoms which penetrated deeply into the human body. He also taught that these atoms escaped at the time of death and scattered, so that an individual soul could not be said to survive death as a distinct thing with some definite structure. Here we have one of the earliest formulations of the kind of materialism that characterizes a significant portion of the intellectual community today. Such a view, of course, is at variance with what most religions, including the Judaeo-Christian faith, have taught about human nature. It helps us understand why philosophy has often been thought to be incompatible with religion.

Not all philosophers, of course, have defended metaphysical monism, that is, the view that there is one kind of basic stuff constituting the universe in its most essential form. Many have been dualists in the sense that they have argued that besides the entities that make up the material world—the world known by the five senses—there is something else not knowable by the senses called soul or spirit or mind. Not all of the philosophers who have defended dualism have done so because they have been religious people eager to defend the view that humans have an immortal soul that survives the death of the body, but clearly a significant number have thought so. The study of metaphysics, then, takes us directly into one of the controversial areas of philosophy.

But not all the issues in metaphysics are as contentious for religion as the one just discussed. Metaphysicians have sought to give adequate accounts of the way in which people see and understand the world. It is common, for instance, to consider the medium-sized objects that surround us on every side—trees, rivers, mountains, chairs, animals, and so on—as substances, or composites of substances, characterized by various properties. (These are medium-sized inasmuch as they are not minute like the atoms of which they are composed or huge like the galaxies that attract the interest of astronomers.) The dog we take for a walk, for instance, is said (and thought) to be solid brown or red or whatever in color, heavy or light in weight, etc. It is a *thing* having properties, some of which are thought essential to its being a dog, such as having a certain shape, while others, like color, are not essential to its being a dog. This view that the world of familiar objects can be broken down into substances having essential and inessential properties is critically examined by metaphysicians.

A final example of metaphysical thought, and perhaps the most important one from a long list of possibilities, is the question of the existence of God. Here, as in most areas of metaphysics, questions of metaphysics join questions of epistemology. This happens because in any attempt to offer an account of what the God might be like whose existence is being discussed, we will raise questions about how propositions about God and God's nature could be known, or whether they could be known. Metaphysics is inextricably woven together with epistemology, and logic of course is a crucial tool used throughout any discussion of such topics.

Values (including Ethics)

The fourth large topical subdivision in the discipline of philosophy has to do with values. We have seen already that to make a knowledge claim is to make an assertion that is implicitly evaluative, for to say that a person knows some proposition is to say that this person is justified in believing or has the right to believe the proposition in question. The mention of values, however, immediately suggests morality and ethics to most people, and they are correct in thinking that this is an important part of philosophy. Debates concerning right and wrong action, good and bad motives, and/or pursuit of the best possible life are philosophical in character insofar as people seek good reasons for positions on these matters and are willing to move beyond tradition.

The question of what it is that makes a right act right has been central to the study of ethics from works of the earliest philosophers. A surprisingly large number of answers has been given to this question by different philosophers in different times and places. We can use a common example in order to illustrate this diversity. Consider the decision to "pull the plug" on some unfortunate person who has been experiencing excruciating pain for months because of an incurable cancer of the throat. Some have suggested that such an act is right because it would bring about the greatest good (however that is understood) to everyone concerned; some say that such an act is right because it is one that God has approved (or would approve if consulted); some think it is right because one could consistently endorse such a response to similar cases of suffering all over the world; some think it is right because people in society have made implicit agreements not to allow a person to have to tolerate interminable suffering; some think it is right because the well-informed conscience of any decent person would approve; etc. All of these accounts purport to give the basis for moral evaluation and thus belong to that branch of philosophy known as ethics.

There are many other branches of value theory, but space prevents me from elaborating on them. They include evaluation of art objects as good or bad and of landscapes or seascapes as beautiful (called aesthetics). Value theory remains one of the very controversial fields of philosophy.

Philosophy of X

The preceding remarks have been essentially introductory, but they indicate that philosophy has long addressed the foundations of intellectual inquiry in general. They demonstrate that philosophy has the capacity to touch on the basic assumptions made by the various subject areas that comprise the modern university—discipline areas that in some cases were once part of philosophy. So we see today such fields of study as philosophy of biology, of medicine, of history, of social sciences, of education, of law, and of religion. These fields are studied by philosophers with interests in the theoretical foundation of biology, medicine, history, for example, or by biologists, physicians, or historians interested in philosophy. Some of the most interesting new work being done in philosophy is found in these areas that form the interface between philosophy and other fields of study.

A CHRISTIAN PERSPECTIVE ON PHILOSOPHY

Anyone with even a modest familiarity with Christianity will realize at once that the kind of topics with which philosophy wrestles can have and often do have a direct bearing on one's personal faith. Christianity, like the other religions found among human cultures, gives expression to a view of life and the world and as such makes explicit or implicit commitment to positions debated in epistemology, metaphysics, and value theory. While not all of the areas in these fields of philosophy are affected by faith, some of them clearly are. Examples can readily be given.

Endorsing the Christian faith does not commit a person to a particular analysis of what it means to know that a particular proposition is true, but endorsing that faith does have implications for whether one thinks that divine revelation might be a source of knowledge. Christianity teaches that God has revealed his nature and his will to humanity through prophets, apostles, holy men who wrote as they were inspired, and through Jesus Christ and the Holy Spirit. While the sources of knowledge concerning mundane things are the senses and the power of reason to reflect on what the senses teach, knowledge about spiritual matters is found, at least in part, through a wisdom that is not of this world. This source of knowledge typically does not replace the ordinary sources we employ in relation to everyday events; rather, it supplements that which is normally available. There does not need to be any conflict between holding that revelation is a source of additional knowledge and believing that most of our knowledge is acquired through the senses and the natural reasoning powers with which people are endowed.

Such belief in the legitimacy of revelation as a source of knowledge demonstrates what Christian philosophy professor Ronald Nash believes to be an important assumption that needs to govern all philosophical conversations: the role of presuppositions. After making reference to Augustine's observation that "before humans can know anything, they must believe something [Nash's words, not Augustine's],"[1] he quotes another Christian philosopher, Thomas Morris (in the latter's 1987 book on the apologetics of Francis Schaeffer), on what such presuppositional contexts usually include: "the most basic and most general beliefs about God, man, and the world that anyone can have. [These presuppositions] . . . are not usually consciously entertained but rather function as the perspective from which an individual sees and interprets both the events of his own life and the various circumstances of the world around him." Nash goes on to list the several presuppositions that all scientists, both theists and non-theists, hold: "that knowledge is possible and that sense experience is reliable (epistemology), that the universe is regular (metaphysics), and that scientists should be honest (ethics)."[2]

I spoke above about the place of logic in philosophy. Some might wonder what relevance a Christian world and life view could have to the study of it. Here we encounter a discipline area that is not altered by embracing the Christian faith. Even the different kinds of logic that have been proposed, from Hegel's dialectical logic to logics that consider propositions as having truth-values other than "true" or "false," are immune to the effects of religious commitment. Religion does not rule on the question of whether one proposition can be inferred from another.

It is apparent, however, that a number of key metaphysical questions have their answers shaped by assumptions or positions of a religious kind.

---

1. Nash, *Life's Ultimate Questions*, 19.
2. Ibid., 20.

Christians are naturally committed to the existence of a Deity—one with a fairly fully specified nature as well—so this topic in metaphysics has already been given an answer. Most Christians also endorse the existence of an immortal soul, so this foundational question is also typically assumed even before it is examined. It is of interest to note that a few Christian scholars are questioning this view, arguing that the biblical position on the question of surviving death is not that our souls survive the death of our bodies but that the Christian hope is that there will be a resurrection of the body sometime in the future. As in epistemology, there are many issues in metaphysics that are not affected by one's religious views.

Finally, a Christian approach to life certainly makes a profound difference on questions of ethics and morals. This is apparent on both practical questions and more abstract ones. For instance, a Christian will not typically endorse a nonchalant attitude toward human life and hence not be casual about capital punishment, abortion, euthanasia (mercy-killing), and suicide. An example of a more abstract issue on which Christians take positions is the question of whether moral judgments are private matters on which a person cannot be correct or incorrect. Christians clearly reject the position that one moral judgment of a particular act or character trait is as good as any other; that is, Christians clearly reject subjectivism in ethics.[3] It is interesting to note, however, that subjectivism in the area of art criticism—another value area—is quite often tolerated by Christians, for it is common to hold that there is no way to judge disputes between two people arguing about a piece of art, one saying it is good art, the other saying it is bad. This ostensible relativity in aesthetic judgment is difficult to understand, for the typical arguments for objectivism in ethics work in favor of objectivism in aesthetics.

Harry Blamires warns against the ethical subjectivism that currently dominates much postmodern (which he calls "post-Christian") discourse as follows:

> [T]he post-Christian mind has divested itself of moral absolutes. It
> can be difficult, therefore, for us to reason with contemporaries who
> lack any such sense of good and evil [as embodied, for example,
> in the Ten Commandments]. . . . There is also increasing inability

---

3. Poe is rather more pointed in this regard when he observes that Christians take an unequivocal stand on the universal reality of human fallenness. For the believer, "[a] theory of ethics that ignores the reality of sin . . . operates from the same disadvantage as a theory of medicine that ignores the reality of germs" (*Christianity in the Academy*, 70).

to make reference to first principles. So far as moral behavioral problems are concerned, the post-Christian mind operates on a level of derivation and subsidiarity. It bypasses the basic rational determinants of the situations it chooses to discuss.[4]

David Claerbaut, in a chapter intriguingly entitled "Down the Intellectual Cul de Sac of Postmodernism" in his 2004 book, observes that postmodernism is essentially "philosophical paganism," with many gods and no basis for choosing between them.[5] Later, in a chapter entitled "Where Does Reason End and Faith Begin," Claerbaut draws attention to the papal encyclical *Fides et Ratio* in which Pope John Paul II observes that postmodernism's influence on philosophy has been to "accentuate the ways in which [the capacity to know truth] is limited and conditional." The Pope urges contemporary thinkers to oppose postmodernism's "emphasis on subjectivity, focus on the self, and concern for the immediate [Claerbaut's words]."[6]

Biola University philosophy professor James P. Moreland is even more unequivocal in his warning to believing members of the academy about the dangers of buying into postmodern thinking. Early in his article (originally a plenary address to the Evangelical Theological Society annual meeting on November 18, 2004), he asserts that "postmodernism is an immoral and cowardly viewpoint that people who love truth and knowledge, especially disciples of the Lord Jesus, should do everything they can to heal."[7] He describes postmodernist epistemology as

> primarily a reinterpretation of what knowledge is and what counts as knowledge. More broadly, it represents a form of cultural relativism about such things as reality, truth, reason, value, linguistic meaning, the self, and other notions.... There is no such thing [for the advocates of postmodernism] as objective reality, truth, value, reason, and so forth. All these are social constructions, creations of linguistic practices, and as such are relative not to individuals, but to social groups that share a narrative.[8]

4. Blamires, *The Post-Christian Mind*, 118.

5. Claerbaut, "Down the Intellectual Cul de Sac," 59.

6. Claerbaut, "Where Does Reason End and Faith Begin?" 115.

7. Moreland, "Truth, Contemporary Philosophy, and the Postmodern Turn," 77.

8. Ibid., 79. Earlier in this article (77), Moreland jestingly suggests that the postmodernist would convert the seminal phrase in the American Constitution "We hold these truths to be self-evident" to "Our socially constructed selves arbitrarily agree that certain chunks of language are to be esteemed in our linguistic community."

Like Claerbaut, Moreland critiques the postmodernist claim that absolute truth does not exist—that it is "simply a contingent creation of language which expresses customs, emotions, and values embedded in a community's linguistic practices."[9] In concluding his response to the postmodern claim that religious, ethical, and metaphysical knowledge is impossible, since it is not verifiable by sense perception, Moreland writes, "I am . . . convinced that postmodernism is an irresponsible, cowardly abrogation of the duties that constitute a disciple's calling to be a Christian intellectual and teacher." He asserts that "postmodernism is a form of intellectual pacifism that, at the end of the day, recommends backgammon while the barbarians are at the gate. It is the easy, the cowardly way out that removes the pressure to engage alternative conceptual schemes, to be different, to risk ridicule, to take a stand outside the gate."[10] Strong words, certainly, but perhaps a more cautious, conciliatory response by a believing philosophy professor (or student) would either be ignored or contemptuously dismissed.

There is much more that could be said in describing philosophy and commenting on the interface between faith and philosophy, but in concluding these remarks I wish to underscore the importance of the issues we have been examining by quoting from an essay by C. S. Lewis, the Oxford professor of English in the earlier part of the twentieth century who did so much to articulate for educated people some of the essential elements of the Christian faith:

> If all the world were Christian, it might not matter if all the world were uneducated. But, as it is, a cultural life will exist outside the Church whether it exists inside or not. To be ignorant and simple now—not to be able to meet the enemies on their own ground— would be to throw down our weapons, and to betray our uneducated brethren who have, under God, no defence but us against the intellectual attacks of the heathen. Good philosophy must exist, if for no other reason, because bad philosophy needs to be answered. The cool intellect must work not only against cool intellect on the other side, but against the muddy heathen mysticisms which deny intellect altogether. Most of all, perhaps, we need intimate knowledge of the past. . . . The learned life then is, for some, a duty.[11]

9. Ibid., 80.

10. Ibid., 88.

11. Lewis, "Learning in War-Time," 51.

WORKS CITED

Blamires, Harry. *The Post-Christian Mind: Exposing Its Destructive Agenda.* Ann Arbor, MI: Servant Publications, 1999.

Claerbaut, David. "Down the Intellectual Cul de Sac of Postmodernism." In his *Faith and Learning on the Edge: A Bold New Look at Religion in Higher Education*, 53–61. Grand Rapids, MI: Zondervan, 2004.

———. "Where Does Reason End and Faith Begin?" In his *Faith and Learning on the Edge: A Bold New Look at Religion in Higher Education*, 115–24. Grand Rapids, MI: Zondervan, 2004.

Lewis, C. S. "Learning in War-Time." In his *Transposition and Other Addresses*, 45–54. London: Geoffrey Bles, 1949.

Moreland, J. P. "Truth, Contemporary Philosophy, and the Postmodern Turn." *Journal of the Evangelical Theological Society* 48.1 (March 2005) 77–88.

Nash, Ronald H. *Life's Ultimate Questions: An Introduction to Philosophy.* Grand Rapids, MI: Zondervan, 1999.

Poe, Harry L. *Christianity in the Academy: Teaching at the Intersection of Faith and Learning.* Grand Rapids, MI: Baker Academic, 2004.

FOR FURTHER READING

Beaty, Michael D., ed. *Christian Theism and the Problems of Philosophy.* Notre Dame, IN: University of Notre Dame Press, 1990.

Brummer, Vincent. *Theology and Philosophical Inquiry: An Introduction.* London: Macmillan, 1981.

Hicks, Peter. *The Journey So Far: Philosophy through the Ages.* Grand Rapids, MI: Zondervan, 2003.

Holmes, Arthur F. "God and Creation: Philosophical." In his *Contours of a Christian World View*, 71–91. Grand Rapids, MI: Eerdmans, 1983.

———. *Philosophy: A Christian Perspective: An Introductory Essay.* Rev. ed. Downers Grove, IL: InterVarsity Press, 1975.

Morelli, Elizabeth M. "An Ignatian Approach to Teaching Philosophy." In *Teaching as an Act of Faith: Theory and Practice in Church-Related Higher Education*, edited by Arlin C. Migliazzo, 233–52. New York: Fordham University Press, 2002.

Morris, Thomas V., ed. *God and the Philosophers: The Reconciliation of Faith and Reason.* New York: Oxford University Press, 1994.

Naugle, David K. "Philosophical Reflections on 'Worldview.'" In his *Worldview: The History of a Concept*, 291–330. Grand Rapids, MI: Eerdmans, 2002.

Neuhaus, Richard J. "Encountered by the Truth" [on Jacques Derrida]. In his *The Best of "The Public Square,"* 174–79. Grand Rapids, MI: Eerdmans, 2001.

Slaatte, Howard A. *Religious Issues in Contemporary Philosophy.* Lanham, MD: University Press of America, 1988.

Wilkens, Steve. *Good Ideas from Questionable Christians and Outright Pagans: An Introduction to Key Thinkers and Philosophies.* Downers Grove, IL: InterVarsity Press, 2004.

Yandell, Keith E. "Christianity and Conceptual Orientation." In *Professors Who Believe: The Spiritual Journeys of Christian Faculty*, edited by Paul M. Anderson, 205–16. Downers Grove, IL: InterVarsity Press, 1998.

———. *Christianity and Philosophy.* Studies in a Christian World View 2. Grand Rapids, MI: Eerdmans, 1984.

23

A Christian Perspective on Physical Education, Health, and Sport

MURRAY W. HALL

INTRODUCTION

WE ALL CARRY WITH us culturally-shaped equipment, based on our upbringing, life experiences, and relationships, which have shaped our values and ethics. The filter you use to view your beliefs and values as they relate to physical education and sport is probably somewhat different than the next person's. Many of us have not had Christian role models in physical education and competitive sport. I never had a single Christian teacher, professor, or coach in eighteen years of formal education. My initial values about physical education and sport were formed largely *outside* of Christian thinking and teaching. Only in recent years have I begun the process of thinking Christianly about the issues in my discipline. I confess that I am still on a pilgrimage to "have the mind of Christ" in these areas. My goal in this chapter is to highlight several biblical principles that should be considered in attempting to formulate a Christian view of physical education, health, and competitive sport.

THE NATURE OF PHYSICAL EDUCATION

Physical Education Historically

Historically, the objective of enhancing physical development and fitness has been basic to physical education for thousands of years. We have a rich heritage of emphasis on the importance of fitness and care of the body. Plato, among the first to recommend accurate planning for the physical education of youth, said in his *Protagoras*, about 350 BC, "send them to the master of physical training so that the body may better minister to the virtuous mind, and that they may not be compelled through bodily weakness to play the coward in war or any other occasion."[1] Plato added that too much physical exercise without the balance of other activities can make one an uncivilized beast, but too little makes one indecently soft. Plato's famous mentor, Socrates, also emphasized the importance of physical development, as follows: "No citizen has a right to be an amateur in the matter of physical training, for what a disgrace . . . to grow old without ever seeing the beauty and strength of which [the] body is capable."[2]

Born a generation earlier than Plato, Hippocrates, the Father of Medicine, said, "That which is used develops; that which is not used wastes away."[3] Emerson's "Essay on Education" advised, "Let us have men whose manhood is only the continuation of their boyhood, natural characters still; such are able for fertile and heroic action; and not that sad spectacle with which we are too often familiar, educated eyes in uneducated bodies."[4]

Physical Education Defined

Defined as "an educational process that has as its aim the improvement of human performance through the medium of physical activities,"[5] physical education involves the acquisition and refinement of motor skills, the development and maintenance of fitness for optimal health and well-being, the attainment of knowledge about and the growth of positive attitudes toward physical activity, and, at institutions where the underlying philosophy is Christian, the interpretation and application of biblical concepts of health and fitness. Its goals include not only the physical outcomes that accrue from participation in activities but also the development of knowledge and attitudes conducive to lifelong learning and active, participatory living.

Physical education is, by its very nature, interdisciplinary. Its ever-changing body of knowledge is borrowed and adapted from three main

1. Voltmer et al., *Organization and Administration of Physical Education*, 101.
2. Ibid.
3. Ibid.
4. Ibid., 104.
5. Wuest and Bucher, *Foundations*, 6.

sources: the *natural sciences* such as biology, anatomy, physiology, kinesiology, computing science, and physics; the *humanities*, including history, political science, and philosophy; and the *social sciences*, including anthropology, psychology, and sociology. The overall subject area therefore includes sub-disciplines such as Psychology of Sport (e.g., violence, aggression, personality development, goal setting, motivation, optimal psychological readiness); Philosophy of Sport (e.g., play and leisure objectives); Sport and Religion; and Sociology of Sport (e.g., group dynamics, crowds, gender issues, riots, hooliganism). This interdisciplinary strength gives physical education a platform to develop leadership traits in students, thereby transcending normal curricular boundaries.

The Focus on Health and Wellness

We now turn our attention to the specific area of health and wellness, a key focus for physical educators nowadays. It has been obvious for some time now that the fitness boom of the 70s was not just a fad. A healthy lifestyle is in vogue. North Americans, especially those at the middle and upper income levels, have taken health more seriously in recent decades than they ever did before. Health professionals have slowly changed from the adoption of a remedial and medical slant to health care to a primarily preventative or "wellness" or "lifestyle" approach.

The Effect of Lifestyle Decisions on Wellness

Society's health needs are being met not only by illness- or disease-treating institutions such as hospitals and clinics but also by wellness-promoting entities like health clubs, counseling agencies, fitness programs, advertising, and even university programs. Physical educator Michael Ellis notes that these health-promoting agencies are assuming an increasingly dominant role, for they

> exist in both the public and private sectors of our economy. They are created by individual action, by businesses for profit, by philanthropic organizations, and by the government. They employ a very large number of people and consume an enormous proportion of the nation's wealth. Known as the *health enhancement industry*, they together share a simple, common goal: improving people's health.[6]

6. Ellis, *The Business of Physical Education*, 4.

Another writer draws attention to the many issues that are now addressed within the field of health and health education, including

> family living, human sexuality, substance abuse, personal health, nutrition, weight control, first aid and safety, consumer health protection, and interpersonal relationships. Over the past several decades, these topical fields have been brought together under the concept of *wellness*, which conveys the broader meaning of promoting a positive, vigorous, healthy lifestyle.[7]

Since it is estimated that over 50 percent of premature deaths are caused by *lifestyle choices*, one can see the importance of an emphasis on total or optimal wellness, encompassing emotional, intellectual, physical, social, and spiritual health. The trend currently is away from just physical fitness and into the broader, all-encompassing concept of wellness.

Holmes, in *The Idea of a Christian College*, cites Aristotle's claim that education should prepare a person for an active life marked by excellence. Excellence here refers to the quality of one's life: "Develop yourself . . . as a human being . . . become a thoroughly responsible agent."[8] This quality is one of the marks of the truly educated person. An educated person will take responsibility for a variety of components that make up health or wellness. In 1975, John H. Knowles, physician and president of the Rockefeller Foundation, convened a group of physicians, philosophers, social scientists, and medical administrators to study health as a means of influencing the quality of American life. The proceedings of this meeting, *Doing Better and Feeling Worse: Health in the United States*, contained strong statements regarding health as both a right and a responsibility. Some thirty years later his words still ring true:

> The cost of sloth, gluttony, alcoholic intemperance, reckless driving, sexual frenzy, and smoking is now a national, and not an individual responsibility. This is justified as individual freedom—but one man's freedom in health is another man's shackle in taxes and insurance premiums. I believe the idea of a "right" to health should be replaced by the idea of an individual moral obligation to preserve one's own health—a public duty if you will. The individual then has the "right" to expect help with information, accessible services of good quality, and minimal financial barriers.[9]

7. Siedentop, *Introduction to Physical Education,* 348.

8. Holmes, *Idea of a Christian College*, 101.

9. Knowles, "Responsibility of the Individual," 59.

Knowles goes on to explain that personal responsibility relating to physical health will include attention to proper nutrition, exercise, weight control, stress management, sleep habits, and avoiding substance abuse and destructive habits.

The Preoccupation with Personal Appearance

Most people today seem to be at one extreme or the other in terms of health and fitness, with very little middle ground between. There seems to be either *an abnormal preoccupation with how we appear*, as witnessed by

- the body-building craze
- increasing incidence of eating disorders such as anorexia, bulimia, bingeing, etc.[10]
- 80% of American women reporting some degree of body image dissatisfaction[11]
- girls as young as nine years old having already dieted (my 9 year old doing leg raises because she is heavier than her friends—in spite of the fact that she is also 4'10" tall)
- media messages constantly conveying to women that they are never good enough, that they must constantly deprive themselves and continually fight the natural size of their bodies—that the feminine physical ideal is flawlessness[12]
- liposuction to surgically remove excess fat

or *a total disregard for physical fitness*:

- 25 to 50% of North Americans are classified as sedentary—they get virtually no exercise
- more than 60% of North American adults do not reach the minimal recommended amount of physical activity
- 80% of Canadians think they are as fit or more fit than others their age

---

10. For a recent comprehensive international treatment of these subjects, see Part II "Eating Disorders," chapters 27 to 67, in Fairburn and Brownall, eds., *Eating Orders and Obesity*.

11. Kilbourne, *Beyond Killing Us Softly* (video).

12. See, for example, *Beauty and the Beach* (video).

- the three most prescribed drugs in Canada are antacids, tranquilizers, and anti-hypertensives
- 80% of all headaches are tension related

Biblical Guidelines for Health

Careful study of the Scriptures will clarify that neither of these extremes is appropriate and that godly concern for the physical body is an essential component of a God-honoring Christian life[13] ("Do everything as unto the Lord," 2 Corinthians 10:31). Do we have a *godly* concern for our bodies? A sobering question. Balance and moderation are required of the obedient Christian. Hiebert notes:

> The weight of Scripture is in fact on *holism*, which is not a platitude of modern humanistic invention but a recurrent theme of Scripture. The Hebrew did not even have an adequate term for the physical body, *basar* being the nearest, because health was considered irreducible, not capable of fragmentation into mental, emotional, social, physical, and spiritual components.[14]

Hiebert continues:

> The New Testament continues this pattern. The description of Jesus in Luke 2:52, which is similar to the description of Samuel in I Samuel 2:26, models holistic health: "And Jesus kept increasing in wisdom [mental health] and stature [physical health], and in favor with God [spiritual health] and man [social health]." I Thessalonians 5:23 reaffirms the link between health and holiness: "Now may the God of peace himself sanctify you entirely; and may your *spirit* and *soul* and *body* be preserved complete without blame at the coming of our Lord Jesus Christ." John's challenge is to match spiritual vigor with holistic health: "I pray that in all respects you may prosper and be in good health, just as your soul prospers" (III John 2). So while Scripture does not argue about or define health, it illustrates and models a holism that serves as a framework from which to construct a physically fit lifestyle.[15]

When you think of the word *stewardship*, you aren't likely to think of your body as one of its objects. In fact, too often we seem to   ⁿe the word *stewardship* comes from a combination of the wo

13. Johnson and Morris, *Physical Fitness and the Christian*, 6.
14. Hiebert, "Glorifying God in the Body," 20.
15. Ibid., 20.

(goulash) and *hardship*! Trying to be good stewards is deemed to be a difficult hardship that we often sooner or later abandon in frustration, leaving our lives in an unholy mess. But that is not stewardship. Being a good steward means recognizing that God created and owns all things and that we are responsible to manage wisely and faithfully, for his glory, what he has given us.

Stewardship is usually thought to involve responsible management of our money and possessions, but every aspect of our lives is to be managed properly—including our spirits, our minds, and our bodies. The Bible repeatedly commands us to control our bodies in God's strength, lest we fall into the evil use of them. Indeed, as the apostle Paul reminds the Corinthian believers in 1 Corinthians 6:20, "You were bought at a price. Therefore honor God with your body" (NIV).

Another reason for being a steward of the body is that it is the "temple" or dwelling place of God's Spirit (1 Corinthians 6:19). Earlier, Paul had asserted, "God's temple is sacred and you are that temple" (3:17). We should therefore value our bodies as much as Israel valued the magnificent temple built during King Solomon's reign. God deserves the regular, healthy upkeep of his habitation! Sire states that as created beings, we are obligated to God in every possible way. We own nothing that is not his: our bodies, souls, minds—everything we are and have belongs to him.[16]

In order to be good stewards, we need to keep our bodies healthy and well. That means keeping them in good physical shape through regular exercise, watching the food and the drink we pour into them, and treating physical problems wisely and expediently. Such activities, however, should not be ends in themselves. They are means to another end—serving God and others.

In Concepts of Physical Fitness courses taught at many Christian institutions, students examine scriptural principles that relate to care of the body such as being created in God's image, the body as the temple of the Holy Spirit, discipline and ambassadorship, and the need for moderation in all things. One such principle is the avoidance of gluttony. Perhaps one of the more explicit biblical teachings on physical health is the stern condemnation of gluttony (Proverbs 23:1). Traditionally considered as one of the seven deadly sins, it is described as a characteristic of the wicked (Philippians 3:18–19). What is notable about gluttony, other than our in-

16. Sire, *Discipleship of the Mind*, 48.

adequate understanding of the point at which we become gluttonous,[17] is our failure to take it seriously. As one speaker I once heard observed, "Christians do not pig out ... they fellowship."

Scripture, while perhaps stopping short of an unequivocal fitness or health mandate, nevertheless *assumes* it. "[N]o one ever hated his own body, but he feeds and cares for it ..." (Ephesians 5:29 NIV). Chafer once commented that "sometimes it is not prayer and Bible study that we need to straighten out our lives, but exercise and proper diet."[18] Not bad advice —and from a theologian! Is God pleased with his temple, our bodies? Are we managing them properly?

A BIBLICAL PERSPECTIVE ON COMPETITIVE SPORT

Competitive Sport and Religion: A Promising Combination?

We now turn our attention to competitive sport, examining key issues and biblical principles that can help us develop our Christian thinking and responses to this area. Prebish, in his book *Religion and Sport*, provides a helpful definition of "sport": "a recreational activity, specifically involving a game, competition, or the like that requires bodily and often mental exertion; abides by fixed rules; aims at fun and/or play; and may be divided into (a) informal sport, (b) organized sport, and (c) corporate sport."[19]

Here is a sample of comments from a variety of individuals as they attempt to reconcile or at least associate religion and sport:

- "To have religion, you need to have heroic forms to try to live up to. ...You need to have a pattern of symbols and myths that a person can grow old with.... You need to have a way to exhilarate the human body, and desire, and will, and the sense of beauty....All these things you have in sports" (Michael Novak, philosopher and theologian).

- "Our Father, we don't want to be mediocre, we don't want to fail. We want to honor you by winning" (Jerry Falwell, former chancellor, Liberty University).

---

17. Hiebert, "Glorifying God in the Body."
18. Cited in Hiebert, "Glorifying God in the Body," 21.
19. Prebish, *Religion and Sport*, xiv.

- "If somebody comes into my territory, my zone, I want to hit him hard. I don't ever want to take a cheap shot, but I'll hit him with all the love of Jesus I can muster" (Gill Byrd, former pro football player for the San Diego Chargers).

- "God is not going to provide any leadership on this basketball team. . . . He is not going to parachute through the roof . . . and score when we need points. . . . God doesn't give a damn what goes on in athletics. Nor should he" (Bobby Knight, former basketball coach, Indiana University).[20]

- "Sport, because of the wholesome elements it gives value to and exalts, may become more and more a vital instrument for the moral and spiritual elevation of the human person and therefore contribute to the construction of an orderly, peaceful, and hard-working society" (Pope John Paul II).[21]

Another evidence of an explicit connection between Christianity and competitive sport is the establishment of many religious organizations that have attempted to use sport to attract more people to Christian beliefs as well as to foster support for Christian athletes. Coakley draws attention to examples of such organizations as the Fellowship of Christian Athletes, Athletes in Action, and Pro Athletes Outreach.[22] He notes that these "sports ministries" sometimes target certain sport events as opportunities to spread Christian beliefs to athletes and spectators alike. Thousands of volunteers traveled to the 1992 Barcelona Olympic Games and distributed 18,000 copies of *Winning for Life*, a 36-page booklet published by the Colorado Springs-based International Bible Society, to athletes and Olympic officials. The volunteers also made an effort to contact each of the 500,000 households in Barcelona. For the 1996 Olympics in Atlanta, over 60 national and international religious groups engaged in a similar massive united outreach effort. Such efforts are becoming increasingly well-organized.[23] Since 1986, the major sport ministries in North America have been linked together through the International

20. All of the above quotations are cited in Coakley, *Sport in Society*, 420.

21. From Pope John Paul II's "Address to Participants in the 33rd Water Skiing Competition of Europe, Africa and the Mediterranean about the Virtue of Sports," on August 31, 1979. Quoted by Kerrigan, "Sports and the Christian Life," 256.

22. Coakley, *Sport in Society*, 431.

23. Mathisen, "Reviving 'Muscular Christianity.'"

Sports Coalition, an umbrella organization designed "to promote unity and cooperation . . . so that together we might follow God's leading in world-wide evangelism."[24]

The Need for Balance

Sports have become almost a national addiction, in both the USA and Canada. Competition, not religion, could be called the opiate of the people. Yet the competitive urge is a two-sided coin—with both benefits and dangers, uses and abuses.[25] For example, Randy Roberts, professor of history at Purdue University, writes about "America's misplaced emphasis and inordinate concern for sports, suggesting that priorities are out of whack with sports increasingly occupying to an unwholesome degree the attention of millions of Americans."[26] He relates the incident of a Denver Broncos fan who watched as his team fumbled seven times in a loss to the Chicago Bears. Apparently it was more than this fan could take, and after the game he attempted suicide. His suicide note read: "I have been a Broncos fan since the Broncos were first organized, and I can't stand their fumbling anymore." The famous scandal of Tonya Harding's involvement in a deliberate attempt to injure her figure-skating rival, Nancy Kerrigan, shows the potentially tragic consequences of this spirit of unbridled competitiveness.

The Problem of Cheating in Competitive Sport

An article appearing some years ago in *Psychology Today* was entitled, "Sport: If You Want to Build Character, Try Something Else."[27] It decried the damage that competitive sport can do to personal development. Some say we have adopted the so-called eleventh commandment: "Do anything to win as long as you don't get caught." This relativistic worldview that there really is no reliable consensual standard of right and wrong permeates much of today's sports activities. The drug-doping scandals that tainted both the 1998 and 2006 French Grand Prix bicycle races are recent painful examples of such moral compromise practiced by some athletes. (The problem of doping in sports is discussed at greater length below.)

24. Ibid., 246.
25. Warner, *Competition*, 53.
26. Roberts and Olson, *Winning*, x.
27. Ogilvie and Tutko, "Sport."

Cheating, or at least bending the rules, is condoned if not often accepted outright now, and practices that were previously regarded as unsportsmanlike are now often accepted as an integral part of the game. In the ancient Olympics, runners who false started were flogged; today, athletes are coached on how to get an advantage by using a rolling start—a practice that is clearly illegal. Athletes unable to stop the clock legally in a game are taught to fake an injury—considered good strategy by some but cheating by others.

Charles W. Eliot, president of Harvard University from 1869 to 1909, once expressed grave misgivings about its baseball program. When asked why, he replied, "Well, this year I'm told the team did well because one pitcher had a fine curve ball. I understand that a curve ball is thrown with a deliberate attempt to deceive. Surely that is not an ability we should want to foster at Harvard."[28] We certainly have come a long way from this form of thinking. Is this progression or regression?

Furthermore, some have commercialized sport so much today that it really is "big business." We bring the latest medical technology to heighten athletic prowess. Indeed, some say that the essential question in world athletic championships is not who has the best athletes but who has the best chemists. Holmes laments that "we have turned play into work, and work into the worst of play, with unbridled competitiveness."[29] Slogans such as Green Bay Packers' coach Vince Lombardi's "Winning isn't everything, it's the only thing"[30] abound.

As a Christian physical educator, what concerns me most is that the church has *not* been sufficiently concerned about such moral deterioration. Church officials regularly used to call attention to the problems and unethical behaviors others have noted in sports for years. Nor have religious sport organizations taken a leadership position in dealing with these problems and unethical behaviors. It appears that few are willing to begin a process for reforming the unethical dimensions of sport.

28. Cited in McAfee, "Quoting Baseball," 82.

29. Holmes, *Contours*, 227.

30. Michener, *Sports*, 420.

Case Studies

The Dubin Inquiry

This last statement may need qualifying in light of two significant reports completed a couple of decades ago. In Canada in October, 1988, following Canadian sprinter Ben Johnson's infamous disqualification as the gold medal winner in the 100-meter final at the Seoul Olympics for anabolic steroid use, a Commission of Inquiry into the "Use of Drugs and Banned Practices Intended to Increase Athletic Performance," headed by Charles Dubin, the Province of Ontario's associate chief justice, was established. The inquiry was very far-ranging, lasting a year and calling 119 witnesses, whose testimony filled approximately 15,000 pages. The final report devotes an entire chapter to ethics and morality in sport. Here is a representative assortment of ethical statements from this comprehensive document on the illegitimate use of performance-enhancing drugs in Canadian athletics:

- "[T]here can be no justification for athletes to cheat in order to win."[31]

- "If the slogan 'winning isn't everything, it's the only thing' is acceptable, then everything is permissible in order to win. If Canadians truly believe that, then, as a society, we are indeed morally bankrupt."[32]

- "The coach is a pivotal character in the moral as well as the physical development of his or her charges."[33]

- "The care, training, and athletic education of an athlete should be in accord with highest standards of ethical behavior and scientific knowledge."[34]

- "Personal integrity cannot be compartmentalized. It is not possible for an individual to act unethically in one area of life without infecting that individual's entire value system."[35]

31. Dubin, *Commission*, 201.
32. Ibid., 504.
33. Ibid., 508.
34. Ibid., 509.
35. Ibid., 511.

- "We must ground the integrity of sport on the firmer base of fair play, ethics, and a sense of what is right."[36]

Several of the final seventy recommendations made by the Dubin Inquiry emphasized the need for ethical direction.

The Knight Foundation Commission on Intercollegiate Athletics

The same month this significant Canadian study was completed, the trustees of the Knight Foundation in the USA created a Commission on Intercollegiate Athletics, directing it to propose a reform agenda for intercollegiate athletics (specifically National Collegiate Athletic Association or NCAA schools). In so doing, they expressed concern that abuses in athletics had reached proportions threatening the very integrity of higher education. The Commission spent more than a year in study and debate, considering suggestions from more than eighty experts. The report was published in March, 1991.[37] What is unique is that for almost three years both Canada and the United States took a hard look at amateur sport and publicized their findings and recommendations. It appeared that both

---

36. Ibid., 523.

37. The 1991 Knight Commission report contained three principal recommendations, described as "one-plus-three": that presidents of all NCAA schools take over the leadership in competitive athletics from athletics directors (the "one") and focus on three broad areas badly in need of reform in order to restore public confidence: academic integrity, financial integrity, and independent certification of all NCAA-related athletic programs. Ten years later, the Knight Commission reconvened to assess the extent to which effective changes had been introduced in NCAA institutions nation-wide. Their 48-page report was published in June, 2001 (see "Works Cited" for internet address). The report noted that while significant progress in correcting abuses had been made during the ten preceding years, significant work yet needed to be done. Indeed, the co-chairmen's covering letter indicated that the problems associated with big-time college sports had, in many respects, grown rather than diminished, threatening the very integrity of US higher education (31). Perpetuating the "one-plus-three" model, the Commission recommended that the NCAA institution presidents establish an Institute for Intercollegiate Athletics (to serve as a watchdog to keep problems in intercollegiate athletics at the forefront of the public mind, including the issuance of periodic report cards on the worst offender institutions), focusing on the continuing need for academic reform (e.g., a woefully low percentage of generously-subsidized athletes ever make it to graduation), the athletics "arms race" of pouring millions of dollars into athletic programs (e.g., only 15% of the NCAA schools were operating in the black financially), and a de-emphasis on the indiscriminant commercialization of college athletics. The Commission underlined the continuing seriousness of the situation by suggesting that unless significant changes were made very soon, "the nation's colleges and universities should get out of the business of big-time sports" (31).

countries had a blueprint for action that addressed the escalated call for reform. The reports clearly spelled out that the problems in athletics are principally ethical ones.

Olympic sports history in the years immediately following the 1988 Seoul games revealed not necessarily a reduction in the use of performance-enhancing drugs but a reduction in the number of athletes getting caught. Pat Lenehan, a private consultant and director of the Drugs and Sport Information Service in Liverpool, UK, reports, "There were no positives for AS [anabolic steroids] in the 1992 games in Barcelona but perhaps that wasn't too much of a shock. While drug testers had been able to work out how to trace steroids, athletes [and usually their coaches, sad to say] had simply moved onto substances that were then, and some still are, undetectable."[38]

The Plot Thickens: The Proliferation of Sports Doping Practices and Efforts to Contain Same

Other sports bodies have adopted anti-doping rules—but not with undue alacrity! The International Olympic Committee initially implemented drug-testing at the 1968 Olympic Games in Grenoble, France, but the National Football League in the U.S. took until 1982 to follow suit, with actual testing not commencing until 1987. Further policy and procedure changes were agreed to by the League and the Players Association in 2005.

The National Basketball Association's first anti-doping policy appeared in 1983; there have been several updates since. The Major Leagues of baseball in North America didn't implement a doping policy until 2003, updating same in 2005 in concert with the Major League Players Association.[39] On December 13, 2007, former U.S. Senate majority leader George J. Mitchell released the first part of his report on doping in major league baseball (commissioned by Baseball Commissioner Bud Selig on March 29, 2006), asserting that at least eighty players (both current and retired) were involved in doping activities, including hitting sensation Barry Bonds (from 1993 until the end of the 2007 season a member of the San Francisco Giants) and superstar pitcher Roger Clemens of the New York Yankees (a seven-time Cy Young award winner). A number of

38. Lenehan, *Anabolic Steroids*, 68.
39. Burns, *Doping in Sports*, 3.

the players so named have acknowledged their culpability, but others—including Clemens—vociferously proclaimed their innocence.

The picture of doping usage by Olympic athletes was further darkened in October 2007 by the admission by retired U.S. medal-winning sprint star Marion Jones (she won three gold and two bronze in the 2000 Sydney Games) of her use of performance-enhancing steroids to help her achieve her superstar status—in spite of both previous protestations of innocence and the absence of any positive tests heretofore.[40] Her admission resulted in her also agreeing that she would forfeit the medals she had won. Ironically, Ben Johnson's former coach, Charlie Francis, had for a while been Jones' trainer. (He had said in 2000 that an Olympic-level athlete could not win without drugs.) Jones' boyfriend, 100-meter record-holder Tom Montgomery, had "tested positive for the banned blood-booster EPO."[41]

Interestingly, this particular instance of cheating occurred soon after the International Olympics Committee established the World Anti-Doping Agency in November 1999 "to support and promote fundamental values in sport."[42] Canada's much-admired former IOC committee member Dick Pound was chosen to chair the WADA. One of its principal goals was to "harmonize rules and regulations regarding doping across all countries and all sports in an attempt to create a level playing field for athletes."[43] As the cases of Jones and Montgomery illustrate, many loopholes in the attempt to eliminate illegal drug use by athletes persist. Off-season unannounced tests can be easily dodged; urine tests can't detect blood doping; therapeutic exemptions can be easily obtained simply by means of a doctor's signature; and evidence of illegal drug use is undetectable if administration of same is stopped several weeks before competition.

In short, in spite of agencies such as the WADA, there seems to be no limit to the creativity of world class athletes and their supporters to resort to illegal performance-enhancing means to win. Australian Commonwealth weightlifting champion Deborah Lovely, who has adamantly refused to depend on any illegal artificial means to increase her

40. See Rowbottom, "Golden Girl of 2000 Olympics Quits."

41. Rowbottom, "Marion Jones: A World Class Cheat."

42. Lenehan, *Anabolic Steroids*, 91.

43. Ibid., 91.

competitive potential, conceded beforehand that she had no chance of winning a medal at the 2008 Beijing Olympics. She stated she was very disillusioned after the 2004 Athens Olympics (she placed twelfth in the 75 kg. class) because of all of the cheating by the athletes in her sport, adding that the use of performance-enhancing drugs was so widespread that it was "not a case of identifying who was doping but rather who was not."[44]

A Chance for Reform?

With both the Knight Commission and the Dubin Inquiry calling for ethical and responsible action, and with the IOC establishing the World Anti-Doping Agency, it appeared that the seemingly unlimited use of illegal drugs in sport might be curtailed. In the past, Christian people were the prime movers and shakers in bringing about positive change through such initiatives as the playground movement, the inception of muscular Christianity, or the development of the YMCA. Evangelical clergymen at the turn of the twentieth century used their pulpits and the editorial page to passionately plead for both recreation facilities and highly participatory, quality sports programs to complement their proclamation of the gospel message. Contrast this with the virtual silence from the pulpit today on matters relating to physical fitness and sport. Will people with a perspective informed by the Christian faith be willing to take the risk of urgently calling for change in this seemingly intolerable situation?

For the Christian the reference point for action must always be scripturally and spiritually based. For too long Christians have been culture followers rather than culture formers[45] or culture transformers.[46] We have a cultural mandate to tend the garden of sports in our society, to be actively involved in shaping competitive athletics from youth to elite levels. In defining our mandate we must constantly ask ourselves "What would Jesus do?" This is the right mindset.

Sire, in *Discipleship of the Mind*, suggests that we all need a "starting place, a place to stand, a ground zero. Ground zero is a *terra firma*, a rock which doesn't shift but stays put."[47] In sport, we need to get back on the solid rock and regain a firm footing. At the same time, "we cannot mar-

---

44. Murdock, "Australian Weightlifter Decries Drugs in Sport."
45. Walsh and Middleton, *Transforming Vision*.
46. Hoffman, "Expressive and Impressive Faces."
47. Sire, *Discipleship of the Mind*, 80–81.

ginalize/compartmentalize God or push him to the edge of our minds when we are involved in sports. He must be the hidden premise of all our work."[48] As either physical educators or participating athletes, our view of competitive sports must be consistent with our faith.

In a 1983 *His* magazine article entitled "Sanctified Sports," Hiebert declared even back then that Christians could no longer identify unequivocally with sport in its current form.[49] Christians' attitudes toward sports should be much different from non-Christians'. Tragically, this intention has often not been realized. Christian hockey and basketball teams are often indistinguishable from secular teams, expressing no commitment to the greater glory of God. The Jekyll and Hyde syndrome of all too many Christian teams must cease.

Issues for the Christian

To summarize, here as I see it are the main issues sincere Christians must come to grips with in their desire to integrate biblical principles with their involvement in sport:

(a) Can a Christian athlete or coach have anything to do with performance-enhancing drugs?

(b) Can/Should Christians participate in violent sports such as football, hockey, etc.?

(c) How can we avoid an over-emphasis on winning?[50]

(d) Surely anything that can be construed as cheating must be absolutely eliminated—e.g., faking an injury near the end of the game to gain some rest for your losing team.

(e) Sunday Play—especially in professional sports? What would happen if all Christian athletes, professional and amateur, refused to play on Sunday?

---

48. Ibid., 48.

49. Hiebert, "Sanctified Sports," 4.

50. Saint Sing makes an excellent comment in this connection when she asserts, "Nothing upsets more than 'cheap shots' taken at weaker opponents, arrogance over winning, anger and tantrums over a loss. Certainly if you win big it is appropriate and great to celebrate and whoop and holler! To feel God's delight inside urging you to feel glee and unabashed joy is fantastic! Go for it! But to learn to lose is also a part of the challenge" (*Spirituality of Sport*, 70).

(f) Player and Spectator Sportsmanship—Is jeering at the other team's mistakes, ridiculing players, trash talk, insulting coaches, and showing disrespect to referees out of line for Christian fans?

(g) Parental Influence and Involvement—What about aggressive parents?

(h) Role Models/Hero Worship—Is it desirable for Christians to idolize sports celebrities like Roger Clemens, David Beckham, or Tiger Woods?

(i) Gender Equity—Imbalance of women in sport and sport leadership and funds spent on female sport; sexism in sport?

(j) Elitism versus Sport for All—Where should government money be spent? Participation for the masses or an elite program? Facilities/clubs—only for the rich?

(k) High Risk Sports—Should Christians participate in bungy-jumping, parachute jumping, football, hockey, or boxing?

(l) High Cost of Medical Care for Athletes?

(m) Racism in Sport?

(n) Leisure Time Use?

(o) Government Policy on Health/Fitness and Sport?

Scriptural Principles in Sport

If involvement in competitive sport is to be seen as worthwhile for Christians, then we need to examine the ingredients that we put into the mix. Our beginning point must be scripturally based. While the Bible does not forbid psychologically intimidating your opponent, it does offer solid life principles that must be carried into the sports arena. The principles need to be blended together in developing a sport ethic that will be God-glorifying. I conclude by suggesting some scriptural passages that could be used to develop our thinking and actions in this area. These principles need to be woven into the fabric of responsible action in sport. Space limitations prevent us from examining each principle, so merely naming them must suffice:

(a) The body as temple of the Holy Spirit (1 Corinthians 6:19)

(b) Parable of the talents (Matthew 25:14–30)

(c) Respect for rules and authority (2 Timothy 2:5)

(d) Striving to do one's best—laying aside besetting weights (Hebrews 12:1) and running for the prize (1 Corinthians 9:24; Philippians 3:14)

(e) Controlling the tongue (Proverbs 21:23; James 3:3–13)

(f) Exhibiting the fruit of the Spirit (Galatians 5:22–23)

(g) Forgiveness (Matthew 6:14–15 and 18:21–22)

(h) Moderation/balance (1 Corinthians 6:12; Philippians 4:5)

(i) Discipline (1 Corinthians 9:26–27)

(j) Being slow to anger (Proverbs 16:32)

(k) Leadership—being a role model (1 Timothy 4:12)

(l) Humility/lack of pride (Proverbs 16:18)

(m) Honesty (Romans 12:17; 2 Corinthians 13:7; 1 Peter 2:12)

(n) Not gloating when an enemy falls (Proverbs 24:17 NIV)

Perhaps the principles implicit in these biblical passages could provide the fabric and thread to weave the banners of Christian Signals and Sentiments that Hoffman[51] thinks should fly high in our stadiums and gymnasiums. Hoffman thinks that when people walk into our facilities they should immediately be aware that they are in a Christian place, that something is unique. Our coaches, athletes, and spectators should be noticeably different.

CONCLUSION

Dubin said that now is the time to act quickly. The 1991 Knight Commission reported that "a great nationwide effort is required to move reform from rhetoric to reality."[52] Individual action is needed but the "lone ranger" approach[53] needs to be supplemented by concerted group action. As Karen Fox explains:

> We need to create a concept of group responsible action where each individual conceives of him/herself as a "stakeholder." It is in

---

51. Hoffman, "Expressive and Impressive Faces."

52. Knight Foundation, *Keeping Faith with the Student Athlete*, 25.

53. See Hiebert, "Sanctified Sports."

collaboration, support and collective projects where we the group develop strength, persistence, and courage. We must not underestimate the difficulty of pursuing a course of responsible action. Such a course takes practice and the perseverance to overcome many obstacles and mistakes. It is the process that is crucial—that we continue to struggle and choose the responsible and ethical channels.[54]

I would simply add that, in my opinion, Christians should be at the forefront of such efforts, leading in both word and deed.

WORKS CITED

Burns, Christopher N., ed. *Doping in Sports.* New York: Nova Science Publishers, 2006.

Coakley, Jay J. *Sport in Society: Issues and Controversies.* 5th ed. St. Louis: Mosby, 1994.

Dubin, Charles. *Commission of Inquiry into the Use of Drugs and Banned Practices Intended to Increase Athletic Performance.* Ottawa: Canadian Government Publishing Centre, 1990.

Ellis, Michael J. *The Business of Physical Education.* Champaign, IL: Human Kinetics, 1988.

Fairburn, Christopher G., and Kelly D. Brownall, eds. *Eating Disorders and Obesity: A Comprehensive Handbook.* 2d ed. New York: Guildford Press, 2002.

Fox, Karen M. "Environmental Ethics and the Future of Parks and Recreation." *Recreation Canada* 49.2 (May 1991) 28–31.

Hiebert, Dennis W. "Glorifying God in the Body." *Christian Educators Journal* 25.2 (1985) 19–21.

———. "Sanctified Sports." *His* 43.8 (May 1983) 1, 4.

Hoffman, Shirl J. "The Expressive and Impressive Faces of Sport and Leisure." Paper presented at the Symposium on Christianity, Sport, and Leisure at Calvin College, Grand Rapids, MI, 1991.

Holmes, Arthur F. *Contours of a World View.* Grand Rapids, MI: Eerdmans, 1983.

———. *The Idea of a Christian College.* Rev. ed. Grand Rapids, MI: Eerdmans, 1987.

Johnson, Pamela S., and L. Delyte Morris. *Physical Fitness and the Christian: Exercising Stewardship.* 2d ed. Dubuque, IA: Kendall/Hunt, 1995.

Kerrigan, Michael P. "Sports and the Christian Life: Reflections on Pope John Paul II's Theology of Sports." In *Sport and Religion,* edited by Shirl J. Hoffman, 253–59. Champaign, IL: Human Kinetics, 1992.

Kilbourne, Jean. *Beyond Killing Us Softly: The Strength to Resist: The Impact of Media Images on Women and Girls* (video). Cambridge, MA: Cambridge Documentary Films, 2000. (33 min. 50 sec.)

Knight Foundation. *Keeping Faith with the Student Athlete: A New Model for Intercollegiate Athletics.* Charlotte, NC: Commission on Intercollegiate Athletics, 1991.

———. "A Call to Action: Reconnecting College Sports and Higher Education." Report of the Knight Foundation Commission on Intercollegiate Athletics. June, 2001. Online: http://www.knightcommission.org/images/uploads/KCfinal-06-2001.pdf.

54. Fox, "Environmental Ethics," 30.

Knowles, John H. "Responsibility of the Individual." *Daedalus* 106.1 (Winter 1977) 57–80. (Note: This entire issue of *Daedalus* is entitled *Doing Better and Feeling Worse: Health in the United States*.)

Lenehan, Pat. *Anabolic Steroids and Other Performance Enhancing Drugs*. London: Taylor & Francis, 2003.

Mathisen, J. "Reviving 'Muscular Christianity': Gil Dodds and the Institutionalization of Sport Evangelism." *Sociological Focus* 23.3 (1990) 233–49.

McAfee, Skip. "Quoting Baseball: The Intellectual Take on Our National Pastime." *NINE: A Journal of Baseball History and Culture* 13.2 (Spring 2005) 82–93.

Michener, James A. *Sports in America*. New York: Random House, 1976.

Murdoch, Alex. "Australian Weightlifter Decries Drugs in Sport." *The Daily Telegraph*, 27 October, 2007. Online: http://www.news.com.au/dailytelegraph/story/O,22049,2265 591-5001023,00.html.

Ogilvie, Bruce C., and Thomas A. Tutko. "Sport: If You Want to Build Character, Try Something Else." *Psychology Today* 5.5 (October 1971) 61–63.

Prebish, Charles S. *Religion and Sport: The Meeting of Sacred and Profane*. Westport, CN: Greenwood Press, 1993.

Prowse, Joan, producer/writer/director. *Beauty and the Beach* (video). CineFocus Canada. Vancouver, BC: BC Learning Connection, 1997. (53 min.)

Roberts, Randy, and James S. Olson. *Winning Is the Only Thing: Sports in America Since 1945*. Baltimore: Johns Hopkins University Press, 1989.

Rowbottom, Mike. "Golden Girl of 2000 Olympics Quits after Drugs Admission." *The Independent on Sunday*, 6 October 2007. Online: http://sport.independent.co.uk/general/article 3033328.ece.

———. "Marion Jones: A World Class Cheat." *The Independent on Sunday*, 6 October 2007. Online: http://sport.independent.co.uk/general/article 3033381.ece.

Saint Sing, Susan. *Spirituality of Sport: Balancing Body and Soul*. Cincinnati, OH: St. Anthony Messenger Press, 2004.

Siedentop, Daryl. *Introduction to Physical Education, Fitness, and Sport*. 2d ed. Mountain View, CA: Mayfield, 1994.

Sire, James. *Discipleship of the Mind: Learning to Love God in the Ways We Think*. Downers Grove, IL: InterVarsity Press, 1990.

Voltmer, E. F., et al. *The Organization and Administration of Physical Education*. 5th ed. Englewood Cliffs, NJ: Prentice-Hall, 1979.

Walsh, Brian J., and J. Richard Middleton. *The Transforming Vision: Shaping a Christian World View*. Downers Grove, IL: InterVarsity Press, 1984.

Warner, Gary. *Competition*. Elgin, IL: David C. Cook, 1979.

Wuest, Deborah A., and Charles A. Bucher. *Foundations of Physical Education and Sport*. 12th ed. St. Louis: Mosby, 1995.

FOR FURTHER READING

Cooper, Kenneth H. *It's Better to Believe*. Nashville: Thomas Nelson, 1995.

Crawford, S. "Values in Disarray: The Crisis of Sport's Integrity." *Journal of Physical Education, Recreation and Dance* 57.9 (1986) 41–44.

Francis, Charlie, with Jeff Coplon. *Speed Trap: Inside the Biggest Scandal in Olympic History*. Toronto, ON: Lester & Orpen Dennys, 1990.

Hall, Murray W. "Christian Ethics in North American Sports." In *Christianity and Leisure: Issues in a Pluralistic Society,* edited by P. Heintzman, G. E. Van Andel, and T. L. Visker, 213–21. Rev. ed. Sioux Center, IA: Dordt College Press, 2006.

———. "Senior College Students' Perspectives on Physical Education and Sport." In *Physical Education, Sport, and Wellness: Looking to God as We Look at Ourselves,* edited by John Byl and Tom Visker, 293–306. [Sioux Center, IA]: Dordt College Press, 1999.

Higgs, Robert J. *God in the Stadium: Sports and Religion in America.* Lexington, KY: The University Press of Kentucky, 1995.

Higgs, Robert J., and Michael C. Braswell. *An Unholy Alliance: The Sacred and Modern Sports.* Macon, GA: Mercer University Press, 2004.

Hoffman, Shirl J., ed. *Sport and Religion.* Champaign, IL: Human Kinetics, 1992.

Kilbourne, Jean. *Killing Us Softly 3* (video). Sut Jhally, producer/director/editor. Northampton, MA: Media Education Foundation, 2000. (34 min.)

Ladd, Tony, and James A. Mathisen. *Muscular Christianity: Evangelical Protestants and the Development of American Sport.* Grand Rapids, MI: Baker, 1999.

Mah, Susie, writer/director. *Thin Dreams* (video). Micheline LeGuillou and Gerry Rogers, producers. [Montreal]: National Film Board of Canada, 1986. (20 min. 38 sec.)

Montgomery, D. J. "Sports." In *The Complete Book of Everyday Christianity: An A-to-Z Guide to Following Christ in Every Aspect of Life,* edited by R. P. Stevens and R. Banks, 953–61. Downers Grove, IL: InterVarsity Press, 1997.

Murray, Melissa A., et al. "The Relationship between Prayer and Team Cohesion in Collegiate Softball Teams." *Journal of Psychology and Christianity* 24.3 (Fall 2005) 233–39.

Pipher, Mary. *Reviving Ophelia: Saving the Selves of Adolescent Girls* (video). Tom Gardner and Sut Jhally, executive producers. Northampton, MA: Media Education Foundation, 1998. (36 min.)

Price, Joseph. L., ed. *From Season to Season: Sports as an American Religion.* Macon, GA: Mercer University Press, 2001.

Schroeder, Peter J., and Jay P. Scribner. "'To Honor and Glorify God': The Role of Religion in One Intercollegiate Athletics Culture." *Sport, Education and Society* 11.1 (Fall 2006) 39–54.

Stewart, Gail B. *Drugs and Sports.* San Diego, CA: Green Haven Press, 1998.

Wiggins, David K., ed. *Sport in America: From Wicked Amusement to National Obsession.* Champaign, IL: Human Kinetics, 1995.

24

A Christian Perspective on Physics

John Byl

INTRODUCTION

How does a Christian perspective make a difference in physics? Answering that question is the prime objective of this chapter. We shall see that worldviews play a major role in physics. I believe a Christian worldview has significant implications for our understanding of both the power and the limitations of physics. First, however, we shall briefly discuss what we understand by *physics*, the importance of studying physics, and how physics works.

PRELIMINARY ISSUES

What Is Physics?

According to Webster's dictionary, *physics* is "the science dealing with the properties, changes, interaction, etc. of matter and energy"; *science* in turn is defined as "systemized knowledge derived from observation, study, and experimentation." Thus physics is concerned with systemized knowledge of matter and energy, as derived from observation and study. Physics is the systematic study of how inanimate objects interact with each other.

Physics above all concerns *mechanics*: the study of motion and the various forces that cause motion. The oldest branch of physics is probably *astronomy*, which deals with the motions of stars and planets. Another ancient part of physics is *optics*, the study of the properties of light. During the nineteenth century the fields of *heat*, *electricity*, and *magnetism* were introduced. In modern times physics has expanded to include also *atomic, nuclear,* and *particle physics.*

In recent years physics has been a particularly exciting discipline, on the very frontiers of the knowledge explosion. Many new discoveries have been made, particularly in astronomy (e.g., via the recent space probes to various planets in our solar system and the Hubble telescope), computer technology, and particle physics (e.g., a host of tiny new particles have been discovered: quarks, pions, muons, etc.). Thus, for example, at the University of British Columbia the Triumf cyclotron is one of the world's foremost tools for studying properties of tiny particles (created by taking larger particles such as protons, smashing them to bits, and looking at the resulting pieces).

Why Study Physics?

Why should you study physics? I believe there are a number of compelling reasons why a study of physics could be of benefit to you.

Important Applications

The success of physics has played a very large role in shaping modern society: it has led to a host of technological wonders such as radios, x-ray machines, satellites, computers, cell-phones, and MP3 players. Because of its great impact on society some appreciation of physics is of great value. To gain insight into the powers and limitations of such gadgets it is advantageous to be familiar with the underlying physical principles. It is important to keep in mind that we are dealing here not with magic black boxes but with definite physical tools.

The Beauty of Physics

A second appealing aspect of physics is its beauty. This beauty lies primarily in the fact that it is possible to explain a wide range of physical phenomena in terms of a small number of physical principles. Not all of you may fully appreciate this beauty because it is essentially mathematical. (It has been said that when students go to university they learn that biology is really chemistry, that chemistry is really physics, that physics is really math, and that math is really tough!). Cambridge University scientist John Polkinghorne comments:

> Time and again it has been our experience in fundamental phys-
> ics that the theories persuading us of their verisimilitude by their
> long-term fruitfulness in explaining phenomena—these are also
> theories whose formulation is characterized by the abstract but
> unmistakable character of mathematical beauty.[1]

Physics has been the most successful of the sciences primarily because its objects of study are accessible enough that they can be represented by simple mathematical equations. Thus, for example, from Newton's
three laws of motion and the law of gravity (four equations) we have the
tools to describe the behavior of a wide collection of objects from rockets
and planets to billiard balls and bicycles. Exactly the same laws apply to
all these objects. Add another four equations and you can describe also all
electro-magnetic phenomena.

The Logic of Physics

The logical, mathematical nature of physics provides a further incentive
for its study. The study of physics provides excellent training in logical
thinking, problem solving, and practical application. If you can't solve
problems in physics, with its relatively simple equations and logical structure, you may have difficulty solving the often more difficult questions
that arise in other fields of study—or even in real life.

HOW DOES PHYSICS WORK?

How do physicists arrive at their knowledge? Let's consider a simple example. Suppose we want to study, say, the motion of the moon. We start
with observations: we observe its position in the sky at various times. To
make sense of our list of observations we next try to fit the observations
into a simple mathematical formula. This allows us to more easily describe
the motion and to summarize our observations. But we would like to do
more. We would like to show that the motion is explicable in terms of a
few basic theoretical concepts such as force, gravity, and conservation of
energy. Hence physics requires observations, mathematics, and theoretical concepts. Let's examine each of these three elements in more detail.

1. Polkinghorne, "Christian Interdisciplinarity," 55.

Observation and Experiment

Experimental data is the basis for all physics. Furthermore, since we want to handle the data using mathematical formulas, the data must be in a suitable, quantified form. Such experiments provide a major constraint on physical theories. The predictions of theories must accord with the observed facts. Often new experiments are devised for the express purpose of testing the predictions of specific theories.

Technological advances are often made possible by the application of theoretical breakthroughs. New technology, in turn, often provides a host of new observations. Consider, for example, the invention of the telescope, space probes to the planets, particle accelerators, and recent data from the Hubble telescope. The new observations are not always easily explicable in terms of current theories. This leads to the construction of newer and better theories, which may result in improved technology. And so the cycle continues.

On the other hand, theory determines how we look at the universe, what we choose to observe, and what kind of measurements are to be made. We view the observational world through theoretical filters. Hence, theory and experiment are intricately linked together.

Mathematical Tools

Also, as I have already indicated, mathematics is crucial to physics. In order to apply abstract, theoretical concepts to the real world of hard data it is necessary to formulate these concepts in terms of mathematical equations appropriate to the physical circumstances. Once posed, the problem must then be solved using the available mathematical tools.

Quite often, new mathematical techniques are invented in order to solve particular problems in physics. Sometimes, however, the mathematical tools have been developed long before being required to explain particular observational data or to solve specific physical problems.

For example, around 1600 Tycho Brahe made very precise observations of the motion of the planet Mars. Johannes Kepler, analyzing this new data a few years later, discovered that it fit the shape of an ellipse, a geometrical shape that had been studied much earlier by the ancient Greeks. Later, towards the end of the seventeenth century, Isaac Newton was able to explain the elliptical shape of planetary orbits by his inverse square law of gravity and his laws of motion. This required more sophisticated mathematical tools, such as differential calculus, which Newton had invented. Similarly, Einstein's theory of general relativity, devised in about 1915, relied heavily on tensor calculus and differential geometry, novel mathematical techniques that had been developed only a few decades earlier.

In our day physicists have to know quite a bit of mathematics, some of which can be very sophisticated. Often their work can be made easier through using computer programs such as MAPLE. Yet even then one must still understand the mathematical principles at work.

Theoretical Principles

Although mathematics forms a major part of theorizing in physics, the bedrock of theory is made up of basic concepts of how nature should behave. These form the fundamental mathematical assumptions or equations from which all else follows. I am thinking here, for example, of Newton's laws of motion, Einstein's principle of relativity that physical laws are not affected by uniform motion, and the notion that matter bends space.

Such theories are very important. In addition to being very useful in summarizing observations and making predictions, they also reflect deep insight into the nature of physical reality. They enable us to explain a wide range of phenomena in terms of just a few basic principles. For example, Newton's laws of motion explained the motion of planets and of earthbound objects. Hitherto it had been thought that heavenly and earthly mechanics were quite different.

Some theoretical concepts such as symmetry, conservation, and invariance are particularly deep and broad. They play a large role in physics, as the renowned physicist Roger Penrose shows in his comprehensive overview of modern physics.[2] These theoretical formulations can be very elegant, evoking a profound sense of beauty.

The Role of Creativity

How are such theories and basic concepts formulated? Unfortunately, they usually cannot simply be logically deduced from a set of data, in a purely objective manner. On the contrary, creativity often plays an essential role in scientific theorizing. The origin of scientific theories is largely subjective. Sir Karl Popper, a prominent philosopher of science, asserts,

2. Penrose, *The Road to Reality*.

"[W]e must regard all laws or theories as hypothetical; that is, as guesses"; he sees theories as "the free creations of our minds."[3] Theories are not so much given to us by nature as they are imposed by us on nature; they are not so much the result of rational thought as they are the creations of our irrational intuition. Thus great physicists are like great artists in their reliance on a fertile imagination.

Unlike in the arts, however, the imaginative products of physicists are not quite free: they must satisfy certain theoretical constraints (e.g., more basic principles such as conservation of energy) and must pass the observational test. Thus theories in physics, although largely subjective, are still objective to the extent that they must reflect, however faintly, some genuine aspect of reality.

Most physicists do not construct new theories but spend their careers applying widely accepted theories to new physical situations where their application has not yet been figured out. This, too, requires a high degree of imagination.

Choosing Theories

Quite often, in physics, there are a number of competing theories that purport to explain all the facts. How can we determine which of these is best? One problem we face here is that often more than one mathematical formula will fit the facts. Just as it is possible to fit an infinite number of different curves through a given set of points, so it is possible to devise an infinite number of theories from a finite set of observations. Furthermore, our observations are often not exact—there may be instrumental limitations, for example—so that we are at times really fitting our curves through a set of very fuzzy points.

Sometimes new, specifically designed experiments can falsify some theories. However, it can often be very difficult to definitely falsify any particular theory. This is because in practice we test not just the theory under consideration but also a host of accompanying, supplementary theories. Hence, any observational failures can be attributed to the secondary theories and can be overcome by suitably modifying these. For example, if the orbit of a planet behaves exactly as predicted by, say, Newtonian mechanics, then this is hailed as a spectacular triumph for the theory. On the other hand, if the predictions are off, it might be conjectured that

3. Popper, *Conjectures and Refutations*, 192.

this is due to tidal distortions, extended atmospheres, or the presence of other objects too faint to be seen. Given enough ingenuity, we can always "save" a favored theory from falsification. Moreover, in practice, even an imperfect theory is not discarded until a better alternative, requiring less *ad hoc* pleading, is devised.

Further, the same mathematical equations can often be explained in terms of different theoretical frameworks. I think here, for example, of quantum mechanics, where Schrodinger's equation defining the energy level of atoms can be interpreted in many ways that differ quite profoundly in their views of reality.

How, then, can we determine which theory is better? It all depends on how we define "better." You may perhaps think that successful theories are more likely to be true. However, consider the example of Newtonian mechanics. This is the most successful scientific theory ever devised. It explained a wealth of physical phenomena. For two centuries it was widely accepted as an indubitable truth. Yet today most physicists would consider it to be false; it has been replaced by Einstein's theory of relativity. And who knows whether a similar fate may not overtake relativity?

We may prefer theories that are useful, simple, beautiful, have broad explanatory powers, or are easily testable. These criteria may seem reasonable enough. But unless we can demonstrate that, say, simple theories are more likely to be true than complex ones, we are simply indulging in knowledge games. Without adequate justification, such criteria are no more than a reflection of our prior religious and philosophical biases. As philosophy of science Professor Del Ratzsch observes, when we choose one particular theory over another, "our choice must depend at least partially on nonempirical factors, whether philosophical, theological, societal . . . [or] personal."[4]

Worldviews and Physics

The bottom line, therefore, is that we construct and choose those theories that accord best with our basic worldview, our deepest convictions about the nature of the universe. Our worldview affects virtually all our thinking. Particularly in physics, theories are closely connected with worldviews. For example, Copernicus's reduction of the earth to an ordinary planet in a heliocentric solar system undermined Aristotelian physics, which postu-

4. Ratzsch, *The Battle of Beginnings*, 111.

lated a fundamental difference between earthly and heavenly mechanics. Later, the success of Newtonian physics caused many people to consider the universe as essentially a clock that ran by itself, without need of a God. Similarly, early in the twentieth century, the new theories of relativity and quantum mechanics contributed greatly to further changes in worldview: relativity in physics was taken by many to support relativism in ethics and philosophy; quantum mechanics was taken to support a holistic universe where the observer and observed were closely intertwined.

Or were the new theories the result of a change of thinking that was already in progress? Cause and effect are sometimes difficult to separate. Suffice it to say that theories in physics are closely linked with worldviews, as is revealed by a close study of the history of physics in its full social context. Therefore, it is important for a physicist to know and appreciate the historical background of the discipline.

In short, the establishment of scientific truth involves more than a mere majority vote. The notion of scientific neutrality and objectivity is largely a myth. We may share the same observational data and the same mathematical tools, but once we attempt to explain and extend this data we depart from our common starting part and view reality through the glasses of our various subjective worldviews.

A CHRISTIAN WORLDVIEW

Since scientific theorizing is heavily dependent on our philosophical and religious presuppositions, the critical question is: What do we choose as our starting point? Modern naturalistic thinkers choose the basis to be themselves, insisting on the autonomy of human reason. Christians, on the other hand, believe in one much greater than themselves: an infinite God who knows all and has communicated truth to us in the form of both special revelation—the Scriptures—and general revelation—the created universe. Let's examine the essentials of a uniquely Christian worldview and how this makes a difference in physics.[5]

A Christian View of Knowledge

A Christian theory of knowledge is grounded upon a proper attitude of obedient submission to God. If we have made a heart commitment to

5. In my book *The Divine Challenge*, I compare the presuppositions and implications of naturalism, relativism, and Christianity.

God then we must think and act accordingly, living obediently in the light of God's Word and striving to do his will.

In my opinion, our submission to God implies that we accept his Word as inerrant—inerrant not because we can prove it to be such, for that would make human reason the final judge—but because it is the Word of him who is truth incarnate (John 14:6). Believing in an inerrant Bible must be our basic presupposition. Further, we must strive to read God's Word with open eyes and hearts, applying proper principles of interpretation that are consistent with this high view of Scripture.

God is the author also both of the physical world and of logic. Hence we expect the Bible, observation of the natural world, and deductive logic to cohere harmoniously. But our reasoning ability includes also the capacity for creative, abstract thought. For this we ourselves are responsible. Our minds are tools that can be manipulated by our inner desires and easily abused: "for out of the heart come evil thoughts" (Matthew 15:19). My point here is that human thought—which includes scientific theorizing—is to be judged in light of Scripture rather than vice versa. The Bible, in my view, must be the ultimate standard by which we assess scientific theorizing.

What is Truth?

Wheaton College philosophy professor emeritus Arthur Holmes, in *The Idea of a Christian College*, has many excellent things to say about Christian higher education. He, too, stresses that Scripture should be our final rule of faith and practice. Further, he argues that because truth is also to be found outside of Scripture, we should approach all truth with reverence since "all truth is God's truth, wherever it may be found."[6]

Here a word of caution is in order, for how are we to recognize the truth as truth when we encounter it? In particular, how can we be sure of the trustworthiness of our theoretical extrapolations beyond our empirical observations? What we believe to be true might turn out to be false. In my opinion, many Christians dealing with the integration of science and Christianity accept too uncritically mere scientific speculation as God's truth. Since God is the author of all truth, and since all truth must therefore form one consistent whole, this frequently results in biblical interpretation being held hostage to naturalistic science. All too often integration

6. Holmes, *Idea of a Christian College*, 52.

consists of little more than an accommodation of biblical revelation to secular science.

For example, theologian Rudolf Bultmann believed science had proven miracles to be impossible. Hence he concluded that all biblical miracles must be "demythologized."[7] He ended up taking Jesus Christ's resurrection as merely a symbol of humans' mastery over their passions. That rationalized dismissal of a fundamental Christian doctrine is what can happen when scientific conjecture is embraced as God's truth.

Those of you who have studied calculus know that integration is studied after differentiation. So also in each discipline the integration of faith and knowledge must be preceded by a proper differentiation. We must test the spirits, discerning carefully between truth and error.

In each field of study, one must look carefully for hidden presuppositions, for the underlying worldview that is rarely explicitly stated. What are the actual assumptions and norms that underpin the conclusions? And how do they square up with scriptural norms? You must strive to consistently think out and work out the consequences of your faith commitment for all of life. Genuine knowledge can be obtained by building on the solid foundation of God's Word.

A Christian View of Reality

What does the Bible tell us about nature? It gives very little information about the physical characteristics of the universe as we currently see it. On the other hand, the Bible says much about the world beyond our observations. First, it tells us about the all-powerful, all-knowing, loving God who created the universe from nothing. This God is quite distinct from his creation, which totally depends upon God not just for its origin but also for its continued existence (Hebrews 1:3).

Second, the Bible tells of the existence of a spiritual realm, wherein are found God, angels, and the souls of the departed. The biblical heaven seems to be a universe parallel to our physical world, but usually invisible to humanity, although at times we are told of the heavens being *opened* and a person seeing into heaven (e.g., 2 Kings 6:16, the story of Elisha and his servant). Modern secularists make the mistake of considering the physical world to be the ultimate reality, with the spiritual world as little more than an idle, unproven abstraction. In actuality, however, it is likely

7. Bultmann, "New Testament and Mythology," 3–5.

that our physical three-dimensional cosmos is no more than a small subspace of a much larger reality.

Third, the Bible tells us about history: the initial "very good" creation of the universe, Adam and Eve's fall into sin, the subsequent redemption of the fallen world through Jesus Christ's sacrificial death on the cross, and the prospective eternal life of joy of the redeemed in a renewed heaven and earth.

PHYSICS IN A CHRISTIAN WORLDVIEW

How does a Christian worldview affect our study of physics? In principle, since one's worldview provides important criteria for choosing among competing theories, a Christian influence should be profound. In practice, however, the Bible generally offers us very little help in constructing specific physical theories. A Christian perspective usually does not affect the actual content of theories. Overall, its main functions are to provide a plausible account for why physics works and to stress the proper limits of scientific theories.

Why Does Physics Work?

As I pointed out earlier, physics has been successful primarily because we can discern basic physical principles that can readily be translated into mathematical equations. Further mathematical manipulations can then lead to a wide range of precise predictions and applications.

But why is it that the universe can be so easily described mathematically? If the universe is merely a chance event and if mathematics is merely a human invention, then this is indeed a mystery. Eugene Wigner, a Nobel Prize winner in physics, has written an essay entitled "The Unreasonable Effectiveness of Mathematics." There he puzzles over this question, coming to the conclusion that the applicability of mathematics to the physical world is a mysterious gift—and an undeserved gift at that.

As Christians we know that Wigner, a non-Christian, was on the right track. The rationality of the universe is indeed a gift: a gift from God. God has created the universe according to a rational plan. Moreover, he has created humanity in his image (Genesis 1), so that people are thinking, conscious, religious beings who can discern the mathematical structures placed in the universe by the Creator.

For physics to be possible there must be a basic mathematically measurable uniformity to nature: the same laws should apply over extended periods of time. Otherwise no predictions are possible. Christianity supplies a basis for such observed regularity: God, in his covenant with Noah after the Flood (Genesis 9), promised the regular flow of times and seasons, until the time comes for a new heaven and a new earth. God has not just started off the universe and then left it to fend for itself; rather, he is continuously upholding his creation.

Miracles

These considerations do not, of course, preclude God from performing miracles. In this respect we should not consider miracles as interventions in a universe otherwise running its own course. Rather, miracles are merely irregular manifestations of God's will, but everything that occurs, both natural and miraculous, is under God's control.

This underscores a fundamental limitation of physics. Physics is concerned with explaining physical phenomena in terms of *natural* causes. It has nothing to say about the existence of a possible *spiritual* realm, nor about the possibility of spiritual causes that have physical effects. On such matters we must take our cue from divinely inspired biblical revelation.

Does God Play with Dice?

According to atomic physics (quantum mechanics), processes involving very small objects such as electrons are not exact but only probabilistic. Thus, for example, we can't predict exactly when a radioactive nucleus will emit a burst of radiation; we can only predict the probability of it occurring at any particular time. One popular interpretation of this phenomenon is that nature is *inherently* probabilistic, so that not even God can predict with certainty the time of the next radioactive emission. A number of theologians, accepting this view of quantum mechanics, have modified their theology accordingly, postulating that God has only limited knowledge of the future. Thus, for example, physicist-theologian John Polkinghorne believes that God has self-limited his divine power in order to let nature develop itself freely.[8]

Albert Einstein, one of the founders of modern physics, objected to such an interpretation of quantum mechanics. Asserting that God

8. Polkinghorne, *Belief in God in an Age of Science,* 13.

does not play with dice, Einstein felt that there must be an underlying determinism so that all physical events do ultimately occur according to precise laws and not by chance. The probabilistic laws can then be seen as exhibiting merely human limitation in observing the very small, rather than as fundamental physical properties of matter itself. Such a deterministic view has recently been defended by the Christian physicist Peter Hodgson in his book *Theology and Modern Physics*. (Note that here the dispute concerns not the *equations* of quantum mechanics but only their proper interpretation.) In this regard I agree with Einstein and Hodgson. The Bible speaks clearly of an all-knowing, all-powerful God who leaves nothing to chance: "The lot is cast in the lap, but the decision is wholly from the Lord" (Proverbs 16:33).

Chaos and Butterflies

Quantum effects apply only to very small objects and are insignificant for larger objects such as billiard balls and planets. There, at least, it seemed as if one could make extremely accurate predictions. In the nineteenth century, a famous French physicist, Pierre LaPlace, boasted that, given the initial positions and speeds of all particles in the universe, he could predict all subsequent events in the universe.[9]

In recent times it has become evident that such accurate predictions are not possible. Many events in nature are what we call "chaotic." For example, try balancing a pencil—point down—on your desk. The direction it falls after you let go is hard to predict, depending very precisely on minute effects such as a small puff of air, a vibration in your desk, or a small initial departure from equilibrium. A tiny change in initial conditions can lead to a very large difference in outcome. It turns out that the equations governing weather are chaotic: they depend very precisely on initial conditions. The disturbance caused by the flight of a butterfly could generate effects eventually culminating in a tornado. Not that I'm suggesting butterflies cause tornados! But it does serve to illustrate that one can predict weather accurately only if one knows the initial conditions with infinitesimal precision—something beyond the capacity of even the most meticulous meteorologist.

In short, even if the world were purely deterministic and naturalistic, there would be limitations in human ability to predict future events. Of

9. LaPlace, *Philosophical Essays on Probabilities*.

course, it may well be that, in the case of the weather, future advances in technology might enable us to effectively predict the weather by controlling it, damping out small disruptive effects before they become significant.

Extrapolations of Physics

Probabilistic laws, chaotic effects, and possible miracles all limit the reliability of scientific predictions. In spite of such current uncertainties, we scientists try to advance scientific knowledge of the distant past and/or the (as yet) unobserved future by extrapolating on the basis of both observed data and our preferred presuppositional theories.

This requires us to make some assumptions regarding the nature of the unobserved universe. It is natural for most scientific theorists to assume the principle of *induction* or *uniformity*: the notion that the laws of nature observed here and now are valid always and everywhere. Consider, for example, the motion of the moon. It is customary to assume that the forces acting on the moon were much the same in the past as they are now. But how do we know that this has really been the case? Perhaps in the past gravity was stronger or weaker, perhaps there have been close encounters with other planets (this is the theory of Velikovsky[10]), or perhaps the moon stood still (as in Joshua 10).

For that matter, some Christian scientists (and I include myself in their number) believe that the entire physical universe might have been created full-blown as recently as some 6,000 years ago. Such a notion, we maintain, has a number of things going for it: it is free from self-contradiction, it can be shown to be consistent with observable facts, and, since it refers to the past, it is beyond any experimental refutation (but this is admittedly true for all theories about the origin of the cosmos). Some of the pros and cons of this "mature creation" thesis are discussed by theologian Vern Poythress.[11] The point is that the universe beyond our observations may well be quite different from what our theories predict.

Naturalists strive to explain the origin and operation of the physical universe in terms of purely natural processes, without acknowledging any involvement of a supernatural being. Obviously such a view may well

---

10. Velikovsky, *Worlds in Collision*.

11. Poythress, *Redeeming Science*, 113–30. I also discuss this viewpoint at some length in my book *God and Cosmos*.

clash with biblical Christianity, particularly when it concerns extensions of physics beyond the presently observable universe.

The most controversial of these extensions are speculations about the origin, destiny, and completeness of the physical universe. Big bang cosmology has become a very popular theory of origins. It purports to explain all of physical reality in terms of the sudden appearance—the Big Bang—of the universe roughly 15 billion years ago and its subsequent manifold evolution. Purely natural causes and random interactions allegedly transformed primordial matter into stars, planets, life and, finally, humans. As to the universe's fate, most advocates of this cosmological thesis prognosticate that presumably all life will eventually be snuffed out (no doubt many millions or even billions of years from now), either in a "Big Crunch" (if the universe is massive enough to turn its expansion into a contraction) or in a "Big Whimper," when energy is spread too thin to support life.

To what extent can Big Bang cosmology be reconciled with the Bible? Usually such a question focuses on origins rather than on the future of the cosmos. Since the Big Bang evolutionary scenario contradicts the traditional reading of Genesis 1–11, many Christian Big Bang exponents (most of whom would also acknowledge themselves to be theistic evolutionists) have been obliged to modify their interpretation of this passage in the Bible.[12] Here a word of caution is in order. Once we permit a scientific theory to modify our understanding of the Bible, where do we stop? What criteria do we have for judging which scientific theories are true and which portions of the Bible are open for revision? Newman comments on the implications of having to re-interpret the opening chapters of Genesis as follows:

> The account of human origins in Genesis 2, taken as a historical account rather than a myth or allegory, is a severe problem for all no-Adam versions of theistic evolution.... The warrant for reading Genesis 2 and 3 [the latter the account of Adam and Eve's fall] as a myth or allegory comes from outside Scripture.... We should not mistake research agendas for empirical results.[13]

---

12 For a detailed look at the issues involved in origins the reader is referred to Ratzsch *The Battle of Beginnings* and Poythress, *Redeeming Science*.

13. Newman, "Some Problems for Theistic Evolution," 28.

A similar question can be raised with respect to the narrative describing God's acts of creation in Genesis 1 or the account of the Noahic flood and its aftermath in Genesis 6–10. No internal evidence exists for interpreting these apparently historical narratives, involving named people, time frames, and places, as mere myths or fictional stories.

I do, of course, recognize that a number of scientists have no difficulty reconciling the Big Bang thesis and/or a belief in theistic evolution with their Christian faith. As I have indicated above, I believe a better alternative, more in line with a high view of the Bible and a recognition of the highly subjective nature of most scientific theorizing, would be to let the Bible speak for itself and to modify our scientific view of origins accordingly.[14] I respectfully "agree to disagree" with Christian scientific colleagues who believe otherwise.

THE TASK OF THE CHRISTIAN IN PHYSICS

We have seen how a Christian worldview makes a difference in physics. What implications does this have for why and how Christians should be involved in physics?

First, we note that a study of physics enables us to better appreciate the wonderful world that God has created, as well as the Creator himself. The beauty, grandeur, coherence, and wisdom in nature reflect the character of its Creator. As we have seen, Christianity gives a plausible explanation as to why the universe exhibits a discernible rational structure. Hence, physics can play an apologetic role, albeit in a rather limited way.

Second, activity in physics finds justification through the cultural mandate to subdue and replenish the earth (Genesis 1:28). Physics provides us with powerful tools that can be applied for the stewardly service of God and our fellow humans. In this regard, physics has yielded many applications—I think here particularly of modern communications, jet travel, and computers—that have not merely benefited humankind in general but also have helped individuals to preach the gospel and thus fulfill the Great Commission.

Third, there is a further, even more important reason why Christians should be involved in physics. We need experts to evaluate and apply the

14. In *God and Cosmos*, I discuss in considerable detail both the case for my belief in a "mature" young earth and why I see as problematic Christians holding to the Big Bang cosmological thesis, with respect to not only the past but also the future, in the light of biblical narratives and teachings.

conclusions of scientific research in a Christian manner. Such experts can guide the Christian community in its interaction with modern society.

A Christian physicist should be fully aware of both the power and limitations of scientific theorizing. In a Christian worldview, we must ensure that our theories, as well as their interpretations and extensions, are consistent with what is revealed to us through the Bible. The Bible (e.g., Psalm 19, Romans 1) does tell us that God reveals himself through nature. However, the knowledge thus revealed is primarily about God's character rather than about origins and other mysteries. Indeed, the Bible (e.g., Job 38–41) often stresses humanity's ignorance regarding origins and deeper questions about nature.

A Christian scientist should therefore be *competent* (know the discipline well), *critical* (be able to discern philosophical presuppositions and implications), and *biblical* (building on a solid scriptural foundation).

CONCLUSION

In summary, I believe a Christian approach to physics will emphasize:

1. the beauty and orderliness of God's creation
2. our responsibility to subdue it as God's stewards
3. the power, as well as the limits, of human theorizing
4. the need to submit all our thinking to the light of the Bible.

A Christian approach to physics may well end up with much the same equations, but it will interpret, apply, and extend these in accordance with God's Word.

Finally, let me stress again the main thesis of this chapter: that in approaching physics—as in any discipline—we must be guided by our fundamental trust in God. As we study his creation we must strive to view it in the light of his inerrant Word, making every thought captive to Christ, "in whom are hid all treasures of wisdom and knowledge" (Colossians 2:3), and applying our knowledge in ways that best serve the advancement of his Kingdom. Above all, we must keep things in a proper perspective. We must not forget that since this world will pass away, along with its physics, we are but pilgrims on our way to an eternal destiny.

WORKS CITED

Bultmann, Rudolf. "New Testament and Mythology." In *Kerygma and Myth*, edited by H. W. Bartsch, 1–44. London: SPCK, 1957.

Byl, John. *God and Cosmos: A Christian View of Time, Space, and the Universe*. Edinburgh: Banner of Truth Trust, 2004.

———. *The Divine Challenge: On Matter, Mind, Math, and Meaning*. Edinburgh: Banner of Truth Trust, 2004.

Hodgson, Peter E. *Theology and Modern Physics*. Burlington, VT: Ashgate, 2005.

Holmes, Arthur F. *The Idea of a Christian College*. Rev. ed. Grand Rapids, MI: Eerdmans, 1987.

LaPlace, P. S. *Philosopical Essays on Probabilities*. Translated by F. W. Truscott and F. L. Emory. New York: Dover, 1986 (1825).

Newman, Robert C. "Some Problems for Theistic Evolution." *Perspectives on Science and Christian Faith* 55.2 (June 2003) 117–28.

Penrose, Roger. *The Road to Reality: A Complete Guide to the Laws of the Universe*. New York: Knopf, 2005.

Polkinghorne, John. *Belief in God in an Age of Science*. New Haven: Yale University Press, 1998.

———. "Christian Interdisciplinarity." In *Christianity and the Soul of the University: Faith as a Foundation for Intellectual Community*, edited by Douglas V. Henry and Michael D. Beaty, 49–64. Grand Rapids, MI: Baker Academic, 2006.

Popper, Karl. *Conjectures and Refutations: The Growth of Scientific Knowledge*. London: Routledge, 1963.

Poythress, Vern S. *Redeeming Science: A God-Centered Approach*. Wheaton, IL: Crossway, 2006.

Ratzsch, Del. *The Battle of Beginnings: Why Neither Side Is Winning the Creation–Evolution Debate*. Downers Grove, IL: InterVarsity Press, 1996.

Velikovsky, Immanuel. *Worlds in Collision*. New York: Dell, 1950.

Wigner, Eugene. "The Unreasonable Effectiveness of Mathematics." *Communications on Pure and Applied Mathematics* 13 (1960) 1–14.

FOR FURTHER READING

Beckman, John C. "Quantum Mechanics, Chaos Physics and the Open View of God." *Philosophia Christi* 4.1 (2002) 204–13.

Berlinski, David. "Was There a Big Bang?" *Commentary* 105 (1998) 28–38.

Claerbaut, David. "Why Is Creation Central to the Faith-and-Learning Enterprise?" In Claerbaut, *Faith and Learning on the Edge: A Bold New Look at Religion in Higher Education*, 146–59. Grand Rapids, MI: Zondervan, 2004.

25

A Christian Perspective on Political Science

MARK W. CHARLTON

INTRODUCTION

SOME TIME AGO I was attending a board meeting for the first time. As we were getting acquainted, someone asked me what I did. After explaining that I taught political science, they caught me off guard by saying, "Oh, you mean there actually is an academic discipline called political science? I thought political science was something that theologians wrote about when they wanted to be relevant." The person was only being facetious, but there is probably more than a grain of truth to the statement. In preparing this chapter, I scanned through the several shelves of books in the library dealing with the Christian and politics, or related topics such as war and peace. Of the several dozen books I reviewed, I found only four written by actual "practicing" political scientists. The rest were in fact written by professors of religious studies or ethics, a few by historians and political activists. And even those written by political scientists barely mentioned, if at all, the question of how one's faith relates to the "doing" of political science as an academic discipline.

Perhaps this should not be surprising given the fact that the study of political science has traditionally been ignored in the curriculum of Christian liberal arts colleges and universities. Even in many American Christian colleges established more than one hundred years ago, you will find that most political science programs are less than twenty years old. While the number of evangelicals with graduate degrees in political science is growing, their ranks are much smaller than those found in other academic disciplines. Thus, in writing about political science, I am in many ways talking about a "new kid on the block" in terms of academic subjects taught at Christian liberal arts institutions. But, given the importance of the topic to our society today, I hope that you will see it as a field that offers unique opportunities for creative Christian discipleship and effective Christian service.

WHAT IS POLITICS?

Politics Defined

John Stott gives us a beautifully simple definition of politics: "Politics is the art of living together in community." Politics is about relating to others, developing a common vision of what is good for society so that we can work together for a common goal. Perhaps more technically, Stott goes on to say that politics can be defined as "the process whereby a group of people, whose opinions or interests are divergent, reach collective decisions which are binding on the whole group and enforced as common policy."[1]

Key Elements of Politics

If we look carefully at this definition, we can see that there are four key elements that help us to understand the nature of politics and why it is so controversial. First, politics assumes a diversity of views about both the ultimate aims of a community and the best method of achieving these aims. If total consensus existed about both these issues, there would be no need for politics. Because politics wrestles with questions concerning the ultimate aims of a community, it is not surprising that it evokes strong disagreement and conflict.

Second, politics is the quest to find a means of settling disagreements without the use of coercive force. The most common means of coming to some collective agreement is through a process of persuasion and bargaining. The political speech or debate, when each side tries to convince the other of the rightness of its position, is the quintessential political event. Bargaining involves the more nitty-gritty business of meeting your opponents' demands part way in order to win concessions from them on your list of demands. Because political persuasion and bargaining can easily be carried out in ways that involve deception and a sacrifice

1. Stott, *Involvement: Being a Responsible Christian in a Non–Christian Society*, 31.

of principle, politics has frequently taken on a negative connotation, especially for Christians. For many, politics is synonymous with deception and compromise.

Third, whatever the nature of the process of persuasion and bargaining that has taken place, the time eventually comes for a decision to be made. This inevitably raises the question about what the best method is for making political decisions that serve the welfare of a political community. Here again, opinions widely vary, from Plato's notion of an enlightened philosopher prince who should make the decisions on behalf of the ignorant and ill-informed masses to an anarchist vision of the individual self being responsible for all decisions with no appeal to some higher authority. But even in cases where a society has tried to strike a balance, as in constitutional democracies, many questions remain: Will simple majority rule provide sufficient protection against the danger of the tyranny of the majority over the minority? Should the right to elect our officials be supplemented by other forms of direct democracy such as referendum and recall?

Finally, once a method of decision-making has been agreed upon, politics assumes that the collective decisions made will now be authoritative, or binding, for the whole community. Since there will always be those that do not want to accept the decisions made by society, politics leads to questions of authority and power. On what basis do we accept and obey decisions made for us by others? To what extent should coercion, or force, be used to impose decisions on citizens? In politics, the temptation has always been great for some to forego the difficult process of persuasion and to use coercion to attain their ends, often for their own benefit. Thus, not surprisingly, politics has been associated with the use of power and coercion. The cynic's definition of politics is "A strife masquerading as a contest of principles. The conduct of public affairs for private advantage."[2]

POLITICAL SCIENCE AS AN ACADEMIC DISCIPLINE

Political science courses are quite different from courses in physics, chemistry, mathematics, or geography, where we may come to the subject material with a sense of indifference. We may learn what H_2SO_4 stands for, but seeing the symbol does not usually invoke any kind of emotional reaction in us. However, we all bring to the study of politics our own

2. Marshall, *Thine Is the Kingdom*, 12.

personal, sometimes intensely held, opinions. The mere mention of a political label (socialism or "Neo-Con") or a name (Osama Bin Laden or George W. Bush) may provoke a heated exchange of opinion between students even before a class begins.

But opinion is not the same as knowledge. What political science tries to do as a field of academic study is to provide the factual background and the theoretical perspectives we need in order to become more effective citizens and advocates for our point of view. But the study of government is not merely an applied discipline, meant only for those seeking a career in public office. The science of politics, like all science, seeks the truth regarding its subject matter. Its study helps us to understand that the question, "How then should I live?" cannot be totally separated from the question, "How then should I live in community?" This is a question relevant for all of us, whether we specifically seek a career in public office or not.

Robert and Doreen Jackson describe political science as "the study of how organized disputes are articulated, and then resolved by public decisions made by governments."[3] Thus, political scientists are concerned about moving beyond the opinions we all have about politics to the empirical task of describing and analyzing the processes and institutions involved in the making of political decisions. At the same time, they are interested in the ethical and normative questions regarding the proper relationship between the institutional structures of politics and the desired aims of political community such as justice, liberty, freedom, and equality. It is not surprising then that political science is a very broad field that goes far beyond the study of constitutions and the organs of government. There are at least four broad ways in which political scientists have approached the study of politics.

Political Science as the Study of Philosophy

From the time of the ancient Greeks, people have wrestled with such questions as "What is the best form of government?" "Is war ever justified?" "How ought leaders to act?" These "ought" questions form the normative questions of political science, as we struggle to answer the most fundamental question, "What is justice?" This approach to political

---

3. Jackson and Jackson, *Contemporary Government and Politics*, 14.

science, tracing its origin back to the ancient Greeks, is strongly rooted in the broader study of philosophy.

Political Science as the Study of Behavior

This approach is interested in asking why people behave politically in the manner that they do. What impact does race or class have on the way people vote? Why do some countries frequently experience military coups when others do not? This approach draws on the methodologies and insights of a variety of social sciences like sociology, psychology, and anthropology to generate insights and provide analytical approaches and models. There are even academic journals entitled *Political Psychology*, *Political Sociology*, and *Political Geography*.

Political Science as the Study of Institutions

This approach is interested in understanding how political institutions and laws develop and evolve. Why is it that Canada and the United States both have an institution called a Senate that has some similar powers but yet is so different in its ability to influence public policy? This approach to political science, with strong roots in the study of history and law, tends to be descriptive in nature.

Political Science as the Study of Public Policy

In recent years there has been a growing interest in making the study of political science more practically oriented by relating it directly to the study of what it is that political institutions and processes produce. Here the study of public policy asks why certain policies have emerged and seeks to evaluate their impact and effectiveness. My own work on Canadian food aid policy would fall in this area. It would seem that providing some of Canada's rich abundance of grain surpluses would be a natural way of resolving some of the world's problems of starvation and malnutrition, but a careful study of food aid programs shows that such programs can have a detrimental effect on those we intend to help. Why is this the case? Why do good intentions sometimes produce bad results? In addressing such issues, policy analysis helps us to understand some of the reasons for the gap between rhetoric and reality that seems so prevalent in the political realm.

PITFALLS IN APPROACHING POLITICS FROM A CHRISTIAN PERSPECTIVE

How should we as Christians approach the subject of politics in a manner that might be different from other approaches? Before trying to answer that question, I think it may be useful to look at two pitfalls that we as Christians, especially evangelicals, are tempted to fall into in addressing this issue.

The Temptation of Isolationism

Throughout most of the nineteenth century, evangelicals promoted social and political reform as an integral part of their evangelical witness. Evangelical Christians played a prominent part in the nineteenth-century movements for prison reform, regulation of child labor, abolition of slavery, and women's suffrage. In the early part of this century, however, with the rise of fundamentalism, many Christians retreated from active involvement in political and social reform. In reacting against the social gospel of liberal Protestants, fundamentalism focused on the preaching of the need for personal salvation. This has given rise to a dualistic thinking among many Christians that sees a clear separation between their public and private lives. They believe that the Christian faith is concerned with our private spiritual life and personal morality. They think the Bible provides guidance for personal spiritual matters but has little to say about the political realm. Politics, being part of the fallen world, outside of God's intended purpose for humankind, is governed by the "worldly" principles of self-interest and power. From this perspective it is tempting to conclude that Christians have no real responsibility towards the political realm. In fact, any involvement in the "messy world" of politics is believed to be detrimental to our higher calling to preach the gospel. For some Christians this has meant a position of *quietism*, in which they think that they have nothing to say at all about political issues and hence no need even to study political science. For others, this has led to a negative critique in which they believe that the Christian task is primarily to demonstrate the utter futility of political involvement.

The Temptation of Political Fundamentalism

Since the early 1970s, there has been a significant move away from the quietism that characterized evangelicals in the first half of the twentieth century. This is especially evident in the growth of what has come to be called the New Religious Right in the United States. Rising out of a reaction to the growing secularization of American society, with its accompanying permissiveness and relativism, the New Right has sought to use political means to restore those traditional values that it believes are under siege. Politics is seen as the last battlefield in the fight to halt the spread of secular humanism.

From this perspective, politics is not seen as a good in itself but as a necessary evil that one must endure to achieve a higher goal. As a result, the tactics and strategies of the New Religious Right often differ little from those of secular interest groups. This approach is based on the hope that by swinging enough votes to pass the right legislation or to elect the right person, or by packing the Supreme Court with the right number of judges, the drift toward secular humanism will be halted. Thus, the rise of the New Right in America is not unlike the rise of Islamic fundamentalism in the Middle East: both seek to seize control of political power to protect or restore the religious values under attack by modernity. This type of political fundamentalism has led to a negative style of engagement that many, even in the New Right movement itself, now admit has been harmful to the Christian cause. Os Guinness reports that after nearly a decade of high-profile political involvement by evangelicals in the United States, "34 per cent of American academics rate evangelicals as a menace to democracy, compared with only 14 per cent who see any danger from racists, the Klu Klux Klan and Nazis."[4] Guinness blames this negative perception on evangelicals themselves, who, he believes, have not taken sufficient care to develop a biblically-rooted philosophy of witness in the public square.

TOWARDS A CHRISTIAN PERSPECTIVE ON POLITICS

How then do we go about the task of developing a biblically-based approach to politics and political science? Nowhere do the Scriptures provide a blueprint or a recipe book for building a model government in a post-industrial, post-Christian, post-modern society at the beginning of the twenty-first century. Rather, what the Bible does provide is an attitude and an approach to dealing with political issues. Indeed, Richard John Neuhaus, late editor-in-chief of the widely-read faith-affirming American

---

4. Guinness, *The American Hour*, 2.

periodical *First Things*, went so far as to observe recently that there is a "growing awareness that we cannot intelligently address the great questions of public life without the wisdom transmitted and proposed by religious faith."[5] World-renowned sociologist of religion from Boston University Peter Berger made a similar comment a couple of years earlier when he said, "Those who neglect religion in their analyses of contemporary affairs do so at great peril [a highly prescient insight in that he made his comment a couple of years prior to the tragedy of the September 11, 2001 terrorist attacks on the World Trade Center in New York and the Pentagon in Washington]."[6]

A Christian approach to politics has as much to do with our *style* of politics as it does with the *substance* of our political beliefs. I propose to list in outline form what I see as the essential building blocks in a Christian approach.

1. It is clear from the Scriptures that God has ordained governments to fulfill a specific purpose in his creation. The Bible clearly shows that God appoints governments to administer justice in society, to protect the weak and vulnerable, and to preserve order, so that the work of his Kingdom can be carried out. Martin Harrison, a British political scientist, remarks that, because governments are ordained by God, "[f]or all their failings, government and politics are to be celebrated, supported and put to constructive use."[7]

2. The goal of Christian political involvement is the pursuit of justice for all people. Although the Bible does not give us a simple definition of justice, the Scriptures contain more than 800 references to justice and righteousness as a promise or obligation in the Bible. As Marshall notes, "The Bible spends more time talking about political doings than it does about charismatic gifts, or the return of Christ."[8] It is clear that political responsibility is a vital part of our religious obligations. In carrying out this responsibility we are seeking justice for all people, not just benefits for our own particular interest group.

---

5. Neuhaus, *The Best of "The Public Square,"* viii.
6. Berger, *The Desecularization of the World*, 18.
7. Harrison, "Authority and Democracy," 148.
8. Marshall, *Thine Is the Kingdom*, 66.

3. If government is indeed God-ordained, and we are called to exercise our responsibility as Christian citizens, then we should also give special attention not only to the *substance* of political issues but to the caring for political *processes* and *institutions* themselves. Harrison points out that even though Christians need not entirely immerse themselves in politics, "but to the extent that they do think or act politically, they can and should adopt an understanding, constructive and caring relationship to government. Too often government is taken for granted; like any human institution it thrives only if it is cared for, nurtured and edified."[9] We must express our views in ways that edify/build up the political system rather than degrade it. As Page has noted in his essay "Shaping Canadian Values,"[10] Christian values of confession, forgiveness, and reconciliation can do much in helping to heal the cynicism and divisions that have torn the political fabric of our country in recent years. As "ministers of reconciliation" we must bring healing to the political process itself.

4. Political evangelism, not imposition, is our starting point. Again to quote Harrison, "securing our political aims is not to be a matter of capturing the formal structures of decision-making through the various techniques of pressure politics; it entails a much broader struggle to change the thinking of society."[11] The approach that Harrison calls for here is similar to one of the distinctive themes of John Paul II's pontificate—that culture, not politics or economics, is the driving force of history.[12] Thus, to bring about political change, we must first focus on bringing about fundamental change within culture itself.

5. Despite what our critics may say, Christianity is not a threat to democratic politics. Nor can we accept that it is simply a matter of private belief with no relevance to public policy. Indeed, as Glenn Tinder, a political scientist at the University of Massachusetts, has argued, Christianity is essential to a humane form of politics.[13] With its view that all people are created in the image of God and that each has val-

9. Harrison, "Authority and Democracy," 169.

10. Page, "Shaping Canadian Values," 25–48.

11. Harrison, "Authority and Democracy," 168.

12. Cf. Weigel, *Witness to Hope*, 295–99 and 792.

13. Tinder, *The Political Meaning of Christianity*.

ue and dignity, Christianity provides the essential basis for a respect for human rights and a check on political ideologies that seek to sacrifice individuals for the sake of some presumably higher goal. At the same time, Tinder notes, the Christian's awareness of sin and of the fallibility of human beings instills in us a healthy scepticism towards political ideologies and programs that promise to provide for us salvation or complete happiness outside of God's Kingdom. Thus, Christianity provides an antidote against any attempt to sacralize politics or transform politics into something more than it is.

6.   We need to learn to read the Bible in a new way. We cannot escape the fact that we live in a democratic political system that is based on the notion that all sovereignty flows from the people. Thus, Harrison argues that in fact we should see ourselves as "citizen-rulers."[14] He suggests that we should thus read the Scriptures very differently. Those Scriptures referring to rulers and leaders, admonishing them to carry out their tasks in justice and righteousness, should be seen as applying to us as we carry out our political responsibilities. Viewed in this light, can we just walk away and ignore what is being carried out in our name, especially if it leads to injustice or oppression?

7.   Finally, our approach to politics will best be described as one of "critical (i.e., careful, discerning) involvement." The Christian is always aware that his/her commitment to any particular political party, program, or agenda can only be a limited and tentative one. Each of us may have to face a time when we will need to break ranks with those around us to give witness to the cause of justice, since our ultimate loyalty is to God's Kingdom.

TOWARDS A CHRISTIAN APPROACH TO POLITICAL ANALYSIS

It would be nice if at this point I could now proceed to outline the basic tools of Christian political analysis. But we as faith-affirming political scientists cannot do that, as Marshall remarks, for "the simple and embarrassing reason that such means do not exist, at least not in any well developed way."[15]

14. Harrison, "Authority and Democracy," 169.
15. Marshall, *Thine Is the Kingdom*, 76.

This situation exists for two basic reasons. First, Christians have frequently avoided the task of developing a distinctive Christian style of political analysis by drawing on convenient existing secular sources. For example, the political analysis of liberation theology draws heavily on Marxist forms of class analysis. The analysis of government's role in the economy by the New Religious Right frequently draws more heavily on the views of the economist Milton Friedman than on biblical sources.

Part of the reason for this lies also in the nature of the Scriptures themselves. They do have much to tell us about political matters and how to live in community. They give us concrete examples of what it means to act with justice, love, and compassion. The Bible does not give us a specific blueprint for building political institutions and policies in this post-industrial, post-modern world, any more than the Scriptures give us guidance on how to build a better car. Inasmuch as the Word of God is "a lamp unto our feet [and] a light on our path" (Psalm 119:105), it helps to set us in the direction we should be going to look for answers. As Marshall observes, "we cannot determine a political policy solely by a process of biblical exegesis."[16] We cannot proof-text a solution to Canada's constitutional impasse or the dilemmas of American foreign policy in the Middle East. But we seek to discover, in the light of our reading of the Scriptures, what it means to do justice and act as stewards in the world as we confront it today. Douglas Johnston's collection of edited articles entitled *Faith-Based Diplomacy: Trumping Realpolitik*, published in 2003, constitutes an impressive attempt by a group of Christian political commentators associated with Johnston's International Center for Religion and Diplomacy to do precisely that. Lee Hamilton, in the book's "Foreword," observes, "The contribution of this book is that it sees religion not as something to overcome or ignore, but as an important part of conflict resolution and the promotion of peace."[17] These contributors focus on the analysis of five areas of world conflict, every one of which is being fueled primarily by extreme religion-based hatred between the principal belligerents: Kashmir, Sri Lanka, the Middle East, Bosnia-Herzegovena and Kosovo, and the Sudan.

These are some ways in which I think that Christian political scientists can approach their task in a distinctive manner. They will always

---

16. Marshall, *Thine Is the Kingdom*, 72.

17. Hamilton "Foreword," ix.

be sensitive to the fact that all areas of life, especially politics, are ultimately fundamentally religious in character. Political institutions and public policies are all rooted in some fundamental set of values about what we hold to be of utmost importance. In cases where these values are given an ultimate importance that transcends all other values, such a response becomes a form of idolatry that distorts our policies and institutions. Thus, a Christian political analysis will seek to uncover those cases of political idolatry. For example, an analysis of foreign policy from a Christian perspective would focus on how a nation's preoccupation with national security, defined purely in terms of military security, has led to the relinquishing of other valid goals that link human rights, democratic freedoms, and economic wellbeing. It will point out how an idolatrous preoccupation with military security, narrowly defined, has itself become the source of new insecurities.

CONCLUSION

Marshall has stated:

> Christian political understanding and action is never an exercise whose answers and strategies are known before we begin. Its end is not predetermined (except in the final sense of Christ's ultimate victory and the renewal of all things). Our politics always involves real questioning, probing, trying, learning and revising as we struggle to learn and to do God's will in the historical situation we are in.[18]

This is an exciting time to be undertaking such a task. Fortunately, there are new opportunities for you as Christians to be involved in this task that were not available at Christian liberal arts colleges and universities in the past. I hope that some of you will join in the interesting but challenging task of seeking God's will in the study of politics.

WORKS CITED

Berger, Peter L., ed. *The Desecularization of the World: Resurgent Religion and World Politics.* Washington, DC: Ethics and Public Policy Center / Grand Rapids, MI: Eerdmans, 1999.

Guinness, Os. *The American Hour: A Time of Reckoning and the Once and Future Role of Faith.* New York: Free Press, 1993.

18. Marshall, *Thine Is the Kingdom*, 73.

Hamilton, Lee H. "Foreword." In *Faith-Based Diplomacy: Trumping Realpolitik*, edited by Douglas Johnston, ix-x. New York: Oxford University Press, 2003.

Harrison, M. "Authority and Democracy: The Political Debate." In *The Year 2000*, edited by John R. W. Stott, 146–79. Basingstoke, England: Marshall, Morgan & Scott, 1983.

Jackson, Robert J., and Doreen Jackson. *Contemporary Government and Politics: Democracy and Authoritarianism*. Scarborough, ON: Prentice Hall Canada, 1993.

Johnston, Douglas, ed. *Faith-Based Diplomacy: Trumping Realpolitik*. New York: Oxford University Press, 2003.

Marshall, Paul A. *Thine Is the Kingdom: A Biblical Perspective on the Nature of Government and Politics Today*. Grand Rapids, MI: Eerdmans, 1986.

Neuhaus, Richard John. *The Best of "The Public Square." Book Two*. Grand Rapids, MI: Eerdmans, 2001.

Page, Don. "Shaping Canadian Values." In *Shaping A Christian Vision for Canada: Discussion Papers on Canada's Future*, edited by Aileen Van Ginkel, 25–48. Markham, ON: Faith Today Publishers, 1992.

Stott, John. *Involvement: Being a Responsible Christian in a Non-Christian Society*. Old Tappan, NJ: Revell, 1985.

Tinder, Glenn E. *The Political Meaning of Christianity: The Prophetic Stance*. San Francisco: HarperSanFrancisco, 1991.

Weigel, George. *Witness to Hope: The Biography of Pope John Paul II, 1920–2005*. New York: Harper, 2001.

FOR FURTHER READING

Carter, Stephen L. *God's Name in Vain: The Rights and Wrongs of Religion in Politics*. New York: Basic Books, 2000.

Chaplin, Jonathan, and Paul Marshall, eds. *Political Theory and Christian Vision*. Lanham, MD: University Press of America, 1994.

Charlton, Mark. "Where's the Political Science Department?" In *Minding the Church: Scholarship in the Anabaptist Tradition*, edited by David Weaver-Zercher, 140–51. Telford, PA: Pandora Press, 2002.

Claerbaut, David. "Reflections for the Christian Political Scientist." In his *Faith and Learning on the Edge: A Bold New Look at Religion in Higher Education*, 245–57. Grand Rapids, MI: Zondervan, 2004.

Ellul, Jacques. *Anarchy and Christianity*. Trans. by Geoffrey W. Bromiley. Grand Rapids, MI: Eerdmans, 1991.

Farrow, Douglas, ed. *Recognizing Religion in a Secular Society: Essays in Pluralism, Religion, and Public Policy*. Montreal, QC: McGill-Queen's University Press, 2005.

Gottwald, Norman K., and Richard A. Horsley, eds. *The Bible and Liberation: Political and Social Hermeneutics*. Rev. ed. Maryknoll, NY: Orbis Press, 1993.

Johnston, Douglas, and Cynthia Sampson, eds. *Religion, the Missing Dimension of Statecraft*. New York: Oxford University Press, 1994.

Kaufman, Peter I. *Redeeming Politics*. Princeton: Princeton University Press, 1990.

Kuipert, H. Martinus. *Everything Is Politics but Politics Is not Everything: A Theological Perspective on Faith and Politics*. Translated by John Bowden. Grand Rapids, MI: Eerdmans, 1986.

Mouw, Richard J. "Alternative Christian Approaches to Political Science: Toward a More Comprehensive Perspective." In *The Reality of Christian Learning: Strategies for*

Faith-Discipline Integration, edited by Harold Heie and David L. Wolfe, 38–52. Grand Rapids, MI: Eerdmans, 1987.

Redekop, John H. *Politics under God.* Waterloo, ON: Herald Press, 2007.

Shriver, Donald W., Jr. *An Ethic for Enemies: Forgiveness in Politics.* New York: Oxford University Press, 1995.

Skillen, James W. "Can There Be a Christian Approach to Political Science?" In *The Reality of Christian Learning: Strategies for Faith-Discipline Integration*, edited by Harold Heie and David L. Wolfe, 17–37. Grand Rapids, MI: Eerdmans, 1987.

Sweetman, Brendan. *Why Politics Needs Religion: The Place of Religious Arguments in the Public Square.* Downers Grove, IL: InterVarsity Press, 2006.

Wogaman, J. Philip. *Christian Perspectives on Politics.* Rev. ed. Louisville, KY: Westminster John Knox Press, 2000.

26

A Christian Perspective on Psychology

Harold W. Faw

INTRODUCTION

M OST COLLEGE OR UNIVERSITY students have some idea what psychology is about, whether they have taken a course in it or not. Typically, my first year students associate it with counseling or clinical practice, an image that the media certainly reinforce, along with a certain naivety portrayed when the psychologist or psychiatrist merely reaffirms the obvious. I'm not about to deny either that counseling is part of psychology or that psychologists sometimes confirm what can be known by common sense, but I do want to demonstrate that the field is much broader than that. Some of my own research has focused on exploring aspects of our memory ability, specifically our capacity to recognize the faces of people we have seen earlier. As a result, I have developed a much greater appreciation for just how complex and remarkable this ability is.

KEY ISSUES AND VIEWPOINTS IN MAINSTREAM PSYCHOLOGY

I first wish to examine psychology more closely by exploring some of the key issues and perspectives it incorporates. To put it rather casually, psychology's purpose is to better understand human behavior and experience. While that statement is true, it is much too general to be helpful, since the whole of one's university education should contribute to this kind of understanding. To appreciate psychology's distinctive contribution, we need to be aware of its unique focus on the self and also to go back to its roots.

For centuries, curious people have pondered the mysteries of human thought, behavior, and experience. Philosophers in particular, right from the time of the ancient Greeks and perhaps even earlier, have been attempting to understand the human mind. So the topic is not at all new. What gave rise to a distinct discipline of psychology was the decision made well over one hundred years ago to explore human experience by applying the empirical methods of science to it. At that time, several German scientists trained in physiology, physics, and medicine began to investigate human behavior through the rigorous experimental methods of science, starting with investigations of our physical senses, those marvelous, intricate capacities that a colleague of mine calls our "windows on the world." Since the discipline's inception, the scientific method of study has been a key distinctive of psychology. Although these methods are now applied somewhat less rigidly than they were during the heyday of Watson, Hull, Skinner, and other behaviorists, it remains true that the understanding of humankind that psychology seeks is based on systematic observation rather than on either casual personal experience or armchair speculation.

When you attempt to apply the methods of science to as complex and elusive a topic as human experience, you have to grapple with some tough questions, as the last century of study has demonstrated. Two of these are: (1) What is the nature of humankind and the meaning of personhood? and (2) How exactly should we go about studying human experience? It is important to note that these questions, significant though they surely are, cannot be addressed by science acting solely on the basis of empirical evidence. Rather, the answers different people give reflect presuppositions shaped by religious and philosophical influences rather than conclusions based on scientific evidence. To help you appreciate the complexity of these issues and the diversity of positions psychologists take on them, let me sketch for you three very different perspectives that have been widely adopted by those seeking to apply science to the understanding of human nature.

Behaviorism

Although he is not its founder, until his death in 1990 B. F. Skinner was the leading spokesman for behaviorism. Skinner had a very religious background. In many of his writings, he makes reference to the work of

Protestant theologians, especially Jonathan Edwards, who seems to have been his favorite. The effects of these ideas are evident in Skinner's emphasis on the strong shaping influence of our environment and, consequently, our own relative lack of freedom in the choices we make.

Skinner conducted extensive research, mostly with animals—rats and pigeons in particular—exploring how behavior could be conditioned through the use of positive reinforcement or rewards. He and others have been able to demonstrate the power of rewards as evidenced, for example, in the remarkable routines circus animals can be trained to perform. I'm sure all of us have marveled at the sight of bears on bicycles, tigers jumping through hoops of fire and dolphins playing basketball, all accomplished through the painstaking and consistent application of techniques examined and refined by behaviorists.

Besides conducting careful studies of how rewards can be used to train animals, Skinner and other behaviorists developed countless human applications of their discoveries. Numerous therapeutic interventions are built on these principles. Pause and picture a behavior therapist attempting to help clients overcome their alcohol problems by conditioning them to strongly dislike the taste or smell of alcohol. Alternatively, consider how Applied Behavior Analysis therapy, a program for delivering strategically timed positive reinforcers, is used to assist children suffering from serious disorders like autism. Interventions such as these have proven to be remarkably effective in changing inappropriate behaviors. While some may question the ethical acceptability of these techniques, you can be assured that they are used only with the consent of the parents (in the case of children) or the clients themselves.

Psychoanalysis

Without doubt, Sigmund Freud is one of the most colorful psychologists of all times and also one of the most influential. Our daily jargon is filled with terms rooted in his theorizing, such as *ego, defense mechanism, unconscious, slips of speech, repression*. In addition, many elements of our cultural understanding have been affected by his views.

Freud worked with some very strange people—even stranger than you and I—seeking a creative explanation for their bizarre and inappropriate actions. He found it in an emphasis on unconscious forces buried deep within the human personality. While earlier thinkers had emphasized our rationality, assuming that we usually behave in a manner dictated by the sober judgments of the mind, Freud was convinced that the majority of our motives and reasons for acting were beyond our conscious awareness—we could not explain our own behavior if we wanted to. Sometimes I find—and you probably do as well—that he was dead right! He developed a picture of the inner personality that was in a constant state of tension. The *ego*, attempting to accommodate reality, had the task of reconciling the strong drives of the *id* with the strict demands of the *superego* or conscience, rooted in parental expectations.[1] Freud was not optimistic about the chances for good adjustment, since he saw these tensions as essentially irresolvable. The best that could be achieved, he believed, was a sort of uneasy and temporary truce.

Granted his belief that much of our experience stems from the unconscious, most people could not be expected to arrive at an accurate self-understanding. For this to be accomplished, he maintained that a skilled and sensitive psychotherapist was needed to help bring into conscious awareness the person's memories, fears, and hurts long buried in the unconscious but still very much alive and powerfully influencing that individual's daily behavior. Freud's view of the person is thus interwoven with his system of therapeutic analysis, which employs such methods as dream interpretation and free association to gain insight into the mysteries of the unconscious.

Reflecting on our two key issues mentioned above, we see that Freud viewed people as victims of strong inner drives, fears, and impulses of which they have little or no understanding. The chief way of gaining insight into the human psyche is through therapy sessions with someone trained to help the individual delve into his/her own past and unconscious self.

Humanism

A third viewpoint that has been very influential, particularly in the more popularized version of the discipline, is humanistic psychology, best

1. Claerbaut observes that Freud's discussion of the conflict between the *id* and the *superego* is portrayed by the apostle Paul in Romans 7, with the former being humankind's fallen nature and the latter being the *imago dei* that gives people an inherent moral sensibility ("Faith Meets the Mental Health Models," 271). He goes on to observe that Freud also agreed with the biblical view of humans as essentially egocentric and self-serving, although he never actually acknowledged the Bible as the source of that viewpoint.

represented by the well-known therapist Carl Rogers. He likewise had a conservative Protestant background, spending a period of time in seminary study before moving away from his religious roots and into secular psychology.[2] The unique brand he developed placed strong emphasis on people's inherent goodness, their creativity, and their positive possibilities. Humanistic psychology's approach is thus ideally suited for upper-middle class North Americans who wish to develop their potential to the maximum. While Rogers' ideas are clearly embodied in his counseling method known as *non-directive therapy*, they also represent a perspective on human nature that has been widely accepted within the discipline as well as in Western society. Terms in common usage such as *self-actualization*, *potential*, and *self-esteem* indicate how much his ideas have been absorbed into our thinking.[3]

In Rogers' view, people are free to choose and create their own futures. This freedom is fundamental to what makes them human. Thus, anything that restricts this freedom to choose and to develop one's potential is seen as negative and inappropriate. Since people are regarded as inherently good, the blame for problems we encounter must be placed outside of ourselves, usually on society in general or on significant others who, failing to appreciate the fragility of human creative potential, restrict or crush it, with devastating consequences. Frequently, a person's difficulties are rooted, so this perspective argues, in a painfully poor self-image, which is in need of strengthening through the work of an accepting, positive therapist or other friend. When our self-concept is healthy, Rogers maintains, most problems of adjustment and living can be readily corrected.

Again, to summarize, people are unique, free to choose, and full of positive potential, according to Rogers and other humanists. It would be demeaning, they say, to study them in controlled experiments as we would animals. Indeed, many of the most human characteristics do not

2. Van Leeuwen suggests that Rogers' Christian background likely accounts for the fact that his theories seem to "[embody] (albeit in secular form) the kind of grace and loving acceptance that the Bible says God extends to all people who are willing to ask for it" ("Scuttling the Schizophrenic Student Mind," 36).

3. Puffer remarks that these optimistic assumptions about human goodness were in large measure undermined by the terrorist attacks on the United States of September, 2001: "since September 11, 2001, Americans have been rudely re-awakened to the wickedness lurking within the human heart" ("Essential Biblical Assumptions about Human Nature," 49).

lend themselves to scientific investigation. Who can define love in laboratory terms or quantify freedom or creativity? Thus, for the humanist,
science in the general sense of observation and systematic study may be
an appropriate method, but people cannot be squeezed into a laboratory straight-jacket or reduced to a set of numbers. With this facet of the
humanist position I suspect that most of us would have a good deal of
sympathy.

PSYCHOLOGY THROUGH THE EYES OF FAITH

Having outlined several influential viewpoints in the field and having
looked briefly at their position on the issues of human nature and appropriate methods of study, I now wish to consider the question, "What
difference does a Christian perspective make in one's approach to the
study of psychology?" If there is any good reason for a Christian college
or university to exist, a Christian perspective surely must make an important difference. Union University Professor of Faith and Culture Harry
Poe explains this role of faith in relation to the disciplines of the academy
as follows:

> Generally speaking, faith intersects an academic discipline at
> the point where it asks its most fundamental questions. . . . Faith
> intersects at the point where a discipline adopts a philosophical
> position to guide it or to provide a structure for its theories, data,
> and explorations. Faith intersects where a discipline establishes
> its core values, upon whatever basis they are founded. One could
> argue that faith is the fundamental basis for all human knowledge,
> without which rationalism and empiricism could not function.[4]

The Value of a Biblical Understanding of Persons

David Myers and Malcolm Jeeves capture the diversity within the field
by calling psychology a "federation of sub-disciplines."[5] What do they
mean by this phrase? They are pointing to the wide range of topics,
approaches, and perspectives adopted by those seeking insight into human experience.[6] In our discussion of the three viewpoints considered

4. Poe, *Christianity in the Academy*, 138.

5. Myers and Jeeves, *Psychology through the Eyes of Faith*, 11.

6. Elaborating on this point, Collins observes that psychology is "worth studying
because more than any other discipline it is committed to understanding people . . . [par-
ticularly how they] live, think, struggle, interact, and act" ("An Integrated View," 110).

above—behaviorism, psychoanalysis, and humanism—we have seen how discrepant the positions taken on fundamental issues concerning humankind's essential nature really are. For example, Skinner and his behaviorist buddies believe that your actions are triggered in reaction to what is going on around you, and that you have little if any real choice in how you will respond. On the other hand, Carl Rogers and his fellow therapists are convinced that you are indeed free to choose which course of action you will take and what you will make of the opportunities before you. Of course, Freud and others of his persuasion have yet another view, although on this particular issue they are much more in agreement with Skinner than with Rogers. The main difference is that psychoanalysts suggest your responses are determined not by outside factors but rather by strong inner forces. Now these three positions seem to be completely at odds with one another, but I would like to suggest that all of them are at the same time both right and wrong. Let me explain—and also clarify what I see as one very significant value provided by a Christian perspective, or what Myers and Jeeves call "the eyes of faith."

Thus far in its 100 plus years of history, psychology has not settled on a unified understanding of essential human nature but has rather explored a variety of possible models. Different people such as Skinner, Rogers, Freud, and others have examined the complexity of our life experience and have been drawn to different aspects of it. Their descriptions have then focused on that particular aspect and have tended to ignore other perspectives. It's a little like the proverbial blind men examining the elephant. One man exploring the elephant's side was convinced the animal was like a wall. Another, who happened on the elephant's tail, found the elephant to be very much like a rope. Yet another, feeling the elephant's leg, described it as a sturdy tree trunk. Now in a sense, these men were all correct and all mistaken at the same time. While human personality is certainly much more complex than the body of an elephant, the analogy still has validity. The viewpoints adopted by various researchers have enabled them to describe accurately what they observed. From the particular perspective each adopted, the characterization was correct. But in another sense, the picture each presents is seriously distorted.

For example, Skinner maintains (and I agree) that we are very powerfully influenced by factors in the environment around us, including, of course, other people as well as physical stimuli. In some cases these factors are so compelling that we have little real freedom to choose a different behavioral option. We have been conditioned to act in a very specific way. Other situations, however, are completely different. We certainly *do* exercise our freedom to choose for reasons of our own and to act on rather than to be molded by our environment. When Rogers claims that our humanity implies the autonomy to reach toward the goals we have selected for ourselves, I believe he is right. It's just that his is not a complete picture either. Likewise, our inner drives may at times be so powerful that, in the grip of rage, fear, lust, or other strong compulsions, we are driven to act in ways we may not really want to but seem to be helpless to curtail. So Freud also characterized accurately a slice of our experience.

It is at this point, then, that bringing a Christian perspective to bear or looking "through the eyes of faith" begins to provide integrity or wholeness for the discipline. A biblical understanding of humans sees persons as uniquely created by God with tremendous potential for good, yet also deeply fallen such that much of that potential is no longer realizable apart from God's redemptive intervention. This view helps us see the larger picture lacking in the fragmented descriptions of various theorists. As Wheaton College psychology professor Robert Roberts reminds us, the Christian church "has had a considerable stake in certain claims about human nature, human motivation, human relationships, human development, healthy and unhealthy formations of character, and about how change from bad to good functioning can be facilitated"[7]—vital concerns, obviously, for the discipline of psychology.

Each of the viewpoints we have examined (as well as others we have not considered) provides valid and significant insight into human functioning, but each is also incomplete. When they are set in the context of the larger picture, we can appreciate the value of each perspective without losing sight of the fact that it is not complete in itself.[8] Thus the truth that we are at times dominated by environmental or inner influences does

7. Roberts, "A Christian Psychology View," 172.

8. Powlison is rather less accommodating about secular psychologies than I try to be with respect to their incomplete understanding of human nature: "Fragmentation happens for a reason. The secular psychologies chase a rainbow: an explanation of what is wrong with us that is anything but sin against God, and a cure for the human condition that is anything but Christ" ("A Biblical Counseling View," 208). I am inclined to side with a more balanced view towards secular psychologies, like David G. Myers, who observes that the Bible does not give answers to such questions as what genes contribute to schizophrenia, or what the functions of dreams are, or how one helps a young person overcome anorexia ("A Levels-of-Explanation Response," 230).

not mean that this is always so or even that it ought to be so in a given situation. By placing each unique insight in the context of a larger and better integrated understanding of total humanity, we can arrive at a more correct understanding of the complexity of our experiences. This is one significant benefit that comes with a Christian perspective.

Psychology professor Gary Collins draws attention to another important dimension of a Christian professor or student's endeavor to think through the impact of her Christian faith on the study of psychology: the fact is that true integration can never be a solely human enterprise. "We have the Holy Spirit," he asserts, "who dwells within, guiding, sustaining, teaching, confronting, challenging, and convicting us." Indeed, he goes on to say, integration is more a verb than a noun. It is ultimately "a Spirit-led activity and a way of life that starts and ultimately takes place in the mind and soul of the integrator."[9]

Incorporating the Perspectives of Theology and Biblical Exegesis

There is a second and related value to be derived from examining psychological insight through eyes of faith. It comes not so much from fitting diverse components into a larger picture but from creating a more holistic understanding of humanity through a union of contributions from Scripture and Christian theology with those based on psychological observation and study. In his book *Integrative Approaches to Psychology and Christianity*, Malone College psychology professor David Entwistle incisively analyzes a number of unsatisfactory ways in which psychologists and theologians have interacted on behalf of their respective disciplines. He goes on to propose the following definition of what true integration between these two subjects should entail:

> . . . the integration of psychology and Christianity is a multifaceted attempt to discern the underlying truths about the nature and functioning of human beings from the unique vantage points of psychology (in its various sub-disciplines, utilizing diverse methodologies) and Christianity (in theology, faith, and practice).[10]

In *The Idea of a Christian College*, Arthur Holmes leaves no room for doubt as to his view of the primary purpose of the Christian university—

---

9. Collins, "An Integrated View," 125–26.

10. Entwistle, *Integrative Approaches*, 242.

this integration of faith and learning.[11] While this purpose obviously applies to other subject areas besides psychology, there is certainly great value in pulling together the insights about human nature and experience to be found, on the one hand, in secular psychology and, on the other, in an understanding of humankind rooted in Scripture and Christian tradition. This is a very large task,[12] one which we are a long way from having completed. Let me try to illustrate with a couple of examples how biblical insights need to be woven into our total understanding.

According to the Genesis account of creation, God made humans to live in the context of the physical world and other forms of life, together with their Creator. Thus we were clearly designed for relationships of various kinds. This emphasis on our relatedness is one that Christians in psychology need to point out in discussions about human nature. While it is true that psychology deals with the influence of other people on our behavior (social psychology is devoted specifically to this topic), there is a strong tendency in all the viewpoints we have considered, but especially in the popular humanistic approach, to stress the individual as an island unto herself. People are seen as making their own individual choices, and needing to do so without regard for what others think or how they may be affected. In other words, the whole idea of community, a prominent theme in Scripture, is almost completely absent in current secular understanding. I believe this distortion is present in the Christian church as well, for we all too often mirror society's views. As an aside, let me cite one illustration of such distortion from how we interpret Scripture.

A familiar passage in Romans 8:28 gives this comforting assurance: "And we know that in all things God works for the good of those who love him, who are called according to his purpose." Now that is a reassuring promise, one that I reflect on frequently when I encounter a situation that is distressing or hard to deal with. My guess is that most of us would interpret this verse as applying individually—God is working for my individual good, to make me stronger, more mature, more Christ-like.

11. Holmes, *Idea of a Christian College*, 18.

12. Eck, in his 1996 article "Integrating the Integrators," identifies no fewer than 27 different models of integration of psychology and the Christian faith! More work still needs to be done, but I also believe (and Eck's article confirms) that psychologists of faith have made considerable progress, particularly during the past two or three decades. See my comments after the "For Further Reading" bibliography (at the end of this chapter) on the important role the Christian Association for Psychological Studies (CAPS) has played in this discourse.

While I don't deny the validity of that view, I believe that if we had a fuller understanding of how God relates with us, we would read this promise as referring also to the corporate good—the benefit of God's kingdom and the church as a whole, and not only to me as an individual. What I am suggesting is that we in Western society are strongly conditioned to think individualistically rather than in terms of community. Our understanding of human nature needs the corrective found in the fact that God created us for relationships rather than for mere individual achievement. This is just one way in which biblical insights can clarify and correct the picture drawn by secular psychologists.[13]

A second aspect fundamental to our humanity according to the Bible is our personal responsibility. We are not independent beings, answering like Robinson Crusoe to no one but ourselves. As Christian psychologist Mary Van Leeuwen puts it, we are accountable stewards with a clear job assignment and someone to whom we must give a performance report.[14] The strong emphasis on human freedom and autonomy found in psychology today desperately needs the corrective of this insight. All the viewpoints we looked at are inclined to remove from us the responsibility for our actions. Freud would blame strong drives we are powerless to control for much of our undesired behavior. Since we can't control them, we can't really be held accountable for the outward actions either, he would maintain. Likewise, Skinner and the behaviorists see us essentially as products of our environment, not truly responsible since we have no real freedom to make choices. While the humanists suggest that we have choice, which seems to imply responsibility, theirs is a perspective that emphasizes making choices to develop one's own potential and exercise one's freedom, with little concern for the impact on others, a position very compatible with a human-rights emphasis. Although this view has merit, it often overlooks our accountability to God as well as to one another. Rogers and his humanist friends are inclined to implicate society for restricting our

---

13. Beck makes the important point that Christian psychologists must be willing to expend extra effort to acquire more that a mere layperson's understanding of the Scriptures—as a prerequisite to undertaking integrative analysis: "Psychologists are in great need of training in how to handle biblical and theological material in an informed manner" ("The Integration of Psychology and Theology," 28). He adds that collaborative projects between psychologists and theologians would constitute an additional helpful approach to responsible integrative analysis.

14. Van Leeuwen, *The Person in Psychology*, 45.

freedom when we do wrong, rather than placing the responsibility where it must go—squarely on the person who made his/her own poor choice.

These two aspects of humanity—our relatedness and our responsibility—represent the kind of corrective that a Christian perspective can provide to the descriptions contained in secular psychology. When these insights are incorporated, the understanding that emerges is much more accurate and complete.

Moving toward a Balanced Viewpoint

Let me briefly mention a third benefit that a Christian perspective can offer, one that is related to both of those we have already considered. It has to do with keeping a balance in our view of humankind. As we have seen, behaviorist, psychoanalytic, and humanist viewpoints each provide useful insights but fail to give the total picture. The understanding derived from Scripture allows us to see value in each position without being carried away by the distortion represented in what each affirms.

Christian psychologist Ron Koteskey describes our nature as having both God-like and animal-like characteristics.[15] In Scripture, we are described as highly significant and of great value but at the same time deeply fallen into sin and unable to redeem ourselves or live as we ought. The Psalmist declares, "You have made him a little lower than the heavenly beings and crowned him with glory and honor" (Psalm 8:5). In the account of creation in Genesis 1, what God made was described as "good" or "very good." On the other hand, Romans 3:10 says, "There is no one righteous, not even one," and the prophet Jeremiah declares, "The heart is deceitful and desperately wicked; who can know it?" (Jeremiah 17:9). Thus humans are clearly presented in Scripture as having this enigmatic dual nature. Both are part of the human condition, and neither can be denied without creating a seriously distorted picture.

Each of the common psychological viewpoints has a strong tendency to emphasize one side of our nature and to downplay if not totally ignore the other. Freud's description of humankind has an amazing similarity to Paul's account of struggling fallen human nature in Romans 7, but it totally misses our positive, creative, and potential-filled side. Rogers and the humanists make exactly the opposite error, effectively capturing our potential for good and for growth while totally ignoring our fallenness

15. Koteskey, *Psychology from a Christian Perspective*, 3.

and our inability to do as we ought. The behaviorist sees humans as morally neutral but certainly as more animal-like and definitely devoid of any God-given potential for creative expression and full humanity. It is by keeping the balance provided through a biblical understanding that we can find the more reasonable middle ground between the two extremes, which Mary Van Leeuwen identifies as the tendency toward either self-deification or reductionism.[16] (Self-deification is thinking too much of ourselves and forgetting the limitations of our fallen nature, while reductionism means losing sight of the fact that we are created in God's image and hence seeing ourselves as little more than machines or animals.) If we can steer clear of both extremes, I believe we will arrive at a more complete and accurate picture of the complexity of humankind.

CONCLUSION

We have considered a few of the key issues and views in current psychological thinking and have also suggested how a Christian perspective can enhance our understanding in our search for the truth about humans. Let me draw this discussion to a close by reflecting on the value of psychology for you.

Because psychology has a large public presence in our society, popular books and magazines are filled with its ideas. A basic understanding of what psychology is and also what it is not—that is, its nature and its limitations—will help you derive insight from these sources without being overwhelmed by ill-founded claims or taken in by all the "hype." You will be a more sophisticated consumer of popularized psychological content as a result of becoming informed as to exactly what it is and what it can offer.

Second, you stand to develop greater self-understanding through your investigation of psychology. Holmes suggests that university is a place to think and explore and raise questions. I believe that the study of psychology will stimulate and enhance this process, since *you* are the subject matter under consideration. You will also grow in appreciation and understanding of others' behavior. As you become more aware of the multiplicity of influences on behavior and the range of ways in which people differ from one another, you will develop tolerance for those who

16. Van Leeuwen, *The Person in Psychology*, 143.

are not like you and may even come to value the characteristics that make them distinct.

Of course, some of you may want to pursue careers in people-related fields. For you, a background in psychology will be very appropriate and perhaps mandatory. Although working with people can be very taxing and emotionally draining, there is tremendous satisfaction in knowing you have been able to assist people to become more fully human, whatever their initial level of functioning may have been. Some of you may even choose a profession for which post-graduate study in psychology is needed. The three editors of a 2007 volume of seminal articles on the integration of psychology and Christianity list a number of leading edge areas of development in psychology—most of them aided by new technology—that will continue to attract and challenge the best minds of future generations of researchers and practitioners. These include cognitive neuroscience, biopsychology, genetics, psychopharmacology, genetically-determined predispositions and neural networks, and the Positive Psychology movement.[17] These areas of inquiry—as well as the more traditional ones—need well-educated but also highly principled and committed Christian researchers and practitioners.

There is one more benefit to be derived from studying psychology at a Christian institution—or at least from a Scripture-informed perspective, one that is perhaps the most important of all. Near the beginning of *The Idea of a Christian College*, in his discussion of the cultural mandate, Holmes makes the statement, "Fallen people, whether they want it or not, and however distortedly, still image their creator."[18] This point is worth pondering. As humans, we are made in the image of God, the majestic Creator and Ruler of the entire universe. We reflect his character and likeness. Certainly sin has distorted our likeness to him, but it has not undone the fact that we remain his image-bearers. Thus as we study people, even with their faults, failures, and inclinations towards evil, there remains something majestic and exalted and God-like in their nature. As we pursue the study of psychology, we have the opportunity of better understanding humankind and in this way of also gaining deeper insight into our great Creator. These outcomes make the pursuit of psychological understanding particularly meaningful and eminently worthwhile.

17. Stevenson, Eck, and Hill, "Postscript: What's Next?" 376–77.

18. Holmes, *Idea of a Christian College*, 21.

WORKS CITED

Allison, Stephen H. "The Christian Association for Psychological Studies: A History (1970–2006)." *Journal of Psychology and Christianity* 25.4 (Winter 2006) 305–10.

Beck, James R. "The Integration of Psychology and Theology: An Enterprise Out of Balance." *Journal of Psychology and Christianity* 22.1 (Spring 2003) 20–29.

Claerbaut, David. "Faith Meets the Mental Health Models." In his *Faith and Learning on the Edge: A Bold New Look at Religion in Higher Education*, 270–78. Grand Rapids, MI: Zondervan, 2004.

———. "Psychology: Need Theory—A Place Where Faith Meets Learning." In his *Faith and Learning on the Edge: A Bold New Look at Religion in Higher Education*, 258–69. Grand Rapids, MI: Zondervan, 2004.

Collins, Gary R. "An Integrated View." In *Psychology and Christianity*, edited by Eric L. Johnson and Stanton L. Jones, 102–29. Downers Grove, IL: InterVarsity Press, 2000.

Eck, Brian E. "Integrating the Integrators: An Organizing Framework for a Multifaceted Process of Integration." *Journal of Psychology and Christianity* 15.2 (Summer 1996) 101–15.

Entwistle, David N. *Integrative Approaches to Psychology and Christianity: An Introduction to Worldview Issues, Philosophical Foundations, and Models of Integration.* Eugene, OR: Wipf and Stock Publishers, 2004.

Holmes, Arthur F. *The Idea of a Christian College.* Rev. ed. Grand Rapids, MI: Eerdmans, 1987.

Koteskey, Ronald L. *Psychology from a Christian Perspective.* 2d ed. Lanham, MD: University Press of America, 1991.

Myers, David G. "A Levels-of-Explanation Response." In *Psychology and Christianity*, edited by Eric L. Johnson and Stanton L. Jones, 226–31. Downers Grove, IL: InterVarsity Press, 2000.

Myers, David G., and Malcolm A. Jeeves. *Psychology through the Eyes of Faith.* Rev. ed. San Francisco: Harper & Row, 2003.

Poe, Harry L. *Christianity in the Academy: Teaching at the Intersection of Faith and Learning.* Grand Rapids, MI: Baker Academic, 2004.

Powlison, David. "A Biblical Counseling View." In *Psychology and Christianity*, edited by Eric L. Johnson and Stanton L. Jones, 196–225. Downers Grove, IL: InterVarsity Press, 2000.

Puffer, Keith A. "Essential Biblical Assumptions about Human Nature: A Modest Proposal." *Journal of Psychology and Christianity* 26.1 (Spring 2007) 45–56.

Roberts, Robert C. "A Christian Psychology View." In *Psychology and Christianity*, edited by Eric L. Johnson and Stanton L. Jones, 148–77. Downers Grove, IL: InterVarsity Press, 2000.

Stevenson, Daryl H., Brian E. Eck, and Peter C. Hill. "Postscript: What's Next?" in *Psychology and Christianity Integration: Seminal Works that Shaped the Movement*, edited by Daryl H. Stevenson, Brian E. Eck, and Peter C. Hill, 375-78. Batavia, IL: Christian Association for Psychological Studies, 2007.

Van Leeuwen, Mary Stewart. *The Person in Psychology: A Contemporary Christian Appraisal.* Grand Rapids, MI: Eerdmans, 1985.

———. "Scuttling the Schizophrenic Student Mind: On Teaching the Unity of Faith and Learning in Psychology." In *Teaching as an Act of Faith: Theory and Practice in*

Church-Related Higher Education, edited by Arlin C. Migliazzo, 21–40. New York: Fordham University Press, 2002.

FOR FURTHER READING

Bourma-Prediger, Steve. "The Task of Integration: A Modest Proposal." *Journal of Psychology and Theology* 18.1 (Spring 1990) 21–31.

Browning, Don S., and Terry D. Cooper. *Religious Thought and the Modern Psychologies.* 2d ed. Minneapolis: Fortress Press, 2004.

Carter, John D., and Bruce Narramore. *The Integration of Psychology and Theology.* Grand Rapids, MI: Zondervan, 1979.

Evans, C. Stephen. *Preserving the Person: A Look at the Human Sciences.* Repr. Vancouver, BC: Regent College Publishing, 1998.

———. *Wisdom and Humanness in Psychology: Prospects for a Christian Approach.* Grand Rapids, MI: Baker, 1989.

Farnsworth, Kirk E. *Wholehearted Integration: Harmonizing Psychology and Christianity through Word and Deed.* Grand Rapids, MI: Baker, 1985.

Faw, Harold W. *Psychology in Christian Perspective: An Analysis of Key Issues.* Grand Rapids, MI: Baker, 1995.

———. *Sharing Our Stories: Understanding Memory and Building Faith.* Belleville, ON: Essence Publishing, 2007.

———. "Wilderness Wanderings and Promised Integration: The Quest for Clarity." *Journal of Psychology and Theology* 26.2 (Summer 1998) 147–58.

Herzfeld, Noreen L. *In Our Image: Artificial Intelligence and the Human Spirit.* Minneapolis: Fortress Press, 2002.

Hodges, B. H. "Faith-Learning Integration: Appreciating the Integrity of a Shop-worn Phrase." *Faculty Dialogue* 22 (Fall 1994) 95–106.

Jeeves, Malcolm A. *Human Nature at the Millennium: Reflections on the Integration of Psychology and Christianity.* Grand Rapids, MI: Baker, 1997.

Johnson, Eric L., and Stanton L. Jones, eds. *Psychology and Christianity.* Downers Grove, IL: InterVarsity Press, 2000.

Jones, Stanton L. "Reflections on the Nature and Future of the Christian Psychologies." *Journal of Psychology and Christianity* 15.2 (Summer 1996) 133–42.

Mathisen, James A. "Integrating World Views with Social Roles: Supplying a Missing Piece of the Discussion on Faith-Learning Integration." *Journal of Psychology and Christianity* 22.3 (Fall 2003) 230–40.

McGrath, Joanna, and Alister E. McGrath. *The Dilemma of Self-Esteem: The Cross and Christian Confidence.* Wheaton, IL: Crossway Books, 1992.

Miller, William R., and Harold D. Delaney, eds. *Judeo-Christian Perspectives on Psychology: Human Nature, Motivation, and Change.* Washington, DC: American Psychological Association, 2005.

Nye, Robert D. *Three Psychologies: Perspectives from Freud, Skinner, and Rogers.* 6th ed. Scarborough, ON: Wadsworth/Thomson Learning, 2000.

Peterson, Gregory R. *Minding God: Theology and the Cognitive Sciences.* Minneapolis: Fortress Press, 2003.

Philipchalk, Ronald P. *Psychology and Christianity: An Introduction to Controversial Issues.* Lanham, MD: University Press of America, 1987.

Roberts, Robert C., and Mark R. Talbot, eds. *Limning the Psyche: Explorations in Christian Psychology*. Grand Rapids, MI: Eerdmans, 1997.

Serrano, Neftali. "Conservative Christians in Psychology: A History of the Christian Association for Psychological Studies (CAPS), 1954–1978." *Journal of Psychology and Christianity* 25.3 (Fall 2006) 293–304.

Sneep, John. "Ecopsychology: An Introduction and Christian Critique." *Journal of Psychology and Christianity* 26.2 (Summer 2007) 166–75.

Van Leeuwen, Mary Stewart. "Five Uneasy Questions, or Will Success Spoil Christian Psychologists?" *Journal of Psychology and Christianity* 15.2 (Summer 1996) 150–60.

Vitz, Paul C. *Psychology as Religion: The Cult of Self-worship*. 2d ed. Grand Rapids, MI: Eerdmans, 1994.

Wolterstorff, Nicholas. "Integration of Faith and Science—The Very Idea." In *Psychology and Christianity Integration: Seminal Works that Shaped the Movement*, edited by Daryl H. Stevenson, Brian E. Eck, and Peter C. Hill, 96–101. Batavia, IL: Christian Association for Psychological Studies, 2007. First appeared in *Journal of Psychology and Christianity* 3.2 (1984) 12–19.

Yangarber-Hicks, Natalia, et al. "Invitation to the Table Conversation: A Few Diverse Perspectives on Integration." *Journal of Psychology and Christianity* 25.4 (Winter 2006) 338–53.

Excellent articles on the integration of psychology and Christianity are regularly published in both the *Journal of Psychology and Theology* and the *Journal of Psychology and Christianity*. (I have listed several of these in the bibliographies above.) The latter journal, the official organ of the Christian Association for Psychological Studies (CAPS) founded in 1956 that began publishing in 1982, has served as a major catalyst to both theoretical and applied reflection on the interaction between psychology and the Christian faith. See the articles by Allison and Serrano listed above that trace the history of CAPS, as well as the book of seminal articles edited by Stevenson, Eck, and Hill that helped to shape the organization.

Principally an American entity at first, CAPS is having an increasingly international impact, eventuating, for example, in the formation of the British Association of Christians in Psychology, whose membership in 2006, including both professionals and students, numbered 280.[19] At the 50th anniversary celebration of CAPS in July, 2006, Executive Director (as of February 2005) Stephen Allison asserted:

> The real strength of CAPS is, and always has been, the association of its members. As we move into the future, I see CAPS continuing to develop as a professional association dedicated to the cross-disciplinary sharing of ideas and experiences, encouragement and

19. Allison, "The Christian Association for Psychological Studies," 309.

spiritual support. With the advent of the internet, email, and other electronic communications, we now have the means of building and sustaining a truly international association of professionals dedicated to the integration of Christian thought and behavioral science, in a way that glorifies God and strengthens the community of faith. And we will continue in our pursuit of excellence in the domains of academia, practice, and spiritual care. . . . [R]esearch and study inform our practice . . . clinical practice illumines our research and study . . . pastoral concern and a Christian worldview give the whole thing a heart and soul.[20]

20. Ibid., 310.

27

A Christian Perspective on Sociology

CRAIG SEATON

INTRODUCTION

THIS CHAPTER ON SOCIOLOGY and the Christian faith is designed (1) to provide a brief overview of several key sociological concepts and (2) to illustrate how biblical truth illuminates a sociological perspective. The sociological concepts to be addressed include *social stratification, social institutions, culture, functionalism,* and *conflict theory.*

Heddendorf, in "Principles of a Christian Perspective in Sociology," begins his article by comparing the observation and analysis of social life with taking a stroll through a forest. He points out that few people are trained to correctly name the different life forms there or are able to identify what is safe to eat and what one should stay away from.[1] You have probably heard the phrase, "He can't see the forest for the trees," indicating that a person lacks an organizing principle or capacity to grasp the "big picture" because of the distracting complexity of details. Our present task is to "look past the trees to find the forest," thereby learning a few fundamentals about the discipline of sociology, and then to briefly consider some of the effects of a biblically informed Christian perspective on this subject area.

Sociology is the "science of society," the study of human behavior in the context of social relationships. Consider a few examples: When a corporation is considering the development of a new product, among the items to be considered is an analysis of the potential customer base and the internal organizational impact of such a change of operations. When

1. Heddendorf, "Principles of a Christian Perspective in Sociology," 113.

elected officials are attempting to determine how to best allocate scarce public tax money, some very serious analysis of the social situation is required. When educational planners are at work on a common curriculum for a public school system, they proceed based upon certain beliefs about basic values concerning humankind and how society works. When a denomination decides it wants to "plant" a church in a given community, it sets about this task by attempting to understand the social characteristics of the people living within a specific area and by trying to understand what special needs characterize these people. The wide-spread alarm across North America about the increasing numbers of broken families gives rise to the questions, "Why has this happened?" and "What can be done to improve the situation?" All of these situations, in the context of the economy, government, education, religion, and the family, reflect the need for sociological understanding and analysis.

By its very nature sociology is an inclusive discipline that freely draws upon findings from other disciplines, including psychology, anthropology, political science, geography, and history. Its setting or laboratory is the larger social world with all of its complexity and color. The sociological perspective has much to offer.

A BRIEF HISTORY OF SOCIOLOGY

In a sense, the specialty of sociologists is generalization. They attempt to find connections that unite the various social sciences into a comprehensive schema or map in order to explain the workings of society and the behavior of individuals. Sociology, literally the science or study of society, is a relatively young discipline. Its roots are traced somewhat differently by different authors, but perhaps the most straight-forward historical lineage leads back to the work of Europeans who studied "moral statistics" in the early nineteenth century. These early thinkers included Adolphe Quetelet, a Belgian; Andre Guerry, a Frenchman; and Henry Morselli, an Italian. When governments began collecting statistics on the causes of death early in the nineteenth century, the rates of suicide became known for the first time. Three patterns were revealed: (a) countries seemed to display consistent rates of death by suicide year after year; (b) the different countries varied greatly in the annual rate of suicide; and (c) all through the century suicide rates were on the increase everywhere. Since this very personal act seemed so patterned, questions began to be raised about the possible contribution of the social context to the act of suicide. Soon statistics were being collected on homicide, theft, rape, illegitimacy, military desertion, and charitable donations. These indices of social behavior displayed the same three patterns that were found with suicide: stability, variation, and increase. The pursuit of greater understanding of these phenomena came to be known as "moral statistics."

Toward the end of the nineteenth century, one of sociology's most prominent thinkers, Emile Durkheim, who called himself a sociologist rather that a moral statistician, published the book *Suicide*. In this work Durkheim argued that modern societies were deficient in the kinds of warm and secure interpersonal relationships that were typical of traditional rural life. Because of this, many people lacked the social support necessary to assist them in times of trouble. Interestingly, while not a Christian believer himself, Durkheim affirmed that a society needed to ascribe to a set of shared moral values in order to survive.[2] This comprehensive emphasis upon the special significance of the social context for defining oneself—as well as reality generally—is the essence of sociology's approach.

Sociology became a part of university life in North America when departments were initiated at the University of Chicago and at Atlanta University in the 1890s. The sociology program at Chicago was the first to offer graduate degrees. That university also produced the first professional sociological journal and the first comprehensive sociology textbook published in North America. The approach at Chicago, and at many universities that followed this model early in the twentieth century, emphasized the importance of analyzing social problems and in designing a better, more equitable society. The "Chicago School" of sociologists pursued the creation of a better society with an almost religious zeal. This was true in part, perhaps, because many of those involved in this movement were ex-clergy or from families of clergy.

In Canada, sociology developed along several somewhat different pathways, beginning about two decades later than the American experience. French-speaking Canadian universities have generally identified with continental Europe and the concerns related to economic trends, political parties, church and state relations, and union movements. English-speaking Canadian universities have followed one of two models. In the

2. Davis, "A Perspective on Human Nature," 194.

1920s, McGill University offered Canada's first sociology major and developed an emphasis that was modeled after the University of Chicago. The University of Toronto followed the British model, emphasizing politics and economics.[3] Today, there are about 2,500 sociologists in Canada and about 20,000 in the United States. The center of the sociological world today, as measured by numbers of sociologists, journals, research projects, and general influence, is without question the United States.

KEY CONCEPTS OF SOCIOLOGY

Social Stratification

The concept of *social stratification* is one of the most significant in sociology. This concept refers to a figurative hierarchical "layering" of people within society. Those who hold positions closer to the "top" of the social system have more power, prestige, and resources. The life experiences of those in the upper class are significantly different from the experiences of those who occupy the lower class. These differences include such things as child-rearing practices, educational expectations and types of schools attended, life style, beliefs about society, and political participation. It has been discovered that virtually all societies have a system of stratification. Some systems are quite rigid; for example, the caste system of India. This system, no longer legal in India, continues to operate in some parts of that country. If you were born as an "untouchable," the lowest caste, your contact with higher level castes and your occupational options would be severely restricted.

In most industrial democracies, the social structure is more open, with the opportunity for upward mobility, usually in connection with additional education, a genuine possibility. One's class position is usually defined as falling within the following classification system:

Upper Class
Middle Class
    Upper-middle class
    Lower-middle class
Lower Class (Working Class)

3. Macionis and Gerber, eds., *Sociology*, 15.

Sociologists have attempted to determine a person's social location or social class in a variety of ways. The most common approach is by utilizing a multiple factor index including objective measures of income, education completed, and occupation. A large body of research has demonstrated that social class identification is a significant influence upon how individuals view the world, and in turn how they are viewed by others. The musical production *My Fair Lady* is a powerful and witty illustration of the impact of social class upon life experience. Sometimes the label given to this concept of stratification is "structured social inequality."

The question that often comes to mind when social stratification is discussed is whether or not it is "fair" or "right" that people are categorized and treated differently based upon class status. This question is at the heart of the divergent perspectives of the two major theoretical perspectives that have dominated sociological thinking, *Functionalism* and *Conflict Theory*. *Functionalism* argues that social inequality is vital for the operation of society. Since social stratification is enduring and is present universally, it presumably must have beneficial effects. The system of differential rewards is seen as the motor that propels the "social machine." Those who perform the most vital and typically most demanding roles do so because they are motivated to fulfill key responsibilities that meet the survival needs of the larger society.

The *Social Conflict* view holds that social stratification ensures that some people gain advantages at the expense of others. Presumably some people are in positions of advantage by virtue of historical coincidence, heredity, or raw power. Society is viewed as an aggregate of people and groups with competing interests. Conflict theorists represent a wide array of views; the thing they share in common is a belief in the injustice of the existing set of social arrangements.

The terms *Functionalism* and *Conflict Theory* are products of the twentieth century, but this difference of opinion has a long history. It is possible to trace this argument back many hundreds of years. Sometimes this issue is described as being the argument between the "conservative thesis" (Functionalism) and the "radical or reform antithesis" (Conflict Theory). In part, this difference of opinion is reducible to differing views about the nature of humankind and the nature of society. However, there are other significant areas of dispute as well.[4] These can be summarized as follows:

Issue	Conservative (Functional)	Radical/Reform (Conflict)
1. Nature of Humanity	There is a belief that humankind is selfish; therefore, there is a need for restraining social institutions (Family, Government, Education, Religion, Economy).	There is a belief that social institutions have less virtue than individuals; they are viewed as oppressive. Humankind is seen as being basically good.
2. Nature of Society	The social system of interactive social institutions and social stratification creates a balance among the different elements of the system while providing for personal needs. The larger system is "good."	Society is only the context within which struggle for ascendancy takes place. There is nothing particularly "good" about any structure as such.
3. Role of Coercion to Maintain the Social Structure	Coercion plays only a minor role. Stratification arises naturally because of individual differences through consensus concerning who the most competent individuals are to fill key roles.	Coercion is the primary shaper and maintainer of the social stratification system.
4. Inequality and the Generation of Conflict in Society	The social class system actually minimizes conflict between different groups by creating social worlds that are largely limited to people with comparable views of social reality and of themselves.	Although conflict is the natural state of things, social class generates antagonism and conflict between natural opponents.

4. Lenski, *Power and Privilege*, 24ff. See also Davis, "A Perspective on Human Nature," 195–96.

5. Acquisition of Rights/Privileges	The rewards and symbols of position are acquired primarily through achievements, training, and experience.	Ultimately, force, fraud, and inheritance are the chief avenues for position acquisition.
6. The Inevitability of Inequality	By virtue of human nature and the nature of society, inequality is inevitable.	Some diversity of thought exists among theorists. Some believe that theoretically it is possible to create a classless society.
7. Nature of the State and the Law	The state and the laws created by the organs of the state act to promote the common good and to protect all members of society.	Both the state and the derived laws are instruments of oppression imposed by the ruling class on those who are unable to prevent it.
8. Understanding of the Concept of Social Class	The concept of class is just that, a concept—a theoretical device that allows for analysis and comparison. It has proven to be a useful framework for understanding the distinctive behavior of people and the structure of society.	Class has "real identity." Groups of people have distinctive interests that inevitably bring them into conflict with other groups. Class is not just a utilitarian descriptive device.

Social Institution

Another key sociological concept is *social institution*. Social institutions are clusters of social groups, activities, and social roles that exist to meet basic needs within society. For example, the Family is one social institution. The Family provides an intimate, accepting environment for the production and socialization of new members of society, ensuring continuity within the culture among different generations.

In addition, there must be arrangements within a society to produce and distribute goods and services, to define relationships and responsibilities, and to provide a sense of stability, identification, and meaning. The social institutions that provide these necessities include the Family, the Economy, Education, Government, and Religion. These various social structures are interdependent and remain in a dynamic balance that varies somewhat from society to society. What is the same in each society, however, is that significant change or disruption in one social institution will have consequences for one or more of the other social institutions. To illustrate, in today's family, women are likely to be working outside the family home. This affects the school system, which is often expected to provide child-care services after school, lunches at noon, and even language and cultural training for new immigrants. Government has also received intense and consistent pressure to provide financial support for child care and for job training opportunities for single parents.

A concept like *social institutions* is sometimes referred to as a *theoretical construct*. Using the theoretical construct of social institutions allows for a simplified model of society, increasing our capacity to understand complex interrelationships. It also allows us to retain an awareness that people, their problems, and their strengths exist together in a powerful interactive association.

Culture

One of the key sociological concepts that describes what people experience throughout their lifespan is that of *culture*. While sociologists use the term *society* to identify a group of people who are defined by their relationships with each other (often within nations), they use the concept of *culture* to identify people with respect to what they believe, what they do, what they know, and how they act. Culture is the amalgamation of everything that is learned and passed on from generation to generation. Astronauts find their experience in space to be a time of new awareness both about "space living" and about similarities and contrasts with daily experience on earth. In a parallel, though perhaps not so dramatic way, when people have a cross-cultural experience—that is, when they go to another country and live there for a while—they become very sensitive to the significance of culture. Culture has the capacity to develop a certain type of character that is uniquely associated with a particular national experience. One of the earliest systematic attempts to chronicle the power of a specific cultural experience to define national character is illustrated in the work of Alexis de Tocqueville. A French intellectual and social critic, he traveled to the United States in the early nineteenth century to try to understand that new experiment in national democracy. He concluded, in his 1835 book *Democracy in America*, that Americans could best be understood by recognizing that they were the products of three primary strands of influence: Biblical Religion, the Republican Tradition, and Individualism. By Biblical Religion he meant a shared belief that absolutes exist, that people are responsible for their own behavior, that they have obligations with respect to the welfare of others, that there is life after death, and that people will face ultimate judgment for how they have lived. The Republican Tradition refers to the extensive role of voluntary associations to meet the needs of the wider community. De Tocqueville was quite impressed that, instead of depending on government to provide all social services, people worked together on a volunteer or privately-funded basis to serve the wider community.

These two rather positive elements were balanced against a potentially negative force that he identified as Individualism. He called attention to the fact that Individualism was not so blatant and destructive a force as the egoism of monarchs or tyrants, but he believed that this tendency to pursue a personal agenda was potentially a destructive element. He saw these three strands of influence woven together in such a way as to be definitive of the kind of society America had produced.

A relatively more recent assessment of the American character by Robert Bellah and his associates, *Habits of the Heart* (1985), concludes that these elements are still definitive of the American character. In his book *Mosaic Madness* (1990), Reginald Bibby argues that the Canadian culture, on the other hand, has produced people who lack a coherent character or national identity. Bibby believes that the dominant strands of influence in Canada are those of Relativism, Pluralism, and Individualism. Both *Habits of the Heart* and *Mosaic Madness* are excellent illustrations of a sociological analysis that focuses upon the primary significance of culture.

THE CHRISTIAN FAITH AND SOCIOLOGICAL UNDERSTANDING

Sociology, like all academic disciplines, is a creation by specific people, shaped by certain historical influences, and operating in keeping with particular methodologies. All of these elements contribute to analysis and application of this specific perspective. Several ideological influences have made an impact on the development of sociology as it is known today. These key emphases include:

1. Evolution—the idea that cultures make positive advances over time from a rather primitive superstitious/religious ethos to a more sophisticated, rational, empirical one.

2. Secularization—the idea that with progress, as described by this evolutionary principle, and with the felt need to accommodate diverse religious ideals so as not to impede action to achieve the common good, there has been movement away from the sectarian toward the secular.[5]

3. Acceptance of the scientific method—although there are a few contemporary reactions against what some have believed to be a mindless "scientism," that is, the attempt to quantify everything or to only study what can be measured objectively.[6] The emphasis upon systematic, replicable studies has a significant factor in the development of sociology. Another consequence of the scientific method in sociological discourse is what Eastern College professors of sociology David Fraser and Tony Campolo describe as "scepticism about appearances," adding, "for that reason [sociology] is a contested and contestable discipline. It participates in a modern world where doubt is more respectable than dogma and where open-mindedness means questioning all beliefs."[7]

4. Activism and personal commitment to values that support reform or renewal—this emphasis was present in the early days of the disci-

5. Union University sociology professor Antonio Chiareli remarks that not once, in all his graduate study in sociology, did he ever meet a Christian sociologist. He describes most U.S. university and college sociology departments as "overwhelmingly secular" and many of those as "deeply antireligious" ("Christian Worldview and the Social Sciences," 241). The primary reason for this widespread antipathy, he later suggests, is the assumption that all religious knowledge is ideological and thus its advocates must inevitably have a political agenda to forcefully foist their perspective on the rest of society (251). Sociology professor Robert Clark expands on this point by asserting that sociology seems to be antagonistic to the Christian faith in particular, mainly because sociology is a product of the Enlightenment [the eighteenth-century European philosophical movement that believed that reason should trump tradition]" ("Sociology and Faith," 71).

6. Sociologist Rodney Stark unequivocally rejects the presupposition that sociological analysis can proceed with complete objectivity: "The image of scientists as neutral, unemotional beings . . . is romantic nonsense. All human beings are inescapably biased; we all have deep personal beliefs. The scientific method does not aim to strip scientists of their fundamental humanity or to make them into computers but rather to prevent our personal biases from distorting our work" (*Sociology*, 25).

7. Fraser and Campolo, *Sociology through the Eyes of Faith*, 68.

pline; it was dominant again early in the twentieth century in North America, and it has resurfaced in recent years in a more pluralistic form.[8] Today, a limited number of sociologists are following an assortment of value commitments and performing social analysis based upon such perspectives as Feminism, Marxism, Ecology, and Christianity.

What can the Christian faith contribute to sociological understanding? I believe that Scripture provides significant information about human nature and about the social order. The Bible does not present a comprehensive description of humankind; rather, it provides us with a picture of God and of his interaction with and concern for humanity. However, the book of Genesis clearly conveys that people have been created as social beings. First and foremost, we need each other to be complete. When God was surveying his creation he observed, "It is not good for the man to be alone. I will make a helper suitable for him" (Genesis 2:18 NIV). Commentators have noted that the Hebrew word translated here as "helper" is actually a term that conveys the idea of bringing to completion or rescuing someone. Even as God was contemplating the creation of humankind, a mysterious sort of mutuality, or of relationship, seems to be illustrated within the persons of the Trinity (God the Father, God the Son, and God the Holy Spirit): "Let *us* make man in *our* image, in *our* likeness . . ." (Genesis 1:26). Holmes suggests that our status as image bearers of God conveys much about our potential as human beings.[9] In addition to being social beings, we are also beings with the special capacity for creativity, rationality, governance or the exercise of authority, and morality (the freedom to choose between right and wrong). Scripture provides many illustrations that support this short list of qualities, but to stay within the Genesis account, note the following:

Humankind Made in the Image of God

Image Quality	Illustration	Reference
1. Sociability	Not good to be alone	Genesis 2:18
2. Rationality	Told not to eat; given a choice	Genesis 2:16, 17
	Allowed to name animals	Genesis 2:19, 20
	Made excuses/disobedience	Genesis 3:9–13

8. See Morgan, "The Development of Sociology," 42–53.

9. Holmes, *Idea of a Christian College*, 15.

3. Creativity	Naming of animals	Genesis 2:19, 20
4. Morality	Allowed a choice to obey/disobey	Genesis 2:16, 17
5. Governance	Subdue the earth Rule over creatures	Genesis 1:28

These are qualities we see in people around us every day. We are beneficiaries of a technological revolution that has been built upon humankind's creativity, intellectual ability, and organizational skills. We seem, however, to be much less able to reach an optimal level in the exercise of our moral capabilities.

Scripture offers insights that allow for a greater understanding of human beings and of our potential. This is reflected in the following summary:

1. People are incapable of living a perfect life (free from sin and selfishness) and are unable to create an ideal society. This follows because of "the fall of humankind," the disobedience of the original couple, Adam and Eve, who passed on through heredity a sinful nature, and because each of us as an individual has made personal choices to sin (Genesis 3; Ecclesiastes 7:20; Isaiah 64:6; Romans 3:23; 5:12).

2. God has provided behavioral absolutes to enhance the quality of individual and group life and to provide direction in human relationships.[10] These guidelines have also been given to demonstrate our inadequacy to meet these expectations, which in turn draws us to a personal commitment to Jesus Christ as a way of superseding the requirements of the Law:

   a. You shall have no other gods before me.

   b. You shall not make an idol.

   c. You shall not misuse the name of the Lord.

   d. Observe the Sabbath day.

   e. Honor your father and mother.

---

10. Clark sees biblical insights into this general area of social ethics (what constitutes healthy relationships both within small groups and within larger and more diverse communities) as one of the principal areas in which the Christian faith can make useful contributions to sociological analyses ("Sociology and Faith," 75).

     f. You shall not murder.

     g. You shall not commit adultery.

     h. You shall not steal.

     i. You shall not give false testimony.

     j. You shall not covet (Exodus 20:1–17; Galatians 3:19–25).

3. God's provision for humans to find fulfilment in personal, social, and spiritual life is premised upon spiritual rebirth, the gift of the Holy Spirit, and growing maturity in the Christian life. A higher, albeit imperfect, morality and social consciousness is the result (John 3:1–21; Romans 8:1–9; Ephesians 4; Romans 7:14–21; Philippians 3:10–14).

4. God's requirement for the believer is a two-fold commitment of oneself to God and then to one's neighbor (i.e., all other people). This two-pronged commitment is to be complete, though performance will fall short until the after-life (Matthew 22:36–40; Luke 10:25–37; 1 Corinthians 15:35–56).

5. The evidence or the confirmation that one is following God's pattern for life is manifested through the demonstration of unity within the church, exercising diverse gifts in service to others, in love, and in the demonstration of certain admirable character qualities (1 Corinthians 12, 13; Galatians 5:22–25).

CONCLUSION

The Christian faith and the discipline of sociology are not comparable systems of thought. The former has to do with the supernatural as well as with the individual and the social. Sociology is merely a perspective, a discipline that attempts to understand social reality, including the relationships of people and groups. While the purpose, the substance, and the methodologies differ, I believe each has something to offer the other.

What does sociology offer Christianity?

1. Christians are instructed by Scripture to advance God's Kingdom in the here and now. This can be facilitated through the use of sociological knowledge and research techniques, involving such things as learning about the context of a particular social setting, training for

new cultural experiences, analyzing of social institutions and organizations, and assessing social need.

2. In Romans 12 believers are instructed to resist conformity to this world's system. Insights provided through sociology increase our awareness of various elements of world influence and thus increase our capacity to resist this type of conformity more effectively.

3. Sociology's focus on real people in real social situations provides a vehicle for moving from merely thinking about spiritual principles to putting them into action.

What does Christianity offer sociology?

1. The Bible provides an accurate picture of humankind's potential, both individually and collectively. No utopian community is possible. But people have value, they are made in God's image, and, though flawed, they have real potential and deserve to receive assistance and encouragement.

2. Sociologists, like all people, maintain certain presuppositions about the world: ideas about what is good, about what is possible, and about priorities and personal commitments. Early in the twentieth century many sociologists were operating within a Christian framework or worldview as they examined society and made suggestions for reform. Christianity has the potential to once again provide an appropriate ideological base for sociology.

WORKS CITED

Bellah, Robert N., et al. *Habits of the Heart: Individualism and Commitment in American Life*. Berkeley: University of California Press, 1985.

Bibby, Reginald W. *Mosaic Madness: The Poverty and Potential of Life in Canada*. Toronto, ON: Stoddart, 1990.

Chiareli, Antonio A. "Christian Worldview and the Social Sciences." In *Shaping a Christian Worldview: The Foundations of Christian Higher Education*, edited by David S. Dockery and Gregory A. Thornbury, 240–63. Nashville: Broadman & Holman, 2002.

Clark, Robert A. "Sociology and Faith: Inviting Students into the Conversation." In *Teaching as an Act of Faith: Theory and Practice in Church-Related Higher Education*, edited by Arlin C. Migliazzo, 70–92. New York: Fordham University Press, 2002.

Davis, Billie. "A Perspective on Human Nature: Sociological Perspectives." In *Elements of a Christian Worldview*, edited by Michael D. Palmer, 192–218. Springfield, MO: Logion Press, 1998.

De Tocqueville, Alexis. *Democracy in America*. Translated by George Lawrence. Edited by J. P. Mayer and Max Lerner. New York: Harper & Row, 1966 (1835).

Durkheim, Emile. *Suicide: A Study in Sociology*. Translated by John A. Spaulding and George Simpson. Glencoe, IL: Free Press, 1951.

Fraser, David A., and Tony Campolo. *Sociology through the Eyes of Faith*. New York: HarperCollins, 1992.

Heddendorf, Russell. "Principles of a Christian Perspective in Sociology." In *A Reader in Sociology: Christian Perspectives*, edited by Charles P. De Santo, Calvin W. Redekop, and William L. Smith-Hinds, 113–24. Kitchener, ON: Herald Press, 1980.

Holmes, Arthur F. *The Idea of a Christian College*. Rev. ed. Grand Rapids, MI: Eerdmans, 1987.

Lenski, Gerhard E. *Power and Privilege: A Theory of Social Action*. New York: McGraw-Hill, 1966.

Macionis, John J., and Linda M. Gerber, eds. *Sociology*. 5th ed. Toronto, ON: Pearson/Prentice-Hall, 2006.

Morgan, J. "The Development of Sociology and the Social Gospel in America." *Social Analysis* 30.1 (Spring 1969) 42–53.

Stark, Rodney. *Sociology*. 5th ed. Belmont, CA: Wadsworth, 1994.

FOR FURTHER READING

Ammerman, Nancy T. "Sociology and the Study of Religion." In *Religion, Scholarship, and Higher Education: Perspectives, Models, and Future Prospects*, edited by Andrea Sterk, 76–88. Notre Dame, IN: University of Notre Dame Press, 2002.

Claerbaut, David. "Sociology: Faith in the Eye of Naturalism." In his *Faith and Learning on the Edge: A Bold New Look at Religion in Higher Education*, 279–94. Grand Rapids, MI: Zondervan, 2004.

Clark, Robert A., and S. D. Gaede. "Knowing Together: Reflections on a Holistic Sociology of Knowledge." In *The Reality of Christian Learning: Strategies for Faith-Discipline Integration*, edited by Harold Heie and David L. Wolfe, 55–86. Grand Rapids, MI: Eerdmans, 1987.

De Santo, Charles P., Zondra G. Lindblade, and Margaret M. Poloma, eds. *Christian Perspectives on Social Problems*. Indianapolis: Wesley Press, 1992.

Grunlan, Stephen A., and Milton Reimer, eds. *Christian Perspectives on Sociology*. Grand Rapids, MI: Zondervan, 1982.

Heddendorf, Russell. "Some Presuppositions of a Christian Sociology." *Journal of the American Scientific Affiliation* 24 (September 1972) 110–17.

———. "What Sociologists Do." *His* 35.4 (January 1975) 12–14.

Leming, Michael R., Raymond G. DeVries, and Brendan F. J. Furnish, eds. *The Sociological Perspective: A Value-Committed Introduction*. Grand Rapids, MI: Academie Books, 1989.

Lyon, David. "The Idea of a Christian Sociology: Some Historical Precedents and Current Concerns." *Sociological Analysis* 44.3 (1983) 227–42.

———. *Sociology and the Human Image*. Downers Grove, IL: InterVarsity Press, 1983.

Mathisen, James A. "The Origins of Sociology: Why No Christian Influence." *Christian Scholar's Review* 19 (September 1989) 49–65.

Naugle, David K. *Worldview: The History of a Concept*. Grand Rapids, MI: Eerdmans, 2002. (See esp. "'Worldview' in Sociology," 222–38.)

Perkins, Richard. "Values, Alienation, and Christian Sociology." *Christian Scholar's Review* 15.1 (1985) 8–27.

————. *Looking Both Ways: Exploring the Interface between Christianity and Sociology.* Grand Rapids, MI: Baker, 1987.

28

A Christian Perspective on Teacher Education

HARRO VAN BRUMMELEN

INTRODUCTION

MOST READERS OF THIS chapter will have attended school for many years. Many students now in college or university will acknowledge that they enjoyed school, but others will feel otherwise. Probably most appreciated some aspects of their school experience but disliked others. No matter how students feel about their elementary or high school education, however, virtually all will acknowledge that their schooling has had a major impact on their lives. Whether a school's climate is warm and supportive or cold and impersonal affects the academic success of many students. Whether or not a school system successfully meets the needs of students with special needs may mean the difference for them being able or not able to function reasonably well in society. Whether or not a school implements a challenging, meaningful program based on clear goals and values may motivate or deter students from using their abilities in constructive, significant ways.

The greatest influence on children's beliefs and behaviors is their home situation. The media, especially television and the Internet, also have a great impact on their lives. Schools, nevertheless, are also important molders of young lives. The Latin word from which "education" is derived means "to lead out." Schools can "lead out" in many different directions. Therefore, in education there are constant debates whose resolution ultimately depends on what we believe about the person and knowledge, and on what values we hold to be important in life. What classroom pedagogy and methods do we use? What content do we choose to teach and how do we organize it? Which textbooks and other resources do we adopt? What are our fundamental goals and aims in education?

I can only begin to answer such questions in the space available here. I also wish to reflect on what it means to teach Christianly, whether such teaching takes place in a public or in a Christian school. In both types of institutions, we need teachers able to nurture young people on the basis of biblical principles. Some of you may have seen the film "Molder of Dreams," in which Guy Doud shared his passion to help his public school students make the right choices in life. We need Guy Douds in our Canadian and American schools—not persons who are all as dynamic and talented as Guy Doud but ones who have a clear vision about what is important in life and are willing and able to share that with their students.

WHAT IS EFFECTIVE TEACHING?

Successful teaching depends, first, on the love and respect that teachers have for their students and the tact with which they approach them. You can't truly teach students unless you first reach them. Good teaching is also based on a desire to enable students to attain goals that the teacher genuinely believes to be important. Teachers foster learning that has intrinsic worth only if they live and share their fundamental convictions. That is why Dudley Plunkett argues that the search for questions of ultimate meaning and purpose must be the central focus of all education, in public as well as in private schools. He adds that teachers and students alike must "reexamine the proposition that there is a source of ultimate values."[1]

Think back for a few moments to your own schooling. Who were the teachers that you appreciated most? Who were the ones that influenced you most? Why? When I pose this question in one of my teacher education classes, the most usual response is to describe teachers who took a warm, personal interest in their students, whose philosophy of life and resulting educational goals came through clearly in their teaching, and who modeled and set high expectations within a caring environment. Research supports that these characteristics lead to meaningful and effective learning.

Let me give two contrasting examples from my own experience. In grade five, I had a principal as a teacher who was respected in our com-

1. Plunkett, *Secular and Spiritual Values*, 124.

munity, mainly because he was a person of strong principles as well as a strict disciplinarian. Most of us in his split grade 5/6 class disliked him, however, because of his coldness and his arbitrariness in meting out discipline. One day he asked me to show the class where various British cities were on a wall map. I didn't know one of the cities. He gave me a detention, even though I could have shown him that that particular city was not on his assigned list. Right there and then, I decided that I would no longer co-operate with him. Sitting near the back of the class, I quietly did all my work and assignments but refused to participate in class discussions, reading the textbooks rather than listening to his lessons. After five or six weeks of this "cold war," the principal contacted my parents, who forced me to go to his office to apologize. I did so reluctantly, in the interest of preventing additional problems, all the while firmly believing that the wrong person was apologizing. During this whole episode he didn't talk to me even once, and, in his office, said only that he accepted my apology. The point here is that his failure to reach me and my classmates and his ineffectiveness in providing a caring environment meant that we participated reluctantly. We learned some skills but did not accept the many valuable insights about life and culture that he did have to offer.

On the other hand, my grade six public school teacher, Miss Milligan, although she taught me for only four months, had a great impact on me. She took personal interest in each of her students. She knew how to draw out the best in each of us. For the first time in my life, I discovered that I had some artistic and writing abilities, that I was able to give leadership in group settings, and that I could use the abilities I had not just for my own benefit but also to help others. Her Christian commitment and values touched all of us. She modeled personal virtues like respect and integrity. She structured the classroom to be a caring community, choosing content that dealt with important issues in life. As a consequence, many of us accepted the values she modeled and taught.

Much later, after I had finished my degree in mathematics and physics and was working in the computer science field, I decided to become a teacher. My motives were not entirely altruistic: I was tired of sitting behind a desk alone, working out programming and analysis problems. I missed working with and helping individuals and groups of people. So I became a high school teacher, mainly in mathematics. Part of the reason I could make that decision was that teachers like Miss Milligan—and I was blessed by having several others like her—had shown me that teachers can make a difference in the lives of their students, that they can teach much more about life than factual subject matter, and that they can help students consider the purpose and meaning of their lives and the importance of making responsible choices.

God calls Christians to be salt and light in the world. Few vocations offer one as much opportunity to influence young persons on a daily basis as teaching. Whether it be in a public or Christian or international school setting, God can use Christian teachers to model and teach what it means to care for a hurting world.

CARING FOR A HURTING WORLD

I was once asked to speak to a group of Christian teachers on the following Bible verses:

> The Spirit of the Lord is on me, because he has anointed me to preach good news to the poor. He has sent me to proclaim freedom for the prisoners and recovery of sight for the blind, to release the oppressed, to proclaim the year of the Lord's favor. (Isaiah 61:1, 2; quoted by Jesus in Luke 4:18–19)

At first, I wondered how I could relate this passage to everyday classroom teaching. I soon began to realize how much this text has to say about the role of Christian teachers. It proclaims God's grace and mercy through the person of Jesus Christ, but not primarily to reasonably comfortable and successful middle class people like most of us, but to the poor, the prisoners, the blind, and the oppressed. In our present day North American society, it seems to me, Christ's love must flow through us to the depressed and chronically unemployed, to the drug junkies that roam our big-city streets, to single mothers whose ex-spouses are not supporting their children, and to First Nations people unable to maintain a responsible way of life in harmony with their own worldview. This means that Christian teachers have a special task to reach the children of these groups, as well as the academically and socially "poor" students frustrated by their school experiences.

Now, *if* we truly believe Peter's and Paul's words that we are a chosen people, a royal priesthood, Christ's ambassadors, and even God's fellow workers, *then* Christian teachers have an obligation to model the unshackling of the bonds of sin in order to live under the sunshine of God's grace and justice within their classrooms. They must be beacons of hope for their students, not because God needs their help, but because God has chosen them and has given them a mandate to proclaim the Lord's favor, binding up the brokenhearted, seeking relief for the oppressed, interceding for the troubled and angry, and providing for the handicapped.

Christian teachers—in both public and Christian schools—must therefore ask themselves: Was this Scripture fulfilled in my classroom today? In what ways did my teaching reflect the love and mercy of God as well as the freedom that Christ has proclaimed? Did the content I taught in social studies or science or physical education this week reflect the intent of this biblical text—or did it put my students even more into the straightjacket of the materialistic individualism of twenty-first century North America?

But some of you may object, suggesting that I am stretching this text too far. Don't teachers just help children function well in society? Don't they just teach the "basics" well, striving for professional competency? Aren't they good teachers as long as they "cover" the curriculum content and keep their classrooms on a quiet, even keel? I agree that these are important aspects of teaching. When teachers contribute to a student functioning with more self-discipline or with improved language or mathematical skills, then they *are* assisting to "release the oppressed."

Yet I believe that this text has more to say about the task of Christian teachers. Critical theorist David Purpel, although influenced by liberation theology and New Age thinking and somewhat naive in his solutions because of his failure to acknowledge the effects of sin, still exhibits helpful insight when he asserts, in his book *The Moral and Spiritual Crisis in Education: A Curriculum for Justice and Compassion in Education*, that North American schools are "intellectually and morally bankrupt."[2] We have replaced, he continues:

1. *humility with arrogance* (e.g., students are taught to believe they can decide their own values autonomously without reference to their cultural tradition or any absolutes other than the current "politically correct" ones);

2. *commitment with alienation* (e.g., students are taught to look mainly after their own welfare and advancement, while our schools fail "to help students to make lasting and profound moral commitments that can energize and legitimate [their] day-to-day lives," with

2. Purpel, *Crisis in Education*, 23.

students becoming alienated from each other and our society rather than committed to serving it);

3. *faith and vision with reason* (e.g., students reason things out for themselves from a smorgasbord of possibilities ranging from faith in reincarnation or the occult to faith in capitalistic self-reliance. Reason is held to be the sole basis for value and meaning, leaving our cultural ship adrift without the rudder of faith and vision);

4. *justice for all with competition* (e.g., we value high marks but often not personal character qualities; we confuse achievement with worth); and

5. *community with individuality* (e.g., our emphasis is on individual achievement rather than on mutual support).[3]

These are serious charges. If they are true, schools are indeed failing to proclaim the year of the Lord's favor. Purpel points to the fact that most teachers arrange learning so that students work individually, all striving for their own self-advancement. The higher the grade level, the more teachers reward student achievement individually with grades (not for effort; we're not very good at assessing effort, as is shown by the very high correlation between achievement and effort columns on report cards that have both). Evaluation, rather than helping students improve, more often pigeonholes and labels students in terms of what the others accomplish (e.g., "below" or "above" average). We will love you, schools say, if you show you deserve it by achieving individual scholastic success—despite the fact that research shows that the relationship between academic "success" in school and later "success" in life is often a tenuous one.

Somehow our culture has influenced teachers to reward "worldly" individual success. The Bible shows a different pattern. As God's story of redemption unfolded, he chose and used Moses, a person who couldn't speak in public; Rahab, a prostitute who likely had no school experience at all; Ruth, an "immigrant" with no "marketable skills" nor any investment funds; David, whom his father Jesse didn't even bother to include when introducing his sons to Samuel; Mary and Joseph, in the eyes of the world an insignificant peasant couple from an unimportant rural village in backward Galilee; and Peter, a rough, impetuous fisherman who likely could never sit still long enough in school to complete a task, but, worse, whose word couldn't be trusted. What was important in all these

3. Purpel, *Crisis in Education*, 31–64.

instances was not as much the quality of the innate gifts these people possessed but their commitment to use their God-given talents to the best of their ability in serving God.

Christian teaching involves providing learning activities and structures that will help the Moseses and Rahabs and Ruths and Peters of our age. Christian teachers can show in the way they go about teaching that they believe that each child is created in God's *image*, that each has a religious heart and a special calling. They can structure their classrooms to be communities where love, concern, justice, and compassion are not only preached but also practiced, and where students learn to work for the welfare of others as well as their own. An *ongoing* aim of Christian teachers must be the nurture of human caring and concern. Students need to learn to cry about the injustice in so many parts of the world as well as in their own communities. They need to support the deprived in their classrooms and in society. Teachers can help students begin to do something about the destruction of God's marvelous creation as our society continues to worship the idol of economic growth. They can challenge their students to begin to make serious commitments to serve God in ways like Mother Teresa did, or like the Mennonite Central Committee worker who gives up comforts and friendships to help aboriginal peoples in isolated communities, or like the businessman who purposely hires ex-convicts to give them a second chance, even when this may negatively affect his profit picture.

Christian teachers are constantly faced with the question: To what end am I preparing my students? How am I affecting Robert, who no longer tries very hard since he realizes that he's no academic match for most of his classmates? How am I helping Stephanie, whom God has blessed with such a large dose of oral communication skills that I'm often totally frustrated with her? How can I even begin to think about helping Karen care for a hurting world when her cynical attitude towards life has been brought about by sexual abuse within her family? How am I helping Jack, who has his parents' materialistic "surpass the Joneses" attitude bred right into him?

The answer does not lie in seemingly never-ending government reports on the future of education, even though they often contain good classroom suggestions. Consider the bold *Year 2000* program that was going to be implemented in British Columbia's classrooms (until it was summarily abandoned by a new, less idealistic government). It tried to accommodate students' diverse learning rates and styles, with the learning rooted in hands-on experiences. It promoted collaborative learning in flexible groups and fostered creative thinking. An integrated curriculum without artificial subject distinctions was supposed to allow children to experience learning as a whole and help them understand connections. Children were to learn writing and reading in purposeful, meaningful contexts. Assessment methods were going to help children improve on the basis of definite criteria, not provide only subjective judgments with vague grades.

But, in spite of a number of positive elements, the proposed program, from a biblical perspective, contained a number of serious deficiencies. *Year 2000* promoted an underlying faith in the basic goodness and autonomy of individuals, and in the power of rationality to solve all humankind's problems. In line with Enlightenment thinking, it assumed that education will always lead to progressive social change and that personal rational thought is the ultimate basis for regulating daily life and choosing values. Yet precisely these assumptions have led our Western culture to become self-centered, hedonistic, riddled with social and ecological problems, ethically and spiritually numb, insensitive to social injustice and alienation, and lacking in a true understanding of community.

Year 2000 listed a number of impressive characteristics of educated persons: creative, self-motivated, productive, co-operative, principled, respectful, able and disposed to think critically, to communicate, and to make independent decisions. But what was the *content* of such terms? "Principled" had no principles attached. A sound basis for making independent decisions was lacking. Yet students were to be taught that they must "construct" their own knowledge and meaning and choose their own values, without any external absolutes to guide them. Further, key biblical traits were totally absent: love, compassion, forgiveness, humility, moral uprightness, truthfulness, self-sacrifice, a search for love, and justice. According to *Year 2000,* in other words, our students were to be molded into autonomous, self-directing individuals who would co-operate only if it was in their own self-interest. *Year 2000* ignored the principle that most knowledge is an integral part of our cultural heritage, and that for society to function well we need to share a basis of such knowledge and a common sense of meaning and commitment. Therefore, in *Year 2000* the *process* of learning became all-important; the *content*, relatively unimportant. The *search* for truth rather than truth itself, *Year 2000* assumed, would set the learner free.

On the other hand, what often replaces programs such as these are ones that emphasize accountability based on a narrow view of the person and of knowledge. High-stakes tests emphasize literacy and numeracy. It is certainly important that students learn to read and write and calculate effectively and efficiently. However, programs affected by testing often begin to teach "to the tests" and consequently downplay the importance of such significant aspects of personhood as critical thinking, discernment, ethical virtues such as the fruit of the Spirit, application in meaningful contexts, service to others, creativity, and even what responsible citizenship entails. Related curricula minimize subjects like the fine arts, physical education, and even social studies so that schools can emphasize the content tested and thus do well on external tests. Even though most teachers try to avoid the extreme of either programs such as *Year 2000* or ones that teach mainly toward tests, they nevertheless do take into account the political winds. Neither of these types of programs takes into account what it means that students and teachers are made in God's image, uniquely gifted but also tainted with sin, and yet called by God to be stewards of his creation to God's glory and for the benefit of their neighbors.

What does all this mean for classrooms of Christian teachers? First, a Christian worldview does not consist of generally accepted platitudes backed by superficial proof-texting. Rather, it requires demanding analysis and astute, knowledgeable discernment of biblical guidelines in the context of today's culture. Scripture also makes clear that such a worldview must impinge on practical living. Paul's letters are powerful because he shows how great truths control our decisions about everyday matters. Christian teachers themselves therefore must have, as Paul put it, *the mind of Christ* and must want to share this with their students. We should not interpret the mind of Christ too narrowly. It encompasses a Christ-like outlook that controls our thinking, our motives, our words, our deeds—our whole praxis. Teachers who want to share this mind of Christ with their students test and approve what God's will is for their lives, and help their students do so also.

Teachers can usually work at this more explicitly and freely in Christian than in public school settings. But in any situation they can do a great deal to help their students develop critical appreciation of the past and discern the spirit of the times. They can explore the values that should undergird thinking and action, encouraging students to commit themselves to a principled way of life and helping them see that knowledge demands committed response in everyday actions. Thomas Rosebrough, Dean of the School of Education and Human Studies at Union University in Tennessee, illuminates the crucial importance of the Christian teacher's role in this regard when he observes, "Students need perspective from their adult teachers. They need reassurances that certain values are timeless, that morality is based on a transcendent standard and that their teacher is committed to holding to that standard."[4] Philosopher Elmer Thiessen shows at length that children need to be initiated into specific traditions and anchored in clearly defined value systems. If not, it is difficult for young people to gain the normal autonomy, the critical openness, and the hope that is necessary for contributing positively to a civilized liberal society.[5] Christian teachers can play a crucial role in this regard.

FOUR DIMENSIONS OF CHRISTIAN TEACHING

I believe there are four dimensions to Christian teaching: guiding, unfolding, structuring, and enabling. I propose to explain these four terms, relating them back to the theme that Christian teaching involves *caring for a hurting world*.

Guiding

First, Christian teachers are called to *guide* young people into the knowledge and discernment that leads to service for God and their fellow human beings—through their modeling, through their informal contact, through their choice of content, and through their pedagogy (i.e., their teaching and learning methods). Teachers lead students astray if they teach that applying the scientific method can solve humankind's problems. They lead them astray if their acid tongue breaks down their pupils' self-concept. They lead them astray if they fail to apply consistent, biblical discipline. But they also lead them astray if they, like many school textbooks, avoid vital issues rooted in religion and moral values, or if they fail to counter our society's prevalent materialistic, entertainment-centered way of life.

To guide children in the truth, Christian teachers must first of all be personally committed to Jesus Christ. They must seek his guidance for their guiding. Their personal commitment to Jesus is the basis for teaching their

4. Rosebrough, "Christian Worldview in Teaching," 296.

5. See, for instance, Thiessen, *Teaching for Commitment*, chapters 5 and 6, and *In Defence of Religious Schools and Colleges*, 249–51.

students to walk in God's ways and delight in his faithfulness. Modeling a Christian way of life is effective only if teachers are committed to it themselves and show this in their dealings with students. They must see their authority as servant authority and thus care for a hurting world in and outside of their classrooms. They must recognize that they need to deal with the hurting hearts of their students with wisdom and responsibility, with empathy and patience, but also with firm action. They should try to see situations through the eyes of their students in order to discover their motives. They should see children not just as objects to be instructed but as people in God's image with their own characteristics, abilities, shortcomings, and pedagogical and psychological needs. Such insights should help them guide their students "in the paths they should go."

Let me give two examples. I remember going into the class of a new grade three teacher a number of years ago. She impatiently lashed out at her children for doing poorly on cursive writing. I remember vividly seeing one little boy with his tongue out of his mouth trying to do his best. He didn't have the muscle co-ordination needed for good work, however, and his best efforts were rewarded only by sharp comments such as "What a mess!" and "Can't you see the lines?" He literally cringed and tried to disappear into his desk every time the teacher came near. I left the room: I could not stomach the deep hurt in his eyes, confirmed by his body language. I talked at length afterwards to the teacher about what was happening in the room, and worked on how she shrilly commandeered rather than guided her charges. After a year, I suggested she tape some of her teaching. Gradually she became convinced that her impatience prevented her from nurturing and guiding her students in a positive and effective way. She went into another line of work where, at last report, she was much happier. Guidance requires understanding and tact, setting high but realistic expectations in an encouraging atmosphere where students are allowed to take risks in their learning.

I also experienced a positive example of guiding some time ago. A grade ten high school English teacher told me enthusiastically about a unit called "Choices" that he had designed and taught. He used a mixture of short stories, poems, news articles, teen-oriented comics, and rock music to discuss how people make choices about sexuality, drugs, suicide, what to do with life. The class discussed the video, "The Man Who Planted Trees," and its implications for their own lives: what it means to "plant trees" and make the world a better place in which to live. The students then chose a "tree planting" organization such as the Red Cross, the Salvation Army, World Vision, or Citizens for Public Justice. They each made contact with one agency and took a school day to visit its office and interview key personnel. They made a report to the class as well as a poster promoting the organization. The unit helped the students, according to the teacher, to become respectful of the people involved, to appreciate how they made choices about their lives, and to consider how they themselves could and must make choices that would affect not only their own lives but the lives of people around them. Through the content and structure, the teacher guided his students into considering important questions about choices in their lives.

Unfolding

Second, effective teaching through biblical servant authority calls Christian teachers to *unfold* the basis, contours, and implications of a Christian vision of life. They are essentially *prophets* in their teaching, proclaiming God's handiwork in creation (e.g., the beautiful intricacies and dependability of scientific laws), the effects of sin (e.g., the tragedy of the holocaust and political and religious persecution), and the possibilities of reconciliation and restoration (e.g., the work of Mother Teresa). Unfolding is the opposite of mere covering of content, when the latter involves teaching much factual material without drawing attention to its meaning and significance or responding to it personally. In this connection, it has been remarked that the real difference between "smart" and "dumb" students in schools too often is that the smart students forget the answers *after* the test. Christian teachers need to unfold God's way of life, leading students to take delight in wholesome living as well as to feel hurt by the effects of sin in the world. Unfolding demands far more than imparting factual information: students evaluate knowledge, think critically about it, solve problems with it, and consciously develop a related value system and disposition.

Christian teachers must constantly ask themselves what content is really meaningful for students in today's society. They must carefully justify what they unfold, on the basis of well-defined aims. When they teach the political history of constitutional development in nineteenth-century Canada, for example, they need to emphasize an understanding of the religious and social contexts and principles that should undergird current constitutional revision (e.g., informed citizenship, responsible stewardship, justice, importance of the family). In grade eleven biology, for instance, they may add units on bioethics as well as responsible stewardship. In grade six or thereabouts, they may teach the principles of loving your neighbor as yourself in operating a business. At the intermediate level, they may show students how work is a calling in and through which we enrich ourselves and our society—and how the biblical principles of justice can be worked out in the workplace. By choosing appropriate literature, they can show the implications of living (or failing to live) according to the biblical norms for friendship, marriage, and family relationships. In geography, they may teach units with the theme, "Am I my Brother's (or Sister's) Keeper?"

When discussing the "unfolding" aspect of effective teaching, I have often asked groups of Christian teachers the following questions: Are we teaching the shocking fact that the USA, with 6 percent of the world's population, consumes 40 percent of the world's resources and still has 15 percent of its population living below the poverty line, with Canadian figures being proportionally just as bad? Are we helping students restructure family and institutional priorities and lifestyles? At higher levels, do we show the need for and involve students in strategies for political and social change that promote justice for the oppressed? Do we deal in our classes with the important social issues raised by organizations such as the Mennonite Central Committee, M2/W2 (a prison ministry), and the Evangelical Fellowship of Canada? Are we doing justice to our mandate to help students care for a hurting world? "Blessed are those who hunger and thirst for *justice*, for they will be filled," Jesus said (Matthew 5:6). Do we help our students confront self-centeredness and injustice that demands a response to the Lord of Life? Do we help our students personally and collectively feed the hungry, welcome strangers, clothe the naked, and visit the sick and those in prison? That's what our risen Lord expects, in and through the unfolding Christian teachers do in schools.

Structuring

Third, there is a *structuring* dimension to teaching. Educators have shown that the "hidden or implicit curriculum"—how we structure our everyday classroom—has as much influence on our students as the content we unfold. The way teachers structure learning activities must proclaim to our students a message of respect and love, of forgiveness and reconciliation, of authenticity, of community, of the need to bear each other's burdens, of the importance of using our unique abilities to contribute to the classroom community, to the Body of Christ in action. I believe there are four more-or-less distinct phases of teaching if learning is to be meaningful (right from kindergarten to post-graduate work): setting the stage, disclosure, reformulation, and transcendence. Each of these phases requires somewhat different approaches, enabling teachers to meet the needs of students with differing learning styles, to forge the classroom into a community where students have both individual and communal responsibilities, to encourage students to use their unique abilities in God-glorifying ways, to build an atmosphere of trust and support—in short, to have students experience what it means to care for each other within the classroom. This is a necessary prerequisite to them being willing and able to care for the hurting outside world. An atmosphere of faith and trust needs to permeate the classroom of the Christian teacher.

This requires, for instance, co-operative group work where pupils must support and care for each other if the task is to be done effectively. Such approaches have become increasingly important, with the prevalence of family breakdown and lack of meaningful communication in many homes. Through co-operative learning, students can learn to experience and contribute mutual support, to value individual differences, to resolve group conflicts, to communicate about meaningful topics, and to evaluate their own contribution to group work. At least in higher grades, typical teachers use 80 percent of class time talking and having students work individually in straight rows. Such teachers, regrettably, tend to prepare students to fit into an individualistic lifestyle where work is a means to an end, where it is everyone for him- or herself, where love and justice are pushed aside by the importance of individual achievement and gain in comparison to others.

Let me clarify what I mean by giving some examples of such structuring. Kindergarteners may draw a picture of what wholesome and gratifying family life can be like. Also, if teachers have structured the classroom to encourage this, pupils may learn to choose their own learning activities responsibly—and also learn justice in the classroom (being on the time-out chair when they do not live up to expectations, for example). Grade Twos may write a story about how we can use plants responsibly, and also how to look after their own plants. Grade Fours may list the differences between an aboriginal way of life and the Western way of life and decide what a sound alternative to the inadequacies of each involves—and how they might make changes in their own lives based on that comparison. Grade Sixes may make a display for parents or write a group response to a local politician about the problems of pollution or aesthetics affecting the local community. Grade Eights may hold a debate about the justice issues involved in native land claims—and contact a government official to discuss the problem, exercising communication and co-operation skills that contribute positively to human relations. Grade Nines may apply science research and investigation skills in new situations. Grade Tens may respond in a personal way to the evil in Golding's novel, *Lord of the Flies*. Grade Elevens may be asked to plan regular entertainment evenings for young offenders as part of a unit on crime and justice. Grade Twelves may be asked to produce poems, stories, videotapes, and art works dealing with their personal beliefs about sexuality and marriage. Throughout this phase, teachers can help students to think through problems they face at home, in school, in their social relations, and, eventually, in the work- and marketplace, encouraging them to apply appropriate norms for morality, for family and social life, for leisure, and for responsible handling of one's financial resources.

Enabling

Finally, through guiding, unfolding, and structuring, teachers can *enable* their students to use their gifts in service to God through service to their fellow creatures. Enabling is a natural consequence of effective unfolding and structuring, and overlaps with these two dimensions of Christian teaching. Such enabling goes much beyond what we have traditionally called the "basics," although it includes them too. It embraces exercising abilities and developing dispositions on the basis of scriptural principles. Enabling takes place especially, though certainly not exclusively, in the transcendence, the response phase of learning. Here theoretical reflection becomes reflective action. Here students develop meaningful products and choose responses that affect their own lives. They commit themselves to certain courses of action and values, setting out their own positions and directions.

TEACHING AS A RELIGIOUS CRAFT

Enabling learners: for that, we need to look at teaching as a *religious craft*. Teaching is, first of all, a craft in that you become more insightful and skillful in it as you apply your knowledge responsibly, and then reflectively and perceptively learn from your experience. In that sense, a good teacher is a personally and socially responsible *reflective practitioner*. But teaching is not just a craft: it involves a crucial religious/moral dimension as well. Even the atheist Bertrand Russell, as we saw earlier, said that teaching must impart what persons believe to be of value, what they consider to be of ultimate worth. If we interpret "religion" in the broad sense, i.e., that it concerns basic beliefs about the cause, nature, and purpose of life, then all teaching is religious.

Christian teaching, therefore, as especially the Old Testament makes clear, points to the marvelous deeds of the Lord (e.g., the awe-inspiring, life-sustaining scientific laws embedded in God's creation) and leads to walking in the paths of the Lord or "the way you should go." To use Parker Palmer's words, "to teach is to create space in which obedience to truth is practiced," so that, ultimately, students allow themselves to be transformed by truth.[6] God calls Christian teachers to create space in their classrooms in which students may practice truth—for instance, to strive for academic excellence in solving and applying mathematical problems, or to knowledgeably care for the disadvantaged and the handicapped. Christian teachers guide, unfold, and structure in order to enable their students to use and develop their own unique gifts in love and compassion for others around them. They want their students not to master truth as much as the Truth that is Christ to master them.

As most of you know, public schools by law and practice have become increasingly secular during the last quarter century. In the province of British Columbia, for example, the banning of prayer and Bible reading in classrooms is just one sign that schools in a pluralistic society are no longer allowed to promote one particular faith. In some jurisdictions, Christian groups may no longer meet on school property. The important influence that Christian teachers still have in public schools is increasingly being curtailed. Parents recognize this, and, as a result, Christian schools have grown by leaps and bounds. In such schools, Christian teachers can be much more explicit about their faith and its implications.

6. Palmer, *To Know as We Are Known*, 105, 124.

Some years ago I wrote a chapter for a book in which I argue that Christian schools should enable their students to be and become *responsive disciples* of Jesus Christ.[7] What do I mean by this term within a school setting? I intend it to be much more encompassing than what evangelical Christianity has often assigned to the so-called "spiritual" dimension of life. Responsive disciples, I believe, go into the heart of our culture's politics and economics and social relations and the media and the arts and sciences, able to contribute to them as Christ-followers.

True, telling others directly about the Good News of Christ is one crucial aspect of responsive discipleship. But discipleship goes much beyond that. It embraces any situation where students—and teachers—use and develop their abilities and talents in God-glorifying ways. The numbers we multiply, the chemicals we mix, the volleyballs we spike, the poems we write, the maps we draw, the textbooks we read, the critical analyses we develop, the procedures we learn, the dispositions we develop—all these are gifts of God to be used as sacramental offerings to him (just as the prophet Zechariah, in Zechariah 14:20, 21, said that the bells of the horses and the cooking pots could be holy to the Lord).

A kindergartener excitedly discovers that 3 + 2 always equals 2 + 3 —and begins to apply that in everyday situations. A student festively paints the stunning beauty of an alpine meadow. A girl ponders in her journal about coping with the anguish of her broken home situation. A class researches and debates how to respond to today's popular music. All these situations exemplify responsive discipleship when we offer back to God the gifts he first gave us. God through his grace then uses our learning activities in the service of advancing his Kingdom, accepting both students and teachers as discipling fellow workers (1 Corinthians 3:9).

Teachers and students who are responsive disciples use Jesus' power and directives to nurture and unfold the potential in themselves, in others, and in God's creation. They believe fervently, care compassionately, love unconditionally, discover breathlessly, evaluate discerningly, create imaginatively—and also grieve profoundly when the power of sin prevents Christ's *shalom*, the biblical peace and justice that heals brokenness and restores creation to what God intended it to be, from breaking through. Developing God-given gifts in a supportive learning community in order

---

7. Stronks and Blomberg, eds., *A Vision with a Task.*

to seek and celebrate God's *shalom* is something that gives purpose and meaning to the whole educational process.

While the foregoing applies more readily to teachers in Christian schools, many aspects can also be implemented by Christian teachers in public schools, even when by law they may not openly promote their faith. All effective education (as opposed to training), after all, involves imparting what we believe to be of value and encourages students to respond to their learning and use their developing insights and abilities to contribute to a compassionate, upright, and just society.

CONCLUSION

There is one final point I need to make about the aforementioned text: "The Spirit of the Lord is on me, because he has anointed me to preach good news." We now know that this description no longer applies only to Jesus Christ. Because of Pentecost, it refers to each one of us if we love and serve the Lord. The Spirit of the Lord *has* been poured out on each one of us who serves Jesus Christ. God *has* anointed us to bring good news. Teachers have remarkable opportunities to do so in their classrooms. They may proclaim that the day of the Lord is at hand and that the hurting world can be healed through Christ's love. They may, in Paul's words, shine like stars in the universe as they hold out God's Word of Life—his Word of liberation—to their students. I hope and pray that many of you who read this may take up that challenge, helping young people care for God's hurting world inside and outside the classroom.

WORKS CITED

Palmer, Parker. *To Know as We Are Known: A Spirituality of Education*. San Francisco: Harper & Row, 1983.

Plunkett, Dudley. *Secular and Spiritual Values: Grounds for Hope in Education*. Granby, MA: Bergin & Garvey, 1989.

Purpel, David E. *The Moral and Spiritual Crisis in Education: A Curriculum for Justice and Compassion in Education*. New York: Routledge, Chapman and Hall, 1990.

Rosebrough, Thomas R. "Christian Worldview and Teaching." In *Shaping a Christian Worldview: The Foundations of Christian Higher Education*, edited by David S. Dockery and Gregory A. Thornbury, 280–97. Nashville: Broadman Press, 2002.

Stronks, Gloria G., and Doug Blomberg, eds. *A Vision with a Task: Christian Schooling for Responsive Discipleship*. Grand Rapids, MI: Baker, 1993.

Thiessen, Elmer J. *In Defence of Religious Schools and Colleges*. Montreal and Kingston: McGill-Queen's University Press, 2001.

————. *Teaching for Commitment: Liberal Education, Indoctrination, and Christian Nurture.* Montreal and Kingston: McGill-Queen's University Press, 1993.

FOR FURTHER READING

Anderson, Ronald. *Religion and Spirituality in the Public School Classroom.* New York: Peter Lang, 2004.

Claerbaut, David. "Education: The Battleground." In his *Faith and Learning on the Edge: A Bold New Look at Religion in Higher Education,* 224–33. Grand Rapids, MI: Zondervan, 2004.

Edlin, Richard J. *The Cause of Christian Education.* 3rd ed. Colorado Springs, CO: Purposeful Design Publications, 1999.

Erickson, Joyce Q. "Parker Palmer's *To Know As We Are Known* Thirteen Years Later—A Review Essay." *Christian Scholar's Review* 26.1 (1996) 72–77.

Graham, Donovan. *Teaching Redemptively: Bringing Grace and Truth into Your Classroom.* Colorado Springs, CO: Purposeful Design Publications, 2003.

Greene, A. *Reclaiming the Future of Christian Education: A Transforming Vision.* Colorado Springs, CO: Purposeful Design Publications, 1998.

Groome, Thomas. *Educating for Life: A Spiritual Vision for Every Teacher and Parent.* Allen, TX: Thomas More, 1998.

Palmer, Parker. *The Courage to Teach: Exploring the Inner Landscape of a Teacher's Life.* San Francisco: Jossey-Bass, 1998.

Parker, Jonathan K. "Effective Stewardship: A Model for Teacher Education Programs in Christian Liberal Arts Colleges." *Faculty Dialogue* 23 (Winter 1995) 177–83.

Shortt, John, and David I. Smith. *The Bible and the Task of Teaching.* Stapleford, England: Stapleford Centre, 2002.

Van Brummelen, Harro. *Steppingstones to Curriculum: A Biblical Path.* 2d ed. Colorado Springs, CO: Purposeful Design Publications, 2002.

————. *Walking with God in the Classroom: Christian Approaches to Learning and Teaching.* 2d ed. Seattle: Alta Vista College Press, 1998.

Wolterstorff, Nicholas. *Educating for Life: Reflections on Christian Teaching and Learning.* Grand Rapids, MI: Baker, 2002.

29

A Christian Perspective on Theater Art

LLOYD A. ARNETT

Three boards, two actors, and a passion. (A description of theater by 16th century playwright Lope de Vega)

Every one whose heart stirred him up to come unto the work to do it. (A description of Israelite artists, Exodus 36:2)

ART AND THE ARTIST IN CHRISTIAN PERSPECTIVE

A CHRISTIAN PERSPECTIVE ON any area of life involves two lines of investigation: divine revelation and human inquiry. An inquiry into the nature of art takes us into the worlds of both biblical literature and the philosophy of art. We turn first to the Bible.

The Bible and Aesthetics

Foremost, and most inescapable, is the first revelation of God in Scripture—indeed, in the very first line—that he is Creator.

Saints Paul and John further encompass all human history by revealing that in God's Son all creation took place and that, in the final analysis, Christ will "make all things new." Christian artists' greatest dignity is that their work, when executed with integrity, is a reflection of their Father in heaven. Indeed, as Wheaton College philosophy professor emeritus Arthur Holmes observes, "The biblical concept of creation imparts sanctity to all realms of nature and to human history and culture."[1]

---

1. Holmes, *Idea of a Christian College*, 15.

Second to the creation, revelation is the understanding the Bible imparts concerning human art. Art is the "wisdom of the heart" in ancient Hebrew culture, artists the "wise of heart," and their product that of the "spirit of wisdom" (Exodus 28:3). In ten chapters of Exodus (28–31 and 35–40), we find theological statements about art and artists within the context of a divine art commission, the Hebrew tabernacle. Artistic ability is referred to as a divine endowment. Artists are presented as having hearts that reflect divine wisdom, hearts that stir them to do their own work and to teach other artists. Women are specifically mentioned as sharing in this endowment. All so gifted are commissioned to create work for "glory and for beauty." The quintessential artist in the passage is one Bezalel, whose name suggests that he and others like him stand "in the shadow of God." God, it seems, has given humankind art and artists as a form of divine wisdom for life in this world. Artists provide another way of knowing: a knowledge of the senses, feelings, emotions—a sensual wisdom. In Genesis 4:21–22, as a corrective for our own society, we find the first biblical references to music and metallurgy; art and technology are introduced side by side. Furthermore, 1 Chronicles 25:1 states that certain members of the Davidic society were set aside for the purpose of "prophesying" with music. In Christian revelation the arts are solidly aligned, in the divine economy,[2] with knowledge and truth.

In turning to human inquiry we find an experiential affirmation of this revelation. The philosophy of art, called "aesthetics," early agreed with the biblical view. The original philosophical definition of the word "aesthetics" was a "theory of sensuous knowledge, as a counterpart to logic as a theory of intellectual knowledge."[3]

The eighteenth-century birth of the discipline of aesthetics coincided with the crisis in Western civilization involving the loss of the arts as part of people's daily lives. There came an awareness of "fragmentation" in culture; human beings were becoming technological specialists and losing an awareness of their full humanity.

It was the German philosopher and artist Friedrich von Schiller who, more than anyone else, spoke to the dangers of this "specializing" phase of social development in a fallen society, a development which resulted in the separation of technical wisdom from heart wisdom. He saw that,

2. For a full treatment of these ideas see Veith, *The Gift of Art*.

3. Kristeller, "The Modern System of the Arts," 152.

in order to advance, human beings had to specialize, but he also noted the rapidly developing cost. He saw that technological advance alone was fragmenting human beings: "Eternally chained to only one single little fragment of the whole, Man himself grew to be only a fragment; with the monotonous noise of the wheel he drives everlastingly in his ears, he never develops the harmony of his being, and instead of imprinting humanity upon his nature he becomes merely the imprint of his occupation, of his science."[4] What Schiller saw happening at the end of the eighteenth century has become a common understanding today: in a technological society, people become indistinguishable from their jobs.

In a striking irony, one of the most influential scientists of the nineteenth century, Charles Darwin, expressed concern over this Schiller-envisioned world that he, Darwin, was helping to create:

> If I had my life to live over again, I would have made a rule to read some poetry and listen to some music at least once a week; for perhaps the parts of my brain now atrophied would have thus been kept alive through use. The loss of these tastes is a loss of happiness, and may possibly be injurious to the intellect, and more probably to the moral character, by enfeebling the emotional part of nature.[5]

Many scholars after Darwin have expressed similar concerns. In a public lecture at the University of Pittsburgh several years ago, Japanese literature expert Thomas Rimer noted that famous Swiss psychologist/psychiatrist Dr. Carl Jung, writing about what he called the "undiscovered self," commented that people who cut themselves off from faith and intuition are consequently deprived of certain important kinds of experience.[6]

Such matters of aesthetics have not traditionally been recognized as vital to Christians. In 1947, Dorothy L. Sayers accurately distilled centuries of church history on the topic, observing, "We have no Christian aesthetic—no Christian philosophy of the arts. The Church has never made up her mind about the arts."[7] In the words of Clyde Kilby, "Our excuse for our esthetic failure has often been that we must be about the

---

4. Schiller, *On the Aesthetic Education of Man*, 40.

5. Darwin, *The Autobiography of Charles Darwin*, 54.

6. Rimer, Lecture at University of Pittsburgh.

7. Sayers, "Towards a Christian Aesthetic," 69.

Lord's business, the assumption being that the Lord's business is never esthetic."[8]

From a Christian perspective, biblically and philosophically, then, God the Creator gave humans the arts as a way of knowing, a door to a sensual wisdom no less important than technology. If we do not step through that door, we are less human, less whole. Professor Norman Jones, chair of the Theater Department at Gordon College at the time, elaborated upon the point this way: "[A]ll art forms, whether music, dance, painting, theater, or any other of the multitude of gifts he has given, are not doomed by being a part of this physical earth. They are good because they are part of God's creation and because they spring directly from the Creator's own image in humans."[9] He goes on to observe that as the director of many plays at Gordon, he is able to approach each exercise of that responsibility as both an incarnational act and an act of worship—a response he endeavors to impart to the actors and technical production people working with him.

Divine Endowment in a Fallen World

So there it is in black and white: God creates, calls, and endows some human beings to be artists. He has seen fit to give human society a cult of muses. Their voices enchant, their art inspires, their drama challenges, their dance gives wing to earthbound spirits, their imaginations carry us forward. Their monuments, cathedrals, paintings, recordings, statues, films, writings, circle the globe. If these things are destroyed by war or natural disaster we all sense loss. It is their reflections of us we cherish, call culture, and save to pass on to our children. It is their products stimulating us, taking us beyond mere survival, that T. S. Eliot described as making "life worth living."[10]

The biblical answer to the student question as to why anyone would want to be an artist is that their "hearts stir them up" to do the work. Among the moments of deep pathos in recent years have been the discoveries of "concentration camp art." On walls in secret places, paintings have been found of ballerinas and scenes that transcended the holocaust experience. In the words of Shakespeare, these were attempts to make "a

8. Kilby, "Christian Imagination," 44.

9. Jones, "The Dramatic Arts and the Image of God," 133.

10. Eliot, *Christianity and Culture*, 100.

heaven of hell." Why? Because artists are created and internally "stirred up" to make objects for "beauty and for glory."

The artist lives in a world of uncommon joys and burdens. On the one hand, the artist can experience the joy of self-expression, using special gifts that both delight others and fascinate the artists themselves. But with this comes the burden of a sensitive vision that can overwhelm the individual in a fallen world. The Italian stage designer and film director, Franco Zeffirelli, once told an American network television interviewer that, if he did not believe in the resurrection of Christ, he would not be able to get out of bed in the morning.[11]

Despite the efforts of some Christian aestheticians to convince us, in recent years, that artists are no different from anyone else, certain biblical claims that would seem to suggest otherwise must be observed. Gifted artists often possess a unique emotional complex with which they and society must come to grips. Behind the myth of the artist as the hypersensitive genius or super-spirit there lies a biblical truth. In the famous Bezalel passages in Exodus we are confronted with the reality of the "heart wisdom" orientation of those whom God has gifted artistically. Very talented artists have and develop aesthetic sensitivity beyond the work-a-day average, sometimes far beyond. Along with these sensitivities and the creations they produce for us, however, comes an emotional price. Artists have been shown in recent studies to be inordinately susceptible to mood shifts, depression, and reliance on therapy and drugs.

The negative effects of this artistic sensitivity are compounded by the spirit of the age. In a fallen world which overvalues some professions and undervalues others, artists seldom receive the encouragement and ego reinforcement they need to keep going. Often members of their own profession are the worst offenders. A New York actor once told me that his greatest obstacles were those people in small administrative power positions in theaters who were themselves failed actors and envied those whom they were forced to supervise.

Commonly, an artist's greatest discouragement comes from within his or her own family. Well-meaning family members, in their concern for the artist's economic future, are among those who discourage survival attempts and tempt to lure the artist into a "safer," more traditional or

---

11. Zeffirelli was being interviewed on a KTCS (Seattle) public television program some time in the 1990s. I fear I cannot document the time of this event more precisely.

acceptable vocational pattern. Such good-intentioned behavior sends out a long-term message which clearly says, "I don't believe in you. Grow up and do something more responsible. Be respectable; you embarrass us." In the final analysis this attitude reflects the ignorance of our need of such people in society, a society sadly bent, so it often seems, on technological and economic self-destruction.

Finally, the gifts of God sometimes run counter to social pressures and expectations. One cannot, for instance, always wait until he or she has a college education, is "safely" married, and has an established family to decide to become a dancer. Tendons set at around age 19 and active dance careers end early. One of my former students, for example, was dancing with the Joffrey Ballet at age 16.

THE HUMAN NATURE OF THEATER ART

Having laid a foundation for understanding the nature and place of art and artists in society (a supplement, I recognize, to earlier chapters on art and music in this collection), I would now like to look at one art specifically, the theater.

The Dignity of Play

When I was a parent of small children I learned more about the place of the arts in human experience, theater in particular, than I have reading a mound of philosophical treatises on aesthetics. I did not need to teach my two young daughters about the kinesthetic relationship between movement and music; as toddlers, they danced to sound and rhythm spontaneously. They sang; they scribbled; they made up stories. And at the age of 1 1/2 years they, like all other children, spontaneously initiated one of the most normal activities to all children: they began to pretend, re-enact, rehearse the common activities of their daily routines as a way of knowing them. They entered, in short, the world of "play."

In a world increasingly technocratic, we have tended as adults to disparage "playing around." But play is the natural occupation of children. It is their work. It is how they learn, socialize, come to grips with their world. We need to acknowledge the dignity of this activity in the divine development of individuals.

Theater, as an art, grows out of this normal developmental activity, which is to say that theater is as natural to humanity as play. In virtually every developed society, as in English speaking ones, the word for play is also the word to describe what happens on the stage of a theater. Our term "role-playing," referring to a natural activity of children and adults alike, comes from the theater. In Elizabethan times actors' parts were not in books but copied out onto scroll-like "roles." As recently as last century, the dominant acting theory of the past eighty years was developed as a result of theorist Constantine Stanislavsky's having watched children absorbed in role-playing at a beach in Finland.

I often ask my students to recall their first date or to remember times when, as adolescents, they had gotten into trouble with authority figures. In virtually all cases students recall "rehearsing" what they would say to others on these occasions. Why? Because role-playing is an inherent attempt at "knowing" how to handle situations for which we have little or no experience. Role-playing is a way of knowing.

While at the University of Pittsburgh, I was a patient-simulator for medical, nursing, and pharmacy schools. Medical students role-played interviews with patient-simulators before being turned loose on real patients in hospitals, clinics, and pharmacies. Even as adults, for them, it was a way of knowing.

Theater as Social Role-Playing

Beyond role-playing, however, is theater as an art. It is so much a "way-of-knowing" in our history that every language is filled with words and phrases that are the evidence of it. We say people are "showing off," "playing it cool," "playing something up (or down)," "making a spectacle of themselves," "playing a role," that they have "an emotional make–up," that they are "acting up," "making a scene." We say "Don't be dramatic," that people are doing "the same old routine, number, bit," that people are "show-offs," or that something is a real "showplace" or is "scenic."[12] Even the Bible uses theatrical terminology. When Saint Paul says, "And my God shall supply all your needs according to his riches in Christ Jesus," he uses the word *choregus,* a Greek theater term for theatrical producer, someone who supplied the actors with all they needed to do a show.

When people come together as a community group to watch theater, certain dynamics instantly go into effect. They are giving themselves to a group of performers to be emotionally entertained and to experi-

---

12. Lahr and Price, *Life Show,* 4–5.

ence something about their world. They bring with them only one thing in common, a knowledge of life. What they see is not a lecture but a multi-dimensional form of moving sound, picture, story, and dialogue. Theologian and play collaborator Ben Quash, in remarking on the fact that the meaning of a play cannot be reduced to a set of propositions—can vary, indeed, with each performance—said, "[D]rama is not a ready-made system of meaning. It's not a logical code of signification, which will always mean the same generally and timelessly. It emerges from a complex interaction between circumstances, actors, text and audience.... It is an *event* of signification, never exactly repeatable a second time."[13]

In addition, theater art often has the effect of intensifying experience for us—of awakening us out of habitual and often semi-conscious states of mind. Many of the most memorable moments of our lives are the ones in which we experience intense consciousness (e.g., a deep religious experience, or the surge of sexual ecstasy, or an adrenalin-inducing threat to life). At its best, theater induces an intense awareness of some aspect of life—a kind of crucible in which everything is unusually focused for a short period of time.

Theater is not an intense awareness of all life, however. It is very selective. An actress in Sartre's play *The Condemned of Altona* says, "Theatre is like life, only compressed and with meaning." Theater historian Peter Arnott writes, "The theater acts as a focusing glass. It reduces complex and momentous issues to manageable proportions, and it allows us to discern patterns that, in the tangle of everyday life, are less clearly visible. ... [Theater] remains a mirror of humanity's state of mind."[14]

The intensity of our response is our "aesthetic experience," our reaction to having taken the beauty of an artistic form into ourselves. It is what makes you cry at the end of a beautiful story and enthusiastically applaud a riotous comedy or great tragedy. It is your part of the process; you are responding to the artists.

Theater as Preserver of Archetypal Truth

From a literary standpoint theater also presents humankind with insights into reality in the form of the genres it presents. To borrow some ideas from Swiss psychotherapist Carl Jung as well as the late Canadian liter-

13. Quash, "The Play beyond the Play," 98.
14. Arnott, *The Theater in Its Time*, 7.

ary critic, Northrop Frye, theater provides a series of vignettes from the panorama of archetypal genres that strive to reflect the totality of human experience. The primary genres of theater are tragedy and comedy. From a Christian perspective these genres and their sub-genres reflect drama-tists' understandings of the universal human condition. Tragedy presents the suffering, decline, and death that are the common experiences of vir-tually all humankind. Violence, murder, death, suicide, and martyrdom are the stuff of tragedy. Tragedy lays bare the human condition. Comedy, on the other hand, is life-affirming, typically speaking to us of food, sex, love, family relations, and the joys of life. To watch a romantic comedy one would think that the be-all and end-all of life was to trundle a couple off to bed. These plays, from Greek times to the present, typically end in a wed-ding, a wedding feast, or a banquet. They celebrate one universal aspect of life: the uniting of men and women at that stage of their development.

In a rephrasing of Justin Martyr and Calvinist ideas from the Reformation, Arthur Holmes affirms, "All truth is God's truth, wherever it be found."[15] Dramatic genres, taken together, both form and reflect our understanding of the common absolutes of human experience. They are one way our culture passes on knowledge of life from one generation to another. In all these things theater takes us beyond individual role-playing to a type of social role-playing that constitutes a communal way of knowing. As Valparaiso University theater professor John Paul ex-presses it, theater art has historically provided audiences with a plethora of "opportunities for theological exploration and spiritual experience . . . [involving] issues of divine intervention, moral action, faith, hope, doubt, death, and redemption."[16]

Theater is in a real sense the art of human nature: it is based in human-ness and is about humanness. I can think of nothing more fascinating.

THEATER AND SOCIETY: BASIC ISSUES OF THE DISCIPLINE

The "issues" of a discipline have a tendency to be its negative or conflict-causing aspects. They are the issues that arise, not from the high calling or inherent goodness of the work, but because the work exists in an imperfect world. There are two categories of issues with which people in theater as a discipline must deal. The first are longstanding issues of

15. Holmes, *Idea of a Christian College*, 17.
16. Paul, "I Love to Tell the Story," 166.

cultural history, where society and the arts find themselves at odds. The second category involves contemporary issues relevant to theater as a discipline in western society.

Philosophical and Religious Issues

In the first category, longstanding philosophical and/or religious issues, there are five recurrent charges laid by those who in virtually every generation wish to attack the theater as a social institution.

1. The first is the charge that acting is, in essence, lying. People have often failed to distinguish between fiction for positive purposes and a lie, which is a deliberate intention to deceive.

2. A second issue has to do with the charge that actors are immoral. In my experience, so are certain doctors, clergymen, business people, female aerobics teachers, and people in almost every other category of persons in society. No one has advocated eradicating them lately. It is true that many actors live libertine lifestyles. But it is also true that many do not. Moreover, in the early years of Western civilization, actors and playwrights were among the most valued members of society (and often were priests, military heroes, etc.). Prominent Greek actors were commonly chosen as ambassadors of state. In the time of the Roman Empire actors were forced into degraded lifestyles and fell under legal restrictions known as the *infamia*. Separated from religion and prey to the whims of deranged emperors, performers were required to present lascivious displays and eventually to even perform live crucifixions on stage. Roman law forbade a person from leaving the acting profession for another; children born under the *infamia* had to enter the profession. In one of the darker decisions of the church, the *infamia* was kept in place in some societies until the French Revolution. Actors were forbidden to take the sacraments and become Christians unless they left their profession, but the *infamia* enforced by the church prohibited them from doing that very thing. The long term effects of such decisions on the acting profession in Western civilization are incalculable.

3. A third issue relates to the problem of "proteanism." Proteus the sea-god could change his appearance to the detriment of others. As Jung and others have pointed out, human beings count on one another

being exactly what they seem to be, for social stability. When one of us tries to leave our assigned place in the world we encounter resistance, from either our families or our community. We don't expect Joe the shoemaker to be a fine poet or Thelma the homemaker to be a great philosopher. In the world of the theater it is the gift of the actor to do just that, however, to regularly become on stage what s/he is not. Psychoanalysts have pointed out that we often think that we cannot know or trust such people. As they change from show to show we think we can never get to know who they really are. A former director with The Lamb's Players in California talked with our students about this a few years ago. She said, "If you don't believe this is true, try applying for a loan or an apartment or house rental, noting your occupation as an actor. You'll discover that lack of trust is a daily part of a performer's experience."

4. A fourth charge is that theater is a spurious activity because its origins can be traced back to pagan religious rituals. It is true that theater seems to originate in religion in most cultures, but this should not, from a Christian perspective, devalue theater. It should, in fact, enhance it. The oldest documents we have discussing the origins of theater (the Indian *Natyasastra*, *The Poetics* of Aristotle in Greece, and *The Kadensho* of Zeami's Medieval Japan) credit it to God (or the gods). Moreover, the darkest days of theater history are those, such as during the Empire period in Rome, when theater was furthest removed from its religious origins.

5. The fifth historical issue has to do with the problem of evil. Historically, two claims concerning the portrayal of evil have generated a lot of controversy. One is that imitating evil makes the imitator evil; the other, that watching portrayals of evil is the same as giving consent to it. For the latter question it should be noted that descriptions or discussions of evil in the Bible have not fallen under the same charge. Concerning the former question, the answer is not so clear. It is a concern Christians have wrestled with since at least the tenth century AD.

Perhaps the best answer was suggested several years ago by David Suchet of the Royal Shakespeare Company and star of the Public Broadcasting System series *Poirot*. An outspoken Christian, Suchet acknowledged that actors, because of complexion and/or dark hair coloring (of whom he is an example), are frequently cast as "dark" or evil characters. He admits that there are days when he has been rehearsing Iago, for instance, that he believes that he must go home and "shake off" the characterization. But, like the playwright-nun Hrotswitha of the Middle Ages, he observes that to exclude evil characters from plays would give an untrue picture of the world, something one does not find in either the Bible or art.[17]

A good actor never becomes his/her character. "Playing" a character is acting; becoming a character is mental illness. (God spent some time with the nation of Israel teaching them that creators and created objects are not the same thing. God created nature, but we are not to worship it. See Romans 1:25.)

Contemporary Issues

The other set of issues in the discipline are both contemporary and somewhat uniquely Western. Among them are:

1. Issues of Neglect, Alienation and Censorship. Because of the neglect of art by much of society, artists often feel alienated from the audiences they wish to attract. In the twentieth century, artists have often consoled themselves by speaking to one another about these matters. When contact is made with the public, that public often finds itself faced with an art that communicates in an apparently elitist language it can no longer understand. If the public takes offense the result is often attempts at censorship; the final arbiter becomes civil courts (which are one of last places one can expect to find a valuable estimation of aesthetic quality!). The final question is always "Who decides?" Who is best qualified to determine the right to existence of controversial art, the society or the artist-as-prophet whose role may sometimes be to offend for the purpose of instigating change?

    The answer is never an easy one. Are there no moral claims on art? Does freedom mean license? Are there no truth claims on the artistic community? Can true art ever be merely bolstering the consensus? Both artists and censorship advocates argue altruistic extremes.

---

17. Suchet made these comments during a televised interview broadcast on KCTS television as part of a PBS promotion for the Agatha Christie Mysteries. Unfortunately, I neglected to record the date and time of this event.

History denies both, revealing that evil has been done in the name of art and likewise revealing evil done against God's gift of art in the name of morality. If it is true that the Nazis used artists to justify the "ultimate solution," it is equally true that so-called moral censorship was leveled by the Russians to prevent Stanislavsky from using any references to God and religion in a play by Tolstoy. If it is true that the Romans used art to persecute Christians, it is equally true that Christian regulation of art by the Puritans nearly sterilized culture on two continents, relieved only by the poetry of Milton and a few colonial writers. The lessons of history are plain: left to their own devices in a fallen world, there are no depths to which artists may not sink nor any outrage against them to which societies may not stoop. Artists must have the freedom to make moral decisions; their audience must be free to make theirs. Neither should be in a position to do violence to the other. Consequently Christians must be prepared to abandon all absolute positions that fail to take into account human imperfection, whether to give all artists *carte blanche* license, on the one hand, or to endorse a "knee-jerk" moralism that owes less to truth than to cultural bias and ignorance of art, on the other.

2. The Problem of North American Capitalism: "Show Business versus Art." The political and economic nature of a society almost always determines the support structure of its art. North American capitalism often requires that art be "profit-making." If there is no other form of support, the profit motive can become paramount and theater can degenerate into "show business." Show business often caters to the lowest common denominator, producing everything from superficial musical theater to "chain-saw" films. Dorothy L. Sayers rightly observed, "This pseudo-art does not really communicate power to us; it merely exerts power over us."[18] The problem for the average member of society is to open the "Arts and Entertainment" section of a Sunday paper and determine which is the art and which is merely cheap entertainment.

Prior to the collapse of the Soviet Union, American theater artists were scandalized by two economic facts: (a) The Soviets spent more money subsidizing theater for children (alone) in a single year than the U.S. National Endowment for the Arts spent on *all* the arts

18. Sayers, "Towards a Christian Aesthetic," 82.

during the same period of time, and (b) while only North Americans who could afford to pay $85 a ticket could see *Les Miserables* (ironically a show about the poor), Soviet citizens in any city could see the best shows with the best actors for one nominal charge.

The point is that a society must decide the value of its artistic institutions and support them accordingly. I once heard the director of the National Theatre of Ireland, The Abbey Theatre in Dublin, say that, without their national subsidy, there would be no national theater in Ireland.

Other issues of concern in the contemporary North American theater, which we do not have space to consider, are:

3. The trend toward the use, in many actor-training programs, of eastern meditation techniques and the spiritual ramifications thereof.

4. The trend toward "using" theater art for political ends, such as a lobbying tool for gay rights, radical feminism, and even Christian propaganda.

5. The trend toward thoughtlessly subscribing to the spirits of the age, cultural pluralism and post-modernism. Some manifestations seem positive, others negative. For instance, many people approve the trend toward the "non-traditional casting" of actors—that is, giving a role to a talented actor regardless of racial compatibility with the text. Others have real reservations about embracing some post-modern themes in literature, such as the possibility of the ultimate meaninglessness of all quests for meaning.

6. The problem of lifestyle. In the past ten years theater people have wrestled with the problems of the eccentric lifestyles and strange hours of the theater. The question: Is it possible to be a performer and have a normal family life? Ironically, economic recession has aided the quest. As rising airfares have made it increasingly more costly for actors to race from city to city for auditions and to relocate from one region to another, they have sought the stability of working in one regional market. Those who have done so find a stable family life a greater possibility.

CHRISTIAN RESPONSES TO THE CHALLENGES
OF THE THEATER

Over the past two or three decades, increasing numbers of North American Christians working in the theater have addressed the challenges of the discipline from a perspective of faith. They have done so in three principal ways:

First, they have worked in colleges and universities and as artists in faith communities, with a purpose to re-educate both the public mind and the Christian mind concerning their artistic calling. Attacking both the secular devaluation of art in a technological society and the religious condemnation of it as non-spiritual, Christian artists and scholars have attempted to distinguish between cultural bias and biblical reality. As Arthur Holmes writes, "Certainly God created our capacity for aesthetic enjoyment, he made the world that delights and awes us, and he made us artistically creative. In this sense, then, all beauty and creativity is God's, to be enjoyed and dedicated to him. None of our cultural endeavors is excluded, nor can they be from education that is Christian."[19] Professor John Paul said he and his department colleagues attempt to foster the integration between faith and the dramatic arts by "assist[ing] our students to see the connection between theater and God by applying to their vocation such Christian values as humility, generosity, responsibility, and community."[20] The characters of the actors, in short, can have an important bearing on the effectiveness of their dramatic portrayals.

Second, Christian artists have tackled the question of the existing institutional models in which performers must work and the influence of these models on the issues facing theater people. Some Christians have investigated ways they can move in secular models and concurrently serve Christ, making daily decisions about suitable work and personal relations. Others have tried to turn art into "ministry," creating a theater that is a religious, vocational hybrid. (Theater becomes a "tool of evangelism" or a "technique of Christian education.") Still others, denying the possibility of doing Christian work in secular models or art in religious models, have attempted to create Christian theater institutions of their own—theaters that *are* theaters but are conducted by biblical ethical standards.

19. Holmes, *Idea of a Christian College*, 19.
20. Paul, "I Love to Tell the Story," 185.

In my view, one useful key to successfully responding to the call of a Christian vocation in the theater is "Christian community." My first attempt at the age of 20 was a miserable failure. I was alone and was nearly swallowed up by the profession. At age 30 I tried again, but this time in the company of about 20 equally dedicated Christian theater artists. I spent ten years of my life learning my profession and dealing with the issues of my discipline—with others, daily. Living in a Christian group-house with other artists, I fellowshipped at church on Sundays with other theater people and met weekly with Christian theater artists to discuss problems and issues and for mutual support—both economic and spiritual.

Having been weaned from that community and city in which I lived, I now move in a larger North American context of Christian theater artists in both universities and the profession. There are even some international efforts among dance and theater artists at cross-cultural networking among Christian professionals. Serious attempts are being made to bring about a resolution of some of the historic tensions between work in the theater and Christian commitment and discipleship.

Involvement, as a Christian, in theater art is simultaneously demanding and rewarding. For those of you whose interest has been piqued by the foregoing discussion, I encourage you to take the next steps towards an investigation of what can be a most worthwhile and fulfilling calling.

WORKS CITED

Arnott, Peter. *The Theater in Its Time*. Boston: Little, Brown, 1981.

Darwin, Charles. *The Autobiography of Charles Darwin*. Edited by F. Darwin. New York: Dover, 1958 (1892).

Eliot, T. S. *Christianity and Culture*. New York: Harper & Row, 1951.

Holmes, Arthur F. *The Idea of a Christian College*. Rev. ed. Grand Rapids, MI: Eerdmans, 1987.

Jones, Norman M. "The Dramatic Arts and the Image of God." In *God through the Looking Glass: Glimpses from the Arts*, edited by William D. Spencer and Aida B. Spencer et al., 129–39. Grand Rapids, MI: Baker, 1998.

Kilby, Clyde S. "Christian Imagination." In *The Christian Imagination: Essays in Literature and the Arts*, edited by Leland Ryken, 37–46. Grand Rapids, MI: Baker, 1981.

Kristeller, Paul Oscar. "The Modern System of the Arts." In *Problems in Aesthetics*, edited by Morris Weitz, 108–64. New York: Macmillan, 1970.

Lahr, John, and Jonathan Price. *Life Show*. New York: Viking Press, 1973.

Paul, John S. "I Love to Tell the Story: Teaching Theater at a Church-Related College." In *Teaching as an Act of Faith: Theory and Practice in Church-Related Higher Education*, edited by Arlin C. Migliazzo, 163–87. New York: Fordham University Press, 2002.

Quash, Ben. "The Play beyond the Play." In *Sounding the Depths: Theology through the* Arts, edited by Jeremy Begbie, 92–104. London: SCM Press, 2002.

Rimer, Thomas. Lecture given for the Asian Studies Program at the University of Pittsburgh, 1990.

Sayers, Dorothy L. "Towards a Christian Aesthetic." In her *Christian Letters to a Post-Christian World*, 69–83. Grand Rapids, MI: Eerdmans, 1969.

Schiller, Friedrich. *On the Aesthetic Education of Man.* Translated by Reginald Snell. New York: Frederick Ungar, 1965.

Veith, Gene Edward, Jr. *The Gift of Art.* Downers Grove, IL: InterVarsity Press, 1983.

FOR FURTHER READING

Arnett, Lloyd. "Evangelical Correctness." *Christian Drama* 17.2 (1994) 3–5.

———. "Problems of Dramaturgy." *Christian Drama* 16.1 (1993) 4–7.

———. "What Hath God Wrought?" *Christian Drama* 18.1 (1995) 3–6.

Barish, Jonas. *The Anti-theatrical Prejudice.* Los Angeles: University of California Press, 1981.

Betti, Ugo. "Religion and Theater." In *The Modern Theater,* edited by Robert W. Corrigan, 624–29. New York: Macmillan, 1964.

Cohen, Robert. *Acting Power.* Palo Alto, CA: Mayfield, 1978.

Elvgren, Gillette. "Christian Theater Artists and Their Culture: The University Experience." *Christian Drama* 17.2 (1994) 20–22.

Forde, Nigel. "The Playwright's Tale." In *Sounding the Depths: Theology through the Arts,* edited by Jeremy Begbie, 59–70. London: SCM Press, 2002.

Kuhn, Bruce. *An Actor Prepares: Life before (and after) Les Miz.* Monographs on Faith and Theater 1. Greenville, SC: Christians in Theater Arts, 1997.

Savidge, Dale, and Lloyd Arnett. "Anti-theatrical Bias." Unpublished paper presented at Christians in Theater Arts Annual Networking Conference, Concordia University, Chicago, June 1992.

Seerveld, Calvin. *Rainbows for the Fallen World.* Toronto, ON: Toronto Tuppence Press, 1980.

Senkbeil, Peter. "Why Christian Theater is Exploding." *Christianity and the Arts* 4.1 (1997) 4–8.

Veith, Gene Edward, Jr. "Playing with Conventions." In *Postmodern Times: A Christian Guide to Contemporary Thought and Culture,* 93–109. Wheaton, IL: Crossway, 1994.

Watts, Murray. *Christianity and the Theatre.* Edinburgh: Handsell Press, 1986.

Modern Authors Index

Scripture Index